Beginning Regular Expressions

Beginning Regular Expressions

Andrew Watt

wrox
Programmer to Programmer™

Beginning Regular Expressions

Published by
Wiley Publishing, Inc.
10475 Crosspoint Boulevard
Indianapolis, IN 46256
www.wiley.com

Copyright © 2005 by Wiley Publishing, Inc., Indianapolis, Indiana

Published simultaneously in Canada

ISBN: 0-7645-7489-2

For general information on our other products and services please contact our Customer Care Department within the United States at (800) 762-2974, outside the United States at (317) 572-3993 or fax (317) 572-4002.

Trademarks: Wiley, the Wiley logo, Wrox, the Wrox logo, Programmer to Programmer, and related trade dress are trademarks or registered trademarks of John Wiley & Sons, Inc. and/or its affiliates, in the United States and other countries, and may not be used without written permission. All other trademarks are the property of their respective owners. Wiley Publishing, Inc., is not associated with any product or vendor mentioned in this book.

Wiley also publishes its books in a variety of electronic formats. Some content that appears in print may not be available in electronic books.

Library of Congress Cataloging-in-Publication Data:

Watt, Andrew, 1953-
  Beginning regular expressions / Andrew Watt.
     p. cm.
  ISBN 0-7645-7489-2 (paper/website)
  1. Text processing (Computer science) I. Title.
  QA76.9.T48W37 2005
  005.52—dc22
                        2004028308

About the Author

Andrew Watt is an independent consultant and experienced author with an interest and expertise in XML and Web technologies. He has written and coauthored more than 10 books on Web development and XML, including *XPath Essentials* and *XML Schema Essentials*. He has been programming since 1984, moving to Web development technologies in 1994. He's a well-known voice in several influential online technical communities and is a frequent contributor to many Web development specifications.

Dedication

I would like to dedicate this book to the memory of my late father, George Alec Watt, a very special human being.

Acknowledgments

Authors often state that a book is the work of a team rather than a single person. There is a good reason for that assertion. It's true.

First, I would like to thank Jim Minatel, the acquisitions editor who put the platform in place to get *Beginning Regular Expressions* off the ground at Wrox/Wiley. His patience, under significant provocation relating to timetable, and his tact, efficiency, and general good nature made those organizational aspects of the book an enjoyable experience to repeat at a future date.

The development editor, Marcia Ellett, was great to work with and did a lot to tidy up my prose to make a better read for all readers of this book. In addition, her eagle eyes spotted some minor slips that had slipped through the authorial net. Thanks, Marcia.

Doug Steele, a fellow Microsoft MVP, was technical editor and carried out a tactful and painstaking job and picked up many little things that the smoke from the author's midnight oil seemed somehow to obscure. Thanks, Doug.

Darren Niemke, another MVP, helped with technical editing of a number of chapters. Thanks, Darren.

My thanks go, too, to the production staff at Wiley who, as is typically the case, the author never meets. Without their efforts in translating a manuscript into a finished product this book would not exist in its current form.

Credits

Acquisitions Editor
Jim Minatel

Development Editor
Marcia Ellett

Technical Editors
Douglas J. Steele
Darren Neimke

Production Editor
Felicia Robinson

Copy Editor
Jeri Freedman/Foxxe Editorial Services

Editorial Manager
Mary Beth Wakefield

Vice President & Executive Group Publisher
Richard Swadley

Vice President and Publisher
Joseph B. Wikert

Project Coordinator
April Farling

Media Development Specialist
Angie Denny

Contents

Contents

Contents

Contents

Contents

Contents

Contents

Contents

Contents

Introduction

...eld as text. As a result, the searching and manipulation of ... any developer undertakes. Regular expressions are one ... and the developer to make finding and manipulating

... expressions intimidating, and this feeling is partly justi-...d, as a result, are often cryptic. Changing a single character ... expression. These difficulties mean that developers often ...wn regular expression code. Worse still, they often feel lost ... expression code written by others, a problem made ...adequately document the regular expression code they ...ons down into their component parts and think carefully ..., they can become a very useful tool, in fact an essential

...dles that make so many developers uncomfortable with ...fective use of the power that is available to the developer ... regular expressions.

...developers who need to manipulate text but are new to reg-...sions in the past but have found that the learning curve, ...eeds of newcomers to the topic, was just too steep to allow

...Windows as their primary or only operating system. You ...ects of Unix to begin to use regular expressions. All of the ...un on Windows, although versions of many are available

Beginning Regular Expressions takes you forward from things you are likely to know already, such as the use of the * and ? characters when doing command line file searching. As you build your knowledge, you see working examples that you can adapt to allow you to explore solutions to the problems that you meet.

Whether you are an occasional programmer or simply one who hasn't used regular expressions yet, you will be shown the component parts of regular expressions, what they mean, how to use them, and pitfalls to be aware of when using them. Working examples form a core part of how you learn to create, under-stand, and use regular expressions. Most of the chapters contain a number of Try It Out sections that show you how to put regular expressions to work. Each Try It Out section is accompanied by a How It Works section or other explanation that explains how a regular expression works.

What This Book Covers

This book introduces the various parts of the construction of a regular expression pattern, explains what they mean, and walks you through working examples showing how they work and why they do what they do. By working through the examples, you will build your understanding of how to make regular expressions do what you want them to do and avoid creating regular expressions that don't meet your intentions.

Beginning chapters introduce regular expressions and show you a method you can use to break down a text manipulation problem into component parts so that you can make an intelligent choice about constructing a regular expression pattern that matches what you want it to match and avoids matching unwanted text.

To solve more complex problems, I encourage you to set out a *problem definition* and progressively refine it to express it in English in a way that corresponds to a regular expression pattern that does what you want it to do.

The second part of the book devotes a chapter to each of several technologies available on the Windows platform. You are shown how to use each tool or language with regular expressions (for example, how to do a lookahead in Perl or create a named variable in C#).

Regular expressions can be useful in applications such as Microsoft Word, OpenOffice.org Writer, Microsoft Excel, and Microsoft Access. A chapter is devoted to each.

In addition, tools such as the little-known Windows `findstr` utility and the commercial PowerGrep tool each have a chapter showing how they can be used to solve text manipulation tasks that span multiple files.

The use of regular expressions in the MySQL and Microsoft SQL Server databases are also demonstrated.

Several programming languages have a chapter describing the metacharacters available for use in those languages together with demonstrations of how the objects or classes of that language can be used with regular expressions. The languages covered are VBScript, JScript, Visual Basic .NET, C#, PHP, Java, and Perl.

XML is used increasingly to store textual data. The W3C XML Schema definition language can use regular expressions to automatically validate data in an XML document. W3C XML Schema has a chapter demonstrating how regular expressions can be used with the `xs:pattern` element.

How This Book Is Structured

Chapters 1 through 10 describe the component parts of regular expression patterns and show you what they do and how they can be used with a variety of text manipulation tools and languages. I suggest that you work through these chapters in order and build up your understanding of regular expressions.

The book then devotes a chapter to each of several text manipulation tools and programming languages. These chapters assume knowledge from Chapters 1 through 10, but you can dip into the tool-specific and language-specific chapters in any order you want.

The book was written in this way so that you could use Chapters 1 through 10 to get a grasp of how to use regular expressions. You can then apply that knowledge by exploring the chapters devoted to technologies you already use or will have to use for specific projects.

Many developers are asked to program in languages in which they are not fully experienced. Each chapter devoted to a programming language provides many examples of working code that you can adapt, as appropriate, to your own needs.

What You Need to Use This Book

Beginning Regular Expressions makes use of a range of tools and programming languages. Examples in Chapters 1 through 10 use a variety of tools ranging from Microsoft Word and OpenOffice.org Writer to PowerGrep, Java, and Perl.

This book is targeted primarily at Windows users and developers. However, developers on other platforms can use much of the book.

It is likely that you won't have all the tools or technologies used in this book. For example, it's unlikely that you'll be programming in JScript, Perl, C#, Java, and PHP on a regular basis. Depending on which languages interest you, it is assumed that you have the necessary tools installed. However, where free trial software or free downloads are available you will be given information about where to obtain them and basic information about how to install them on Windows.

Conventions

To help you get the most from the text and keep track of what's happening, a number of conventions are used throughout the book.

Try It Out

The *Try It Out* is an exercise you should work through, following the text in the book.

1. They usually consist of a set of steps.
2. Each step has a number.
3. Follow the steps in order.

How It Works

After most *Try It Outs*, the code you've typed is explained in detail.

> **Boxes like this one hold important, not-to-be-forgotten information that is directly relevant to the surrounding text.**

Tips, hints, tricks, and asides to the current discussion are offset and placed in italics like this.

As for styles in the text:

- ❏ Important words are *highlighted* when introduced.
- ❏ Keyboard strokes are shown like this: Ctrl+A.
- ❏ Filenames, URLs, and code within the text appear like this: `persistence.properties`.
- ❏ Code is presented in two different ways:

```
In code examples new and important code is highlighted with a gray background.
```

The gray highlighting is not used for code that's less important in the present context or that has been shown before.

Source Code

As you work through the examples in this book, you may choose either to type in all the code manually or to use the source code files that accompany the book. All of the source code used in this book is available for download at `www.wrox.com`. Once at the site, simply locate the book's title (either by using the Search box or by using one of the title lists), and click the Download Code link on the book's detail page to obtain all the source code for the book.

> *Because many books have similar titles, you may find it easiest to search by ISBN; for this book the ISBN is 0-7645-7489-2.*

Once you download the code, just decompress it with your favorite compression tool. Alternately, you can go to the main Wrox code download page at `www.wrox.com/dynamic/books/download.aspx` to see the code available for this book and all other Wrox books.

Errata

We make every effort to ensure that there are no errors in the text or code. However, no one is perfect, and mistakes do occur. If you find an error in one of our books, such as a spelling mistake or faulty piece of code, we would be grateful for your feedback. By sending in errata you may save another reader hours of frustration, and you will be helping us provide even higher quality information.

To find the errata page for this book, go to `www.wrox.com` and locate the title using the Search box or one of the title lists. Then, on the book details page, click the Book Errata link. On this page, you can view all errata that has been posted for this book. A complete book list including links to each book's errata is also available at `www.wrox.com/misc-pages/booklist.shtml`.

If you don't spot "your" error on the Book Errata page, go to `www.wrox.com/contact/tech support.shtml` and complete the form there to send us the error you have found. We'll check the information and, if appropriate, post a message to the book's errata page and fix the problem in subsequent editions of the book.

p2p.wrox.com

For author and peer discussion, join the P2P forums at p2p.wrox.com. The forums are a Web-based system for you to post messages relating to Wrox books and related technologies and interact with other readers and technology users. The forums offer a subscription feature to e-mail you topics of interest of your choosing when new posts are made to the forums. Wrox authors, editors, other industry experts, and your fellow readers are present on these forums.

At http://p2p.wrox.com you will find a number of forums that will help you not only as you read this book, but also as you develop your own applications. To join the forums, just follow these steps:

1. Go to p2p.wrox.com, click the Register link, and read the terms of use and click Agree.

2. Complete the required information to join as well as any optional information you wish to provide and click Submit.

3. You will receive an e-mail with information describing how to verify your account and complete the joining process.

You can read messages in the forums without joining P2P but to post your own messages, you must join.

Once you join, you can post new messages and respond to messages other users post. You can read messages at any time on the Web. If you would like to have new messages from a particular forum e-mailed to you, click the Subscribe to this Forum icon by the forum name in the forum listing.

For more information on how to use the Wrox P2P, be sure to read the P2P FAQs for answers to questions about how the forum software works and many common questions specific to P2P and Wrox books. To read the FAQs, click the FAQ link on any P2P page.

Introduction to Regular Expressions

Text is a crucial part of many people's work with computers. From writing documents to editing code, text is almost everywhere. Web pages commonly consist largely of text, some of which is Hypertext Markup Language (HTML) or Extensible Hypertext Markup Language (XHTML) markup and some of which is regular text, but all of it consists of sequences of characters that can be matched using regular expressions. Forms on the Web accept text as input, which can be matched against allowable input. Business documents consist of text, and searches for specific sequences of characters can be made using regular expressions. E-mail messages consist of text. Developers' code consists of text. And regular expressions can be beneficially used in many situations where text is used.

Not only is text everywhere, but there also is lots of it, and increasingly, text must be updated or aggregated. As the volume of text created or to which you have access increases, you need efficient and effective ways to find text of particular interest or to change specific pieces of text.

Finding and changing individual pieces of text can be straightforward if you are dealing with a single document only a page or two in length. It becomes a more daunting task, potentially prone to human error, if you are dealing with dozens of documents, each hundreds of pages in length, or with thousands of relatively short documents. It is for tasks such as this that regular expressions are used, because regular expressions allow automation of many useful types of text processing.

For example, in a Web form you will want to check that a credit card number is correctly structured or that a postal code is correctly formed. In a lengthy document, you might want to find a hazily recalled URL for an important source of information. You might want to convert HTML code so that it conforms to the rules of Extensible Markup Language (XML) syntax and complies with company policy to use XHTML code. You might want to check that user input into a Windows application satisfies necessary criteria to allow correct processing.

In this chapter, you will learn the following:

- ❏ What regular expressions are
- ❏ What regular expressions can be used for
- ❏ Why regular expressions can seem daunting

The list of possible uses for a tool that allows the manipulation of text is almost endless, with text being so widespread. Sadly, many computer users and developers have little or no knowledge of regular expressions and how they can help in working with text. This book aims to change that.

What Are Regular Expressions?

Regular expressions are patterns of characters that match, or fail to match, sequences of characters in text. To allow developers to create regular expression patterns, certain characters and combinations of characters have special meanings and uses, and this book spends considerable time looking at those. But first, here are some more basic ideas.

Regular expressions, at the most basic level, allow computer users and developers to find desired pieces of text and, often, to replace those pieces of text with something that is preferred. At other times, regular expressions are used to test whether a sequence of characters that might be intended to be a credit card number or a Social Security number has an allowed pattern of characters. Whether it's finding existing sequences of characters or testing sequences of characters for their suitability (or not) for storage, the key aspect of regular expressions is matching a pattern against a sequence of characters.

It is reasonable, in a broad sense, to refer to a regular expression language, but strictly speaking, there is no regular expression language. Like scripting languages such as JavaScript and VBScript, which can be used only in the context of another application or language, regular expressions can be used only in the context of a "proper" programming language, including scripting languages, or as part of an application such as Microsoft Word and OpenOffice.org Writer or a command-line utility such as the `findstr` utility. Regular expressions can be discussed in an abstract way, but they are *used* together with another language or application.

This chapter focuses on very simple examples of regular expressions. Chapter 2 takes a closer look at regular expression tools. For the moment, either download the latest version of OpenOffice.org from `www.openoffice.org` to try out the simple examples in this chapter or simply read the text and examine the figures carefully. I encourage you to download OpenOffice.org, because it is a very simple tool to allow you to explore many aspects of regular expression syntax.

Try It Out   Matching Literal Characters

The simplest type of regular expression pattern is a sequence of characters. For example, if you want to find the sequence of three characters `car`, you can use a regular expression pattern `car` to find those characters.

First, try to express the problem in plain English:

Match a sequence of characters; first match the letter c, followed by the letter a, followed by the letter r.

Suppose that you had the following text in a document, `Car.txt`:

```
Carl spilt his carton of orange juice on the carpet of his new car.
If he had taken more care when opening the carton he wouldn't have had this
annoying and disappointing accident.
Some car shampoo would, Carl hoped, make the carpet look as good as new.
```

There are many occurrences of the sequence of characters `car`, as shown in a simple regular expressions search in OpenOffice.Org Writer in Figure 1-1. To try it out for yourself, follow these steps:

1. Open `Car.txt` in OpenOffice.org Writer (regular expressions are supported in version 1.1 and above).

2. Use Ctrl+F to open the Find and Replace dialog box.

3. Check the Regular Expressions check box.

4. Enter **car** in the Search For text box.

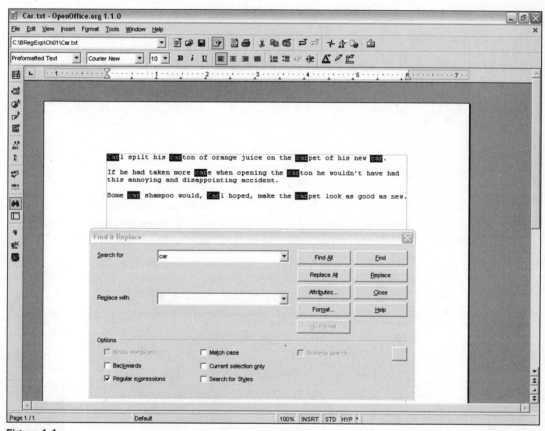

Figure 1-1

As you can see in Figure 1-1, the sequences of characters `car` have been selected whether or not they formed a word and whether the initial character of the sequence was uppercase or lowercase.

The following table shows a more formal breakdown for the very simple regular expression pattern `car`.

When you have simple literal patterns such as `car`, a formal layout of the meaning of a regular expression seems like overkill, but when you begin to create significantly more complex regular expression patterns later in the book, laying out each part of a regular expression helps you keep track of the pieces.

Letter	Instruction
c	Match the letter c
a	Match the letter a
r	Match the letter r

In short documents, as in this example, whether matches that are whole words or simply character sequences, if you use the Find All option in a search in OpenOffice.org Writer, you can quickly scan all the matches by eye, because they are shown in reversed highlight.

However, regular expressions can be used to tighten up the match. For example, you might want to find occurrences of the sequence of characters car that make up a word, but you don't want to find it when it is part of another word. And you might also want to make the search case sensitive.

You can do both in OpenOffice.org Writer by using the regular expression \<car\> and checking the Match Case check box, as shown in Figure 1-2. The \< and \> metacharacters simply match the boundary of a word.

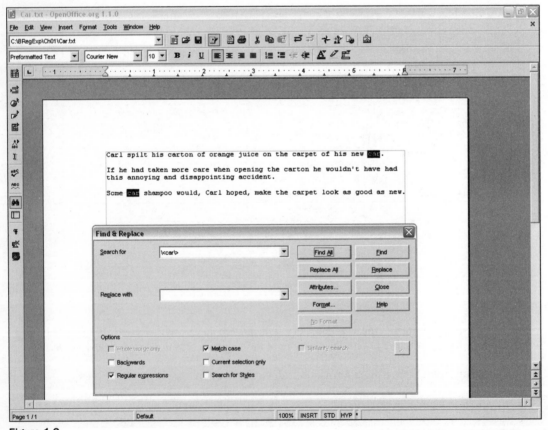

Figure 1-2

Don't worry too much about the syntax for matching the positions at the beginning and end of words for the moment. You'll see the various forms of syntax for that in Chapter 6.

What Can Regular Expressions Be Used For?

The potential number of uses for regular expressions is enormous. This section briefly describes some examples of what regular expressions can be used for.

Finding Doubled Words

Regular expressions can be used to find text where words have been doubled. In some text, such as the following sentence, a doubled word may be intentional:

It is for tasks such as that that regular expressions are used.

The doubling of the word *that* is how I wanted to express an idea. In other situations, the doubling of a word is inappropriate and undesired, as in the following:

Paris in the the Spring

The techniques to find doubled words are described in detail in Chapter 7.

In some settings, you don't need regular expressions to identify doubled words. In the preceding phrase, the second `the` is often underlined with a wavy red line in Microsoft Word, for example (depending on settings).

Checking Input from Web Forms

Another common use of regular expressions is to check that data entered in Web forms conforms to a structure that will be acceptable to the server-side process to which the form data will be submitted. For example, suppose someone attempts to enter the following as a supposed U.S. Social Security number (SSN):

```
Fred-123-4567
```

You can be confident that it isn't a valid SSN, and you want to be sure that it isn't entered into a back-end database. If you want to check the supposed SSN client side, you could use JavaScript and its `RegExp` object to check whether a string entered by a user conforms to a pattern that is a valid SSN.

One of the reasons for checking input from Web forms is that the data collected will be sent to a database, likely a relational database. If the wrong datatype is entered in a field in a form, you might end up with an attempt being made to enter a name into a date column in the database, which will likely cause an error when the attempt is made to write the data to the database. You also need to be able to make checks to ensure that you don't allow dates such as 2005-02-31, because there are never 31 days in February. The data you collect from a form is simply a sequence of characters; therefore, regular expressions are ideal to ensure that inappropriate data is detected on the client side and that the user is asked to enter appropriate data in place of the erroneous data.

Changing Date Formats

Imagine that you are "translating" a business document from U.S. English to British English. One of the components of the document's text may represent dates, and you will need to locate and, very possibly, change those dates, because the conventional representation of dates in the United States and in the U.K. differs. For example, in the United States, the date for Christmas Day 2001 would be written as 12/25/2001. In the U.K., this might be written as 25/12/2001. If you also had to represent dates for Japanese customers, you might express the same date as 2001-12-25.

Assuming that you had a document with dates using the U.S. English conventions, you could create a regular expression to detect those sequences of characters wherever they occurred in the document. Depending on what the desired output format is, you could also replace a U.S. English date on the input side with a British English or Japanese date on the output side.

Finding Incorrect Case

Because there are a lot of jargon and acronyms associated with computing, it is very easy for incorrect case to creep into documents. This can happen either because of a word processor attempting to autocorrect what it imagines (wrongly) are incorrect doubling of uppercase (capital) letters. The sample document shown here, XPath.txt, is designed to illustrate one of the problems that can creep into technical documents.

```
Xpath is an abbreviation for the XML Path Language.

XPath is used to navigate around a tree model of an XML document.

There are significant differences in the data model of XpatH 1.0 and Xpath 2.0.

XSLT is one of the technologies with which xpath is often used.
```

The correct way to write XPath is with two uppercase initial letters. As you can see, the sample document has several incorrect forms of the word due to errors in the case of one or more characters.

The sensible approach to a problem like this depends, in part, on whether the word at issue can also be used in normal English. In the case of XPath there is only one correct form, and it doesn't occur as a word in normal English. That allows you to simply find all occurrences of the characters xpath, whether upper- or lowercase, and replace them with the correct sequence of characters, XPath.

There are several possible approaches to problems of this type, and you will see many examples of them later in the book.

Adding Links to URLs

Suppose that you have URLs located in a document that you want to convert for displaying on the Web. If the URL is stored in a separate column in a relational database, it may be straightforward just to place the URL in the column as the value of the href attribute of an HTML/XHTML a element. However, if the URL is included in a piece of text such as the following, the problem of recognizing a URL becomes a little tougher.

```
The World Wide Web Consortium, the W3C, has developed many specifications for
XML and associated languages. The W3C's home page is located at
http://www.w3.org and its technical reports are located at
http://www.w3.org/tr/.
```

Finding URLs depends on being able to recognize a URL as it occurs anywhere in what might potentially be a very long document. In addition, you don't know what the actual titles of the Web pages are to which the URLs point, so you can't supply the page title as text but have to use the URL both as the value of the `href` attribute of an XHTML a element and also as the text contained between the start tag and end tag of the a element. What you want to do is locate each URL and then replace it with a new piece of text constructed like this (the italicized *theURL* stands for the actual URL that you find inside the text):

```
<a href="theURL">theURL</a>
```

Regular Expressions You Already Use

If you have used a computer for any length of time, you very likely are familiar with at least some uses of regular expressions, although you may not use that term to describe the text patterns that you use in word processors or directory listings from the command line, for example.

Search and Replace in Word Processors

Most modern word processors have some sort of regular expression support, although for some word processors the term *regular expressions* is not used. In Microsoft Word, for example, the limited regular expression support available in the word processor itself uses the term *wildcards* to describe the supported regular expression patterns.

The simplest *pattern* is literal text. So if you want to find a text pattern of `Star`, you can enter those four characters in the Find What box in the Find and Replace dialog box in Microsoft Word. As you will see a little later in this chapter, an approach like that can have its problems when you're handling substantial quantities of text.

Directory Listings

If you have done any work at the command line, you have probably used simple regular expressions when doing directory listings. Two metacharacters are available: * (the asterisk) and ? (the question mark).

For example, on the Windows platform, if you want to find the executable files in the current directory you can use the following command from the command line:

```
dir *.exe
```

The `dir` command is an instruction to list all files in the current directory and is equivalent to entering the following at the command line:

```
dir *.*
```

The *.exe pattern matches any sequence of zero or more characters followed by a period followed by the literal sequence of characters exe in a filename. Similarly, the *.* pattern indicates zero or more characters followed by a period followed by zero or more characters.

> The syntax of wildcards in directory paths differs significantly from that of regular expressions, so the intention of this section is not to focus on the details of path wildcards, but to remind you that you likely already apply patterns to find suitable pieces of text (in this case, filenames).

On other occasions, when searching a directory you will know the exact number of characters that you want to match. Suppose that you have a directory containing multiple Excel workbooks, each of which contains monthly sales. If you know that the filename consists of the word *Sales* followed by two digits for the year followed by three alphabetic characters for the month, you could search for all sales workbooks from 2004 by using this command:

```
Dir Sales04???.xls
```

This would display the Excel workbooks whose filenames are constructed as just described. But if you had some other workbooks named, for example, Sales04123.xls and Sales04234.xls, the command would also cause those to be displayed, although you don't necessarily want to see those.

The ways in which regular expressions can be used together with the dir command are, as you can see, very limited due to the provision of only two metacharacters in path wildcards.

Online Searching

Another scenario where regular expressions, although admittedly simple ones, are widely used is in online searching. The search box on eBay.com, for example, will accept the asterisk wildcard so that photo* matches words such as photo, photos, photograph, and photographs.

Why Regular Expressions Seem Intimidating

There are several reasons why many developers find regular expressions intimidating. Among the reasons are the compact, cryptic syntax of regular expressions. Another is the absence of a standards body for regular expressions, so that the regular expression patterns for a particular meaning vary among languages or tools that support regular expressions.

Compact, Cryptic Syntax

Regular expressions syntax is very compact and can seem totally cryptic to those unfamiliar with regular expressions. At times it seems as if there are backslash characters, parentheses, and square brackets everywhere. Once you understand what each character and metacharacter does in a regular expression pattern, you will be able to build your own regular expressions or analyze those created by other developers.

> A **metacharacter** is a character, or combination of characters, that have a special meaning when they are contained in a regular expression pattern.

Whitespace Can Significantly Alter the Meaning

Placing unintended whitespace in a regular expression can radically alter the meaning of the regular expression and can turn what ought to be matches into nonmatches, and vice versa. When creating regular expression patterns, you need to be meticulous about handling whitespace.

For example, suppose that you want to match the content of a document that stores information about people. A sample document, `People.txt`, is shown here:

```
Cardoza, Fred
Catto, Philipa
Duncan, Jean
Edwards, Neil
England, Elizabeth
Main, Robert
Martin, Jane
Meens, Carol
Patrick, Harry
Paul, Jeanine
Roberts, Clementine
Schmidt, Paul
Sells, Simon
Smith, Peter
Stephens, Sheila
Wales, Gareth
Zinni, Hamish
```

Assuming that each name is laid out in the preceding format, you can use a regular expression to locate all names where the surname begins with an uppercase *S* by using the following regular expression:

```
^S.*
```

Figure 1-3 shows the result of using that regular expression in OpenOffice.org Writer in `People.txt`. Notice that all the names where the surname begins with *S* are selected.

However, if you insert a single space character between the ^ and the S in the regular expression pattern, as follows, there is no match at all, as illustrated in Figure 1-4.

```
^ S.*
```

This occurs because the ^ metacharacter is a marker for the beginning of a line (or paragraph in OpenOffice.org Writer). So inserting a space character immediately after the caret, ^, means that the regular expression is searching for lines that begin with a space character. Because each of the lines in `People.txt` has an alphabetic character at the beginning of the line, there is no line that begins with a space character, and therefore, there is no match for the regular expression pattern.

Spotting an error like the existence of the inadvertent space character can be tough. I recommend that you always look carefully at the data you are going to manipulate so that you understand its characteristics and know that at least some matches for the regular expression should be present. If you follow that advice (which I discuss in more detail in Chapter 2), you will know that there are some surnames beginning with *S*, and therefore, you should be aware that something is wrong with the regular expression pattern if the regular expression is returning zero matches.

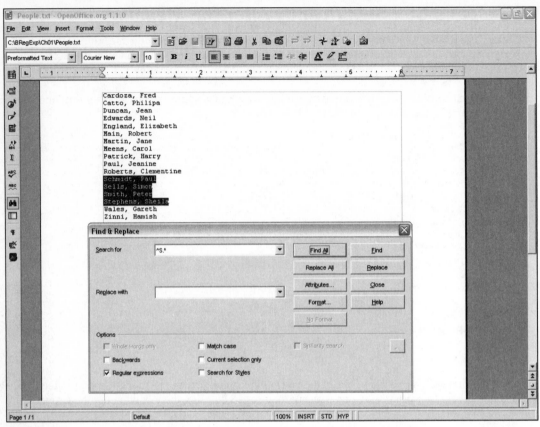

Figure 1-3

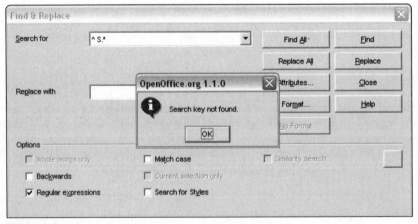

Figure 1-4

However, when a regular expression returns some matches, you might overlook the undesired effects of inadvertently introduced whitespace. Suppose that you want to find names where the surname begins with *C*, *D*, *R*, or *S*. You could do that with the following regular expression pattern:

```
^(C|D|R|S).*
```

What if you accidentally introduce a space character after the *D*, giving the following regular expression?

```
^(C|D |R|S).*
```

You might not see the space character, or you might not realize the change in meaning introduced by a space character, and you might easily be fooled because there are a good number of names returned, although there is no name returned where the surname begins with *D*, as you can see in Figure 1-5.

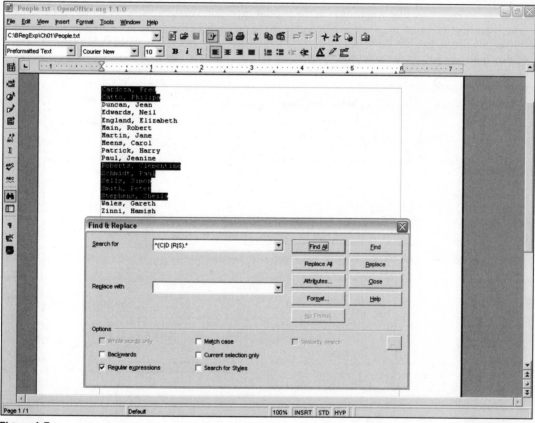

Figure 1-5

With the small amount of ordered data in `People.txt` you might easily notice the absence of expected names with surnames starting with *D*. In larger documents where the data is not ordered, however, it might be a different story.

The use of whitespace inside regular expression patterns is discussed in Chapter 4.

No Standards Body

One reason for the variation in regular expressions is that there is no standards body to define the syntax for regular expressions. Regular expressions first came to prominence in the Perl language and were adopted, with varying degrees of exactness, in various other languages and applications over an extended period.

Without a formal standards body for regular expressions, variation in implementations is substantial.

Differences between Implementations

Regular expressions and wildcards have a lot in common among many of the various implementations, but many implementations are quite visibly nonstandard.

You saw in Figure 1-2 that you could use the regular expression pattern \<car\> to find occurrences of the sequence of characters car only when they made up a whole word. However, if you want to do the same functional search — that is, find occurrences of car only as a whole word in Microsoft Word — you would use the regular expression pattern <car>, as shown in Figure 1-6.

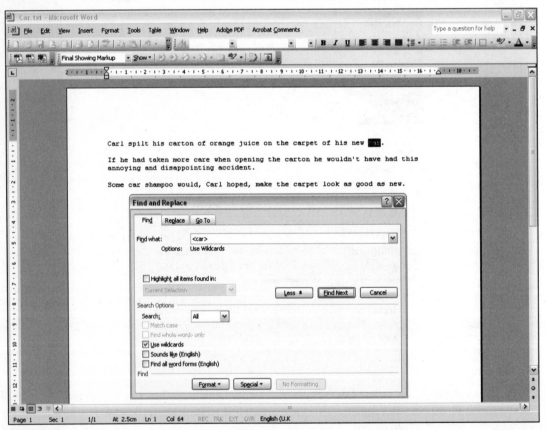

Figure 1-6

Similarly, if you want to match any single alphabetic character, you use the . (period) metacharacter in OpenOffice.Org Writer and several scripting languages such as Perl. But we must use the ? (question mark) character in Word for exactly the same function. In that aspect Word is distinctly nonstandard, resembling file path usage rather than true regular expression patterns.

Differences in the implementation of regular expressions will be discussed as you progress through the fundamental techniques in each of the next several chapters. In addition, later chapters of this book are dedicated to specific languages and applications, and characteristics of the implementation of regular expressions syntax are discussed in detail.

Characters Change Meaning in Different Contexts

Another reason why people find regular expressions confusing is that individual characters, or metacharacters, can have significantly different meanings depending on where you use them.

For example, the ^ metacharacter can signify the beginning of a line in regular expressions in some languages. However, in those same languages the same ^ metacharacter can, when used inside a character class, signify negation. So the regular expression pattern ^and matches the sequence of characters and at the beginning of a word, but the regular expression [^and] signifies a character class that must not include any of the characters a, n, and d.

Character classes are introduced and described in detail in Chapter 5.

The test document, And.txt, is shown here:

```
and
but
and
Andrew
sand
button
but
band
hand
```

If you use the regular expression pattern ^and in OpenOffice.org Writer, you expect to select all the occurrences when the beginning of a line, indicated by the ^ metacharacter, is followed by the exact sequence of characters a, n, and d (regardless of case of those characters). Figure 1-7 shows the application of this regular expression in OpenOffice.Org Writer.

The regular expression selects the word and when it occurs at the beginning of a line (twice) and the first three characters of the word Andrew. The first three characters of Andrew are selected because the search is case insensitive.

However, if you use the ^ metacharacter as the first character inside a character class in the regular expression pattern .[^and].*, the sequences of characters shown in Figure 1-8 are selected.

What the regular expression pattern .[^and].* means is a single character followed by a character that is *not* a or n, or d, followed by zero or more characters.

13

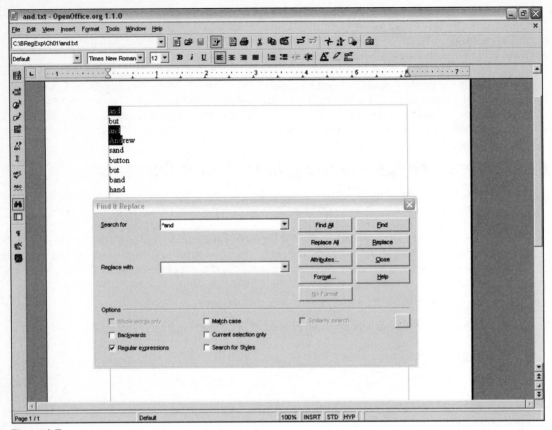

Figure 1-7

If the ^ is used inside a character class in any position other than the first character, it has the normal meaning that it has outside a character class. The caret functions as a negation metacharacter only when it is the first character inside the opening square bracket of a character class. Don't worry about the detail of the interpretation at this stage. The relevant issues are discussed in detail in Chapter 5.

Another character that can have different meanings inside and outside character classes is the hyphen. Outside a character class, a dash simply represents itself, for example, in a date value:

```
2004-12-25
```

However, inside a character class, when it isn't the first character the dash indicates a range. For example, to specify a character class that has all lower- and uppercase alphabetic characters, you could use the following pattern:

```
[a-zA-Z]
```

The character class is short for the following:

```
[abcdefghijklmnopqrstuvwxyzABCDEFGHIJKLMNOPQRSTUVWXYZ]
```

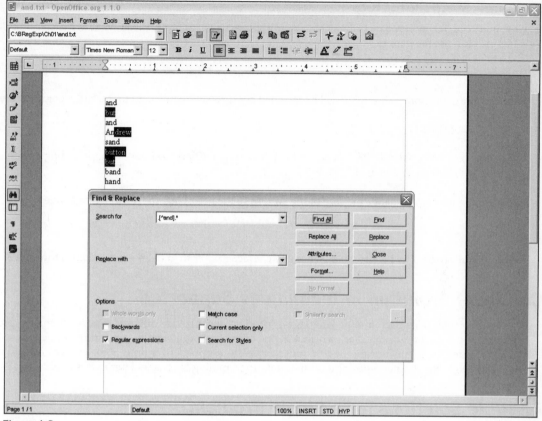

Figure 1-8

Regular Expressions Can Be Case Sensitive

A further complicating aspect of using regular expressions is that in some circumstances regular expressions are case sensitive. Case sensitivity has two aspects, one related to whether matching is carried out in a case-sensitive or case-insensitive fashion, and the other being the different, indeed opposite, meaning of metacharacters of different case.

Case-Sensitive and Case-Insensitive Matching

Individual regular expression implementations handle case differently. For example, OpenOffice.org Writer provides a Match Case check box in the Find and Replace dialog box that you saw in examples earlier in this chapter. The default behavior is case-insensitive matching.

By contrast, the default matching in programming languages is often case sensitive. Many programming languages provide switches that indicate whether use of a regular expression pattern is in case-sensitive mode or case-insensitive mode. These issues are discussed in Chapter 4. In addition, use of case-sensitive and case-insensitive searches is demonstrated in many of the chapters dedicated to individual programming languages.

Case and Metacharacters

Case is crucial in how some metacharacters are interpreted. For example, if you want to match numeric digits you can use the pattern

```
\d
```

and numeric digits from 0 through 9 will be matched because \d is equivalent to the fairly lengthy pattern

```
(0|1|2|3|4|5|6|7|8|9)
```

which also selects numeric digits. By adding the relevant quantifiers to either of the preceding patterns, any integer value can be matched.

However, if you simply change the case of the pattern to the following, the meaning is changed:

```
\D
```

In fact, it is reversed. The pattern \D matches any character other than the numeric digits 0 through 9.

Continual Evolution in Techniques Supported

Different versions of a programming language or product may provide different types of regular expression functionality. For example, Perl, which was one of the first languages to support regular expressions, has added new functionality to its regular expression support over time. Some of those differences are discussed in the chapters specific to individual programming languages later in this book.

Multiple Solutions for a Single Problem

Frequently, there are multiple regular expression solutions for any particular problem. For example, if you want to specify that a part number in a warehouse parts inventory must begin with an uppercase alphabetic character followed by two numbers, you could use any of the following patterns. The first is pretty lengthy due to using multiple possible options inside parentheses, the options being mutually exclusive:

```
(A|B|C|D|E|F|G|H|I|J|K|L|M|N|O|P|Q|R|S|T|U|V|W|X|Y|Z)\d\d
```

The numeric part of the pattern could use a quantifier for the \d metacharacters:

```
(A|B|C|D|E|F|G|H|I|J|K|L|M|N|O|P|Q|R|S|T|U|V|W|X|Y|Z)\d{2}
```

Or you could use a much more succinct pattern that makes use of a character class, which is much shorter and easier to read:

```
[A-Z]\d{2}
```

The flexibility of regular expression syntax can be useful to experienced users, but to beginners, the fact that such different regular expression patterns will match the same sequences of characters is potentially confusing.

What You Want to Do with a Regular Expression

The right regular expression to use depends on what it is you are trying to do and the source data you are attempting to do it on. It also depends on how well you know the data and how precisely you can define what you want to find.

If, for example, you had a document that you knew contained several URLs, you might not need to use a regular expression at all, but simply a plain-text search, using the characters http as a proxy for all URLs. For example, that approach works well if the World Wide Web Consortium's home page is expressed as http://www.w3.org/ but will fail completely if it happens to be expressed as www.w3.org/. The data determines the matching behavior of a pattern.

If you think that the W3C's home page URL is expressed as either www.w3.org or www.w3c.org but can't remember which it is in a particular document, you could do a single search with this regular expression pattern:

```
\.w3c?\.org
```

This would match the literal period character in a URL using the metacharacter \. followed by the literal characters w3, followed optionally by the literal character c, followed by the literal period identified by the \. Metacharacter, followed by the literal characters org.

Metacharacters are discussed in detail in Chapter 4, where there are many examples of how they are used in regular expressions.

The Languages That Support Regular Expressions

There is a huge range of tools and languages that support regular expressions, ranging from text editors through word processors to scripting languages and full-featured programming languages. Several of those applications and languages are described in detail later in this book.

To conclude this chapter, take a look at a problem that you might be faced with and for which regular expressions, correctly used, could be very useful.

Replacing Text in Quantity

One use of regular expressions is to replace quantities of text, possibly across many thousands of documents. Things can very easily go wrong if you don't understand what you are doing, as the following simple example shows.

Imagine that you have just joined the fictional Star Training Company as a summer intern. Just before you start with the company, someone decides that Star Training Company should become the equally fictional Moon Training Company, possibly as a result of a recent takeover or change in corporate focus. One result of that name change is that the company's Web site needs to reflect the new naming scheme, and a large number of internal and public documents must be updated, too. Because you are at the bottom of the pecking order, that job is given to you.

On the first day of your internship, you are asked to update Moon Training Company's documents and Web site to show the new name consistently throughout the hundreds of existing company documents.

The first document you open, StarOriginal.doc, looks like this:

```
Star Training Company

Starting from May 1st  Star Training Company is offering a startling special offer
to our regular customers - a 20% discount when 4 or more staff attend a single Star
Training Company course.

In addition, each quarter our star customer will receive a voucher for a free
holiday away from the pressures of the office. Staring at a computer screen all day
might be replaced by starfish and swimming in the Seychelles.

Once this offer has started and you hear about other Star Training customers
enjoying their free  holiday you might feel left out. Don't be left on the outside
staring in. Start right now building your points to allow you to start out on your
very own Star Training holiday.

Reach for the star. Training is valuable in its own right but the possibility of a
free holiday adds a startling new dimension to the benefits of Star Training
training.

Don't stare at that computer screen any longer. Start now with Star. Training is
crucial to your company's well-being. Think Star.
```

It's your first day, and you haven't done anything like this before. So you open the document, open up Search and Replace in your favorite word processor, and elect to replace Star with Moon. You choose Replace All.

And here is the result: StarSimpleReplace.doc. Read the following carefully to see the effect of the chosen find-and-replace strategy.

```
Moon Training Company

Moonting from May 1st Moon Training Company is offering a Moontling special offer
to our regular customers - a 20% discount when 4 or more staff attend a single Moon
Training Company course.

In addition, each quarter our Moon customer will receive a voucher for a free
holiday away from the pressures of the office. Mooning at a computer screen all day
might be replaced by Moonfish and swimming in the Seychelles.

Once this offer has Moonted and you hear about other Moon Training customers
enjoying their free  holiday you might feel left out. Don't be left on the outside
Mooning in. Moont right now building your points to allow you to Moont out on your
very own Moon Training holiday.

Reach for the Moon. Training is valuable in its own right but the possibility of a
free holiday adds a Moontling new dimension to the benefits of Moon Training
training.

Don't Moone at that computer screen any longer. Moont now with Moon. Training is
crucial to your company's well-being. Think Moon.
```

As you can see from the resulting text, quite a few things have gone wrong. While you have replaced every occurrence of the word `Star` in the original document, lots of undesired changes have also occurred. The first sentence shouldn't start `Moonting from May 1st`. There are several other problems in the document, too, including the creation of words that don't exist in English and the inappropriate introduction of uppercase initial letters in the middle of several sentences.

As you progress through the next several chapters, you will look at approaches that will yield better results when applied to the test document `Star.txt`.

Regular Expression Tools and an Approach to Using Them

This chapter takes a preliminary look at many of the tools with which you can use regular expressions. That basic familiarity with the tools will allow for a progressive development of a range of examples over the next several chapters, so that the individual aspects of regular expressions can be demonstrated in examples drawn from several possible usage scenarios.

Many tools that can be used on the Windows platform have at least some support for regular expressions — or, to use a term found in Word and some other programs, *wildcards*. The tools described in the following sections are discussed in more detail in later chapters of this book.

The second part of the chapter takes you step by step through a pretty rigorous approach to using regular expressions. A systematic approach to regular expressions, other than the very simplest ones, can help you ensure that the regular expressions that you create do what you want them to do. It also helps make maintenance of those regular expressions easier and more efficient, particularly when you carefully document the regular expressions that you create.

In this chapter, you will learn the following:

❑   How to use some regular expression tools

❑   How regular expressions are used in some popular programming languages and database management systems

Regular Expression Tools

This section introduces several utilities, tools, and languages with which you can use regular expressions on the Windows platform. Some of the tools mentioned (for example, MySQL) can be used on several platforms, not only on Windows. The brief introductory descriptions in this chapter apply to the behavior of those tools on the Windows platform. Note that different versions of some tools differ a little in their behavior between versions designed for particular platforms.

> In the examples that follow, it is assumed that you have downloaded the sample code for the book and have installed it in the directory C:\BRegExp\Ch02. If you have installed the code in some other location, you will need to make appropriate adjustments to the instructions given.

One of the issues discussed on many occasions in this book is the variation among tools in how they implement regular expressions. These introductory descriptions mention some variations in implementations or nonstandard usages, but fuller descriptions of these differences are found in later chapters.

findstr

The findstr utility is a command-line utility found in several versions of Windows. To run the findstr utility in Windows XP, simply open a command prompt window and type the following at the command-line prompt:

```
findstr /?
```

You should see an image similar to that shown in Figure 2-1.

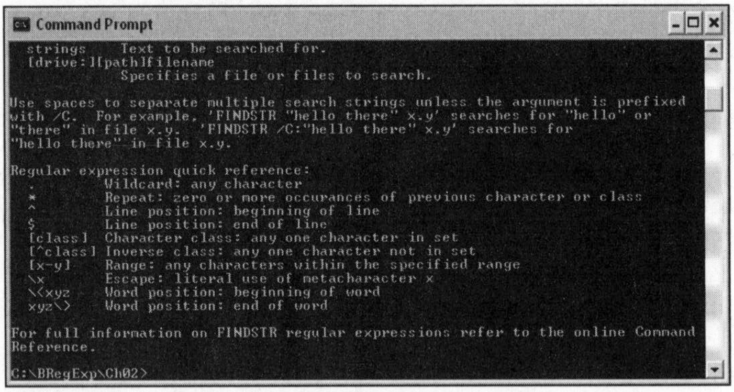

Figure 2-1

If you attempt to type simply findstr at the command line, you will likely receive a bad-command-line error message, because you haven't supplied necessary command-line parameters.

In the C:\BRegExp\Ch02 directory are a couple of test files that you can use. The first is named Test.txt, and its contents are shown here:

```
test
text
tent
teat
```

You can use the findstr utility to locate any line in the same directory that contains the text tent using the following command:

```
findstr /N tent *.*
```

Strictly speaking, the tent on the command line is a regular expression pattern. The /N switch causes the line number to be displayed for each line that contains a match, together with the filename and the matching text. So the result for the preceding command is shown in Figure 2-2.

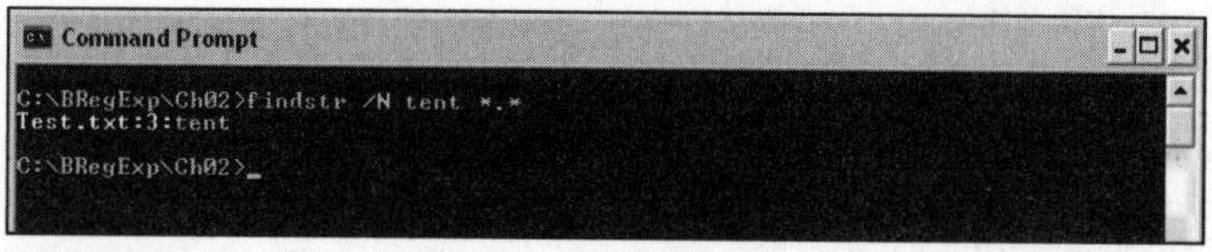

Figure 2-2

As you can see in Figure 2-2, the filename is displayed first, followed by the number of the line that contains a match for the literal regular expression pattern tent, followed by the text contained on the line that has a match for the regular expression pattern tent.

There are some limitations in how you can use regular expressions with the findstr utility. For example, the findstr utility lacks a metacharacter that quantifies a single optional occurrence of a character. For some purposes, the metacharacter that specifies an optional character but allows that character to occur more than once will provide appropriate functionality. At other times, it may allow undesired matches.

The use of regular expressions with the findstr utility is described in more detail in Chapter 13.

Microsoft Word

Microsoft Word provides *wildcards,* which are an incomplete and nonstandard implementation of a few fairly simple pieces of regular expression functionality.

> **Wildcards differ from many regular expression implementations in the range of metacharacters that are supported, for example, but wildcards have the same purpose of attempting to match patterns of characters in text.**

To make use of wildcard functionality in Microsoft Word, use the keyboard shortcut Ctrl+F to open the Find and Replace dialog box. By default, search functionality in Word simply uses literal text for search. Turn on the wildcard functionality by checking the appropriate check box. To access that check box you need to click the More button in the Find and Replace window (see Figure 2-3, which shows its appearance in Word 2003).

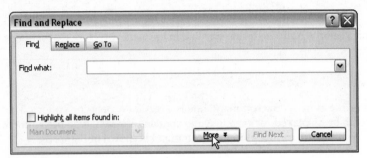

Figure 2-3

Further options are then displayed in the Find and Replace dialog box. To use the wildcard functionality, click the Use Wildcards check box, as shown in Figure 2-4.

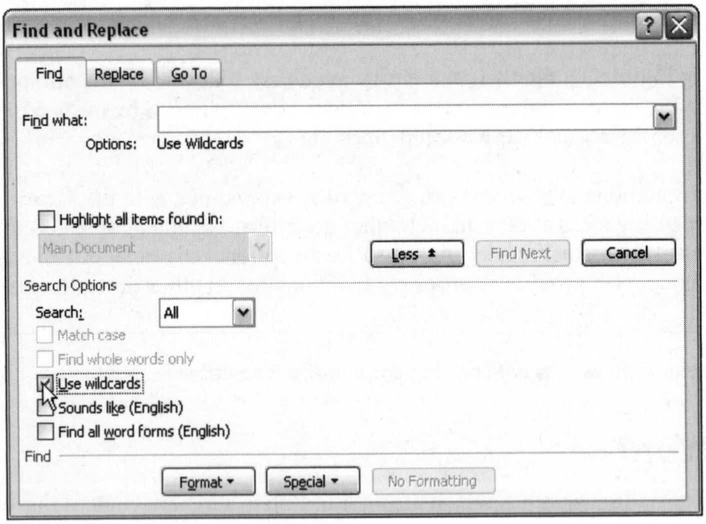

Figure 2-4

For example, you can search for sequences of characters where there is a single different character between words. You might want to find the following words, which are contained in the sample file ight.txt:

```
right

sight

might

light
```

You could find them all in a Microsoft Word document using the following regular expression pattern:

```
?ight
```

The question mark is a nonstandard Word wildcard that stands for a single alphanumeric character.

Word allows only one match to be highlighted at a time. Figure 2-5 shows the result of using the regular expression pattern ?ight to search the document one match at a time. Figure 2-6 shows the match of sight, which is highlighted after you click the Find Next button twice.

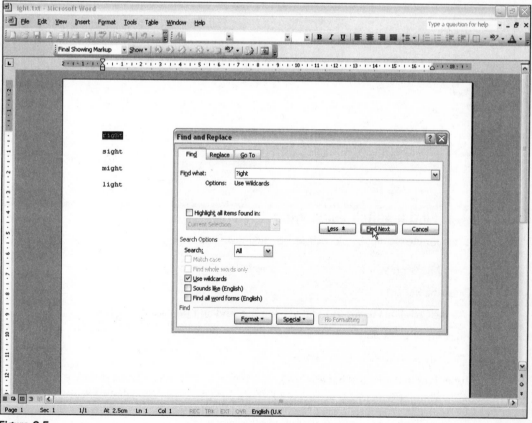

Figure 2-5

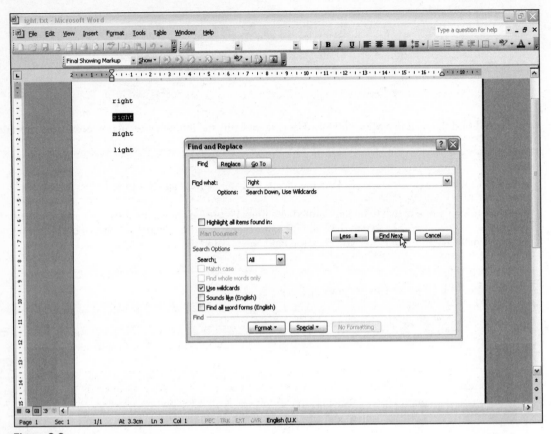

Figure 2-6

Try It Out Find a Match Using Word

To try out this simple example, follow these instructions:

1. Open Microsoft Word.

2. Open the file ight.txt.

3. Use the Ctrl+F keyboard shortcut to open the Find and Replace dialog box

4. Click the More button.

5. Check the Use Wildcards check box.

6. Type **?ight** in the Find What text box.

7. Click the Find Next button to highlight the first match.

8. Click the Find Next button again to find other matches.

Each of the four words in the file ight.txt is matched in turn.

How It Works

The regular expression engine in Word attempts to find matches for the following pattern:

```
?ight
```

The ? metacharacter in Word matches any single alphanumeric character but doesn't match other ASCII characters— for example, the newline character that is also contained in the file ight.txt. If a matching character is found for the ? metacharacter, an attempt is made to match the next character against the pattern i (lowercase i). If there is a match for that, an attempt is made to match the next character against the pattern g (lowercase g). Then an attempt is made to match the next character against the pattern h (lowercase h). If all four attempts at matching have been successful, an attempt is made to match against the pattern t (lowercase t). If all attempts at matching are successful, the match is highlighted in Word (as you saw in Figures 2-5 and 2-6). In this example, the first match is the word right, and that is highlighted after you click the Find Next button for the first time.

When you click the Find Next button a second time, Word attempts to find another match. The next match occurs when the attempt to match is made on the initial s of the word sight and the four characters that follow that s.

Many more wildcard options are available in Microsoft Word. For example, the pattern h?nd would match the sequences of characters hand and hind but would not match hound, because there are two characters between the h and the nd of hound. The ? metacharacter matches exactly one alphanumeric character in Word.

> In most regular expression implementations the ? metacharacter is a quantifier, which specifies that the character or group that it qualifies occurs zero times or one time (meaning that it is optional).

However, another Word wildcard, the asterisk, matches zero or more alphanumeric characters, so the pattern h*nd would match hand, hind, and hound.

The use of regular expressions (wildcards) in Word is described in more detail in Chapter 11.

StarOffice Writer/OpenOffice.org Writer

Regular expressions are supported in OpenOffice.org Writer from version 1.1 and in Sun StarOffice Writer version 6 and above. OpenOffice.org is the official name of an open-source package consisting of word processor, spreadsheet, and presentation packages.

Many of the examples provided in the early parts of this book will show sample documents open in OpenOffice.org Writer, because the regular expressions implementation in OpenOffice.org Writer is standard in many respects, and it provides a convenient and useful way to demonstrate regular expression patterns without assuming that you have knowledge of particular programming languages. OpenOffice.org Writer is a particularly useful teaching tool because its regular expression implementation is mostly standard. It has a significant advantage in that it has an option to display all matches at once for a specified regular expression pattern.

The use of regular expressions in OpenOffice.org is described in more detail in Chapter 12.

Komodo Rx Package

Active State, whose Web site is located at www.ActiveState.com, produces the Komodo developer's editor. One tool in that editor is the Komodo Regular Expressions Toolkit, which allows regular expression patterns to be easily tested against sample sequences of characters.

The Komodo Regular Expressions Toolkit allows the developer to test regular expressions against a test string.

Figure 2-7 shows the Komodo Regular Expressions Toolkit being used to find matches for the pattern .ight. In most regular expression implementations, the period character (also called the dot character) can match a single character (with the exception of newline and similar characters, but even that depends on specific settings in some situations).

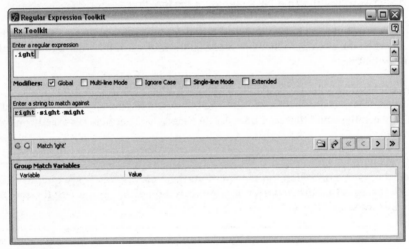

Figure 2-7

Komodo Regular Expressions Toolkit version 2.5 is used in the examples in this chapter and following chapters. Version 3.0 of Komodo is used in Chapter 26.

PowerGrep

PowerGrep is a powerful, flexible, and educational tool because it implements many pieces of regular expression functionality. However, it also allows real-life search-and-replace use of regular expressions that can be targeted using the Folder and File mask, shown in Figure 2-8.

The use of regular expressions in PowerGrep is described in Chapter 14.

Microsoft Excel

Microsoft Excel supports limited use of wildcards. The use of wildcards in Excel is described in Chapter 15.

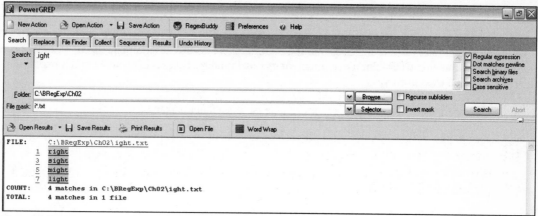

Figure 2-8

Language- and Platform-Specific Tools

The next few sections briefly describe the regular expression support at your disposal in several programming and scripting languages that are available on the Windows platform.

JavaScript and JScript

JavaScript was the original client-side scripting language from Netscape. Officially, we are now expected to refer to ECMAScript, because JavaScript was submitted to ECMA for recognition as an official standard. Support for regular expressions is significantly more complete in JavaScript 1.5 than in JavaScript 1.2.

Support for regular expression functionality is available in the RegExp and String objects.

The use of regular expressions in JavaScript is described in more detail in Chapter 19.

VBScript

Visual Basic Scripting Edition, often referred to simply as VBScript, has similarities to the regular expression support that exists in JScript. However, the object model underlying VBScript isn't the same. Nonetheless, you can use techniques similar to those in JScript in many situations.

The use of regular expressions in VBScript is described in more detail in Chapter 20.

Visual Basic.NET

Regular expression support in Visual Basic .NET makes use of classes in the System.Text.RegularExpressions namespace of the .NET Framework.

The use of regular expressions in Visual Basic .NET is described in more detail in Chapter 21.

C#

C# is a new language, similar to Java, that Microsoft introduced as part of its .NET platform. C#, like VB.NET, makes heavy use of the classes in the `System.Text.RegularExpressions` namespace from the .NET Foundation Class Library for much of its functionality. There is extensive regular expression support in that class library.

The use of regular expressions in C# is described in more detail in Chapter 22.

PHP

PHP (PHP Hypertext Processor) is widely used on Web servers for the processing of data submitted from forms in Web pages. PHP has extensive regular expression support, which is largely standard.

The use of regular expressions in PHP is described in more detail in Chapter 23.

Java

Java is a full-featured, object-oriented programming language developed under the guidance of Sun Microsystems. Like Microsoft's C# language, Java has ancestry in the C language.

Regular expression support in the Java language is focused in the `java.util.regex` pattern, which was introduced in Java version 1.4.

The use of regular expressions in Java is described in more detail in Chapter 25.

Perl

Regular expressions were first seriously applied in Perl in part because Perl was designed as a text manipulation language. Any programming language that is targeted at text processing will almost certainly have a significant need for regular expression functionality.

The range of regular expression support in Perl is enormous, often with several ways to achieve the same thing. Because both Perl code and regular expression syntax can be compact and cryptic, using regular expressions in Perl can be daunting at first for newcomers to the language. However, the power that is there makes the effort to master at least the basics well worthwhile.

The use of regular expressions in Perl is described in more detail in Chapter 26.

MySQL

MySQL is a relational database management system available on Windows and on Unix and Linux.

MySQL supports the SQL LIKE keyword. In addition, it supports a REGEXP keyword, which provides additional options for applying regular expressions.

The use of regular expressions in MySQL is described in more detail in Chapter 17.

SQL Server 2000

Microsoft's SQL Server 2000 is, at the time of this writing, the flagship database management system product from Microsoft. SQL Server 2005 is scheduled to be released a few months after this book is published.

The use of regular expressions in SQL Server is described in more detail in Chapter 16.

W3C XML Schema

W3C XML Schema is a language that specifies the permitted structure of classes of XML documents. The W3C XML Schema element, `xs:pattern`, allows the use of regular expressions to constrain the values allowed in XML documents.

The use of regular expressions in W3C XML Schema is described in more detail in Chapter 24.

An Analytical Approach to Using Regular Expressions

This section explains in some detail an approach that I think can help you considerably in thinking about, designing, and maintaining regular expressions in your code.

The approach shouldn't be applied mechanically. When you are creating simple regular expressions, such a full-featured approach is pretty evidently overkill. In other situations, you won't be able to apply all the suggested components because a language or tool may not, for example, support the desired approach to documentation. However, for anything but pretty simple use of regular expressions, making use of an approach like the one I am about to describe will help you create regular expression patterns that achieve exactly what you want and help make maintenance of those regular expressions significantly easier.

The approach is described in several parts. First, here is a list of the components of the approach that I suggest that you take:

❑   Express and document what you want to do in English.

❑   Consider the data source and its likely contents.

❑   Consider the regular expression options available to you.

❑   Consider sensitivity and specificity.

❑   Create appropriate regular expressions.

❑   Document all but simple regular expressions.

❑   Use whitespace to aid in clear documentation of the regular expression.

❑   Test the results of a regular expression.

If you are planning to use a simple regular expression to carry out a search and replace in Microsoft Word, you almost certainly won't want to bother with such a detailed approach. However, as the complexity of what you are attempting to achieve increases, a systematic approach such as the one just listed becomes increasingly useful.

Let's look at each of the components of the suggested approach.

Express and Document What You Want to Do in English

In almost any type of programming that goes beyond the trivial, a fairly formal expression of the problem to be solved is of great importance. The same principle applies to the use of any but the simplest regular expressions.

Just as planning and developing an application may take several iterations, during which you refine the detail of the application's design, you may need several iterations to get the description of what you want to do correct.

In the Star Training Company example in Chapter 1, the new recruit might have made the following first attempt at defining in English what he wanted to achieve:

Replace every occurrence of Star with Moon.

As you saw in Chapter 1, that simple approach, particularly when the default behavior is that the pattern Star is applied in a case-insensitive way, leads to a mess in the document where the blanket replacement has been carried out. The problem with that simple approach is that there are many undesired matches.

The inappropriate replacements result because the definition of what is to be matched isn't sufficiently precise. The result is a regular expression of low specificity, a problem that is discussed in more detail in Chapter 8.

What is needed is to make the specification of the problem more precise. A second attempt to specify what is desired might be the following:

Replace every occurrence of Star that has an initial uppercase S with Moon.

That removes some of the undesired matches, such as starfish and stare, in the file StarOriginal.doc.

An alternative approach to the problem might be this:

Replace every occurrence of Star, when Star is a word, with Moon.

That is an improvement over the initial problem definition, because undesired matches such as startling and stare are averted.

You can make the problem definition even more precise by combining the last two definitions:

Replace every occurrence of Star with Moon when Star is a word and Star also has an initial letter that is an uppercase S.

You can attempt to make the problem definition even more precise, as follows:

Replace every occurrence of Star with Moon when Star is a word and Star also has an initial letter that is an uppercase S and when Star is also followed by a single space character and the word Training (with an initial uppercase T).

But a definition as precise as this will cause you to miss desired matches. For example, in the file StarOriginal.doc, the match in the sentences.

```
    Start now with Star.
```

and

```
    Think Star.
```

should be matched but won't be.

The definition is now *too* precise. You are losing matches to the regular expression pattern that you want to identify. In that situation, the *sensitivity* of the regular expression isn't what you want.

> *The issues surrounding sensitivity of a regular expression pattern are discussed in more detail in Chapter 8.*

One approach to that inadequate sensitivity is to widen the problem definition a little, as follows:

Replace every occurrence of Star with Moon when Star is a word and Star also has an initial letter that is an uppercase S and when Star is also followed by a period character (a full stop) or is followed by a single space character and the word Training (with an initial uppercase T).

That problem definition, when correctly translated into a regular expression pattern, will match Star pretty precisely and will also cut out many of the undesired matches mentioned earlier. Chapter 8 will look at this problem of balancing specificity and sensitivity in a regular expression. In addition, using the various regular expression techniques that you will learn in Chapters 3 to 7 will allow you to translate the various versions of the problem definition into regular expression patterns that you can test against the sample text.

I hope you have noticed that the basis on which the problem definition was revised was an understanding of the data sources that you want to use and their likely contents.

Consider the Data Source and Its Likely Contents

In the Star Training Company example in Chapter 1, you saw how a failure to consider the data source led to many problems in the document created by using a simplistic search and replace. It was, for example, undesirable to replace startling so that the pseudoword Moontling appeared in the middle of a sentence after the search and replace had been carried out. One of the causes of such inappropriate results is a failure to seriously consider the data source to which a regular expression is to be applied.

For example, when the data source is a structured comma-delimited file you may find that the data has very few variations in its structure. On the other hand, when you have word-processed documents as the data source you will need to think carefully about issues such as different word forms.

A regular expression that matches the sequence of characters `ball` may or may not match the plural form `balls` or the possessive form `ball's`, depending on how the pattern is constructed. Similarly, it may or may not match related words such as `balloon`, `balloons`, and `ballooned`.

In addition, you may have similar words, some of which you want to match while avoiding matching others. In real life, you may also have to consider the issue of whether it is appropriate to spend time trying to match words that are incorrectly spelled.

When validating data entered by a user in a form on a Web page, you will need to consider possible ways the user might enter data. For example, will a user enter the 16 digits of a credit card number with or without spaces? In that situation and others, it makes sense to allow for all reasonable variants that a user might enter and provide additional code to carry out any necessary conversions into the type you desire.

Consider the Regular Expression Options Available

As mentioned in Chapter 1, not every language or application has the same set of regular expression tools available to users or developers. So when faced with a practical problem for which regular expressions might be a suitable solution, you need to consider carefully what regular expression tools are available.

One of the situations where use of regular expressions is limited is when you use regular expressions in Microsoft Word. OpenOffice.org Writer is significantly less limited in regular expression support. Programmer's editors such as ActiveState Komodo, Microsoft Visual Studio, and the Microsoft Visual Basic for Applications Editor all have different levels of regular expression support.

> **Be careful to distinguish the regular expression support in a programmer's editor from the regular expression support in the languages that a programmer's editor may support.**

Frequently, you will be in a situation where the language to be used for a programming project has already been decided, probably for reasons unrelated to the regular expression functionality supported by the language. In that situation, you will quite possibly need to make the best use of the regular expression functionality of the language for the project. However, in some situations you will have more flexibility. For example, it may be possible or desirable to manipulate input files using a language different from the primary language used in the project.

If your task is to manipulate static text files, it is likely that you won't be constrained by the language(s) used by others on the same project. However, be aware of issues such as differences in newline characters (sometimes called *line terminators*), which differ between operating systems. If your regular expression patterns depend on a particular type of newline character, and you are using text files from a different operating system, you may run into unexpected and undesired behavior.

Consider Sensitivity and Specificity

The concepts of sensitivity and specificity are explained in detail in Chapter 8. However, they will be briefly described here.

Suppose that you use a simple regular expression to look for a word such as `ball`; then it will always match.

```
.*
```

Because that regular expression, simply stated, says, "Match zero or more alphanumeric characters," it will match any word or sequence of characters. It has 100 percent sensitivity in that it will always match any occurrence of the word `ball` but essentially 0 percent specificity because it will match a host of undesired words.

Toward the other end of the spectrum, suppose that you want to match all occurrences of all forms of the word `ball`, including the plural form, `balls`, and the possessive form, `ball's`. In that situation, using the following regular expression pattern will match only the singular form `ball` if it is in a context where only whole words are matched.

```
ball
```

Or it may match the first four letters of `balls` and `ball's`, which may not be what you want.

To be able to discuss this topic in detail, you will need to understand more about regular expression syntax so that you can try out various options and show the effect of choices that you might make in designing your regular expression patterns.

Create Appropriate Regular Expressions

Once you have given careful thought to precisely what it is you want to do and have studied the data source sufficiently to give you a good understanding of what it contains, you are in a good position to create regular expression patterns appropriate to your needs. There is no magic formula that is appropriate for all situations. Only you, the developer, can decide precisely what you want to match and want not to match. To get the desired results you may need to carry out text manipulation in two steps. However, often you will be able to carry out a match or replace in one step by combining regular expression constructs.

Document All but Simple Regular Expressions

If you are creating regular expression patterns that go beyond simple patterns, I suggest that you seriously consider documenting the regular expression. Why do that? Think about the possible situation in 6 or 12 months' time when you come back to your code, perhaps because it isn't behaving exactly as users expect, and you can't decipher the precise purpose of the regular expression. It's in these situations that the truism that regular expressions can be difficult to decipher becomes very real. The existence of clear and complete documentation can prevent a lot of wasted time and frustration.

Several of the language-specific chapters later in this book will show you how you can document regular expression code. Some languages (for example, Perl) allow you to specify a mode that enables you to include inline comments about your regular expressions. Documenting each component of a regular expression pattern in that way makes it much easier to follow the intentions of the original developer and either spot any flaws in the approach or analysis, or adapt it more easily to an altered business need.

When you are using regular expressions interactively (such as in Microsoft Word or OpenOffice.org Writer), it makes little sense to document a regular expression, in part because typically when you use regular expressions (wildcards) interactively in a word processor, you use fairly simple regular expressions, and in part because a word processor doesn't provide any standard way for you to document the regular expressions you use.

When creating more complicated regular expressions, there are three aspects of the regular expression that I suggest you consider documenting:

❑ What you expect the regular expression to do

❑ What you want to select

❑ What you want not to select

The more complex the problem you are seeking to define and the more complex the regular expression pattern(s) you create, the more likely it is that you will want to take time to document each of these aspects.

Each of these aspects is discussed in the following sections.

Document What You Expect the Regular Expression to Do

Documenting the intention of a regular expression is useful particularly when you are creating a regular expression that is intermediate or higher in complexity. Of course, your perception of what is advanced or complex will change as your experience and skills in writing and interpreting regular expressions increase. You may well find, like many other users of regular expressions, that your intuitive feel for a regular expression and what you intended it to do fall off severely after a few weeks or months. To minimize the effects of that falloff in understanding, it is better to err on the side of too much documentation rather than too little.

How might you document a regular expression? Let's return to the Star Training Company example. Depending on how you iterate through refinement of the problem definition, you may also find that you need to refine the documentation comments you include in your code.

I will make the assumption that for this project, you are working in Visual Basic .NET. A first attempt at documentation might look like this:

```
'Replace Star with Moon
```

At first sight, this seems straightforward but, as you saw in Chapter 1, it is documenting an approach that can result in a messed-up document when it is applied without due attention to refining that initial thought.

Another attempt at defining what ought to be done might be the following:

```
'Replace Star with Moon when it occurs as a whole word but leave Star
'unchanged when it occurs as part of a word.
```

If you iterate through the problem definition several times and choose to create the documentation comments early in that iteration process, be sure to update the documentation comments when you make any changes to the regular expression pattern. If you forget to update the documentation comments, you can end up with documentation comments describing something that you no longer intend to do. And that, in my experience, is one of the few situations where having documentation can be worse than having no documentation at all.

In more formal or more complex situations, you may also want to create paper documentation, as part of the documentation of a project, that describes in detail what the regular expressions were intended to do.

Document What You Want to Match

Express as precisely as you can what patterns of characters you want to match. The more formally you make it your habit to express this notion, the more likely you are to fully understand what it is that you *really* want to do.

Because the effect of a regular expression is to match some sequence of characters, it can be helpful to spell out precisely what sequence(s) of characters it is that you intend to match.

So continuing with the fictional Star Training Company example, you might add these comments to the code:

```
'Match Star each time it occurs as part of Star Training Company
'Match Star when it is standalone but refers to Star Training Company
'for example in phrases like "Star is the best"
'Match any occurrence of the possessive form Star's
```

After you document clearly what your aim is, you are in a better position to create a regular expression pattern that does exactly what you intended it to do.

Document What You Don't Want to Select

This may seem the oddest part of the suggested process because, by definition, the text that you don't want to match is probabl — at first sight, anyway — of least interest to you. However, making mistakes so that you match and change undesired text can give you "moontling" results, as you saw with the Star Training Company example, where the word startling was inappropriately replaced by the sequence of characters Moontling due to a search and replace that wasn't sufficiently specific.

If the new recruit for Star Training Company had taken time to document words that he didn't want to change (such as the following), the result of the search and replace might have been less obviously bad:

```
'Don't match any occurrence of words like start, startling
```

The better you understand your data source and the effects of regular expression patterns that you are considering creating, the more specific you can be in your comments.

Use Whitespace to Aid in Clear Documentation of the Regular Expression

In several languages, such as Perl, you can spread a regular expression over several lines. That allows you to use whitespace intelligently together with comments for each logical component of the regular expression, so that you achieve a much clearer set of comments. Because each part of the regular expression has its own comments, ambiguity is reduced or avoided.

In some other languages (JavaScript is an example), you cannot use whitespace in this way because all JavaScript statements must be written on a single line. When writing complex regular expressions in a language such as JavaScript, I suggest you consider writing a copy of the regular expression pattern as components with explanation on the lines immediately following the regular expression pattern itself.

In the short term, it adds to your tasks, but it can save time because you are forced to make explicit what you are trying to do. Down the road, it can help you or another developer modify the code with a fuller understanding of the original objectives.

By adding comments in that fashion, you gain many of the benefits of the detailed documentation when patterns are split over several lines. The key difference is that in languages such as Perl and Java you can add comments inside the regular expression on live components of a pattern, whereas in JavaScript you are adding comments to a text copy of components of the code, which is treated by the JavaScript interpreter as comments.

Of course, one risk of doing that is that the working copy of the regular expression is different from the componentized documentation copy.

Test the Results of a Regular Expression

When you are working on a single, fairly simple document, you probably don't need to test a regular expression other than interactively. Most of the examples in this book, for practical reasons of space, use short, simplified documents. Depending on what you want to use a regular expression to do, you will probably find that you can often carry out regular expression matching interactively when using the examples from this book. That is no more than a simple form of testing. Does the pattern select what you want and avoid selecting undesired matches? Then use it there and then.

However, that interactive approach doesn't scale. When you are using regular expressions on dozens, hundreds, or perhaps hundreds of thousands of documents or documents that may be many megabytes, you want to be sure that you don't create a mess like the one shown in the Star Training Company example in Chapter 1, but on a much larger scale.

Therefore, it makes a lot of sense to carefully test a complex regular expression on some appropriate test data to make sure that you find all the character sequences that you want to find and that you don't inadvertently change character sequences that you don't want to be changed.

The short sample documents in this book may give you ideas about the kind of test documents you will need to create. But simply copying example documents from this book will very likely not work. You must carefully consider the data that you want to select and possibly also similar data that you want to be sure not to select. Only careful thought about the actual data that you are processing and what changes you want to make will allow you to craft a really useful test document.

If you follow the steps suggested here about how to handle nontrivial regular expression tasks, you should be in good shape to create test documents that are relevant and helpful. Because you should also have a good understanding of the desired text manipulation task, you should be able to take your problem definition and translate that into an appropriate and accurate regular expression pattern to achieve what you want. Testing that regular expression on carefully chosen test data will give you confidence that the large-scale manipulation of textual data will also succeed.

When you are intending to manipulate large amounts of data, always make sure that you have good backups of the data. If you plan the text manipulation task well, everything ought to go smoothly, and you are unlikely to need to make use of the backups. But undoing an incorrectly designed regular expression task that has been carried out on many megabytes of data is not a desirable situation to get yourself into.

Having backups is one thing. Having backups that you know can be used to restore data is another. The only way you can be totally sure that your backups work is to test that they can be read and used to restore a configuration. That should be a routine quality assurance procedure for valuable data. It is too late to find out that your backups don't work at the time when you really need them to rescue you from some disaster, whether caused by badly crafted regular expressions or some other cause.

Simple Regular Expressions

This chapter takes a closer look at some basic aspects of constructing some simple regular expressions. One reason for working through the simple regular expressions examined in this chapter is to reinforce the approach described in Chapter 2 and look at how it can be applied to fairly simple regular expressions.

The examples used are necessarily simple, but by using regular expressions to match fairly simple text patterns, you should become increasingly familiar and comfortable with the use of foundational regular expression constructs that can be used to form part of more complex regular expressions. Later chapters explore additional regular expression constructs and address progressively more complex problems.

One of the issues this chapter explores in some detail is the situation where you want to match occurrences of characters other than those characters simply occurring once.

This chapter looks at the following:

- ❑ How to match single characters
- ❑ How to match optional characters
- ❑ How to match characters that can occur an unbounded number of times, whether the characters of interest are optional or required
- ❑ How to match characters that can occur a specified number of times

First, let's look at the simplest situation: matching single characters.

Matching Single Characters

The simplest regular expression involves matching a single character. If you want to match a single, specified alphabetic character or numeric digit, you simply use a pattern that consists of that character or digit. So, for example, to match the uppercase letter L, you would use the following pattern:

```
L
```

The pattern matches any occurrence of the uppercase L. You have not qualified the pattern in any way to limit matching, so expect it to match any occurrence of uppercase L. Of course, if matching is being carried out in a case-insensitive manner (which is discussed in Chapter 4), both uppercase L and lowercase l will be matched.

Try It Out   Matching a Single Character

You can apply this pattern to the sample document UpperL.txt, which is shown here:

```
Excel had XLM macros. They were replaced by Visual Basic for Applications in later
versions of the spreadsheet software.

CMLIII

Leoni could swim like a fish.

Legal difficulties plagued the Clinton administration. Lewinski was the source of
some of the former president's difficulties.
```

1. Open OpenOffice.org Writer, and open the file UpperL.txt.

2. Use the Ctrl+F keyboard shortcut to open the Find and Replace dialog box, and check the Regular Expressions check box and the Match Case check box in the Options section.

3. Enter the regular expression pattern L in the Search For text box at the top of the Find and Replace dialog box, and click the Find All button.

If all has gone well, each occurrence of an uppercase L should be highlighted.

Figure 3-1 shows the matching of the pattern L in OpenOffice.org Writer against the sample document UpperL.txt. Notice that there are five matches contained in the sequences of characters XLM, CMLIII, Leoni, Legal, and Lewinski.

How It Works

The default behavior of OpenOffice.org Writer is to carry out a case-insensitive match. As you can see in Figure 3-1, I have checked the Match Case check box so that only the same case as specified in the regular expression is matched.

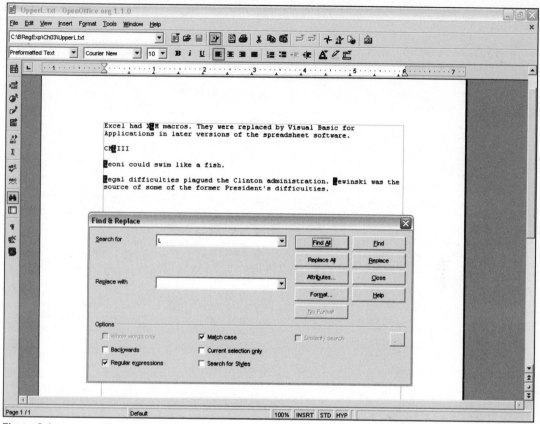

Figure 3-1

For each character in the document, OpenOffice.org Writer checks whether that character is an upper-case L. If it is, the regular expression pattern is matched. In OpenOffice.org Writer, a match is indicated by highlighting of the character(s) — in this case, a single character — for each match, assuming that the Find All button has been clicked.

How can you match a single character using JavaScript?

Try It Out   Matching a Single Character in JavaScript

You want to find all occurrences of uppercase L. You can express the simple task that you want to use regular expressions to do as follows:

Match any occurrence of uppercase L.

You can see, using JavaScript as a sample technology, how most regular expression engines will match the pattern L using the XHTML file UpperL.html, shown here:

```
<html>
<head>
<title>Check for Upper Case L</title>
<script language="javascript" type="text/javascript">
var myRegExp = /L/;

function Validate(entry){
return myRegExp.test(entry);
} // end function Validate()

function ShowPrompt(){
var entry = prompt("This script tests for matches for the regular expression
pattern: " + myRegExp + ".\nType in a string and click on the OK button.", "Type
your text here.");
if (Validate(entry)){
alert("There is a match!\nThe regular expression pattern is: " + myRegExp + ".\n
The string that you entered was: '" + entry + "'.");
} // end if
else{
 alert("There is no match in the string you entered.\n" + "The regular expression
pattern is " + myRegExp + "\n" + "You entered the string: '" + entry + "'." );
} // end else

} // end function ShowPrompt()

</script>
</head>
<body>
<form name="myForm">
<br />
<button type="Button" onclick="ShowPrompt()">Click here to enter text.</button>
</form>
</body>
</html>
```

1.   Navigate in Windows Explorer to the directory that contains the file UpperL.html, and double-click the file. It should open in your default browser.

2.   Click the button labeled Click Here to Enter Text. A prompt window is shown, as you can see in Figure 3-2.

3.   Type a character or a string in the text box that contains the default text *Type your text here*, and the JavaScript code will test whether or not there is a match for the regular expression pattern, in this case L. Click the OK button.

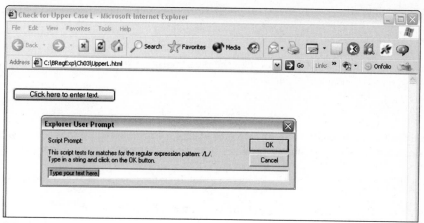

Figure 3-2

4. Inspect the alert box that is displayed to assess whether or not a match is present in the string that you entered. Figure 3-3 shows the message when a successful match is made. Figure 3-4 shows the message displayed when the string that you enter does not match the regular expression pattern.

Figure 3-3

Figure 3-4

How It Works

The simple Web page contains JavaScript code.

The JavaScript variable myRegExp is assigned the literal regular expression pattern L, using the following declaration and assignment statement:

```
var myRegExp = /L/;
```

In JavaScript, the forward slash is used to delimit a regular expression pattern in a way similar to how paired quotes are used to delimit a string. There is an alternate syntax, which is not discussed here.

When you click the button labeled Click Here to Enter Text, the ShowPrompt() function is called.

The entry variable is used to collect the string you enter in the prompt box:

```
var entry = prompt("This script tests for matches for the regular expression
pattern: " + myRegExp + ".\nType in a string and click on the OK button.", "Type
your text here.");
```

The output created depends on whether or not the text you entered contains a match for the regular expression pattern. Once the text has been entered and the OK button clicked, an if statement is executed, which checks whether or not the text you entered (and which is stored in the entry variable) contains a match for the regular expression pattern stored in the variable myRegExp:

```
if (Validate(entry)){
```

The if statement causes the Validate function to be called:

```
function Validate(entry){
return myRegExp.test(entry);
} // end function Validate()
```

The test() method of the myRegExp variable is used to determine whether or not a match is present.

If the if statement:

```
if (Validate(entry))
```

returns the Boolean value true, the following code is executed

```
alert("There is a match!\nThe regular expression pattern is: " + myRegExp + ".\n
The string that you entered was: '" + entry + "'.");
```

and uses the myRegExp and entry variables to display the regular expression pattern and the string that you entered, together with explanatory text.

If there is no match, the following code is executed, because it is contained in the else clause of the if statement:

```
alert("There is no match in the string you entered.\n" + "The regular expression
pattern is " + myRegExp + "\n" + "You entered the string: '" + entry + "'." );
```

Again, the `myRegExp` and `entry` variables are used to give feedback to the user about what is to be matched and the string that he or she entered.

Of course, in practice, you typically want to match a sequence of characters rather than a single character.

Matching Sequences of Characters That Each Occur Once

When the regular expression pattern L was matched, you made use of the default behavior of the regular expression engine, meaning that when there is no indication of how often a character (or sequence of characters) is allowed to occur, the regular expression engine assumes that the character(s) in the pattern occur exactly once, except when you include a quantifier in the regular expression pattern that specifies an occurrence other than exactly once. This behavior also allows the matching of sequences of the same character.

To match two characters that are the same character and occur twice without any intervening characters (including whitespace), you can simply use a pattern with the desired character written twice in the pattern.

Try It Out   Matching Doubled Characters

As an example, look at how you can match sequences of characters where a character occurs exactly twice — for example, the doubled r that can occur in words such as `arrow` and `narrative`.

A problem definition for the desired match can be expressed as follows:

Match any occurrence of the lowercase character r immediately followed by another lowercase r.

An example file, `DoubledR.txt`, is shown here:

```
The arrow flew through the air at great speed.

This is a narrative of great interest to many readers.

Apples and oranges are both types of fruit.

Asses and donkeys are both four-legged mammals.

Several million barrels of oil are produced daily.
```

The following pattern will match all occurrences of rr in the sample file:

```
rr
```

1. Open OpenOffice.org Writer, and open the sample file `DoubledR.txt`.
2. Use the keyboard shortcut Ctrl+F to open the Find and Replace dialog box.
3. Check the Regular Expressions check box and the Match Case check box.
4. Enter the pattern **rr** in the Search For text box, and click the Find All button.

Figure 3-5 shows `DoubledR.txt` opened in OpenOffice.org Writer, as previously described. Notice that all occurrences of `rr` are matched, but single occurrences of `r` are not matched.

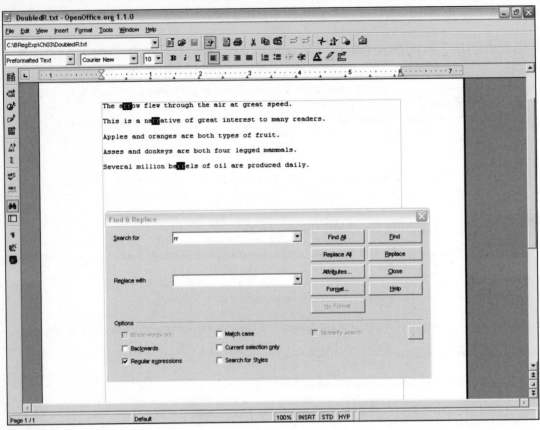

Figure 3-5

How It Works

The pattern `rr` indicates to the regular expression engine that an attempt should be made to match the lowercase alphabetic character `r`; then, if that first match is successful, an attempt should be made to match the next character. The entire match is successful if the second character is also a lowercase `r`.

If the attempt to match the first character fails, the next character is tested to see if it is a lowercase `r`. If it is not a lowercase `r`, the match fails, and a new attempt is made to match the following character against the first `r` of the regular expression pattern.

You can also try this out in the Komodo Regular Expression Toolkit, as shown in Figure 3-6, which matches successive lowercase `m`s. The latest trial version of the Komodo IDE, which includes the Regular Expression Toolkit, can be downloaded from `http://activestate.com/Products/Komodo`. Komodo version 2.5 is used in this chapter. Clear the regular expression and the test text from the Komodo Toolkit. Enter **mammals** in the area for the string to be matched, and type **m** in the area for the regular expression. At that point, the initial m of mammals is matched. Then type a second **m** in the area for the regular expression, and the highlight indicating a match moves to the mm in the middle of mammals, as you can see in Figure 3-6.

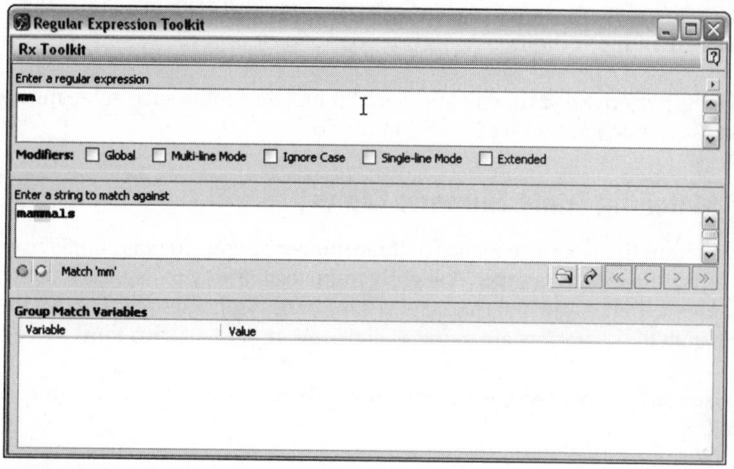

Figure 3-6

These two examples have shown how you can match doubled characters using one of the syntax options that are available. Later in this chapter, you will look at an alternative syntax that can match an exact number of successive occurrences of a desired character, which can be exactly two or can be a larger number. The alternative syntax uses curly braces and, in addition to allowing matches of an exact number of occurrences, allows variable numbers of occurrences to be matched.

Introducing Metacharacters

To match three characters, you can simply write the character three times in a row to form a pattern. For example, to match part numbers that take the form ABC123 (in other words, three alphabetic characters followed by three numeric digits, which will match the alphabetic characters AAA), simply use the following pattern:

```
AAA
```

To match the other part of such part numbers, you need to introduce the concept of a *metacharacter*. The patterns you have seen so far include characters that stand, literally, for the same character. A metacharacter can be a single character or a pair of characters (the first is typically a backslash) that has a meaning other than the literal characters it contains.

There are several ways in which you can match the 123 part of a part number of the form ABC123. One is to write the following:

```
\d\d\d
```

Each \d is a metacharacter that stands for a numeric digit 0 through 9, inclusive. The \d metacharacter does *not* stand for a backslash followed by a lowercase d.

Notice that the \d metacharacter differs significantly in meaning from the literal characters we have used in patterns so far. The character L in a pattern could match only an uppercase L, but the metacharacter \d can match *any* of the numeric digits 0, 1, 2, 3, 4, 5, 6, 7, 8, or 9.

A metacharacter often matches a *class* of characters. In this case, the metacharacter \d matches the class of characters that are numeric digits.

When you have the pattern \d\d\d, you know that it matches three successive numeric digits, but it will match 012, 234, 345, 999 and hundreds of other numbers.

Try It Out   Matching Triple Numeric Digits

Suppose that you want to match a sequence of three numeric digits. In plain English, you might say that you want to match a three-digit number. A slightly more formal way to express what you want to do is this: Match a numeric digit. If the first character is a numeric digit, attempt to match the next character as a numeric digit. If both the characters are numeric digits, attempt to match a third successive numeric digit.

The metacharacter \d matches a single numeric digit; therefore, as described a little earlier, you could use the pattern:

```
\d\d\d
```

to match three successive numeric digits.

If all three matches are successful, a match for the regular expression pattern has been found.

The test file, ABC123.txt, is shown here:

```
ABC123

A234BC

A23BCD4

Part Number DRC22

Part Number XFA221

Part Number RRG417
```

For the moment, let's aim to match only the numeric digits using the pattern \d\d\d shown earlier.

For this example, we will use JavaScript, for reasons that will be explained in a moment.

1. Navigate to the directory that contains the file ABC123.txt and ThreeDigits.html. Open ThreeDigits.html in a Web browser.

2. Click the button labeled Click Here to Enter Text.

3. When the prompt box opens, enter a string to test. Enter a string copied from ABC123.txt.

4. Click the OK button and inspect the alert box to see if the string that you entered contained a match for the pattern \d\d\d.

Figure 3-7 shows the result after entering the string Part Number RRG417.

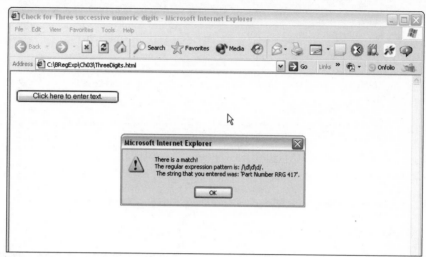

Figure 3-7

Try each of the strings from ABC123.txt. You can also create your own test string. Notice that the pattern \d\d\d will match any sequence of three successive numeric digits, but single numeric digits or pairs of numeric digits are not matched.

How It Works

The regular expression engine looks for a numeric digit. If the first character that it tests is not a numeric digit, it moves one character through the test string and then tests whether that character matches a numeric digit. If not, it moves one character further and tests again.

If a match is found for the first occurrence of \d, the regular expression engine tests if the next character is also a numeric digit. If that matches, a third character is tested to determine if it matches the \d metacharacter for a numeric digit. If three successive characters are each a numeric digit, there is a match for the regular expression pattern \d\d\d.

You can see this matching process in action by using the Komodo Regular Expressions Toolkit. Open the Komodo Regular Expression Toolkit, and clear any existing regular expression and test string. Enter the test string **A234BC**; then, in the area for the regular expression pattern, enter the pattern **\d**. You will see that the first numeric digit, 2, is highlighted as a match. Add a second **\d** to the regular expression area, and you will see that 23 is highlighted as a match. Finally, add a third **\d** to give a final regular expression pattern \d\d\d, and you will see that 234 is highlighted as a match. See Figure 3-8.

You can try this with other test text from ABC123.txt. I suggest that you also try this out with your own test text that includes numeric digits and see which test strings match. You may find that you need to add a space character after the test string for matching to work correctly in the Komodo Regular Expression Toolkit.

Why did we use JavaScript for the preceding example? Because we can't use OpenOffice.org Writer to test matches for the \d metacharacter.

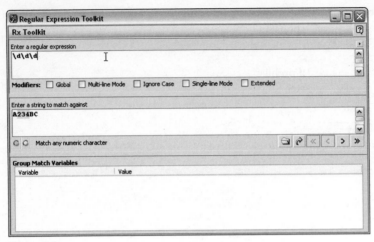

Figure 3-8

Matching numeric digits can pose difficulties. Figure 3-9 shows the result of an attempted match in ABC123.txt when using OpenOffice.org Writer with the pattern \d\d\d.

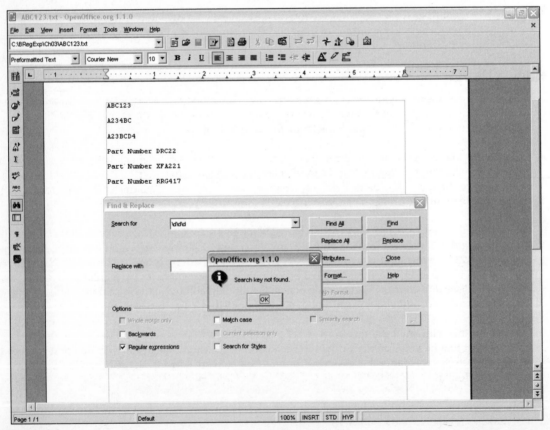

Figure 3-9

As you can see in Figure 3-9, no match is found in OpenOffice.org Writer. Numeric digits in OpenOffice.org Writer use nonstandard syntax in that OpenOffice.org Writer lacks support for the \d metacharacter.

One solution to this type of problem in OpenOffice.org Writer is to use character classes, which are described in detail in Chapter 5. For now, it is sufficient to note that the regular expression pattern:

```
[0-9][0-9][0-9]
```

gives the same results as the pattern \d\d\d, because the meaning of [0-9][0-9][0-9] is the same as \d\d\d. The use of that character class to match three successive numeric digits in the file ABC123.txt is shown in Figure 3-10.

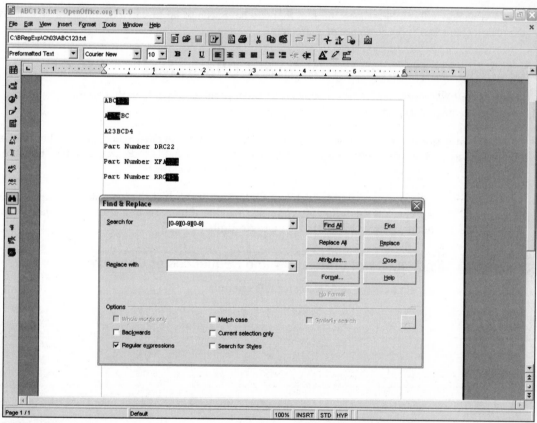

Figure 3-10

Another syntax in OpenOffice.org Writer, which uses POSIX metacharacters, is described in Chapter 12.

The findstr utility also lacks the \d metacharacter, so if you want to use it to find matches, you must use the preceding character class shown in the command line, as follows:

```
findstr /N [0-9][0-9][0-9] ABC123.txt
```

You will find matches on four lines, as shown in Figure 3-11. The preceding command line will work correctly only if the ABC123.txt file is in the current directory. If it is in a different directory, you will need to reflect that in the path for the file that you enter at the command line.

Figure 3-11

The next section will combine the techniques that you have seen so far to find a combination of literally expressed characters and a sequence of characters.

Matching Sequences of Different Characters

A common task in simple regular expressions is to find a combination of literally specified single characters plus a sequence of characters.

There is an almost infinite number of possibilities in terms of characters that you could test. Let's focus on a very simple list of part numbers and look for part numbers with the code DOR followed by three numeric digits. In this case, the regular expression should do the following:

Look for a match for uppercase D. If a match is found, check if the next character matches uppercase O. If that matches, next check if the following character matches uppercase R. If those three matches are present, check if the next three characters are numeric digits.

Try It Out	Finding Literal Characters and Sequences of Characters

The file PartNumbers.txt is the sample file for this example.

BEF123

RRG417

DOR234

DOR123

CCG991

First, try it in OpenOffice.org Writer, remembering that you need to use the regular expression pattern [0-9] instead of \d.

1. Open the file `PartNumbers.txt` in OpenOffice.org Writer, and open the Find and Replace dialog box by pressing Ctrl+F.

2. Check the Regular Expression check box and the Match Case check box.

3. Enter the pattern **DOR[0-9][0-9][0-9]** in the Search For text box, and click the Find All button.

The text DOR234 and DOR123 is highlighted, indicating that those are matches for the regular expression.

How It Works

The regular expression engine first looks for the literal character uppercase D. Each character is examined in turn to determine if there is or is not a match.

If a match is found, the regular expression engine then looks at the next character to determine if the following character is an uppercase O. If that too matches, it looks to see if the third character is an uppercase R. If all three of those characters match, the engine next checks to see if the fourth character is a numeric digit. If so, it checks if the fifth character is a numeric digit. If that too matches, it checks if the sixth character is a numeric digit. If that too matches, the entire regular expression pattern is matched. Each match is displayed in OpenOffice.org Writer as a highlighted sequence of characters.

You can check the `PartNumbers.txt` file for lines that contain a match for the pattern:

```
DOR[0-9][0-9][0-9]
```

using the `findstr` utility from the command line, as follows:

```
findstr /N DOR[0-9][0-9][0-9] PartNumbers.txt
```

As you can see in Figure 3-12, lines containing the same two matching sequences of characters, DOR234 and DOR123, are matched. If the directory that contains the file `PartNumbers.txt` is not the current directory in the command window, you will need to adjust the path to the file accordingly.

Figure 3-12

The Komodo Regular Expression Toolkit can also be used to test the pattern DOR\d\d\d. As you can see in Figure 3-13, the test text DOR123 matches.

Now that you have looked at how to match sequences of characters, each of which occur exactly once, let's move on to look at matching characters that can occur a variable number of times.

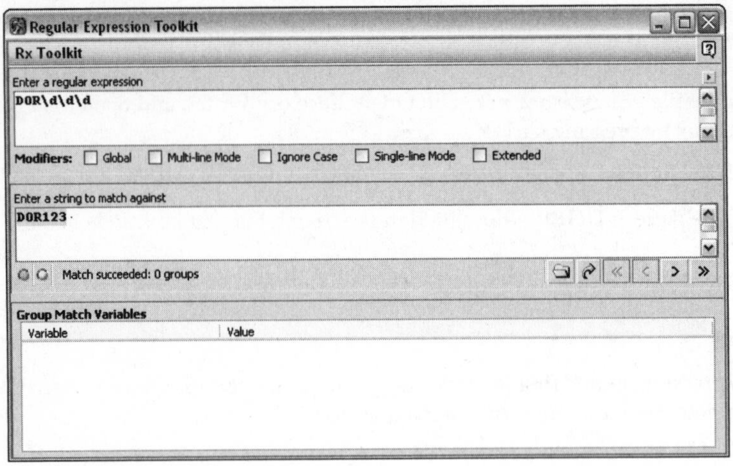

Figure 3-13

Matching Optional Characters

Matching literal characters is straightforward, particularly when you are aiming to match exactly one literal character for each corresponding literal character that you include in a regular expression pattern. The next step up from that basic situation is where a single literal character may occur zero times or one time. In other words, a character is optional. Most regular expression dialects use the question mark (?) character to indicate that the preceding chunk is optional. I am using the term "chunk" loosely here to mean the thing that precedes the question mark. That chunk can be a single character or various, more complex regular expression constructs. For the moment, we will deal with the case of the single, optional character. More complex regular expression constructs, such as groups, are described in Chapter 7.

For example, suppose you are dealing with a group of documents that contain both U.S. English and British English.

You may find that words such as color (in U.S. English) appear as colour (British English) in some documents. You can express a pattern to match both words like this:

```
colou?r
```

You may want to standardize the documents so that all the spellings are U.S. English spellings.

Try It Out   **Matching an Optional Character**

Try this out using the Komodo Regular Expression Toolkit:

1. Open the Komodo Regular Expression Toolkit ,and clear any regular expression pattern or text that may have been retained.

2. Insert the text colour into the area for the text to be matched.

3. Enter the regular expression pattern colou?r into the area for the regular expression pattern. The text colour is matched, as shown in Figure 3-14.

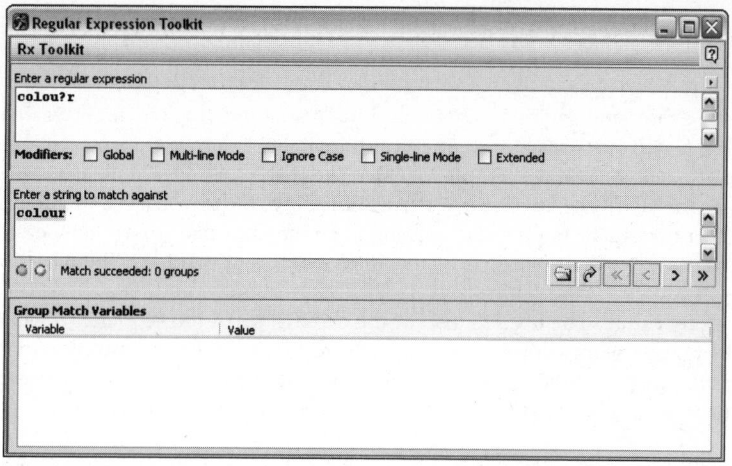

Figure 3-14

Try this regular expression pattern with text such as that shown in the sample file `Colors.txt`:

```
Red is a color.

His collar is too tight or too colouuuurful.

These are bright colours.

These are bright colors.

Calorific is a scientific term.

"Your life is very colorful," she said.
```

How It Works

The word `color` in the line `Red is a color.` will match the pattern `colou?r`.

When the regular expression engine reaches a position just before the `c` of `color`, it attempts to match a lowercase `c`. This match succeeds. It next attempts to match a lowercase `o`. That too matches. It next attempts to match a lowercase `l` and a lowercase `o`. They match as well. It then attempts to match the pattern `u?`, which means zero or one lowercase `u` characters. Because there are exactly zero lowercase `u` characters following the lowercase `o`, there is a match. The pattern `u?` matches zero characters. Finally, it attempts to match the final character in the pattern — that is, the lowercase `r`. Because the next character in the string `color` does match a lowercase `r`, the whole pattern is matched.

There is no match in the line `His collar is too tight or too colouuuurful`. The only possible match might be in the sequence of characters `colouuuurful`. The failure to match occurs when the regular expression engine attempts to match the pattern `u?`. Because the pattern `u?` means "match zero or one lowercase `u` characters," there is a match on the first `u` of `colouuuurful`. After that successful match, the regular expression engine attempts to match the final character of the pattern `colou?r` against the second lowercase `u` in `colouuuurful`. That attempt to match fails, so the attempt to match the whole pattern `colou?r` against the sequence of characters `colouuuurful` also fails.

What happens when the regular expression engine attempts to find a match in the line These are bright colours.?

When the regular expression engine reaches a position just before the c of colours, it attempts to match a lowercase c. That match succeeds. It next attempts to match a lowercase o, a lowercase l, and another lowercase o. These also match. It next attempts to match the pattern u?, which means zero or one lowercase u characters. Because exactly one lowercase u character follows the lowercase o in colours, there is a match. Finally, the regular expression engine attempts to match the final character in the pattern, the lowercase r. Because the next character in the string colours does match a lowercase r, the whole pattern is matched.

The findstr utility can also be used to test for the occurrence of the sequence of characters color and colour, but the regular expression engine in the findstr utility has a limitation in that it lacks a metacharacter to signify an optional character. For many purposes, the * metacharacter, which matches zero, one, or more occurrences of the preceding character, will work successfully.

To look for lines that contain matches for colour and color using the findstr utility, enter the following at the command line:

```
findstr /N colo*r Colors.txt
```

The preceding command line assumes that the file Colors.txt is in the current directory.

Figure 3-15 shows the result from using the findstr utility on Colors.txt.

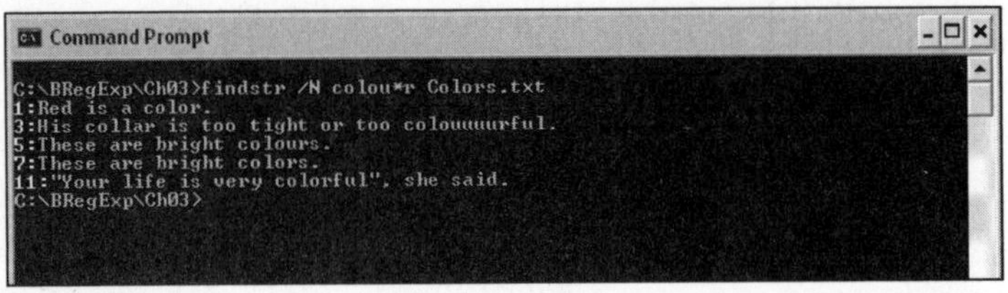

Figure 3-15

Notice that lines that contain the sequences of characters color and colour are successfully matched, whether as whole words or parts of longer words. However, notice, too, that the slightly strange "word" colouuuurful is also matched due to the * metacharacter's allowing multiple occurrences of the lowercase letter u. In most practical situations, such bizarre "words" won't be an issue for you, and the * quantifier will be an appropriate substitute for the ? quantifier when using the findstr utility. In some situations, where you want to match precisely zero or one specific characters, the findstr utility may not provide the functionality that you need, because it would also match a character sequence such as colonifier.

Having seen how we can use a single optional character in a regular expression pattern, let's look at how you can use multiple optional characters in a single regular expression pattern.

Matching Multiple Optional Characters

Many English words have multiple forms. Sometimes, it may be necessary to match all of the forms of a word. Matching all those forms can require using multiple optional characters in a regular expression pattern.

Consider the various forms of the word `color` (U.S. English) and `colour` (British English). They include the following:

```
color (U.S. English, singular noun)

colour (British English, singular noun)

colors (U.S. English, plural noun)

colours (British English, plural noun)

color's (U.S. English, possessive singular)

colour's (British English, possessive singular)

colors' (U.S. English, possessive plural)

colours' (British English, possessive plural)
```

The following regular expression pattern, which include three optional characters, can match all eight of these word forms:

```
colou?r'?s?'?
```

If you tried to express this in a semiformal way, you might have the following problem definition:

Match the U.S. English and British English forms of `color` (`colour`), including the singular noun, the plural noun, and the singular possessive and the plural possessive.

Let's try it out, and then I will explain why it works and what limitations it potentially has.

Try It Out   **Matching Multiple Optional Characters**

Use the sample file `Colors2.txt` to explore this example:

```
These colors are bright.

Some colors feel warm. Other colours feel cold.

A color's temperature can be important in creating reaction to an image.

These colours' temperatures are important in this discussion.

Red is a vivid colour.
```

To test the regular expression, follow these steps:

1. Open OpenOffice.org Writer, and open the file `Colors2.txt`.

2. Use the keyboard shortcut Ctrl+F to open the Find and Replace dialog box.

3. Check the Regular Expressions check box and the Match Case check box.

4. In the Search for text box, enter the regular expression pattern **colou?r'?s?'?**, and click the Find All button. If all has gone well, you should see the matches shown in Figure 3-16.

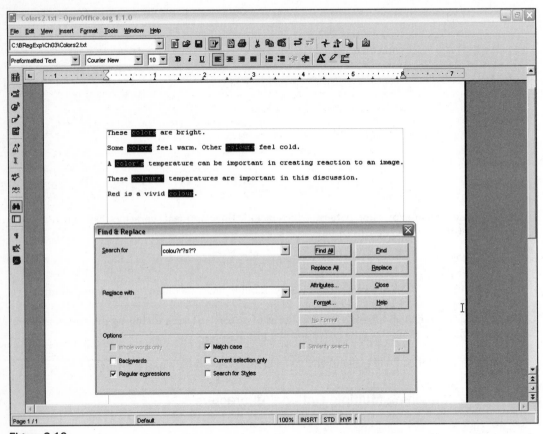

Figure 3-16

As you can see, all the sample forms of the word of interest have been matched.

How It Works

In this description, I will focus initially on matching of the forms of the word `colour/color`.

How does the pattern `colou?r'?s?'?` match the word `color`? Assume that the regular expression engine is at the position immediately before the first letter of `color`. It first attempts to match lowercase c, because one lowercase c must be matched. That matches. Attempts are then made to match a subsequent lowercase o, 1, and o. These all also match. Then an attempt is made to match an optional lowercase u. In other words, zero or one occurrences of the lowercase character u is needed. Because there are zero occurrences of lowercase u, there is a match. Next, an attempt is made to match lowercase r. The lowercase r in `color` matches. Then an attempt is made to match an optional apostrophe. Because there is no occurrence of an apostrophe, there is a match. Next, the regular expression engine attempts to match an optional lowercase s — in other words, to match zero or one occurrence of lowercase s. Because there is no occurrence of lowercase s, again, there is a match. Finally, an attempt is made to match an optional apostrophe. Because there is no occurrence of an apostrophe, another match is found. Because a match exists for all the components of the regular expression pattern, there is a match for the whole regular expression pattern `colour?r'?s'?`.

Now, how does the pattern `colou?r'?s?'?` match the word `colour`? Assume that the regular expression engine is at the position immediately before the first letter of `colour`. It first attempts to match lowercase c, because one lowercase c must be matched. That matches. Next, attempts are made to match a subsequent lowercase o, 1, and another o. These also match. Then an attempt is made to match an optional lowercase u. In other words, zero or one occurrences of the lowercase character u are needed. Because there is one occurrence of lowercase u, there is a match. Next, an attempt is made to match lowercase r. The lowercase r in `colour` matches. Next, the engine attempts to match an optional apostrophe. Because there is no occurrence of an apostrophe, there is a match. Next, the regular expression engine attempts to match an optional lowercase s — in other words, to match zero or one occurrences of lowercase s. Because there is no occurrence of lowercase s, a match exists. Finally, an attempt is made to match an optional apostrophe. Because there is no occurrence of an apostrophe, there is a match. All the components of the regular expression pattern have a match; therefore, the entire regular expression pattern `colour?r'?s?'?` matches.

Work through the other six word forms shown earlier, and you'll find that each of the word forms does, in fact, match the regular expression pattern.

The pattern `colou?r'?s?'?` matches all eight of the word forms that were listed earlier, but will the pattern match the following sequence of characters?

```
colour's'
```

Can you see that it does match? Can you see why it matches the pattern? If each of the three optional characters in the regular expression is present, the preceding sequence of characters matches. That rather odd sequence of characters likely won't exist in your sample document, so the possibility of false matches (reduced specificity) won't be an issue for you.

How can you avoid the problem caused by such odd sequences of characters as `colour's'`? You want to be able to express is something like this:

Match a lowercase c. If a match is present, attempt to match a lowercase o. If that match is present, attempt to match a lowercase 1. If there is a match, attempt to match a lowercase o. If a match exists, attempt to match an optional lowercase u. If there is a match, attempt to match a lowercase r. If there is a match, attempt to match an optional apostrophe. And if a match exists here, attempt to match an optional lowercase s. If the earlier optional apostrophe was not present, attempt to match an optional apostrophe.

With the techniques that you have seen so far, you aren't able to express ideas such as "match something only if it is not preceded by something else." That sort of approach might help achieve higher specificity at the expense of increased complexity. Techniques where matching depends on such issues are presented in Chapter 9.

Other Cardinality Operators

Testing for matches only for optional characters can be very useful, as you saw in the `colors` example, but it would be pretty limiting if that were the only quantifier available to a developer. Most regular expression implementations provide two other cardinality operators (also called *quantifiers*): the * operator and the + operator, which are described in the following sections.

The * Quantifier

The * operator refers to zero or more occurrences of the pattern to which it is related. In other words, a character or group of characters is optional but may occur more than once. Zero occurrences of the chunk that precedes the * quantifier should match. A single occurrence of that chunk should also match. So should two occurrences, three occurrences, and ten occurrences. In principle, an unlimited number of occurrences will also match.

Let's try this out in an example using OpenOffice.org Writer.

Try It Out   Matching Zero or More Occurrences

The sample file, `Parts.txt`, contains a listing of part numbers that have two alphabetic characters followed by zero or more numeric digits. In our simple sample file, the maximum number of numeric digits is three, but because the * quantifier will match three occurrences, we can use it to match the sample part numbers. If there is a good reason why it is important that a maximum of three numeric digits can occur, we can express that notion by using an alternative syntax, which we will look at a little later in this chapter. Each of the part numbers in this example consists of the sequence of uppercase characters ABC followed by zero or more numeric digits:

```
ABC

ABC123

ABC12

ABC889

ABC8899

ABC34
```

We can express what we want to do as follows:

Match an uppercase A. If there is a match, attempt to match an uppercase B. If there is a match, attempt to match an uppercase C. If all three uppercase characters match, attempt to match zero or more numeric digits.

Because all the part numbers begin with the literal characters ABC, you can use the pattern

```
ABC[0-9]*
```

to match part numbers that correspond to the description in the problem definition.

1. Open OpenOffice.org Writer, and open the sample file, `Parts.txt`.

2. Use Ctrl+F to open the Find and Replace dialog box.

3. Check the Regular Expression check box and the Match Case check box.

4. Enter the regular expression pattern **ABC[0-9]*** in the Search For text box.

5. Click the Find All button, and inspect the matches that are highlighted.

Figure 3-17 shows the matches in OpenOffice.org Writer. As you can see, all of the part numbers match the pattern.

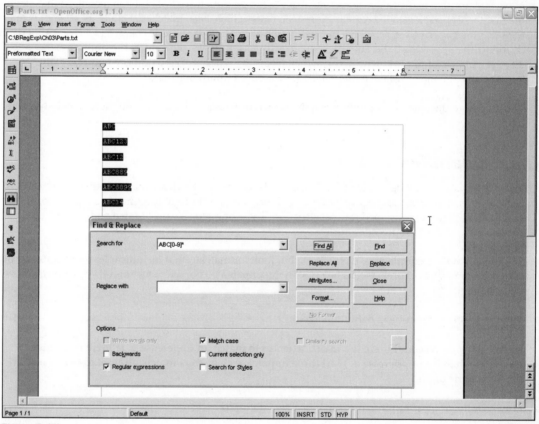

Figure 3-17

How It Works

Before we work through a couple of the matches, let's briefly look at part of the regular expression pattern, `[0-9]*`. The asterisk applies to the character class `[0-9]`, which I call a *chunk*.

Why does the first part number `ABC` match? When the regular expression engine is at the position immediately before the `A` of `ABC`, it attempts to match the next character in the part number with an uppercase

A. Because the first character of the part number ABC is an uppercase A, there is a match. Next, an attempt is made to match an uppercase B. That too matches, as does an attempt to match an uppercase C. At that stage, the first three characters in the regular expression pattern have been matched. Finally, an attempt is made to match the pattern [0-9]*, which means "Match zero or more numeric characters." Because the character after C is a newline character, there are no numeric digits. Because there are exactly zero numeric digits after the uppercase C of ABC, there is a match (of zero numeric digits). Because all components of the pattern match, the whole pattern matches.

Why does the part number ABC8899 also match? When the regular expression engine is at the position immediately before the A of ABC8899, it attempts to match the next character in the part number with an uppercase A. Because the first character of the part number ABC8899 is an uppercase A, there is a match. Next, attempts are made to match an uppercase B and an uppercase C. These too match. At that stage, the first three characters in the regular expression pattern have been matched. Finally, an attempt is made to match the pattern [0-9]*, which means "Match zero or more numeric characters." Four numeric digits follow the uppercase C. Because there are exactly four numeric digits after the uppercase C of ABC, there is a match (of four numeric digits, which meets the criterion "zero or more numeric digits"). Because all components of the pattern match, the whole pattern matches.

Work through the other part numbers step by step, and you'll find that each ought to match the pattern ABC[0-9]*.

The + Quantifier

There are many situations where you will want to be certain that a character or group of characters is present at least once but also allow for the possibility that the character occurs more than once. The + cardinality operator is designed for that situation. The + operator means "Match one or more occurrences of the chunk that precedes me."

Take a look at the example with Parts.txt, but look for matches that include at least one numeric digit. You want to find part numbers that begin with the uppercase characters ABC and then have one or more numeric digits.

You can express the problem definition like this:

Match an uppercase A. If there is a match, attempt to match an uppercase B. If there is a match, attempt to match an uppercase C. If all three uppercase characters match, attempt to match one or more numeric digits.

Use the following pattern to express that problem definition:

```
ABC[0-9]+
```

Try It Out   **Matching One or More Numeric Digits**

1. Open OpenOffice.org Writer, and open the sample file Parts.txt.

2. Use Ctrl+F to open the Find and Replace dialog box.

3. Check the Regular Expressions and Match Case check boxes.

4. Enter the pattern **ABC[0-9]+** in the Search For text box; click the Find All button; and inspect the matching part numbers that are highlighted, as shown in Figure 3-18.

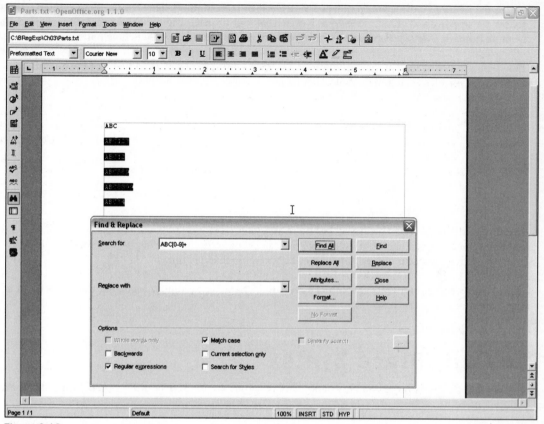

Figure 3-18

As you can see, the only change from the result of using the pattern ABC[0-9]* is that the pattern ABC[0-9]+ fails to match the part number ABC.

How It Works

When the regular expression engine is at the position immediately before the uppercase A of the part number ABC, it attempts to match an uppercase A. That matches. Next, subsequent attempts are made to match an uppercase B and an uppercase C. They too match. At that stage, the first three characters in the regular expression pattern have been matched. Finally, an attempt is made to match the pattern [0-9]+, which means "Match one or more numeric characters." There are zero numeric digits following the uppercase C. Because there are exactly zero numeric digits after the uppercase C of ABC, there is no match (zero numeric digits fails to match the criterion "one or more numeric digits," specified by the + quantifier). Because the final component of the pattern fails to match, the whole pattern fails to match.

Why does the part number ABC8899 match? When the regular expression engine is at the position immediately before the A of ABC8899, it attempts to match the next character in the part number with an uppercase A. Because the first character of the part number ABC8899 is an uppercase A, there is a match. Next, attempts are made to match an uppercase B and an uppercase C. They too match. At that stage, the first three characters in the regular expression pattern have been matched. Finally, an attempt is made to match the pattern [0-9]+, which means "Match one or more numeric characters." Four numeric digits follow the uppercase C of ABC, so there is a match (of four numeric digits, which meets the criterion "one or more numeric digits"). Because all components of the pattern match, the whole pattern matches.

Before moving on to look at the curly-brace quantifier syntax, here's a brief review of the quantifiers already discussed, as listed in the following table:

Quantifier	Definition
?	0 or 1 occurrences
*	0 or more occurrences
+	1 or more occurrences

These quantifiers can often be useful, but there are times when you will want to express ideas such as "Match something that occurs at least twice but can occur an unlimited number of times" or "Match something that can occur at least three times but no more than six times."

You also saw earlier that you can express a repeating character by simply repeating the character in a regular expression pattern.

The Curly-Brace Syntax

If you want to specify large numbers of occurrences, you can use a curly-brace syntax to specify an exact number of occurrences.

The {n} Syntax

Suppose that you want to match part numbers with sequences of characters that have exactly three numeric digits. You can write the pattern as:

```
ABC[0-9][0-9][0-9]
```

by simply repeating the character class for a numeric digit. Alternatively, you can use the curly-brace syntax and write:

```
ABC[0-9]{3}
```

to achieve the same result.

Most regular expression engines support a syntax that can express ideas like that. The syntax uses curly braces to specify minimum and maximum numbers of occurrences.

The {n,m} Syntax

The * operator that was described a little earlier in this chapter effectively means "Match a minimum of zero occurrences and a maximum occurrence, which is unbounded." Similarly, the + quantifier means "Match a minimum of one occurrence and a maximum occurrence, which is unbounded."

Using curly braces and numbers inside them allows the developer to create occurrence quantifiers that cannot be specified when using the ?, *, or + quantifiers.

The following subsections look at three variants that use the curly brace syntax. First, let's look at the syntax that specifies "Match zero or up to [a specified number] of occurrences."

{0,m}

The {0,m} syntax allows you to specify that a minimum of zero occurrences can be matched (specified by the first numeric digit after the opening curly brace) and that a maximum of m occurrences can be matched (specified by the second numeric digit, which is separated from the minimum occurrence indicator by a comma and which precedes the closing curly brace).

To match a minimum of zero occurrences and a maximum of one occurrence, you would use the pattern:

```
{0,1}
```

which has the same meaning as the ? quantifier.

To specify matching of a minimum of zero occurrences and a maximum of three occurrences, you would use the pattern:

```
{0,3}
```

which you couldn't express using the ?, *, or + quantifiers.

Suppose that you want to specify that you want to match the sequence of characters ABC followed by a minimum of zero numeric digits or a maximum of two numeric digits.

You can semiformally express that as the following problem definition:

Match an uppercase A. If there is a match, attempt to match an uppercase B. If there is a match, attempt to match an uppercase C. If all three uppercase characters match, attempt to match a minimum of zero or a maximum of two numeric digits.

The following pattern does what you need:

```
ABC[0-9]{0,2}
```

The ABC simply matches a sequence of the corresponding literal characters. The [0-9] indicates that a numeric digit is to be matched, and the {0,2} is a quantifier that indicates a minimum of zero occurrences of the preceding chunk (which is [0-9], representing a numeric digit) and a maximum of two occurrences of the preceding chunk is to be matched.

Try It Out	Match Zero to Two Occurrences

1. Open OpenOffice.org Writer, and open the sample file `Parts.txt`.

2. Use Ctrl+F to open the Find and Replace dialog box.

3. Check the Regular Expressions and Match Case check boxes.

4. Enter the regular expression pattern **ABC[0-9]{0,2}** in the Search For text box; click the Find All button; and inspect the matches that are displayed in highlighted text, as shown in Figure 3-19.

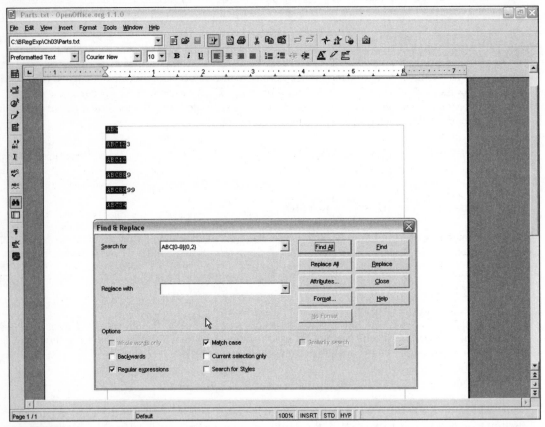

Figure 3-19

Notice that on some lines, only parts of a part number are matched. If you are puzzled as to why that is, refer back to the problem definition. You are to match a specified sequence of characters. You haven't specified that you want to match a part number, simply a sequence of characters.

How It Works

How does it work with the match for the part number ABC? When the regular expression engine is at the position immediately before the uppercase A of the part number ABC, it attempts to match an uppercase A. That matches. Next, an attempt is made to match an uppercase B. That too matches. Next, an attempt is made to match an uppercase C. That too matches. At that stage, the first three characters in the regular expression pattern have been matched. Finally, an attempt is made to match the pattern [0-9]{0,2}, which means "Match a minimum of zero and a maximum of two numeric characters." Zero numeric digits follow the uppercase C in ABC. Because there are exactly zero numeric digits after the uppercase C of ABC, there is a match (zero numeric digits matches the criterion "a minimum of zero numeric digits" specified by the minimum-occurrence specifier of the {0,2} quantifier). Because the final component of the pattern matches, the whole pattern matches.

What happens when matching is attempted on the line that contains the part number ABC8899? Why do the first five characters of the part number ABC8899 match? When the regular expression engine is at the position immediately before the A of ABC8899, it attempts to match the next character in the part number with an uppercase A and finds is a match. Next, an attempt is made to match an uppercase B. That too matches. Then an attempt is made to match an uppercase C, which also matches. At that stage, the first three characters in the regular expression pattern have been matched. Finally, an attempt is made to match the pattern [0-9]{0,2}, which means "Match a minimum of zero and a maximum of two numeric characters." Four numeric digits follow the uppercase C. Only two of those numeric digits are needed for a successful match. Because there are four numeric digits after the uppercase C of ABC, there is a match (of two numeric digits, which meets the criterion "a maximum of two numeric digits"), but the final two numeric digits of ABC8899 are not needed to form a match, so they are not highlighted. Because all components of the pattern match, the whole pattern matches.

{n,m}

The minimum-occurrence specifier in the curly-brace syntax doesn't have to be 0. It can be any number you like, provided it is not larger than the maximum-occurrence specifier.

Let's look for one to three occurrences of a numeric digit. You can specify this in a problem definition as follows:

Match an uppercase A. If there is a match, attempt to match an uppercase B. If there is a match, attempt to match an uppercase C. If all three uppercase characters match, attempt to match a minimum of one and a maximum of three numeric digits.

So if you wanted to match one to three occurrences of a numeric digit in Parts.txt, you would use the following pattern:

```
ABC[0-9]{1,3}
```

Figure 3-20 shows the matches in OpenOffice.org Writer. Notice that the part number ABC does not match, because it has zero numeric digits, and you are looking for matches that have one through three numeric digits. Notice, too, that only the first three numeric digits of ABC8899 form part of the match.

The How It Works explanation in the preceding section for the {0,m} syntax should be sufficient to help you understand what is happening in this example.

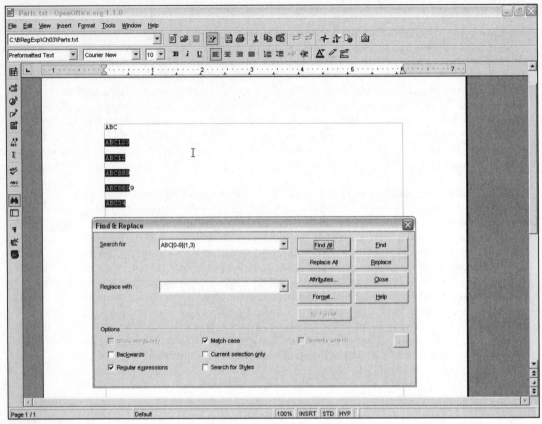

Figure 3-20

{n,}

Sometimes, you will want there to be an unlimited number of occurrences. You can specify an unlimited maximum number of occurrences by omitting the maximum-occurrence specifier inside the curly braces.

To specify at least two occurrences and an unlimited maximum, you could use the following problem definition:

Match an uppercase A. If there is a match, attempt to match an uppercase B. If there is a match, attempt to match an uppercase C. If all three uppercase characters match, attempt to match a minimum of two occurrences and an unlimited maximum occurrences of three numeric digits.

You can express that using the following pattern:

```
ABC[0-9]{2,}
```

Figure 3-21 shows the appearance in OpenOffice.org Writer. Notice that now all four numeric digits in ABC8899 form part of the match, because the maximum occurrences that can form part of a match are unlimited.

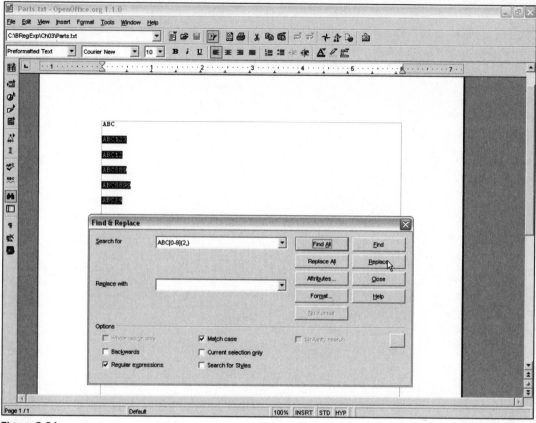

Figure 3-21

Exercises

These exercises allow you to test your understanding of the regular expression syntax covered in this chapter.

1. Using `DoubledR.txt` as a sample file, try out regular expression patterns that match other doubled letters in the file. For example, there are doubled lowercase s, m, and l. Use different syntax options to match exactly two occurrences of a character.

2. Create a regular expression pattern that tests for part numbers that have two alphabetic characters in sequence — uppercase A followed by uppercase B followed by two numeric digits.

3. Modify the file `UpperL.html` so that the regular expression pattern to be matched is `the`. Open the file in a browser, and test various pieces of text against the specified regular expression pattern.

Metacharacters and Modifiers

This chapter moves on to look at several regular expression metacharacters and modifiers. Metacharacters can be combined with literal characters and quantifiers, which were discussed in Chapter 3, to create more complex regular expression patterns. Using metacharacters allows you to release more of the power and flexibility of regular expressions.

A *metacharacter* is a character that is used to convey a meaning other than itself. For example, the period character (also called a *full stop*) is a metacharacter that can signify any alphanumeric character — that is, any uppercase or lowercase character used in English or any alphabetic character used in other languages or any numeric digit 1 through 9. Other regular expression metacharacters allow ASCII alphabetic characters and numeric digits to be specified separately. In addition, there are metacharacters that match whitespace characters, such as the space character, or other invisible characters, such as line feeds.

> This chapter does not attempt to cover all metacharacters. Several metacharacters — such as those that signify the beginning and end of lines (^ and $), the beginning and end of words (\< and \>), and word boundaries (\b) — are described and demonstrated in Chapter 6. The metacharacters considered in Chapter 6 signify *position*. The metacharacters described in this chapter signify *classes* of characters.

A modifier, not surprisingly, modifies how a regular expression is applied. Depending on the language or tool being used, there are modifiers to specify whether a regular expression pattern is to be interpreted in a case-sensitive or case-insensitive way and how lines or paragraphs are to be handled.

The following metacharacters are introduced in this chapter:

- ❑ The . metacharacter
- ❑ The \w and \W metacharacters
- ❑ The \d and \D metacharacters
- ❑ Metacharacters that match whitespace characters, such as the space character

Regular Expression Metacharacters

You saw in Chapter 3 how literal characters can be combined with quantifiers to create useful but fairly simple regular expression patterns. However, literal characters are pretty restrictive in what they match. Sometimes, it is desirable or necessary to allow more flexible matching. Several metacharacters match a class of characters rather than simply a single literal character. That wider scope can be very useful.

Many of the metacharacters referred to and demonstrated in this chapter consist of two characters. The term metasequence is sometimes used to refer to such pairs of characters that, taken together, convey the meaning of a metacharacter. I use the terms metacharacter and metasequence interchangeably.

For example, consider a parts inventory, `Inventory.txt`, such as the following:

```
D99C44

A9DC55

CODD29

RT2C23

MNZC55

UVCC83
```

Notice the variability in how the first three characters of the sample part numbers are structured. For example, the first part number has an alphabetic character followed by two numeric digits. However, the second part number has a single alphabetic character followed by a single numeric digit, followed by a single alphabetic character. The techniques you have used previously won't allow you to specify a suitable regular expression pattern, because the structure of a part number is too variable to allow you to easily address the problem using literal characters in a regular expression pattern. The task you want to carry out is to achieve matches to correspond to the following problem definition:

Match part numbers where the fourth character is an uppercase C and the fifth and sixth characters are numeric digits.

If the data is simple, with a relatively small number of options for any individual character, it might be possible to provide a solution using the alternation techniques described in Chapter 7. However, for the purposes of this chapter, assume that the data is so varied that other techniques should be used.

Thinking about Characters and Positions

One of the important basic concepts that you need to grasp is the difference between a character and a position.

To make the distinction between a character and a position clear, look at the following sample text:

```
This is a simple sentence.
```

The first character in the sample text is the uppercase T of This. However, there is a position immediately before the uppercase T. The position is not visible and does not match any of the literal characters discussed in Chapter 3. However, there are metacharacters that match a position, such as the ^ metacharacter, which matches the position immediately before the uppercase T in the sample text. Metacharacters that match positions rather than characters are introduced in detail in Chapter 6.

The second character in the sample text is the lowercase h of This. Between the initial uppercase T and the lowercase h, there is a position. Often, such positions between the letters of a sequence of characters (in other words, positions inside words) are not of specific interest to a developer. However, positions at the beginning of a string, at the end of a string, and at the beginning and end of a sequence of alphabetic characters are often of more interest to developers, which is why there are metacharacters that correspond to such positions. The so-called word-boundary metacharacters (strictly speaking, they match the boundaries of a sequence of alphabetic or alphanumeric characters) match a position between an alphabetic character and a nonalphabetic character. In many situations, those boundaries will correspond to the boundaries of a word. Those metacharacters are introduced in Chapter 6.

Metacharacters that match classes of characters are also very useful, and it is those that this chapter tackles.

The Period (.) Metacharacter

The period is one of the most broadly scoped metacharacters. It can match any alphabetic character, whether lowercase or uppercase, as well as any numeric digit. This can be an advantage, because the . metacharacter will match almost anything, which can be useful if you aren't too concerned about exactly what you match or how many matches you end up with. The disadvantage of the . metacharacter is the same — it will match almost anything. For example, in a search-and-replace operation, replacing the sequence of characters that match the . metacharacter can be very dangerous, with results similar to, but potentially wider in scope than, the replacement of startling by Moontling that you saw in the Star Training Company example in Chapter 1.

Try It Out   The Period (.) Metacharacter

Using the Komodo Regular Expression Toolkit, you can experiment with using the period and then entering alphabetic and numeric characters as test text. Remember that the Komodo Regular Expression Toolkit matches only the first occurrence of any character.

1. Open the Komodo development environment.

2. Click the button for the Komodo Regular Expressions Toolkit, and clear any regular expression and test string in the toolkit.

3. Enter a test string in the Enter a String to Match Against area. The test string is Andrew.

4. Enter a period in the Enter a Regular Expression area of the toolkit, and inspect the result, which is displayed immediately below the Enter a String to Match Against area.

The result in this case is Match succeeded: 0 groups. The concept of groups is discussed in Chapter 7.

The . metacharacter matches any alphabetic character used in English, any numeric digit, whitespace characters such as the space character, and a very large number of alphabetic characters used in languages other than English. Figure 4-1 shows the . metacharacter in the Komodo Regular Expression Toolkit matching an uppercase A.

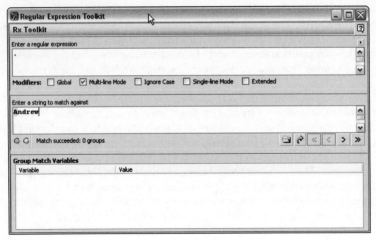

Figure 4-1

How It Works

When the . metacharacter occurs in a regular expression pattern, the regular expression engine attempts to match it against any uppercase or lowercase English alphabetic character or any numeric digit. In addition, a very large number of non–English-language characters will match.

The regular expression engine begins attempting to find a match at the position immediately before the initial A of Andrew. The first character of the test text, A, is tested as a possible match for the . metacharacter. It matches. So the initial A is outlined in pale green, indicating that it is the first match.

The . metacharacter also matches alphabetic characters in languages other than English.

Try It Out   The . Metacharacter Matching Non-English Characters

If you have closed the Komodo Regular Expression Toolkit, follow all of the following steps. If you have kept the toolkit open, start at Step 2.

1. Open the Komodo development environment, and click the button for the Komodo Regular Expressions Toolkit.

2. Clear any regular expression and/or test string in the toolkit.

3. Open the Windows Character Map. In Windows XP, you can do that by selecting Start ⇨ All Programs ⇨ Accessories ⇨ System Tools and, finally, selecting Character Map.

4. Click once on the scroll bar to the right of the Character Map window. Click the uppercase Ω character (omega), and you should see something similar to that shown in Figure 4-2.

5. With the uppercase Ω selected, click the Select button. The Ω character should appear in the Character Map window's Characters to Copy text box.

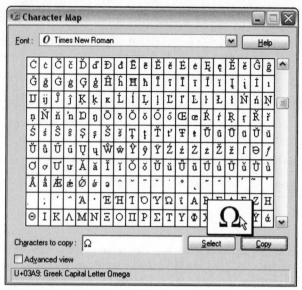

Figure 4-2

6. Click the Copy button in the Character Map window.

7. Enter a test string in the Enter a String to Match Against area of the Komodo Regular Expression Toolkit by clicking in the Enter a String to Match Against area and pressing Ctrl+V to paste. The test string is Ω.

8. Enter a period in the Enter a Regular Expression area of the toolkit, and inspect the result, which is displayed immediately below the Enter a String to Match Against area. Notice, too, that the uppercase omega is highlighted in pale green on-screen, indicating that it is a match for the . metacharacter.

How It Works

The regular expression engine attempts to match the . metacharacter against any character that is not a newline. An attempt at matching begins at the position immediately before the uppercase omega. The first character, the uppercase omega, matches the . metacharacter. Because the uppercase omega is a character that isn't a newline, there is a match. Because the entire regular expression is matched (there is only a single metacharacter on this occasion), matching is complete and successful.

Referring back to Figure 4-2, you can see the . metacharacter matching the Greek uppercase letter omega.

You can also try the . metacharacter with any numeric digit or sequence of numeric digits — for example, 234 — and you will see that the . metacharacter matches any numeric digit from 0 through 9.

Using the . metacharacter with any English text is very straightforward. In most circumstances, it will match anything except a newline. However, the matching characteristics of the . metacharacter can be modified to match a newline. In the Komodo Regular Expression Toolkit, this can be done using the single-line mode.

The . Metacharacter Matching a Newline Character

1. Open the Komodo development environment, and click the button for the Komodo Regular Expressions Toolkit.

2. Clear any regular expression and test string in the toolkit.

3. Check the Global check box and the Single-Line Mode check box.

4. Click in the Enter a String to Match Against area. Press the Return key once. This causes the first character in the test area to be a newline character.

5. Enter the . metacharacter in the Enter a Regular Expression area, and inspect the results.

There is pale green highlighting on the first (newline) character in the test text area. The gray area below the Enter a String to Match Against area should read `Match succeeded: 0 groups`.

How It Works

The regular expression engine matches a newline character, as well as the other characters it normally matches, when the Global and Single-Line Mode check boxes are checked. Modifiers are discussed in more detail later in this chapter. Therefore, when the regular expression engine starts attempts at matching at the position before the initial newline character, the first attempt to match is successful.

Because the period has very broad scope, it risks matching unintended characters, particularly when it is followed by the * or + quantifier, both of which allow unlimited numbers of potentially matching characters. In many situations, a regular expressions engine will match "greedily," meaning that it will match as many characters as possible. Patterns such as .* and .+ can match many paragraphs or pages of text, which may not be what you intend.

Having looked at what the . metacharacter does, let's return to the parts inventory problem briefly touched on at the beginning of this chapter.

Matching Variably Structured Part Numbers

The problem definition is as follows:

Match part numbers where the fourth character is an uppercase C and the fifth and sixth characters are numeric digits.

Whether the . metacharacter is an ideal component of a regular expression pattern depends, in part, on the structure of the data. If the data is as shown in the sample file `Inventory.txt`, you can use the following pattern to satisfy the problem definition

```
...C[0-9][0-9]
```

(three periods followed by an uppercase C, followed by two numeric digits), which is equivalent to the following:

```
.{3}C[0-9][0-9]
```

I have used the character class [0-9] for numeric digits because this example is tested using OpenOffice.org Writer, which does not support the \d metacharacter to match a numeric digit.

Try It Out   **Using the . Metacharacter to Match Inventory**

1.   Open OpenOffice.org Writer, and open the sample file `Inventory.txt`.

2.   Use Ctrl+F to open the Find and Replace dialog box.

3.   Check the Regular Expressions and Match Case check boxes, and enter the pattern **...C[0-9][0-9]** in the Search For text box.

4.   Click the Find All button to display all matches in highlighted text, and inspect the results, as shown in Figure 4-3. Notice that the second part number is not matched.

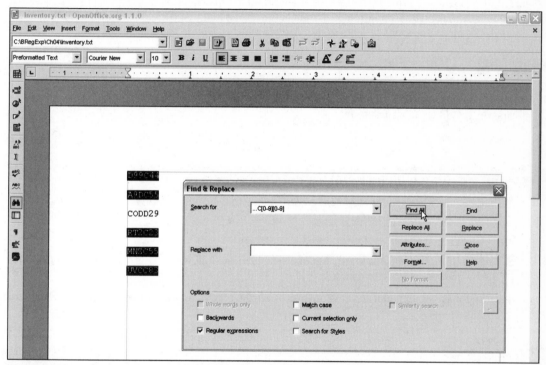

Figure 4-3

How It Works

Look at why the pattern `...C[0-9][0-9]` matches the part number D99C44 but fails to match the part number CODD29. In the descriptions that follow, I refer to part numbers, but strictly speaking, the regular expression engine matches a sequence of characters because it has no knowledge of what is or is not a part number.

Assuming that the regular expression engine is at the position immediately before the initial D of D99C44, it first attempts to match the . metacharacter with the D. That matches. Next, it attempts to match the second . metacharacter. Because the second character of the part number is 9, the . metacharacter matches. Similarly, the third . metacharacter matches the second 9. The fourth character in the regular expression pattern is an uppercase C. That matches the fourth character of the part number, which is C.

# Chapter 4

Next, the regular expression engine attempts to match a numeric digit. Because the first 4 of the sequence of characters D99C44 matches the pattern [0-9], there is a match for the fifth character. Finally, an attempt is made to match the second [0-9], which matches because the sixth character is a numeric digit, 4. Because all components of the regular expression pattern match, the pattern as a whole matches. The text is therefore highlighted in OpenOffice.org Writer.

If the regular expression engine is at the position immediately before the initial A of CODD29, it first attempts to match the first . metacharacter with the initial C of CODD29. That matches. Next, it attempts to match the second . metacharacter with the O of CODD29. That also matches. Then it attempts to match the third . metacharacter with the third character in CODD29. That also matches. Next, it attempts to match the uppercase C with the D of CODD29. That does not match. Because one part of the pattern has failed to match, the whole pattern fails to match. Assuming that you clicked the Find All button, the regular expression engine then attempts to find further matches later in the test document.

Matching a Literal Period

Given the existence of the . metacharacter, you cannot use a period as a literal character in a pattern to selectively match a period in a target document. To match a period in a target document, you must escape the period using a backslash:

```
\.
```

Try It Out   Matching a Literal Period Character

1. Open the Komodo development environment, and click the button to open the Komodo Regular Expression Toolkit.

2. Clear any residual test text and regular expression.

3. In the Enter a String to Match Against area enter the following: **This sentence has a period at the end. We will try to match it.**

4. In the Enter a Regular Expression area, enter the pattern \. and inspect the results, as shown in Figure 4-4.

How It Works

The regular expression engine starts at the position before the uppercase T of This and attempts to match each character in turn against the pattern \.. The first character that matches is the period that follows the word end.

As you have seen, the . metacharacter matches an extremely wide range of characters. The following sections look at metacharacters that allow a little more specificity, examine metacharacters that match only ASCII alphabetic characters (upper- and lowercase A through Z), and that match only numeric digits.

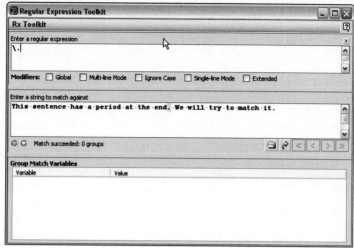

Figure 4-4

The \w Metacharacter

The \w metacharacter matches only characters in the English alphabet, plus numeric digits and the underscore character. Thus, it differs from the . metacharacter because it does not match symbols; punctuation; or, in some implementations, alphabetic characters from languages other than English.

> In some settings, the \w metacharacter is interpreted in the context of Unicode rather than ASCII. In those cases, the matching is wider than described in the preceding paragraph.

Try It Out **Matching Using the \w Metacharacter**

1. Open the Komodo Regular Expression Toolkit, and clear any residual regular expression and test text.

2. In the Enter a String to Match Against area, type **This sentence has a period at the end.**

3. In the Enter a Regular Expression area, enter the regular expression **\w{3}**.

4. Inspect the results in the Enter a String to Match Against area and in the gray area below it. The three characters Thi should be highlighted (in pale green, if you're looking at it on-screen).

   Figure 4-5 shows the results of this step.

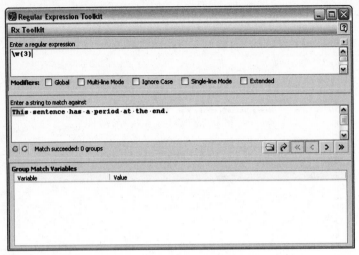

Figure 4-5

How It Works

The pattern \w indicates that an ASCII alphabetic character (upper- or lowercase A through Z or a through z), a numeric digit, or an underscore is to be matched. The quantifier {3} indicates that three successive "word" characters are to be matched.

The regular expression engine starts its attempts at matching at the position before the T of This. It first attempts to match a word character. Because the uppercase T is an alphabetic character, there is a match. It next attempts to find another word character. Because the h of This is an alphabetic character that too matches. Finally, it attempts to match a third word character. Because the i of This is also an alphabetic character, there is a third match. Because all components of the pattern match, the whole pattern matches. The sequence of three word characters Thi is therefore highlighted in pale green.

> The term *word character* used to refer to the characters matched by the \w metacharacter is potentially misleading, because for many people, numeric digits and the underscore character won't be thought of as word characters.

The \W Metacharacter

The \W metacharacter matches characters that are not matched by the \w metacharacter. In other words, the \W metacharacter matches any character other than ASCII alphabetic characters, numeric digits, or the underscore character.

Try It Out   ### Matching Using the \W Metacharacter

1. Open the Komodo Regular Expression Toolkit, and delete any residual regular expression pattern and test text.

2. In the Enter a String to Match Against area, enter the text **This sentence has a period at the end.**

3. In the Enter a Regular Expression area, enter the pattern **\W**.

4. Inspect the results in the Enter a String to Match Against area and in the gray area below it. The expected result is that the space character after `This` and before `sentence` should be highlighted in pale green when viewed on-screen (see Figure 4-6).

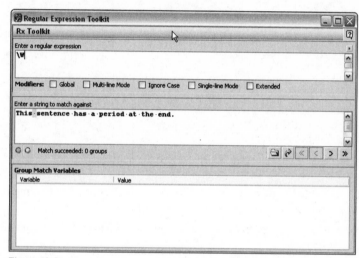

Figure 4-6

How It Works

The regular expression engine starts at the position before the uppercase `T` of `This`. It first attempts to match the uppercase `T` of `This` against the pattern \W. There is no match. It attempts to match each of the remaining characters of `This` in turn, but none of them matches the \W pattern, because each of those characters are "word characters." When the regular expression engine reaches the position after the final `s` of `This`, the match succeeds because the space character that follows is not a word character and therefore matches the \W metasequence. Therefore, the matching character (the space character that follows `This` and precedes `sentence`) is highlighted.

Digits and Nondigits

Many regular expression implementations have characters that signify numeric digits or characters other than numeric digits.

The metacharacter \d is widely used to signify numeric digits. The metacharacter \D is used to signify nondigits in implementations that support the \d metacharacter.

> OpenOffice.org Writer does not support the \d and \D metacharacters and so can't be used to demonstrate these features.

The \d Metacharacter

The \d metacharacter matches one numeric digit 0 through 9.

A sample file, Digits.txt, is shown here:

```
D1
AB8
DE9
7ED
6py
0EC
E3
D2
F4
GHI5
ABC89
```

Try It Out   Matching against the \d Metacharacter

1. Open the Komodo Regular Expressions Toolkit, and clear any residual regular expression and test text.

2. In the Enter a String to Match Against area, enter the first two lines from Digits.txt.

3. In the Enter a Regular Expression area, type the pattern **\d**.

4. Inspect the results in the Enter a String to Match Against area and in the gray area below it. Figure 4-7 shows the appearance expected after this step.

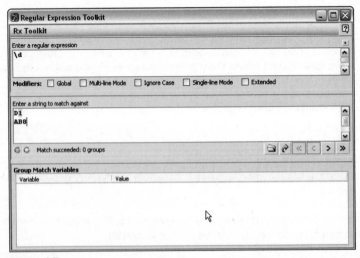

Figure 4-7

How It Works

The \d metacharacter matches a numeric digit. The regular expression engine starts matching at the position before the D of D1. The first character, D, is not a numeric digit, and therefore, there is no match. The regular expression engine moves on to the position after the D and attempts to match the character that follows that position. Because the next character is the numeric digit 1, there is a match.

Canadian Postal Code Example

Canadian postcodes take the form A1A 1A1, with an alphabetic character preceding a numeric digit, which in turn is followed by an alphabetic character. That in turn is followed by a space character (usually one), which is followed by one numeric digit, followed by one alphabetic character, followed by a numeric digit.

To match a Canadian postal code, you can use the following problem definition:

Match an ASCII alphabetic character, followed by a numeric digit, followed by an ASCII alphabetic character, followed by an optional space character, followed by a numeric digit, followed by an ASCII alphabetic character, followed by a numeric digit.

The sample file CanPostcodes.txt has sample sequences of characters, some of which take the format just described, which are consistent with the structure of Canadian postal codes (although the examples in the file are simply character sequences). Not all alphabetic characters are currently used in the first position in a Canadian postal code. Further information is available at www.canadapost.com.

```
T3Z 3N7
D8R 8C4
RR4 88D
P9C 3Q4
V2X 3RU
V5R8S4
M8N 7LK
J1M6U4
S1B 2R9
88B U2L
D7R 7L2
F9Z6G4
```

A careful look at the sample data indicates that some lines have sequences of three alphanumeric characters, followed by a space character, followed by three more alphanumeric characters. Other lines have no space character. So if you are to detect all valid character sequences, you must allow for the optional nature of the space character.

First, let's design a pattern that will match the sequences of characters that omit the space character. You want to match an alphabetic character first, which you can express using the metacharacter \w, followed by a numeric digit, which is matched by the metacharacter \d. If you don't make allowance for the optional existence of a space character, you could use the following pattern:

```
\w\d\w\d\w\d
```

It matches the character, digit, character, digit, character, digit sequence that forms a Canadian postal code.

To allow for an optional space character, you can simply add a space character to the pattern with a ? quantifier, if you assume that only a single space character is possible, or a * quantifier if you assume that optionally, there may be multiple space characters. Assuming that there is no space character or a single space character, you would have the following pattern:

```
\w\d\w ?\d\w\d
```

Try It Out   **Matching Canadian Postcode 1**

1. Open the Komodo Regular Expression Toolkit, and clear any residual regular expression and test text.

2. In the Enter a String to Match Against area, enter the first two lines of CanPostcodes.txt as the test string.

3. In the Enter a Regular Expression area, enter the pattern **\w\d\w ?\d\w\d**.

4. Inspect the results in the Enter a String to Match Against area and in the gray area below it, as shown in Figure 4-8.

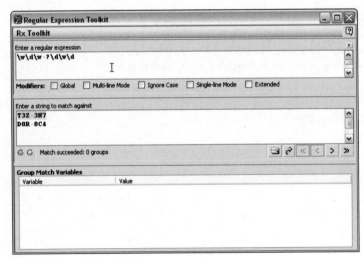

Figure 4-8

How It Works

The text T3Z 3N7 matches. The regular expression engine starts at the position before the uppercase T and attempts to match the character following that position against the first metacharacter, \w. That matches because T is an ASCII alphabetic character. It next attempts to match the \d metacharacter against the numeric digit 3. That too matches. The next attempt is to match the pattern \w against the uppercase character Z. That too matches. Next, an attempt is made to match the pattern ? (a space character followed by the ? quantifier) against a single space character (displayed as a mid dot in the Komodo Regular Expression Toolkit). That matches. Next, it attempts to match the pattern \d against the second numeric digit 3. That too matches. Next, it attempts to match the pattern \w against the uppercase N. Because that is an alphabetic character, there is a match. Finally, it attempts to match the metacharacter \d against the numeric digit 7. Because all components of the regular expression pattern match, the whole pattern matches. The matching text is highlighted in pale green in the Komodo Regular Expression Toolkit.

If you wish to match characters sequences that require at least one space character, you can use the + quantifier, which matches one or more occurrences of the preceding character or group.

Some regular expression implementations (for example, OpenOffice.org Writer) don't support the \w and \d metacharacters and require the use of character classes, which are described in more detail in Chapter 5.

The following character class corresponds to the metacharacter \w:

```
[A-Za-z0-9_]
```

And the following character class corresponds to the metacharacter \d:

```
[0-9]
```

Assume that Canadian postal codes use only uppercase alphabetic characters. Using character classes, the following pattern would give the same results as the previous pattern, except that only uppercase alphabetic characters are matched:

```
[A-Z][0-9][A-Z] ?[0-9][A-Z][0-9]
```

Try It Out Alternative Approach to Canadian Postcodes

1. Open OpenOffice.org Writer, and open the test file CanPostcodes.txt.

2. Use the Ctrl+F keyboard shortcut to open the Find and Replace dialog box.

3. Check the Regular Expressions and Match Case check boxes.

4. Enter the pattern **[A-Z][0-9][A-Z] ?[0-9][A-Z][0-9]** in the Search For text box.

5. Inspect the highlighted text, which indicates matches for the regular expression pattern. Figure 4-9 shows this pattern used in OpenOffice.org Writer on CanPostcodes.txt.

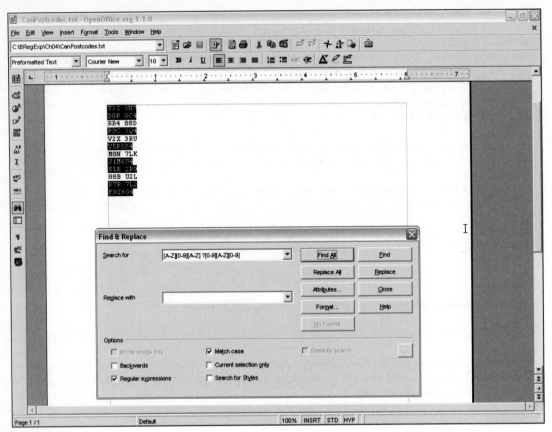

Figure 4-9

How It Works

The text T3Z 3N7 matches. The regular expression engine starts at the position before the uppercase T and attempts to match the character following that position against the first metacharacter, [A-Z]. That matches. It next attempts to match the [0-9] character class metacharacter against the numeric digit 3. That too matches. The next attempt is to match the pattern [A-Z] against the character Z. That too matches. Next, an attempt is made to match the pattern   ? (a space character followed by the ? quantifier) against a single space character. That matches. Next, it attempts to match the pattern [0-9] against the second numeric digit 3. That too matches. Next, it attempts to match the pattern [A-Z] against the uppercase N. Because that is an alphabetic character, there is a match. Finally, it attempts to match the metacharacter [0-9] against the numeric digit 7. Because all components of the regular expression pattern match, the whole pattern matches. The matching text is highlighted in OpenOffice.org Writer.

If you assumed that lowercase alphabetic characters were also allowed, a pattern like this would be required to allow for the possible existence of upper- and lowercase characters:

```
[A-Za-z][0-9][A-Za-z] ?[0-9][A-Za-z][0-9]
```

The \D Metacharacter

The \d metacharacter, as you have seen, matches a numeric digit, 0 through 9. The \D metacharacter matches characters that don't match the \d metacharacter. So the characters that match the \D metacharacter include alphabetic characters (both English-language and non–English-language alphabetic characters) and whitespace characters such as space characters.

Try It Out   The \D Metacharacter

1. Open the Komodo Regular Expression Toolkit, and clear any residual regular expression patterns and test text.

2. Enter sample text **321ABC** in the Enter a String to Match Against area.

3. Enter the regular expression pattern **\D** in the Enter a Regular Expression area.

4. Inspect the results in the area below and within the Enter a String to Match Against area. Below the area, the message `Match succeeded: 0 groups` is expected. Within the area, the A of 321ABC should be highlighted.

    Figure 4-10 shows the result's appearance in the Komodo Regular Expression Toolkit.

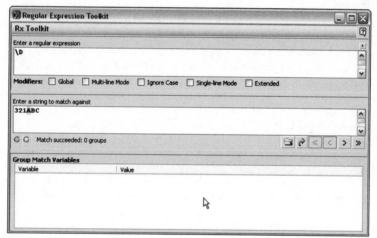

Figure 4-10

5. In the Enter a String to Match Against area, click the mouse between 321 and ABC of 321ABC, and press the spacebar once.

6. Inspect the results in the Enter a String to Match Against area and in the gray area below it. In the former, the space character between the 1 and A of 321ABC should be highlighted in pale green (on-screen). In the latter, the message `Match succeeded: 0 groups` should be displayed.

    Figure 4-11 shows the result.

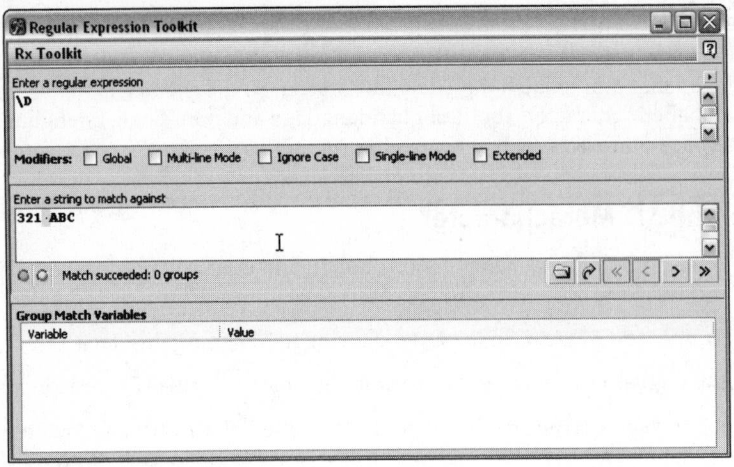

Figure 4-11

How It Works

First, consider what happens when the test text is 321ABC. The regular expression engine starts at the position before the 3 of 321ABC and attempts to find a match. There is no match because the next character, the numeric digit 3, does not match the pattern \D (which matches characters that are not numeric digits). So the regular expression engine moves to the position after the 3 of 321ABC and again attempts to find a match. That too fails. When the regular expression engine moves to the position before the A of 321ABC and attempts a match, it is successful, because uppercase A is not a numeric digit and, therefore, is a match for the \D pattern. As mentioned earlier, in the Komodo Regular Expression Toolkit, matching characters are highlighted in pale green on-screen.

After Step 5, there is a space character between the 1 and A of the test text 321ABC. The regular expression fails to match when the starting position is any of the positions before the position immediately before the space character. When the regular expression engine starts at that latter position the next character, a space character, is not a numeric digit and therefore matches the \D pattern.

Alternatives to \d and \D

The \d metacharacter matches numeric digits 0 through 9. It is possible to match the same digits using other, less succinct regular expression patterns. The techniques to do this involve *alternation*, which is described in Chapter 7, or *character classes*, which are described in Chapter 5. You saw an example of using a character class a little earlier in this chapter. However, a couple of simple examples using alternation are shown here so you can see how to handle the matching of digits or nondigits in implementations that do not support the \d and \D metacharacters.

The \d metacharacter is a succinct way of expressing the notion of "0 or 1 or 2 or 3 or 4 or 5 or 6 or 7 or 8 or 9." That notion can be expressed in a closely corresponding way using the following pattern, where the vertical bar (sometimes called a *pipe*) signifies logical OR:

```
(0|1|2|3|4|5|6|7|8|9)
```

Figure 4-12 shows the use of the preceding pattern in OpenOffice.org Writer, which does not support the \d metacharacter.

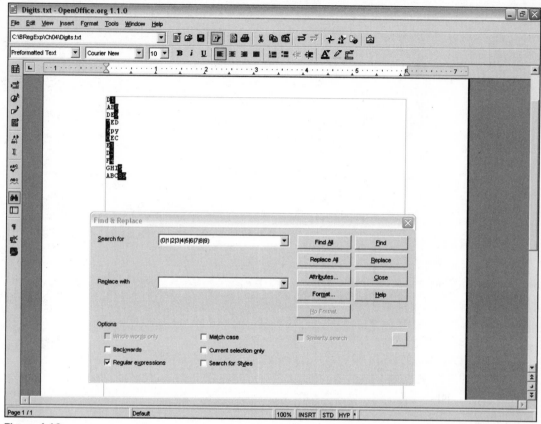

Figure 4-12

A more succinct way to express the same idea is to use a character class, where the start and the end of the character class are expressed using the [and] metacharacters, respectively. To express a character class containing the numeric digits, you could write the following pattern:

```
[0123456789]
```

Or, more succinctly, use a range in a character class, as shown here:

```
[0-9]
```

Figure 4-13 shows the [0-9] character class used to match all numeric digits in the sample file, Digits.txt.

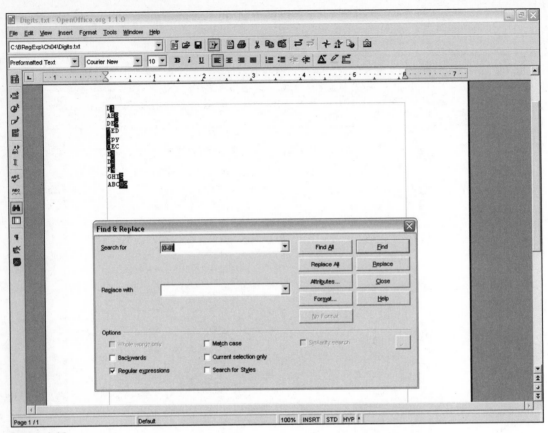

Figure 4-13

Whitespace and Non-Whitespace Metacharacters

Whitespace characters may often occur in significant places in data. For example, in XML it is common to have whitespace inside the start tag of an XML element. Suppose you had a simple XML document that contained data about a person, `Person.xml`:

```
<?xml version='1.0'?>
<Person DateOfBirth="1970/01/12">
 <FirstName>John</FirstName>
 <LastName>Scoliosis</LastName>
</Person>
```

The `DateOfBirth` attribute has a single space character before it; otherwise, the element type name would be incorrectly read as `PersonDateOfBirth`. In addition, after the closing double quote that follows the value of the `DateOfBirth` attribute, there is no whitespace, but the rules of XML allow the use of whitespace such as space characters, tab characters, or any mix of those characters before the right-angled bracket, >. So you cannot assume that there is no whitespace there and should allow for the possibility of whitespace existing.

The rules of XML also allow the use of newline characters inside the start tag of an element. In the file Person2.xml, two newline characters are used to lay out the start tag of the Person element in a potentially more readable way. As far as an XML parser is concerned, this is the same document as Person1.xml, because the logical structure is the same. But as far as a regular expressions engine is concerned, it is different because it contains a different sequence of characters in the start tag of the Person element.

```
<?xml version='1.0'?>
<Person
 DateOfBirth="1970/01/12"
 >
 <FirstName>John</FirstName>
 <LastName>Scoliosis</LastName>
</Person>
```

If you are to be able to use regular expressions to match sequences of characters inside XML documents, you need to allow for such use of whitespace inside start tags and elsewhere in XML documents.

Similar considerations regarding whitespace apply to HTML and XHTML documents.

Many regular expression implementations provide one or more characters, which can match some or all of the likely whitespace characters. First, let's look at the \s metasequence.

The \s Metacharacter

The \s metacharacter is the least specific of the metacharacters that can match any single whitespace character. The \s metacharacter can match a space character, a tab character, or a newline character.

Try It Out   **The \s Metacharacter**

1. Open the Komodo Regular Expressions Toolkit, and clear any residual regular expression and test text.

2. In the Enter a String to Match Against text area, type **ABC**, press the Return key, and then type **DEF**.

3. In the Enter a Regular Expression area, type the pattern \s.

4. Inspect the result in the Enter a String to Match Against area and the gray area below it. Notice that the invisible character (which is a newline character) immediately after the C of ABC is highlighted in pale green on-screen.

   Figure 4-14 shows the expected appearance. At this point, the \s metacharacter matches a newline character.

5. Delete the regular expression and the test text. (The reason for doing so is that sometimes in Komodo version 2.5, the highlighting is misplaced after editing.)

6. In the Enter a String to Match Against area, type the string **ABC DEF** (that is, ABC, then a space character, then DEF).

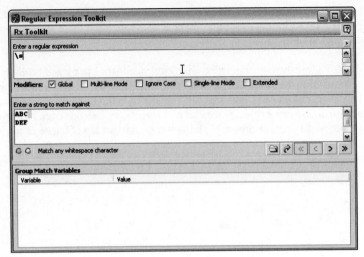

Figure 4-14

7. In the Enter a Regular Expression area, type the pattern \s, and inspect the results.

   Figure 4-15 shows the expected appearance of the result. At this point, the \s metacharacter matches a space character (shown in Komodo Regular Expression Toolkit as a mid dot).

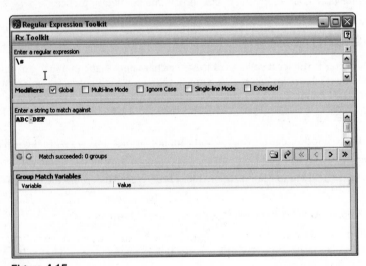

Figure 4-15

It isn't possible to type a tab character in the Enter a String to Match Against area, but it can be pasted into the area.

8. Delete the regular expression and test text.

9. Open Notepad, and type **ABC**, followed by a tab character, followed by **DEF**.

10. Use the Ctrl+A keyboard shortcut to select all the text in Notepad, and use the Ctrl+C keyboard shortcut to copy the selected text.

11. In the Enter a String to Match Against area of the Komodo Regular Expression Toolkit, use the Ctrl+V keyboard shortcut to paste the copied text (including the tab character). In the Komodo Regular Expression Toolkit, the tab character is shown as a right-pointing arrow (which can be seen in Figure 4-16).

12. In the Enter a Regular Expression area, type the regular expression pattern \s, and inspect the results.

Figure 4-16 shows the expected results. Note that the right-pointing arrow (which represents a tab character) between ABC and DEF is highlighted as a match.

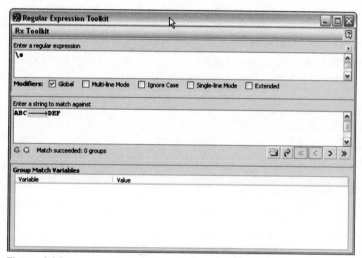

Figure 4-16

How It Works

The \s metacharacter matches any kind of whitespace character.

With the test text specified in Step 2 (which includes a newline character) matching fails until the regular expression engine reaches the position after the C of ABC. At that position, the character that follows is a newline character. That matches the \s metacharacter. The matching character is indicated by pale green highlighting on-screen immediately after the C of ABC.

With the test text specified in Step 6 (which includes a space character), matching fails until the regular expression engine reaches the position after the C of ABC. At that position, the character that follows is a space character. A space character is a match for the \s metacharacter. The matching space character is indicated by pale green highlighting on-screen after the C of ABC.

Handling Optional Whitespace

Matching optional whitespace is a task that is commonly required when dealing with HTML, XHTML, and XML documents.

For the purposes of the following example, assume that only paired double quotation marks are used in the test text to delimit the value of the DateOfBirth attribute (XML syntax also allows paired apostrophes).

Try It Out   **Matching Optional Whitespace**

1. Find the file CheckWhitespace.html in Windows Explorer, and double-click the file to open it in the default browser.

2. Click the Click Here to Enter Text button, and in the alert window that opens, type the test text **<Person DateOfBirth="AnythingGoesHere" >**. Be sure not to have any space characters on either side of the = character.

3. Click the OK button, and inspect the alert window that is displayed. Figure 4-17 shows the expected result after Step 3 using the Firefox browser.

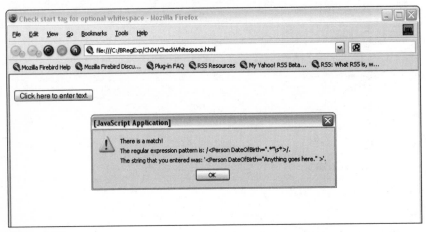

Figure 4-17

How It Works

The test file CheckWhitespace.html is shown here:

```
<html>
<head>
<title>Check start tag for optional whitespace</title>
<script language="javascript" type="text/javascript">
var myRegExp = /<Person DateOfBirth=".*"\s*>/;
```

```
function Validate(entry){
return myRegExp.test(entry);
} // end function Validate()

function ShowPrompt(){
var entry = prompt("This script tests for matches for the regular expression
pattern:\n " + myRegExp + ".\nType in a string and click on the OK button.", "Type
your text here.");
if (Validate(entry)){
alert("There is a match!\nThe regular expression pattern is: " + myRegExp + ".\n
The string that you entered was: '" + entry + "'.");
} // end if
else{
 alert("There is no match in the string you entered.\n" + "The regular expression
pattern is " + myRegExp + "\n" + "You entered the string: '" + entry + "'." );
} // end else

} // end function ShowPrompt()

</script>
</head>
<body>
<form name="myForm">
<br />
<button type="Button" onclick="ShowPrompt()">Click here to enter text.</button>
</form>
</body>
</html>
```

Notice the line where the variable myRegExp is declared:

```
var myRegExp = /<Person DateOfBirth=".*" *>/;
```

Remember that forward slashes are used in JavaScript to delimit a regular expression. So the regular expression pattern to be matched is as follows:

```
<Person DateOfBirth=".*"\s*>
```

Most of the characters in the pattern are literal characters. Notice that the value of the DateOfBirth attribute is to match the pattern .*; in other words, it will match zero or more characters (matching almost anything other than a newline character). After the second of the paired double quotation marks around the value of the DateOfBirth attribute, the pattern is \s* (a whitespace character followed by the asterisk quantifier), meaning a match of zero or more whitespace characters.

Test the regular expression by entering test text several times, using different numbers of spaces before the > character. You won't be able to directly test that the \s metacharacter matches the tab character or newline character. Attempting to enter a tab character will shift the focus away from the line where you enter text. Attempting to enter a newline character is equivalent to clicking the OK button. However, you can paste text containing tab or newline characters into the dialog box.

Using the period metacharacter is acceptable here because you are testing user-entered text. As mentioned earlier, greedy matching can cause problems when using the period metacharacter because it can match many lines or pages of text.

The \S Metacharacter

The \S metacharacter matches any character that is not a whitespace character. Characters from languages other than English will also match the \S metacharacter. The \S metacharacter does not match quite as many characters as the period metacharacter (which matches all characters with the possible exception of the newline character, depending on settings).

The \t Metacharacter

The \t metacharacter matches a tab character.

It is not possible to use the Komodo Regular Expression Toolkit unless you paste in the text containing a tab character, because typing a tab character in the Enter a String to Match Against area causes the focus to move away from that area instead of adding a tab character to the area.

The sample file, Tabs.txt, contains words that are separated from one another by tab characters:

```
Words      separated     by      tabs.

Some       more       tab-separated     words.
```

Try It Out   The \t Metacharacter

1. Open OpenOffice.org Writer, and open the test file Tabs.txt in OpenOffice.org Writer.

2. Press Ctrl+F to open the Search & Replace dialog box, and check the Regular Expressions and Match Case check boxes.

3. Enter the pattern \t in the Search For text box; click the Find All button; and inspect the highlighted text that matches the pattern \t, as shown in Figure 4-18.

How It Works

The regular expression engine begins at the position before the W of Words. Each character is tested in turn to determine whether it matches the \t pattern — in other words, whether it is a tab character. Each tab character in the document is highlighted.

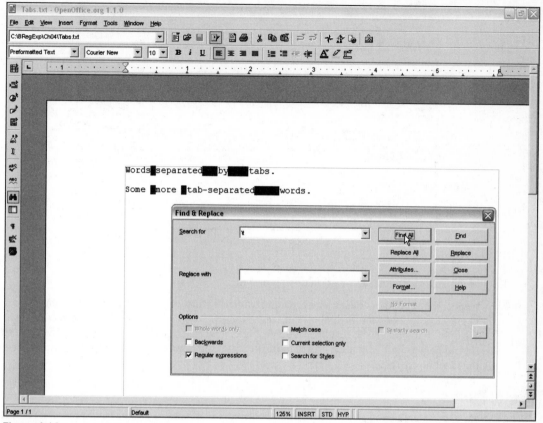

Figure 4-18

The \n Metacharacter

The \n metacharacter matches a newline character — in other words, it matches the character that you add to a text file when you press the Return key.

The \n Metacharacter

1. Open the Komodo Regular Expression Toolkit, and clear any existing regular expression pattern and sample text.

2. In the Enter a String to Match Against area, enter the following test text:

```
Andrew
Watt
```

In other words, type **Andrew**, then press the Return key, then type **Watt**. The text in the Enter a String to Match Against area should look like the text shown in Figure 4-19.

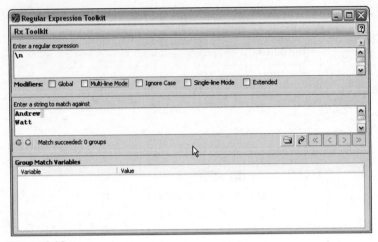

Figure 4-19

3. In the Enter a Regular Expression area, type **\n**.

4. Inspect the area below the Enter a String to Match Against area. The Komodo Regular Expression Toolkit should show Match succeeded: 0 groups. In addition, immediately after the final character on the first line of the test text, a whitespace character (the newline character) should be highlighted in pale green, indicating that the regular expression pattern has matched the newline character.

How It Works

The regular expression engine starts at a position before the A of Andrew and tests whether the character that follows is a newline character. If not, it moves to the position after the tested character and tests the character immediately following that new position. If that character is a newline character, there is a match. As mentioned earlier, in the Komodo Regular Expression Toolkit, a match is indicated by pale green highlighting. Because the newline character is an invisible character (other than the characters that follow it being on a new line), a seemingly blank character is highlighted.

<hr>

Try It Out   **The \n Metacharacter in Visual Studio**

The \n metacharacter is also supported in the Microsoft Visual Studio 2003 editor. If you have a copy of Visual Studio 2003, you can work through the following example:

1. Open Microsoft Visual Studio 2003, and open the Person2.xml test file.

2. Use Ctrl+F to open the Find window, and check the Use check box.

3. In the drop-down list toward the bottom-left corner of the Find window, select the Regular Expressions option.

4. Enter the pattern **\n** in the Find What text box, and click the Find Next button.

5. Inspect the highlighting of the first match. If the cursor was initially at the beginning of the file, the first match for the pattern \n should occur at the end of the first line.

Figure 4-20 shows the appearance in the Visual Studio 2003 editor after following the preceding steps.

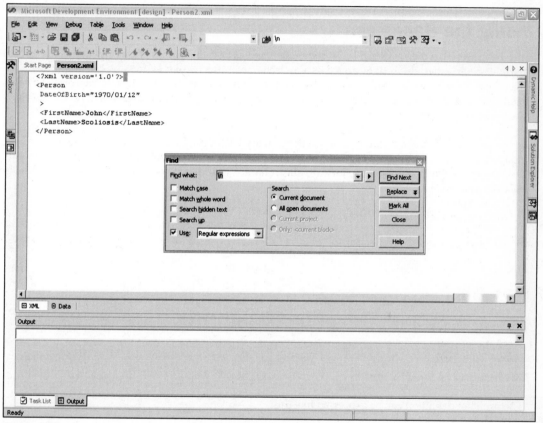

Figure 4-20

How It Works

With the cursor at the beginning of the file Person2.xml, the regular expression engine in Visual Studio 2003 checks each character in turn to see if it matches the pattern \n — in other words, whether it is a newline character. The first matching character is highlighted, as shown at the end of the first line in the sample file.

Escaped Characters

Some characters, such as the . character, must be escaped if you want to use them to match the corresponding literal character. You saw earlier in the chapter the use of the \. metasequence to match a period.

Another character that requires special treatment is the backslash.

Finding the Backslash

You have seen that the backslash (\) is frequently used as part of a pair of characters that *escape* a character that would otherwise be interpreted as a metacharacter in a regular expression pattern, or the backslash is used together with another character to form a character pair, which is interpreted as a metacharacter inside a regular expression pattern. The question, therefore, arises as to how you select the backslash character literally.

Suppose that you have a document that contains many URLs. A URL should contain only forward slash characters (/) and never any backslash characters. The sample document URLS.txt contains several URLs, some of which correctly use forward slash characters and some of which have residual undesired backslash characters:

```
http://www.w3.org/

http://www.amazon.com/

http://www.w3.org\tr/

http://www.XMML.com\default.svg

http://www.wiley.com/

http:\\www.wrox.com/

http://www.example.org/
```

The problem definition can be expressed like this:

Find any backslash character in the file URLS.txt.

Assume that all the URLs that you are interested in begin with the four-character sequence http. What you need to find is any occurrence of the backslash character following that initial sequence of characters.

The following regular expression pattern finds all occurrences of the initial four-character sequence followed by zero or more characters, indicated by the pattern .*, followed by a single backslash, indicated by the pattern \\, followed by zero or more characters, indicated by the pattern .*.

```
http.*\\.*
```

Figure 4-21 shows the result of using that pattern in searching the sample file URLS.txt in OpenOffice.org Writer.

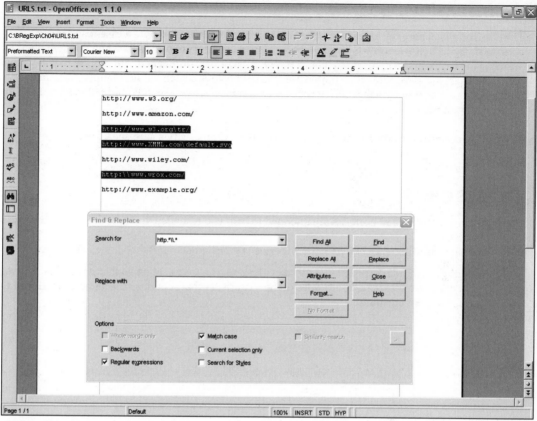

Figure 4-21

Modifiers

Modifiers, as their name suggests, modify how a search is carried out. The description here focuses on the tools that are being used in demonstrating regular expression examples. Similar modifiers are available in the programming languages considered later in this book.

Global Search

The global search modifier determines whether a single match is found or whether all matches should be looked for. When used as part of search-and-replace functionality, the global modifier determines whether one occurrence of the target text is replaced (with the global modifier off) or whether all are (with the global modifier on). Individual programming languages have their own syntax for expressing a global search.

Case-Insensitive Search

The Star Training Company example in Chapter 1 showed a situation where a case-insensitive search produced results that weren't what was wanted. However, there are occasions when you will want to search using a case-insensitive search. For example, a list of part numbers might require that any alphabetic characters in a part number be uppercase. A case-sensitive search would identify part numbers with a lowercase character inappropriately used. A case-insensitive search would fail to identify such malformed part numbers.

In OpenOffice.org Writer, the Match Case check box is used to specify a case-sensitive search.

Exercises

The following questions and exercises are intended to help you test what you have learned in this chapter.

1. What is the difference between the . (period) metacharacter and the \w metacharacter?

2. Modify the regular expression pattern in CheckWhitespace.html so that it will match strings that allow whitespace on both sides of the = character that separates the name and value of the DateOfBirth attribute.

Character Classes

Character classes are used when you want to match any one of a collection of characters. The need for character classes may, for example, occur when you are matching certain parts in a parts catalog or certain names in an employee listing.

Some character classes correspond to widely used collections of characters. For example, the character class [A-Z] corresponds to uppercase ASCII characters, and the character class [0-9] matches a numeric digit.

This chapter looks at the following:

- ❑   How character classes work
- ❑   How to use quantifiers with character classes
- ❑   How to use ranges inside character classes
- ❑   How to use negated character classes

Introduction to Character Classes

A character class is a nonordered grouping of characters from which one character is chosen to provide a match for a regular expression pattern. If none of the characters specified in the character class matches the character currently being matched, the match fails.

The following pattern containing the character class [yi] would match the surnames Smith and Smyth because the third character of each of those sequences of characters is contained in the specified character class.

```
Sm[yi]th
```

When a character class has no associated quantifier, the pattern specifies that exactly one character from the character class is to be matched. So the following pattern would match pear, peer, and peir but would not match per, because there is no match in per for either of the characters contained in the character class:

```
pe[aei]r
```

*The term **character set** is sometimes used to refer to the notion for which I use the term **character class**. The term character class seems to be more widely used and is the one I use consistently in this chapter and elsewhere in this book.*

Examine the following problem definition:

Match an uppercase A, followed by an uppercase B, followed by either the numeric digit 1 or the numeric digit 2, followed by another numeric digit.

To select part numbers AB10 to AB29 given this definition, you could use the following pattern:

```
AB[12][0123456789]
```

The first character class, [12], indicates that the third character in a sequence of characters can be the numeric digit 1 or the numeric digit 2. The character class [0123456789] indicates that the fourth character in a sequence of characters must be a numeric digit, 0 through 9.

The sample data is in the file ABPartNumbers.txt:

```
AB31

AB2D

AB10

AB18

AB44

AB29

AB24
```

Try It Out   Character Class

1. Open OpenOffice.org Writer, and open the test file ABPartNumbers.txt.
2. Use Ctrl+F to open the Find & Replace dialog box.
3. Check the Regular Expressions and Match Case check boxes.
4. Enter the pattern **AB[12][0123456789]** in the Search For text box, and click the Find All button.
5. Inspect the sample text, shown in Figure 5-1, to see which sequences of characters have been highlighted. Notice that neither of the first two sequences of characters is matched.

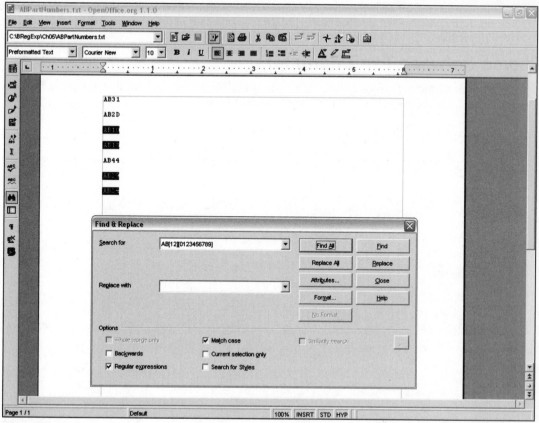

Figure 5-1

How It Works

The regular expression engine begins matching at the position immediately before the A of AB31. It attempts to match the uppercase A in the pattern against the uppercase A in the sample text. There is a match. It next attempts to match the second character in the pattern, uppercase B, against the next character in the sample text, which is an uppercase B. That too matches. Next, it attempts to match the third component of the pattern (which is the character class [12] rather than a single literal character) against the third character of the sequence, the numeric digit 3. There is no match. Because one component of the pattern fails to match, the entire pattern fails to match.

The sequence of characters AB2D also fails to match. The first two characters in the sequence match against the first two characters, AB, in the pattern. The third character in the sequence of characters, 2, matches against the character class [12]. However, the fourth character in the sequence of characters, D, does not match against the character class [0123456789]. Because one component of the pattern fails to match, the entire pattern fails to match.

However, the sequence of characters AB10 does match. The first character in the sequence of characters, A, matches the first character in the pattern, A. The second character in the sequence of characters, B, matches the second character in the pattern, B. The third character of the sequence of characters, the numeric digit 1, matches the third component of the pattern, the character class [12], because the numeric digit 1 is contained in the character class. The fourth character in the sequence of characters, the numeric digit 0, matches because the numeric digit 0 is contained in the character class `[0123456789]`.

Choice between Two Characters

You can use a character class for a choice as simple as that between two characters. However, for that scenario you can just as easily use parentheses to enclose two options.

Parentheses and how they can be used in alternation are described in more detail in Chapter 7.

Suppose that you want to select people in a listing represented by the sample document `People.txt`, shown here:

```
Cardoza, Fred
Catto, Philipa
Duncan, Jean
Edwards, Neil
England, Elizabeth
Main, Robert
Martin, Jane
Meens, Carol
Patrick, Harry
Paul, Jeanine
Roberts, Clementine
Schmidt, Paul
Sells, Simon
Smith, Peter
Stephens, Sheila
Wales, Gareth
Zinni, Hamish
```

Assume that all names are laid out as shown, on separate lines, and that the surname is first, followed by a comma, then a space, then the first name. If you wanted to select people whose surname begins with C or D, you could use the following problem definition:

Match an uppercase C or an uppercase D, followed by any number of successive ASCII lowercase alphabetic characters.

The following pattern could be used to express a solution to the problem definition:

```
[CD][a-z]+
```

However, that pattern is not specific enough. If you use it to test `Roberts,  Clementine` you will find that there is an undesired match in the first name `Clementine`, and you want to match last names. So you need a more specific pattern. In this case, you can simply modify the problem definition to the following:

Match an uppercase C, followed by any number of successive ASCII lowercase alphabetic characters, followed by a comma.

This results in a more specific pattern:

```
[CD][a-z]+,
```

An alternative approach is to use parentheses to express the problem definition with the same results, as shown here:

```
(C|D)[a-z]+,
```

Now try it out.

Try It Out   Selecting Specified Surnames

1. Open OpenOffice.org Writer, and open the test file `People.txt`.

2. Use the Ctrl+F keyboard shortcut to open the Find & Replace dialog box.

3. Check the Regular Expressions and Match Case check boxes.

4. Enter the pattern **[CD][a-z]+,** in the Search For text box, and click the Find All button.

5. Inspect the results. Figure 5-2 selects all three names in `People.txt` where the surname begins with C or D. Notice that with the comma included in the regular expression pattern, the test text `Meens, Carol` and `Roberts, Clementine` does not match.

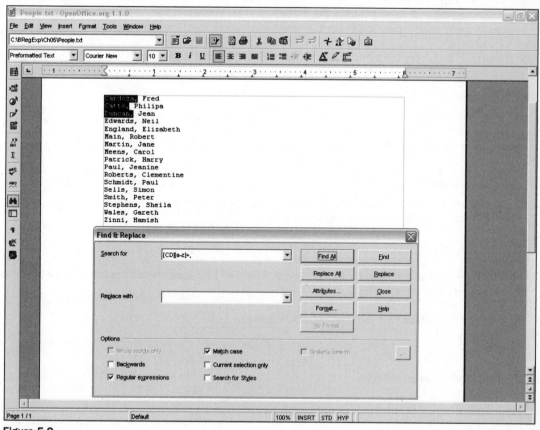

Figure 5-2

6.   Delete the final comma from the regular expression pattern.

7.   Click the Find All button, and inspect the matches. Notice that now, when the final comma is removed, the character sequences Meens, Carol and Roberts, Clementine are matches.

How It Works

When the regular expression engine begins to match, it starts at the position before the initial C of Cardoza, Fred. It attempts to match the first component of the pattern, the character class [CD], against the first character of the test text, an uppercase C. There is a match. Next, it attempts to match the second component of the pattern, the pattern [a-z]+ (meaning one or more lowercase ASCII characters), against the second and subsequent characters of the test text. Each of the characters a, r, d, o, z, and a matches. The final comma does not match the pattern [a-z]+ but does match the final component of the regular expression pattern, which is a literal comma. So there is a match for each of the components of the regular expression. The uppercase C matches [CD], the sequence of lowercase characters ardoza matches [a-z]+, and the final comma in the test text matches the comma in the regular expression pattern.

When the regular expression engine comes to the position before the C or Carol in the test text Meens, Carol, it attempts to match the [CD] character class as before against the uppercase C. That matches. The following test text, arol, matches the pattern [a-z]+. However, there is no match for the final comma in the regular expression pattern, so there is no match for the entire pattern.

A character class is very flexible and can be changed or extended as needed. For example, you could extend the selection to include people whose surname begins with C or D or S by modifying the pattern as follows:

```
[CDS]\w+,
```

Of course, you could also write that using parentheses, as shown here:

```
(C|D|S) \w+,
```

In some situations only a single letter differs in correct spellings of words. One example is the spelling of grey (in British English) and gray (in U.S. English).

The problem definition can be expressed as follows:

Match a lowercase g, followed by a lowercase r, followed by a choice of either lowercase e or lowercase a, followed by lowercase y.

A pattern that expresses that problem definition follows:

```
gr[ae]y
```

It can also be written as follows:

```
gr[ea]y
```

Figure 5-3 shows the use of the former pattern to match the test text grey in Komodo Regular Expression Toolkit.

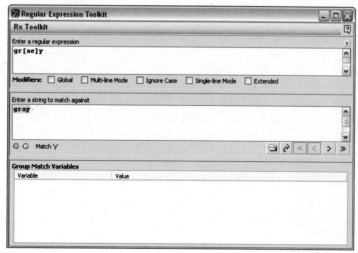

Figure 5-3

The first two characters of the pattern gr[ae]y match the literal characters g and r. The character class [ae] matches the third character of the test text, a lowercase a. The final y of the pattern is matched by the final y of gray.

Using Quantifiers with Character Classes

So far, you have seen how a simple character class can be used when no quantifier is specified. Just like a single character, the absence of a quantifier indicates that a character from the character class can occur exactly once.

However, the ?, *, and + quantifiers and the curly-brace quantifier syntax can be used with a character class just as they are used with a single character.

For example, you could use the {2} quantifier in the following pattern to match against the test text in ABPartNumbers.txt:

```
[AB]{2}[12][0-9]
```

Figure 5-4 shows the results using the Find All button in OpenOffice.org Writer.

As you can see, all sequences of part numbers between AB10 and AB29 in the sample text are matched.

However, using the character class [AB] with the quantifier {2} can cause undesired matches. For example, if the test text contained a part number AA23 or BB19, each of those would match, although they are not desired matches according to the problem definition that was expressed earlier in this chapter.

Think about how it works. If the regular expression engine is at the position before the initial B of BB19, it attempts to match the character class [AB] against the uppercase B. That matches. Next, because of the {2} quantifier, it attempts to match the character class [AB] against the second B. That too matches. Then the character class [12] is matched against the numeric digit 1. That matches. Finally, the character class [0-9] is matched against the numeric digit 9, which matches. Because all components of the pattern have a corresponding match in the test text, the test text matches.

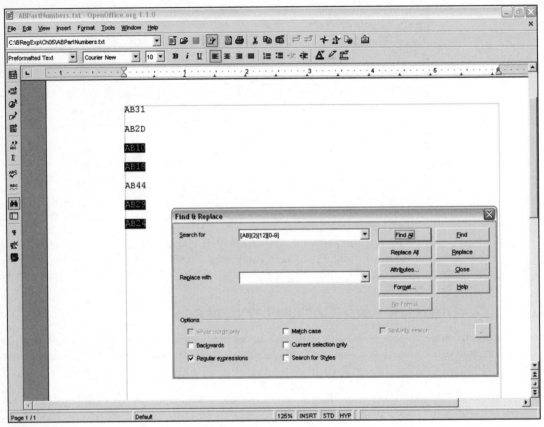

Figure 5-4

Using the \b Metacharacter in Character Classes

One metacharacter, which you will read about in Chapter 6, that has a different meaning inside a character class than it has outside a character class is the \b metacharacter.

Inside a character class the \b metacharacter represents a backspace character. Outside a character class the \b metacharacter signifies a word boundary; at least, it does in several regular expression implementations.

The use of the \b metacharacter outside a character class is described in Chapter 6.

The \b metacharacter isn't the only metacharacter that has one meaning inside a character class and another meaning outside. The hyphen (-) and caret (^) metacharacters have special meanings inside characters, as explored later in this chapter. Inside a character class the $ character simply matches itself. Outside a character class the $ metacharacter matches a position rather than a character, as is discussed in Chapter 6.

Selecting Literal Square Brackets

You have probably realized that if you use the [and] metacharacters to define the boundaries of a character class you cannot at the same time use those characters to select themselves literally. The text file SquareBrackets.txt, shown here, illustrates some situations in which square brackets may occur literally:

```
These are alphabetic characters [A to Z and a to z].

myVariable = myArray[3];

Character[7]

The first five characters in the ASCII character set after uppercase Z are [, \, ],
^, and _.
```

To select either square-bracket character you must *escape* the corresponding literal square-bracket character. Escaping, in this context, simply means preceding the square bracket by a backslash character. So to select the left square-bracket character, [, use the following pattern:

```
\[
```

And use the following to select the right square-bracket character,]:

```
\]
```

Figure 5-5 shows the use, in OpenOffice.org Writer, of the \[pattern to select the left square-bracket character.

> The backslash (\) character can be used to escape most metacharacters. To use the backslash literally you must escape it, too. So the pattern \\ selects a single backslash character.

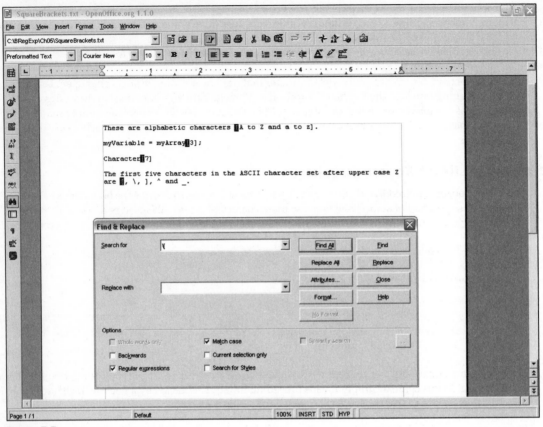

Figure 5-5

Using Ranges in Character Classes

Using character class ranges is much more succinct and less error-prone than specifying a large number of individual characters. For example, if you want to select all alphabetic characters used in English (both lowercase and uppercase) you could write the following character class:

```
[abcdefghijklmnopqrstuvwxyzABCDEFGHIJKLMNOPQRSTUVWXYZ]
```

However, you could express the same character class by using the character class:

```
[a-zA-Z]
```

or:

```
[A-Za-z]
```

each of which uses two character class ranges: a-z for lowercase ASCII characters and A-Z for uppercase ASCII characters. Depending on the data set and the problem definition, it may not be appropriate simply to write [A-z] because that does not restrict characters in the character class to ASCII alphabetic characters. Due to the ASCII ordering of characters, several nonalphabetic characters, such as square brackets, come after uppercase Z and before lowercase a.

Ranges in character classes allow you to customize a character set to your own needs. For example, if you want to select surnames beginning with A, B, C, D, and E, the character set [A-E] can be used to match the first character of a surname.

Alphabetic Ranges

Look at a simple use of ranges in character classes using the example document Light.txt, which is shown here:

```
fight
light
sight
right
night
delight
plight
tight
fights
height
lightning
might
quite
rights
weight
bite
quite
```

If you want to select the sequences of characters right, sight, and tight, you can use the following regular expression:

```
[rst]ight
```

This simply enumerates three literal characters in a character class.

However, you can take advantage of the fact that the initial character of each of the three sequences of characters you are interested in follow each other in the alphabet. So you can use a range in a character class, like this:

```
[r-t]ight
```

The pattern [r-t] is a character class; the r is a literal character in the character class, the hyphen is a metacharacter indicating a range, and the t is a literal character. Figure 5-6 shows that the pattern selects the character sequences right, sight, and tight.

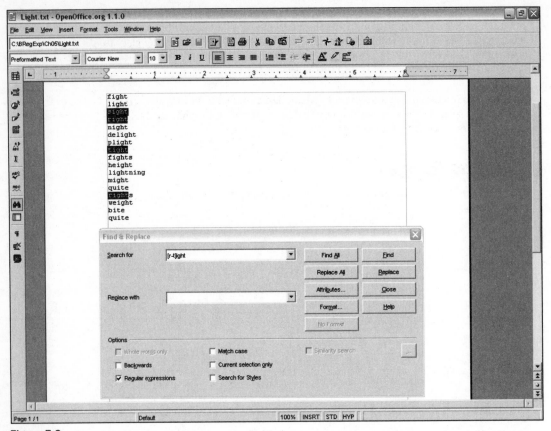

Figure 5-6

Use [A-z] With Care

If you want to select all English-language alphabetic characters you might be tempted to use the regular expression pattern:

```
[A-z]
```

expecting it to be equivalent to the character class:

```
[A-Za-z]
```

but that is not the case. The ASCII and Unicode characters sets don't express the uppercase and lowercase alphabetic characters in one continuous sequence of characters, as you can see in Figure 5-7, which shows the Windows Character Map utility.

Six characters, each of which is not alphabetic, follow z and precede lowercase a. They are [(left square bracket), \ (backslash),] (right square bracket), ^ (caret), _ (underscore), and the grave accent. In Figure 5-7 the cursor is on the] character.

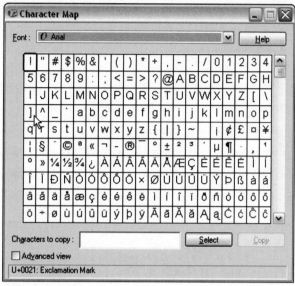

Figure 5-7

Digit Ranges in Character Classes

Numeric digits are widely used. One such use is in constructing part numbers. The file `PartNums.txt` shows some possible part numbers:

```
DB992
AX891
FG339
GE919
GE442
FG935
DB882
AX717
AX803
FG919
GE604
```

Notice that the part numbers consist of two alphabetic characters followed by three numeric digits. The alphabetic characters are of four sequences: AX, DB, FG, and GE. The data for the numeric digits suggests that all digits from 0 to 9 are used.

In implementations that support it, the `\d` metacharacter can be used to represent the class of numeric digits. An alternative is to use the character class `[0-9]` to represent a numeric digit.

Try It Out   **Matching Numeric Digits Using a Character Class**

If you assume that the first two characters are uppercase alphabetic characters, as described earlier, you can represent them using the first character using the character class `[ADFG]`, and you can represent the

117

second character using the character class [XBGE]. Similarly, each numeric digit can be matched using the character class [0-9].

The pattern, therefore, would be as follows:

```
[ADFG][XBGE][0-9]{3}
```

1. Open OpenOffice.org Writer, and open the test file, PartNums.txt.
2. Use Ctrl+F to open the Find & Replace dialog box.
3. Check the Regular Expressions and Match Case check boxes.
4. Type the pattern **[ADFG][XBGE][0-9]{3}** in the Search For text box, and click the Find All button.
5. Inspect the results, as shown in Figure 5-8 (all part numbers are highlighted).

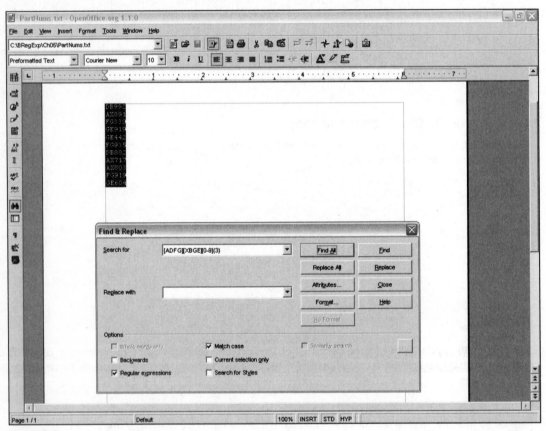

Figure 5-8

How It Works

Look at how the first part number, DB992, matches. The regular expression will start matching from the position immediately before the D. First, it attempts to match the first component of the pattern, the character class [ADFG], with the first character of DB992, which is D. That matches. Next, it attempts to match the second component of the pattern, the character class [XBGE], with the second character of the test text, B. That too matches. Next, the third component of the pattern, the character class [0-9] with the quantifier {3}, attempts to match three successive numeric digits. Because the third, fourth, and fifth characters of the test text are the numeric digits 9, 9, and 2, there is a match. Because all components of the regular expression pattern match, the entire pattern matches.

If, however, you wanted not to match a hypothetical sequence of characters AG123, using the first two character classes would give undesired matches because the pattern [ADFG][XBGE] would match the first two characters of AG123.

Hexadecimal Numbers

One situation when character ranges are useful is when identifying hexadecimal numbers. As you probably know, hexadecimal numbers represent numerical values to the base 16 rather than normal, decimal arithmetic where numbers are expressed to base 10. To enable display of numbers from 0 to 15 the alphabetic characters A through F or a through f (either case is acceptable) are used to represent numbers 10 through 15 using a single character. The following table shows decimal numbers and hexadecimal numbers representing 10 through 15, in case you are not familiar with the notation. Numbers from 0 through 9 in hexadecimal are represented in the same way as in decimal numbers.

Decimal	Hexadecimal
10	A or a
11	B or b
12	C or c
13	D or d
14	E or e
15	F or f

Hexadecimal numbers are natural in many computing uses because 16 is 2 to the power of 4. One situation where hexadecimal numbers are used is in defining color values in some HTML/XHTML or Scalable Vector Graphics (SVG) attribute values.

In SVG, for example, a color value is often expressed as three successive two-character hexadecimal numbers. Each sequence of characters is written as a literal #, followed by six characters, each pair of which should be a valid hexadecimal number.

Several values, some of which contain correctly written hexadecimal values and some of which do not, are contained in the file Numbers.txt, shown here:

```
#DE88D9
#DE88D9
#DG3399
#0099FF
#99FG00
#CCCCCC
#669933
#66330
#8i8824
#902332
#8F8F8F
#2099CC
#88CCFF
#CFE
#994488
#CFEE
```

Some of the sequences of characters contain characters outside the ranges 0 through 9 and A (or a) through F (or f). Some don't contain exactly six characters or digits.

You could express the problem definition as follows:

Match a literal # character, followed by matching six successive characters, each of which can represent a hexadecimal number from 0 through 15 (decimal) — that is, 0 through F (hexadecimal).

The following regular expression pattern selects valid character sequences:

```
#[0-9a-fA-F]{6}
```

Figure 5-9 shows the result in of applying the pattern to Numbers.txt.

Rather than select valid hexadecimal numbers, you might wish to select all numbers that are not valid for one reason or another. Later in this chapter, you will examine how you might approach that after the concept of negated character ranges is introduced.

IP Addresses

Another example where you might benefit from regular expressions is in using IP addresses. IP addresses are used to locate servers on the World Wide Web. When you type www.WhereIWantToGo.com in your browser, that is translated to an IP address, which takes a form such as 123.2.234.23, where you have groups of one, two, or three digits separated by period characters.

Strictly speaking, values such as 002 are allowed in IP addresses. However, leading zeros are not commonly used. For the purposes of this example, I will assume that leading zeros don't occur in the sample data.

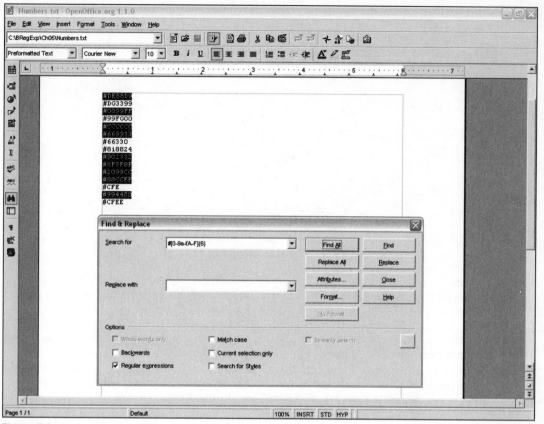

Figure 5-9

Describing the structure of an IP address in English, you might attempt to express the problem definition as follows:

Match between 1 and 3 numeric digits followed by a period character, followed by between 1 and 3 numeric digits, followed by a period character, followed by between 1 and 3 numeric digits, followed by a period character, followed by between 1 and 3 numeric digits.

Based on that description, a first attempt to create a regular expression pattern to identify IP addresses might look like this:

```
[0-9]{1,3}\.[0-9]{1,3}\.[0-9]{1,3}\.[0-9]{1,3}
```

Remember that you need to use the escape sequence \. to match a period.

The sample file to test is `IPLike.txt`, which includes numbers that are valid IP addresses and others that are not:

```
12.12.12.12

255.255.256.255

12.255.12.255

256.123.256.123

8.234.88.55

196.83.83.191

8.234.88,55

88.173.71.66

241.92.88.103
```

Figure 5-10 shows the results of a match on `IPLike.txt` in OpenOffice.org Writer using the pattern just mentioned.

Only one of the strings, `8.234.88,55`, in `IPLike.txt` fails to match the pattern because it contains a comma, whereas from the description we are using, it ought to contain a period.

However, so far, the fact that IP addresses may contain numbers with a maximum value of 255 has been overlooked. So although your pattern matches the second string in `IPLike.txt`, `256.123.256.123`, that sequence of characters is not a valid IP address.

The pattern `[0-9]{1,3}\.[0-9]{1,3}\.[0-9]{1,3}\.[0-9]{1,3}` matches IP addresses but also matches things that are not valid IP addresses.

Take a closer look at how a valid IP address is made up. First, look at the situation where you a have single-digit number. You could describe those as being "a single numeric digit between 0 and 9." That fits neatly with the following character class:

```
[0-9]
```

That character class matches numbers such as 1, 3, 4, 6, and 9, which is what you want.

In the next scenario you have numbers with two digits. Those are in the range 10 to 99. So again, a character class can be used to express each of the two digits, like this:

```
[1-9][0-9]
```

You use the character class `[1-9]`, not `[0-9]`, for the first of the two character classes because numbers less than 10 are written as single-digit numbers and are covered by the previously defined character class, `[0-9]`. However, the second digit of a two-digit number can be 0, such as in 10 or 50, or 9, such as in 29 or 79, so the character class `[0-9]` is appropriate for the second of the two digits.

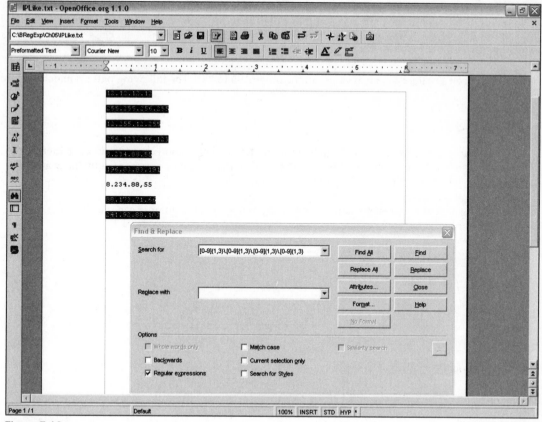

Figure 5-10

You have found patterns made up from character classes that match one-digit or two-digit values contained in IP addresses. Now look at a situation where one of the numeric values is a three-digit number. For clarity, this explanation is split into two parts. The first is creating a pattern that matches numbers from 100 to 199; the second is creating a pattern that matches numbers from 200 to 255.

First, a pattern to match numbers from 100 to 199 is shown here:

```
1[0-9][0-9]
```

You know that all the numbers you are interested in begin with a 1, so you can include it literally as the first character in the pattern. The second digit can be anything from 0, as in 103 or 106, to 9, as in 191 or 197, so the character class [0-9] is appropriate for the second digit. Similarly, the third digit can be from 0 to 9, so the character class [0-9] is appropriate.

Next, look at the situation where you have three-digit values in the range from 200 to 249. The following pattern matches those values:

```
2[0-4][0-9]
```

The first character in the pattern, 2, is the same for all values in that range, such as 202, 226, and 241. The second character in the pattern is a numeric digit that can be represented by the character class [0-4], and the third character in the pattern can be represented by the character class [0-9], as in 203, 228, or 249.

Next, you need a pattern to match values in the range 250 to 255. The following pattern matches those values:

```
25[0-5]
```

The first character is always a 2, so it can be written literally. The second character in the pattern is always a 5, so it, too, can be written literally. The third character can be represented by the character class [0-5], which matches 250, 253, and 255, for example.

So let's bring all that together. To match numbers from 0 to 255, the number can match any of the following patterns:

```
[0-9]
```

when it's a single-digit value, or:

```
[1-9][0-9]
```

when it's a value between 10 and 99, or:

```
1[0-9][0-9]
```

when it's a value between 100 and 199, or:

```
2[0-4][0-9]
```

when it's between 200 and 249, or:

```
25[0-5]
```

when it's between 250 and 255.

If you try to express that in a problem definition, you have a definition that is considerably longer than any you have seen so far:

Match any of the following:

1. **If a numeric value is a single digit, match any number from 0 through 9.**

2. **If the numeric value is a two-digit number, match 1 through 9 for the first character and 0 through 9 for the second character.**

3. If the numeric value is a three-digit numeric value, it matches if it matches any of the following:

   a. Match the numeric digit 1, followed by a numeric digit 0 through 9, followed by a numeric digit 0 through 9, or

   b. Match the numeric digit 2, followed by a numeric digit 0 through 4 followed by a numeric digit 0 through 9, or

   c. Match the numeric digit 2, followed by a numeric digit 5, followed by a numeric digit 0 through 4.

To put the preceding five patterns together, you need to use parentheses, and because the patterns are mutually exclusive options, use the pipe character, |, to separate one option from another. So to match a single value from 0 to 255 and only values in that range, you have the following pattern:

```
([0-9]|[1-9][0-9]|1[0-9][0-9]|2[0-4][0-9]|25[0-5])
```

Imagine coming back to this six months later, or maintaining someone else's code if there is no documentation that describes what he or she intended to do. Ideally, you can see the value of good documentation for problems like this.

This has been a bit more complicated than anything tackled so far in this book, so for further practice, try it out in OpenOffice.org Writer.

Try It Out   Attempting to Match a Numeric Value up to 255

1. Open OpenOffice.org Writer, and open the test file IPLike.txt.

2. Open the Find & Replace dialog box, using Ctrl+F, and check the Regular Expressions and Match Case check boxes.

3. Enter the pattern ([0-9]|[1-9][0-9]|1[0-9][0-9]|2[0-4][0-9]|25[0-5]) in the Search For text box. Be careful not to include any whitespace inside the parentheses.

4. Click the Find All button, and inspect the results, as shown in Figure 5-11. You may be surprised to see that the value 256 is still matched.

How It Works

When you look closely at Figure 5-11, you will see that there are matches in both the second and fourth lines on the values 256. Because you've just spent quite a bit of time carefully crafting a regular expression that matches values only up to 255, what is happening?

For a hint about what is happening, let's switch to the Komodo Regular Expression Toolkit. Apply the following pattern to the test value 256:

```
([0-9]|[1-9][0-9]|1[0-9][0-9]|2[0-4][0-9]|25[0-5])
```

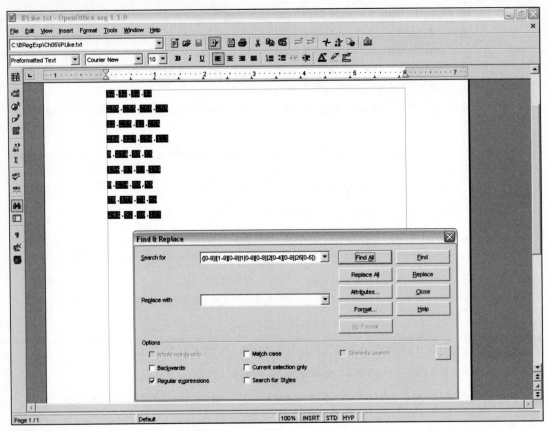

Figure 5-11

Figure 5-12 shows the results.

The first digit, 2, of 256 is matched. In other words, the 2 of 256 matches the first option inside the parentheses. This provides a clue as to what is happening in OpenOffice.org Writer. The first option in the pattern, the character class [0-9], matches the 2 of 256 in IPLike.txt, and that same pattern, from the available pattern options inside the parentheses, also matches the 5 of 256 and the 6 of 256. So in OpenOffice.org Writer, when you seem to have a match for 256, you actually have three separate matches: one for 2, one for 5, and one for 6. The way those three consecutive characters are highlighted makes it look as though there is a problem with the regular expression pattern when, in fact, that isn't the problem.

What happens if you modify the ordering of the options inside the parentheses? First, modify the regular expression pattern so that the [0-9] is moved to the end:

```
([1-9][0-9]|1[0-9][0-9]|2[0-4][0-9]|25[0-5]|[0-9])
```

If you try to edit the regular expression pattern inside the Find & Replace dialog box of OpenOffice.org Writer 1.1, you may run into some bugs in the editor, which can lead to overwriting of existing characters or a failure to accept new characters. If you do find that you can't edit correctly inside the Search For text box, I suggest that you edit the pattern elsewhere, such as in Notepad, for example, and paste the edited pattern into the Search For text box.

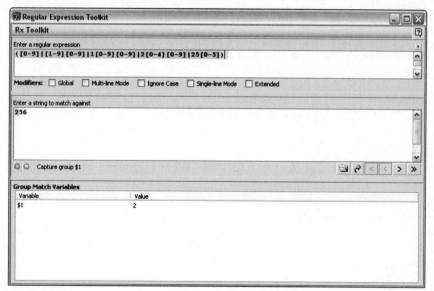

Figure 5-12

If you then click the Find All button, the values 256 of the sample text is highlighted. If you take time to use the Find button (rather than the Find All button) to step through the matches, you will see that first 25 is matched (that matches the [1-9][0-9] pattern, which is now the first option inside the parentheses) and then 6 matches (which matches the [0-9] character class, which is now the last option inside the parentheses).

Even if you reverse the order of all the options inside the parentheses, all occurrences of 256 are matched:

```
(25[0-5]|2[0-4][0-9]|1[0-9][0-9]|[1-9][0-9]|[0-9])
```

What you need to be able to take this example to a successful conclusion is a regular expression pattern that allows you to specify that all characters up to the first period must match in a single chunk, that the digits between two periods must match as a single chunk, and the digits between the final period and the end of the string also match in a single chunk. You will return to this problem in Chapter 6 after you have looked at the meaning and usage of the ^ and $ metacharacters.

Just in case you want to try out a solution right now, here is a pattern that will do what you want — that is, it will not match any IP-like sequence of characters that contain values of 256 or more.

```
^((25[0-5]|2[0-4][0-9]|1[0-9][0-9]|[1-9][0-9]|[0-9])\.){3}(25[0-5]|2[0-4][0-9]|1[0-9][0-9]|[1-9][0-9]|[0-9])$
```

The way the preceding pattern works is explained in Chapter 6.

Reverse Ranges in Character Classes

The ranges you have looked at so far follow alphabetic or numeric order. However, it is possible, at least using some tools, to write ranges that are in reverse alphabetic or numeric order, for which I use the term *reverse ranges*.

When you use character ranges inside a character class, you must be careful if you attempt to use a reverse range because different products and languages are inconsistent in how they handle that syntax.

For example, examine the following regular expression:

```
[t-r]ight
```

OpenOffice.org Writer will interpret the regular expression pattern not as you might expect, selecting r, s, and t as the initial characters in the desired character sequence, but interpreting the t and r as literal characters in a character class and ignoring the hyphen. You can see this in action in Figure 5-13. Notice that the character sequence -ight, which is included in the file Light2.txt, is not selected by the regular expression pattern.

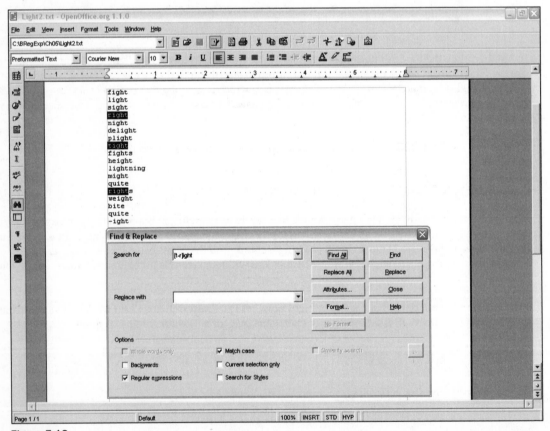

Figure 5-13

However, in PowerGrep, the regular expression pattern [t-r]ight won't compile and produces the error shown in Figure 5-14.

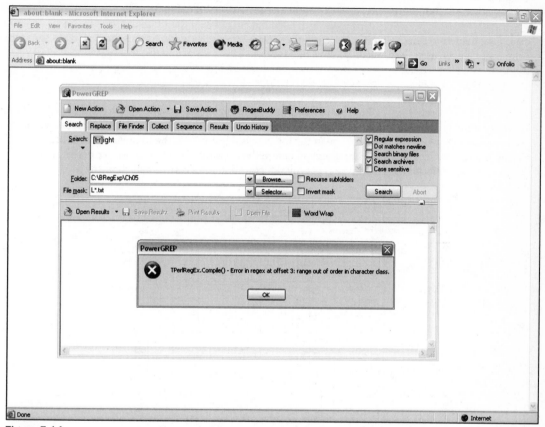

Figure 5-14

There is, typically, no advantage in attempting to use reverse ranges in character classes, and I suggest that you avoid using these.

A Potential Range Trap

Suppose that you want to allow for different separators in dates occurring in a document or set of documents. Among the issues this problem throws up is a possible trap in expressing character ranges.

As a first test document, we will use Dates.txt, shown here:

```
2004-12-31
2001/09/11
2003.11.19
2002/04/29
2000/10/19
2005/08/28
2006/09/18
```

As you can see, in this file the dates are in YYYY/MM/DD format, but sometimes the dates use the hyphen as a separator, sometimes the forward slash, and sometimes the period. Your task is to select all occurrences of sequences of characters that represent dates (assume for this example that dates are expressed only using digits and separators and are not expressed using names of months, for example).

So if you wanted to select all dates, whether they use hyphens, forward slashes, or periods as separators, you might try a regular expression pattern like this:

```
(20|19)[0-9]{2}[.-/][01][0-9][.-/][0123][0-9]
```

In the character class `[.-/]`, which you attempt to use to match the separator, the sequence of characters (period followed by hyphen followed by forward slash) is interpreted as the range from the period to the forward slash. However, as you can see in the top row of Figure 5-15, the hyphen is U+002D, and the period (U+002E) is the character immediately before the forward slash (U+002F). So, undesirably, the pattern `.-/` specifies a range that contains only the period and forward-slash characters.

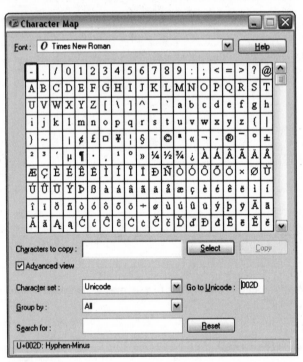

Figure 5-15

> **Characters can be expressed using Unicode numeric references. The period is U+002E; uppercase A is U+0041. The Windows Character Map shows this syntax for characters if you hover the mouse over characters of interest.**

To use the hyphen without creating a range, the hyphen should be the first character in the character class:

```
[-./]
```

This gives a pattern that will match each of the sample dates in the file Dates.txt:

```
(20|19)[0-9]{2}[-./][01][0-9][-./][0123][0-9]
```

Try It Out   Matching Dates

1. Open PowerGrep, and enter the regular expression pattern **(20|19)[0-9]{2}[-./][01][0-9][-./][0123][0-9]** in the Searc text box.

2. Enter **C:\BRegExp\Ch05** in the Folder: text box, assuming that you have saved the Chapter 5 files from the download in that directory.

3. Enter **Dates.txt** in the File Mask text box.

4. Click the Search button, and inspect the results shown in Figure 5-16. Notice particularly that the first match, 2004-12-31, includes a hyphen confirming that the regular expression pattern works as desired.

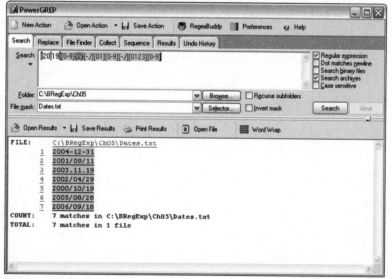

Figure 5-16

How It Works

The first part of the pattern, (20|19), allows a choice of 20 or 19 as the first two characters of the sequence of characters being tested. Next, the pattern [0-9]{2} matches two successive numeric digits in the range 0 through 9. Next, the character class pattern [-./] matches a single character, which is a hyphen, a period, or a forward slash.

The next component of the pattern, [01], matches the numeric digits 0 or 1, because months always have 0 or 1 as the first digit in this date format. Similarly, the next component, the character class [0-9], matches any number from 0 through 9. This would allow numbers for the month such as 14 or 18, which are obviously undesirable. One of the exercises at the end of this chapter will ask you to provide a more specific pattern that would allow only values from 01 to 12 inclusive.

Next, the character class pattern [-./] matches a single character that is a hyphen, a period, or a forward slash.

Finally, the pattern [0123] [0-9] matches days of the month beginning with 0, 1, 2, or 3. As written, the pattern would allow values for the day of the month such as 00, 34 or 38. A later exercise will ask you to create a more specific pattern to constrain values to 01 through 31.

Finding HTML Heading Elements

One potential use for characters classes is in finding HTML/XHTML heading elements. As you probably know, HTML and XHTML 1.0 have six heading elements: h1, h2, h3, h4, h5, and h6. In XHTML the h must be lowercase. In HTML it is permitted to be h or H.

First, assume that all the elements are written using a lowercase h. So it would be possible to match the start tag of all six elements, assuming that there are no attributes, using a fairly cumbersome regular expression with parentheses:

```
<(h1|h2|h3|h4|h5|h6)>
```

In this case the < character is the literal left angled bracket, which is the first character in the start tag. Then there is a choice of six two-character sequences representing the element type of each HTML/ XHTML heading element. Finally, a > is the final literal character of the start tag.

However, because there is a sequence of numbers from 1 to 6, you can use a character class to match the same start tags, either by listing each number literally:

```
<h[123456]>
```

or by using a range in the character class:

```
<h[1-6]>
```

The sample file, HTMLHeaders.txt, is shown here:

```
<h1>Some sample header text.</h1>

<h3>Some text.</h3>

<h6>Some header text.</h6>

<h4></h4>

<h5>Some text.</h5>

<h2>Some fairly meaningless text.</h2>
```

There is an example of each of the six headers.

Try It Out   **Matching HTML Headers**

1. Open PowerGrep, and enter the regular expression pattern **<h[1-6]>** in the Search: text box.

2. Enter **C:\BRegExp\Ch05** in the Folder text box, assuming that you have saved the Chapter 5 files from the download in that directory.

3. Enter **HTMLHeaders.txt** in the File Mask text box.

4. Click the Search button, and inspect the results, as shown in Figure 5-17.

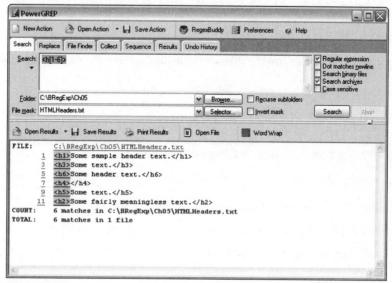

Figure 5-17

Metacharacter Meaning within Character Classes

Most, but not all, single characters have the same meaning inside a character class as they do outside.

The ^ metacharacter

The ^ metacharacter (also called a caret), when it is the first character after the left square bracket, indicates that any other cases specified inside the square brackets are not to be matched. The use of the ^ metacharacter is discussed in the section on negated character classes a little later.

If the ^ metacharacter occurs in any position inside square brackets other than the character that immediately follows the left square bracket, the ^ metacharacter has its literal meaning—that is, it matches the ^ character.

A test file, `Carets.txt`, is shown here:

```
14^2 expresses the idea of 14 to the power 2.

The ^ character is called a caret.

The _ character is called an underscore or underline character.

3^2 = 9

Eating ^s helps you see in the dark. At least that's what I think he said.
```

The problem definition can be expressed as follows:

Match any occurrence of the following characters: the underscore, the caret, or the numeric digit 3.

The character class to satisfy that problem definition is as follows:

```
[_^3]
```

Try It Out   Using the ^ Inside a Character Class

This example matches the three characters mentioned in the preceding problem definition:

1. Open OpenOffice.org Writer, and open the test file `Carets.txt`.

2. Use the Ctrl+F keyboard shortcut to open the Find & Replace dialog box.

3. Check the Regular Expressions and Match Case check boxes, and enter the pattern [_^3] in the Search For text box.

4. Click the Find All button, and inspect the results, as shown in Figure 5-18.

5. Modify the regular expression pattern so that it reads [^_3].

6. Click the Find All button, and compare the results shown in Figure 5-19 with the previous results.

How It Works

When the pattern is [_^3], the meaning is simply a character class that matches three characters: the underscore, the caret, and the numeric digit 3.

When the ^ immediately follows the left square bracket, [, that creates a negated character class, which in this case has the meaning "Match any character except an underscore or the numeric digit 3."

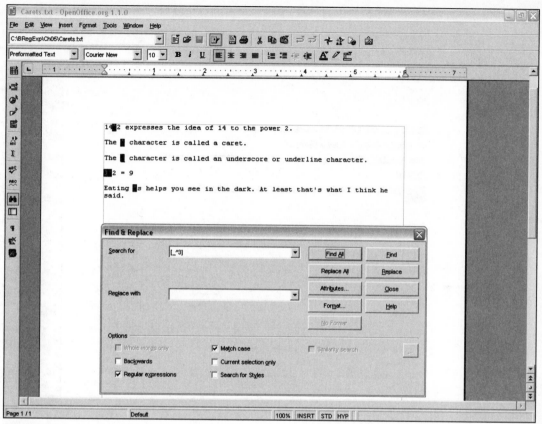

Figure 5-18

How to Use the - Metacharacter

You have already seen how the hyphen can be used to indicate a range inside a character class. The question therefore arises as to how you can specify a literal hyphen inside a character class.

The safest way is to use the hyphen as the first character after the left square bracket. In some tools, such as the Komodo Regular Expressions Toolkit, you can also use the hyphen as the character immediately before the right square bracket to match a hyphen. In OpenOffice.org Writer, for example, that doesn't work.

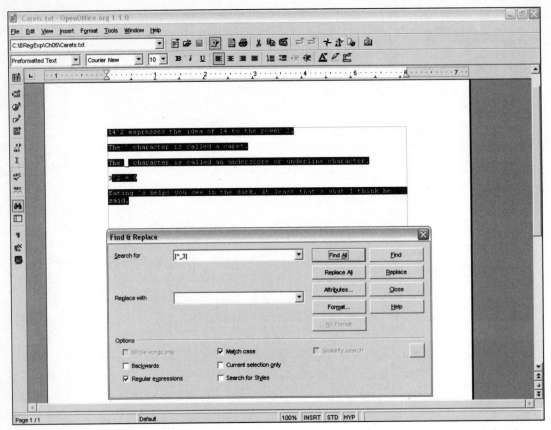

Figure 5-19

Negated Character Classes

Negated character classes always attempt to match a character. So the following negated character class means "Match a character that is not in the range uppercase A through F."

```
[^A-F]
```

Using that pattern, as follows, will match AG and AZ because each is an uppercase A followed by a character that is not in the range A through F:

```
A[^A-F]
```

The pattern will not match A on its own because, while the match for A succeeds, there is no match for the negated character class [^A-F].

Combining Positive and Negative Character Classes

Some languages, such as Java, allow you to combine positive and negative character classes.

The following example shows how combined character classes can be used. The problem definition is as follows:

Match characters A and D through z.

An alternative way to express that notion is as follows:

Match characters A through z but not B through D.

You can express that in Java by combining character classes, as follows:

```
[A-Z&&[^B-D]]
```

Notice the paired ampersands, which means logical AND. So the pattern means "Match characters that are in the range A through Z AND are not in the range B through D."

A simple Java command-line program is shown in `CombinedClass2.java`:

```java
import java.util.regex.*;

public class CombinedClass2{
  public static void main(String args[])
  throws Exception{

  String TestString = args[0];

  String regex = "[A-Z&&[^B-D]]";

  Pattern p = Pattern.compile(regex);

  Matcher m = p.matcher(TestString);
  String match = null;

  System.out.println("INPUT: " + TestString);
  System.out.println("REGEX: " + regex);
  while (m.find())
        {
         match = m.group();
         System.out.println("MATCH: " + match);
        } // end while

        if (match == null){
         System.out.println("There were no matches.");
        } // end if


  } // end main()
}
```

Try It Out   Combined Character Classes

These instructions assume that you have Java 1.4 correctly installed and configured. This example demonstrates how to use combined character classes in Java:

1. Open a command prompt window, and at the command –line, type **javac CombinedClass2.java** to compile the source code.

2. Type **java CombinedClass2.java "A C E G"** to run the program and supply a test string **"A C E G"**.

3. Inspect the results, as shown in Figure 5-20. Notice that A, E, and G are matches, but C is not a match.

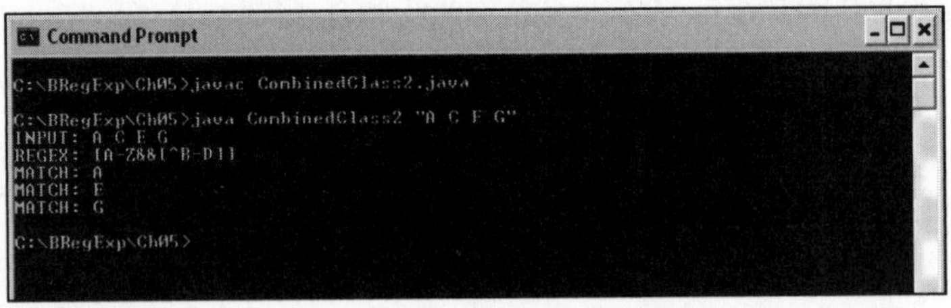

Figure 5-20

How It Works

You supply a test string at the command line. The test string is assigned to the variable TestString:

```
String TestString = args[0];
```

A regular expression is assigned to the variable regex:

```
String regex = "[A-Z&&[^B-D]]";
```

The regular expression is the combined character class described earlier.

The compile() method of the Pattern object is executed with the regex variable as its argument:

```
Pattern p = Pattern.compile(regex);
```

Next, the matcher() method of the Pattern object, p, is executed with the TestString variable as its argument:

```
Matcher m = p.matcher(TestString);
```

A new variable, match, is assigned the value null:

```
String match = null;
```

The simple output shows the test string that was supplied on the command line; the regular expression pattern that was used; and, if there are one or more matches, a list of each match or, if there was no match, a message indicating that no matches were found:

```
System.out.println("INPUT: " + TestString);
System.out.println("REGEX: " + regex);
while (m.find())
        {
        match = m.group();
        System.out.println("MATCH: " + match);
        } // end while

        if (match == null){
        System.out.println("There were no matches.");
        } // end if
```

Try it out with strings containing other uppercase characters as input on the command line.

POSIX Character Classes

Some regular expression implementations support a very different character class notation: the POSIX character class notation. The POSIX approach uses a naming convention for a number of potentially useful character classes instead of specifying character classes in the way you saw earlier in this chapter. For example, instead of the character class [A-Za-z0-9], where the characters are listed, the POSIX character class uses [:alnum:], where alnum is an abbreviation for alphanumeric. Personally, I prefer the syntax used earlier in this chapter. However, because you may see code that uses POSIX character classes, this section gives brief information about them.

As an example, the [:alnum:] character class is shown.

> *The POSIX syntax is dependent on locale. The syntax described in this section relates to English-language locales.*

The [:alnum:] Character Class

The [:alnum:] character class varies in how it is implemented in various tools. Broadly speaking, the [:alnum:] class is equivalent to the following character class:

```
[A-Za-z0-9]
```

However, there are different interpretations of [:alnum:].

Try It Out   The [:alnum:] Class in OpenOffice.org Writer

In OpenOffice.org Writer it is necessary to add a ? quantifier (or other quantifier) to successfully use the
[:alnum:] character class:

1. Open OpenOffice.org Writer, and open the sample file AlnumTest.txt.

2. Use the Ctrl+F keyboard shortcut to open the Find & Replace dialog box.

3. Check the Regular Expressions and Match Case check boxes, and enter the pattern **[:alnum:]?** in
    the Search For text box.

4. Click the Find All button, and inspect the highlighted text, as shown in Figure 5-21, to identify
    matches for the pattern [:alnum:]?.

Notice that the underscore character, which occurs twice in the final line of text in the sample file, is not
matched by the [:alnum:]? pattern.

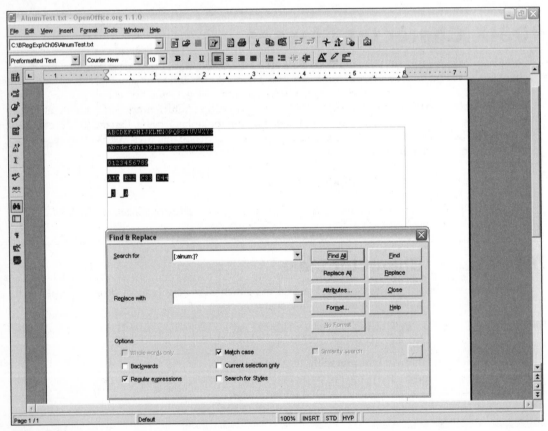

Figure 5-21

If Step 4 is replaced by clicking the Find button, assuming that the cursor is at the beginning of the test
file, the initial uppercase A will be matched, because that is the first matching character.

How It Works

If the regular expression engine starts at the position immediately before the A of the first line of the test file, the A is tested against the pattern [:alnum:]?. There is a match because uppercase A is an alphabetic character. The matched text is highlighted in reverse video.

When the Find All button is used, after that first successful match the regular expression engine moves to the position between A and B and attempts to match against the following character, B. That matches, and so it, too, is highlighted in reverse video. The regular expression engine moves to the next position and then matches the C, and so on. When the newline character is reached, there is no match against the pattern [:alnum:]?, and the regular expression engine moves on to the position after the newline character and attempts to match the next character.

When the regular expression engine reaches the position before the underscore character and attempts to match that character, there is no match, because the underscore character is neither an alphabetic character nor a numeric digit.

Exercises

1. You have a document that contains American English and British English. State a problem definition to locate occurrences of license (U.S. English) and licence (British English). Specify a regular expression pattern using a character class to find both sequences of characters.

2. The pattern (20|19)[0-9]{2}[-./][01][0-9][-./][0123][0-9] was used earlier in this chapter to match dates. As written, this pattern would allow months such as 00, 13, or 19 and allow days such as 00, 32, and 39. Modify the relevant components of the pattern so that only months 01 through 12 and days 01 through 31 are allowed.

String, Line, and Word Boundaries

This chapter looks at metacharacters that match positions before, between, or after characters rather than selecting matching characters. These *positional metacharacters* complement the metacharacters that were described in Chapter 4, each of which signified characters to be matched.

For example, you will see how to match characters, or sequences of characters, that immediately follow the position at the beginning of a line. In normal English you might, for example, say that you want to match a specified sequence of characters only when they immediately follow the beginning of a line or the beginning of the whole test text. The implication is that you don't want to match the specified sequence of characters if they occur anywhere else in the text. So using a positional character in this way can significantly change the sequences of characters that match or fail to match.

Equally, you might want to look for whole words rather than sequences of characters or sequences of characters when they occur in relation to the beginning or end of a word. Many regular expression implementations have positional metacharacters that allow you to do that.

This chapter provides you with the information needed to make matches based on the position of a sequence of characters.

The term *anchor* is sometimes used to refer to the metacharacters that match a position rather than a character.

In some documentation (for example, the documentation for .NET regular expression functionality), these same positional metacharacters are termed *atomic zero-width assertions*.

# Chapter 6

This chapter looks at how to do the following:

❑ Use the ^ metacharacter, which matches the position at the beginning of a string or a line

❑ Use the $ metacharacter, which matches the position at the end of a string or a line

❑ Use the \< and \> metacharacters to match the beginning and end of a word, respectively

❑ Use the \b metacharacter, which matches a word boundary (which can occur at the beginning of a word or at the end of a word)

String, Line, and Word Boundaries

Metacharacters that allow you to create patterns that match sequences of characters that occur at specific positions can be very useful.

For example, suppose that you wanted to find all lines that begin with the word The. With the techniques you have seen and used in earlier chapters, you can readily create a literal pattern to match the sequence of characters The, but with those techniques you haven't been able to specify where the sequence of characters occurs in the text, nor whether it is a whole word or forms part of a longer word. The relevant pattern, written as The, would match sequences of characters such as There, Then, and so on at the beginning of a sentence in addition to the word The and would also match parts of personal or business names such as Theodore or Theatre.

Similarly, assuming that you used the pattern The in a case-insensitive mode, you would also (possibly as an undesired side effect) match sequences of characters such as the in the word lathe. At other times, you might want to find a sequence of characters only when they occur at the end of a word (again for example, the the in lathe).

The ^ and $ metacharacters, which are used to specify a position in relation to the beginning and end of a line or string, are discussed and demonstrated first.

The ^ Metacharacter

The ^ metacharacter causes matching to target characters that occur immediately after the beginning of a line or string.

So the pattern.

```
The
```

when applied to the test text.

```
The Thespian Theatre opens at 19:00.
```

would match the sequence of characters The in the words The, Thespian, and Theatre.

However, the same pattern preceded by the ^ metacharacter

```
^The
```

when applied to the same test text would match only the sequence of characters The in the word The because that sequence of characters occurs immediately after the start of the string.

> The ^ metacharacter, when used outside a character class, does not have the negation meaning that it has when used as the first character inside a character class.

Try It Out   Theatre Example

Use the very simple test text in the file Theatre.txt:

```
The Thespian Theatre opens at 19:00.
```

1. Open PowerGrep, and check the Regular Expression check box.

2. Enter the pattern **The** in the Search text box.

3. Enter **C:\BRegExp\Ch06** in the Folder text box.

4. Enter **Theatre.txt** in the File Mask text box.

5. Click the Search button, and inspect the results in the Results area, as shown in Figure 6-1. Notice that the information in the Results area indicates three matches for the pattern The.

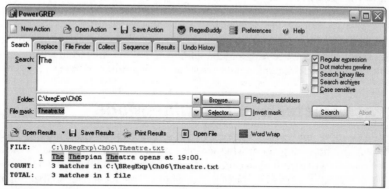

Figure 6-1

6. Edit the regular expression pattern so that it reads ^The.

7. Click the Search button, and inspect the results in the Results area, as shown in Figure 6-2. Notice that there is now only one match, in contrast to the three matches before you edited the regular expression pattern.

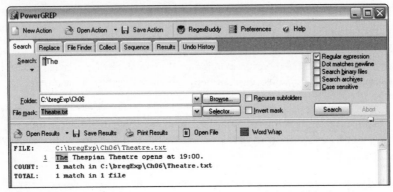

Figure 6-2

How It Works

The regular expression engine starts at the position before the first character in the test file. The first metacharacter in the pattern, the ^ metacharacter, is matched against the regular expression engine's current position. Because the regular expression engine is at the beginning of the file, the condition specified by the ^ metacharacter is satisfied, so the regular expression engine can proceed to attempt to match the other characters in the regular expression pattern. The next character in the pattern, the literal uppercase T, is matched against the first character in the test file, which is uppercase T. There is a match, so the regular expression engine attempts to match the next character in the pattern, lowercase h, against the second character in the test text, which is also lowercase h. The literal h in the pattern matches the literal h in the test text. Then the regular expression engine attempts to match the literal e in the pattern against the third character in the test text, lowercase e. There is a match. Because all components of the regular expression match, the entire regular expression matches.

If the regular expression attempts a match when the current position is anything other than the position before the first character of the test text, matching fails on that first metacharacter, ^. Therefore, the pattern as a whole cannot match. Matching fails except at the beginning of the test text.

The ^ Metacharacter and Multiline Mode

In the preceding example, the test text is a single line, so you were able to examine the use of the ^ metacharacter without bothering about whether the ^ metacharacter would match the beginning of the test text or the beginning of each line, because the two concepts were the same. However, in several tools and languages, it is possible to modify the behavior of the ^ metacharacter so that it matches the position before the first character of each line or only at the beginning of the first line of the test file.

When using the Komodo Regular Expression Toolkit, for example, the following test text.

```
This

Then
```

will fail to find a match when the pattern is as follows:

```
^The
```

Figure 6-3 shows the failure to match.

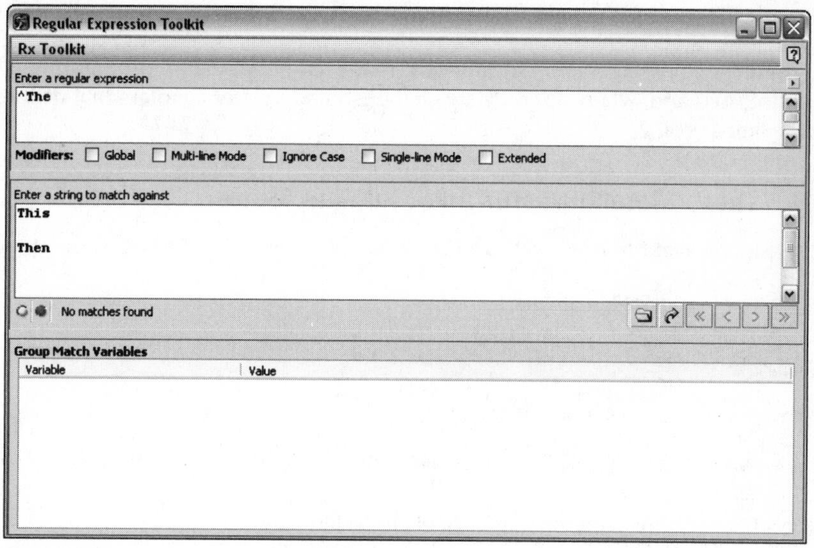

Figure 6-3

However, if you check the Multi-Line Mode check box, the sequence of characters The on the second line is highlighted and in the gray area below the message Match succeeded: 0 groups is displayed, as you can see in Figure 6-4.

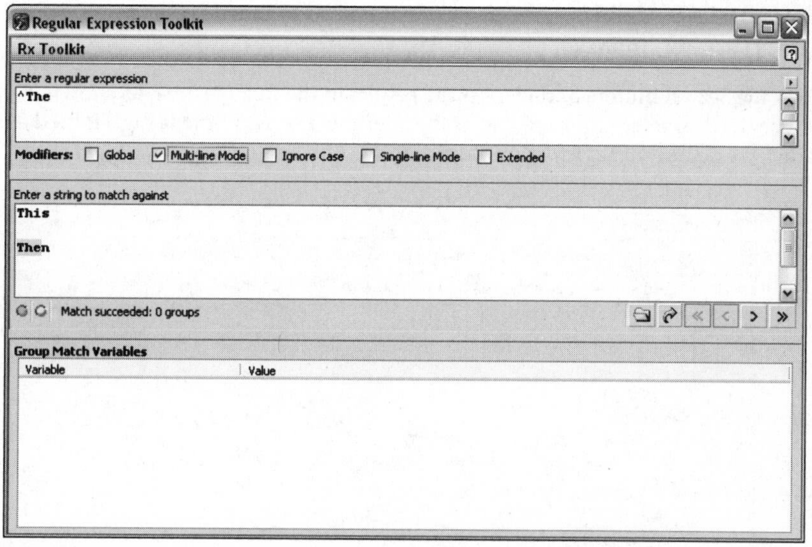

Figure 6-4

When multiline mode is used, the position after a Unicode newline character is treated in the same way as the position that comes at the beginning of the test file. A Unicode newline character matches any of the characters or character combinations that can be used to express the notion of a newline.

Not all programming languages support multiline mode. How individual programming languages treat this issue is discussed and, where appropriate, demonstrated in later chapters that deal with individual programming languages.

Try It Out   The ^ Metacharacter and Multiline Mode

This exercise uses the test file TheatreMultiline.txt:

```
The Thespian Theatre opens at 19:00.

Then theatrical people enter the building.

They greatly enjoy the performance.

The interval is the time for liquid refreshment.
```

Notice that each line begins with the sequence of characters The.

Some tools, such as PowerGrep, are in multiline mode by default, as shown here.

1. Open PowerGrep, and check the Regular Expressions check box.

2. Enter the regular expression pattern **^The** in the Search text box.

3. Enter **C:\BRegExp\Ch06** in the Folder text box. Adjust this if you chose to put the download files in a different folder.

4. Enter **TheatreMultiline.txt** in the File Mask text box.

5. Click the Search button, and inspect the results in the Results area, as shown in Figure 6-5. Notice the character sequence The at the beginning of each line is highlighted as a match, indicating the default behavior of multiline mode.

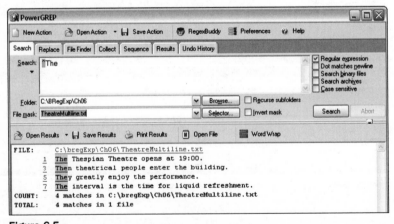

Figure 6-5

The $ Metacharacter

The ^ metacharacter allows you to be specific about where a matching sequence of characters occurs at the beginning of a file or the beginning of a line. The $ metacharacter provides complementary functionality in that it specifies matches in a sequence of characters that immediately precede the end of a line or a file.

First, look at a simple example that uses a test text containing a single line, Lathe.txt:

```
The tool to create round wooden or metal objects is the lathe
```

As you can see, the sequence of characters the occurs more than once in the sample text. The period that might naturally come at the end of the sample sentence has been omitted to illustrate the effect of the $ metacharacter. The following pattern should match only when the sequence of characters occurs immediately before the end of the test string:

```
the$
```

Try It Out   **The $ Metacharacter**

This example demonstrates the use of the pattern the$:

1. Open PowerGrep, and check the Regular Expressions check box.
2. Enter the pattern **the$** in the Search text box.
3. Enter **C:\BRegExp\Ch06** in the Folder text box.
4. Enter **Lathe.txt** in the File Mask text box.
5. Click the Search button, and inspect the results displayed in the Results area, as shown in Figure 6-6.

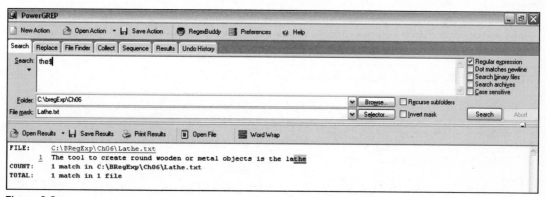

Figure 6-6

Notice that there is only one match and that the sequence of characters The at the beginning of the line does not match nor does the word the, which precedes the word lathe.

6. Delete the $ metacharacter in the Search text box.
7. Click the Search button, and inspect the revised results in the Results area.

Notice that with the $ metacharacter deleted the pattern now has three matches (not illustrated). The first is the The at the beginning of the test text. That matches because the default behavior in PowerGrep is a case-insensitive match. The second is the word the before the word lathe. The third is the character sequence the, which is contained in the word lathe.

How It Works

The default behavior of PowerGrep is case-insensitive matching. When the regular expression engine starts to match after Step 6, it starts at the position before the initial The. The regular expression engine attempts to match The and succeeds. Finally, the regular expression engine attempts to match the $ metacharacter against the position that follows the lowercase e in the test text. That position is not the end of the test string; therefore, the match fails. Because one component of the pattern fails to match, the whole pattern fails to match.

Attempted matching progresses through the test text. The first three characters of the pattern match when the regular expression engine is at the position immediately before the word the. However, as described earlier, the $ metacharacter fails to match; therefore, there is no match for the whole pattern.

However, when the regular expression engine reaches the position after the a of lathe and attempts to match, there is a match. The first character of the pattern, lowercase t, matches the next character, the lowercase t of lathe. The second character of the pattern, lowercase h, matches the h of lathe. The third character of the pattern, lowercase e, matches the lowercase e of lathe. The $ metacharacter of the pattern does match, because the e of lathe is the final character of the test string. Because all components of the pattern match, the whole pattern matches, and the character sequence the of lathe is highlighted as a match in Figure 6-6.

The $ Metacharacter in Multiline Mode

Like the ^ metacharacter, the $ metacharacter can have its behavior modified when it used in multiline mode. However, not all tools or languages support multiline mode for the $ metacharacter.

Tools or languages that support the $ metacharacter in multiline mode use the $ metacharacter to match the position immediately before a Unicode newline character. Some also match the position immediately before the end of the test string, but not all do, as you will see later.

The sample file, ArtMultiple.txt, is shown here:

```
A part for his car

Wisdom which he wants to impart

Leonardo da Vinci was a star of medieval art

At the start of the race there was a false start
```

Notice that to make the example a test of the $ metacharacter, the period that might be expected at the end of each sentence has been omitted.

The $ Metacharacter in Multiline Mode

This example demonstrates the use of the $ metacharacter with multiline mode:

1. Open PowerGrep, and check the Regular Expressions check box.

2. Enter the pattern **art** in the Search text box.

3. Enter the text **C:\BRegExp\Ch06** in the Folder text box.

4. Enter the text **ArtMultiple.txt** in the File Mask text box.

5. Click the Search button, and inspect the results in the Results area, as shown in Figure 6-7. Notice that occurrences of the sequence of characters art are matched when they occur at the end of a line and at other positions — in this example, part in Line 1 and the first occurrence of start in Line 7.

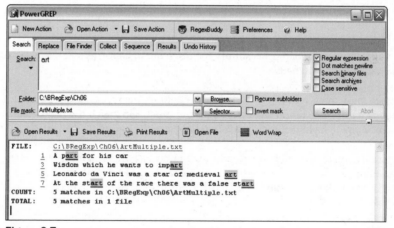

Figure 6-7

6. Edit the regular expression pattern to add the $ metacharacter at the end, giving art$.

7. Click the Search button, and inspect the results in the Results area, as shown in Figure 6-8. Notice that the matches for the pattern art that were previously present in the words part in Line 1 and the first occurrence of start in Line 7 are no longer present, because they do not occur at the end of a line. The $ metacharacter means that matches must occur at the end of a line.

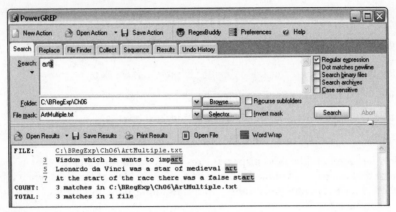

Figure 6-8

How It Works

When the regular expression pattern is simply the three literal characters art, any occurrence of those three literal characters is matched.

However, when the $ metacharacter is added to the pattern, the regular expression pattern engine must match the sequence of three literal characters art and must also match the position either immediately before a Unicode newline character or immediately before the end of the test string.

When an attempt is made to match art in part in the first line, the first three characters of the regular expression pattern match; however, the final $ metacharacter of the pattern art$ fails to match. Because a component of the pattern has failed to match, the entire pattern fails to match.

When the regular expression engine has reached a position immediately before the a of impart, it can match the first three characters of the pattern art$ successfully against, respectively, the a, r, and t of impart. Finally, an attempt is made to match the $ metacharacter against the position immediately following the t of impart. Because that position immediately precedes a Unicode newline character (that is it is the final position on that line), there is a match. Because all the components of the pattern match, the entire pattern matches.

When the regular expression engine has reached a position immediately before the a of the second start on the final line, it can match the first three characters of the pattern art$ successfully against, respectively, the a, r, and t of start. Finally, an attempt is made to match the $ metacharacter against the position immediately following the t of start. Because that position immediately precedes the end of the test string (that is, it is the final position of the test file), there is a match. Because all the components of the pattern match, the entire pattern matches.

Using the ^ and $ Metacharacters Together

Using the ^ and $ metacharacters together can be useful to identify lines that consist entirely of desired characters. This can be very useful when validating user input, for example.

The sample text, `ABCPartNumbers.txt`, is shown here:

```
ABC123

There is a part number ABC123.

ABC234

A purchase order for 400 of ABC345 was received yesterday.

ABC789
```

Notice that some lines consist only of a part number, whereas other lines include the part number as part of some surrounding text.

The intention is to match lines that consist only of a part number. The problem definition is as follows:

Match a beginning of line position, followed by the literal sequence of characters A, B, and C, followed by three numeric digits, followed by a position that is either the end-of-line position or an end-of-string position.

Try It Out   Matching Part Numbers

This example demonstrates using the ^ and $ metacharacters in the same pattern:

1. Open OpenOffice.org Writer, and open the test file `ABCPartNumbers.txt`.

2. Open the Find & Replace dialog box, using the Ctrl+F keyboard shortcut, and check the Regular Expressions and Match Case check boxes.

3. Enter the pattern **^ABC[0-9]{3}$** in the Search For text box.

4. Click the Find All button, and inspect the highlighted text, as shown in Figure 6-9. Notice how three occurrences of a sequence of characters representing a part number are highlighted as matches, while two occurrences of a part number are not highlighted because they are not matches.

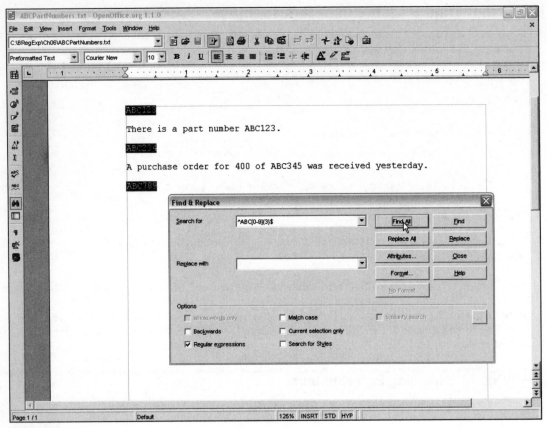

Figure 6-9

How It Works

The regular expression engine begins the matching process at the start of the test file. It attempts to match the ^ metacharacter against the current position. There is a match. It next attempts to match the literal character A in the pattern against the first character in the line, which is uppercase A. There is a match. The matching process is repeated successfully for the literal characters B and C. Then the regular expression engine attempts to match the pattern [0-9]{3}. It attempts to match the character class [0-9] against the character 1 in the test text. That matches. It then proceeds to match the character class [0-9] a second time, this time against the character 2. That also matches. It next proceeds to match the character class [0-9] for a third time, as indicated by the {3} quantifier, against the character 3. That too matches. Finally, it attempts to match the $ metacharacter against the position following the character 3. That matches because it immediately precedes a Unicode newline character. Each component of the pattern matches; therefore, the entire pattern matches.

At the beginning of the second line, the regular expression successfully matches the ^ metacharacter. It next attempts to match the literal character A in the pattern against the first character on the line, an uppercase T. The attempt at matching fails. Any subsequent attempt to match on that line fails when the attempt is made to match the ^ metacharacter because the position is not at the beginning of the line.

Matching Blank Lines

One of the potential uses of the ^ and $ metacharacters together is to match blank lines. The following pattern should match a blank line, because the ^ metacharacter signifies the beginning of the line and the $ metacharacter signifies the position immediately either before a Unicode newline character or the end of the test string.

```
^$
```

However, not all tools support this pattern.

The test file, WithBlankLines.txt, is shown here:

```
Line 1

Line 3 which follows a blank line

Line 5 which follows a second blank line

Line 7 which follows a third blank line
```

After Line 7, there are two further blank lines to end the test file.

Try It Out   **Replacing Blank Lines**

1. Open OpenOffice.org Writer, and open test file WithBlankLines.txt.

2. Open the Find & Replace dialog box using the Ctrl+F keyboard shortcut, and check the Regular Expressions and Match Case check boxes.

3. Enter the pattern ^$ in the Search For text box.

4. Click the Find All button, and inspect the results, as shown in Figure 6-10.

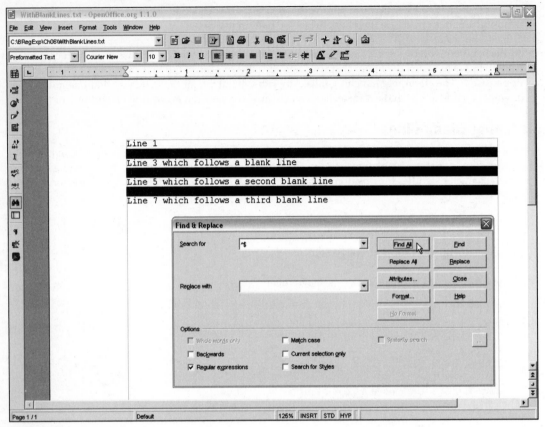

Figure 6-10

Each blank line, except the last two, is highlighted as a match. If you try to scroll down, you will find that OpenOffice.org Writer has lost one of the blank lines that is present if you open the `WithBlankLines.txt` file in Notepad. If you manually reenter one of the blank lines that OpenOffice.org Writer strips out, an additional blank line will match. A blank line at the end of a file seems not to match in OpenOffice.org Writer.

5. Click the Replace All button, and inspect the results, as shown in Figure 6-11. Notice that the three previously highlighted blank lines have been deleted.

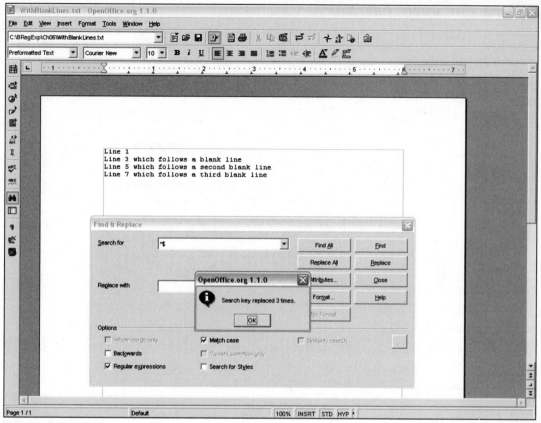

Figure 6-11

How It Works

The second line of the original test file is a blank line. When the regular expression engine is at the position at the beginning of that blank line, matching is attempted against the ^ metacharacter. There is a match. Without moving its position, the regular expression engine then attempts to match the $ metacharacter against the same position. Because that position immediately precedes a Unicode newline character, there is a match for the $ metacharacter, too. Therefore, the entire pattern matches. In OpenOffice.org Writer, the matching of the blank line leads to the entire width of the text area on that line being highlighted.

When the regular expression engine is at the beginning of the third line of the original file, it first attempts to match the ^ metacharacter. That matches. It next attempts to match the $ metacharacter against the same position. Because the position is followed by the character uppercase L, it is not the position that precedes a Unicode newline character. Therefore, the attempt at matching fails.

Working with Dollar Amounts

Because the $ metacharacter in a regular expression pattern indicates the end-of-line (or end-of-string) position, you cannot use that metacharacter to match the dollar currency symbol in a document. To match the dollar sign in a string, you must use the \$ escape sequence.

The sample file, `DollarUsage.txt`, is used to explore how to use the \$ escape sequence:

```
The pound, £, and US dollar, $, are major global currencies.

$99.00

99,00$

$1,000,000

$1000

$1,000

$1,000.00

$0.50

$2 # A Perl variable

$ 0.99

$myVariable

$2.25
```

As you can see, the $ sign may occur in situations other than simply being at the beginning of a sequence of numeric digits. For example, the first line indicates how the dollar sign might appear in a piece of narrative text. The third line, 99,00$, indicates how a dollar amount might be written in a non-English locale or, perhaps, how it might be written by someone who is not a native speaker of English.

Matching a literal $ sign is straightforward; you can simply use the following regular expression pattern, which will match all occurrences of the dollar sign in text:

```
\$
```

Figure 6-12 shows the application of that simple pattern in PowerGrep.

Suppose that you want to detect a dollar sign only when the dollar sign is followed by numeric digits. Even something seemingly this simple may not be entirely straightforward. For example, the third-to-last line has a space character following the $ sign, which you need to take into account if you want to match all relevant occurrences of the $ sign:

```
$ 0.99
```

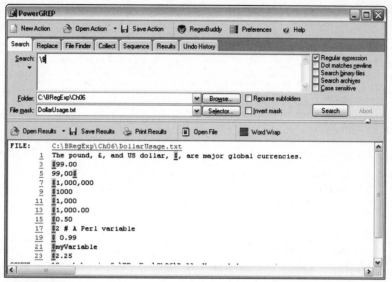

Figure 6-12

Notice in the fourth-to-last line that a dollar sign may be followed by a numeric digit in a way that is acceptable as a dollar amount, yet has quite a different meaning:

```
$2 # A Perl variable
```

To know whether a problem like that is relevant to the data you are working on, you need to know your data and what is in it. For simplicity at the moment, assume that you want to match all occurrences of the $ sign that are followed by numeric digits with or without intervening whitespace.

Depending on the regular expression implementation, you can express a pattern for numeric digits in several ways: \d, [0-9], and [:digit:].

First, try to match situations where a dollar sign is followed by one or more numeric digits, followed by a period, followed by zero or more numeric digits. The following pattern expresses that:

```
\$[0-9]+\.[0-9]*
```

The \$ matches a literal dollar sign. The character class [0-9] matches a numeric digit, and the + quantifier indicates that there is at least one numeric digit. Following that is a literal period character indicated by the escape sequence \.. Finally, the pattern [0-9]* indicates that zero or more numeric digits can occur after the period.

Figure 6-13 shows this pattern applied against DollarUsage.txt when using OpenOffice.org Writer. Notice that only three of the examples in DollarUsage.txt are matched. Can you see, for example, why the examples $1,000,000 and $1000 have not been matched?

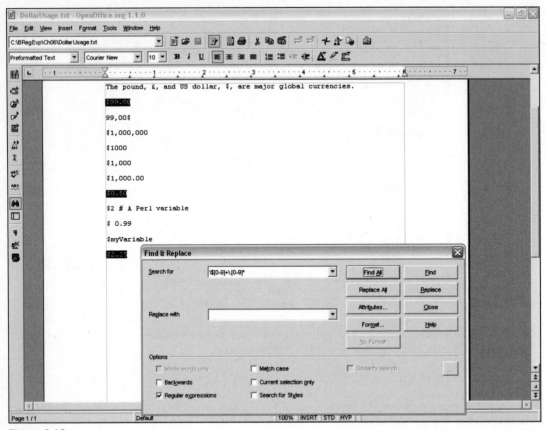

Figure 6-13

Let's deal with $1000 first. This doesn't match because the pattern \. (which matches a period) does not have a match in the text. So to allow for dollar values that do not include a decimal point, you must add a ? quantifier to indicate that the decimal point is optional. The amended pattern, \.?, matches zero or one decimal points.

So if you run the amended pattern against DollarUsage.txt, you will see the result shown in Figure 6-14.

```
\$[0-9]+\.?[0-9]*
```

Notice that for dollar values that include commas as thousand separators or million separators, the comma prevents the pattern from matching all of the dollar value. Adding the following pattern allows for one or more space characters to give a final pattern for this chapter:

```
\$ *[0-9]+\.?[0-9]*
```

By using the * quantifier after the space character in the preceding pattern, you can allow for situations where there is more than a single space character after the dollar sign.

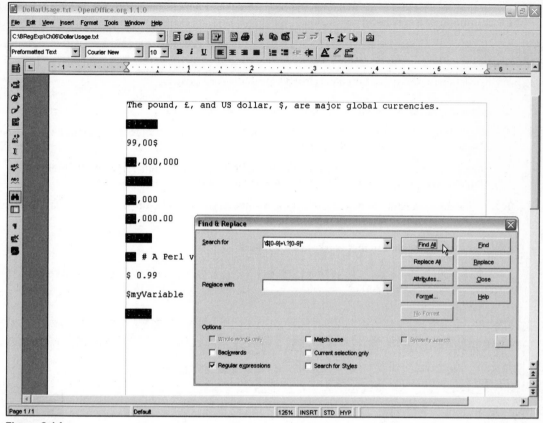

Figure 6-14

Revisiting the IP Address Example

In Chapter 5, we spent some time looking at how you could use character classes to match IP addresses, using the following sample file, IPLike.txt:

```
12.12.12.12

255.255.256.255

12.255.12.255

256.123.256.123

8.234.88.55

196.83.83.191

8.234.88,55

88.173.71.66

241.92.88.103
```

Now that you have looked at the meaning and use of the ^ and $ metacharacters, you are in a position to take that example to a successful conclusion.

Try It Out   **Matching IP Addresses**

These instructions assume that you have closed OpenOffice.org Writer.

1. Open OpenOffice.org Writer, and open the test file IPLike.txt.

2. Open the Find & Replace dialog box using the Ctrl+F keyboard shortcut, and check the Regular Expressions and Match Case check boxes.

3. Enter the regular expression pattern **^((25[0-5]|2[0-4][0-9]|1[0-9][0-9]|[1-9][0-9]|[0-9])\.) {3}(25[0-5]|2[0-4][0-9]|1[0-9][0-9]|[1-9][0-9]|[0-9])$** in the Search For text box.

4. Click the Find All button, and inspect the results, as shown in Figure 6-15. Notice that the lines containing a value of 256 are not matched, which is what you wanted.

The regular expression pattern that works is shown here:

```
^((25[0-5]|2[0-4][0-9]|1[0-9][0-9]|[1-9][0-9]|[0-9])\.){3}(25[0-5]|2[0-4][0-9]|1[0-
9][0-9]|[1-9][0-9]|[0-9])$
```

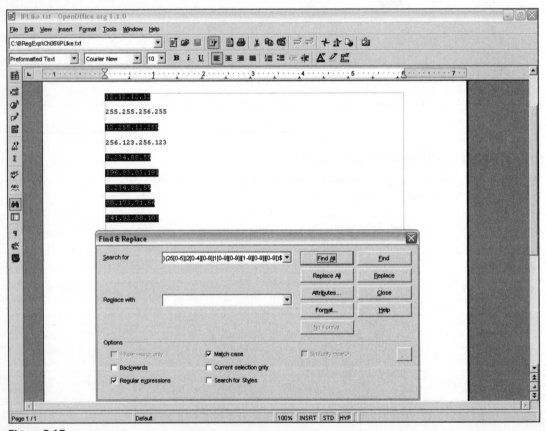

Figure 6-15

How It Works

First, let's break the regular expression down into its component parts.

The initial ^ metacharacter indicates that there is a match only when matching is being attempted from a position at the beginning of a line.

The following component indicates several options for numeric values, each of which is followed by a literal period in the test text:

```
((25[0-5]|2[0-4][0-9]|1[0-9][0-9]|[1-9][0-9]|[0-9])\.){3}
```

Remember that the escape sequence that matches a literal period is \.. If you had used a period in the pattern, the test text would have matched, but so would any alphanumeric character. This would have led to undesired matches such as the following, which is clearly not an IP address:

```
12G255F12H255
```

Using the . metacharacter would have lost much of the specificity that you obtain by using the \. metacharacter.

The first time the following pattern is processed, it immediately follows the position that indicates the start of a line:

```
((25[0-5]|2[0-4][0-9]|1[0-9][0-9]|[1-9][0-9]|[0-9])\.){3}
```

That means a match succeeds if any of the options inside the nested parentheses are found between the start-of-line position and a literal period character. Given the way the options are constructed, only numeric values from 0 to 255 are matched.

The second time the following pattern is matched, you know that it is preceded by a literal period character (because the second attempt at matching follows the first attempt, which you know ends with a literal period):

```
((25[0-5]|2[0-4][0-9]|1[0-9][0-9]|[1-9][0-9]|[0-9])\.){3}
```

In other words, you are looking for a numeric value from 0 to 255 that is preceded by a literal period character and followed by a literal period character.

Similarly, the third time an attempt is made to match, it is preceded by a literal period character (which matches the \. metacharacter from the second time of matching) and is followed by a period character.

If all preceding components of the pattern match, the regular expression engine attempts to match the pattern:

```
(25[0-5]|2[0-4][0-9]|1[0-9][0-9]|[1-9][0-9]|[0-9])$
```

Because the pattern ends in a $ metacharacter, you know that it matches only a numeric value from 0 to 255 only when it follows a literal period character (which was the final character to match the third attempt to use the earlier component of the pattern) and when it is followed by a Unicode newline character.

What Is a Word?

The notion of what constitutes a word might seem, at first sight, to be obvious. But if you were asked to say which of the sequences of characters on the following lines were words, what would your answer be? And what criteria would you use to arrive at your opinion?

```
cat
ja
jar
Nein
parr
smolt
pomme
Claire
spil
```

How many words did you identify? Probably cat and jar were on your list. But what about ja and Nein? If you know German, you almost certainly would classify both those as words. Similarly, if you know French, you would identify pomme as a word, but if you had no knowledge of French, you might take the opposite view. And an English speaker familiar with the life cycle of the Atlantic salmon would have no difficulty in identifying parr and smolt as stages in that life cycle, but some other English speakers might not be familiar with those words.

Clearly, it isn't realistic to expect a text processor to have knowledge about what is or isn't a word in English, French, German, or any of a host of other languages. Similarly, you can't expect a text processor to have knowledge in all technical areas. So you need another technique—a more mechanistic technique—to allow identification of word boundaries.

Identifying Word Boundaries

A word boundary can be viewed as two positions: one at the beginning of a sequence of characters that form a word and one at the end of a sequence of characters that form a word.

Depending on which tools or languages you use, there are metacharacters that match a word-boundary position occurring at the beginning of a word, a word-boundary position occurring at the end of a word, or both.

The \< Syntax

The \< metacharacter identifies a word-boundary position occurring at the beginning of a word. It is preceded by a character that is not an alphabetic character (for example, a space character) or is a beginning-of-line position.

A simple sample file, BoundaryTest.txt, is shown here:

```
ABC DEF GHI
GHI ABC DEF
ABC DEF GHI
CAB CBA AAA
```

The problem definition is as follows:

Match an uppercase A when it occurs immediately following a word boundary.

In other words, match an uppercase A when it is preceded by a nonword character or by a start-of-string or start-of-line position.

Try It Out   Matching a Beginning-of-Word Word Boundary

1. Open OpenOffice.org Writer, and open the file BoundaryTest.txt.

2. Open the Find & Replace dialog box using the Ctrl+F keyboard shortcut, and check the Regular Expressions and Match Case check boxes.

3. Enter the pattern \<A in the Search For text box.

4. Click the Find All button, and inspect the results, as shown in Figure 6-16.

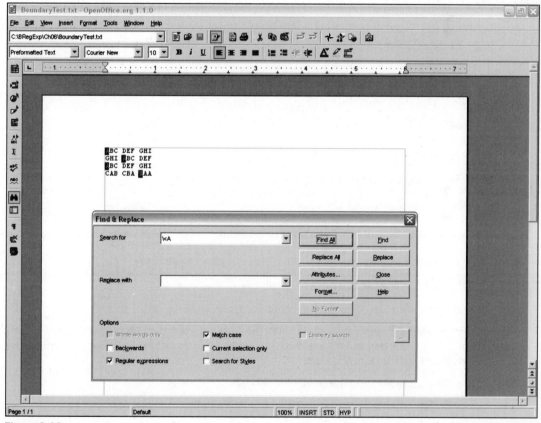

Figure 6-16

How It Works

On the first line, the A of ABC follows the start-of-text position, so there is a match.

On the second line, the A of ABC follows a space character (which is a nonword character), so there is a match.

On the third line, the A of ABC follows a start-of-line position, so there is a match for the pattern \<A.

On the final line, the A of CAB has an alphabetic character before it, so the pattern \<A does not match. The A of CBA is followed by a nonword character but is preceded by an alphabetic character, so the pattern \<A does not match.

The first A of AAA is preceded by a nonword character, so the pattern \<A matches. However, the second and third A of AAA is preceded by an alphabetic character and does not match.

The \>Syntax

The \> metacharacter signifies a word boundary that occurs at the end of a sequence of word characters. In other words, it matches a word boundary that occurs at the end of a word.

The test file, EndBoundary.txt, is shown here:

```
Theodore said "This is a lathe

I shaved today and my new shaving cream made a good lather.

A lathe is a tool for turning wood or metal.

The Thespian Theatre is something I am loathe to attend.

The quick brown fox jumped over the lazy dog.
```

The task is to match the sequence of characters the when they occur before a word boundary at the end of a word.

Try It Out   The \> Metacharacter

1. Open OpenOffice.org Writer, and open the file EndBoundary.txt.

2. Open the Find & Replace dialog box using the Ctrl+F keyboard shortcut, and check the Regular Expressions check box, but do not check the Match Case check box, because you want a case-insensitive search on this occasion.

3. Enter the pattern **the\>** in the Search For text box.

4. Click the Find All button, and inspect the results, as shown in Figure 6-17.

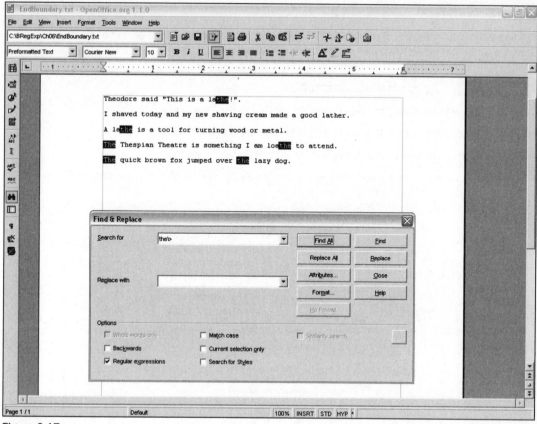

Figure 6-17

How It Works

The matching sequence of characters the in the first line comes immediately before an exclamation mark, which is not an alphabetic character. Therefore, the sequence of characters the precedes a word boundary and matches the pattern the\>.

On the second line, the sequence of characters the in lather is followed by an alphabetic character, a lowercase r. There is no word boundary after the sequence of characters the and, thus, no match.

The matching occurrences later in the test file each precede a space character that is a nonword character, so each sequence of characters precedes an end-of-word word boundary. Each matches the pattern the\>.

The \b Syntax

The \b metacharacter can match a word boundary at either the beginning or end of a word, as illustrated in the following Try It Out section.

The \b Metacharacter

1. Open PowerGrep, and enter the pattern **\bA** in the Search text box.

2. Enter the text **C:\BRegExp\Ch06** in the Folder text box.

3. Enter the filename **BoundaryTest.txt** in the File Mask text box.

4. Click the Search button, and inspect the results in the Results area, as shown in Figure 6-18.

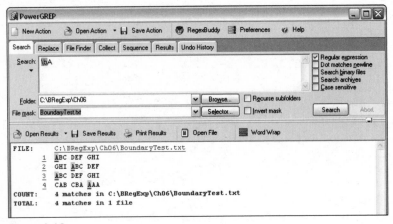

Figure 6-18

How It Works

The pattern \bA is identical in effect to \<A. It means a word boundary followed by an uppercase A. In theory, the meaning isn't identical, because \<A means the following:

Match a beginning-of-word word boundary followed by an uppercase A.

Whereas \bA means the following:

Match a word boundary that can be a beginning-of-word word boundary or an end-of-word word boundary followed by an uppercase A.

In practice, a word boundary followed by an alphabetic character must be a beginning-of-word word boundary. One of the exercises will ask you to match end-of-word word boundaries using the \b metacharacter.

The \B Metacharacter

The \B metacharacter is the opposite of the \b metacharacter. The \B metacharacter matches a position that is not a word boundary.

Less-Common Word-Boundary Metacharacters

Other word-boundary metacharacters that mark either a beginning-of-word or end-of-word word boundary are available in some languages or tools.

Exercises

These exercises allow you to test your understanding of some of the information in this chapter.

1. You learned that the \b metacharacter can match a word boundary at the beginning of a word or the end of a word. What pattern, using the \b metacharacter, will match the same text as the pattern the\>?

2. Create a pattern that will match the sequence of characters the in lather but that won't match the same sequence of characters in then or in lathe.

Parentheses in Regular Expressions

Parentheses are powerful tools when you are using regular expressions. They can be used to group characters for several purposes, each of which will be explained later in the chapter. Parentheses can, for example, be used to express simple alternatives or to express multiple options.

Parentheses create one or more groups. Groups of matched characters can then be used later in the manipulation of text — for example, in the construction of replacement text for specified pieces of matched text.

In this chapter, you will learn how to do the following:

- ❑ Use parentheses for grouping
- ❑ Use quantifiers with groups of characters and/or metacharacters
- ❑ Match literal opening and closing parenthesis characters
- ❑ Provide alternatives or multiple options in regular expression patterns
- ❑ Use capturing and non-capturing parentheses
- ❑ Use back references

Grouping Using Parentheses

Parentheses inside regular expression patterns are used to group characters and remember matched text. Often, the group(s) of characters created by using parentheses are used for text manipulation purposes. This section looks at what grouping is and how it is achieved.

To create a group of characters, simply precede the character group with an opening parenthesis character and follow the group with a closing parenthesis character. For example, examine the following pattern:

```
United States
```

Containing only literal characters, this pattern could be used to match the text United States. Now examine the following pattern:

```
(United)( )(States)
```

It would match the same text but would, at the same time, create three groups: the first for the sequence of characters United, the second for a space character, and the third for the sequence of characters States. If, for example, you wanted to replace the group United with an uppercase U, the group containing the space character with nothing, and the group States with the uppercase character S, you could by a slightly cumbersome process replace the string United States with the abbreviation US.

Parentheses allow you to group sequences of characters. What you do with the groups depends on your text manipulation task.

When using parentheses in patterns, be careful that you don't inadvertently include any whitespace inside the parentheses, because if you do include whitespace, the regular expression engine will attempt to match that whitespace as part of the sequence of characters. If it fails to match the whitespace, you might find that you fail to get the desired matches.

Try It Out   Grouping Characters

This example demonstrates simple grouping in action:

1.   Open the Komodo Regular Expressions Toolkit, and delete any regular expression pattern and/or test text left over from previous use.

2.   In the Enter a String to Match Against text area, enter the test text **The hot water**.

3.   In the Enter a Regular Expression area, enter the pattern **hot**.

4.   Inspect the matched text (which is the string hot), and notice the message in the gray area below the Enter a String to Match Against text area: Match succeeded: 0 groups.

5.   Change the regular expression pattern to read (hot), inspect the matched text (it is still the string hot), and notice that the message in the gray area below the Enter a String to Match Against text area has changed. It now reads Match succeeded: 1 group.

Figure 7-1 shows the appearance after Step 6. By adding parentheses to a simple regular expression pattern you have, as indicated by the message mentioned in Step 7, created a group. Notice that in the Group Match Variables area, the value $1 appears in the Variable column, and the value hot appears in the Value column, indicating that the group can be referenced as $1 and that its value is the sequence of characters hot. This topic is further discussed later in the chapter.

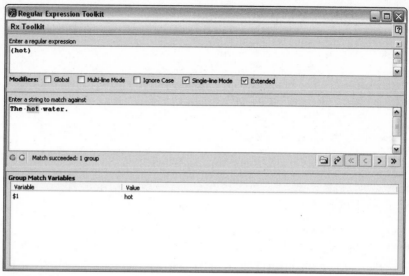

Figure 7-1

How It Works

The first pattern hot contains only three literal characters and simply matches a sequence of characters: hot.

When the matched parentheses enclose the hot component of the pattern, those three literal characters form a group.

Parentheses and Quantifiers

One basic use for parentheses is in grouping characters and/or metacharacters so that a quantifier can be applied to the group contained by the parentheses.

For example, if you expect that a group of characters occurs more than once in succession, the relevant characters and/or metacharacters can be enclosed in parentheses and an appropriate quantifier used immediately following the closing parenthesis.

For example, suppose that you want to match a sequence of characters that consists of an uppercase A, followed by a numeric digit, followed by another uppercase A and another numeric digit. You can use the following pattern to match the described sequence of characters:

```
(A\d){2}
```

The (A\d) component of the pattern matches an uppercase A followed by a numeric digit. The parentheses do not match anything — neither a character in the test text nor a position. The quantifier {2} indicates that everything contained in the parentheses must occur exactly twice if there is to be a match.

Try It Out   **Parentheses and Quantifiers**

A test file, `QuantifierTest.txt`, is shown here:

```
A3A4CDE

B9B6XYZ

A2A9RTE

B4B4UIO

G2H1WEQ
```

1.   Open PowerGrep, and enter the regular expression pattern **(A\d){2}** in the Search Text area.

2.   Enter the text **C:\BRegExp\Ch07** in the Folder text box. Amend this if you installed the code download in some other location.

3.   Enter the filename **QuantifierTest.txt** in the File Mask text box; click the Search button; and inspect the outcome in the Results area, as shown in Figure 7-2.

4.   Click the Search button, and inspect the outcome in the Results area.

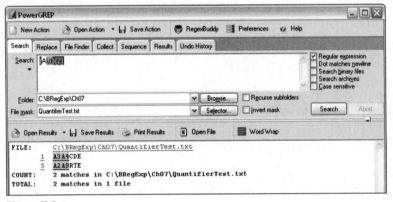

Figure 7-2

How It Works

The pattern `(A\d){2}` has the same meaning, in terms of the sequence of characters that it matches, as the pattern `A\dA\d`. In other words, it matches an uppercase A, followed by a numeric digit, followed by another uppercase A and a numeric digit.

PowerGrep indicates that there are matches on lines 1 and 5.

When the regular expressions engine is at the position before the first A on line 1, it first attempts to match the first A on the line against the first character inside the parentheses, an uppercase A. There is a match. It next attempts to match the second component inside the parentheses, the metacharacter \d, against the numeric digit 3. There is a match. All the components inside the parentheses have been matched once. Because there is a {2} quantifier, the regular expressions engine next attempts to match the first component inside the parentheses, the literal character A, against the third character of line 1, the uppercase A. There is a match. It next attempts to match the second component inside the parentheses, the metacharacter \d, against the fourth character of line 1, the numeric digit 4. There is a match. The components inside the parentheses have been matched twice, so matching is complete, and all components of the pattern have matched. Therefore, the entire pattern has matched, and the sequence of characters A3A4 is highlighted in PowerGrep.

Matching Literal Parentheses

Because the opening (and closing) parentheses characters have special functions in regular expression patterns, they cannot be used to match the corresponding literal characters. To match an opening parenthesis, the following pattern is used:

```
\(
```

To match a closing parenthesis, the pattern needed is:

```
\)
```

Suppose that you want to match the text (Home) in the following:

```
Tel. 123 456 7890 (Home)
```

You would use this pattern:

```
\(Home\)
```

U.S. Telephone Number Example

One practical use for metacharacters that match literal parentheses is in matching sequences of characters that form U.S. telephone numbers.

Several formats can be used for U.S. telephone numbers. For the purpose of this example, assume that the following format is the one that the data source should contain:

```
(123) 123-4567
```

A problem definition for that structure could read as follows:

Match an opening parenthesis, followed by three numeric digits, followed by a closing parenthesis, followed by a space character, followed by three numeric digits, followed by a hyphen, followed by four numeric digits.

If you use a character class to match numeric digits, the following pattern can be used:

```
\(\d{3}\) \d{3}-\d{4}
```

Try It Out   Phone Number Example

This example tests the preceding pattern to match the specified U.S. telephone number format.

The test file, PhoneNumbers.txt, is shown here:

```
(987) 133-4477

(123) 876-3456

123-456-7890

(898 123-1234

879) 345-8765
```

Only the first two telephone numbers correspond to the problem definition previously stated.

1. Open PowerGrep, and enter the regular expression pattern **\(\d{3}\) \d{3}-\d{4}** in the Search text area.

2. Enter the folder name **C:\BRegExp\Ch07** in the Folder text box.

3. Enter the filename **PhoneNumbers.txt** in the File Mask text box.

4. Click the Search button, and inspect the outcome displayed in the Results area.

Figure 7-3 shows the appearance after Step 4.

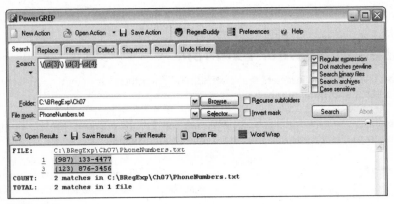

Figure 7-3

How It Works

First, let's look at how the test text (987) 133-4477 on the first line matches. Assuming that the regular expression engine is at the position immediately before the opening parenthesis, it attempts to match the \(metacharacter against the opening parenthesis character, (. There is a match. Next, the pattern \d{3} is matched. Because the second, third, and fourth characters of the test string are numeric digits, there is a match. Then the literal) matches the pattern \). Next, the literal space character is matched against the sixth character of the test string, which is a space character. There is a match. Next, the pattern \d{3} is matched against the seventh, eighth, and ninth characters of the test string, 133. Because each of those characters is a numeric digit, there is a match. Next, a literal hyphen in the pattern is matched against a hyphen in the test string, which, of course, matches. Finally, the pattern \d{4} is matched against the final four characters of the test string, 4477. Because each of those is a numeric digit, there is a match. All components of the regular expression match; therefore, the whole regular expression matches.

There is no match for the test string 123-456-7890, because the first metacharacter in the regular expression, \(, has no match.

There is no match for the test string (898 123-1234. Assuming that the regular expression engine is at the position immediately before the opening parenthesis, the metacharacter \(is matched successfully, and the pattern \d{3} is matched by the sequence of characters 898. However, there is no match for the \) metacharacter; therefore, matching of the whole regular expression fails.

Alternation

One important and straightforward use of parentheses is in expressing alternatives. Making choices among alternatives involves using the parentheses metacharacters and the | metacharacter, sometimes called the bar metacharacter, which expresses the idea of the logical OR.

Strictly speaking, you can have no more than two alternatives. When there is a choice of three or more choices, those are options, not alternatives. However, the term alternation is well established in regular expression terminology for options of two or more, so the term alternative or alternation will be used in this section whether there are two options or more.

The simplest usage is to select either of two literal options. For example, you might have to deal with documents in U.S. and British English, where the color gray is spelled two different ways: gray in U.S. English and grey in British English.

The problem definition could be expressed as follows:

Match a lowercase g, followed by an r, followed by either an a OR an e, followed by a y.

You might wonder why I specify lowercase for the initial g. If, for example, your data contains the surnames Grey or Gray, or the name of a place beginning with either combination of four letters, you don't want to replace the e in text such as Mr. Grey to achieve consistent U.S. spelling, because changing someone's surname will likely have undesired effects.

You could express the problem definition as the following pattern:

```
(gray|grey)
```

Or as follows:

```
gr(a|e)y
```

These have the same logical meaning. In fact, you could equally use a character class in the following pattern, if you wished. Using a character class rather than alternation typically will offer efficiency benefits:

```
gr[ae]y
```

Try It Out   Choosing Two Literal Alternatives

This example demonstrates how to choose between two alternatives expressed literally. Suppose that you want to make selections from a list of part numbers, as shown in the sample document, PartNums.txt:

```
ABC03
ABC08
ABC11
ABC13
ABC18
ABC25
ABC45
ABC12
ABC19
ABC88
ABC71
ABC04
ABC02
ABC55
```

As you can see, the part numbers are not ordered. Suppose that you want to select part numbers between ABC01 and ABC19. One way to do that is to use parentheses in the following regular expression pattern:

```
ABC(0|1)[0-9]
```

1. Open OpenOffice.org Writer, and open the test file PartNums.txt.
2. Open the Find & Replace dialog box using the Ctrl+F keyboard shortcut.
3. Check the Regular Expressions and Match Case check boxes.
4. Enter the pattern **ABC(0|1)[0-9]** in the Search For text box.
5. Click the Find All button, and inspect the result. As you can see in Figure 7-4, all the part numbers in the sample document that lie between ABC01 and ABC19 (there are gaps in the data) are highlighted.

Part numbers with a first numeric digit that is neither 0 nor 1 are not matched.

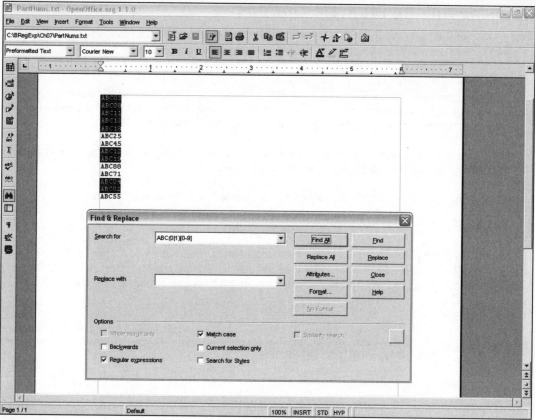

Figure 7-4

How It Works

Matching of ABC03 in the first line is achieved as follows. Assuming that the regular expression engine is starting at the position before the initial A of ABC03, it first attempts to match the first character in the pattern, A, against the first character in the test text, A. There is a match. Matches also are achieved when attempting to match the second character, B, and the third character, C. Next, a match is sought for the pattern (0|1). This is tested against the fourth character of the test text, the numeric digit 0. There is a match. Finally, the character class [0-9] is matched against the numeric digit 3. There is a match. Because all components of the regular expression match, the whole regular expression matches.

The test text ABC11 matches. The first three characters match as described in the preceding paragraph. When the pattern (0|1) is matched against the numeric digit 1, there is a match. The character class [0-9] matches the numeric digit 1, the fifth character of the test text.

The test text ABC25 does not match, because the pattern (0|1) cannot successfully be matched against the numeric digit 2.

Choosing among Multiple Options

Suppose that you have some text about people, including information about individuals who practice medicine. You want to find all references to individuals who are doctors.

You may find text that uses the term Doctor (or doctor) or that uses one or both of the abbreviations Dr. (with a period) and Dr (without a period). Whether or not you want to include the word doctor in your search depends on its purpose. Assume that you only want to find mention of doctors when the word has an uppercase initial D. The problem definition could be stated as follows:

Match the sequence of characters D, o, c, t, o, and r OR match the sequence of characters D and r OR match the sequence of characters D, r, and . (a period).

The following pattern will satisfy the requirements specified in the problem definition:

```
(Doctor|Dr|Dr\.)
```

Remember that the period in a pattern is a metacharacter that matches a wide range of alphanumeric characters. To restrict the match to the literal period character in the test text, you must escape the period character in the pattern \.. An alternative pattern to match the same options is as follows:

```
(Doctor|Dr\.?)
```

Try It Out   Matching Multiple Options

The test text, Doctors.txt, is shown here:

```
Doctor

Drf

Dr

Dr.

Drs

Doctors
```

1.   Open OpenOffice.org Writer, and open the test file Doctors.txt.

2.   Open the Find & Replace dialog box using the Ctrl+F keyboard shortcut.

3.   Check the Regular Expressions and Match Case (choosing not to match the text doctor) check boxes.

4.   Enter the pattern **(Doctor|Dr\.|Dr)** in the Search For text box.

5.   Click the Find All button, and inspect the results, as shown in Figure 7-5. Notice that only the Dr of Dr. is matched.

6.   Add the test text **Drive** at the end of the test file, and click the Find All button.

7. Inspect the results. Notice that the Dr of Drf is matched, reflecting our earlier attempt at a problem definition, but as you can see, undesired text is matched. A revised and more specific problem definition is shown here:

> **Match the sequence of characters D, o, c, t, o, and r OR match the sequence of characters D and r OR match the sequence of characters D, r, and . (a period). Following the previously described options, there must be a word-boundary position.**

However, there is a subtle trap in the preceding problem definition, because the period character is a nonword character. So a better problem definition is as follows:

> **Match the sequence of characters D, o, c, t, o, and r OR match the sequence of characters D and r. Following the previously described options, there must be a word-boundary position.**

The problem definition could have been more precise and specified an *end* word boundary position. However, because it specified that the options that precede the word boundary are all alphabetic (word) characters, it can only be an end-of-word boundary.

8. Modify the pattern so that it reads (Doctor|Dr)\>.

9. Click the Find All button, and inspect the results. Notice that the initial Dr of Drive is no longer matched. Notice, too, that the whole of Dr. is now matched.

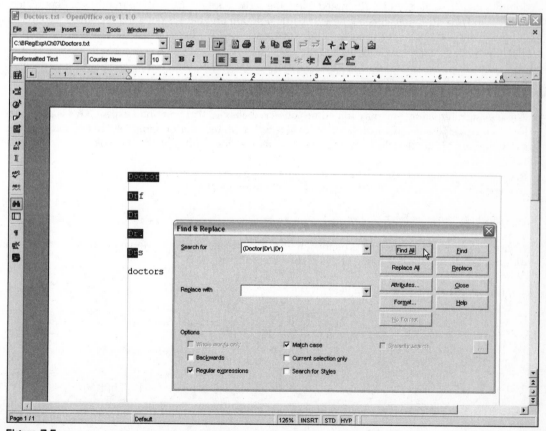

Figure 7-5

How It Works

First, consider some aspects of the situation after Step 4.

The text Doctor in Line 1 matches because the pattern Doctor is the first option inside the parentheses. Each literal character in the pattern matches the corresponding literal character in the test text.

The text Dr in Line 3 matches because the pattern Dr, the third option in the parentheses, matches the test text character for character.

In Line 4, the sequence of two characters, Dr., matches.

The Dr of Drive is matched — because it matches the third option inside the parentheses.

Now let's look at the change in matches after adding the end-of-word boundary metacharacter after the closing parenthesis.

Previously, the Dr of Drf on Line 2 matched. Now there is no match because, although the Dr of Drf continues to be matched by the third option inside the parentheses, the following character is an f, and the position before the f is not an end-of-word word-boundary position.

On Line 4, there is now a two-character sequence that matches. The first option inside the parentheses does not match, so matching is attempted using the second option inside the parentheses. That matches the first and second characters on Line 4. The literal period on Line 4 is not a word character, so the position following the r of Dr is an end-of-word word boundary. The boundary occurs because of the period that follows it, not because of the space character that follows the period.

Unexpected Alternation Behavior

When using alternation, you may sometimes observe behavior that you don't expect. This is particularly likely to happen if you have options of unequal length with the shorter option on the left and with the shorter option included in the longer option. That may sound confusing, so let's look at an example.

Suppose that you want to match either the single lowercase character a or the lowercase character sequence ab. You could express that desire in the following pattern:

```
(a|ab)
```

Notice that the shorter option, a, is on the left and that it is also part of the longer option, ab. So the conditions described at the beginning of this section are both satisfied.

The sample file, ab.txt, is shown here:

```
a

ab

ac ab

ba

bab
```

Notice that on three lines, the sequence of characters ab is present.

Try It Out   Unequal Alternation

First, try it out, using the following pattern:

```
(a|ab)
```

1. Open the file ab.txt in OpenOffice.org Writer.

2. Open the Find & Replace dialog box by pressing Ctrl+F, and check the Regular Expressions and Match Case check boxes.

3. Enter the regular expression pattern **(a|ab)** in the Search For text box.

4. Click the Find All button, and inspect the results, as shown in Figure 7-6.

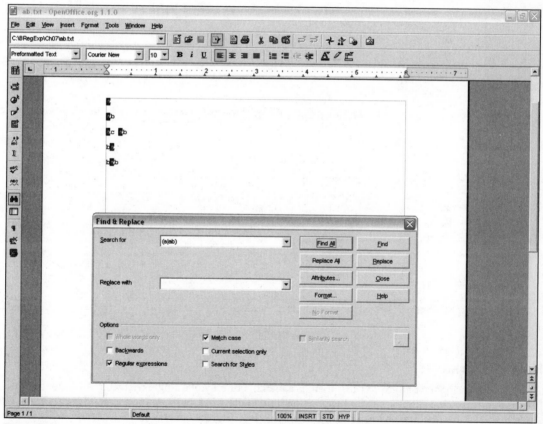

Figure 7-6

Notice that each of the highlighted matches is only a single character in length and matches the lowercase character a.

5. Now reverse the alternation options and use the following pattern:

```
(ab|a)
```

Edit the pattern in the Search For text box to read `(ab|a)`.

6. Click the Find All button, and inspect the results in Figure 7-7. Notice that there are now three matches that are two characters in length and that match the sequence of lowercase characters ab.

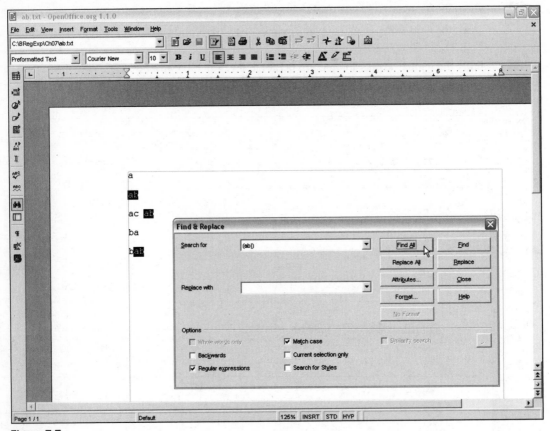

Figure 7-7

How It Works

On Line 2, using the pattern `(a|ab)`, there is a match, but only of a single character. Assume that the regular expression engine starts at the position immediately before the a. It attempts a match of the first option a against the first character on the line, also an a. There is a match for that character. Because the first option is a single character, an option matches. The regular expression engine doesn't attempt to match the second option. It moves to the position after the match it has found (the position between a and b). It then attempts to match again, but neither option, a or ab, matches the character b, so there is no match.

Using the pattern `(a|ab)`, there will never be a match for the sequence of characters ab, because the first option will always match an a, meaning that the second option is never evaluated.

However, when you change the pattern to (ab|a), there is a two-character match on Line 2. The first option, ab, is evaluated first. Assuming that matching starts from the position before the a, the first option matches, because the pattern ab is matched by the sequence of characters ab. Because the first option matches, the second option is not evaluated.

Capturing Parentheses

The uses of parentheses you've looked at have routinely *captured* the content between the opening and closing parentheses. As you saw in Figure 7-1, there was a group of characters, with the value of hot, captured and assigned to a variable $1.

Numbering of Captured Groups

Numbering of captured groups is determined by the order of the opening parentheses in a regular expression pattern.

For example, use the following pattern:

```
(United) (States)
```

Match it against the following test text:

```
The United States
```

The sequence of characters United (which follows the first opening parenthesis) is the value of the variable $1, and the sequence of characters States (which follows the second opening parenthesis) is the value of the variable $2. Figure 7-8 shows this in the Komodo Regular Expressions Toolkit.

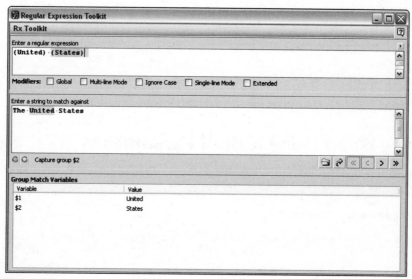

Figure 7-8

Suppose that you modify the pattern so that the space character is also inside parentheses, as follows:

```
(United)( )(States)
```

Then there are three groups, as shown in Figure 7-9.

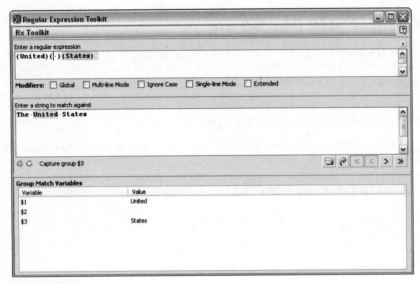

Figure 7-9

If you are wondering why you might want to capture a whitespace character, think of how you might combine two names:

```
([A-Za-z])( )([A-Za-z])
```

as a filename such as the following:

```
FirstWord_SecondWord.html
```

You might specifically want to replace the space character with an underline character.

Numbering When Using Nested Parentheses

When you use nested parentheses, the same rule applies. Variables are numbered in accordance with the order in which the opening parentheses characters occur.

You have the following sample text:

```
A22 33
```

And you want to match it against the following rather confusing pattern:

```
((\w(\d{2}))(( )(\d{2}))))
```

The first question that might occur to you is why might you want to do this. Also, you may want to use the documentation techniques mentioned in Chapter 10 and illustrated in several of the language-specific chapters later in the book.

To get a hint as to why nested parentheses can be useful, take a look at Figure 7-10.

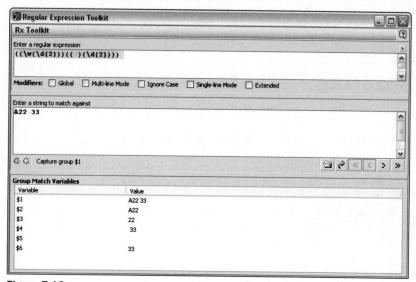

Figure 7-10

If you want to use different parts of the test text A22 33 for different programmatic purposes, you are now in a position to do so. The variable $1 has the value A22 33. So you can use all six characters (including the space character) for some purpose. However, if you want to reuse the three-character sequence A22 for some purpose, the variable $2 exists and can be used in your code.

Other variables have been created with values that correspond to different chunks of the test text.

Named Groups

Python and the .NET languages allow named groups to be created. The syntax:

```
(?<GroupName>Pattern)
```

or:

```
(?'GroupName'Pattern)
```

is used in .NET languages, whereas the pattern:

```
(?P<GroupName>Pattern)
```

is used in Python.

So if you had data that included the form:

```
Temperature:22.2
```

and you wanted to capture the temperature in a variable named `MeanTemp`, you could use the following pattern, assuming that temperature is in the range 10 to 99 degrees and is recorded to one decimal place:

```
Temperature:(?<MeanTemp>\d{2}\.\d
```

Non-Capturing Parentheses

Some regular expression implementations provide support for non-capturing parentheses.

Another term for non-capturing parentheses is grouping-only parentheses.

Suppose that you want to capture two sequences of characters, the first sequence of interest being a form of `Doctor` and the second being the doctor's surname. Assume that the data is structured as follows:

```
Doctor Firstname LastName
Dr FirstName LastName
Dr. FirstName LastName
```

You can use the following pattern to capture the form of `Doctor` or one of its abbreviations and have the form of address as `$1` and the surname as `$2`, as you can see in Figure 7-11:

```
(Doctor|Dr.|Dr)(\s\w{1,}\s)(\w{1,})
```

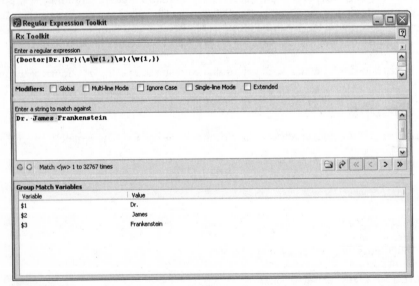

Figure 7-11

The pattern `(Doctor|Dr.|Dr)` has created the group `$1` and has captured the form of `Doctor` or its abbreviation. The pattern `(\s\w{1,}\s)` has created the group `$2` and has captured a space character, the doctor's first name, and another space character. The pattern `(\w{1,})` creates the group `$3` and has captured the doctor's surname.

The pattern to create non-capturing parentheses is as follows:

```
(?:the-non-captured-content)
```

In other words, when an opening parenthesis is followed by a question mark, then followed by a colon character, the parentheses do not capture the content.

If you modify the pattern to:

```
(Doctor|Dr.|Dr)(?:\s\w{1,}\s)(\w{1,})
```

`$1` is the form of doctor and `$2` is the surname, as you can see in Figure 7-12. The pattern `(?:\s\w{1,})` does not capture a group containing the first name.

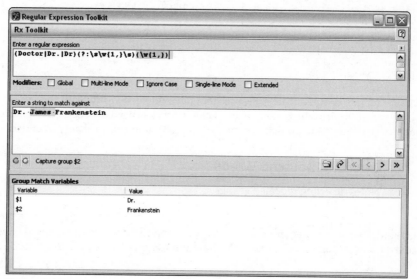

Figure 7-12

Non-capturing parentheses do make the pattern look more complex. But in complex situations, they can reduce the number of groups that you work with and can make programming a little easier.

In addition, when the regular expression engine has fewer groups to keep track of, there can be an efficiency gain.

Back References

A common use of capturing parentheses is in back references, which is also sometimes written as one word, backreferences.

One situation where back references come in handy is where you have inadvertently doubled the the definite article in a sentence, as I have deliberately done in this sentence. In documents of significant length, it can be a fairly major task to pick up doubled words.

A sample document, `DoubledWords.txt`, is shown here:

```
Paris in the the spring.

The theoretical viewpoint is of little value here.

I view the theoretical viewpoint as being of little value here.

I think that that is often overdone.

This sentence contains contains a doubled word or two two.

Fear fear is a fearful thing.

Writing successful programs requires that the the programmer fully understands the
problem to be solved.
```

Included in the sample document are sentences that have doubled words with the same case and with different case and examples where a sequence of characters has been doubled but legitimately so. In the fourth sentence is a doubled word that is entirely acceptable and was probably intended.

Try It Out   Detecting Doubled Words

This exercise explores detecting repeated strings.

> **In OpenOffice.org Writer, the variable representing the first group captured is designated \1 rather than $1 as it was in the Komodo Regular Expression Toolkit.**

The following regular expression pattern uses parentheses to capture sequences of alphabetic characters, defined by the character class `[A-Za-z]`:

```
([A-Za-z]+) +\1
```

After one or more matches for the character class, there follows a space character with the quantifier +, indicating that there must be one or more space characters between the content of the parentheses and what is to follow. The final part of the regular expression pattern is \1, which is a back reference to the contents of the first pair (in this example the only pair) of capturing parentheses.

1. Open `DoubledWords.txt` in OpenOffice.org Writer.

2. Open the Find & Replace dialog box, and check the Regular Expressions and Match Case check boxes.

3. Enter the pattern **([A-Za-z]+) +\1** in the Search For text box.

4. Click the Find All button, and inspect the results. Figure 7-13 shows the result of applying the regular expression pattern to `DoubledWords.txt` in OpenOffice.org Writer.

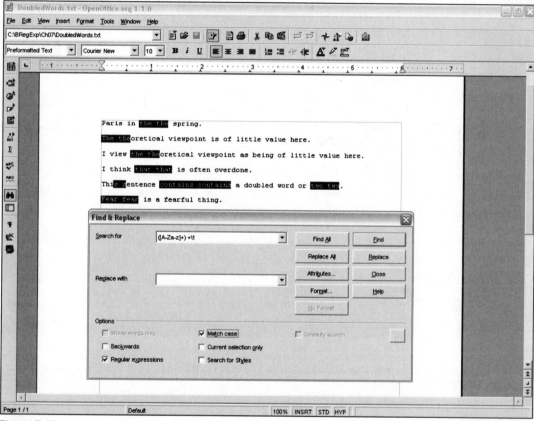

Figure 7-13

As you can see from the figure, you have some undesired matches in `DoubledWords.txt`, principally because the chosen regular expression pattern selects repeated character sequences rather than repeated words.

So you need to modify the pattern so that the beginning of the first word is made explicit and the end of the possibly repeated word is made explicit, too. The following pattern achieves this:

```
\<([A-Za-z]+) +\1\>
```

5. Modify the pattern in the Search For text box to \<([A-Za-z]+) +\1\>.

6. Click the Find All button, and inspect the results. As you can see in Figure 7-14, the selection now focuses only on repeated words and ignores repeated sequences of characters that are not words.

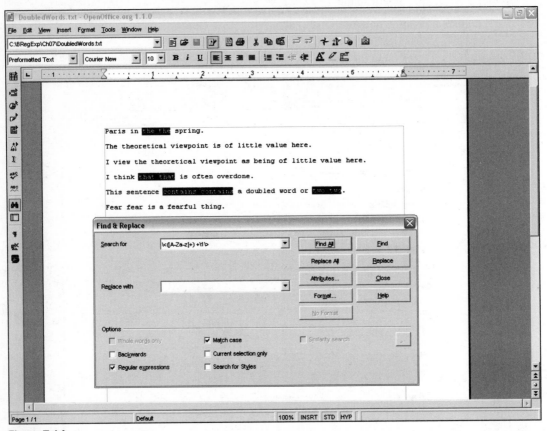

Figure 7-14

How It Works

First, let's look at what happens with the pattern ([A-Za-z]+) +\1.

The problem definition that corresponds to this pattern could be expressed as follows:

Match one or more ASCII alphabetic characters followed by one or more spaces. Then attempt to match the preceding sequences of ASCII alphabetic characters.

There is nothing that specifies that the sequence of alphabetic characters is a word. So you find that in Line 3 the sequence of characters the, which occurs in the word the, also occurs as the first three characters of the word theoretical. That is a match, but an undesired match.

Similarly, on Line 5, the final s of This is repeated in the initial s of sentence.

Because the search was conducted in a case-sensitive way (remember that the Match Case check box was checked), the word Fear, which is doubled as fear on Line 6, is not detected.

When you modify the pattern so that word-boundary metacharacters are included, the undesired matches of part words, such as the and theoretical, no longer match.

You could have made the beginning and the end of the first word and the beginning and the end of the second word explicit by using the following pattern:

```
\<([A-Za-z]+)\> +\<\1\>
```

However, the requirement for at least one space character after the first sequence of characters already achieves that. Either pattern will achieve the same results.

Exercises

Test your understanding of the material in this chapter using the following exercises:

1. Specify three patterns that will match the sequences of characters license and licence.

2. Find a solution that will identify the repeating of the word fear, irrespective of whether fear occurs at the beginning of a sentence. Assume that exactly one space character separates the two words.

Lookahead and Lookbehind

Chapter 7 looked briefly at back references, which allow a very specific form of coordinated testing or examination of related parts of test text, as you saw in the doubled words example in that chapter. A back reference allows you to test whether a sequence of characters has already occurred in the test text and use that previously occurring sequence of characters for some specified purpose. That is very helpful for a narrow range of uses, such as finding doubled words, but a more general form of awareness of preceding or following text allows the developer to express ideas such as "Match a word if it is preceded by a specified sequence of characters" or "Match a sequence of characters if it is followed by a specified sequence of characters."

Matching a character sequence when you know what does or doesn't follow or precede it allows you to get rid of many potentially undesired matches. This can be particularly useful when you have to process large amounts of data and the risk of undesired matches in a search-and-replace operation is significant.

Matching using patterns to implement such problem definitions enables matching to be carried out in a way that depends on the context of words or sequences of characters that are of interest.

> *The term lookaround is sometimes used to refer to both lookahead and lookbehind.*
>
> *Lookahead and lookbehind are each split into positive and negative types. So, lookaround consists of positive lookahead, negative lookahead, positive lookbehind, and negative lookbehind.*

In this chapter, you will learn the following:

- ❑ What type of situations might benefit from lookahead and lookbehind
- ❑ How to use positive and negative lookahead
- ❑ How to use positive and negative lookbehind

Why You Need Lookahead and Lookbehind

Chapter 1 looked at a fairly clumsy first attempt to modify one of the documents of the fictional Star Training Company. One of the problems in that first attempt at text replacement was an inability to express an idea such as "Match the word Star only when it is followed by the word Training." That notion is lookahead.

As a further attempt at making the replacement of text in the Star Training Company documents more specific, you could create the following problem definition:

Match the sequence of Characters s, t, a, and r when it is followed by a space character and also followed by the sequence of characters T, r, a, i, n, i, n, and g.

In other words, you would match the word Star only when it is followed, with an intervening space character, by the word Training. This allows matching to be much more specific than any of the techniques used in earlier chapters.

The following pattern implements the preceding problem definition:

```
Star(?= Training)
```

Strictly speaking, when using the preceding pattern, you are matching Star when it is followed by a space character and the sequence of characters Training. If you want to ensure that only the word Training is in the lookahead, you can include the \b word boundary or the \> end-of-word metacharacter, depending on which metacharacters your tool supports:

```
Star(?= Training\b)
```

The characters that follow the (?= and precede the) are not captured.

The (? metacharacters

Several metacharacters can be considered special kinds of opening parentheses, each of which begins with the sequence of characters (?. Several of those are briefly described here, because many developers find them fairly difficult to distinguish, and it may help you grasp which combination does what by seeing them together.

In Chapter 7, you saw the (?: form, which carries the idea of non-capturing grouping. The other special opening parentheses that apply to lookahead and lookbehind are described in this chapter. together with several examples of how they are used.

The combination (?= is used for positive lookahead. The syntax for positive lookahead, negative lookahead, positive lookbehind, and negative lookbehind is summarized in the following table for easy comparison.

Metacharacter	Meaning
(?: ...)	Non-capturing grouping
(?= ...)	Positive lookahead
(?! ...)	Negative lookahead
(?<= ...)	Positive lookbehind
(?<! ...)	Negative lookbehind

Lookahead

Lookahead allows you to make a match conditional on the matching sequence of characters being followed by (positive lookahead) or not being followed by (negative lookahead) a specified sequence of characters.

> Some documentation (the .NET documentation is an example) refers to lookahead as zero-width lookahead assertion. This chapter will generally use the shorter term, *lookahead*, with the same meaning. Where relevant, the terms *positive* and *negative* will be used as qualifiers of the term *lookahead*.

A key point to appreciate about lookahead is that the characters that occur later than the specified match are not consumed by the regular expression engine.

This can become quite abstract, so a simple example follows to help clarify what the regular expression engine is doing.

Suppose that you have a document containing part numbers of the form alphabetic character, alphabetic character, numeric digit, numeric digit, as follows:

```
BC99
```

However, you are interested only in the alphabetic characters. The problem definition can be expressed as follows:

Match two consecutive alphabetic characters if they occur at the beginning of a line and are immediately followed by two numeric digits.

The matching takes place only on the alphabetic characters. The pattern that implements this problem definition never matches any numeric digits. A pattern to implement the problem definition is as follows:

```
^[A-Za-z]{2}(?=\d\d)
```

The ^ metacharacter indicates the beginning of line position. The two \w metacharacters indicate ASCII alphabetic characters. The (?=\d\d) pattern is the lookahead, which specifies that after the two alphabetic characters, there must be two numeric digits.

A simple test file, PartNumbers.txt, is shown here:

```
AB21

AB1

CD8D3

RD/25
```

Only one of the four parts numbers will match.

Try It Out   **Part Numbers Example**

1. Open PowerGrep, and in the Search Text area, enter the pattern **^[A-Za-z]{2}(?=\d\d)**.

2. In the Folder text box, enter the folder name **C:\BRegExp\Ch08**. Amend the folder name if you downloaded the example code to a different directory.

3. In the File Mask text box, enter **PartNumbers.txt**, and click the Search button.

4. Inspect the results in the Results area, as shown in Figure 8-1. Notice that only one of the four part numbers matches the pattern.

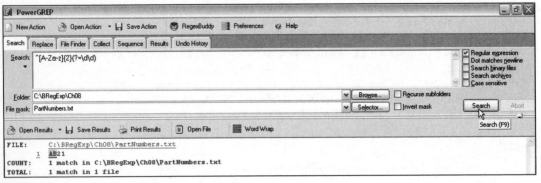

Figure 8-1

How It Works

Assume that the regular expression engine starts at the position before the A on the first line. It first attempts to match its current position against the ^ metacharacter. There is a match. Next, it attempts to match the first [A-Za-z] character class against the first character on the first line. The uppercase A matches the character class. Next, it attempts to match the character class again against the second character of the test text, B. There is a match. To that point in the processing, the regular expression engine has carried out a match in the way that you have seen previously. However, the pattern (?=\d\d) tells the regular expression engine that it must check what the following sequence of characters is and match the two alphabetic characters only if two numeric digits, as indicated by the \d\d specified inside the lookahead, are present. The first \d metacharacter matches the 2 of 21. The second \d metacharacter matches the 1 of 21. So there is a sequence of two numeric digits following the two alphabetic characters; the constraint imposed by the lookahead pattern, (?=\d\d), is satisfied. Therefore, the whole pattern matches.

When the regular expression reaches the position at the start of the second line, the test text on that line is AB1. The regular expression engine attempts to match the ^ metacharacter. Because the regular expression engine is at the beginning of line position, there is a match. Subsequent match attempts for the A and B of AB1 are successful. Matching is complete, so the lookahead part of the regular expression pattern is processed. The lookahead (?=\d\d) does not match, because there is only one numeric digit. All the characters you wanted to match have been matched, but the lookahead has failed; therefore, the whole regular expression fails.

Positive Lookahead

Positive lookahead is the process of matching a sequence of characters constrained by a requirement that the sequence must be followed by some other sequence of characters (which is usually different).

As with many other techniques in regular expressions, there is often more than one way to use lookahead with the same result. For example, to match the character sequence State only when it occurs in States, you could use:

```
(?=States)State
```

or

```
State(?=s)
```

The first option means "Find a position that is followed by the character sequence States. If such a position exists, attempt to match the character sequence State." The second option means "Match the character sequence State only if it is followed by a lowercase s." Both patterns will match the same character sequence.

Positive Lookahead — Star Training Example

Now that you understand how to use positive lookahead, let's revisit the Star Training Company example and improve the specificity of the processing.

The most straightforward way to approach the problem, assuming for the moment that you will use only lookahead, is the following problem definition:

Match the sequence of characters, s, t, a, and r when they are followed by a single space character and then followed by the sequence of characters T, r, a, i, n, i, n, and g.

The following pattern implements the problem definition:

```
Star(?= Training)
```

Positive Lookahead — Star Training Example

1. Open PowerGrep, and type the pattern **Star(?= Training)** in the Search text area.

2. Type the folder name **C:\BRegExp\Ch08** in the Folder text box. Amend the folder name if you downloaded the sample files for this chapter to a different location.

3. Type the filename **StarOriginal.txt** in the File Mask text box, and click the Search button.

4. Inspect the results in the Results area, as shown in Figure 8-2. Notice that all six occurrences of the character sequence Star, which precedes Training (with an intervening space character), are matched. Due to the way that PowerGrep displays text, you will likely need to scroll horizontally to see some of the matching character sequences.

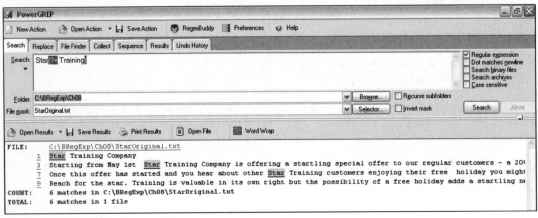

Figure 8-2

How It Works

The regular expression engine starts at the beginning of the test document, attempting to match the character sequence Star. Matching of Star takes place in the normal way. However, each time the character sequence Star is matched, the regular expression engine also looks ahead to find out whether or not Star is followed by a space character and the character sequence Training.

The occurrence of Star on the first line is followed by the specified sequence, so there is a match.

However, in the second line, Star, which is part of Starting, is matched by the pattern Star, but matching fails when the lookahead is evaluated.

Positive Lookahead — Later in Same Sentence

Positive lookahead can find occurrences of two words of interest in the same sentence. This section looks at how you can match a word if a second word occurs later in the same sentence. The assumption is made that the data does not contain a number that includes a decimal point (which is indistinguishable from a period character) and does not include an ellipsis made of a short sequence of period characters.

The test file, Sentence.txt, is shown here:

```
Here is a sentence where one can look ahead to interesting character sequences.

This sentence does not contain interesting characters.

Here is a sequence of characters.

Which sequence of characters is contained in this sentence?
```

The problem definition is as follows:

Match the character sequence sentence only when it is followed by the character sequence sequence in the same sentence.

Only one of the lines, the first, contains the sequence of characters sentence with the sequence of characters sequence later in the same sentence.

Try It Out   Positive Lookahead — Later in the Same Sentence

1.   Open PowerGrep, and type the pattern **sentence(?=.*sequence.*\.)** in the Search text area.

2.   Type the folder name **C:\BRegExp\Ch08** in the Folder text box. Amend the folder name if you downloaded the test files for this chapter to another folder.

3.   Type the filename **Sentence.txt** in the File Mask text box, and click the Search button.

4.   Inspect the results displayed in the Results area, as shown in Figure 8-3.

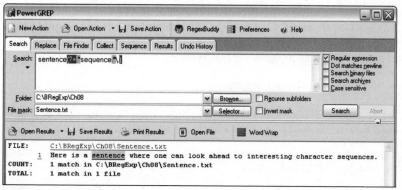

Figure 8-3

How It Works

The regular expression engine looks for the character sequence sentence. If it finds that character sequence, it tests to see if the lookahead condition is satisfied. The lookahead pattern, (?=.*sequence.*\.), tests, from the position that follows the final e of sentence, for the occurrence of the character sequence sequence with any number of intervening characters, as indicated by .*. It then tests for the later occurrence of a period character, as indicated by the \. metacharacter, with any number of intervening characters as indicated by the pattern .*.

In the first line, all parts of the regular expression, including the lookahead, are satisfied, so there is a match.

In the second line, although the character sequence sentence can be matched, the lookahead fails. With no occurrence of the character sequence sequence, there is no match on that line.

On the third line, the character sequence sentence cannot be matched, so there is no match on that line.

On the fourth line, both sentence and sequence occur, but in the wrong order to satisfy the constraint imposed by the lookahead.

Negative Lookahead

Negative lookahead is the process of matching a sequence of characters constrained by an additional requirement that the sequence must *not* be followed by some other sequence of characters.

For example, in the Star Training Company example, you might want to find occurrences of the sequence of characters s, t, a, and r when they are not followed by a space character and the word Training. That would allow you to find occurrences of the sequence of characters s, t, a, and r that are less likely to refer to Star as part of the name of Star Training Company.

Negative lookahead is written as an opening parenthesis followed by an exclamation point; then the string to be looked for; and, finally, the closing parenthesis. So if you wanted to match a sequence of characters not followed by the word Training, you could use the following as the lookahead part of the regular expression when using tools and languages that support the \b metacharacter:

```
(?!\bTraining\b)
```

Negative lookahead can be usefully combined with other constraints. For example, by specifying that the matching process is case-sensitive and using the pattern (lowercase) star, you can keep occurrences of Star from successfully matching the supplied pattern.

The problem definition can be stated as follows:

Match the sequence of character s, t, a, and r, but only when that sequence of characters is not followed by a space character and the sequence of characters T, r, a, i, n, i, n, and g.

Try It Out   Negative Lookahead

1. Open PowerGrep, and enter the pattern **Star(?! Training)** in the Search text area.

2. In the Folder text box, enter the folder name **C:\BRegExp\Ch08**.

3. In the File Mask text, box enter the filename **StarOriginal.txt**, and click the Search button.

4. Inspect the results in the Results area, as shown in Figure 8-4. (Due to the way that PowerGrep interprets line breaks, you will likely find lines that scroll off the screen in a way similar to that shown in the figure.)

Notice that none of the six occurrences of Star before a space character followed by the character sequence Training matches.

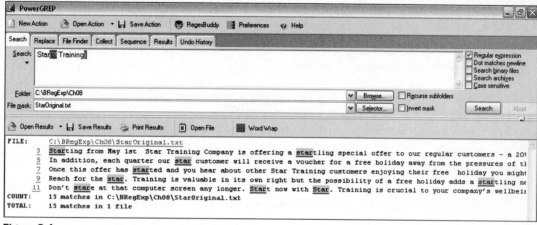

Figure 8-4

How It Works

The character sequence Star is matched in the normal way. If a match for Star is found, the regular expression engine tests the lookahead. If the character sequence following Star is a space character followed by Training, the lookahead fails (because it is a negative lookahead). If the negative lookahead is successful, the Star is a match.

On Line 1, Star is followed by a space character, then Training Company. Because the character sequence specified by the negative lookahead is found, the lookahead fails. Therefore, Star in Line 1 is not matched.

On Line 2, Star occurs as part of Starting. The regular expression engine matches Star. It then tests to see if the next character is a space character. In this case, the character is the second t of Starting. The pattern specified in the lookahead is not found. Because it is a negative lookahead, the lookahead constraint is satisfied. Therefore, the match of Star in Starting does match, even after the lookahead constraint is evaluated.

Positive Lookahead Examples

The following section works through some potential uses of positive lookahead.

You may at some point need to test a document to find if some selected text is present with some additional text of interest somewhere later in the document.

Positive Lookahead in the Same Document

Suppose that you have a document, Databases.txt, and you want to test whether Microsoft SQL Server is mentioned and to find out whether the MySQL database product is mentioned later in the document. The test file, Databases.txt, is shown here:

The current version of Microsoft SQL Server is SQL Server 2000. However a new version, SQL Server 2005 is scheduled for release for the calendar year 2005. The MySQL database product lacks some of the features of big commercial database products like SQL Server but the product team is working hard to provide an improved set of features.

Try It Out   **Lookahead in the Same Document**

1. Open RegexBuddy, and select the Match tab in the upper pane.

2. Enter the regular expression pattern **SQL Server(?:.*MySQL)** in the Match tab, and select the Test tab in the middle pane.

3. Click the Open File option, navigate to C:\BRegExp\Ch08, and open the Databases.txt file. Adjust the navigation if you installed the code downloads elsewhere.

4. Click the Find First button, and inspect the highlighted text in the lower pane.

    Figure 8-5 shows the results. Notice that RegexBuddy highlights the whole text from the match of SQL Server to the first appearance of the sequence of characters MySQL. Strictly speaking, only the string SQL Server is matched by the regular expression. The highlighted area, in a convention that is also followed by PowerGrep, also highlights the text specified by the look-ahead component.

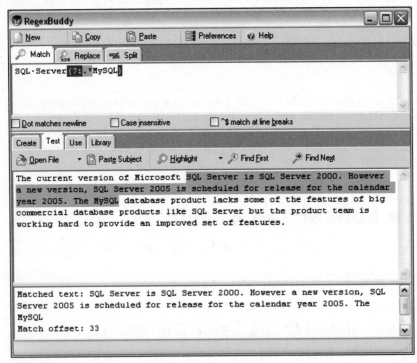

Figure 8-5

How It Works

The matching process takes place on a literal sequence of characters, SQL Server, in the normal way. The regular expression engine starts its attempts to match that sequence of characters from the position before the word The on the first line. The first occurrence of the pattern SQL Server matches. The regular expression engine then attempts to satisfy the lookahead constraint. It looks for any occurrence of the character sequence MySQL. The pattern . * indicates that the character sequence MySQL can occur anywhere later in the document than the occurrence of the character sequence SQL Server.

Inserting an Apostrophe

This example adds an apostrophe in places where it may have been inadvertently omitted. With increasing use of texting via mobile phones, some misspellings and inappropriate abbreviations are sometimes carried over into more formal documents. The test text is shown here:

```
This is not Andrews first book.

This book is Andrews.
```

In both lines of the test text, there should be an apostrophe between the w and s of Andrews, because it is being used as a possessive. You can assume that the sequence of characters Andrews is unlikely to be part of a longer sequence of alphabetic characters, and it seems reasonable that the character following the character sequence Andrews is likely to be a space character or a period character.

However, it is possible that, for example, a question mark could follow the character sequence Andrews, as in the following:

```
Is this book Andrews?
```

So you need to allow for other possible characters following the lowercase s. One solution is to specify that the character s must be followed by a word boundary. This would allow for either whitespace characters or punctuation characters following the s.

The problem definition can be expressed as follows:

Match the sequence of characters A, n, d, r, e, w IF it is followed by a lowercase s that is followed by a word-boundary position.

This problem definition can be expressed using the following pattern:

```
Andrew(?=s\b)
```

If you wanted to constrain matching to the situation where the s is followed only by a space character or a period character, you could use this pattern, which uses alternation to specify two alternate lookahead constraints:

```
Andrew((?=s )|(?=s\.))
```

Try It Out   Inserting an Apostrophe

This example demonstrates the effect of the two preceding patterns.

1. Open RegexBuddy, and enter the pattern **Andrew((?=s)|(?=s\b))** in the Match tab.

2. In the Test tab, enter the following test text:

```
This is not Andrews first book.

This book is Andrews.

Is this book Andrews?
```

3. Click the Find First icon, and inspect the matched character sequence.

4. Click the Find Next button twice, observing whether or not there is a match after each click.

Figure 8-6 shows the results. There is a match on the first occurrence of the character sequence Andrews. However, after the second click of the Find Next button, there is no match. This is because the character sequence Andrews, which is followed by the question mark, does not match the lookahead.

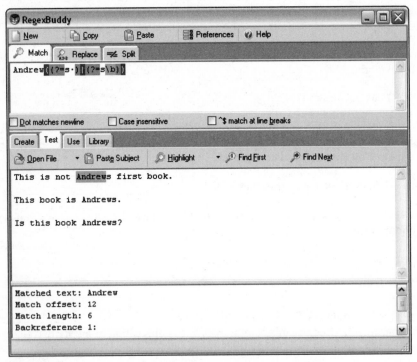

Figure 8-6

5. Edit the regular expression in the Match tab to Andrew(?=s\b).

6. Click the Find First icon and then click the Find Next icon twice, observing each time what character sequence is or is not matched.

Figure 8-7 shows the appearance after the Find Next icon has been clicked twice. With the modification of the regular expression, all three occurrences of the character sequence `Andrew` now match.

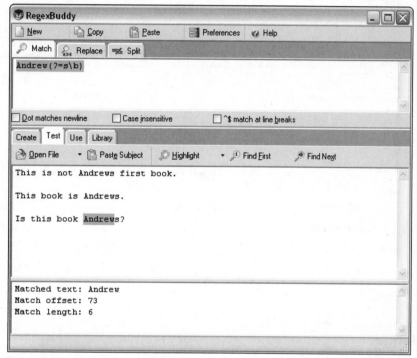

Figure 8-7

7. Now that you know that each occurrence of the relevant string matches, you can modify the regular expression to create two groups between which you can insert the desired apostrophe to make `Andrew's` possessive.

Modify the regular expression in the Match tab to `(Andrew)(s)(?=\b)`.

8. Using the Find First and Find Next icons, confirm that all three occurrences of the slightly modified desired character sequence `Andrews` match.

9. Click the Replace tab. In the lower pane on the Replace tab, type **$1'$2**.

10. On the Test tab, click the Replace All icon, and inspect the results in the lower pane on the Test tab. (You may need to adjust the window size to see all the results.)

Figure 8-8 shows the appearance after this step.

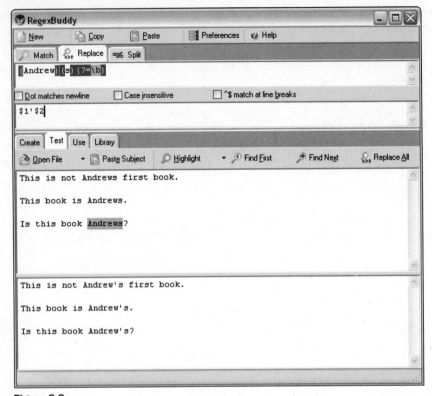

Figure 8-8

How It Works

The pattern Andrew((?=s)|(?=s\b)) matches the character sequence Andrew followed by either s and a space character or by s and a word boundary.

In the first line, the character sequence Andrew is followed by s and a space character, so it satisfies the first lookahead constraint. Because the match is successful and the lookahead constraint is satisfied, there is a match for the whole regular expression.

In the second line, the character sequence Andrew is followed by s and a period character. The second lookahead constraint is satisfied.

On the third line, the character sequence Andrew is followed by an s and then a question mark. Because the question mark is in neither lookahead, the lookahead constraint is not satisfied.

When the regular expression pattern is changed to Andrew(?=s\b), when Andrew is matched, the lookahead constraint is an s followed by a word boundary. There is a word boundary following each Andrews and the following character on all three lines. In Line 1, there is a word boundary before the space character. In Line 2, there is a word boundary before the period character. In Line 3, there is a word boundary before the question mark. So each occurrence of Andrew matches.

When the regular expression is modified to `(Andrew)(s)(?=\b)`, you capture the character sequence `Andrew` in $1 and capture the s in $2. The lookahead does not capture any characters. So to insert an apostrophe, you want $1 (`Andrew`) to be followed by an apostrophe to be followed by $2 (a lowercase s).

Lookbehind

Lookbehind tests whether a sequence of characters that is matched is preceded (positive lookbehind) or not preceded (negative lookbehind) by another sequence of characters.

For example, if you wanted to match the surname `Jekyll` only if it is preceded by the sequence of characters `Dr.` (an uppercase D, a lowercase r, a period, and a space character), you would use a pattern like this:

```
(?<=Dr. )Jekyll
```

The component `(?<=Dr. )` indicates the sequence of characters that is tested for as a lookbehind, and the component `Jekyll` matches literally.

Positive Lookbehind

A positive lookbehind is a constraint on matching. Matching occurs only if the pattern to be matched is preceded by the pattern contained in the lookbehind assertion.

Try It Out   **Positive Lookbehind**

1. Open the Komodo Regular Expression Toolkit, and delete any residual regular expression and sample text.

2. In the Enter a String to Match Against area, enter the test text, **Mr. Hyde and Dr. Jekyll are characters in a famous novel**.

3. In the Enter a Regular Expression area, enter the pattern **(?<=Dr.)Jekyll**.

4. Inspect the highlighted text in the String to Match Against area and the description of the results in the gray area below, `Match succeeded: 0 groups`.

    Figure 8-9 shows the appearance. Notice that the sequence of characters `Jekyll` is highlighted.

5. Edit the regular expression pattern to read `(?<=Mr. )Jekyll`.

6. Inspect the description of the results in the gray area, `No matches found`.

7. Edit the regular expression pattern to read `((?<=Mr. )|(?<=Mister ))Hyde`. Ensure that there is a space character after the r of `Mister`. If that is omitted, there will be no match.

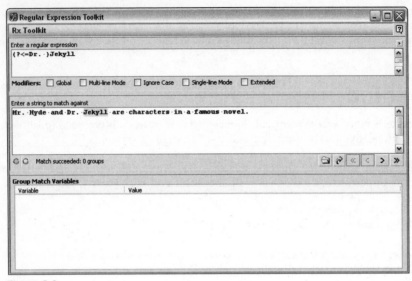

Figure 8-9

8. Inspect the description of the results in the gray area, Match succeeded: 1 group. Also notice that the character sequence Hyde is highlighted.

9. Edit the Mr. in the test text to read Mister.

10. Inspect the gray area again. Again, the description is Match succeeded: 1 group. Figure 8-10 shows the appearance.

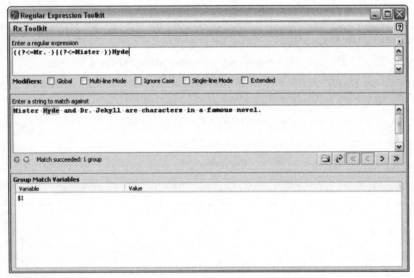

Figure 8-10

How It Works

The following description of how the regular expression engine operates is a conceptual one and may not reflect the approach taken by any individual regular expression engine. The text matched is the sequence of characters Jekyll.

Matching starts at the beginning of the test text. The character following the regular expression's position is checked to see whether it is an uppercase J. If so, that is matched, and an attempt is made to match the other characters making up the sequence of characters Jekyll. If any attempt to match fails, the whole pattern fails, and the regular expression engine moves forward through the text attempting to match the character sequence Jekyll.

If a match is found for the character sequence Jekyll, the regular expression engine is at the position immediately before the J of Jekyll. It checks that the immediately preceding character is a space character. If so, it then tests if the character before that is a period character. If so, it tests if the character before that is a lowercase r. Finally, it tests if the character before that is an uppercase D. Because matching of Jekyll was successful, and the constraint that the character sequence Jekyll be preceded by the character sequence Dr. (including a space character) was satisfied, the whole regular expression succeeds.

When you edit the pattern to read (?<=Mr.)Jekyll, the character sequence Jekyll is successfully matched as before. However, when the regular expression engine checks the characters that precede that character sequence, the constraint fails, because despite the fact (reading backward) that the space character, the period character, and the lowercase r are all present, there is no preceding uppercase D. Because the lookbehind constraint is not satisfied, there is no match.

It is possible to express alternatives in lookbehind. The problem definition might read as follows:

Match the character sequence Hyde if it is preceded by EITHER the character sequence Mr. (including a final space character) OR by the character sequence Mister (including a final space character).

After changing the pattern to read ((?<=Mr.)|(?<=Mister))Hyde, the regular expression engine attempts to match the character sequence Hyde. When it reaches the position immediately before the H of Hyde it will successfully match that character sequence. It then must also satisfy the constraint on the sequence of characters that precedes Hyde.

The pattern ((?<=Mr.)|(?<=Mister))Hyde uses parentheses to group two alternative patterns that must precede Hyde. The first option, specified by the pattern (?<=Mr.), requires that the sequence of four characters M, r, a period, and a space character must precede Hyde. At Step 8, that four-character sequence matches.

After the edit has been made to the test text, replacing Mr. with Mister, the other alternative comes into play. The pattern (?<=Mister) requires that a seven-character sequence (Mister plus a space character) precedes Hyde.

The positioning of the lookbehind assertion is important, as you will see in the next example.

Positioning of Positive Lookbehind

1.   Open RegexBuddy, click the Match tab, and enter the regular expression **(?<=like)SQL Server**.

2.   Click the Test tab, click the Open File icon, and open the `Databases.txt` file.

3.   Click the Find First icon, and inspect the highlighted text in the pane in the Test tab, as shown in Figure 8-11.

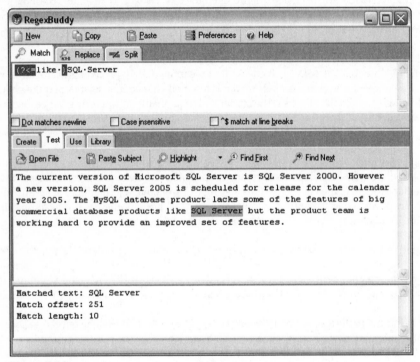

Figure 8-11

4.   Edit the regular expression in the Match tab so that it reads `SQL Server(?<=like )`.

5.   Click the Find First icon in the Test tab. Confirm that there is no now no highlighted text.

6.   Edit the regular expression in the Match tab so that it reads `SQL Server(?<=like SQL Server)`.

7.   Click the Find First icon in the Test tab. Confirm that there is again a match in the test text, as shown in Figure 8-12.

How It Works

When the pattern is `(?<=like )SQL Server`, the lookbehind looks behind, starting from the position immediately before the `S` of `SQL`. Because the character sequence `like SQL Server` exists in the test text, there is a match. When the pattern is `SQL Server(?<=like )`, the lookbehind starts from the position after the `r` of `Server`. Because that position is preceded by `Server`, not `like`, and the lookbehind is attempting to match the character sequence `like`, there is no match.

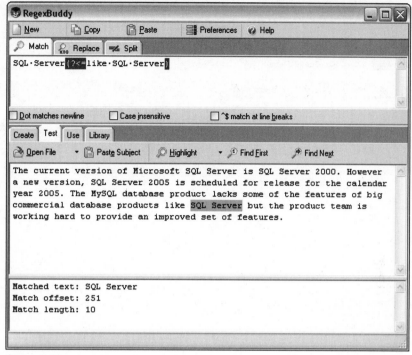

Figure 8-12

Negative Lookbehind

Negative lookbehind is a constraint on matching. Matching occurs only if the pattern to be matched is *not* preceded by the pattern contained in the lookbehind assertion.

Try It Out   Negative Lookbehind

Find occurrences of the character sequence SQL Server that are not preceded by the character sequence like followed by a space character.

1.   Open RegexBuddy, click the Match tab, and enter the regular expression **(?<!like)SQL Server**.

2.   Click the Test tab, click the Open File icon, and open the Databases.txt file.

3.   Click the Find First icon, and inspect the highlighted text in the pane in the Test tab, as shown in Figure 8-13.

4.   Look for other matches by clicking the Find Next icon several times. Note which occurrences of SQL Server match or don't match.

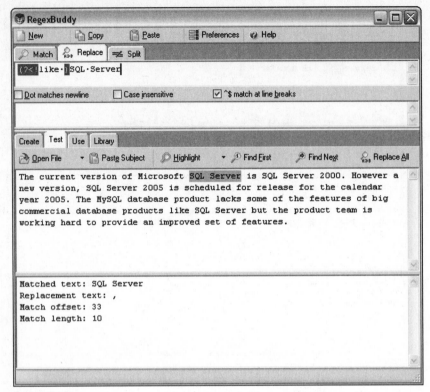

Figure 8-13

How It Works

When the regular expression engine matches the character sequence SQL Server, it checks whether the preceding characters correspond to the pattern specified in the lookbehind.

The first occurrence of SQL Server is not preceded by the character sequence like followed by a space character. The negative lookbehind is, therefore, satisfied. Because the character sequence SQL Server matches and the negative lookbehind constraint is satisfied, the whole regular expression matches.

The only occurrence of the character sequence SQL Server that fails to match is the occurrence preceded by the word like. The occurrence of the character sequence like followed by a space character does not satisfy the constraint imposed by the lookbehind. Therefore, although the character sequence SQL Server matches, the failure to satisfy the lookbehind constraint means that the whole regular expression fails to match.

How to Match Positions

By combining lookahead and lookbehind, it is possible to match positions between characters. For example, suppose that you wanted to match a position immediately before the Andrew of the following sample text:

```
This is Andrews book.
```

You could state the problem definition as follows:

Match a position that is preceded by the character sequence is followed by a space character and is followed by the character sequence Andrew.

You could match that position using the following pattern:

```
(?<=is )(?=Andrew)
```

Matching a Position

1. Open RegexBuddy. On the Match tab, type the regular expression pattern **(?<=is)(?=Andrew)**. If you used RegexBuddy for the replace example earlier in this chapter, delete the replacement text on the Replace tab.

2. On the Test tab, enter the sample text **This is Andrews book.**

3. Click the Find First icon, and inspect the information in the lower pane of the Test tab, as shown in Figure 8-14. On-screen, you can see the cursor blinking at the position immediately before the initial A of Andrews.

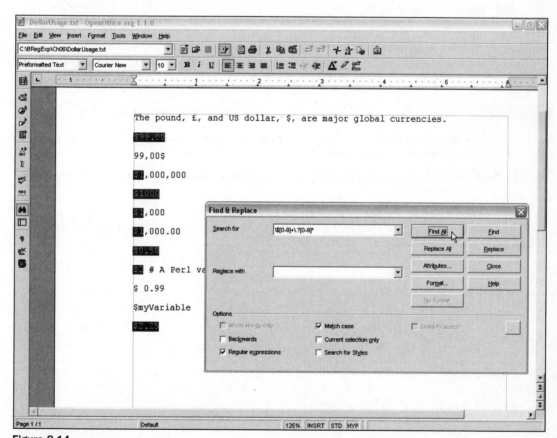

Figure 8-14

How It Works

The regular expression engine starts at the beginning of the document and tests each position to see whether both the lookbehind and lookahead constraints are satisfied. In the test text, only the position immediately before the initial A of Andrews satisfies both constraints. It is, therefore, the only position that matches.

Adding Commas to Large Numbers

One of the useful ways to apply a combination of lookbehind and lookahead is adding commas to large numbers.

Assume that the sales for the fictional Star Training Company are $1,234,567. The data would likely be stored as an integer without any commas. However, for readability, commas are usual in many situations where financial or other numerical data is presented.

The process of adding commas to a large numeric value is essentially to match the position between the appropriate numeric digits and replace that position by a comma.

In some European languages, the thousands separator, which is a comma in English, is a period character. Such periods can be added to a numeric value by slightly modifying the technique presented below.

First, let's look at a numeric value of 1234 and how you can add a comma in the appropriate place. You want to insert the comma at the position between the 1 and the 2. The reason to insert a comma in that position is that there are three numeric digits between the desired position and the end of the string.

Try It Out   Adding a Comma Separator to a Four-Digit Number

1. Open RegexBuddy. On the Replace tab, enter the pattern (?<=\d)(?=\d\d\d) in the upper pane and a single comma character in the lower pane.

2. On the Test pane, click the Find First icon. Confirm that there is a match, as described in the lower pane on the Test tab.

3. Click the Replace All icon, and check the replacement text shown in the lower pane on the Test tab (see Figure 8-15). The replacement text is 1,234, which is what you want. The regular expression pattern works for four-digit numbers.

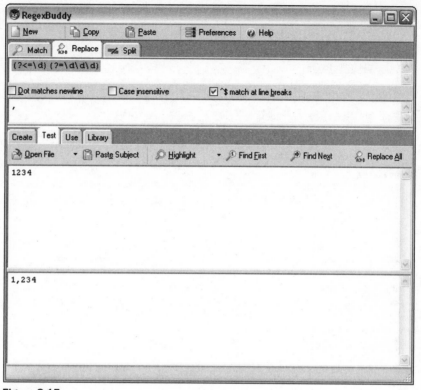

Figure 8-15

4. Edit the test text in the upper pane of the Test tab to read `1234567`.

5. Click the Replace All icon, and inspect the replacement text in the lower pane of the Test tab. The replacement text is `1,2,3,4,567`, which is not what you want. All the positions that have at least three numeric digits to the right have had a comma inserted, as shown in Figure 8-16.

6. Edit the pattern to `(?<=\d)(?=(\d\d\d)+)`.

7. Click the Replace All icon, and inspect the replacement text in the lower pane of the Test tab. The undesired commas are still there.

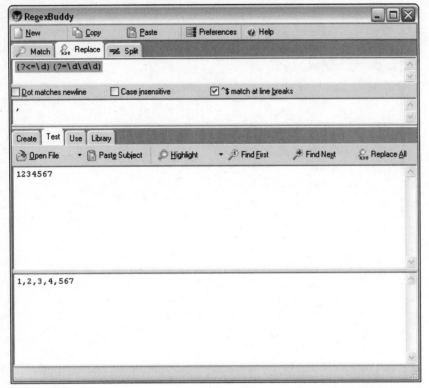

Figure 8-16

8. Edit the pattern to `(?<=\d)(?=(\d\d\d)+$)`.

9. Click the Replace All icon, and inspect the replacement text in the lower pane of the Test tab (see Figure 8-17). This is `1,234,567`, which is what you want.

10. Depending on your data source, the pattern `(?<=\d)(?=(\d\d\d)+$)` may not work. Imagine if a single character — for example, a period character — follows the last digit of the number to which you wish to add commas. Edit the test text to read `Monthly sales figures are 1234567.`

11. Edit the regular expression on the Replace tab to read `(?<=\d)(?=(\d\d\d)+\W)`.

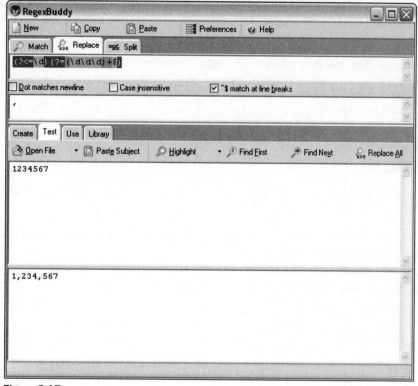

Figure 8-17

How It Works

The pattern `(?<=\d)(?=\d\d\d)` looks for a position that follows a single numeric digit and precedes three numeric digits. In the sample text `1234`, there is only one position that satisfies both the lookbehind and lookahead constraints: the position after the numeric digit `1`.

When the test text is changed to `1234567`, the pattern `(?<=\d)(?=\d\d\d)` matches several times. For example, the position following the numeric digit `2` is preceded by a numeric digit and is followed by three numeric digits. That position therefore satisfies both the lookbehind and lookahead constraints.

You need to group the numeric digits into groups of three to attempt to get rid of the undesired comma replacements. The pattern `(?<=\d)(?=(\d\d\d)+)` groups the numeric digits in the lookahead into threes but fails, as you saw in Figure 8-16, to prevent the unwanted commas. At the position following the numeric digit 2, there is still a sequence of three digits following that position, so the position matches. A comma is therefore inserted (although that is not appropriate to formatting norms for numbers).

When the pattern is edited to `(?<=\d)(?=(\d\d\d)+$)`, you get the results you want. The position following the numeric digit 2 now fails to satisfy the lookahead constraint. It is followed by five numeric digits, which does not match the pattern `(\d\d\d)+`.

However, the position after the numeric digit 1 still matches. It is followed by six numeric digits, which matches the pattern `(\d\d\d)+`. Similarly, the position after the numeric digit 4 is matched, because it is followed by three numeric digits, which matches the pattern `(\d\d\d)+`. In both those positions that match, a comma is inserted.

Exercises

These exercises allow you to test your understanding of some of the techniques for lookahead and lookbehind that were introduced in this chapter:

1. Specify a pattern that will match a sequence of one or more alphabetic characters only if they are followed by a comma character.

2. Create a pattern, using lookbehind and lookahead, to match the word sheep. Do not use the word-boundary metacharacters in your pattern.

Sensitivity and Specificity of Regular Expressions

This chapter discusses the issues of sensitivity and specificity of regular expression patterns. Sensitivity and specificity relate to two fundamental tasks in all uses of regular expressions: trying to ensure that you match all the text that you want to match and trying to avoid matching text that you don't want to match.

Assuming that you typically want to manipulate the data that you match in some way, failing to match desired data will mean that part of your intended task remains undone. If you don't have a good appreciation of your data and the effect on it of the regular expression that you are using, you can be completely unaware that you have missed some data. At least, you are unaware that you have missed it until your manager or a customer calls and complains.

Conversely, matching and manipulating undesired data may well corrupt parts of your data. Whether that data corruption leads to minor typos or more serious problems depends on your data, what its intended use is, and the extent and severity of the undesired changes you unintentionally make to it. Again, the undesired effects can impact adversely on customer satisfaction. So sensitivity and specificity are issues to take seriously.

In this chapter, you will learn the following:

- ❑ What sensitivity and specificity are

- ❑ How to work out how far you should go in investing time and effort in maximizing sensitivity and/or specificity

- ❑ How to use regular expression techniques to give an optimal balance of sensitivity and specificity

- ❑ How the detail of the data source can affect sensitivity and specificity

- ❑ How to gain a better balance of sensitivity and specificity in the Star Training Company example

What Are Sensitivity and Specificity?

Sensitivity is the capacity to match the pattern that you want to match. *Specificity* is the capacity to limit the character sequences selected by a pattern to those character sequences that you want to detect.

> Sensitivity and specificity are terms derived from quantitative disciplines such as statistics and epidemiology. Broadly, *sensitivity* is a measure of the number of true hits you find divided by the total number of true hits you ought to find if you match all occurrences of the relevant character sequences, and *specificity* is the number of hits you find that are true hits divided by the total number of hits you find. The higher the sensitivity, the closer you are, in the context of regular expressions, to finding all true matches, and the higher the specificity, the closer you are to finding only true matches.

The definitions given may feel a little abstract, so the following examples are provided to develop a clearer understanding of the ideas of sensitivity and specificity.

Extreme Sensitivity, Awful Specificity

Suppose that you want to match the character sequence ABC. It is very easy to achieve 100 percent sensitivity using the following pattern:

```
.*
```

It selects sequences of zero or more alphanumeric characters.

A sample document, `ABitOfEverything.txt`, is shown here:

```
ABC123

DEF9FR

Mary had a little lamb.

var x = 234 / 1.56;

<html><body></body></html>

<book></book>

This is a random 58#Gooede garbled piece of 8983ju**nk but it is still selected.
```

As you can see, there is a pretty diverse range of content, not all of which is useful. However, if you apply the regular expression pattern .* you achieve 100 percent sensitivity, because the only occurrence of the character sequence ABC is matched. However, you also select every other piece of text in the sample document, as you can see in Figure 9-1 in OpenOffice.org Writer.

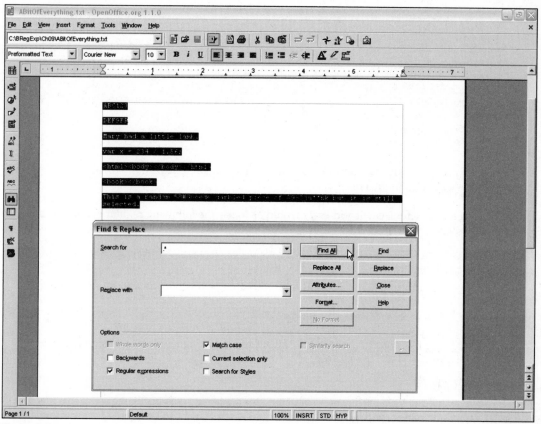

Figure 9-1

I introduced this slightly silly example to make an important point. It is possible to create very sensitive regular expression patterns that achieve nothing useful. Of course, you are unlikely to use .* as a standalone pattern, but it is important to carefully consider the usefulness of the regular expression patterns you create when, typically, the issues will be significantly more subtle.

Useful regular expressions keep the 100 percent sensitivity (or something very close to 100 percent) of the .* pattern but combine it with a high level of specificity.

Email Addresses Example

Suppose that you have a large number of documents or an email mail file that you need to search for valid email addresses. The file `EmailOrNotEmail.txt` illustrates the kind of data that might be contained in the material you need to search. The content of `EmailOrNotEmail.txt` is shown here:

```
@Home
@ttitude
John@somewhere.invalid
Peter@example.org
Peter@example.info
John@Smith@example.com
20 @ $10 each
@@@ This is a comment @@@
Jane@example.net
Peter.Smith@example.net
```

You will see pretty quickly that some of the character sequences in `EmailOrNotEmail.txt` are valid email addresses and some are not.

One approach to matching email addresses would be to use the following regular expression to locate all email addresses:

```
.*@.*
```

If you try that pattern using the `findstr` utility, you can type the following at the command line:

```
findstr  /N /i  .*@.* EmailOrNotEmail.txt
```

You search a single file, `EmailOrNotEmail.txt`, for the following regular expression pattern:

```
.*@.*
```

The `/N` switch indicates that the line number of any line containing a character sequence that matches the regular expression pattern will be displayed. The `/i` switch, which isn't essential here, indicates that the pattern will be applied in a case-insensitive way. Figure 9-2 shows the result of running the specified command.

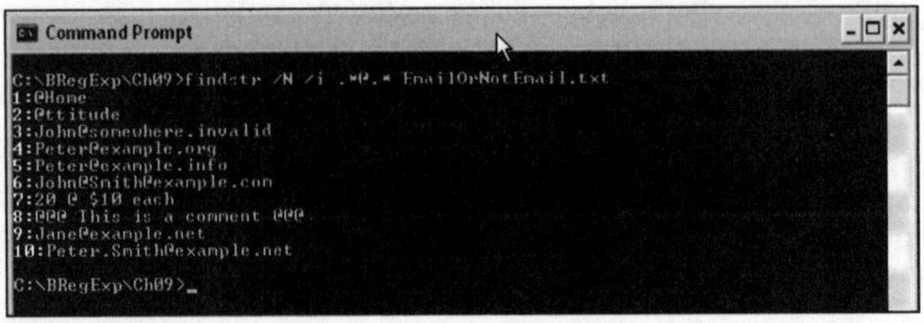

Figure 9-2

As the figure shows, all the valid email addresses (which are on lines 4, 5, 9, and 10) are selected. This gives you 100 percent sensitivity, at least on this test data set. In other words, you have selected every character sequence that represents a valid email address. But you have, on all the other lines, matched character sequences that are pretty obviously not email addresses. You need to find a more specific pattern to improve the specificity of matching.

Look a little more carefully at how an email address is structured. Broadly, an email address follows this structure:

```
username@somehostname
```

To achieve a better match, you must find patterns that match the username and the hostname but are more specific than your previous attempt.

The structure of the username can be simply a sequence of alphabetic characters, as here:

```
AWatt@XMML.com
```

Or it can include a period character, such as the following:

```
A.Watt@XMML.com
```

Therefore, you need to allow for the possibility of a period character occurring inside the username part of the email address. The following pattern matches, at a minimum, a single alphabetic character due to the \w+ component of the pattern:

```
\w*\.?\w+
```

The \w*\.? allows the mandatory alphabetic character(s) to be preceded by zero or more optional alphabetic characters followed by a single optional period character.

You probably don't want to match an email address that begins with a period character, as in the following:

```
.Watt@XMML.com
```

So you could use a lookbehind to allow a match for a period character only when it has been preceded by at least one alphabetic character. This pattern would allow matching of a period character only when it is preceded by an alphabetic character:

```
\w*(?<=\w)\.?\w+
```

Try It Out Email Address

1. Open PowerGrep, and enter the pattern **\w*(?<=\w)\.?\w+@.*** in the Search text area.

2. Enter the folder name **C:\BRegExp\Ch09** in the Folder text box. Amend, as appropriate, if you downloaded the sample files to a different directory.

3. Enter the filename **EmailOrNotEmail.txt** in the File Mask text box, and click the Search button.

4. Inspect the results in the Results area. Compare the matches shown in Figure 9-2 with the matches now shown in Figure 9-3, particularly noting the character sequences that no longer match.

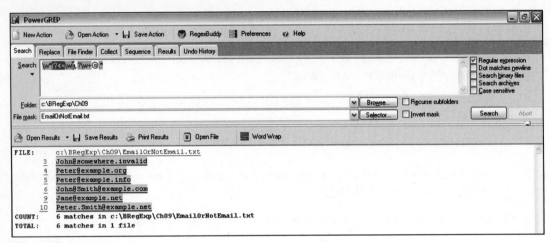

Figure 9-3

This is an improvement. The pattern is more specific. You no longer match the undesired character sequences on lines 1, 2, 7, and 8. However, the character sequence on Line 3, John@somewhere.invalid, is not a valid email address.

You can remove that undesired match by making the hostname part of the email address more specific. How specific you want to be is a matter of judgment. You know that all hostnames will have a sequence of alphabetic characters, followed by a period character, followed by three (com, net, org, or biz) or four (info) alphabetic characters. For the purposes of this example we won't consider hostnames like example.co.uk. The following pattern would be an appropriate pattern to match hostnames that correspond to the structure just described:

```
\w+\.\w{3,4}
```

The \w+ will match even single character domain names (which are allowed with .com, .net, and .org domains). The \. metacharacter matches a single period character, and the \w{3,4} component matches either three or four alphabetic characters.

Combining that pattern with your earlier one gives you the following:

```
\w*(?<=\w)\.?\w+@\w+\.\w{3,4}
```

5. Enter the pattern **\w*(?<=\w)\.?\w+@\w+\.\w{3,4}** in the Search text area, and click the Search button.

6. Inspect the results. Notice that the undesired match on Line 3 is no longer matched. However, a problem on Line 6, not mentioned earlier, is brought to the surface. On Line 6, the seeming email address has two @ characters, which is not allowed.

One way to approach this is to use a lookahead to specify that following the first match for an @ character, another @ character does not occur. If you continue to assume that only alphabetic characters are allowed in an email address, you can specify that you look ahead from the first @ character matched to the first match for a character that is not an alphabetic character or a period character.

You can do that using the following pattern:

```
\w*(?<=\w)\.?\w+@(?=[\w\.]+\W)\w+\.\w{3,4}
```

7. Edit the pattern in the Search text area to be
`\w*(?<=\w)\.?\w+@(?=[\w\.]+\W)\w+\.\w{3,4}`, and click the Search button.

8. Inspect the results. Figure 9-4 shows the appearance.

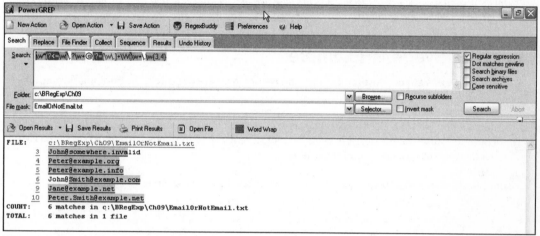

Figure 9-4

Unfortunately, the lookahead has not solved the problem with the undesired matches on lines 3 and 6. You need to specify that the pattern is the whole text on a line. In other words, you add a ^ metacharacter to specify the position at the start of the line and the $ metacharacter to specify the position at the end of the line.

9. Modify the pattern in the Search area to be
`^\w*(?<=\w)\.?\w+@(?=[\w\.]+\W)\w+\.\w{3,4}$`, and click the Search button.

10. Inspect the results. Figure 9-5 shows the appearance.

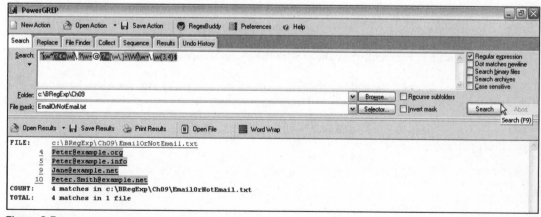

Figure 9-5

Happily, you have now succeeded in avoiding matching the undesired matches on lines 3 and 6. At least on this simple test data, you have achieved 100 percent sensitivity and 100 percent specificity.

The terms sensitivity and specificity come from quantitative sciences, such as statistics and epidemiology. In those contexts, both the sensitivity and specificity are expressed numerically, often as percentages. So for the preceding example, you have a sensitivity of 100 percent because all true email addresses are detected using your first attempt at a regular expression pattern, and you initially have a specificity of 40 percent because 6 of the 10 matches are false matches (in the sense that they are not valid email addresses). By the end of the Try It Out example, the specificity has risen to 100 percent on the test data.

Replacing Hyphens Example

This example looks at another problem that can occur if you are not careful in thinking through the meaning of a regular expression.

Assume that you have a collection of text documents that have to be converted into HTML/XHTML. This example focuses on the possible need for replacing a line of hyphens with the HTML/XHTML <hr> element to create a horizontal ruled line.

A simplified sample document, HyphenTest.txt, is used in this example:

```
something
not much
----
a little text
Fred
-------------
-Fred
```

A first attempt at expressing the problem definition might be as follows:

Replace any hyphens that occur with the character sequence <hr>.

However, that is too imprecise. For example, the third line would be replaced with the following:

```
<hr><hr><hr><hr>
```

A more precise statement of the problem definition would be as follows:

Replace any group of consecutive hyphens with the character sequence <hr>.

Assume that you will omit the end tag of the hr element, because many Web browsers have problems if you use the empty element tag, <hr/>.

If you use the following regular expression pattern to express the idea of one or more hyphens, you can run into problems for two reasons:

```
-*
```

First, not all regular expression engines interpret that pattern correctly. The pattern -* means "Match zero or more hyphens," which means that the occurrence of *zero* hyphens is a match. Therefore, the text Fred ought to match, which may not be what you expected. Why does Fred match? Because there are zero hyphens.

OpenOffice.org Writer implements the -* pattern as you might intuitively expect, because it matches only when at least one hyphen occurs, as shown in Figure 9-6, when it ought to match on each line because each line has zero hyphens at the beginning.

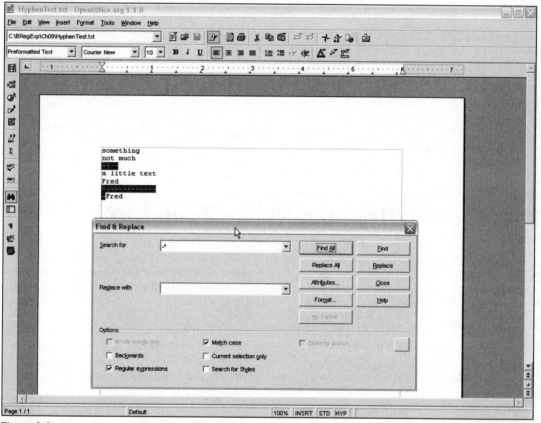

Figure 9-6

The Komodo Regular Expressions Toolkit interprets the regular expression pattern correctly — for example, detecting a match for the text Fred, as you can see in Figure 9-7.

Of course, the pattern -+ is more appropriate because you want at least one hyphen to be present before you expect a match. However, the fact that the * quantifier matches even the absence of the character or metacharacter that it refers to can cause confusion in some situations.

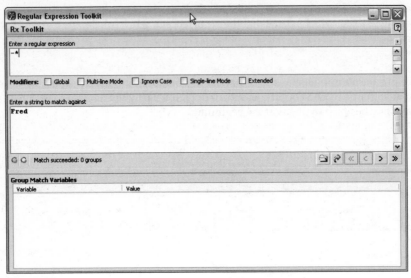

Figure 9-7

The Sensitivity/Specificity Trade-Off

Sensitivity and specificity are always part of a trade-off. Sensitivity and specificity are components of the trade-off, but the amount of effort required to get 100 percent sensitivity and 100 percent specificity may not be practical in some situations. Some undefined "good" specificity may be enough. It's a trade-off in that, in the end, only you can judge how much effort is appropriate for the task that you are using regular expressions to achieve.

How important are sensitivity and specificity? The answer is, "It depends." There are many times when you will need high sensitivity, 100 percent sensitivity ideally, and at the same time you also need high specificity. At other times, one or the other may be less important. This section looks at some of the factors that influence how much importance it is relevant to place on sensitivity and specificity.

It depends to a significant extent on who the customer is. If you are using regular expressions to achieve something for your own use, you may not worry too much if you miss one or two matches. On the other hand, if you are conducting a replacement of every occurrence of a company name after a takeover, for example, it would be serious if sensitivity fell below 100 percent.

How Metacharacters Affect Sensitivity and Specificity

In general, the more metacharacters you use, the more specific a pattern becomes. The pattern `cat` matches that sequence of characters whether they refer to a feline mammal or form character sequences in words such as `cathode` and `caterpillar`.

Adding further metacharacters, such as the \b word boundary, makes the use of the character sequence cat in a pattern much more specific. The pattern \bcat\b will match only the word cat (singular).

When using specific patterns like that, you need to watch carefully for the possibility of reducing sensitivity. The pattern \bcat\b will match cat but won't match cats, for example. If you are interested in finding all references in the document to feline mammals, the \bcat\b pattern may not be the best option. You may want to allow for the occurrence of the plural form, cats, and the possessive form, cat's, too. The pattern \bcat'?s?'?\b would match cat, cats, cats' (plural possessive), and cat's (singular possessive) but would also match cat', which is unlikely to be a desired match. If your data is unlikely to contain the character sequence cat', the pattern \bcat'?s?'?\b may be sufficient. But if, for some reason, you want to match only cat, cats, cat's, and cats', some other, more specific pattern will be needed. One simple option is as follows:

```
(cat|cats|cat's|cats')
```

An alternative follows:

```
ca(t|ts|t's|ts)
```

Similar issues apply whatever the word or sequence of characters of interest.

Sensitivity, Specificity, and Positional Characters

The positional characters explored in Chapter 6 can be expected in many cases to affect both sensitivity and specificity.

In the following example, an initial version of the problem definition can be expressed as follows:

Match all occurrences of the sequence of characters t, h, and e case insensitively.

The pattern the will match twice in the following text:

```
Paris in the the spring.
```

It will match once in the following text:

```
The spring has sprung.
```

However, suppose you modify the problem definition to the following:

Match the position at the beginning of a string; then match the sequence of characters t, h, and e case insensitively.

The pattern ^the now has no match in the first sample text but still has a single match in the second. The effect of adding one or more positional metacharacters depends on the data the pattern is being matched against.

Sensitivity, Specificity, and Modes

When you specify that a regular expression is to be executed in a case-insensitive or case-sensitive mode, you affect the matches that will be returned. Continuing with the preceding example, the pattern ^the applied case sensitively has no match in either of the two test pieces of text. In the second sample text, the ^ metacharacter matches the position at the beginning of the string, but the lowercase t of the pattern does not match the uppercase T of the test text.

Similarly, the use of the period metacharacter (which matches a large range of characters) can be switched to match or not match a newline character.

Sensitivity, Specificity, and Lookahead and Lookbehind

When you add lookahead or lookbehind to an existing regular expression, you may have no effect on sensitivity ,or you may adversely impact it. Equally, you may improve specificity or, less likely, it may stay the same.

If a lookbehind is carefully crafted, it won't reduce sensitivity. However, if you make an error in the pattern inside the lookbehind, you will fail to match when you intended to match, reducing sensitivity. Suppose that you wanted to find information about Anne Smith. The following pattern would match when the spelling of Anne is correct, and it is followed by exactly one space character:

```
(?<=Anne )Smith
```

However, if Anne is spelled as Ann somewhere in the document you may miss intended matches, because the pattern (?<=Anne)Smith will no longer match.

Equally, if the person's name were written as A. Smith somewhere in the data, there would be no match. More detailed understanding of the data would be needed to know whether a match was intended or not. The character sequence A. Smith might refer to the person of interest, Anne Smith, but alternatively might refer to Adam Smith or some other person.

Similarly, lookahead can reduce sensitivity. For example, suppose that you want to match all occurrences of the character sequence John. The following pattern would match a word boundary, then the desired character sequence John, and then check if the following character is a space character:

```
\bJohn(?= )
```

However, if the test text is as follows, the lookahead is too specific and causes what is likely to be a desired match to fail:

```
I went with John, and Mary on a trip.
```

Modifying the lookahead to (?=\b) or (?=\W) would prevent the problem caused by the occurrence of an unanticipated comma.

How Much Should the Regular Expressions Do?

Most of the examples earlier in this book use a range of tools with regular expression functionality to apply regular expressions. That's great when teaching regular expressions, but when you use regular expressions as a developer, you will typically be using regular expressions inside code written in Java, JavaScript, VB.NET, and so on, or you may be applying regular expressions to data retrieved from a relational database. So how much should you expect the regular expressions to do, and how much can you safely assume that your other code or the error checking in a database already does?

For example, suppose you have a collection of HTML documents that include IP addresses, and your task is to amend the style that the IP addresses are displayed in. Suppose that initially, IP addresses are nested inside the start and end tags for HTML b elements, as in the following:

```
<b>1.12.123.234</b>
```

What pattern should you use to find such IP addresses? Should you just assume that the data you receive will be correctly formed (including having no values of 256 or more), or should you include a more complex pattern so that the regular expression will match only correctly formed IP addresses?

If you assume that the IP addresses are already correctly formed or are checked by some other part of your code, you could use a fairly simple pattern such as the following:

```
<b>([0-9]+(\.[0-9]+){3})</b>
```

This would match character sequences that are not IP addresses, such as the following:

```
<b>1234.2345.5678.9999999</b>
```

If you can be sure that your data doesn't include undesired values such as the preceding one, the simple pattern shown might be enough. Without much work, you can adapt the pattern so that only between one and three numeric digits can be included before or after a period character:

```
<b>([0-9]{1,3}(\.[0-9]{1,3})</b>
```

Inappropriate character sequences such as the following would still be matched, but at least you improve the specificity a little by excluding false matches with multiple numeric digits, as shown earlier:

```
<b>999.256.789.1</b>
```

If, however, you can't be sure that the supposed IP addresses are correctly formatted, you may need to develop a longer, more complex pattern. On the other hand, it may not matter for a particular purpose whether the supposed IP addresses are valid IP addresses or not. If that is the situation, the simplest regular expression is likely to be an appropriate option to use.

Knowing the Data, Sensitivity, and Specificity

One of the key issues that affect how well you achieve sensitivity and specificity is how well you understand the data to which you are applying regular expressions. Of course, your understanding of the regular expression syntax and techniques supported by your chosen language or tool is important, too.

But if you don't really understand the data you are working with, even a regular expression with correct syntax can turn up unexpected results, by lowering either sensitivity or specificity.

Abbreviations

Abbreviations can pose significant potential for lowering the sensitivity of a regular expression. For example, titles such as `Dr` (with no period character) and `Dr.` (with a period character) are frequently used as abbreviations for `Doctor`. In some circumstances, you may be confident that only one form is used in the data source. If all three forms occur in the data, a pattern like the following will be necessary to avoid missing some desired matches:

```
(Doctor|Dr.|Dr)
```

Similar issues arise when handling data that includes information about qualifications. For example, if a `Doctor of Philosophy` degree is of interest, it will often be written as `PhD` (no space character or period character), `Ph.D.` (two period characters), or `Ph. D.` (one space character, two period characters).

To match the options just mentioned, a pattern such as the following would be satisfactory:

```
Ph\. ?D\.?
```

It includes the `\.` metacharacter twice with a `?` quantifier, which matches each of the optional period character(s) that can occur in some of the options. Depending on where the degree was obtained, the form `D.Phil.` (two period characters) with option `DPhil` (no period characters) can also occur. To allow for these additional forms, a pattern such as the following would be needed:

```
(Ph\.?D\.?|D\.?Phil\.?)
```

Characters from Other Languages

The focus of this book is the use of regular expressions with English, including U.S. English and British English. However, with the increasing globalization of trade, the inclusion of words and characters from other languages commonly occurs in documents that are, for the most part, written in English.

In Canada, many official documents are in French. Therefore, many characters with accents will be routinely encountered.

In documents written in English, there can be differences in how words are written. For example, the test text.

```
"Nostalgia is not what it used to be." That is my favorite cliche.
```

might equally have been written as follows:

```
"Nostalgia is not what it used to be." That is my favorite cliché.
```

The second version includes the acute character é just before the period, which concludes the sentence. To match both forms, you would need to use a pattern such as the following:

```
clich(e|é)
```

Foreign characters introduce other issues when they occur in HTML. The sample document, EAcute.html, uses the notation é instead of the literal character:

```
<h2>"Nostalgia is not what it used to be." That is my favorite clich&eacute;.</h2>
```

Yet as you can see in Figure 9-8, the correct character is displayed on the Web page.

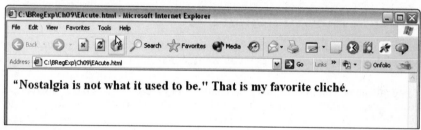

Figure 9-8

Foreign characters may be expressed as Unicode numbers inside some documents, adding another consideration to be remembered when attempting to match those characters.

Names

As people become more mobile, for example, in employment, it is likely that names originating in languages that don't use Roman script will often form part of human resources data and so on. For example, the Indian first name that is sometimes spelled Saurav is also spelled Saurabh and, less commonly, Surav. The pattern Saurav would fail to match the latter two spellings, although quite possibly, it would be your intent to match all occurrences of the name. To match all spellings, you would need a pattern such as the following:

```
Sa?ura(v|bh)
```

Similar considerations apply in other foreign names. The Russian name for Peter, sometimes transliterated as Pyotr, may also be found spelled as Petr or Pëtr, or even translated as Peter, and may need to be matched in all instances. To match all these possible forms of the name, you might use a pattern like this:

```
P(yo|e|ë)tr
```

Some European surnames have variant spellings too. For example, the surnames `Van Nistelrooy` (with an intermediate space character) can also be spelled `Van Nistelrooij` or `VanNistelrooy` (with no intermediate space character). So a pattern such as the following would be needed to match these three spelling variants:

```
Van *Nistelroo(ij|y)
```

Of course, because some such surnames may sometimes be spelled with a lowercase v in van, the following pattern might be more sensitive in some situations:

```
[vV]an *Nistelroo(ij|y)
```

Sensitivity and How to Achieve It

To achieve maximum sensitivity, you must be aware of all the variant character sequences that can be used to express the character sequence that you want to match.

Each time you add some component to a pattern that makes it more specific, you need to carefully consider whether, given the data you are working with, it might also cause some desired matches to fail.

Specificity and How to Maximize It

Conceptually, the way to maximize specificity is to make the regular expression as specific as possible. There are many techniques to cut out unwanted matches, several of which have been discussed earlier in this chapter.

When attempting to maximize specificity, it is important to give careful consideration to situations that you don't want to match and constructing a pattern that excludes those unwanted character sequences from matching. Achieving high specificity involves having an understanding of regular expression syntax and the effects of the techniques available to you, and understanding how those techniques affect the data you are working with.

Revisiting the Star Training Company Example

In Chapter 1, you looked at an example that posed a challenge to a new recruit to the fictional Star Training Company. Having learned a range of techniques in Chapters 2 through 7, you are now in a much better position to avoid many of the pitfalls that occurred when a simple find and replace was attempted in Chapter 1.

For convenience, the sample text, `StarOriginal.txt`, is reproduced here:

```
Star Training Company

Starting from May 1st  Star Training Company is offering a startling special offer
to our regular customers - a 20% discount when 4 or more staff attend a single Star
Training Company course.

In addition, each quarter our star customer will receive a voucher for a free
holiday away from the pressures of the office. Staring at a computer screen all day
might be replaced by starfish and swimming in the Seychelles.

Once this offer has started and you hear about other Star Training customers
enjoying their free  holiday you might feel left out. Don't be left on the outside
staring in. Start right now building your points to allow you to start out on your
very own Star Training holiday.

Reach for the star. Training is valuable in its own right but the possibility of a
free holiday adds a startling new dimension to the benefits of Star Training
training.

Don't stare at that computer screen any longer. Start now with Star. Training is
crucial to your company's wellbeing. Think Star.
```

The problem definition can be expressed as follows:

Match all occurrences of the character sequence s, t, a, and r when that character sequence refers to the Star Training Company. Replace each occurrence of the preceding character sequence with the character sequence M, o, o, and n.

The objective is to replace all references to the fictional Star Training Company with corresponding references to the equally fictional Moon Training Company.

When faced with a task like this in real life, it can be helpful to view a few sample documents in a text editor or word processor with search facilities. That allows you to enter a pattern to look for occurrences of character sequences that might be relevant. In this case, you can use the simple literal pattern star (all lowercase) and use regular expressions matching in a case-insensitive way.

Try It Out	Replacing Star with Moon

1. Open the file StarOriginal.txt in OpenOffice.org Writer.

2. Open the Find & Replace dialog box using Ctrl+F.

3. Check the Regular Expressions check box, but leave the Match Case check box unchecked, because you want to find all occurrences of the specified pattern in a case-insensitive way.

4. Type the pattern **star** in the Search For text box, and click the Find All button.

5. Inspect the matches shown in Figure 9-9, paying careful attention to any occurrences of the character sequence star that refer to the Star Training Company.

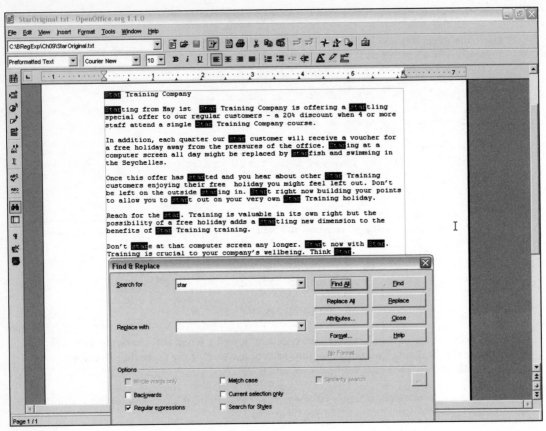

Figure 9-9

How It Works

The matching in the preceding example is straightforward and matches all occurrences of the literal character sequence that constituted the pattern.

OpenOffice.org Writer is convenient to do this on single documents. However, when dealing with multiple documents, a tool such as PowerGrep will allow you to look for matches in several documents at the same time, highlighting each match for your convenience. This can save a lot of time in getting a feel for the data that you have to manipulate.

Let's take time to list the character sequences that you want to match. You want to match star in the following:

```
Star Training
Star.
```

You want to avoid matching `star` in the following character sequences:

```
Starting
startling
star customer
Staring
starfish
started
Start right
start out
star.
startling
stare
Start now
```

I don't routinely take time to lay out desired matches in a list and undesired matches in a second list. But particularly when you need to get things as close to 100 percent sensitivity and 100 percent specificity as possible, it makes a lot of sense to make lists like this.

Splitting character sequences into desired matches and undesired matches can be really helpful in working out how sensitive and specific any pattern will prove to be.

If you decide that a lookahead is the way to proceed (as it probably is), you could try to match all desired matches using the following pattern:

```
Star(?= Training)
```

However, if you look at the list of desired matches, you can see immediately that the preceding pattern will fail in a sentence such as `Think Star`. That's one of the occurrences of `Star` followed by a period character.

The following pattern, which offers alternation of two lookaheads, fits all the desired matches that you have seen in the sample text:

```
Star((?= Training)|(?=\.))
```

Thus, as judged by the sample text, you have 100 percent sensitivity. Figure 9-10 shows the preceding pattern being tested against the character sequence `Star`.

It is always wise to consider that the test data you have looked at doesn't hold all the likely or possible character sequences that you need to think about. One of the exercises in this chapter asks you to modify the preceding pattern to allow for other possible occurrences that might be relevant to the uses of `Star` that are of interest.

The patterns that you want to match are, in general, different from those that you want not to match. So it is generally straightforward to be sure that the pattern does not match any of the undesired character sequences, with one exception: You want to match the five-character sequence of characters `Star.` (with an initial uppercase `S`) but not match the five-character sequence of characters `star.` (with an initial lowercase `s`).

If you use the preceding pattern in matching that is case sensitive, there is no problem. The undesired character sequence star. does not match. However, if the matching is case insensitive, the undesired character sequence star. will match, lowering the specificity of the chosen pattern.

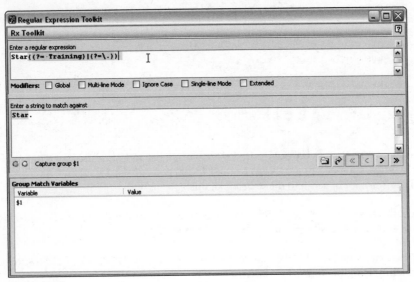

Figure 9-10

Exercises

Test your understanding of the material in this chapter using the following exercises:

1. Modify the pattern `^\w*(?<=\w)\.?\w+@(?=[\w\.]+\W)\w+\.\w{3,4}$`, which was developed earlier in the chapter for matching email addresses, so that it matches only hostnames in the .com, .net, and .org domains.

2. Modify the pattern in the Star Training Company example to match the character sequence star so that it also matches in data like the following:

```
What do you think of Star?
The best training company is Star!
```

Documenting and Debugging
Regular Expressions

Because you are reading this book, you have in all likelihood already discovered that regular expressions can be hard to write. Regular expressions can also be hard to read, whether they were written by somebody else or by you, even a short time ago. When regular expressions are used in a project over a period of time, you come face to face with a third truism: Regular expressions are hard to maintain. The purpose of this chapter is to help you take steps to minimize the effects of these three truisms.

A basic consideration that is important not to forget is that regular expressions never occur in isolation. They are always used to work on data, whether simple or extensive, and are used in the context of a tool or a programming language. In addition, the developer has a specific purpose, sometimes a complex or subtle business purpose, for the regular expressions that he writes.

The problems that arise when using regular expressions can be due simply to being unable to write patterns that express the matching characteristics that you want. Ideally, as you work through this book, that problem will become less and less common.

In this chapter, you will learn the following:

- ❑ How to document regular expressions
- ❑ How to explore the data you are working with
- ❑ How to create test cases for regular expressions
- ❑ How to debug regular expressions

Documenting Regular Expressions

Any programming project of significant size can benefit from good documentation. It makes the purpose of many aspects of the project clear and can assist in further development of the code at a future date. Given the compact, cryptic nature of regular expression syntax, it makes good sense seriously to consider documenting your approach to the creation of a particular regular expression and what you expect the parts of the regular expression to do.

In many circumstances, your use of regular expressions may be on a very small scale, where it is tempting to avoid any documentation. Sometimes, no documentation is the only sensible approach. For example, in some situations, such as using regular expressions in Microsoft Word or OpenOffice.org Writer, documenting a regular expression is overkill. You want to find or replace a character sequence there and then in a single document. Formal documentation is unnecessary.

However, in more significant tasks or projects, creating documentation can be a useful discipline, serving to make explicit aspects of the task that you might otherwise be tempted to allow to remain ambiguous.

Document the Problem Definition

The problem definition is a key component in recording your thought process while designing a regular expression pattern. As mentioned in earlier chapters, you may well not get the problem definition sufficiently precise the first time round. If the problem is a complex one, it may be worth recording a problem definition that isn't what you want so that if you come back to the code in a few months' time, you will be reminded of the work you needed to do while designing the regular expression pattern.

A first attempt at a problem definition might be very nonspecific or expressed in a way that doesn't immediately allow definition of a pattern to match what it is hoped to do.

A first attempt at a problem definition to solve the Star Training Company problem in Chapter 1 might be as follows:

Replace `Star` with `Moon`.

A brute-force search and replace can cause a substantial number of inappropriate changes. If you made such inappropriate changes across a large number of documents in the absence of recent backups, it could take a considerable amount of time to rectify the problems that poor use of a literal regular expression caused.

Refining a problem definition depends on an understanding of the data. You might have text like the following:

```
Star Training Company ...

... I highly recommend Star.

Why not accept this special offer from Star?

... recent course with Star - which was great!
```

You can see the different ways in which desired matches can be expressed. You must understand the data to be able to construct a pattern that will match (and then replace) all of these.

On the other hand, there may be text that contains similar text, which is text that you want to leave alone:

```
The trainer was good - a real star!

The training was excellent - star training.

Star performer among the trainers ...
```

Again, if you don't take time to understand undesired possible matches, you may end up making inappropriate changes to the documents you are working with.

Add Comments to Your Code

Adding comments to your code is a basic task. Try to make comments as meaningful as possible, and try to make them express what the pattern you create is expected to do.

Comments such as the following are pretty useless, particularly when you come back to the code to find out why it isn't doing that:

```
// This will replace Star with Moon
```

Make the comments meaningful, such as in the following example:

```
// This matches Star case sensitively, avoiding words like start and star

//It matches when Star is followed by a space character and the character sequence
Training

//or followed by a period (full stop)

//or followed by a question mark
```

Comments like these give a much clearer idea of what was intended and should correspond pretty closely to components of the regular expression pattern.

If you make a false start of some kind in attempting to solve a problem, it can also be useful to include a comment about what doesn't work and why. While it can be embarrassing to admit a mistake in your thinking, being upfront about the problem is better than wasting time a few weeks later by going down the same blind alley.

Making Use of Extended Mode

When I write code in JavaScript, Java, Visual Basic .NET, and various other programming languages. I space the components of the code out and indent nested components so that the structure of the code is easily discerned. I would never consider jamming sizeable chunks of code onto a single line if it was avoidable, because that is much harder to read. Making code readable and adding comments where they are most relevant make the coding and maintenance experience a much smoother one.

One of the key advantages of comments on ordinary code is that you can place the comments right next to the component of the code to which the comments relate. It's far less useful to have comments that are a screen or two away from the code to which they refer. A similar problem can occur in many regular expression implementations, where you simply cannot put the comments adjacent to the code that they refer to.

Extended mode is available in languages such as Perl, Java, and PHP. It allows you to include comments on the same line as the pattern component that they describe. Keeping a piece of code right next to its description helps cut down on occurrences of misunderstanding code.

Extended mode in Perl is indicated by the x modifier following the second forward slash of the m// operator.

To match input from two known users, you could use a simple program such as JimOrFred.pl:

```perl
#!/usr/bin/perl -w
use strict;
print "This program will say 'Hello' to Jim or Fred.\n";
my $myPattern = "^(Jim|Fred)\$";
# The pattern matches only 'Jim' or 'Fred'. Nothing else is allowed.
print "Enter your first name here: ";
my $myTestString = <STDIN>;
chomp ($myTestString);
if ($myTestString =~ m/$myPattern/x)
{
 print "Hello $myTestString. How are you today?";
}
else
{
 print "Sorry I don't know you!";
}
```

The program simply accepts input from the user. If the name entered is Jim or Fred, a Hello message is displayed; otherwise, the user is told that the system doesn't recognize the name.

Figure 10-1 shows the appearance after both the desired names have been entered.

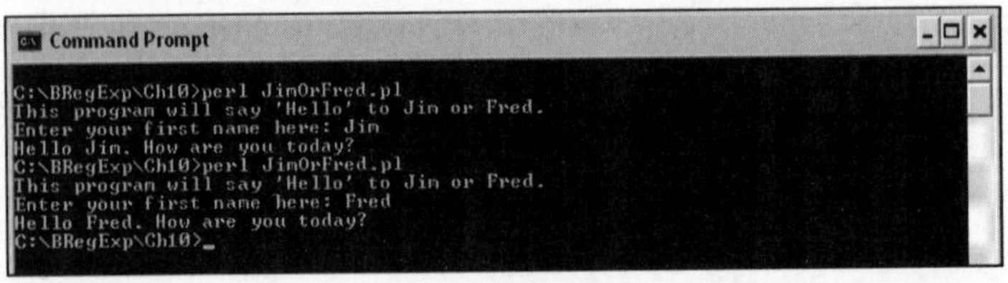

Figure 10-1

The following single comment is reasonably informative:

```
# The pattern matches only 'Jim' or 'Fred'. Nothing else is allowed.
```

Extended mode allows you to give much more detail inside the code about what each part of the pattern actually does.

The file JimOrFred2.pl shows the same code using extended mode. Notice that the assignment statement for the $myPattern variable is spread over several lines:

```perl
#!/usr/bin/perl -w
use strict;
print "This program will say 'Hello' to Jim or Fred.\n";
my $myPattern = "
^      # Matches the position before the first character on the line
(Jim # Literally matches 'Jim'
|      # The alternation character
Fred)# Literally matches 'Fred'
\$"  # Matches the position after the last character on the line
;
# The pattern matches only 'Jim' or 'Fred'. Nothing else is allowed.
print "Enter your first name here: ";
my $myTestString = <STDIN>;
chomp ($myTestString);
if ($myTestString =~ m/$myPattern/x)
{
 print "Hello $myTestString. How are you today?";
}
else
{
 print "Sorry I don't know you!";
}
```

What was previously written on a single line in JimOrFred.pl

```perl
my $myPattern = "^(Jim|Fred)\$";
```

is now written across several lines in JimOrFred2.pl, each of which includes a comment describing what that component of the pattern does:

```perl
my $myPattern = "
^      # Matches the position before the first character on the line
(Jim # Literally matches 'Jim'
|      # The alternation character
Fred)# Literally matches 'Fred'
\$"  # Matches the position after the last character on the line
;
```

In addition to the comments allowed by extended mode, you can still include the following overall comment, which makes clear the purpose of the whole regular expression pattern:

```perl
# The pattern matches only 'Jim' or 'Fred'. Nothing else is allowed.
```

The x modifier means that the whitespace used for layout in JimOrFred2.pl is ignored inside the value of $myPattern:

```perl
if ($myTestString =~ m/$myPattern/x)
```

Know Your Data

When you are using regular expressions, it is crucial that you really understand the data you are working with.

The following sections illustrate the type of problem that may lie in your data.

Abbreviations

If you are handling large volumes of text, you may find that abbreviations for a term of interest can cause problems in matching.

Suppose that you want to locate information about Dr. Victor Smith. Among the forms you might find are:

```
Dr. Smith
Dr. V. Smith
Victor Smith
Doctor V. Smith
Doctor Victor Smith
Dr Victor Smith
```

As you can see, the appellation can be written as `Doctor`, `Dr` (with no period character), or `Dr.` (with a period character).

Technical terms are also often abbreviated and raise similar issues. For example, if you wanted to find information about Microsoft's Most Valuable Professionals, you would need to match forms such as the following:

```
MVP
MVPs
Most Valuable Professional
```

Proper Names

If the relevant part of the data involves proper names, whether of people, businesses, or places, all sorts of problems can arise.

If, for example, you are interested in the work of the famous artist Leonardo da Vinci, you might find any of the following variants in the data:

```
Leonardo Da Vinci
Leonardo da Vinci
Leonardo DaVinci
Leonardo daVinci
```

Notice the variations in case among the four examples and the variations in whether or not there is a space character before `Vinci`.

You cannot safely try to match only the preceding variants of `Leonardo da Vinci`, because you might find phrases such as the following:

```
the great da Vinci
sgnr da Vinci
Sgnr da Vinci
Mr. da Vinci
```

You might try a very nonspecific literal pattern such as `vinci` used with case-insensitive matching to gain an impression of what variety of usage there is in the data you are working with. Inevitably, such a nonspecific pattern will return undesired matches, such as `vinci` in words such as `invincible`. In this exploratory phase, undesired matches don't matter. What is important is that you see all likely forms of the name you want to match.

Once you see the range of spelling variants in the data, you can start the process of designing an appropriate regular expression pattern.

Incorrect Spelling

People make mistakes when spelling words, even sometimes when spelling familiar words. Unless you are very lucky, incorrect spelling will be present if you are manipulating large quantities of text. To maximize sensitivity and specificity, you need to make allowance for such misspellings, at least in important or extensive text manipulation.

To allow for misspelling, it can be helpful to use exploratory patterns such as the following:

```
\b\w+\s+Training
```

and:

```
Star\s+T\w+g
```

The former pattern will detect words that precede `Training`. So you might pick up variants such as `Satr` and `Star`. The latter pattern will pick up many possible misspellings of `Training`.

Spell checking can prevent some problems but can introduce others. Recently, I saw someone post information about a book by an author whose surname was, supposedly, `Debate`. It wasn't. The problem arose because a spell checker had changed a surname that it didn't recognize into a word with which it was familiar.

Creating Test Cases

Creating test cases can be a very useful approach when you are using regular expressions on multiple documents. As mentioned in Chapter 2, it is important that you understand the data source that you are working with. The larger the number of documents or the more extensive the database that you are trying to search or manipulate, the more important it becomes that you take time to thoroughly understand the data that is being addressed using regular expressions.

The creation of a suitable test case depends on understanding your data source. To test whether or not you detect all references to Star Training, you might include lines with words such as the following:

```
Star Training
Star.
Star?
```

And to ensure that you don't match undesired character sequences, also include text such as the following:

```
Star performer
Starting from the beginning
```

Making sure that you succeed in matching desired text and avoid matching undesired text will give you increased confidence in your pattern if it behaves as expected on the test data or reveal problems in your approach if desired matches fail to match or undesired matches do match.

When your pattern doesn't behave as expected, first look at the unexpected results to see if you can quickly spot why the behavior differs from the results you expect. In examples in earlier chapters, I stepped through explanations character by character. If you understood those, it should help you interpret what you expect to happen with your own patterns. If that analysis doesn't work, you may need to go back to the beginning of the process and create a problem definition which you then refine, as well as invest more time in understanding the data source.

Debugging Regular Expressions

The first thing to say about debugging regular expressions is that you should avoid it if at all possible. Debugging regular expressions can be time-consuming and intensely frustrating.

The more time you invest in stepping through the refinement of a problem definition, the clearer your ideas of what you need the regular expression to do should be. If you also clearly document in your code what you expect each component of the regular expression pattern to achieve, you should substantially reduce the number of times you have thoroughly puzzling behavior from your regular expression code.

However, even when your code is thoroughly thought out, a few problems can crop up.

Treacherous Whitespace

Whitespace is a treacherous commodity in regular expressions; it can be so difficult in modern, high-resolution monitors to be sure whether a whitespace character, particularly a single space character, is in the pattern or not. It can also occur when there is uncertainty about whitespace in relevant parts of the test text.

Problems due to whitespace can occur both when expected whitespace is missing from the pattern and when unexpected whitespace characters are present.

A common error by relatively inexperienced regular expression programmers is including a space character next to the pipe character (|), which separates options in a regular expression. Superficially, it makes the pattern easier to read, but at the cost of changing the meaning of the pattern.

If you are using extended mode, which was described earlier in this chapter, any whitespace characters in your pattern will be ignored. So if your pattern requires you to match a character sequence that depends on whitespace characters, such as a space character, you must specify the whitespace character(s) using metacharacters such as \s, which matches any whitespace character.

The file `JimOrFred3.pl` has an unwanted single space character after the pipe character in the following line:

```
my $myPattern = "^(Jim| Fred)\$";
```

Otherwise, `JimOrFred3.pl` is identical to `JimOrFred.pl`. The effect of that single whitespace character is that `Jim` still matches, but `Fred` does not, because the regular expression engine is trying to match the pattern space character followed by the character sequence `Fred`, which wasn't entered by the user, so matching fails. Figure 10-2 shows the character sequence `Fred` failing to match.

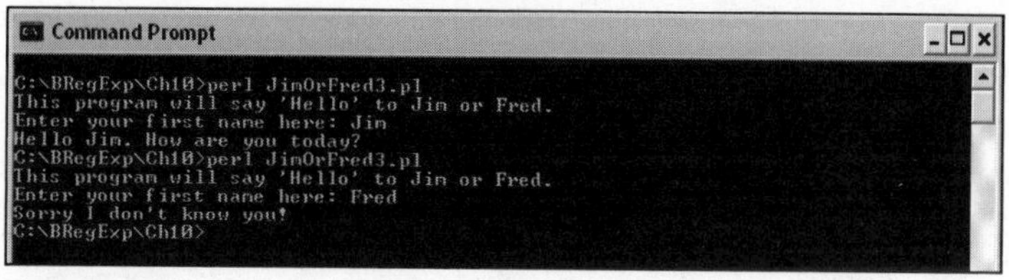

Figure 10-2

> If you don't have Perl installed on your development machine, visit Chapter 26 and review the download and installation information there if you want to run this code.

Try It Out   Basic Alternation Example

This example asks the user to type his or her first name and then displays a message depending on whether or not the name the user entered was recognized by this very simple system.

The code uses simple alternation (`Jim| Fred`) to accept the name `Jim` or the name `Fred` as user input. The positional metacharacters `^` and `$` are also used to specify that no input other than the desired choice of first name will be matched.

1.   Type the following Perl code into your favorite text editor, or use the file `JimOrFred3.pl` in the code download for this chapter.

```
#!/usr/bin/perl -w
use strict;
print "This program will say 'Hello' to Jim or Fred.\n";
my $myPattern = "^(Jim| Fred)\$";
print "Enter your first name here: ";
my $myTestString = <STDIN>;
chomp ($myTestString);
if ($myTestString =~ m/$myPattern/)
{
 print "Hello $myTestString. How are you today?";
}
else
{
 print "Sorry I don't know you!";
}
```

2. Run the code at the command line, using the command perl JimOrFred3.pl.

3. At the prompt, enter **Jim**, and press the Return key.

4. Inspect the displayed result.

5. Run the code again, and enter **Fred**; then press the Return key.

6. Inspect the displayed result. (Figure 10-2 shows the appearance after this step.)

How It Works

When the pattern is ^(Jim| Fred)$, the character sequence Jim matches because that character sequence is the one that precedes the pipe character. However, after the pipe character, the required character sequence is space character, then Fred. Unless the user types a space character, then Fred, there will be no match.

You may also be wondering about the \$ in the pattern in JimOrFred3.pl. That issue is discussed in a moment.

Intermittent problems can also occur due to whitespace characters. One possibility is caused by the user, not the developer.

Suppose that you run JimOrFred.pl again, which as you saw in Figure 10-1 matches both the character sequences Jim and Fred. However, Fred may phone you up, telling you that he is locked out of the program when he attempts to log in. What might be happening is that he types Fred Schmidt and then deletes the Schmidt but leaves the space character. That won't match, because the space character is not allowed. He can send you a screen shot, like that shown in Figure 10-3, which shows the failed login.

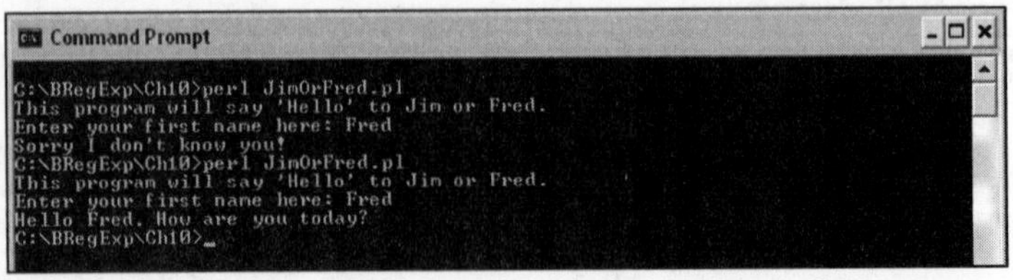

Figure 10-3

Admittedly, that example is a little forced. The point that is important to take away is that user actions can be odd. If you don't code to take those actions into account, you can have an intermittent problem that you never track down, because there is nothing "wrong" with your code, except that it didn't allow for the user doing something unexpected some of the time.

Backslashes Causing Problems

In some settings, the omission or addition of a backslash character can change the meaning of your regular expression pattern. If the pattern is attempting to match a character sequence that is different from the one you want to match, you will get different matches from those you expected.

In Perl, one such situation occurs when you use the $ metacharacter. Notice that when a value was assigned to the $myPattern variable in JimOrFred3.pl, it was written as follows:

```
my $myPattern = "^(Jim| Fred)\$";
```

In this situation, omitting the backslash will mean that your code won't compile. However, the need to use \$ in this setting to specify the $ metacharacter can be confusing.

However, in other situations you may find that a lookahead or lookbehind fails but without any compilation errors. You may intend the regular expression engine to match a metacharacter, while it is attempting to match a character instead. The result is a puzzling failure to match when you are sure that the pattern is correct.

Considering Other Causes

Complex regular expressions undoubtedly have significant potential for producing unexpected and undesired results. However, the complexity and cryptic nature of a lengthy regular expression pattern should not blind you to the possibility that the cause of undesired results is a flaw somewhere else in your analysis or code.

The range of possible problems depends on what you are doing with your code. Just keep in mind that problems with regular expression code are a complex interaction between the regular expression pattern, the data source, and the surrounding code. Each possibility needs to be examined in a systematic way if the problem persists.

Regular Expressions in Microsoft Word

Regular expressions can be very useful when carrying out searches in Microsoft Word or when carrying out search and replace operations. However, the regular expression syntax used in Microsoft Word differs significantly from that in most programming languages. Microsoft Word refers to regular expressions as wildcards and, unfortunately, has many nonstandard features. So if you have been using regular expressions in other languages or tools, you may have significant adjustments to make, in part because of nonstandard syntax in Word and in part because of the fairly limited functionality. There is, for example, no lookbehind or lookahead functionality.

In this chapter, you will learn the following:

❑ How to access regular expression functionality in Microsoft Word

❑ The regular expression functionality supported in Microsoft Word, and its differences from standard regular expression syntax

❑ How to use Microsoft Word wildcards in a range of example scenarios

The User Interface

The interface to use regular expressions in Microsoft Word is straightforward. To use regular expressions (wildcards) in Word 2003, simply select the Edit menu; then select Find. Alternatively, you can use the equivalent keyboard shortcut Ctrl+F. The Find and Replace dialog box opens. If you have not used regular expressions or other advanced search functionality in Word, the appearance expected is shown in Figure 11-1.

To access regular expression functionality, click the More button. Further options are displayed, as shown in Figure 11-2.

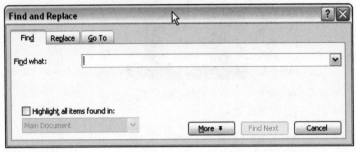

Figure 11-1

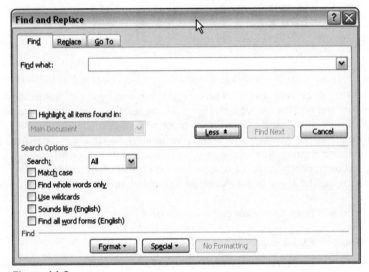

Figure 11-2

To use Word regular expression functionality, click the Use Wildcards check box.

Try It Out   Word Wildcards

1. With Microsoft Word open, open the test file `Apple.doc`.

The content of the test file is shown here:

```
The skin of the apple is green.

The apple's flavor was fantastic.

Apples grow on trees.
```

2. Type Ctrl+F to open the Find and Replace dialog box. If necessary, click the More button to display the Use Wildcards check box.

3. Check the Use Wildcards check box. When you click the Use Wildcards check box, the Match Case and Find Whole Words Only check boxes are grayed out. The Sounds Like and Find Whole Words Only check boxes cannot be checked at the same time as the Use Wildcards check box. Those three options, although displayed as check boxes in Word, function more like a set of radio buttons in a Web form, because you can select only one option at any one time.

4. Enter the pattern **apple** in the Find What text box, and click Find Next three times, inspecting the highlighted text after each click.

Figure 11-3 shows the appearance after clicking Find Next twice in Step 4. After the third click, a dialog box should display, indicating that the end of the file has been reached: "Word has finished searching the document."

How It Works

The matching of the character sequence apple in the first line is straightforward. The character sequence Apple in the third line does not match, because the default behavior in Microsoft Word, when wildcards are used, is to match case sensitively. The character sequence Apple fails to match the pattern apple because the first character of the character sequence is an uppercase a, and the first character of the pattern is a lowercase A.

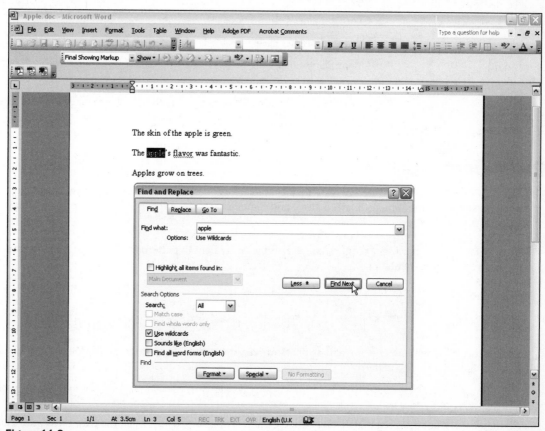

Figure 11-3

Metacharacters Available

The following table shows the metacharacters available in Word 2003. The functionality relating to what each metacharacter does in Word is described in more detail in the following sections of this chapter.

Metacharacter	Description
?	Nonstandard usage (in Word, it is not a quantifier). Matches a single character. Broadly equivalent to the dot metacharacter (.) in standard syntax.
*	Nonstandard usage. Matches zero or more characters. Broadly equivalent to .* in standard syntax.
<	Matches the position between a nonalphabetic character and a following alphabetic character. Effectively, a beginning-of-word position metacharacter.
>	Matches the position between an alphabetic character and a following nonalphabetic character. Effectively, an end-of-word position metacharacter.
[...]	Character class delimiters.
!	Used in character classes as the character class negation metacharacter.
{n,m}	Quantifier syntax.
@	Quantifier. Nonstandard syntax, to match one or more occurrences of the preceding character or group. Equivalent to the + metacharacter in standard syntax.

Quantifiers

Microsoft Word does not use the ?, *, or + metacharacters as quantifiers in the way typical of most regular expression implementations. Instead, the ? and * metacharacters are used in the same way as they are in DOS filenames.

The ? metacharacter signifies a single character and is equivalent to patterns such as . or \w in most regular expression implementations.

So the pattern:

```
so?t
```

in Microsoft Word will match `soft` and `sort`. However, the ? metacharacter in Word does not carry the notion of optionality. The pattern:

```
sa?t
```

will match `salt` but does not match `sat`, because there is no character between the a and t in sat. The ? metacharacter in Word always matches exactly one character.

The * metacharacter in Word signifies zero or more characters and is roughly equivalent to `.*` or `\w*` in most implementations. Notice that while the ? metacharacter does not have the notion of optionality, the * metacharacter does signify an optional character. So the pattern:

```
se*t
```

will match `set` (the letter between the `e` and `t` is optional), `seat`, `sect`, and `sent`. However, the effect of the * metacharacter in Word may occasionally surprise you with unexpected matches when it matches zero characters. For example, the pattern:

```
s*t
```

will match words such as `sit` and `sat`, but will also match the character sequence `st` in words such as `first` and `best`. Figure 11-4 shows an example with the `st` character sequence in `first` matching. The test text is as follows:

```
sit
sat
first
```

The pattern is `s*t`.

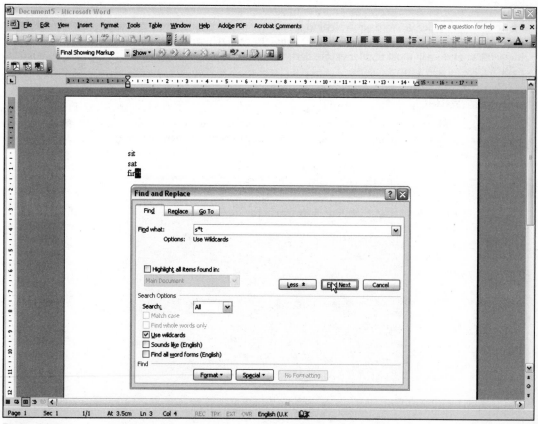

Figure 11-4

If you are carrying out a search and replace, such undesired matches can cause significant oddities in the text following the replacement operation.

> The use of the * metacharacter in Word can lower the specificity of a search substantially. So replacement operations using the * metacharacter are, in general, to be avoided.

The following table summarizes the support for quantifiers in Microsoft Word:

Metacharacter	Comment
?	The ? metacharacter in Word is *not* a typical quantifier. It matches a single character and is not a quantifier at all.
*	The * metacharacter in Word is *not* a typical quantifier. It matches zero or more characters.
@	The @ metacharacter.
{n,m}	The {n,m} syntax is a quantifier in Word.

There is no quantifier in Word equivalent to the zero or more occurrences ? metacharacter in most regular expression implementations. Neither is there a quantifier that matches zero or more occurrences as the * metacharacter does in most regular expression implementations. In Word, the {n,m} syntax cannot be used to provide equivalent functionality.

The @ Quantifier

The only true quantifier metacharacter in Microsoft Word is the @ metacharacter. It is equivalent to the + metacharacter in most implementations, matching one or more occurrences of the character or group that precedes it.

Try It Out   The @ Quantifier

The test file is Hot.doc, whose content is shown here:

```
hot
hoot
host
holt
shoot
ht
```

1. Open Hot.doc in Microsoft Word, and open the Find and Replace dialog box using the Ctrl+F keyboard shortcut.

2. Check the Use Wildcards check box, and type the pattern **ho@t** in the Find What text box.

3. Click Find Next three times. After each click, inspect the text that is highlighted.

   Figure 11-5 shows the appearance after Step 3, when the Find Next button has been clicked three times. After the first click, the character sequence hot is highlighted. After the second click, the character sequence hoot is highlighted. After the third click, the character sequence hoot in shoot is highlighted. Notice that the character sequence ht on the final line is not highlighted if you click the Find Next button again, because zero occurrences of o between the h and t of ht does not match the o@ component of the pattern.

4. Create a new blank Word document, and type the test text **AABABABABAAAAAAA** in it.

5. If necessary, open the Find and Replace dialog box, and check the Use Wildcards check box.

6. Type the pattern **A(AB)@** in the Find What text box; click the Find Next button; and inspect the highlighted text, as shown in Figure 11-6.

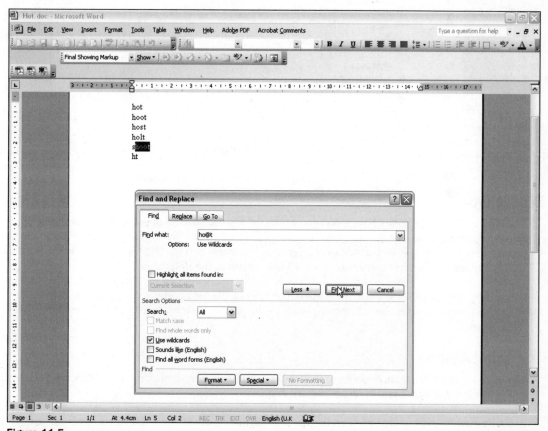

Figure 11-5

259

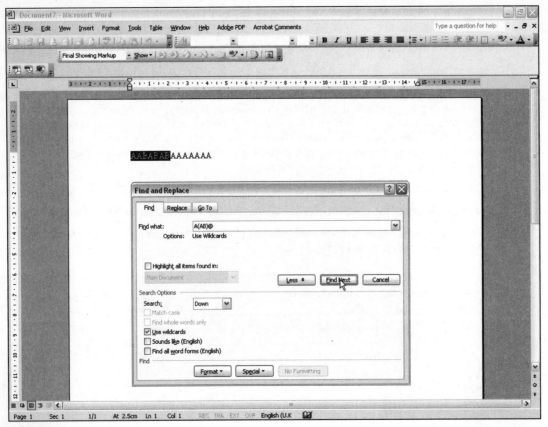

Figure 11-6

How It Works

The pattern o@ matches one or more occurrences of the lowercase o. So in the test document hot.doc, the first click matches hoot because two occurrences of lowercase o match the pattern o@. Similarly, the second click matches hot because one occurrence of lowercase o in the test text matches the pattern o@. The third click matches hoot in shoot for the same reason as the first match.

When the pattern A(AB)@ is used, the @ quantifier refers to the preceding group, not simply a single character. In the example, the (AB)@ component of the pattern matches three occurrences of the character sequence AB.

The {n,m} Syntax

The {n,m} quantifier syntax is available in Word but, unfortunately, cannot provide quantifiers equivalent to the ? and * metacharacters in typical regular expression syntax.

Some limitations exist in how you can use the {n,m} syntax in Word. You cannot, for example, use {0,} or {0,*} to create a quantifier exactly equivalent to the * metacharacter in typical regular expression syntax. In fact, you can't use 0 as the first numeric digit inside curly braces at all. The lack of support for 0 as a minimum occurrence constraint means that neither the ? nor * metacharacters can be mimicked using the {n,m} syntax.

Try It Out   **The {n,m} Syntax**

The test document, `Zeros.doc`, is shown here:

```
AB1
AB10
AB100
AB1000
AB10000
```

1.   Open `Zeros.doc` in Word, and open the Find and Replace dialog box using Ctrl+F.

2.   Enter the pattern **AB10{1,100}** in the Find What text box, and click Find Next four times, inspecting the text highlighted after each click.

      Figure 11-7 shows the text's appearance after the first time that the Find Next button is clicked.

3.   Edit the pattern in the Find what text box to `AB10{3,100}`, click the Find Next button three times, and inspect the text that is highlighted each time.

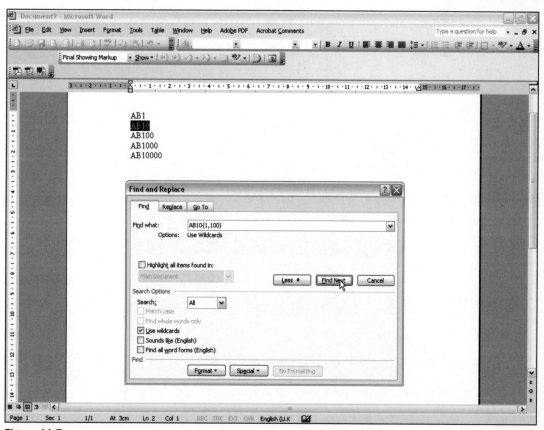

Figure 11-7

How It Works

The {n,m} syntax works as in other implementations. The n specifies the minimum number of occurrences that match. The m specifies the maximum number of occurrences that match.

When the pattern is AB10{1,100}, the first match is the character sequence AB10, because the first three characters of the pattern match literally, and there is one occurrence of the numeric digit 0, which fits with the minimum occurrence constraint.

The other matches for the pattern AB10{1,100} occur because the number of occurrences of the numeric digit 0 is between 1 and 100, the minimum occurrence constraint and maximum occurrence constraint, respectively.

When the pattern is altered to AB10{3,100}, the first match is AB1000, which has three occurrences of the numeric digit 0. The character sequences AB1, AB10, and AB100 have too few occurrences of the numeric digit 0.

Modes

The choice of modes in Microsoft Word is nil. There is no way to use wildcards in a case-insensitive way.

Applying the pattern:

```
Staff
```

to the test text, Staff.doc

```
Staff is an archaic word for a long walking stick.

The Staff party takes place on Friday.

I spoke yesterday with senior staff.
```

will find a match on the lines containing:

```
Staff is an archaic word for a long walking stick.
```

and

```
The Staff party takes place on Friday.
```

but will find no match on the line:

```
I spoke yesterday with senior staff.
```

because the pattern Staff matches only a sequence of characters that begins with an uppercase S.

There is a workaround to achieve case-insensitive matching: Use a character class for each literal character in the pattern to be matched. That approach can be tedious, but it allows things to be done that cannot be done in Word any other way. The test text, Star.doc, is shown here:

```
sTar

star

Star

STAR
```

Notice how the case of some characters differs among the sample lines.

Character Classes to Match Case Insensitively

1. Open `Star.doc` in Microsoft Word, and use the Ctrl+F keyboard shortcut to open the Find and Replace dialog box.

2. Check the Use Wildcards check box, and enter the pattern **star** in the Find What text box.

3. Click the Find Next button, and inspect the results.

4. Click the Find Next button again, and inspect the results, as shown in Figure 11-8.

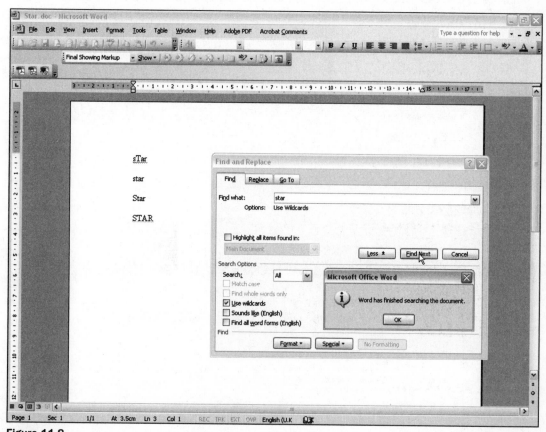

Figure 11-8

Notice that the line containing star (all lowercase) is the first (and only) line that matches. When you click Find Next again, the message window shown in Figure 11-8 is displayed.

5. Edit the pattern in the Find What text box to [Ss][Tt][Aa][Rr].

6. Ensure that the cursor is at the beginning of the test document. Click the Find Next button four times.

Figure 11-9 shows the text's appearance after clicking Find Next once in Step 6.

How It Works

The pattern star matches case sensitively. The character sequence sTar does not match because its second character is an uppercase T, which does not match the corresponding character in the pattern, a lowercase t, when matching is case sensitive.

The character sequence star on the second line matches because each character in the pattern matches the corresponding character in the test character sequence.

The character sequence Star does not match because the first character is uppercase. The character sequence STAR does not match the pattern star because matching will fail on the first character, which is uppercase.

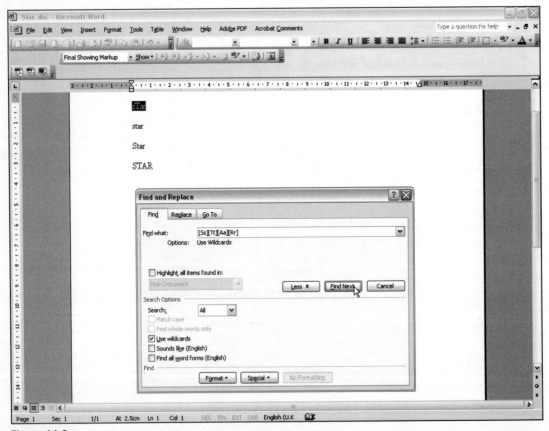

Figure 11-9

264

When the pattern is [Ss][Tt][Aa][Rr], all of the test character sequences will match, because for each character in a test character sequence, both uppercase and lowercase options are provided.

Character Classes

Microsoft Word provides support for character classes. The most important variation from standard syntax is that the ! metacharacter is used to negate a character class (in place of the ^ character typically used in other implementations).

Back References

Back references can be used successfully in Microsoft Word by grouping character sequences using paired parentheses in the normal way. An example using back references is provided later in this chapter.

Lookahead and Lookbehind

Microsoft Word does not support lookahead or lookbehind.

Lazy Matching versus Greedy Matching

Another difference between the default behavior of most regular expression implementations and frequent behavior of the regular expression implementation in Microsoft Word is that Word tends to default to lazy matching. Most other regular expression implementations default to greedy matching (with many languages providing a special syntax to be used for lazy matching).

However, Word conducts greedy matching in some circumstances. Recall the pattern A(AB)@ in the example earlier in this chapter. It matched the maximum available occurrences.

Word usually matches as few characters as possible, consistent with matching a pattern. Let's look at an example to make the concept clearer. The test file, ABC123.doc, is shown here:

```
ABC123

ABC123456

ABC123456
```

| Try It Out | Lazy Matching in Microsoft Word |

1. Open the file ABC123.doc in Microsoft Word, and use the Ctrl+F keyboard shortcut to open the Find and Replace dialog box.

2. Check the Use Regular Expressions check box, and enter the pattern * in the Find What text box.

3. Click the Find Next button, and inspect the results. In Figure 11-10, notice that one character, the first uppercase A, is highlighted.

4. Click the Find Next button a few more times, each time inspecting the result.

5. Modify the pattern in the Find What text box to A*.

6. Click at the beginning of the file to ensure that the cursor is at the position before the first uppercase A. Click the Find Next button, and inspect the results.

7. Click the Find Next button twice more, inspecting the result each time.

    Notice in Figure 11-11 that each time, only the first uppercase A on the relevant line is highlighted.

8. Modify the pattern in the Find What text box to A*{2,5}.

9. Click at the beginning of the file to ensure that the cursor is at the position before the first uppercase A. Click the Find Next button, and inspect the results, as shown in Figure 11-12.

10. Click the Find Next button twice more, inspecting the result each time. Each time, the initial ABC on each line is highlighted.

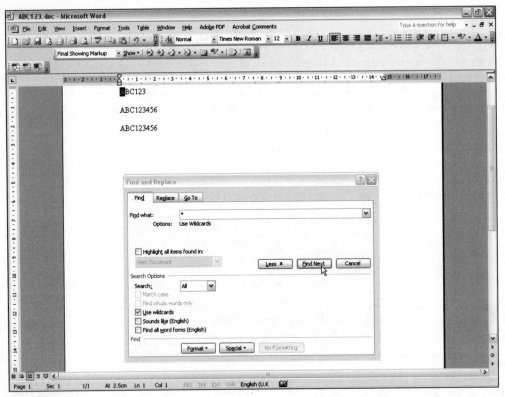

Figure 11-10

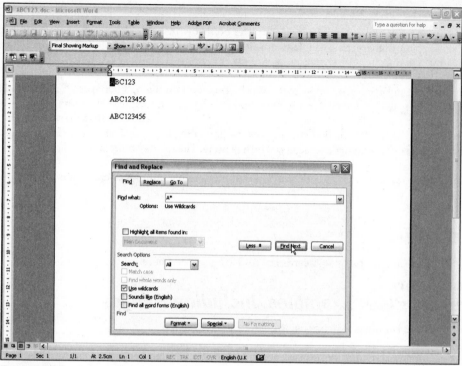

Figure 11-11

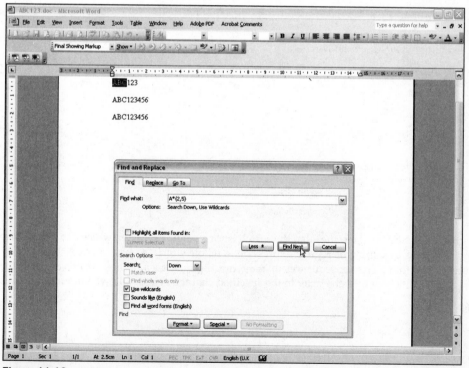

Figure 11-12

How It Works

The behavior when matching the * metacharacter on its own is odd. The * metacharacter is supposed to match zero or more characters, so if lazy matching were applied to the letter, it would match zero characters. In fact, it matches one character, as you saw in Figure 11-10.

If you use the * metacharacter on its own, which you won't do often, it behaves as anticipated for lazy matching. The pattern A* matches only the initial character A on each line. Assuming that the regular expression starts matching at the beginning of the first line, it matches the first character in the pattern, a literal uppercase A, with the first character of the line in the test text. Then it matches the minimum possible number of following characters, which is none. That is lazy matching.

Similarly, in the pattern A*{2,5}, only the minimum possible number of characters, BC, are matched.

Examples

Some further examples using wildcards in Word are provided here.

Character Class Examples, Including Ranges

Microsoft Word supports searches using character classes.

Word uses standard regular expression syntax for positive character classes. For example, to find the character sequences gray and grey in a document, gray.doc, you could use the following regular expression:

```
gr[ae]y
```

The content of gray.doc is shown here:

```
gray
grey
greying
greyed
grapple
grim
goat
filigree
great
groat
gloat
```

The character class [ae] specifies that the search is for a single character, which can be either a or e. There is nothing to restrict the regular expression to whole words, so you can expect the search to return the first four character sequences in gray.doc, because each of those words contains the literal characters gr followed by a character in the specified character class, followed in turn by the literal character y.

Whole Word Searches

It is a common requirement to find a sequence of characters that constitutes a whole word. You might, for example, search for the words (not merely the character sequences) gray and grey. The word boundary metacharacters < and > can be combined with other regular expression components.

Try It Out   **Whole Word Searches**

The preceding test document, Gray.doc, will be used.

1.   Open Gray.doc in Microsoft Word, and open the Find and Replace dialog box.

2.   Check the Using Wildcards check box, and type the pattern **<gr[ae]y>** in the Find What text box.

3.   Click the Find Next button three times, inspecting the text that is or is not matched each time. Figure 11-13 shows the appearance after Find Next is clicked the first time.

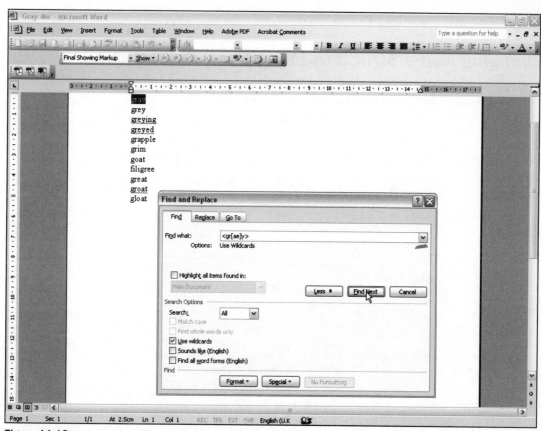

Figure 11-13

How It Works

The character sequence gray is matched because it is a word, rather than simply a character sequence. The < metacharacter matches the position before the g of gray. The literal g matches, as does the literal r. The character class [ae] includes a match for the e, which is the third character of the test text. The final y of the pattern matches the final y of the character sequence. After the y matches, the > metacharacter matches the end-of-line position.

The word grey matches for reasons explained in the preceding paragraph. However, the words greying and greyed do not match. The <gr[ae]y component of the regular expression matches, but matching fails on the > metacharacter. The character following the y in greying and in greyed is an alphabetic character, so there is no end-of-word boundary position.

Search-and-Replace Examples

The following examples illustrate how wildcards can be useful in a search-and-replace operation.

Changing Name Structure Using Back References

In Microsoft Word, you can use wildcards to reverse the structure of all the names in a document. For example, a name that originally appears as:

```
Fred Smith
```

becomes the following, after the use of wildcards, in a search-and-replace operation:

```
Smith, Fred
```

Achieving this depends on using back references.

The content of the sample document, Names.doc, is shown here:

```
Fred Smith
Alice Green
Barbara Kaplan
Ali Hussein
Paul Simenon
```

Notice that each name appears as a first name followed by a space character, followed by a surname. The consistency of that structure is important in the find operation.

Try It Out   Changing Name Structure

1. Open Names.doc in Microsoft Word, and use the Ctrl+F keyboard shortcut to open the Find and Replace dialog box.

2. If the Search Options part of the Find and Replace window is not visible, click the More button to display the Search Options area. Check the Use Wildcards check box.

3. In the Find What text box, type the pattern **(<*>) (<*>)** (make sure that there is a space character between the first closing parenthesis and the second opening parenthesis).

4. In the Replace With text box, type the pattern **\2, \1** (make sure that there is a space character after the comma in the pattern).

5. Click the Find Next button. (The text `Fred Smith` should be highlighted.)

6. Click the Replace button. Inspect the result of the first replace operation. (The text `Fred Smith` should be replaced by `Smith, Fred`, as shown in Figure 11-14.)

7. Click the Replace All button, and inspect the results, as shown in Figure 11-15. All the names should be in the following form:

```
Surname, FirstName
```

How It Works

Let's look at how the pattern `(<*>) (<*>)` works. The two pairs of parentheses are there for grouping. The < metacharacter matches the position at the beginning of a sequence of alphabetic characters. The * metacharacter matches zero or more characters (equivalent to `.*` in more standard regular expression syntax). And the > metacharacter matches the position between the end of a sequence of alphabetic characters and the beginning of a sequence of nonalphabetic characters. So <*> matches a word of any length. When that is contained inside paired parentheses, grouping takes place.

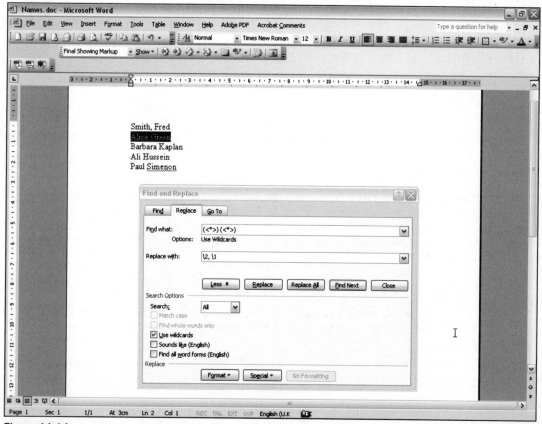

Figure 11-14

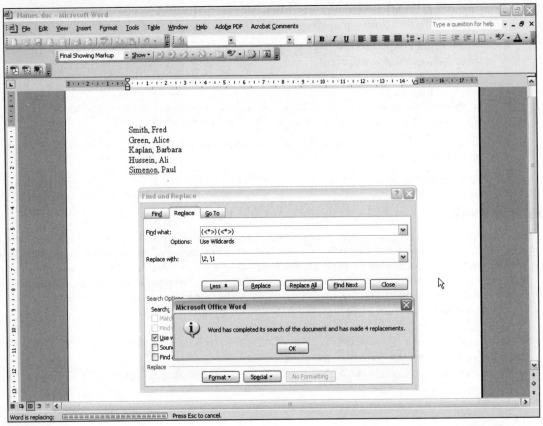

Figure 11-15

Because there is a space character between the first (<*>) pattern and the second, the pattern:

```
(<*>) (<*>)
```

matches two words separated by a single space character, which is the structure of the names in the file Names.doc. It also captures two groups, \1 and \2, which are available for use in the replace operation.

The parentheses create two groups: \1 contains the word before the space character, and \2 contains the word that follows the space character. So the pattern:

```
\2, \1
```

replaces what had been two words separated by a space character, with the second word (indicated by \2), followed by a comma, followed by a space character, followed by what had been the first word (indicated by \1).

Manipulating Dates

Just as words such as gray (grey) and license (licence) differ in individual dialects of English, so does the structure of dates. In the United States, dates in numeric form are typically written as MM/DD/YYYY. In the United Kingdom, dates are written in the DD/MM/YYYY format. In Japan, the format YYYY/MM/DD is used. I have shown those formats using a forward slash as a separator, but other separators, such as a hyphen (dash) or a period character, are also used. In this example, I assume that the dates you want to manipulate are not written in the format 25 December 2005, 25 Dec 2005, or other similar formats.

The test document, Dates.doc, is shown here:

```
2005-12-25
12/11/2003
01.25.2006
03-18-2007
07-19-2004
2006/09/18
```

The dates in the test document consist of some in the International date format, YYYY-MM-DD, and some in U.S. date format, MM/DD/YYYY (with a range of separators). The task is to match U.S. date formats and replace them with the international date format equivalent. Because the international date format is used in XML, it is likely that an increasing amount of date-related information will be stored in that format.

We will assume that no dates are in U.K. date format, because the date on the second line would be ambiguous if U.K. dates were present. In U.S. date format, it would mean December 11, 2003, while in U.K. date format, it would mean 12 November 2003.

Try It Out   Conversion to International Date Format

1. Open Dates.doc in Microsoft Word.

2. Open the Find and Replace dialog box using Ctrl+F, and check the Use Wildcards check box.

   First, we will check whether we can create a regular expression to find the dates that are in U.S. date format.

3. Type the pattern ([0-9]{2})[./-]([0-9]{2})[./-]([0-9]{4}) in the Find What text box, click the Find Next button four times, and inspect the highlighted text.

   If all has gone well, the pattern should match the dates that are in U.S. format but not those that are already in international date format. We have assumed that all entries are valid dates. The pattern shown would also match nonsense character sequences such as 44/12/5432.

   Figure 11-16 shows the text's appearance after Step 3, when the Find Next button has been clicked four times.

4. Switch to the Replace tab of the Find and Replace dialog box, and type the pattern \3-\1-\2 in the Replace With text box.

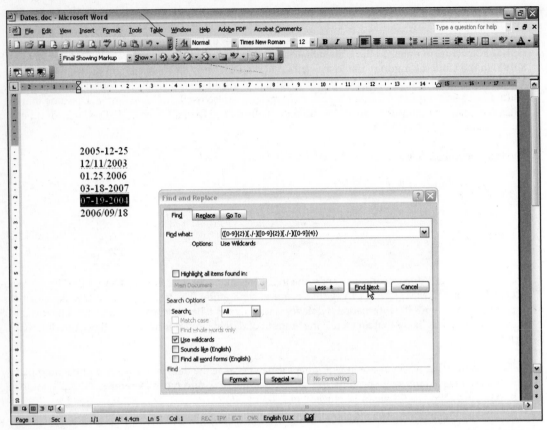

Figure 11-16

5. Click Find Next. Click Replace. Confirm that the change has produced an appropriately formatted date — that is, a date in international date format.

6. Repeat Step 5 three times to replace all occurrences of dates in U.S. date format. Figure 11-17 shows the appearance after Step 6 has been completed.

How It Works

Let's break the pattern ([0-9]{2})[./-]([0-9]{2})[./-]([0-9]{4}) into its component parts to understand what it is doing.

The ([0-9]{2}) component matches a character sequence made up of two successive numeric digits. We have to use the character class [0-9] to match numeric digits, because Microsoft Word wildcards don't have a metacharacter that is specific to numeric digits. The parentheses are grouping parentheses, creating the group \1, which contains the date's month component.

The [./-] component will match dates that use the hyphen, forward slash, or period character as the separator. Be careful not to write this character class as [.-/], because written that way, the hyphen creates a range that won't give you the desired results.

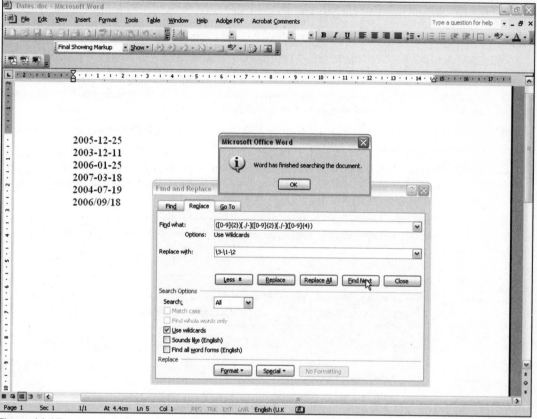

Figure 11-17

The components ([0-9]{2})[./-] do the same as the first two components of the pattern, except that the grouping parentheses create group \2, which contains the date's day component.

The ([0-9]{4}) component of the pattern matches a character sequence of four numeric digits. The grouping parentheses create group \3, which contains the date's year component.

The replacement pattern, \3-\1-\2, reorders the date. The \3 group, which contains the year component, is followed by a literal hyphen, which is in turn followed by the \1 group, which contains the month component of the date. Another literal hyphen follows and, finally, the \2 group containing the date's day component.

The Star Training Company Example

Microsoft Word has no lookahead functionality, so we can't use that to carry out a search and replace of the Star Training Company document in Word. However, we can make use of back references to achieve what we want, although not quite so elegantly as we might have if lookahead were available in Word.

Try It Out   **Star Training Company Example**

1. Open `StarOriginal.doc` in Microsoft Word, and open the Find and Replace dialog box.

2. Switch to the Replace tab. Because of the absence of alternation (there is no | metacharacter available in Word), we have to carry out the replacement in two stages.

3. In the Find What text box, type the pattern **(Star)(Training)**, making sure that there is a space character inside the parentheses before the uppercase T of `Training`.

4. Click Find Next several times, inspecting the result each time. Confirm that each occurrence of the character sequence `Star Training` is matched.

5. In the Replace With text box, type the pattern **Moon\2**. Be careful to avoid inserting a space character between `Moon` and `\2`. The space character was captured inside the group `\2`, so you don't need to add one here.

6. Use the Find Next and Replace buttons to step through the document, replacing each occurrence of the character sequence `Star Training`. Figure 11-18 shows the screen's appearance when the first occurrence of `Star Training` has already been replaced.

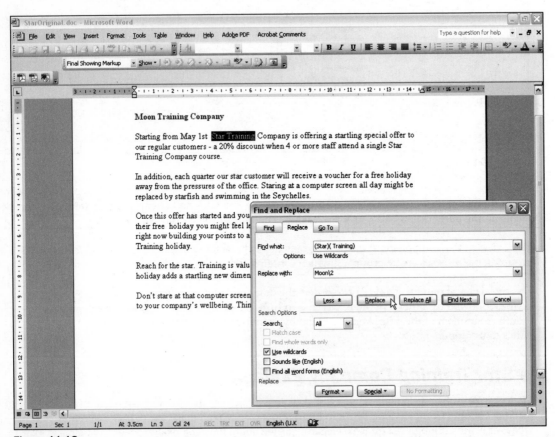

Figure 11-18

7. Edit the pattern in the Find What text box to (Star)([.]). This slightly unusual pattern is necessary in Word, as explained later.

8. You can leave the pattern in the Replace With text box unchanged. Use the Find Next and Replace buttons to replace the pattern Star. with Moon.. Figure 11-19 shows the appearance when the first occurrence of the character sequence Star. is about to be replaced.

How It Works

First, let's look at how the pattern (Star)(Training) matches. Two groups are created using this approach. We have created a group with (Star) and a second group that contains a space character followed by the character sequence Training. By capturing group \2 and simply putting it in the replace string we are, in effect, creating a workaround for the lack of lookahead functionality. The character sequence Star is replaced with Moon, and we replace the content of \2 with itself.

The pattern (Star)([.]) creates two groups. The first contains the character sequence Star, and the second, a period character. In most regular expression implementations, you wouldn't have to enclose the period character inside a character class. You would likely use the \. metacharacter instead. However, in Word you have to enclose the period character inside a character class to avoid an error message. Occurrences of Star before a period character are replaced by Moon.

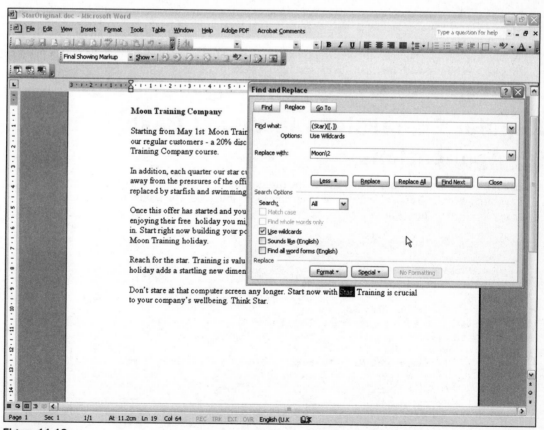

Figure 11-19

The resulting document, `StarWhichIsNowMoon.doc`, with all relevant occurrences of the character sequence `Star` replaced using the two-step replace just described, is shown here:

```
Moon Training Company

Starting from May 1st  Moon Training Company is offering a startling special offer
to our regular customers - a 20% discount when 4 or more staff attend a single Moon
Training Company course.

In addition, each quarter our star customer will receive a voucher for a free
holiday away from the pressures of the office. Staring at a computer screen all day
might be replaced by starfish and swimming in the Seychelles.

Once this offer has started and you hear about other Moon Training customers
enjoying their free  holiday you might feel left out. Don't be left on the outside
staring in. Start right now building your points to allow you to start out on your
very own Moon Training holiday.

Reach for the star. Training is valuable in its own right but the possibility of a
free holiday adds a startling new dimension to the benefits of Moon Training
training.

Don't stare at that computer screen any longer. Start now with Moon. Training is
crucial to your company's wellbeing. Think Moon.
```

We have replaced all the relevant occurrences of `Star`. It's a big improvement over the novice attempt in Chapter 1, achieved with high sensitivity and high specificity.

Regular Expressions in Visual Basic for Applications

Visual Basic for Applications (VBA) allows the programmatic use of regular expressions (wildcards) in ways similar to those available from the Microsoft Word interface. The following Word macro, `StarToMoon`, does the same:

```vba
Sub StarToMoon()
'
' StarToMoon Macro
' Macro recorded 19/07/2004 by Andrew Watt
'
    Selection.Find.ClearFormatting
    Selection.Find.Replacement.ClearFormatting
    With Selection.Find
        .Text = "(Star)( Training)"
        .Replacement.Text = "Moon\2"
        .Forward = True
        .Wrap = wdFindContinue
        .Format = False
        .MatchCase = False
        .MatchWholeWord = False
        .MatchAllWordForms = False
```

```
                .MatchSoundsLike = False
                .MatchWildcards = True
        End With
        Selection.Find.Execute Replace:=wdReplaceAll
        With Selection.Find
            .Text = "(Star)(.)"
            .Replacement.Text = "Moon\2"
            .Forward = True
            .Wrap = wdFindContinue
            .Format = False
            .MatchCase = False
            .MatchWholeWord = False
            .MatchAllWordForms = False
            .MatchSoundsLike = False
            .MatchWildcards = True
        End With
        Selection.Find.Execute
        With Selection
            If .Find.Forward = True Then
                .Collapse Direction:=wdCollapseStart
            Else
                .Collapse Direction:=wdCollapseEnd
            End If
            .Find.Execute Replace:=wdReplaceOne
            If .Find.Forward = True Then
                .Collapse Direction:=wdCollapseEnd
            Else
                .Collapse Direction:=wdCollapseStart
            End If
            .Find.Execute
        End With
        With Selection
            If .Find.Forward = True Then
                .Collapse Direction:=wdCollapseStart
            Else
                .Collapse Direction:=wdCollapseEnd
            End If
            .Find.Execute Replace:=wdReplaceOne
            If .Find.Forward = True Then
                .Collapse Direction:=wdCollapseEnd
            Else
                .Collapse Direction:=wdCollapseStart
            End If
            .Find.Execute
        End With
    End Sub
```

It isn't the purpose of this chapter to teach how to create Word macros, but it can be useful to have find-and-replace functionality inside a Word macro.

The file `StarOriginalWithMacro.doc` contains the preceding macro, which you can execute.

The file `StarAfterMacro.doc` contains the file after replacement of the text using the macro.

> To run the `StarToMoon` macro, you may need to adjust your macro security settings in Word.
>
> Please note that the machine on which the macro was created was believed to be free of viruses. However, you may wish to check using your own antivirus software to ensure that it remains virus free.

Exercises

The following exercises allow you to test your understanding of the material introduced in this chapter:

1. Create a pattern, that, in Word, will match the character sequences peak and peek.

2. Modify the date example so that it will take dates in U.K. date format and convert them to international date format.

Regular Expressions in StarOffice/OpenOffice.org Writer

Microsoft Office has, for many years, been the preeminent office system available for use on the Windows platform. In recent years, in part because of price advantage, the StarOffice and OpenOffice.org office suite members have become increasingly popular as alternatives to Microsoft Word and Microsoft Excel. This chapter focuses on the use of regular expressions in the word processor component of the OpenOffice.org suite, OpenOffice.org Writer.

The support for regular expressions in OpenOffice.org is better than in Microsoft Word. More metacharacters are supported, and the regular expression syntax used in OpenOffice.org Writer is more standard than the syntax used in Microsoft Word. Of course, that difference in functionality is only one of many factors that you will likely consider if you are choosing between these popular word processors.

One piece of functionality in OpenOffice.org Writer that I find very useful is the Find All button. You have seen the use of the Find All button in many examples in the early chapters of this book. I find it a quick and useful way to see which test character sequences match a regular expression that I am testing. In a few situations, which are discussed later in this chapter, you do need to take care when interpreting the results shown by the Find All button.

OpenOffice.org version 1.0 does not support regular expressions. To make use of regular expressions, you will need OpenOffice.org version 1.1 or later.

In this chapter, you will learn the following:

- ❏ How to use the OpenOffice.org Writer interface to employ regular expressions when searching for and replacing text

- ❏ The regular expression syntax supported in OpenOffice.org Writer

❑ How to carry out search operations and search-and-replace operations in OpenOffice.org Writer

❑ How to use the POSIX character classes, which are supported in OpenOffice.org Writer

The User Interface

OpenOffice.org Writer's user interface is different in a number of ways from that of Microsoft Office. However, as in Word, the Ctrl+F shortcut brings up the Find & Replace dialog shown in Figure 12-1.

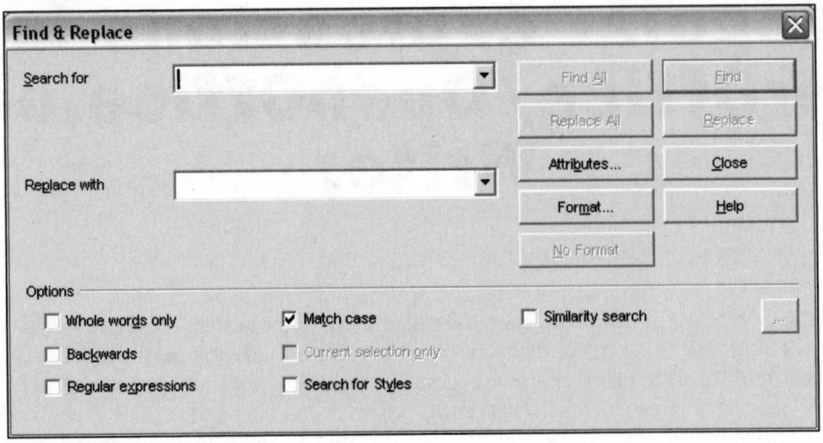

Figure 12-1

To use regular expressions in OpenOffice.org Writer, you have to check the Regular Expressions check box toward the bottom-left corner of the dialog box. OpenOffice.org's default behavior is to conduct case-insensitive regular expression matches. To match regular expressions case sensitively, you must check the Match Case check box as well as the Regular Expressions check box. Depending on what you have been doing in OpenOffice.org Writer, you may sometimes find that the Match Case check box is checked when you open the Find & Replace dialog box. If you expect a default case-insensitive match and don't notice that the Match Case check box is checked, the matches may not be those you expect. The Regular Expressions check box is, in my experience, always unchecked when you first open the Find & Replace dialog box. However, if you have several OpenOffice.org windows open, the settings in the Find & Replace dialog box for one document may carry over when you open the Find & Replace dialog box in another document.

If the Regular Expressions check box is checked, the Whole Words Only check box is grayed out. OpenOffice.org Writer provides metacharacters, described later in the chapter, which match the beginning-of-word position and the end-of-word position, allowing matches using regular expressions to be made only on whole words (more strictly, on sequences of word characters).

As you have seen in examples in earlier chapters, the Find All button is a very convenient way to find all matches for a particular regular expression pattern. However, you must be careful in interpreting the effect of the Find All button in certain circumstances. For example, suppose that you have multiple successive numeric digits, as in several lines in the following sample (Numbers.txt):

```
A123

2345

9876

12ABC345

999
```

When Find All is clicked, the pattern [0-9]+ in the Search For text box will cause all numeric digits to be matched, as shown in Figure 12-2. However, using the Find All button doesn't make it clear whether matching is greedy or lazy — in other words, whether a single matching process matches one digit or several.

Interpreting the matches is uncertain if you are unaware that in OpenOffice.org Writer matching is always greedy. If you are uncertain about exactly what is being matched by a pattern, successive clicks of the Find button are useful to help you be sure what the pattern is matching on any one occasion.

This uncertainty is present only when using simple patterns. In most (perhaps all) real-life patterns, the ambiguity isn't a problem.

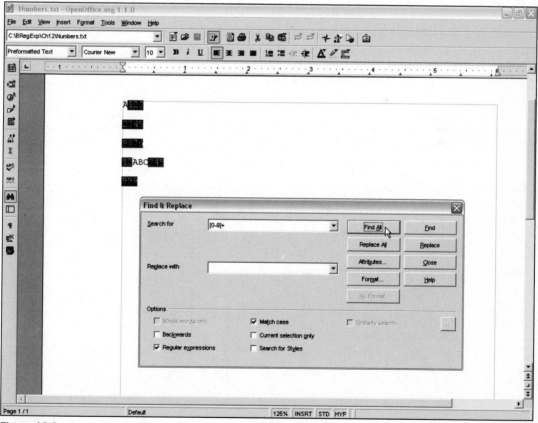

Figure 12-2

Metacharacters Available

The metacharacters used in OpenOffice.org Writer have similarities to those used in Microsoft Word but are not identical to the range of wildcards in Word; neither are the metacharacters used in OpenOffice.org Writer identical to those found, for example, in Perl regular expressions. The following table summarizes the metacharacters supported in OpenOffice.org Writer. POSIX character classes that are supported in OpenOffice.org Writer are described separately in a later section.

In the following table, the term chunk *is used to refer to a single character or a group contained in paired parentheses.*

Metacharacter	Description
.	Matches almost any character, including many symbols and characters not used in English. Used alone or with the ?, *., or + quantifiers.
?	A quantifier indicating zero or one occurrence of the preceding chunk.
*	A quantifier indicating zero or more occurrences of the preceding chunk.
+	A quantifier indicating one or more occurrences of the preceding chunk.
\n	Nonstandard usage. It matches a new line only when it was created using Shift+Enter.
^	The beginning-of-line position.
$	The end-of-line position.
\t	Matches a tab character.
\<	Matches the beginning-of-word position.
\>	Matches the end-of-word position.
&	Nonstandard. Behaves similarly to a back reference.
[ ]	Character class.
|	Alternation. Matching is of the chunk that precedes or follows the | metacharacter.
{n,m}	Quantifier syntax.

The following metacharacters are *not* supported:

- ❑ \b
- ❑ \s
- ❑ \w
- ❑ \d

Quantifiers

The use of quantifiers in OpenOffice.org Writer is standard. The ?, *, +, and {n,m} quantifiers are all available.

The test file, AandSomeBs.txt, is shown here:

```
ABC

ABBC

AC

A3C

ABBBBBBC

AbbCC
```

The pattern AB?C matches the character sequences ABC and AC, as shown in Figure 12-3. Each of the matched character sequences consists of an uppercase A, followed by zero or one uppercase B, followed by an uppercase C.

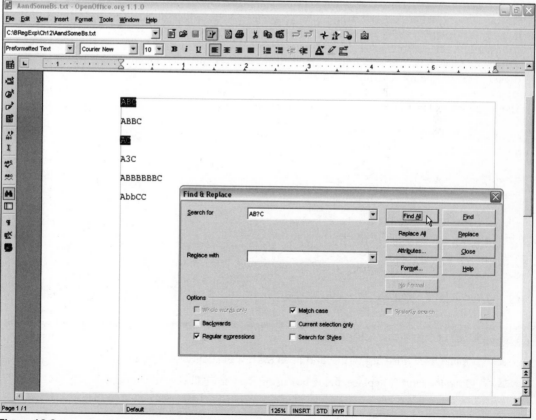

Figure 12-3

# Chapter 12

If the pattern is edited to AB*C, the character sequences matched are ABC, ABBC, AC, and ABBBBBBC. Each of the matched character sequences consists of an uppercase A, followed by zero or more uppercase Bs, followed by an uppercase C.

If the pattern is edited to AB+C, the character sequence AC no longer matches, because it does not have an uppercase B. The pattern AB+C means "Match an uppercase A, followed by one or more uppercase Bs, followed by an uppercase C."

If the pattern is edited to AB{2,4}C, only the character sequence ABBC matches, because it is the only character sequence in the test text that has an uppercase A, followed by between two and four uppercase Bs, followed by an uppercase C.

Modes

OpenOffice.org Writer supports both case-insensitive (the default) and case-sensitive matching. The Match Case check box is the interface tool that controls which mode is used in matching.

Character Classes

The implementation of character classes in OpenOffice.org Writer is pretty much standard. Ranges are supported, as are negated character classes.

OpenOffice.org Writer does not support the \d metacharacter, which matches numeric digits, or the \w metacharacter, which matches word characters. Therefore, the regular expressions author must use the corresponding character classes, [0-9] to match a numeric digit and [A-Za-z] to match both cases of alphabetic characters. The preceding character classes can be qualified by any of the quantifiers mentioned in the preceding "Quantifiers" section.

The following test text, ClassTest.txt is used in the Try It Out exercise that follows:

```
AB1

RD2

K9

993ABC

ABCDEFGHIJKLMNOPQRSTUVWXYZ

abcdefghijklmnopqrstuvwxyz

0123456789
```

Try It Out   Character Classes

1. Open OpenOffice.org Writer, and open the test file ClassTest.txt.

2. Open the Find & Replace dialog box using the Ctrl+F keyboard shortcut.

3. Check the Regular Expressions and Match Case check boxes.

4. In the Search For text box, type the pattern **[0-9]**.

5. Click the Find All button, and inspect the results. As shown in Figure 12-4, all the numeric digits in the test document match the character class [0-9].

6. Edit the pattern in the Search For text box to [A-Z].

7. Click the Find All button, and inspect the results. As shown in Figure 12-5, all the uppercase alphabetic characters in the test document match the character class [A-Z].

8. Edit the pattern in the Search For text box to [a-z].

9. Click the Find All button, and inspect the results. All lowercase alphabetic characters should now be highlighted as matches of the new pattern.

10. Uncheck the Match Case check box.

11. Click the Find All button, and inspect the results. As shown in Figure 12-6, both lowercase and uppercase alphabetic characters are now highlighted as matches.

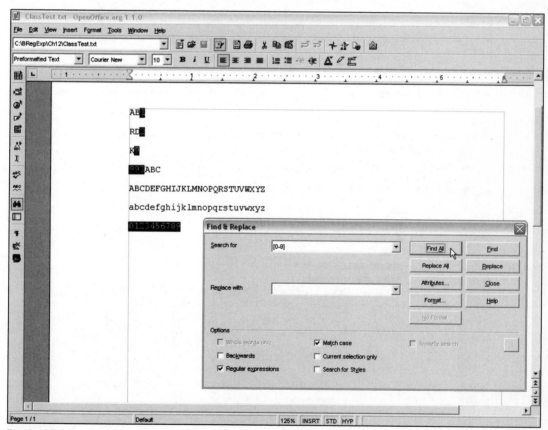

Figure 12-4

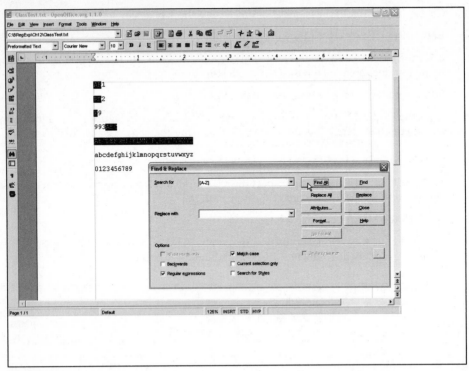

Figure 12-5

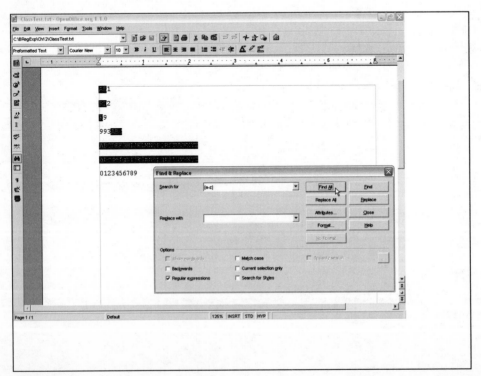

Figure 12-6

How It Works

The initial character class, `[0-9]`, matches the same characters as the character class `[0123456789]`. The dash in `[0-9]` represents a range, so `[0-9]` represents the range of numeric digits from 0 to 9 inclusive. Because OpenOffice.org Writer does not support the `\d` metacharacter, which in most regular expression implementations matches numeric digits, the use of a character class to match numeric digits is needed.

The character class `[A-Z]`, similarly, matches the same characters as the character class as the pattern `[ABCDEFGHIJKLMNOPQRSTUVWXYZ]` but is much more succinct. Because the Match Case check box is checked (see Step 3), only uppercase alphabetic characters are matched.

The character class `[a-z]` matches the same characters as the character class `[abcdefghijklmnopqrs tuvwxyz]`. With the Match Case check box checked, only lowercase alphabetic characters are matched.

When the Match Case check box is unchecked in Step 10, the pattern `[a-z]` matches all alphabetic characters, both lowercase and uppercase.

Alternation

OpenOffice.org Writer supports the | character (often called the pipe character), which conveys the notion of alternation or the logical OR.

A test document, `Licenses.txt`, is shown here:

```
This licence has expired.

Friday is the day that the licensing authority meets.

Licences are essential before you can do that legally.

License is morally questionable.

Licensed practitioners only should apply.
```

The aim is to match any occurrence of `licence`, `license`, or `licensing` while allowing for the possibility (not occurring in the test document) that the form `licencing` might also be used.

The problem definition can broadly be expressed as follows:

Match any occurrence of the word licence or licensing, allowing for possible variations in how each word is spelled.

Refining that initial attempt at a problem definition would give something like the following:

Match, case insensitively, the literal character sequence l, i, c, e, n followed by either c or s, in turn followed by e or the character sequence i, n, and g.

A pattern that would, when applied case insensitively, satisfy the problem definition follows:

```
licen(c|s)(e|ing)
```

So let's try it out.

Try It Out   Alternation

1. Open OpenOffice.org Writer, and open the test file `Licenses.txt`.

2. Check the Regular Expressions check box. Because the aim is case-insensitive matching, ensure that the Match Case check box is unchecked.

3. In the Search For text box, enter the pattern **licen(c|s)(e|ing)**.

4. Click the Find All button, and inspect the highlighted text. Figure 12-7 shows the appearance after Step 4.

You can see that the d or s at the end of `Licensed` and `Licenses`, respectively, are not matched. If the desire is to match the whole word, the pattern can be modified to achieve that. When the character sequences `licens` or `licenc` are followed by an e, you want to allow an optional choice of d or s. So `licence`, `license`, `licenced`, `licensed`, `licences`, and `licenses` would all be matched. However, when the match is `licensing` or `licencing`, you don't want to allow an s or a d as the following character.

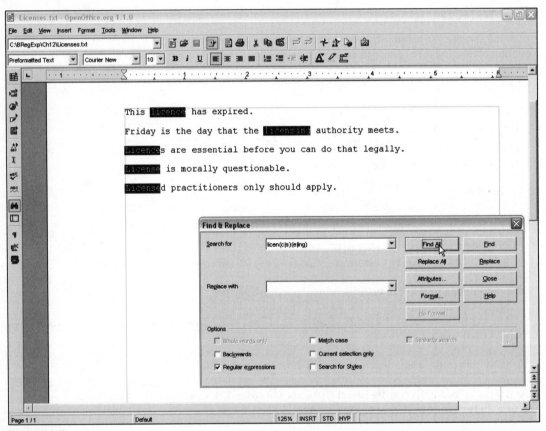

Figure 12-7

The problem definition would be modified like this:

Match, case insensitively, the literal character sequence l, i, c, e, n followed by either c or s, in turn followed by either e followed by a choice of d or s, each of which is optional, or the character sequence i, n, and g.

So the pattern is modified to `licen(c|s)(e(s|d)?|ing)` to express the preceding problem definition.

As you can see from the preceding problem definition and pattern, it can become difficult to clearly express nested options.

5.   Edit the pattern in the Search For text box to `licen(c|s)(e(s|d)?|ing)`.

6.   Click the Find All button, and inspect the results Figure 12-8 shows the appearance after this step.

How It Works

Let's look at how the pattern `licen(c|s)(e(s|d)?|ing)` matches in each of the lines of the test text.

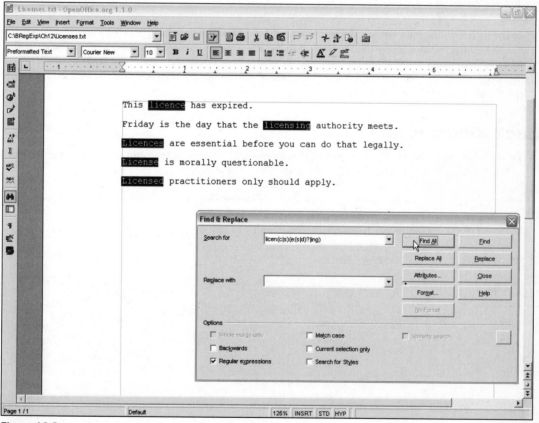

Figure 12-8

In the first line, the relevant text that matches is `licence`. When the regular expression engine reaches the position immediately before the initial `l` of `licence`, the first five characters of the word match the first five literal characters of the pattern. Then the second `c` of `licence` matches the first option in `(c|s)`. And the final `e` of `licence` matches the first option in `(e(s|d)?|ing)` — in other words, `e(s|d)?`, which is an `e` followed optionally by an `s` or a `d`.

In the second line, the relevant text that matches is `licensing`. When the regular expression engine reaches the position immediately before the initial `l` of `licensing`, the first five characters of the word match the first five literal characters of the pattern. Then the `s` of `licensing` matches the second option in `(c|s)`. Then the final character sequence `ing` matches the second option in `(e(s|d)?|ing)`, which is the sequence of literal characters `ing`.

In the third line, the relevant text that matches is `Licences`. Remember that the matching is being carried out case insensitively, so the initial `licen` of the pattern matches the initial character sequence `Licen`. The second `c` in `Licences` matches the first option in `(c|s)`. The final `es` matches the first of the two options in `(e(s|d)?|ing)`. In other words, it matches a literal `e` followed by zero or one `s`.

The matching in the fourth line is the same, except that there is no final `s` to be matched. Because the `(s|d)?` means that the `s` or `d` is optional, there is a match.

In the fifth line, the relevant text that matches is `Licenced`. The matching is being carried out case insensitively, so the initial `licen` of the pattern matches the initial character sequence `Licen`. The second `c` in `Licenced` matches the first option in `(c|s)`. The final `ed` matches the first of the two options in `(e(s|d)?|ing)`. In other words, it matches a literal `e` followed by zero or one `d`. So in this line, `e(s|d)?` matches the character sequence `ed`.

Back References

OpenOffice.org Writer doesn't support back references in a standard way, but the `&` metacharacter provides a limited back-reference-like functionality, which can be used in search and replace.

Suppose that you want to modify all occurrences of words such as `walk` and `sulk` with `walking`, `sulking`, and so on. You can match on the literal character sequence `lk` and then add `ing` to each such matched character sequence. The `&` metacharacter allows you to do that.

The test file, `Walk.txt`, is shown here:

```
Walk

talk

sulk

milk
```

The & Metacharacter

1. Open OpenOffice.org Writer, and open the test file `Walk.txt`.

2. Use the Ctrl+F keyboard shortcut to open the Find & Replace dialog box.

3. Check the Regular Expressions check box. Leave the Match Case check box unchecked.

4. Enter the literal pattern **lk** in the Search For text box.

5. In the Replace With text box, enter the pattern **&lk**.

6. Click the Replace All button, and inspect the result.

Figure 12-9 shows the appearance after Step 6. As you can see, each word that has the character sequence `lk` in it has had the character sequence `ing` added to it.

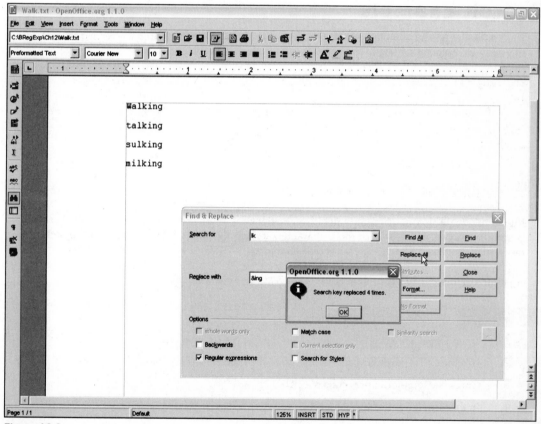

Figure 12-9

How It Works

The & metacharacter matches the text matched in the pattern in the Search For text box. In each case in this example, the matched text is the character sequence lk. That character sequence is replaced by the same character sequence, followed by the character sequence ing, so sulk becomes sulking and milk becomes milking after the replacement. As with any pattern, you must be careful to assess whether the pattern is suitable for the test data. If the test data included a word such as walks, it would be changed to walkings.

Lookahead and Lookbehind

Neither lookahead nor lookbehind is supported in OpenOffice.org Writer.

Search Example

The following search example finds occurrences of the words (strictly, the character sequences) Heaven and Hell in the same sentence.

The sample file, Heaven.txt, is shown here:

```
This sentence contains both the words Heaven and Hell.

This sentence does not contain those two words and therefore is not matched.

This paragraph has Heaven in the first sentence. And Hell in the second.
```

The problem definition can be expressed as follows:

Match the beginning-of-paragraph position, match zero or more characters, match the character sequence Heaven, match zero or more characters, match the character sequence Hell, match zero or more characters, and match a literal period character.

A pattern to implement the problem definition is ^.*Heaven.*Hell.*\..

Try It Out　　**Words in Proximity**

1. Open OpenOffice.org Writer, and open the test file Heaven.txt.

2. Use the Ctrl+F keyboard shortcut to open the Find & Replace dialog box.

3. Check the Regular Expressions check box.

4. In the Search For text box, enter the pattern **^.*Heaven.*Hell.*\..**

5. Click the Find All button, and inspect the results.

   Figure 12-10 shows the appearance after Step 5. You may be surprised to see that both sentences in the third paragraph are highlighted as matches. That will be explained in the How It Works section in a moment.

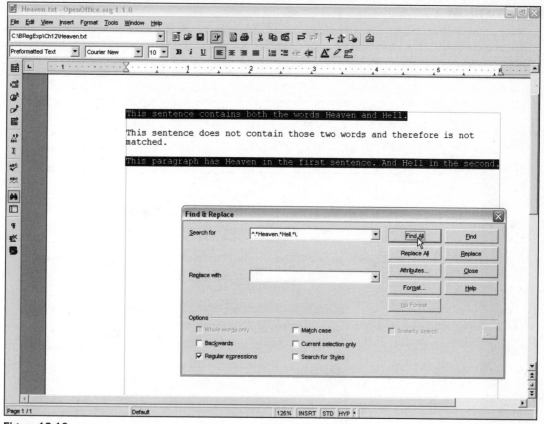

Figure 12-10

If you want to match only occurrences in the same sentence, the current pattern is not suffi-ciently specific. You can modify the pattern to `^.*Heaven[^.]*Hell.*\.`.

6. Edit the pattern in the Search For text box to read `^.*Heaven[^.]*Hell.*\.`.

7. Click the Find All button, and inspect the results.

   Figure 12-11 shows the appearance after Step 7. Notice that now, only the sentence in the first paragraph is highlighted as a match.

8. If the desire is to match two words only in the same paragraph, there is an alternate pattern that can be used. Edit the pattern in the Search For text box to `^.*Heaven.*Hell.*$`.

9. Click the Find All button, and inspect the results. In the sample text, the highlighted text after Step 9 is the same as shown in Figure 12-10.

How It Works

The pattern used up to Step 5 is `^.*Heaven.*Hell.*\.`. The `^` metacharacter matches the beginning-of-paragraph position. The `.*` matches zero or more characters, and the `Heaven` matches the literal character sequence `Heaven`; the `.*` matches zero or more characters, and the `Hell` matches the literal character sequence `Hell`; the `.*` matches zero or more characters, and the `\.` matches a literal period character.

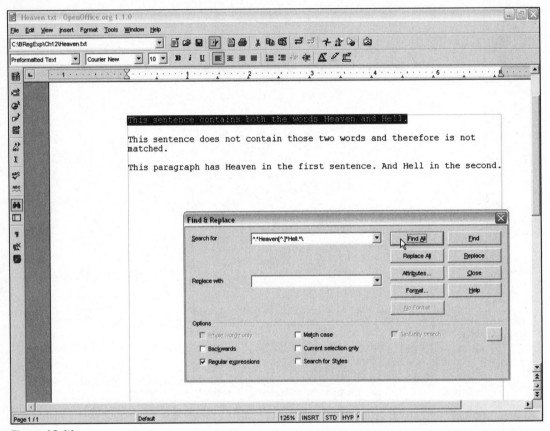

Figure 12-11

The match in the first paragraph is straightforward. However, the match in the third paragraph may be less obvious. The key part of the regular expression is the `.*` that follows `Heaven` and precedes `Hell`. Because OpenOffice.org Writer matches greedily, the `.*` can match the period character that occurs at the end of the first sentence. So it can match the occurrence of `Heaven` and `Hell` in two different sentences, as long as there is a period character following the character sequence `Hell`. If you delete the final period character in the third paragraph, the pattern `^.*Heaven.*Hell.*\` no longer matches.

The pattern in Step 6, `^.*Heaven[^.]*Hell.*\.`, has the pattern `[^.]*` between `Heaven` and `Hell`. That means that only characters that are not the period character can occur between the character sequences `Heaven` and `Hell`. A match is present only when the two character sequences occur in the same sentence, assuming that the period character is not omitted.

The pattern in Step 8, `^.*Heaven.*Hell.*$`, uses the `$` metacharacter, which matches the end of a paragraph in OpenOffice.org Writer. The `^` metacharacter matches the beginning-of-paragraph position, the `.*` matches zero or more characters, the `Heaven` matches literally, the `.*` matches zero or more characters, the `Hell` matches literally, the `.*` matches zero or more characters, and the `$` metacharacter matches the end-of-paragraph position. In effect, this means that if `Heaven` precedes `Hell` in a paragraph, there is a match.

Search-and-Replace Example

The following example illustrates a very practical use of regular expressions in OpenOffice.org Writer.

Online Chats

Information tools are changing very fast. Online chats can be one of the most useful places to keep up with cutting-edge information. However, unedited transcripts of many online chats are very difficult to read because the actual chat is often swamped by information about which chat participants are joining or leaving. Regular expressions can be useful to quickly clean such documents.

A highly simplified sample document, `Interesting Chat.sxw`, is shown here:

```
Some interesting chat
A welcome message.
Some interesting information.
Somebody says something interesting.
(Andrew Smith has joined the conversation
(Jane Callander has left the conversation.

Another piece of real chat.

(Harry Danvers has joined the conversation
(Carol Clairvoyant has left the conversation
(Ceridwen Davies has joined the conversation.
Another real comment.
```

The 8 in the preceding sample is the representation of the nonalphabetic character used by the chat software to flag the joining and leaving actions.

On a really busy chat, the joining and leaving information can totally dominate the real information. For example, when applying this technique to a real chat on a day I was writing this chapter. there were over 1,200 lines replaced in one chat transcript.

Figure 12-12 shows the visual appearance of the sample document. Notice the right-pointing arrow at the beginning of lines that contain information about joining and leaving.

The aim is to remove the extraneous information about joining and leaving, making the document easier to read so the theme of the chat can be better assimilated. The problem definition is as follows:

Delete all lines that contain information about individuals joining or leaving the chat.

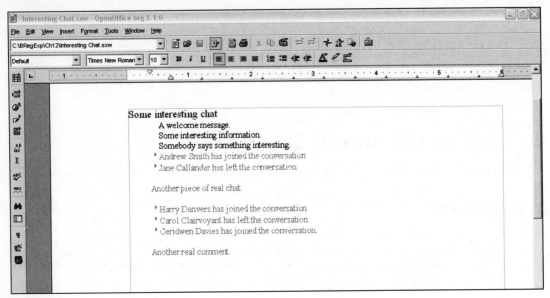

Figure 12-12

The chat software conveniently presents all joining and leaving information on a separate line, making the task straightforward. The problem definition for the sample chat transcript can be refined as follows:

Match all lines that begin with a special character that the chat software uses, followed by zero or more characters of any kind, followed by an end-of-line position. Replace all matches with nothing.

The real-life example I mentioned earlier was in a Microsoft Word document. Because Microsoft Word has no metacharacter to match a beginning-of-line or end-of-line character, it was more convenient to carry out the search and replace in OpenOffice.org Writer. I opened the document in OpenOffice.org Writer and used Writer's more complete regular expression support to do what I wanted.

> *The default behavior of Writer when opening a Word document is to open it read-only. To edit the document, simply click the Edit button in the toolbar, and you will be asked if you want to edit the document. Choosing Yes opens a new Writer (.sxw) document on which you can use Writer regular expressions to clean up. You can then save the cleaned document in Word format, using the Save As option in Writer.*

Try It Out   Tidying Up an Online Chat Transcript

1. Open OpenOffice.org Writer; then open the test file `Interesting Chat.sxw`.

2. Open the Find & Replace dialog box using the Ctrl+F keyboard shortcut.

3. Check the Regular Expressions and Match Case check boxes.

4. Highlight the right-arrow symbol on one line of text.

5. In the Search For text box, type the ^ character, paste in the right-arrow symbol, and then type .*$. You should see the pattern shown in Figure 12-13 in the Search For text box. Notice that the pasted right arrow is displayed as a hollow square. Although the display is ambiguous, the matching proceeds correctly. Leave the Replace With text box blank.

6. Click the Find button once. The first line containing the right-arrow symbol is highlighted.

7. Click Replace once. The line that was highlighted after Step 6 is now blank.

8. Click the Replace All button once. All lines that contain the right-arrow symbol are now blank.

Figure 12-14 shows the appearance after Step 8. Notice that all the lines that previously contained the right-arrow symbol have been deleted.

9. In the Search For text box, enter the pattern ^$. Leave the Replace With text box blank.

10. Return the cursor to the beginning of the document. Click the Find button. The first blank line is now highlighted.

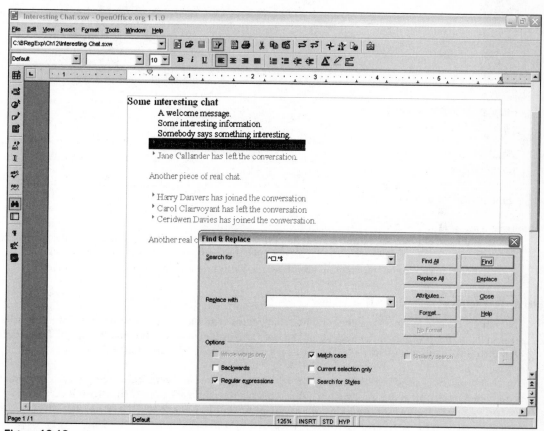

Figure 12-13

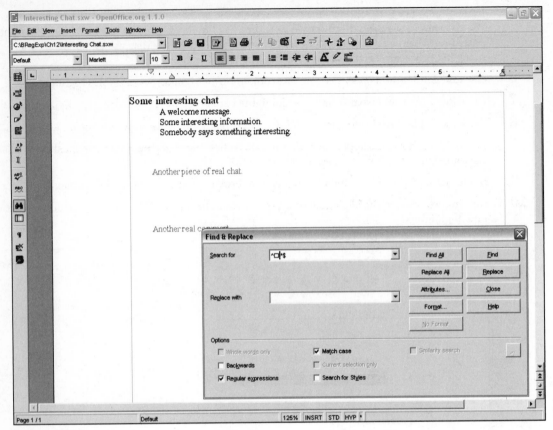

Figure 12-14

11. Click the Replace All button so that all blank lines are now replaced, and inspect the results, as shown in Figure 12-15. Notice that all the lines that contained the right-arrow symbol (and therefore contained information about people joining or leaving) have now been deleted.

How It Works

The pattern created in Step 5 matches any line that begins with the right-arrow symbol. The ^ metacharacter matches the position at the beginning of a line. The right-arrow symbol matches itself. The pattern . * matches zero or more characters. The $ metacharacter matches the position at the end of a line.

The chat transcript I used in real life had the right-arrow symbol as the first character of each line that contained joining or leaving information. Other chat clients may vary in how they treat lines that only contain joining or leaving information. You might, for example, have to insert a space character after the ^ metacharacter if the right-arrow symbol is preceded by a space.

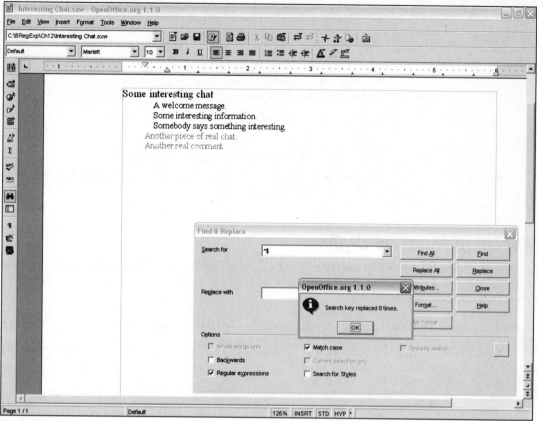

Figure 12-15

POSIX Character Classes

In addition to support for conventional regular expression character classes, OpenOffice.org Writer version 1.1 supports a subset of the POSIX character classes. The supported classes and their interpretation are listed in the following Table. The ? character is part of the POSIX character class syntax. It is not a quantifier indicating that a preceding character class is optional.

Character Class	Meaning
`[:digit:]?`	Matches a single numeric digit when used alone. When used as part of a longer pattern, it matches an optional numeric digit.
`[:digit:]*`	Matches zero or more numeric digits.
`[:space:]?`	Finds space characters.

Table continued on following page

Character Class	Meaning
[:print:]?	Matches a single character that prints, including space characters. When used as part of a longer pattern. it matches an optional printable character.
[:alnum:]?	Matches a single alphabetic character or a numeric digit. As part of a longer pattern, it matches an optional alphanumeric character.
[:alpha:]?	Matches an alphabetic character but not a numeric digit.
[:lower:]?	Matches a lowercase character if the Match Case check box is checked. Otherwise, it behaves as [:alpha:]?.
[:upper:]?	Matches an uppercase character if the Match Case check box is checked. Otherwise, it behaves as [:alpha:]?.

Matching Numeric Digits

As mentioned in the preceding table, the POSIX have some idiosyncracies when used alone. The example in this section walks you through a test file to clarify how the POSIX [:digit:]? character class behaves in OpenOffice.org Writer.

The test text is contained in the test file ADigitsB.txt, whose content is shown here:

```
A123B

AB

A8B

A1234567890B
```

As you can see, all the test strings have an uppercase A, followed by zero or more numeric digits, followed by an uppercase B.

Try It Out   **The [:digit:] POSIX Character Class**

1. Open the file ADigitsB.txt in OpenOffice.org Writer.

2. Open the Find & Replace dialog box using the Ctrl+F keyboard shortcut.

3. Check the Regular Expressions check box.

4. In the Search For text box, type the pattern **[:digit:]?**.

5. Click the Find button (not the Find All) button several times, each time inspecting the character that is highlighted.

    You should see that only a single numeric digit is highlighted each time. When used alone, the pattern [:digit:]? matches exactly one numeric digit. The standalone pattern [:digit:] is not recognized by OpenOffice.org Writer; you can test this by deleting the ? in the pattern.

6. Click before the first character of the test file. Edit the pattern in the Search For text box to [:digit:].

7. Click the Find button once, and observe the result.

You should see the dialog box shown in Figure 12-16. The message indicates that OpenOffice.org Writer has searched the entire document and found no match.

The quantifiers * and + produce the same matches when they are used alone. Each pattern [:digit:]* and [:digit:]+ matches one or more numeric digits.

8. Click before the first character of the file. Edit the regular expression pattern to [:digit:]*.

9. Click the Find button several times, inspecting the highlighted characters, until the end of the document is reached.

10. Modify the regular expression pattern to [:digit:]+.

11. Click the Find button several times, inspecting the highlighted characters, until the end of the document is reached.

12. When used in a longer pattern, the pattern [:digit:] behaves in slightly different ways. Click before the first character of the file. Edit the regular expression pattern to A[:digit:]B.

13. Click the Find button twice, each time observing the result. In this situation, [:digit:] behaves as you might have expected it to earlier — it matches exactly one numeric digit. Similarly, when [:digit:] forms part of a longer pattern, the ? quantifier operates as an indicator that the character class is optional.

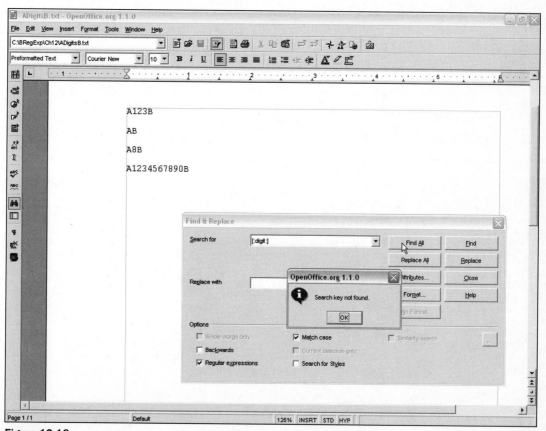

Figure 12-16

How It Works

In Step 4. you specify the pattern `[:digit:]?`. Each time you click the Find button, a single numeric digit is matched. If you delete the `?` character, there is no match.

When the pattern is `[:digit:]*`, the character sequences 123, 8, and 1234567890 are matched because the `*` character acts as a quantifier. The same character sequences are matched by the pattern `[:digit:]+`.

However, when the pattern is `A[:digit:]B`, the `?` character is no longer needed for the POSIX character class to match a single numeric digit. The pattern matches the character sequence A8B only in the test text. If the `?` character is added, as in the pattern `A[:digit:]?B`, both A8B and AB match.

Exercises

These exercises are intended to allow you to test your understanding of some of the material that you learned in this chapter:

1. Specify a character class that will match all uppercase alphabetic characters except W, X, Y, and Z.

2. Specify a character class that will match lowercase characters a through h and t through z.

Regular Expressions Using findstr

The findstr utility is a command-line utility that can be used to find files containing a particular string pattern. The findstr utility allows searches similar to those carried out using Windows Search but also supports more specific searches that include regular expressions.

The findstr utility makes use of parameters supplied on the command line, as well as some standard and nonstandard regular expression syntax.

In this chapter, you will learn the following:

❑ How to use findstr from the command line

❑ How to use the regular expression metacharacters supported by findstr

Introducing findstr

The findstr utility is available on many recent versions of Windows and can be used, for example, from a Windows XP command line without having to set paths or environment variables.

The description of the findstr utility in this chapter is based on findstr in Windows XP Professional.

To confirm the presence and functioning of the findstr utility on your version of Windows simply type findstr /? at the command prompt. If all is well, as it should be, you will see a considerable amount of help information scrolling past in the command window. Figure 13-1 shows the final part of the help information to be displayed. Approximately another full screen of help information has scrolled out of sight.

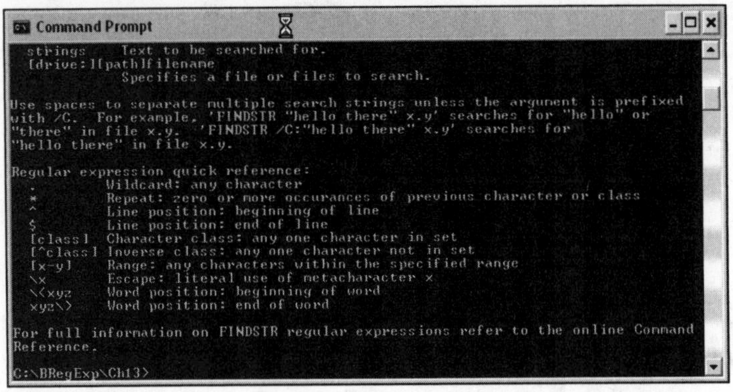

Figure 13-1

You cannot use the following command on its own from the command line, or you will receive a bad command error, as shown in Figure 13-2:

```
findstr
```

Figure 13-2

It is essential that you use one or more of the command-line switches and parameters that specify what findstr is to do.

Finding Literal Text

One of the simplest tasks that findstr can be used for is to match literal text. The general form of a findstr command to perform simple literal matching in a single file is as follows:

```
findstr "Text of interest" Filename.suffix
```

Strictly speaking, you supply a regular expression pattern that consists only of literal characters to be matched.

The test file, Hello.txt, is shown here:

```
Hello world!

Hello with initial upper-case.

hello with initial lower case.

Goodbye!
```

Notice that two lines have Hello with an initial uppercase H, and one line has hello with an initial lowercase h.

Finding Literal Text

1. Open a command window, and navigate to the directory into which you downloaded the test file Hello.txt.

2. Type the following command at the command line:

```
findstr "Hello" Hello.txt
```

3. Press Return, and inspect the results returned by findstr. Figure 13-3 shows the result. The two lines containing Hello (initial uppercase H) are displayed, while the line containing hello (initial lowercase h) is not. This is because the default behavior of findstr is to match case sensitively.

   Notice that the content of two lines is displayed, but no indication of the file they come from or the line number is given. When you use findstr to examine multiple files, that additional information is useful.

Figure 13-3

4. The sample file, Hello.txt, has everything neatly on separate lines, but not all documents are so simply structured. Therefore, it is often useful to have line numbers displayed along with the text on a particular line, because that allows you to scan to roughly the right point in a long document to see what the context is. To display line numbers from findstr, use the /n switch.

   Type the following command on the command line, and press Return:

```
findstr /n "Hello" Hello.txt
```

5. Inspect the results returned when the /n switch was added to the command. Figure 13-4 shows the result. Notice that the line number is now displayed for each line of the test file that contains matching text.

> Particularly when the command line has been repeated using F3 and then edited, the findstr utility can sometimes fail to find any matches even though matches exist. If you find an unexpected failure to match any results, I suggest that you type the desired command afresh. This, in my experience, fixes the problem.

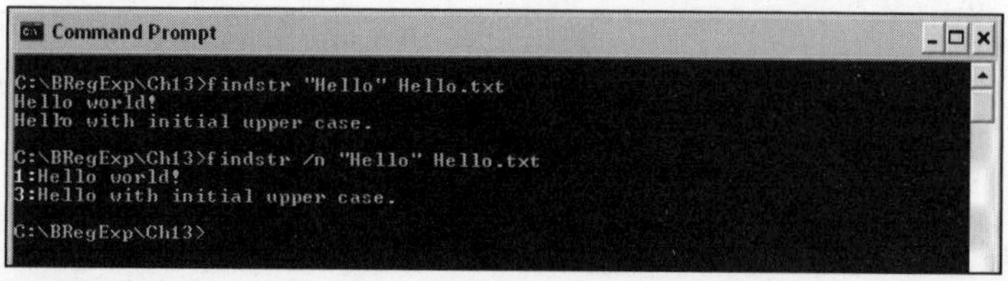

Figure 13-4

6. If you wish matching to be carried out case insensitively, you can use the /i switch. Type the following command at the command line, and press Return:

```
findstr /i /n "Hello" Hello.txt
```

Figure 13-5 shows the results. Notice that all three lines containing Hello or hello are now displayed.

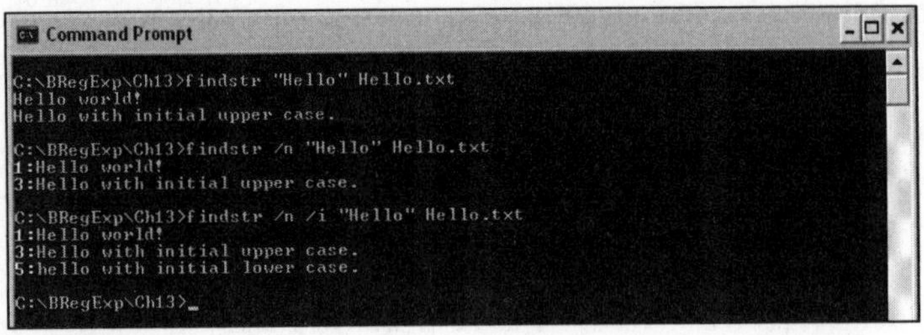

Figure 13-5

There are some findstr command-line switches that substitute functionally for regular expressions' metacharacters. They will be discussed in the relevant place when the supported metacharacters are covered in the next section.

Metacharacters Supported by findstr

The findstr utility supports many regular expression patterns, but perhaps because it is used on the command line, the utility has many nonstandard pieces of regular expression syntax (refer to the following table).

Metacharacter	Meaning
.	Any character
*	Quantifier indicating zero or more occurrences
?	Not supported
+	Not supported
{n,m}	Not supported
^	Beginning-of-line position
$	End-of-line position
[...]	Character class
\<	Beginning-of-word position
\>	End-of-word position

As noted in the preceding table, some metacharacters are not supported. The following table lists findstr command-line switches that perform functions similar to regular expression metacharacters in many other settings, as well as command-line switches with other meanings. Command-line switches that take arguments are described in a separate table.

Command-Line Switch	Equivalent Metacharacter or Other Meaning
/b	Matches when the following character(s) are at the beginning of a line. Equivalent to the ^ metacharacter.
/e	Matches when the following character(s) are at the end of a line. Equivalent to the $ metacharacter.
/p	Specifies that files containing nonprintable characters are skipped.
/offline	Specifies that only files with the offline attribute set are processed.
/o	Prints the offset of the character from the beginning of the file.
/m	Prints the filename if the file contains a match.
/n	Displays the line number for each line that matches and is displayed.
/v	Displays lines that do not contain a match.
/x	Constrains matches to match only if the whole line matches the regular expression. Similar to using the ^ and $ metacharacters in other implementations.
/i	Specifies that regular expression matching is case insensitive. The default matching is case sensitive.
/s	Means that the current directory and all its subdirectories are searched for files that meet the file specification part of the command line.
/r	Specifies that the text inside paired double quotes is to be interpreted as regular expressions. This is the default behavior even if the /r switch is not specified.
/l	Means that regular expressions cannot be interpreted as regular expressions. Instead, matching is literal.

The following command-line switches each take an argument that affects their behavior:

Command-Line Switch	Description
/f:file	The argument file is the name of a file that contains a list of files to be searched.
/c:string	The argument string is a search string to be used literally.
/g:file	The argument file is the name of a file that contains a list of search strings.
/d:dirlist	The argument dirlist is a comma-separated list of directories to be searched.
/a:colorattribute	The argument colorattribute specifies a color attribute using two hexadecimal digits.

Quantifiers

Support for quantifiers in findstr is limited. The * quantifier is supported with the standard meaning of zero or more occurrences. However, neither the ? quantifier nor the + quantifier is supported; neither is the {n,m} quantifier notation supported.

The test files Order1.txt and Order2.txt show how the * quantifier can be used.

The content of Order1.txt is shown here:

```
This is an order for Part No. ABC123.

Blah blah.  As easy as ABC.

2004/08/20
```

The content of Order2.txt is here:

```
This is an order for Part No. ABC456.

Blah blah.

2003/07/18
```

For the purposes of this example, the part number is the focus of interest. In many regular expression implementations you would use ABC\d{3} or ABC[0-9]{3} to match exactly three digits, but findstr does not support that syntax.

Try It Out   **The * Quantifier**

1. Open a command window, and type the following command at the command prompt:

```
findstr /n "ABC [0-9]*" Order*.txt
```

2. Inspect the results returned, as shown in Figure 13-6. Notice that three lines contain a match. The second of the displayed lines is undesired because the occurrence of ABC with no following numeric digit is not a part number.

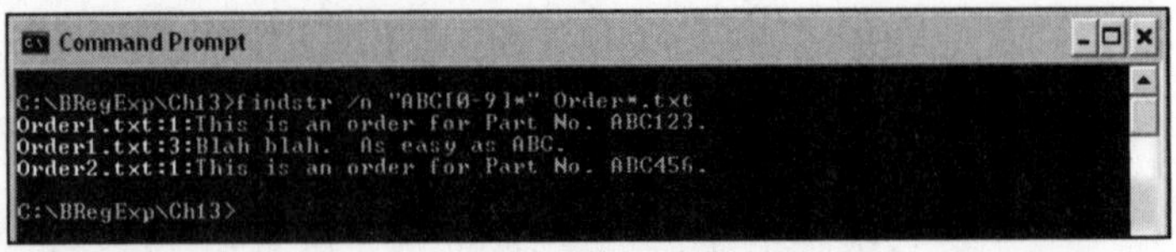

```
Command Prompt                                                    _ □ ×
C:\BRegExp\Ch13>findstr /n "ABC[0-9]*" Order*.txt
Order1.txt:1:This is an order for Part No. ABC123.
Order1.txt:3:Blah blah.  As easy as ABC.
Order2.txt:1:This is an order for Part No. ABC456.

C:\BRegExp\Ch13>
```

Figure 13-6

3. To match the desired number of numeric digits, exactly three, use the following pattern:

```
ABC[0-9][0-9][0-9]
```

4. At the command line, enter the following command:

```
findstr /n "ABC[0-9][0-9][0-9]" Orders*.txt
```

Figure 13-7 shows the results.

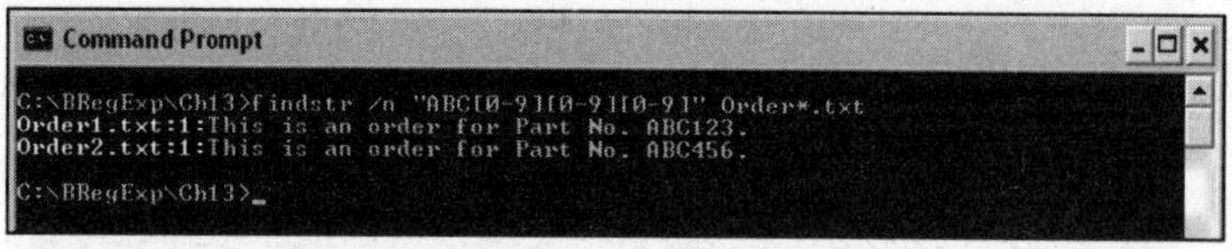

Figure 13-7

How It Works

After Step 2, the two lines that contain part numbers consisting of the character sequence ABC followed by three numeric digits are matched, which is what you want. However, the second line in Orders1.txt is also matched, because the pattern [0-9]* matches zero or more occurrences of the character class that matches numeric digits. Because ABC in As easy as ABC. has zero occurrences of a numeric digit, the pattern ABC[0-9]* is matched, because the character sequence ABC is present together with zero occurrences of a numeric digit.

> Back references, lookahead, and lookbehind are not supported in the findstr utility.

Character Classes

As you saw in an earlier example in this chapter, the character class [0-9] is supported in findstr. In fact, the character class [0-9], or one of the alternative ways of defining a character class, [0123456789], is needed because findstr does not support the \d metacharacter.

The following text, contained in the file PartNums.txt, is the test file:

```
ABC123

DEF890

GHI234

HKO838

RUV991

ILR246

UVW991

ADF274

DRX119
```

In findstr ranges are supported, as are negated character classes.

Try It Out   **Character Classes**

1. Open a command window, and navigate to the directory containing the file PartNums.txt.

2. Type the following at the command line:

```
findstr /n "A[A-Z][A-Z][0-9][0-9][0-9]" PartNums.txt
```

3. Inspect the results, as shown in Figure 13-8. The lines containing part numbers that begin with uppercase A, have two uppercase letters following, and have three numeric digits are displayed.

Figure 13-8

Because of the way that findstr works, you could have used a simpler pattern, A[A-Z] [A-Z][0-9], given the sample data. If there were part numbers such as ABC1 in the test text, the preceding pattern would match lines containing part numbers like that, which may not be what you want.

4. Type the following command at the command line:

```
findstr /n "A[A-Z][A-Z][0-9]" PartNums.txt
```

5. Inspect the results. (Notice that the same lines are matched.)

6. If you want to match part numbers that begin with an uppercase A but that do not have an uppercase B as the second character in the part number, you can use the negated character class [^B] to achieve that.

At the command line, type the following command:

```
findstr /n "A[^B][A-Z][0-9]" PartNums.txt
```

7. Inspect the results (notice that Line 1 no longer matches), as shown in Figure 13-9.

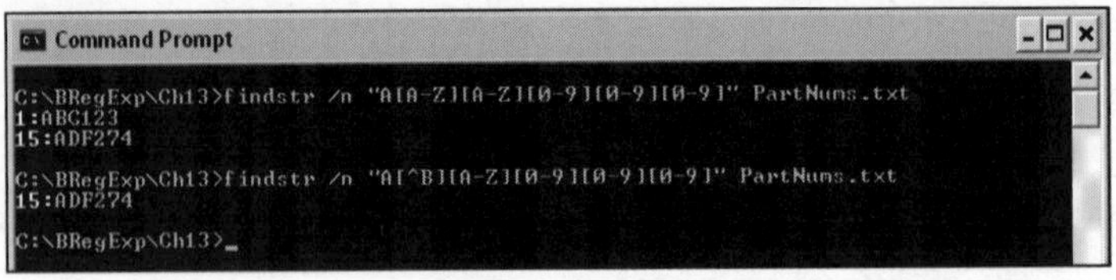

Figure 13-9

How It Works

In Step 2, the pattern A[A-Z][A-Z][0-9][0-9][0-9] is used. The A matches uppercase A literally. Because only Line 1 and Line 15 contain a part number beginning with A, only those lines are possible matches for the rest of the regular expression. The character class [A-Z] matches any alphabetic character, matching B on Line 1 and D on Line 15. The second occurrence of the character class [A-Z] in the regular expression matches C on Line 1 and F on Line 15. The three character classes [0-9][0-9][0-9] match three successive numeric digits, 123 on Line 1 and 274 on Line 15. So there are matches on lines 1 and 15.

In Step 6, the pattern A[^B][A-Z][0-9] is used. The initial A matches on lines 1 and 15 as before. The character class [^B] matches any character except uppercase B. So there is no match for A[^B] on Line 1. However, on Line 15, D is a match for [^B], so matching continues on Line 15. The [A-B] pattern matches the F on Line 15, and [0-9][0-9][0-9] matches 274 on Line 15. So the only match is on Line 15.

There is a risk in having a character class such as [^B] in a pattern, because that is almost equivalent to the dot character. So if a malformed part number A$C123 were in the test file, it would match the pattern [A-Z][^B][A-Z][0-9][0-9][0-9]. If the intent was that any uppercase character except B was desired, a more specific character class would be [AC-Z]. So the regular expression would be

```
A[AC-Z][A-Z][0-9][0-9][0-9]
```

with [AC-Z] having the same meaning as [ACDEFGHIJKLMNOPQRSTUVWXYZ].

Word-Boundary Positions

The findstr utility supports separate metacharacters that match the beginning-of-word position and the end-of-word position. The \< metacharacter matches the beginning-of-word position, and the \> metacharacter matches the end-of-word position.

A test file, Word.txt, has the following content:

```
Swords are sharp, typically.

Words are powerful things. They can wound.

Churchill is a byword for wartime persistence.

Do you have a favorite word?

His surname is Answord.

Wordsworth was a famous English poet.

Word by word is, typically, not a good method of translation.
```

Notice that the character sequence word occurs at the beginning or end of a sequence of alphabetic characters or embedded inside a longer character sequence. Notice, too, that sometimes an uppercase character is part of word or Word, so you must take care in how you use case-sensitive or case-insensitive search.

Try It Out   Beginning- and End-of-Word Positions

1. Open a command window, and navigate to the directory containing the Word.txt test file.

2. At the command prompt, enter the following command:

```
findstr /n "Word" Word.txt
```

3. Inspect the results, as shown in Figure 13-10. Notice that only three of the seven lines containing text are displayed. This is so because the default behavior of findstr is case-sensitive matching.

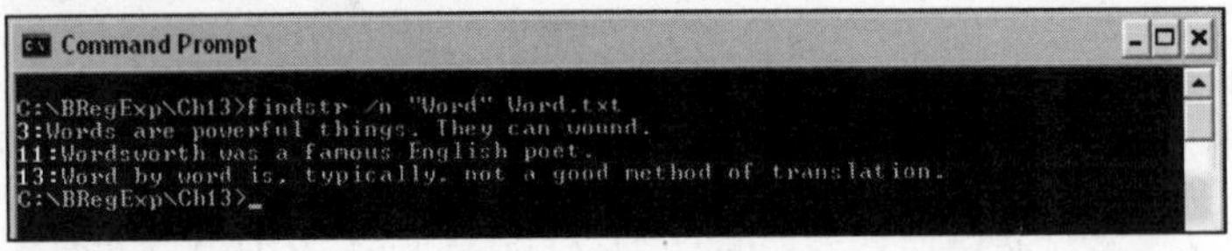

Figure 13-10

4. To ensure that all occurrences of the character sequence word are displayed, you can use the /i command-line switch.

    At the command line, enter the following command:

```
findstr /n /i "Word" Word.txt
```

5. Inspect the results. Now all seven lines containing text are displayed. So you can be confident that all occurrences of the character sequence word are now displayed.

6. Next, let's look at the effect of the beginning-of-word position metacharacter, \<.

    At the command prompt, enter the following command:

```
findstr /n /i "\<Word" Word.txt
```

7. Inspect the results, as shown in Figure 13-11. As you can see, only four of the seven lines that contain text are displayed. Each of the lines contains the character sequence word or Word (remember the matching is case insensitive) with that character sequence at the beginning of an alphabetic character sequence (in effect, at the beginning of what you would typically call a "word").

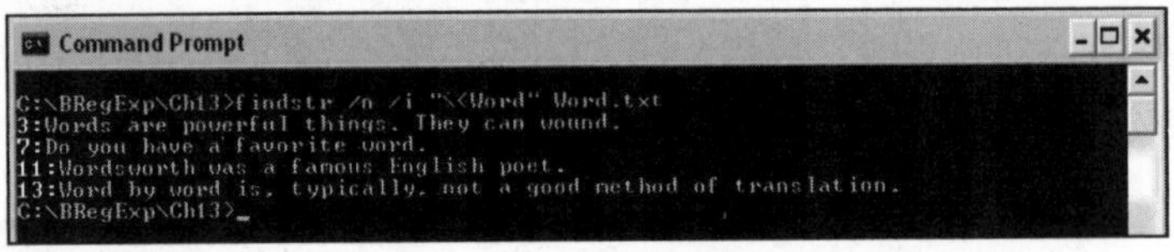

Figure 13-11

8. You can add the end-of-word position metacharacter, \>, to the regular expression to make the matching more specific, matching only when the character sequence word or Word is preceded by a beginning-of-word position and followed by an end-of-word position.

    At the command prompt, enter the following command:

```
findstr /n /i "\<Word\>" Word.text
```

9. Inspect the results, as shown in Figure 13-12. Now only two lines are displayed. On each line the character sequence word is actually just that—a word. Strictly speaking, the beginning-of-word position and end-of-word position metacharacters mark the beginning and end of an alphabetic sequence, respectively. For many practical purposes, they signify the beginning and end of a word.

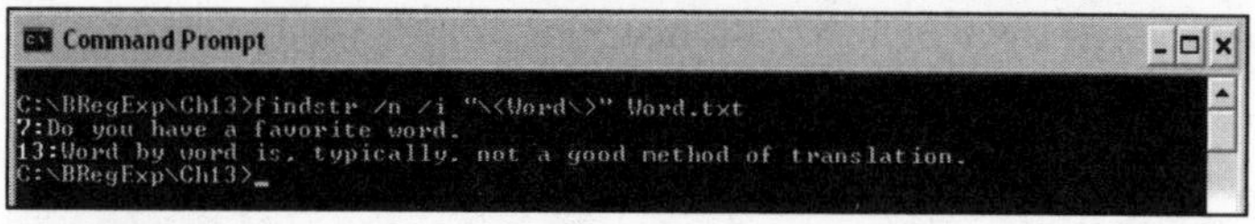

Figure 13-12

Beginning- and End-of-Line Positions

The findstr utility offers two quite distinct ways to specify that matching is to take place at the beginning or end of a line. First, there are the /b and /e switches, which specify matching at the beginning and end of a line, respectively. Second, there are the ^ and $ metacharacters.

The content of the test file, Low.txt, is shown here:

```
Low is the opposite of high.

A Ferrari isn't usually thought of as slow.

Slow, slow, quick, quick, slow

Slow, slow, quick, quick, slow.

Allow me to to pass please.

Lowering sky over a blackened sea.
```

Try It Out   Beginning- and End-of-Line Positions

1. Open a command window, and navigate to the directory containing the file Low.txt.

2. At the command prompt, enter the following command:

```
findstr /n /i "Low" Low.txt
```

3. Inspect the results. All six lines that contain text are displayed because the character sequence low, matched case insensitively (notice the /i switch), is present on all six lines.

4. Next, test the /b switch, which limits matching to the beginning of a line.

    At the command line, enter the following command:

```
findstr /n /i /b "Low" Low.txt
```

5. Inspect the results, as shown in Figure 13-13. Now only two lines are displayed, each of which has the character sequence Low as its first three characters.

Figure 13-13

6. Next, test the /e switch, which limits matching to the end of a line.

   At the command line, enter the following command:

```
findstr /n /i /e "Low" Low.txt
```

7. Inspect the results, as shown in Figure 13-14.

Figure 13-14

Only one line is displayed. If you expected three lines to be displayed, take a closer look at the lines. On two lines, where `low` is the last alphabetic character sequence, there is a period character after that sequence. In other words, `low` isn't at the end of the line. That is the reason those two lines don't match successfully.

8. You can achieve the same effects using more conventional metacharacters. To match only at the beginning of a line, you can use the ^ metacharacter.

   Type the following command at the command line:

```
findstr /n /i "^Low" Low.txt
```

9. Inspect the results. The lines that were displayed in Figure 13-13 are again displayed.

10. Finally, you can use the $ metacharacter to match only at the end of the line.

    At the command line, type the following command:

```
findstr /n /i "Low$" Low.txt
```

11. Inspect the results. Only one line is displayed — the same one as in Figure 13-14. The period character at the end of two lines prevents a successful match for the pattern Low$.

Command-Line Switch Examples

This section looks at the effects of several of the `findstr` command-line switches. Some produce direct effects on regular expressions — for example, the /i switch causes matching to be carried out case insensitively.

The /v Switch

The /v switch causes only lines that do *not* match to be displayed. This can be useful when you want to test for data that fails to correspond to the standards you expect.

For example, if you know that parts listed in a parts-number inventory should all consist of three alphabetic characters followed by three numeric digits, it is straightforward to find lines where a malformed part number is present.

The content of the test file, PartNums2.txt, is shown here:

```
ABC876

A2D993

AB2882

AEJ88

KHD945

HEW78R

H
```

As you work through the following example, assume that case-sensitive matching is needed.

Try It Out The /v Switch

1. Open a command window, and navigate to the directory where PartNums2.txt is located.

2. At the command prompt, enter the following command:

```
findstr /n /v "[A-Z][A-Z][A-Z][0-9][0-9][0-9]" PartNums2.txt
```

3. Inspect the results, as shown in Figure 13-15. Notice that several lines are displayed, which have supposed part numbers that do not match the pattern [A-Z][A-Z][A-Z][0-9][0-9][0-9].

Figure 13-15

4. To confirm that all lines have either matched or failed to match, you can run findstr again, omitting the /v switch.

   At the command prompt, type the following command:

```
findstr /n "[A-Z][A-Z][A-Z][0-9][0-9][0-9]" PartNums2.txt
```

5. Inspect the results, as shown in Figure 13-16. Compare Figure 13-15 and Figure 13-16, and you will see that all lines appear in one or the other window, but no line is displayed in both.

Figure 13-16

How It Works

When the /v switch is used, several blank lines are displayed. Because none of those lines contains the desired pattern [A-Z][A-Z][A-Z][0-9][0-9][0-9], there is no basis for a match. They are, therefore, displayed as lines not containing a match.

On Line 3, the text A2D993 does not match because the second character is a numeric digit, which does not match the [A-Z] character class that is second in the regular expression pattern.

On Line 5, the text AB2882 does not match because the third character is a numeric digit, which does not match the [A-Z] character class that is third in the regular expression pattern.

On Line 7, the text ABJ88 does not match because there are only two numeric digits and, therefore, no match for the third [0-9] character class.

On Line 11, the text HEW78R does not match because the sixth character is an uppercase R, which does not match the character class [0-9].

Turning to Step 4 and the results shown in Figure 13-16, lines 1 and 9 match because each contains a part number consisting of three uppercase alphabetic characters followed by three numeric digits, which matches the pattern [A-Z][A-Z][A-Z][0-9][0-9][0-9].

The /a Switch

The /a switch is followed by a colon and either one or two hexadecimal numbers. If a single hexadecimal number is used, that controls the text (or foreground) color for the information about line numbers and filenames returned by findstr. If two hexadecimal numbers are used, the first specifies the background color, and the second specifies the text color.

Hexadecimal Number	Color Specified
0	Black
1	Blue
2	Green
3	Aqua
4	Red
5	Purple
6	Yellow
7	White
8	Gray
9	Light blue
A	Light green

Hexadecimal Number	Color Specified
B	Light aqua
C	Light red
D	Light purple
E	Light yellow
F	Bright white

Some combinations either make no sense, such as white text on a white background, or are ignored. For example, if you type

```
findstr /n /i /a:00 "ABC[0-9]" Orders*.txt
```

which specifies black text on a black background, the normal white on black is used. Some other combinations, such as the following for blue text on a blue background

```
findstr /n /i /a:11 "ABC[0-9]" Order*.txt
```

are allowed but are essentially useless, unless you simply want a block of color to be displayed at the beginning of a line that contains a match.

Figure 13-17 shows the on-screen appearance of some of the possible arguments for the /a switch.

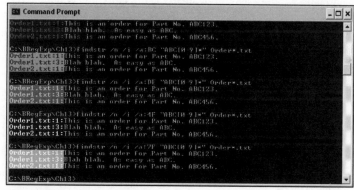

Figure 13-17

Single File Examples

The following examples also illustrate usage of the findstr utility. The findstr utility is limited in the quantifiers that it supports, which tends to limit what it can effectively be used for.

Simple Character Class Example

This example will use the sample file `gray.txt` to demonstrate the use of the `findstr` utility. The content of `gray.txt` is shown here:

```
gray
grey
greying
greyed
grapple
grim
goat
filigree
great
groat
gloat
Gray
Grey
```

The problem definition is as follows:

Match a g followed by an r, followed by a choice of e or a, followed by y.

The pattern `gr[ae]y` contains a simple character class that allows the desired text to be matched.

Try It Out   **Simple Character Class Example**

1. Open a command window, and navigate to the directory that contains `Gray.txt`.

2. At the command prompt, type the following command:

```
findstr /n "gr[ae]y" Gray.txt
```

3. Inspect the results, as shown in Figure 13-18.

Figure 13-18

Find Protocols Example

This example illustrates a simple technique to find Internet protocols. The content of the sample text `Protocols.txt` is shown here:

```
http://www.w3.org/

ftp://www.XMML.com/

mailto:someone@example.org
```

At the command line, enter the following command:

```
findstr /n "://" Protocols.txt
```

It will display all lines that contain an Internet protocol — in this case, lines 1 and 2.

Multiple File Example

One of the most useful aspects of the `findstr` utility is that from the command line, you can search across several files at once. This can save time compared to, for example, opening each file in an editor or word processor.

This example looks at how `findstr` can be used to find occurrences of HTTP URLs across multiple files. There are three short test files. `URL1.txt` contains the following:

```
I found interesting information at http://www.w3.org/ on the XQuery specification.
```

`URL2.txt` contains the following:

```
I wanted to find information about Microsoft SQL Server 2005 and the site at
http://www.microsoft.com/sql/ was very useful.
```

And `URL3.txt` contains the following:

```
This document shouldn't be detected because the protocol, http, is omitted. The
site that I

visited was www.w3.org.
```

The problem definition can be stated as follows:

Match the character sequence `http` followed by a colon character, followed by two forward-slash characters.

Try It Out   Finding URLs

1. Open a command window, and navigate to the directory that contains the files `URL1.txt`, `URL2.txt`, and `URL3.txt`.

2. At the command line, type the following command:

```
findstr /n "http://" URL*.txt
```

3. Inspect the results, as shown in Figure 13-19. Notice a limitation of `findstr` in the layout of results in Figure 13-19, where results from one file run on into results from another. This happens when the test text is not tidily line based but, instead, is paragraph based. Because `findstr` displays text in which a match is contained, rather than specifically the matched text, this imprecision can become a problem. When you see such results running into one another, the need for the `/a` switch, for which an example was shown earlier, becomes clearer.

Figure 13-19

A Filelist Example

The relatively simple examples in this chapter have used filenames where they can be expressed on the command line using a wildcard, such as in URL*.txt. However, sometimes you will want to search several files for which no such wildcard exists. The /f command-line switch allows this to be done.

The content of the file, Targets.txt, contains a list of files:

```
URL1.txt
URL2.txt
URL3.txt
```

The file Data.txt contains a very simple regular expression to find

```
http://
```

To put these together, you need to use the /g and /f findstr command-line switches. The argument to the /g switch is a filename for the file that contains the data to be searched for. The argument to the /f switch is a filename for a list of files that are to be searched. In addition, a list of the files with matches can be piped to a results file.

Try It Out   The /g and /f Switches

1. Open a command window, and navigate to the directory that contains Data.txt, Targets.txt, URL1.txt, URL2.txt, and URL3.txt.

2. At the command prompt, enter the following command:

```
findstr /g:Data.txt /f:Targets.txt > Results.txt
```

3. Then, at the command prompt, enter the following command:

```
Type Results.txt
```

4. Inspect the results. The results are the same as in the preceding example, but this time they have been piped to an output file where they are listed rather than, as in previous examples, being simply echoed to the screen.

How It Works

The argument /g:Data.txt specifies that the regular expression pattern is contained in the file Data.txt. The argument /f:Targets.txt specifies that the file Targets.txt contains the names of files to be searched. The results are redirected to the file Results.txt, as indicated by > Results.txt in the command line.

Exercises

The following exercises are intended to help reinforce some of the material presented in this chapter:

1. What findstr command would display lines that contain part numbers whose second character is any uppercase character except L, M, or N? Assume a structure of three alphabetic characters, three numeric digits, and that the files to be checked can be expressed as filename*.extension.

2. Give two possible findstr commands that would display lines beginning with either the or The.

PowerGREP

PowerGREP is a powerful regular expressions tool. It is a commercial Windows product that provides a tool with a graphical user interface (GUI) that implements much of the functionality that is available with grep, egrep, and similar tools on the Unix and Linux platforms. Further information about PowerGREP is available at www.powergrep.com.

Compared to the findstr utility, PowerGREP avoids the need to learn command string arguments. PowerGREP also has a much more complete implementation of regular expression functionality. In addition, it can carry out replace operations that are beyond the capabilities of findstr.

In this chapter, you will learn the following:

❑   How to use the PowerGREP interface

❑   How to use the extensive range of regular expressions functionality that PowerGREP supports

❑   How to use PowerGREP to perform example search or search-and-replace operations, some across multiple files

Examples in this chapter were checked using PowerGREP version 2.3.1.

The PowerGREP Interface

If you haven't used PowerGREP before, the appearance on first starting the program will be like that shown in Figure 14-1. If you have used PowerGREP before, the most recently used regular expression pattern, folder choice, and file mask will be displayed. If you have used PowerGREP at all, you will find residual results in the results pane, as you can see in Figure 14-1.

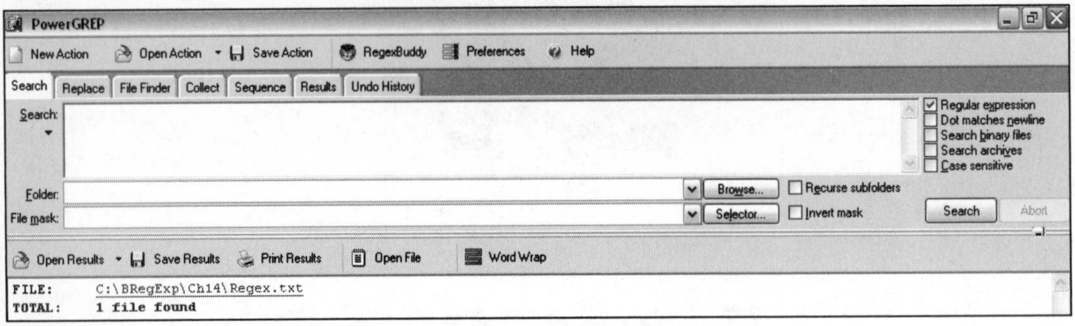

Figure 14-1

A Simple Find Example

The following example uses the test text, `Regex.txt`, shown here:

```
This is regular but not an expression.

Here is a simple regular expression pattern: \d.

Regex is an abbreviation for regular expression.

Some people use the abbreviation regexp.

The plural of regex is regexes.
```

The test text contains various words that refer to regular expressions. Notice that sometimes the term `regular expression` is used; sometimes it's the abbreviation `regex`; and sometimes the less common abbreviation, `regexp`, is used.

The problem definition can be stated as follows:

Match any occurrence of the text regular expressions or its abbreviations.

Of course, to meaningfully translate that into a regular expression, you need to refine the problem definition to achieve more precision. One possible refinement is the following:

Match any of the following:

❑ **The literal character sequence regular expression**

❑ **The literal character sequence regex**

❑ **The literal character sequence regexp**

There are various options for expressing this as a regular expression. One option is simple alternation:

```
(regular expression|regex|regexp)
```

This option has the advantage of simplicity and readability.

Another option, exploiting the common characters among the desired matches, is as follows:

```
reg(ular expression|ex|exp)
```

It's slightly shorter but arguably less readable.

If you wish for maximum succinctness, you could use the following:

```
reg(ular expression|(ex)p?)
```

However, again, readability is less than with the longer simple alternation option.

Try It Out   **Simple Find**

1.   Open PowerGREP, and in the Search text area, type **(regular expression|regex|regexp)**.

2.   Ensure that the Regular Expressions check box is checked.

3.   In the Folder text box, type **C:\BRegExp\Ch14**, assuming that you downloaded the code file to the C: drive and unzipped it into the BRegExp directory. Adjust accordingly if you downloaded and unzipped it to another location.

4.   In the File Mask text area, type **Regex.txt**, and click the Search button.

5.   Inspect the results, as shown in Figure 14-2. Notice that there are six matches. If you compare the content of Regex.txt with results displayed in PowerGREP, you will see that all occurrences of regular expression, regex, or regexp have been matched.

6.   In the Search text area, type the alternate regular expression, **reg(ular expression|ex|exp)**, and inspect the results.

7.   In the Search text area, type the alternate regular expression, **reg(ular expression|(ex)p?)**, and inspect the results.

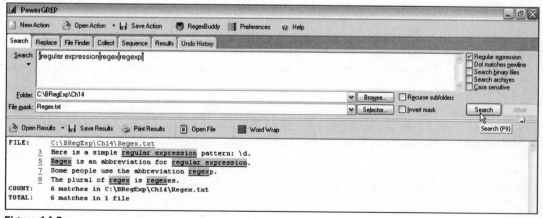

Figure 14-2

The results in the results pane should be identical to those shown in Figure 14-2. The regular expression pattern in the Search area is, of course, different, as described in Steps 6 and 7.

How It Works

Look at the first regular expression, `(regular expression|regex|regexp)`. Matching is achieved in a straightforward way, because you have three literal strings to be matched, each of which is an option. The regular expression engine first attempts to match `regular expression`; if that's unsuccessful, it attempts to match `regex`; if that's unsuccessful, it attempts to match `regexp`.

On Line 1, the character sequence `regular` and `expression` both occur, but there are intervening characters, so the pattern does not match.

On Line 3 and Line 5, `regular expression` is matched.

On Line 5 (once), on Line 7 (once), and on Line 9 (twice) `regex` is matched.

The pattern `regexp` is never matched (see the comment at the end of this section).

Now look at matching the first alternate regular expression, `reg(ular expression|ex|exp)` and, with the second alternate regular expression, `reg(ular expression|(ex)p?)`.

On Line 1, the character sequence `reg` matches, but none of the three options can be matched against the characters that follow in the pattern, so there is no match on Line 1.

On lines 3 and 5, the character sequence `reg` matches; therefore, the options are tested. The first option, `ular expression`, matches on those lines for both patterns.

On Line 5 (once), Line 7 (once), and Line 9 (twice), the character sequence `reg` matches. The first option, `ular expressions`, doesn't match, but the second option `ex` or `(ex)` does match. So the character sequence `regex` is matched on each line.

> There is a flaw in the matching strategy in this example. If you spotted it as you worked through the example, you will have the opportunity to correct the problem in an exercise later in this chapter.

The Replace Tab

Among the tabs in PowerGREP is the Replace tab, which allows the user to define how text replacement is to take place.

Figure 14-3 shows the Replace tab just after the example in the preceding section has run. Notice that the results from the Find tab are still displayed. That can be useful because, for example, the results from the Find tab allow you to see what matches and, therefore, what may be changed.

The following exercise tests the possible replacement of any occurrence of the character sequences `regular expression`, `regex`, or `regexp` with the character sequence `regex`.

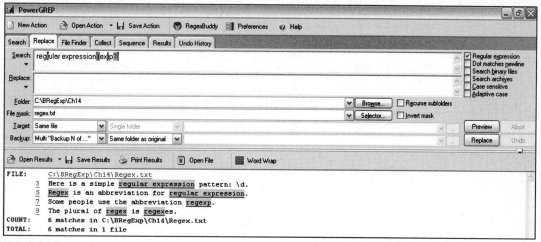

Figure 14-3

Try It Out   Replace Tab

1. Click the Replace Tab once. The screen should appear as shown in Figure 14-3.

2. In the Replace text area, type the text **regex**, and click the Preview button.

3. Inspect the appearance in the results pane, as shown in Figure 14-4. If you view this on-screen, the original text is by default displayed in yellow, and the potential replacement text is displayed in green. In Line 3, for example, the original text, regular expression, is highlighted in yellow, and the potential replacement text, regex, is highlighted in green.

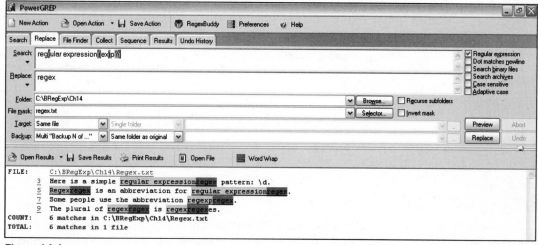

Figure 14-4

The File Finder Tab

The File Finder tab allows you to search for files in a chosen folder that contain a specified regular expression.

Immediately after running the Replace-tab example, the appearance in the File Finder tab is as shown in Figure 14-5. The results in the result pane are not those you would expect in the File Finder tab's result pane. Data carries over from the previous activity.

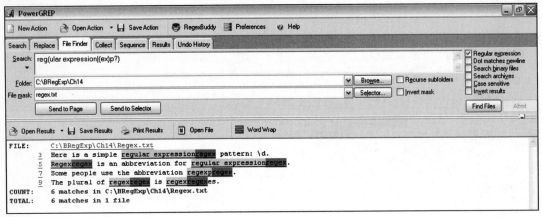

Figure 14-5

Simply click the Find Files button, and the results appropriate to the File Finder tab are displayed, as you can see in Figure 14-6.

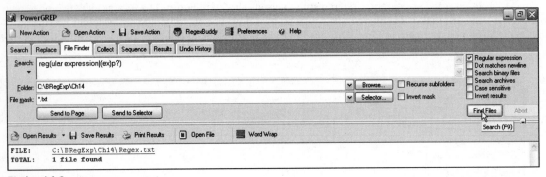

Figure 14-6

In this case, there is only a single file, Regex.txt, which contains matches to the specified regular expression reg(ular expression|(ex)p?).

Syntax Coloring

I will briefly mention one configuration option in PowerGREP that I find useful to turn off. By default, PowerGREP applies syntax coloring to regular expressions. Some of the screen shots in this chapter have syntax coloring turned on. However, as regular expressions become complex, I find the coloring can become confusing.

To turn off syntax coloring, click the Preferences icon in the PowerGREP toolbar. On the Search Boxes tab, uncheck the Apply Syntax Coloring to Regular Expressions check box. Now regular expressions will be displayed as plain text.

Other Tabs

The Collect and Sequence tabs allow other uses of regular expressions but won't be described further in this chapter. The Results tab simply displays the results information that is also displayed in the results pane of other tabs. The Undo History tab, depending on backups made, allows changes to be undone when carrying out replacements. Again, this facility won't be considered further in this chapter. But these additional facilities give you a very powerful tool to apply regular expressions without your having to be familiar with the programming languages described later in this book.

Metacharacters Supported

Compared to Microsoft Word, PowerGREP has vastly more support for regular expressions. It also has more supported options than either OpenOffice.org Writer or the `findstr` utility. Its regular expression support is comparable to the Komodo Regular Expressions Toolkit. PowerGREP has the advantage that you can use it as a utility to apply regular expressions to achieve practical tasks without programming.

The following table summarizes the metacharacters that are supported in PowerGREP. Most of the metacharacters listed are described further or used in examples later in this section or later in the chapter.

Metacharacter	Description
. (the dot character)	Matches almost any character.
\w	Matches an alphabetic character, numeric digit, and the underscore character.
\W	Matches any character except alphabetic characters, numeric digits, and the underscore character.
\d	Matches a numeric digit.
?	Quantifier; matches if the character or chunk that it qualifies occurs zero or one time.
*	Quantifier; matches if the character or chunk that it qualifies occurs zero or more times.
+	Quantifier; matches if the character or chunk that it qualifies occurs one or more times.
{n,m}	Quantifier; matches if the character or chunk that it qualifies occurs a minimum of n and a maximum of m times.
{n,}	Quantifier; matches if the character or chunk that it qualifies occurs a minimum of n times. Maximum occurrences are unbounded.

Table continued on following page

Metacharacter	Description
[...]	Character classes are supported.
[^ ...]	Negated character classes are supported.
(|)	Alternation is supported.
\1 etc	Back references are supported.
^	Positional metacharacter. Matches the position before the first character on a line.
$	Positional metacharacter. Matches the position after the last character on a line.
\b	Word-boundary position.
\<	Beginning-of-word position. Not supported.
\>	End-of-word position. Not supported.

Numeric Digits and Alphabetic Characters

PowerGREP supports the \w, \W, and \d metacharacters.

The test file, AlphaNumTest.txt, is shown here:

```
This line contains numbers, 1 2 3, and text . . . Blah, blah.

ABC

DEF 890

The next line has nonalphabetic characters.

?!"£$%^&*()_

1234567890
```

Try It Out   **Matching Numeric Digits and Alphanumeric Characters**

1. Open PowerGREP, and navigate to the Search tab. Ensure that the Regular Expression check box is checked.

2. In the Search text area, enter the simple regular expression **\w**.

3. In the Folder text box, type **C:\BRegExp\Ch14**, assuming that you downloaded the code file to the C: drive and unzipped it into the BRegExp directory. Adjust accordingly if you downloaded and unzipped it to another location.

4. In the File Mask text box, type **AlphNumTest.txt**, and inspect the results, as shown in Figure 14-7. As you can see, alphabetic characters, numeric digits, and the underscore character are matched by the \w metacharacter. Each match is a single character or digit.

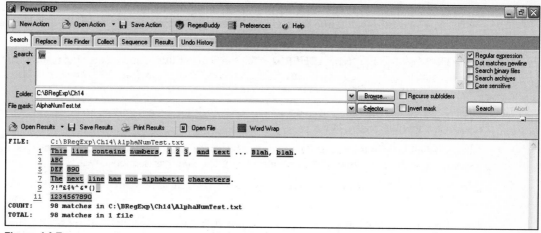

Figure 14-7

5. Edit the pattern in the Search area to \d, and inspect the results. You will see that the \d meta-character matches the numeric digits in the sample file, each match being a single numeric digit.

Quantifiers

PowerGREP supports the ?, * and + quantifiers, as well as the {n,m} syntax.

The test file, ABDEF.txt, is shown here:

```
AB123DEF

AB1DEF

ABDEF

AB12DEF

AB1234567890DEF
```

Notice that each line has the character sequence AB, followed by zero or more numeric digits, followed by the character sequence DEF.

Try It Out   **Quantifiers**

1. Open PowerGREP, and navigate to the Search tab. Ensure that the Regular Expression check box is checked.

2. In the Search text area, type **AB\d?DEF**.

3. In the Folder text box, type **C:\BRegExp\Ch14**, assuming that you downloaded the code file to the C: drive and unzipped it into the BRegExp directory. Adjust accordingly if you downloaded and unzipped it to another location.

4. In the File Mask text box, type **ABDEF.txt**, click the Search button, and inspect the results. The text that matches is ABDEF (zero occurrences of a numeric digit) and AB1DEF (one occurrence of a numeric digit).

5. Edit the Search text area content to read AB\d*DEF, click the Search button, and inspect the results, as shown in Figure 14-8.

   Notice that all lines in the test text are matched because each has the character sequence AB, followed by zero or more numeric digits, followed by the character sequence DEF.

6. Edit the content of the Search text area to read AB\d+DEF, click the Search button, and inspect the results.

   The + quantifier matches one or more occurrences. Therefore, the former match ABDEF (on Line 5 in Figure 14-8) no longer matches because it has zero occurrences of a numeric digit. The other lines in Figure 14-8 continue to match because they contain one or more occurrences of a numeric digit.

7. Edit the content of the Search text area to read AB\d{0,3}DEF, click the Search button, and inspect the results.

   Notice in Figure 14-9 that there is no match on Line 9, because AB1234567890DEF contains 10 numeric digits, and the maximum the pattern AB\d{0,3}DEF will match is three.

8. Edit the content of the Search text box to read AB\d{2,}DEF, click the Search button, and inspect the results.

   The matching text is AB123DEF, AB12DEF, and AB1234567890DEF. Each match has a minimum of two occurrences of a numeric digit. The maximum number of permitted occurrences is unbounded.

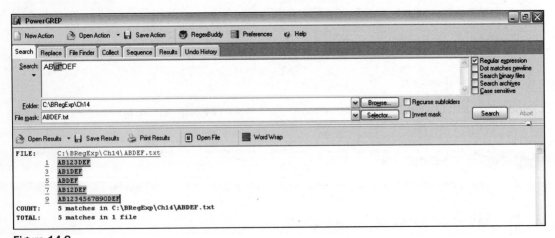

Figure 14-8

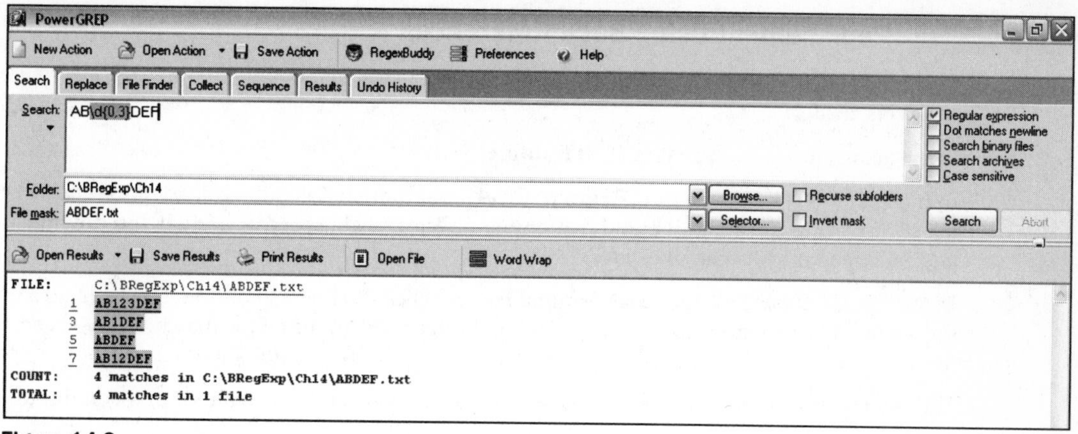

Figure 14-9

Back References

PowerGREP supports the use of back references. Each pair of parentheses in a regular expression creates a group. Each group captured by parentheses in the regular expression is captured in numerical order and can be referenced by using \1, \2, and so on.

The following example uses PowerGREP and back references to replace all occurrences of Star in the term Star Training with Moon. For convenience, the test file StarOriginal.txt, is reproduced here. Take careful note of each occurrence of Star Training.

```
Star Training Company

Starting from May 1st  Star Training Company is offering a startling special offer
to our regular customers - a 20% discount when 4 or more staff attend a single Star
Training Company course.

In addition, each quarter our star customer will receive a voucher for a free
holiday away from the pressures of the office. Staring at a computer screen all day
might be replaced by starfish and swimming in the Seychelles.

Once this offer has started and you hear about other Star Training customers
enjoying their free  holiday you might feel left out. Don't be left on the outside
staring in. Start right now building your points to allow you to start out on your
very own Star Training holiday.

Reach for the star. Training is valuable in its own right but the possibility of a
free holiday adds a startling new dimension to the benefits of Star Training
training.

Don't stare at that computer screen any longer. Start now with Star. Training is
crucial to your company's wellbeing. Think Star.
```

You replace Star only when it precedes Training.

Try It Out   Replacement Using Back References

1. Open PowerGREP, and navigate to the Replace tab. Ensure that the Regular Expression check box is checked.

2. In the Search text area, type **(Star)(*)(Training)**.

3. In the Folder text box, type **C:\BRegExp\Ch14**, assuming that you downloaded the code file to the C: drive and unzipped it into the BRegExp directory. Adjust accordingly if you downloaded and unzipped it to another location.

4. In the File Mask text box, type **StarOriginal.txt**, and click the Preview button. Figure 14-10 shows the results. You may need to scroll the window horizontally to see all the matches. On-screen, the text that matches is shown in yellow. The potential replacement text is shown in green.

The suggested replacements look good. So we are in good shape to go ahead and commit to the replacement.

In PowerGREP terminology the "target" is a file after an attempted search-and-replace operation. There are many options, only some of which are demonstrated here.

5. In the first drop-down list in the Target section, select Copy Only Modified Files.

6. In the second drop-down list in the Target section, select Single Folder.

7. In the third text area drop-down list in the Target section, enter **C:\BRegExp\Ch14\Changed**. Alternatively, you can browse to a desired folder destination.

8. In the first drop-down list in the Backup section, select ***.bak**.

9. In the second drop-down list in the Backup section, select Single Folder.

10. In the third text area drop-down list in the Backup section, enter **C:\BRegExp\Ch14\Changed**. Figure 14-11 shows the appearance after this step.

Steps 5 to 7 place modified files into the C:\BRegExp\Ch14\Changed directory, giving them the same names as the originals.

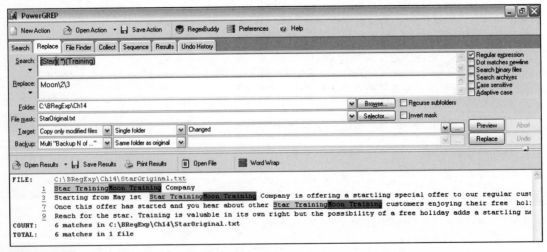

Figure 14-10

Steps 8 to 10 make a backup of the original file in the folder C:\BRegExp\Ch14\Changed and give it a .bak file extension. The files added to the Changed folder are shown in Figure 14-12.

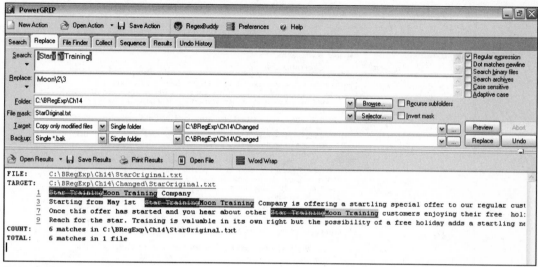

Figure 14-11

The use of relative paths for targets and backups in PowerGREP can be quite confusing. If you attempt to use the . abbreviation, thinking that this will save a backup in the same directory as the original file, you will be disappointed. It will result in the files being saved in the directory into which PowerGREP is installed, rather than where you probably intended.

The safest technique is to avoid relative paths entirely and to use only absolute paths.

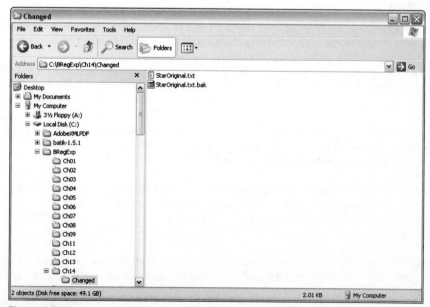

Figure 14-12

The file, after replacement, is located at C:\BRegExp\Ch14\Changed\StarOriginal.txt. Its content is shown in the Komodo 2.5 editor (to show the full path) in Figure 14-13.

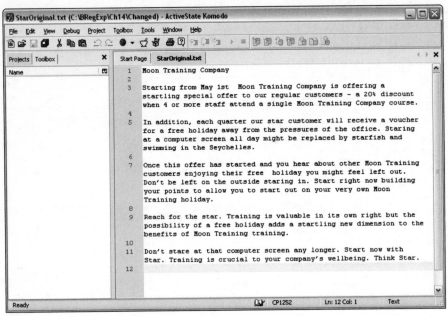

Figure 14-13

Notice that each of the occurrences of the character sequence Star, which were found in the Preview, has been replaced by the character sequence Moon.

How It Works

This section focuses only on how the back reference works. Explanation of the aspects that relate specifically to PowerGREP is found within the steps in the preceding Try It Out section.

The pattern to be matched is (Star)(*)(Training). This will match the character sequence Star, zero or more whitespace characters (one or more is likely in the test text), and the character sequence Training.

The first component of the regular expression, (Star), matches the character sequence Star and also captures it into \1. You won't use \1 in the replace part of the search and replace. The character sequence Moon is used in the replace where \1 occurred.

The second component of the regular expression, (*), will match and capture zero or more space characters in \2. Any whitespace captured will be used in the replace exactly as it occurred in the original text. An alternative approach would have been to replace one or more space characters with a single literal space character.

The third component of the regular expression, (Training), matches and captures the character sequence Training in \3. The \3 in the replace simply copies the character sequence Training from the original to the changed text.

The overall effect is that if `Star` occurs before zero or more spaces and then the character sequence `Training`, it is replaced by the character sequence `Moon`.

Alternation

Alternation is supported by PowerGREP. An example was shown in the first example in this chapter, using `Regex.txt` as a sample file.

Line Position Metacharacters

PowerGREP supports both line-end positional metacharacters ^ and $. The ^ metacharacter matches the position before the first character in a line. The $ metacharacter matches the position after the last character in a line.

The test file, `LineEndTest.txt`, is shown here:

```
This is here.

Look at this.

This is a theatre.

Theatre is as stimulating as this.
```

Try It Out   Line Position Metacharacters

1. Open PowerGREP, and ensure that the Regular Expression check box is checked.

2. In the Search text area, type the pattern **^This**.

3. Ensure that the Folder text box contains `C:\BRegExp\Ch14` or adapt this path if you downloaded code to a different directory.

4. In the File Mask text box, type **LineEndTest.txt**; click the Search button; and inspect the results, as shown in Figure 14-14. Remember that the default matching in PowerGREP is case insensitive. Notice that the character sequence `This` is matched only at the beginning of a line.

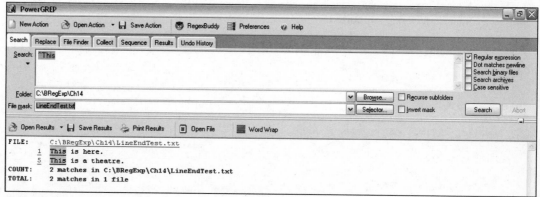

Figure 14-14

5. Modify the pattern in the Search text area to this\.$. Remember that if the period character is the last character on the line, the pattern this$ will never match with the test text for this example.

6. Click the Search button, and inspect the results, as shown in Figure 14-15. Both of the occurrences of the character sequence this. at the end of a line are matched.

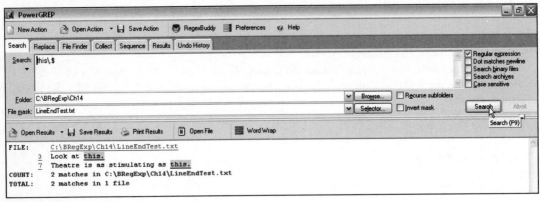

Figure 14-15

How It Works

First, let's look at matching with the pattern ^This. This matches the position before the first character on a line and then attempts to match the character sequence This. This means that it matches the character sequence This at the beginning of a line.

When the pattern is this\.$, this followed by a period character, followed by the $ metacharacter, the character sequence this followed by a period character is first matched; then an attempt is made to match the end-of-line position. That only succeeds when this. makes up the final five characters on a line.

Word-Boundary Metacharacters

Only the \b word-boundary character is supported in PowerGREP. Neither the \< nor the \> word-boundary metacharacters is supported.

The test text for this example, Cat.txt, is shown here:

```
Catalonia is a region of Spain.

"Scat," he said.

A caterpillar later becomes a butterfly.

I love my cat.

The cat sat on the mat.
```

Try it Out   Word-Boundary Position Metacharacters

1. Open PowerGREP, and ensure that the Regular Expression check box is checked.

2. In the Search text area, type the pattern **\bcat**.

3. In the Folder text box, type **C:\BRegExp\Ch14**, adjusting the folder if you downloaded files to some other location.

4. In the File Mask text box, type **Cat.txt**; click the Search button; and inspect the results, as shown in Figure 14-16. Notice that the character sequence cat is matched only when it is the first three characters of an alphabetic character sequence — colloquially, a word.

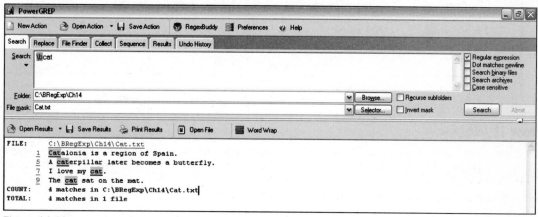

Figure 14-16

5. Modify the pattern in the Search text area to cat\b; click the Search button; and inspect the results, as shown in Figure 14-17. Notice that the character sequence cat is matched only when it is the last three characters of an alphabetic character sequence.

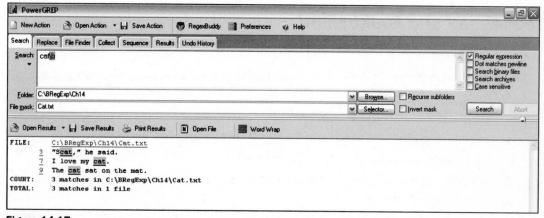

Figure 14-17

6. Modify the pattern in the Search text area to \bcat\b; click the Search button; and inspect the results, as shown in Figure 14-18.

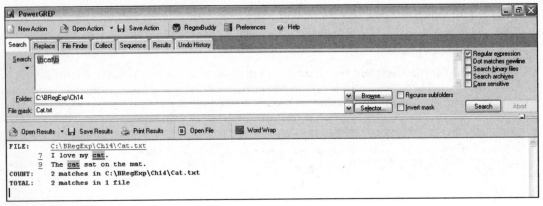

Figure 14-18

How It Works

The pattern \bcat first matches a boundary between nonalphabetic and alphabetic characters. Because the \b metacharacter is followed by a sequence of alphabetic characters, it is, in that context, functioning as a beginning-of-word position metacharacter. Therefore, \bcat matches the three-character sequence of characters cat when it occurs at the beginning of a word.

The pattern cat\b matches the three-character sequence of characters cat when the sequence is followed by a word-boundary position. Therefore, cat\b matches the character sequence when it occurs at the end of a word, as in cat or Scat.

The pattern \bcat\b matches only when there is a word-boundary position before the character sequence cat and immediately after it. In other words, the pattern \bcat\b matches only the word cat.

Lookahead and Lookbehind

Lookahead and lookbehind are supported in PowerGREP.

The following example uses the StarOriginal.txt file, which was used earlier in the chapter.

Try It Out Lookahead and Lookbehind

1. Open PowerGREP, and ensure that the Regular Expression check box is checked.

2. In the Search text area, type the pattern **Star(?=.)**.

3. In the Folder text box, type **C:\BRegExp\Ch14** or adapt the path if you downloaded sample files to another location.

4. In the File Mask text box, type **StarOriginal.txt**; click the Search button; and inspect the results, as shown in Figure 14-19.

5. Edit the pattern in the Search text area to (?<=with)Star, click the Search button, and inspect the results.

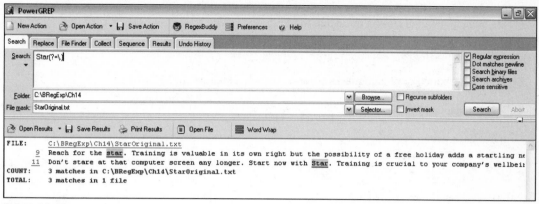

Figure 14-19

How It Works

First, let's look at the pattern Star(?=\.). First, the pattern Star is matched literally. Because the default behavior of PowerGREP is case insensitive, the character sequences star and Star will match. In fact, STAR and sTar would match too, although neither is present in the test text. However, a constraint is applied on the matching by the lookahead. The pattern (?=\.) is a lookahead that means after Star is matched literally, matching may fail if Star (of whatever case) is not followed immediately by the period character, as indicated by the \. metacharacter.

The pattern (?<=with)Star includes a lookbehind that specifies the character sequence Star (whatever case) matches only if it is preceded by the character sequence with followed by a space character.

Longer Examples

This section looks at some longer examples that apply some of the regular expression functionality found in PowerGREP. One of the most useful aspects of PowerGREP is that it finds matches across multiple text files. For reasons of space, the examples use only two files, each of which is short.

Finding HTML Horizontal Rule Elements

This example aims to find all occurrences of the HTML rule element, <hr>, across multiple documents.

A first attempt at a problem definition would be as follows:

Match all HTML/XHTML horizontal rule elements.

Clearly, you need to understand the permitted structure of an hr element to refine this further.

The form may be as simple as:

```
<hr>
```

which can also be written as uppercase. The latter is often found in HTML. Or it can have attributes in HTML style, without enclosing quotation marks:

```
<hr width=50% color=#990066 size=4 />
```

Or it can have paired quotation marks around attribute values, as in XHTML:

```
<hr width="50%" color="#990066" size="4" />
```

Or it can have paired apostrophes:

```
<hr width='50 %' color='#990066' size='4' />
```

Notice, too, that in the XHTML form there is a forward slash before the right-angled bracket at the end of the element.

A more detailed attempt at a problem definition would be the following:

Match a < character followed by the character sequence hr (either case), followed by optional white-space characters, followed by zero or more characters, followed by optional whitespace characters, followed by an optional forward slash, followed by a > character.

A pattern corresponding to the preceding problem definition is shown here:

```
<hr *.* */?>
```

The simple sample documents are shown here. First, `HorizRule1.html`:

```
<html>
<head>
<title>Horizontal Rule 1</title>
</head>
<body>
<p>This file contains a horizontal rule with no attributes.</p>
<hr />
</body>
</html>
```

Then `HorizRule2.html`:

```
<html>
<head>
<title>Horizontal Rule 1</title>
</head>
<body>
<p>This file contains a horizontal rule with three attributes.</p>
<hr width="50%" color="#990066" size="4" />
</body>
</html>
```

Horizontal Rules

1. Open PowerGREP, and ensure that the Regular Expression check box is checked.

2. In the Search text area, type the pattern **<hr *.* */?>**.

3. Ensure that the Folder text box contains `C:\BRegExp\Ch14` or adapt the path if you downloaded code to a different directory.

4. In the File Mask text box, type **Horiz*.html**; click the Search button; and inspect the results, as shown in Figure 14-20.

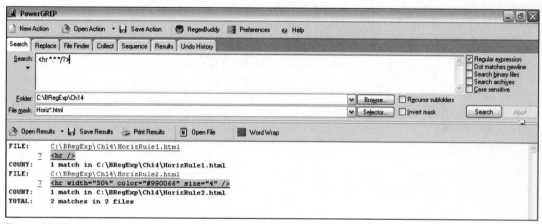

Figure 14-20

How It Works

The pattern `<hr *.* */?>` matches a < character followed by the character sequence hr (either case), followed by optional space characters, followed by zero or more characters, followed by zero or more space characters, followed by an optional forward-slash character, followed by a > character.

If you simply want to find all correctly structured hr elements, this pattern should be close to 100 percent sensitive. If the element is spread over several lines:

```
<hr
 width="50%"
 color="#990066"
 size="4" />
```

the pattern could be usefully modified to the following:

```
<hr\s*.*\s*/?>
```

The \s metacharacter ensure that tab characters or newline characters are also matched.

The pattern will also find some incorrectly formed character sequences that are likely intended to be hr elements For example:

```
<hr width=="50%" />
```

has two consecutive = signs, which is not allowed. Using the . * pattern, you could match all sorts of illegal character sequences. Although this lowers the specificity of the pattern, it might be useful because it would ensure that all hr elements were matched, even if they contained slight syntax errors.

If the files of interest contain HTML or XHTML markup, this type of loss of specificity is unlikely to be a significant problem.

Matching Time Example

This example looks at how you can match data that makes up a time of day. The first attempt at a problem definition can be expressed as follows:

Match any time of day, whether expressed as 12-hour clock notation or 24-hour clock notation.

To refine what's needed, you must fully understand each of the notations and how it is written.

The 12-hour notation might have values like this:

```
9:31 am
```

or:

```
09:31am
```

or:

```
09:31 pm
```

or:

```
09:31pm
```

An optional first digit can be a 0 or 1. When there is a 0, the next digit can be 0 to 9 inclusive, but when the first digit is a 1, the next digit can only be a 0, 1, or 2 in 12-hour notation.

The following pattern would match hours up to 09:

```
[0]?[0-9]
```

Hours from 10 to 12 would be matched by the following pattern:

```
1[0-2]
```

So for the part of the pattern before the colon character, you can use the following pattern:

```
([0]?[0-9]|1[0-2])
```

If you test that out on illegal "times" such as 18:88pm, it will match, but that is a problem that goes away after you add a colon character at the end of the pattern.

Matching the remainder of the 12-hour time is straightforward:

```
:[0-5][0-9] ?[ap]m
```

Putting those parts together, you have the following pattern to match times in 12-hour time notation:

```
\b([0]?[0-9]|1[0-2]):[0-5][0-9] ?[ap]m
```

Twenty-four-hour time can be expressed using the following pattern:

```
([01][0-9]|2[0-4]):[0-5][0-9]
```

Putting those two patterns together using alternation, you have the following pattern:

```
(\b([0]?[0-9]|1[0-2]):[0-5][0-9] ?[ap]m|([01][0-9]|2[0-4]):[0-5][0-9])
```

Test file `Time1.txt` contains a range of 12-hour–format times:

```
08:22 pm
08:37 am
19:88 am
12:00 am
11:39pm
7:28 am
8:19 am
```

Test file `Time2.txt` contains a range of 24-hour–format times:

```
06:31
19:15
18:12
23:59
00:03
19:54
03:00
10:49
```

Try It Out   Matching Times

1. Open PowerGREP, and ensure that the Regular Expression check box is checked. First, you will match 12-hour times in `Time1.txt`.

2. In the Search text area, enter the pattern **\b([0]?[0-9] | 1[0-2]):[0-5][0-9] ?[ap]m**.

3. In the Folder text box, type **C:\BRegExp\Ch14** or adapt the path according to your folder structure.

4. In the File Mask text box, type **Time1.txt**; click the Search button; and inspect the results, as shown in Figure 14-21. Notice that all the legal times in the test file are matched, but the illegal "time" 19:88 am is not matched.

    Next, you will attempt to match the 24-hour–format times in `Time2.txt`.

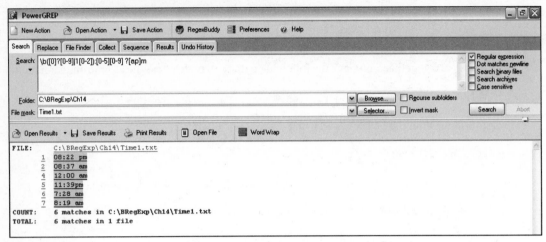

Figure 14-21

5. Edit the content of the Search text area to `([01][0-9]|2[0-4]):[0-5][0-9]`.

6. Edit the file mask to `Time2.txt`; click the Search button; and inspect the results, as shown in Figure 14-22. Notice that all 24-hour–format times are matched.

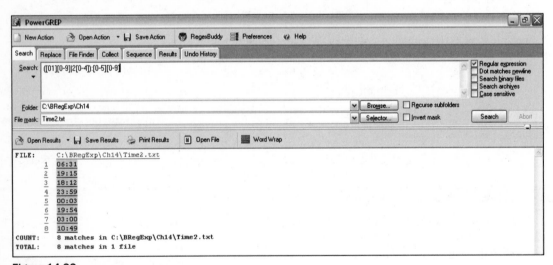

Figure 14-22

Finally, you will attempt to match times in the formats in both `Time1.txt` and `Time2.txt`.

7. Edit the content of the Search text area to `(\b([0]?[0-9]|1[0-2]):[0-5][0-9]`
`?[ap]m|([01][0-9]|2[0-4]):[0-5][0-9])`.

8. Edit the file mask to `Time*.txt`; click the Search button; and inspect the results, as shown in Figure 14-23. Notice that all valid 12-hour–format and 24-hour–format times in the test files are matched.

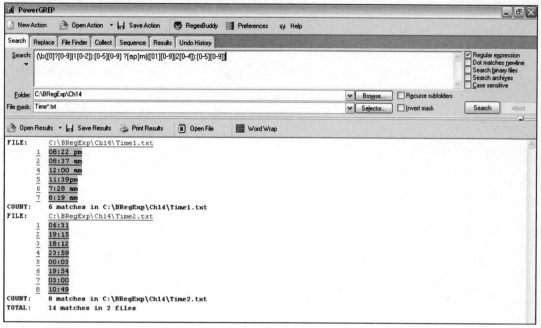

Figure 14-23

Exercises

1. In the first example in this chapter, the character sequence regexp was never matched, although the character sequence regexp does occur in the sample file Regex.txt, and the pattern regexp is one of the options in each of the patterns tested. Provide an improved pattern that will match all occurrences of the character sequence regexp.

2. Create a pattern to match dollar values with two digits before the decimal point and two after it. A sample value is $88.23.

Wildcards in Microsoft Excel

Microsoft Office Excel is one of the most successful applications in the Microsoft Office suite. Much of the data held in Excel worksheets is text that is searchable. Excel provides a search facility on formulas, values, or comments in a worksheet or workbook.

Excel does not have full regular expression support. Like Microsoft Word, Excel has limited support for regular expressions, by means of wildcards. The range of wildcards in Excel is significantly more limited than in Word, but as you'll see, the wildcard functionality that is provided can, when used together with other Excel tools, provide useful productivity gains.

In this chapter, you will learn the following:

- ❏ The interface to Excel wildcard functionality in the Find and Replace dialog box
- ❏ The wildcards that Excel supports
- ❏ How to use those wildcards in searches
- ❏ How to use wildcards in data forms
- ❏ How to use wildcards in filters

> **The wildcard functionality described in this chapter was tested on Microsoft Office Excel 2003.**

The Excel Find Interface

The Excel interface for using wildcards has similarities to the interface in Microsoft Word. The Find and Replace dialog box, which is shown in Figure 15-1, is central to the process.

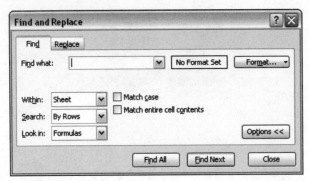

Figure 15-1

A sample spreadsheet, Months.xls, will be used to explore how the Find and Replace dialog box works. The appearance of Months.xls is shown in Figure 15-2. Notice that it contains simple text values in several cells and a sum in cell B15.

	A	B	C	D
1				
2	Jan	100		Jan Sales
3	Feb	223		Feb Sales
4	Mar	224		Mar Sales
5	Apr	883		Apr Sales
6	May	914		May Sales
7	Jun	770		Jun Sales
8	Jul	77		Jul Sales
9	Aug	234		Aug Sales
10	Sep	945		Sep Sales
11	Oct	881		Oct Sales
12	Nov	377		Nov Sales
13	Dec	388		Dec Sales
14				
15	Total	6016		
16				
17				

Cell B15 = SUM(B2:B13)

Figure 15-2

Try It Out   The Find and Replace Interface

1. Open the worksheet Months.xls in Excel, and use the Ctrl+F keyboard shortcut to open the Find and Replace dialog box.

2. In the Find What text box, type the character sequence **Jan**; click the Find Next button; and inspect the results, as shown in Figure 15-3. The cell A2, which contains the literal character sequence Jan, is highlighted.

3. The Find and Replace dialog box in Excel has a Find All button, a feature that is absent from Microsoft Word. Click the Find All button, and inspect the results, as shown in Figure 15-4. Notice that a list of matches is displayed in the lower part of the Find and Replace dialog box. Only one match is highlighted: the first cell in the search order, which in this case is again cell A2.

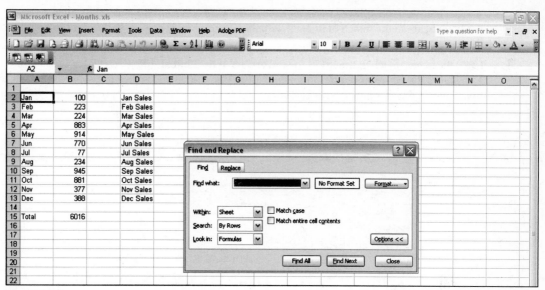

Figure 15-3

The reason for the list displayed in the lower part of the Find and Replace dialog box is that some matches may not be on the currently displayed screen. Particularly in large spreadsheets, there may be multiple matches, likely spread over several screens of information.

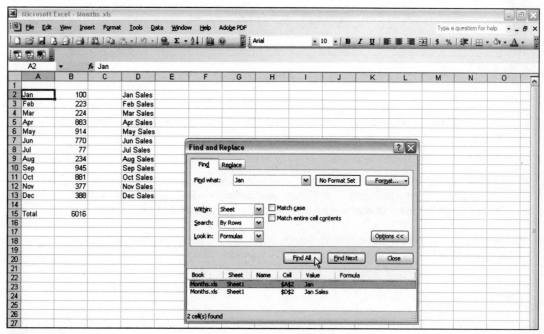

Figure 15-4

The list of matches displayed in the bottom of the Find and Replace dialog box allows you to easily navigate to the match of interest, whether or not it is on-screen. In this simple example, there are only two matches.

4. Click the lower match in the list in the lower part of the Find and Replace dialog box. Figure 15-5 shows the appearance after this step. Notice that the cell D2 is now highlighted because it, too, contains the character sequence Jan.

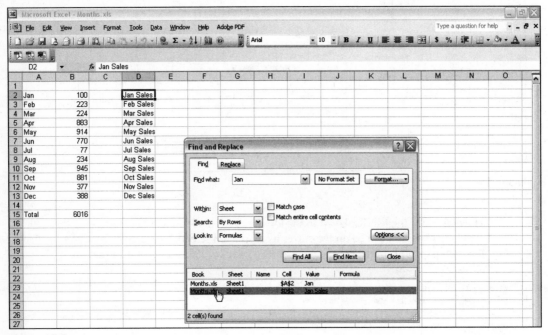

Figure 15-5

The Find and Replace dialog box has a Match Case check box that does what you would expect. If checked, it converts the default case-insensitive matching to case-sensitive matching.

The Match Entire Cell Contents check box, if checked, means that the literal pattern Jan will match only if Jan is the whole content of a cell.

5. Check the Match Entire Cell Contents check box; click the Find All button; and inspect the results, as shown in Figure 15-6. Notice that now only one match is listed. Cell D2 is no longer included in the list of matches because Jan is only a part of that cell's content.

Before looking at the effect of the Within, Search, and Look In drop-down lists, look at the limited range of regular expression–like functionality provided by Excel wildcards.

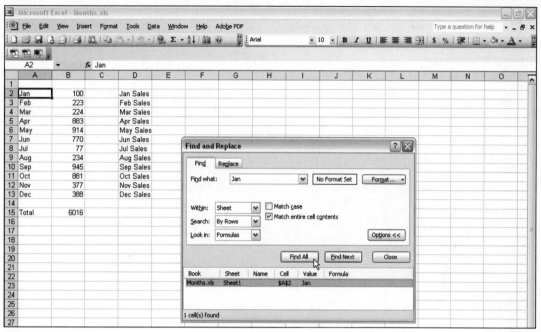

Figure 15-6

The Wildcards Excel Supports

Excel supports fewer wildcards than any other tool described in this book. It supports only three metacharacters, which are listed in the following table.

Metacharacter	Meaning
?	Matches any single character
*	Matches any sequence of 0 or more Characters
~	The escape character

Try It Out   The Excel Wildcards

1. Open Months.xls in Excel. Ensure that the Match Entire Cell Contents check box is unchecked.

2. In the Find box, type the pattern **J?n**. The pattern will match character sequences such as Jan and Jun, each of which occurs twice in Months.xls.

3. Click the Find All button, and inspect the results displayed in the lower part of the Find and Replace dialog box, as shown in Figure 15-7.

   Clicking any of the items listed in the lower part of the Find and Replace dialog box allows you to navigate to any desired value, whether it is currently visible on-screen or not.

4. Click the third line, whose value is Jan Sales. Figure 15-8 shows that the chosen cell is now highlighted.

355

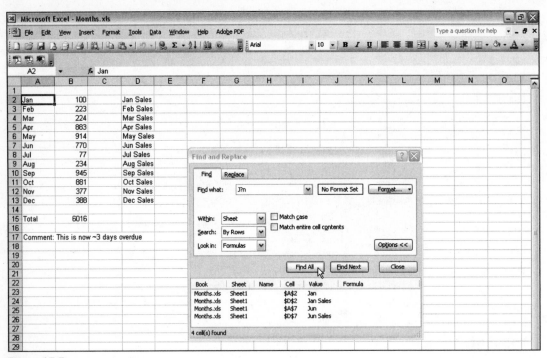

Figure 15-7

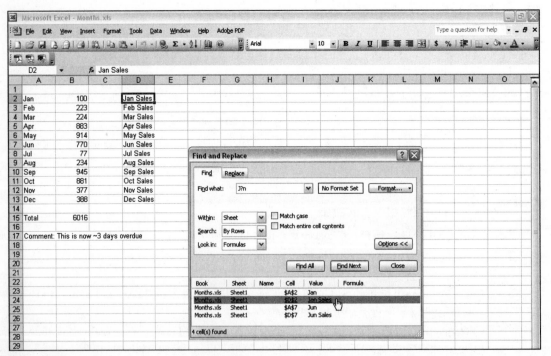

Figure 15-8

5. Click other matches in the lower part of the Find and Replace dialog box to confirm that you navigate to the chosen cell.

6. Edit the pattern in the Find What text box to A*; click the Find All button; and inspect the results, as shown in Figure 15-9. Notice that every occurrence of the alphabetic character A or a is matched.

The number of matches for the pattern A* is unacceptably large even for the small amount of data in Months.xls. Excel has no notion of positional metacharacters such as the beginning-of-line metacharacter, ^, so you can't narrow down the matches using that technique. In this example, you can remove the undesired matches due to the word sales by specifying a case-sensitive match. In Excel, the default is a case-insensitive match.

7. Check the Match Case check box; click the Find All button; and inspect the results, as shown in Figure 15-10. Notice that now only matches that have an uppercase A are in the cell.

This example illustrates a general problem with matching using the limited wildcards in Excel, which is that specificity can sometimes be very low.

Don't close Excel, because you will continue from this point in the next example.

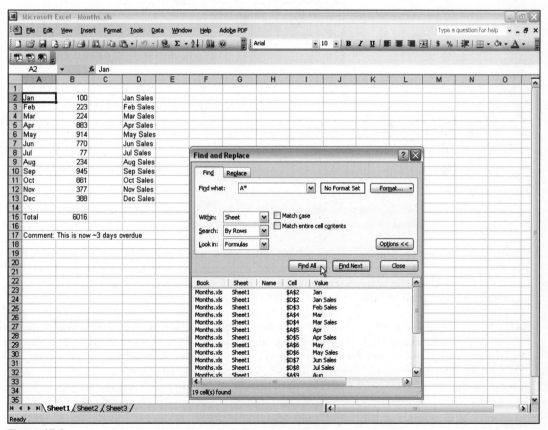

Figure 15-9

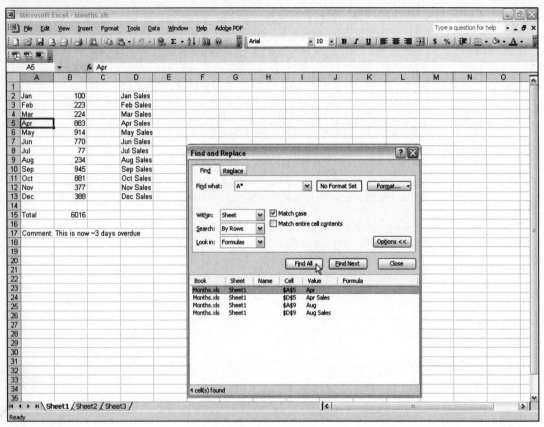

Figure 15-10

How It Works

The pattern `J?n` matches any character sequence that begins with a `J` and is followed by any character which, in turn, is followed by an `n`. In the sample data, the character sequences `Jan` and `Jun` match.

The pattern `A*`, when the Match Case check box is unchecked, will match any character sequence that contains `A` or `a` followed by any number of characters. The biggest source of undesired matches is the word `sales`, which occurs 12 times. That matches because it contains an `a` that isn't the final character of the word, and the matching is being carried out case insensitively.

In large worksheets the number of matches could be overwhelming if you chose a pattern as nonspecific as `A*`. Another technique to narrow the matches is to add further characters in the pattern; for example, `Ap*` would match character sequences such as `April` but not `August`. Another option is to use multiple `?` metacharacters, each of which would match a single character, so that you specify the number of characters that you want to match; for example, the pattern `Ap???` would match `April`.

Escaping Wildcard Characters

There may be times that you want to match the * or ? metacharacters not as metacharacters, but literally. To escape those metacharacters in Excel you need to use the ~ character (tilde).

So to match a literal ? character you use ~?, and to match a literal * character you use the pattern ~*. To match the literal tilde character you use the pattern ~~.

Try It Out   Escaping Wildcards

1. Edit the pattern in the Find What text box to ~~.

2. Click the Find Next button, and inspect the results, as shown in Figure 15-11. Notice that cell A17 is highlighted. Notice, too, that the list of matches in the lower part of the Find and Replace window is still displayed, which is potentially misleading.

3. The problem of the carried-over results from previous use of the Find All button can be avoided by clicking the Find All button again with the new pattern. If there is more than one match, you can use the navigation facility in the lower part of the Find and Replace dialog box to navigate to the desired cell. Click the Find All button.

4. Inspect the Find and Replace dialog box to confirm that carried-over results have been replaced by results relevant to the current search.

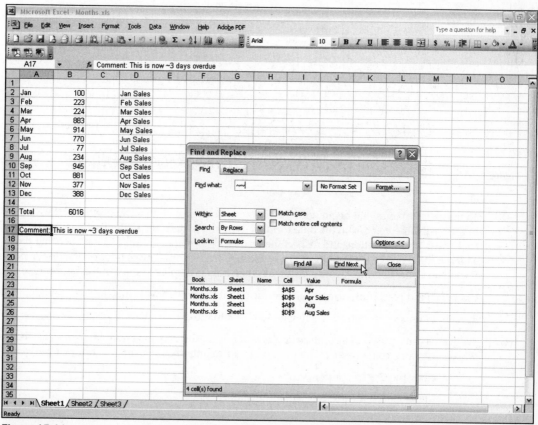

Figure 15-11

Using Wildcards in Data Forms

Tabular data in Excel can be held in a list. The sample file, Names.xls, contains a simple list that contains last name, first name, and date of birth for several people.

Try It Out   Using Wildcards in Data Forms

1. Open Names.xls in Excel.

2. From the Data menu, select Form. Inspect the display of the list data. The data form, titled Sheet 1, opens. Notice that there is a slider in the middle of the data form.

3. Click the Criteria button. Figure 15-12 shows the appearance after this step. The Criteria button is replaced by the Form button. You can now enter criteria to match data in the data form.

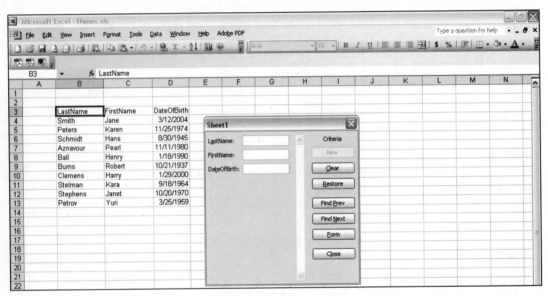

Figure 15-12

4. To match last names that begin with the character sequence St you can use the pattern St* in the LastName text box in the data form. So type the pattern **St*** in the LastName text box; click the Find Next button; and inspect the results, as shown in Figure 15-13. Notice that the slider in the center of the data form is now close to the bottom. This is because the first match is the eighth of the ten rows. Notice, too, that when data is displayed the Criteria button reappears.

5. Click the Find Next button again, and confirm that the ninth row is matched.

   The Find Previous button allows navigation back to the eighth row.

6. Wildcards can be used in a combination of text boxes. You can, for example, search for people whose last name contains St and whose first name contains kar using the following steps:

   a. Click the Criteria button.

   b. In the LastName text box, enter the pattern **St***.

c. In the FirstName text box enter the pattern **Kar?**.

d. Click the Find Next button, and inspect the appearance of the data form. Figure 15-14 shows the appearance after this step. In this limited data set there is only one match, Kara Stelman.

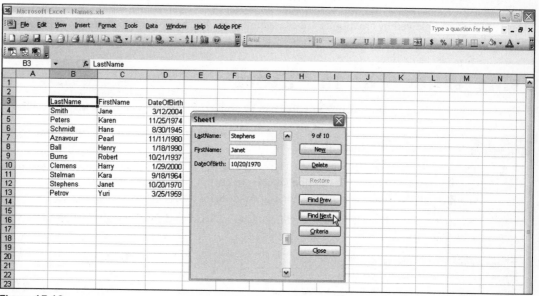

Figure 15-13

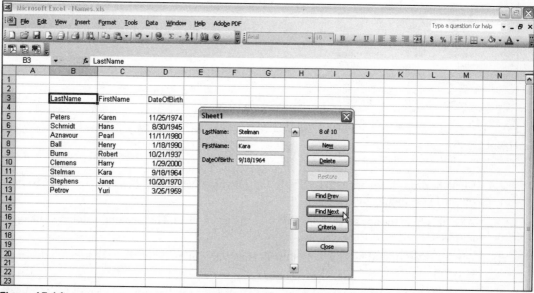

Figure 15-14

How It Works

With the pattern St* in the LastName text box, surnames that contain the character sequence St or st are matched.

With the pattern St* in the LastName text box and Kar? in the first name text box, only names that contain the character sequence Kar followed by one character in the first name and that contain the character sequence St followed by any number of characters in the last name are matched.

Using Wildcards in Filters

Excel contains powerful filter functionality that can be applied to tabular data that constitutes a list.

Try It Out   **Using Wildcards in Excel Filters**

1. Open Names.xls in Excel. From the Data menu select Filter, and then select AutoFilter. You should see something similar to that shown in Figure 15-15. The file NamesWithFilter.xls is made available should you have difficulty creating the AutoFilter.

    Notice the drop-down lists contained inside cells B3, C3, and D3. They give access to the AutoFilter functionality.

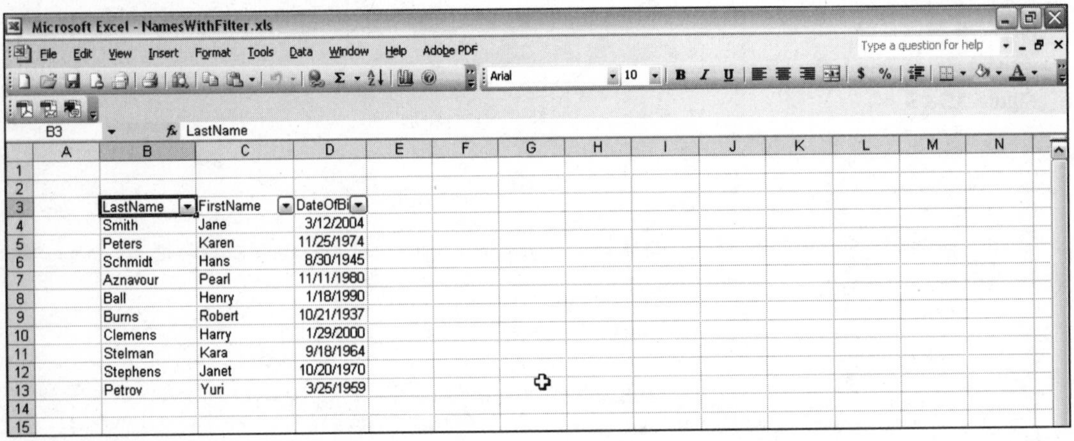

Figure 15-15

2. Click the drop-down list in the cell with the value LastName (cell B3), and click the Custom option in the menu offered.

    After this step, the appearance should be as in Figure 15-16. The Custom AutoFilter dialog box allows selected rows to be displayed.

3. In the top-left drop-down list, select the Begins With option (you will have to scroll down to select it).

4. In the top-right text box, enter the pattern **St***; click the OK button; and inspect the results, as shown in Figure 15-17. Notice that now only two of the ten rows are displayed. The displayed rows are those where the last name begins with the character sequence St.

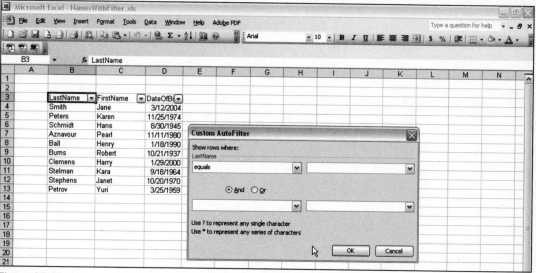

Figure 15-16

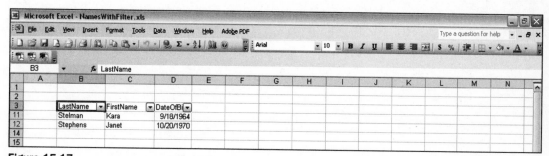

Figure 15-17

The Custom AutoFilter offers advantages over the data form in some respects. For example, it allows the user to specify that a pattern occurs at the beginning or end of a cell's value. This gives functionality similar to the ^ and $ metacharacters. In addition, AND or OR logic can be used to create two rules.

However, the Custom AutoFilter allows patterns to be defined for only one column. The data form criteria can be defined on any combination of the columns in the list.

Exercises

1. How can you display in NamesWithFilter.xls only names where the first name begins with Kar?

2. In Months.xls, describe how you would match only cells that contain the character sequence Jun or the character sequence Jul.

Regular Expression Functionality in SQL Server 2000

Vast quantities of business and other data are stored in SQL Server, Microsoft's premier relational database product. Most administrators and developers who use SQL Server are familiar with the problems that can occur when retrieving data from a very large data store. The better a developer or user understands the data, the better the retrieval of data is achieved. The sensitivity and specificity of the retrieval of desired data from SQL Server can be improved by using regular expression functionality.

Regular expression–like functionality can be achieved using the LIKE keyword in a WHERE clause or by using SQL Server's full-text indexing and search capability.

> **This chapter describes functionality in SQL Server 2000. Similar functionality is present in the beta of SQL Server 2005.**

In this chapter, you will learn the following:

- ❑ Which metacharacters are supported in SQL Server 2000
- ❑ How to use the supported metacharacters with the LIKE keyword
- ❑ How to achieve regular expression–like functionality using full-text search

The examples in this chapter assume that you have SQL Server 2000 installed as a local, unnamed instance. If you are running SQL Server 2000 as a named instance, modify the connection information accordingly, if necessary.

Metacharacters Supported

SQL Server 2000 supports a limited number of metacharacters, some of which have nonstandard usage and meaning. Each of the four metacharacters is used in the context of the LIKE keyword.

The metacharacters supported in SQL Server 2000 are listed in the following table.

Metacharacter	Meaning
%	Matches zero or more characters. % is not a quantifier.
_	The underscore character matches a single character. It is not a quantifier.
[...]	Matches a character class. Character class ranges are supported.
[^...]	Matches any character except those in the character class.

Many aspects of regular expressions are not supported for use with the LIKE keyword. The following table lists regular expressions features that are not supported.

Metacharacter or Functionality	Comment
\d	Not supported
\w	Not supported
Back references	Not supported
?	Not supported
*	Not supported; the % metacharacter is not a quantifier
+	Not supported
{n,m}	Not supported
Lookahead	Not supported

Using LIKE with Regular Expressions

The LIKE keyword is used in a WHERE clause which, in turn, is part of a SELECT statement. The LIKE keyword allows the WHERE clause to filter on a regular expression pattern, rather than simply on a literal character sequence.

The Try It Out sections that follow look at examples that make use of the limited collection of metacharacters that SQL Server 2000 supports.

The % Metacharacter

The % metacharacter matches zero or more characters. The % metacharacter is equivalent to the metasequence . * in more standard regular expression implementations.

Try It Out   **The % Metacharacter**

1. Open Query Analyzer. In Windows XP, select Start ➪ All Programs ➪ SQL Server ➪ Query Analyzer.

2. From the Connect to SQL Server dialog box, connect to the appropriate SQL Server. The Query Analyzer should open with an appearance similar to that shown in Figure 16-1. The appearance may vary depending on previous use of Query Analyzer and option settings.

3. In the first query, you will use the pubs sample database and will select authors whose last name begins with B. You can do this by using the pattern B%, where the metacharacter % matches any number of any character or combination of characters.

    Type the following Transact-SQL code into the query pane of the Query Analyzer:

```
USE pubs
SELECT au_lname, au_fname FROM dbo.authors
WHERE au_lname LIKE 'B%'
ORDER BY au_lname
```

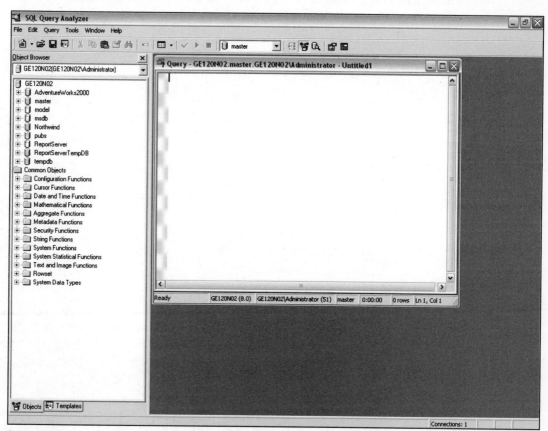

Figure 16-1

4. Press F5 or click the blue right-pointing arrow above the query pane to run the Transact-SQL code. Figure 16-2 shows the appearance after Step 4. Notice that the last name and first name of authors whose surname begins with B are displayed in the results pane, in the lower part of the figure.

If you have mistyped the Transact-SQL code, an error message may appear in the results pane. If you cannot find the error, the code is included in the file BSurnames.sql.

5. To match surnames that contain the letter B, either case, occurring at the beginning of the surname or later, you can use the pattern %b%.

Type the following Transact-SQL code into the query pane of the Query Analyzer:

```
USE pubs
SELECT au_lname, au_fname FROM dbo.authors
WHERE au_lname LIKE '%b%'
ORDER BY au_lname
```

6. Press F5 or click the blue right-pointing arrow above the query pane to run the Transact-SQL code. Figure 16-3 shows the appearance. Notice that the last names of the authors in the result set each contain a letter b, either at the beginning of the word or later in the word.

If you have difficulty when you type the code in, you can use the file BAnywhere.sql as an alternative way to run the code.

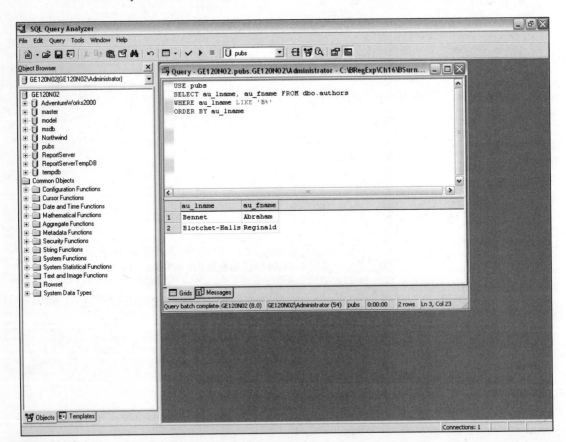

Figure 16-2

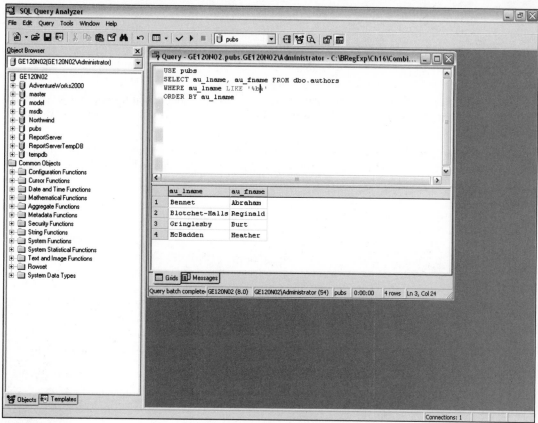

Figure 16-3

7. To find last names that contain the character sequence nt, you can use the pattern %nt%.

Type the following Transact-SQL code into the query pane of the Query Analyzer:

```
USE pubs
SELECT au_lname, au_fname FROM dbo.authors
WHERE au_lname LIKE '%nt%'
ORDER BY au_lname
```

8. Press F5 or click the blue right-pointing arrow above the query pane to run the Transact-SQL code. Figure 16-4 shows the appearance. Notice that each of the surnames contains the character sequence nt.

The file NTanywhere.sql contains the code if you prefer not to type it into the query pane.

9. The LIKE keyword can be used more than once in the same WHERE clause. For example, if you wanted to find authors with surnames that begin with R and a first name that begins with the character sequence Al, you could use the pattern R% in relation to the au_lname column and the pattern Al% in relation to the au_fname column.

Type the following code into the query pane in Query Analyzer:

```
USE pubs
SELECT au_lname, au_fname FROM dbo.authors
WHERE au_lname LIKE 'R%' AND au_fname LIKE 'Al%'
ORDER BY au_lname
```

10. Press F5 or click the blue right-pointing arrow above the query pane to run the Transact-SQL code. Figure 16-5 shows the appearance. On this occasion, only one name is returned that satisfies both criteria.

11. You can combine the LIKE keyword with the NOT keyword. For example, to select authors whose surname does not begin with B, you can use a WHERE clause like this:

```
WHERE au_lname NOT LIKE 'B%'
```

Type the following code into the query pane of the Query Analyzer:

```
USE pubs
SELECT au_lname, au_fname FROM dbo.authors
WHERE au_lname NOT LIKE 'B%'
ORDER BY au_lname
```

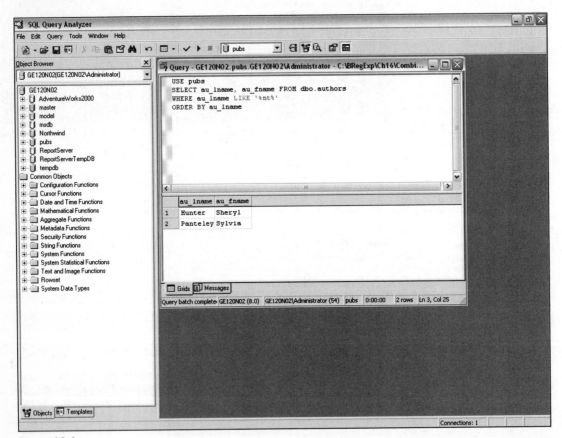

Figure 16-4

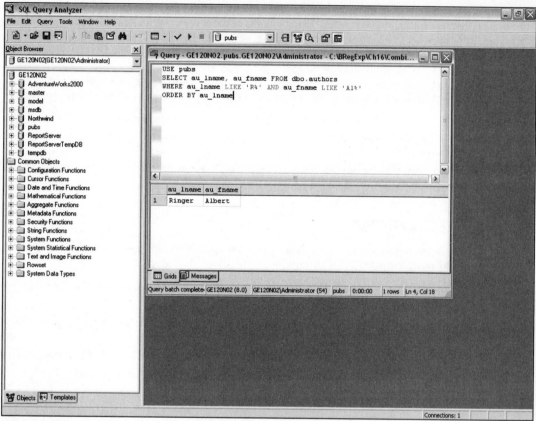

Figure 16-5

12. Press F5 or click the blue right-pointing arrow above the query pane to run the Transact-SQL code. When the code is run, all authors in the pubs database are returned except for those whose surname begins with B.

How It Works

The pattern B% matches the character B or b when it occurs at the beginning of a value and is then followed by any number of any characters. Occurrences of the character b, either case, that occur after the beginning of the word are not matched.

The pattern %b% matches the character B or b anywhere in a last name. The % at the beginning of %b% matches zero or more characters. When it matches zero characters, it can match surnames beginning with B.

The pattern %nt% combines a character sequence nt with a preceding % metacharacter and a following % metacharacter. Any surname containing the character sequence nt is matched.

When the pattern R% is used in relation to the au_lname column and the pattern A1% is used in relation to the au_fname column, any row where the au_lname column begins with R is matched. From those matches, any row where the au_fname column begins with A1 is matched. Only rows where both attempts at matching succeed are displayed.

When the NOT keyword is used together with the LIKE keyword and a pattern as, for example, in the following WHERE clause, only rows where the last name *fails* to match the value of the pattern are matched:

```
WHERE au_lname NOT LIKE 'B%'
```

In this case, the pattern matches last names that begin with the character B. So only last names beginning with a character other than B are matched.

The _ Metacharacter

The _ metacharacter matches exactly one character. It is similar to the dot metacharacter in more standard regular expression syntax.

Try It Out   Using the _ Metacharacter

1. Open the Query Analyzer. Type the following Transact-SQL code into the query pane of the Query Analyzer:

```
USE Northwind
SELECT SupplierID, ProductID, ProductName FROM dbo.products
WHERE SupplierID LIKE '1%'
ORDER BY SupplierID
```

Notice that you are now using the Northwind sample database, as specified by the first line of the Transact-SQL code. Using the pattern 1% in the third line will show you that there are some SupplierID values consisting only of the character 1.

2. Press F5 or click the blue right-pointing arrow above the query pane to run the Transact-SQL code. Figure 16-6 shows the appearance after this step. Notice that the first Supplier ID values displayed consist of the character 1 only. When you use the _ metacharacter later in this Try It Out, those rows should not be displayed.

3. Type the following code into the query pane of Query Analyzer:

```
USE Northwind
SELECT SupplierID, ProductID, ProductName FROM dbo.products
WHERE SupplierID LIKE '1_'
ORDER BY SupplierID
```

You can simply replace the pattern 1% with the pattern 1_ in the third line of the Transact-SQL code.

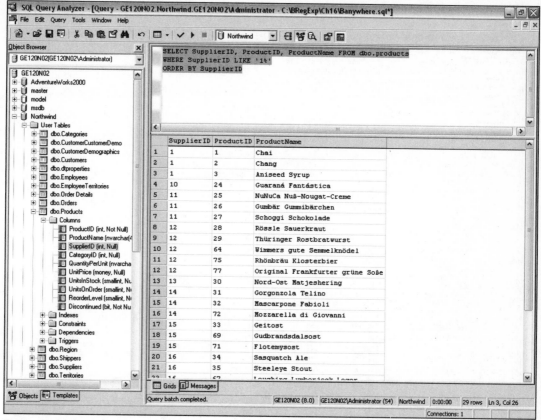

Figure 16-6

4.   Press F5 or click the blue right-pointing arrow above the query pane to run the Transact-SQL code. Figure 16-7 shows the appearance after this step. Notice that the first three rows that were displayed in Figure 16-6 are no longer displayed.

How It Works

The pattern 1% matches SupplierID values that begin with the numeric digit 1 followed by zero or more characters. So it matches values such as 1 and 10.

The pattern 1_ matches SupplierID values only if they begin with the numeric digit 1 followed by exactly one character. Thus, the value 1 does not match, because 1 is followed by zero characters. However, values such as 10 do match, because the 1 is followed in the value by exactly one character.

Character Classes

Support for character classes in SQL Server 2000 provides the behavior that you are familiar with in other implementations. Character class ranges are supported.

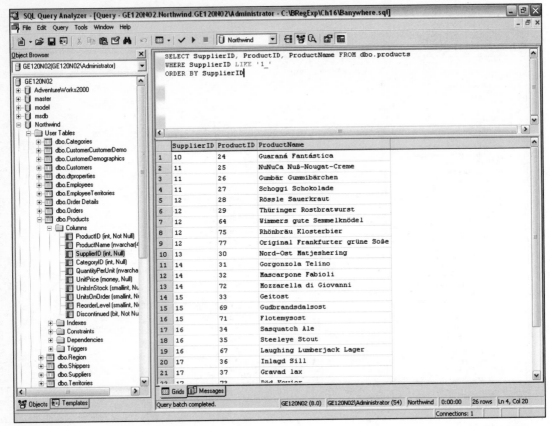

Figure 16-7

Character classes provide useful functionality that complements usage of the % and _ metacharacters. For example, you can use the character class [ABC] in the pattern [ABC]% to match authors whose last name begins with A or B or C.

Character Classes

1. Open Query Analyzer, and type the following code in the query pane of Query Analyzer:

```
USE pubs
SELECT au_lname, au_fname from dbo.authors
WHERE au_lname LIKE '[ABC]%'
ORDER BY au_lname
```

2. Press F5 or click the blue right-pointing arrow above the query pane to run the Transact-SQL code. Figure 16-8 shows the appearance after this step. Because no author last names begin with A, only those last names beginning with B or C are displayed.

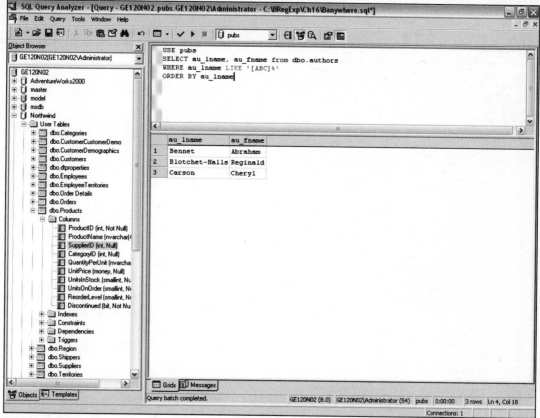

Figure 16-8

3. Character class ranges can also be used. For example, to display rows containing last names that begin with characters in the range N through Z, you can use the character class [N-Z] in the pattern [N-Z]%.

Type the following code in the query pane of the Query Analyzer:

```
USE pubs
SELECT au_lname, au_fname from dbo.authors
WHERE au_lname LIKE '[N-Z]%'
ORDER BY au_lname
```

4. Press F5 or click the blue right-pointing arrow above the query pane to run the Transact-SQL code. Figure 16-9 shows the appearance after this step.

How It Works

The character class [ABC] matches a single character that is A or B or C. The pattern [ABC]% is thus equivalent to the combination of the patterns A%, B%, and C%. The pattern A% matches authors whose last name begins with A. The patterns B% and C% match last names beginning with B and C, respectively. Putting all three together, the pattern [ABC]% matches last names beginning with A, B, or C.

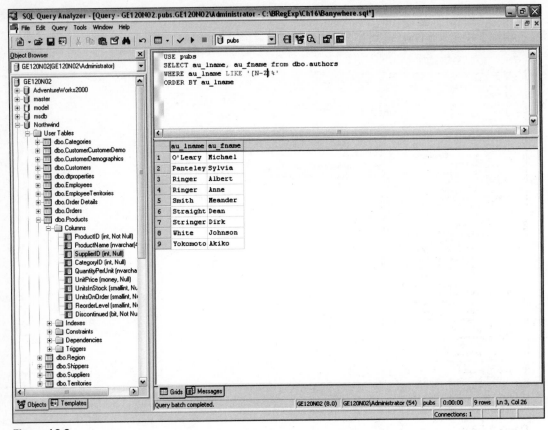

Figure 16-9

The character class [N-Z] is equivalent to the character class [NOPQRSTUVWXYZ]. Thus, last names that begin with any character from N through Z are matched by the pattern [N-Z]%.

Negated Character Classes

Negated character classes are supported in SQL Server 2000. The ^ metacharacter is used immediately following the initial square bracket to signify that a negated character class is being specified.

Negated character classes can be used together with ranges in a character class.

Try It Out   Negated Character Classes

1. Open Query Analyzer, and in the query pane, type the following Transact-SQL code:

```
USE AdventureWorks2000
SELECT LastName, FirstName from dbo.contact
WHERE LastName LIKE 'Ad%'
ORDER BY LastName, FirstName
```

This example uses the `AdventureWorks2000` database. Be careful about the capitalization of the database name `AdventureWorks2000`. Also ensure that you don't insert a space into the database name. The preceding code matches last names that begin with `Ad`. When you use a negated character class in a moment, you will see that those rows are not matched.

2. Press F5 or click the blue right-pointing arrow above the query pane to run the Transact-SQL code. Figure 16-10 shows the appearance after this step. Notice that there are, for example, four rows where the surname `Adams` is displayed.

3. Type the following code into the query pane:

```
USE AdventureWorks2000
SELECT LastName, FirstName from dbo.contact
WHERE LastName LIKE 'A[^d]%'
ORDER BY LastName, FirstName
```

4. Press F5 or click the blue right-pointing arrow above the query pane to run the Transact-SQL code. Figure 16-11 shows the appearance after this step. Notice that the rows containing the last name `Adams` are not displayed. They would be displayed between rows 6 and 7 if they had been matched, given the `ORDER BY` clause.

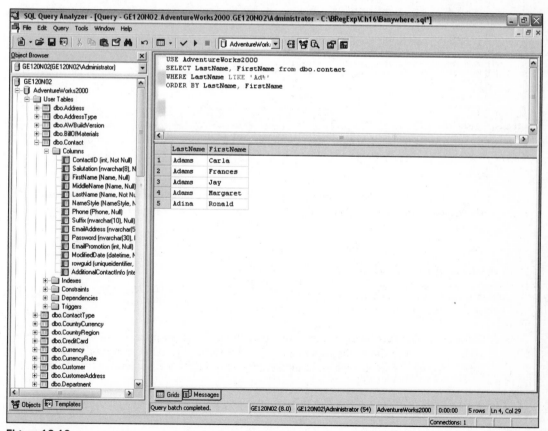

Figure 16-10

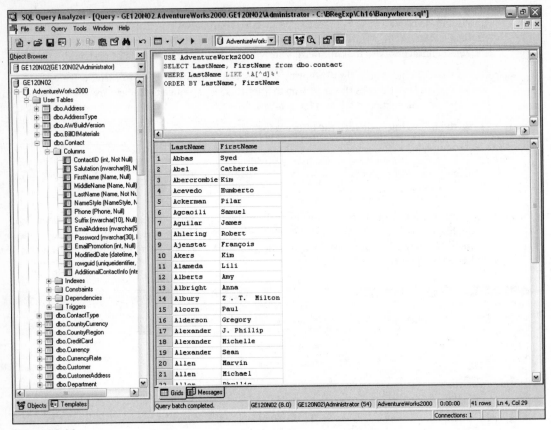

Figure 16-11

5. Negated character classes can be used with ranges. For example, if you wanted to match last names that begin with A where the next character is not in the range a through k, you can use the pattern A[^a-k]%.

Type the following code into the query pane:

```
USE AdventureWorks2000
SELECT LastName, FirstName from dbo.contact
WHERE LastName LIKE 'A[^a-k]%'
ORDER BY LastName, FirstName
```

6. Press F5 or click the blue right-pointing arrow above the query pane to run the Transact-SQL code. Figure 16-12 shows the appearance after this step. Notice that no last name that begins with A and has its second character in the range a through k is displayed in the results pane.

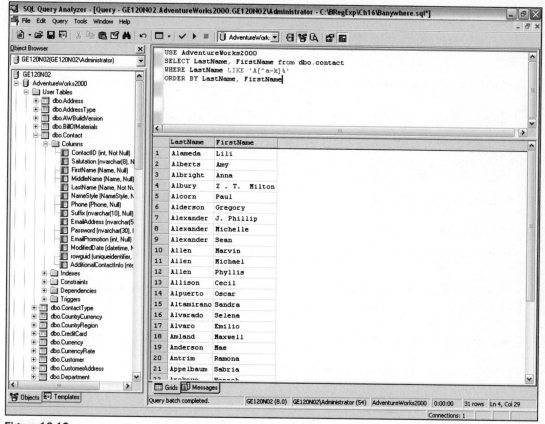

Figure 16-12

How It Works

The pattern Ad% matches last names that begin with the character A, followed by the character d.

The pattern A[^d]% matches last names that begin with the character A followed by any character but d. The character class [^d] signifies any character but d.

The pattern A[^a-k]% matches last names that begin with A and have a second character not in the range a through k. The % metacharacter matches zero or more characters of any kind in the third and later characters of the last name.

Using Full-Text Search

SQL Server Full-Text Search was introduced in SQL Server 7.0. Full-Text Search isn't an integral part of SQL Server 2000 at all, because it uses the MSSearch service component, originally derived from Indexing Server, to create indexes that are external to SQL Server. Because the full-text indexes are external to SQL Server, they are not updated automatically in the way that regular indexes are updated.

A full-text index is contained in a full-text catalog. A full-text catalog is stored in the file system, not in a SQL Server database, although the catalog and its indexes are administered through the database. The full-text catalog for an instance of SQL Server 2000 must reside on the hard disk that is local to the SQL Server instance.

The following table summarizes a comparison between full-text indexes and SQL Server indexes.

Full-Text Index	SQL Server 2000 Index
Grouped into full-text catalogs. Only one catalog per SQL Server database that s full-text indexed.	Not grouped.
Stored in the file system. Administered through the relational database with which they are associated.	Stored in connection with the database with which they are associated.
Maximum of one full-text index per SQL Server table.	More than one index is permitted per table.
Population of the full-text index can occur on a scheduled basis, in response to change of data, or manually.	Updated automatically when data is inserted, deleted, or updated.
SQL Server 2000 Enterprise Manager, wizards, or stored procedures are used to create, manage, or drop full-text indexes.	SQL Server 2000 Enterprise Manager, wizards, or Transact-SQL statements are used to create and drop regular indexes.

To use full-text search functionality, the relevant full-text indexes must first be created. In this example, you will add full-text indexing related to the pubs database. You can use several techniques to create full-text indexing. The technique using the SQL Server 2000 Enterprise Manager is described here.

Try It Out   Enabling and Creating a Full-Text Index

1. Open SQL Server 2000 Enterprise Manager, and in the left pane, navigate to the pubs database so that it is highlighted as shown in Figure 16-13.

2. Double-click the Full-Text Catalog icons to confirm whether or not any full-text catalogs already exist on the pubs database. The likelihood is that there are none.

3. Click the Back button (a left-pointing arrow) situated near the top-left corner of the Enterprise Manager, and click the titles table.

4. From the Tools menu, select Full-Text Indexing. The initial screen of the Full-Text Indexing Wizard, shown in Figure 16-14, is displayed.

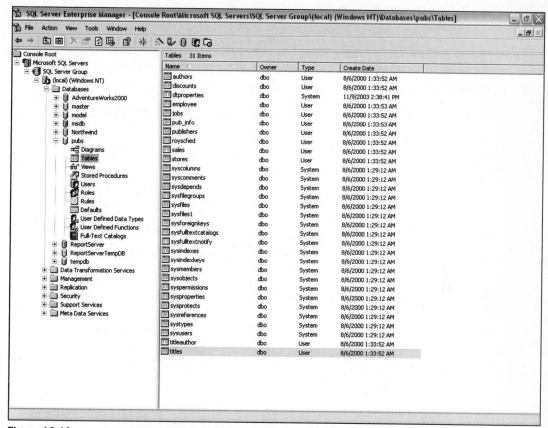

Figure 16-13

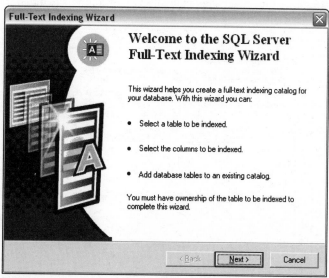

Figure 16-14

5. Click the Next button. There is only one possible index on the `titles` table, so no other option is available from the drop-down list.

Figure 16-15 shows the screen where you may be offered a choice about which column to use for indexing. (As previously noted, in the `titles` table of the `pubs` database, there is only one option.)

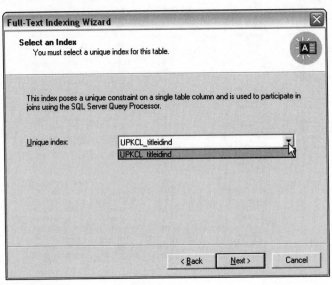

Figure 16-15

6. On the next screen, check the check boxes for the `title` and `notes` columns, and click the Next button.

Figure 16-16 shows the screen where the selection of columns to index is made.

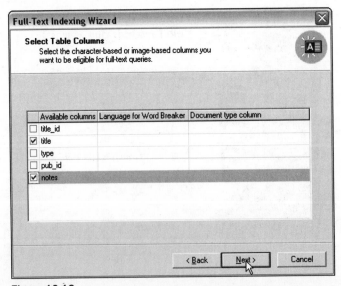

Figure 16-16

7. Choose a name for the catalog. I called the one I created on my machine Chap16.

8. Optionally, you can choose a location for the catalog that is different from the default location.

9. Click the Next button. So far, you have specified the creation of a catalog and index, and what they will contain. Now you need to specify when they are to be populated with the indexing information.

10. On the next screen, you are asked to specify options for populating the index. Click the New Catalog Schedule button. Figure 16-17 shows the appearance.

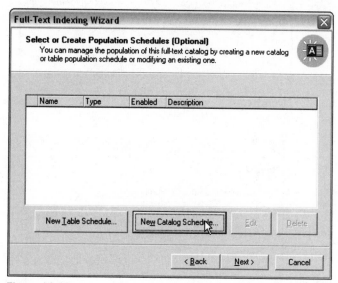

Figure 16-17

11. In the next window, specify a time to populate the index. Select the Full Population and One Time radio buttons.

12. Assuming that you want to populate the index straight away, choose an appropriate time a few minutes later than the current time. Figure 16-18 shows the appearance.

13. Click OK; then click Next; and finally, click Finish.

    You will see some messages as the Full-Text Indexing Wizard attempts to implement the choices you have made on the various screens of the wizard. Assuming that there are no errors, you should see a screen that appears similar to Figure 16-19.

    The message tells you that the index has not yet been populated. Assuming that you have opted in Step 11 to do a full population at a time only a few minutes away, you may want to wait until that time arrives and the population takes place.

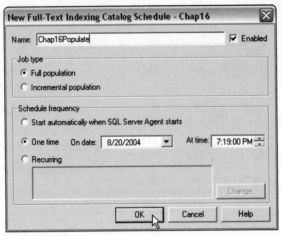

Figure 16-18

Figure 16-19

14. With the `pubs` database selected in Enterprise Manager, double-click the Full-Text Indexes option. If `Chap16` (or whatever you chose to call your index) has been created correctly, it will be displayed there. If population hasn't started, you will see `Idle` in the Status column, and the Last Population Date column will be blank.

You have the option to carry out a full population under manual control.

15. Right-click the `Chap16` catalog, and in the context menu, click the Start Full Population option, which is shown in Figure 16-20.

The `pubs` database is small, so on a fast machine, full population is almost instantaneous. Once the catalog has been populated, you will see a date and a time displayed in the Last Population Date column. Figure 16-21 shows the appearance when population has completed.

The description of the process of full-text indexing has been pretty detailed, because if you fail to set the catalog and index up correctly, you won't be able to work through the following examples. Assuming that all has gone well, you are now ready to explore full-text search functionality.

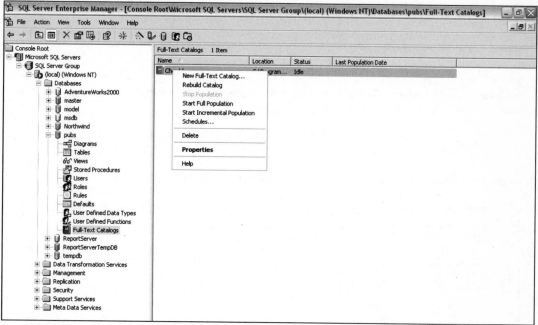

Figure 16-20

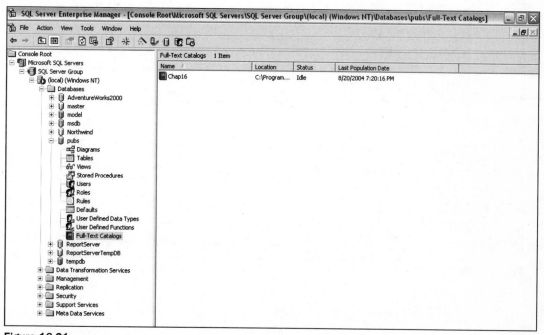

Figure 16-21

Using The CONTAINS Predicate

The CONTAINS predicate, which is part of SQL Server Full-Text Search, is used in the WHERE clause of a Transact-SQL SELECT statement.

You will use the CONTAINS predicate on the titles table, paying particular attention to the title and notes columns. If you haven't already looked at the content of those columns, you can use the following Transact-SQL code to view the relevant information:

```
USE pubs
SELECT title_id, title, notes FROM titles
```

Figure 16-22 shows the appearance after the preceding code has been run.

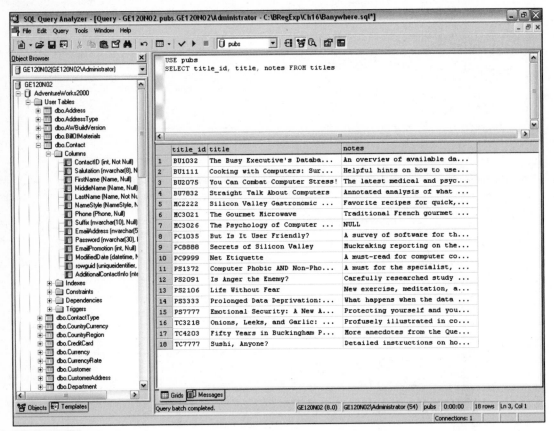

Figure 16-22

The following exercise searches for titles that contain the word `computer`.

Try It Out   The CONTAINS Predicate

1. Open Query Analyzer, if it is not already open, and type the following code into the query pane:

```
USE pubs
SELECT title_id, title, notes FROM titles
WHERE CONTAINS(title, ' "computer" ')
```

2. Press F5 or click the blue right-pointing arrow to run the code. Figure 16-23 shows the appearance after this step. Notice that now only three titles are displayed. As you see in Figure 16-23, each of the titles contains the word `computer`.

The CONTAINS predicate takes two arguments. The first argument is the name of the column of interest. The second argument is the full-text search condition. In this example, the full-text search condition is very simple, being a literal string.

You could have achieved similar, but not identical, results using LIKE, as in the following code:

```
USE pubs
SELECT title_id, title, notes FROM titles
WHERE title LIKE '%computer%'
```

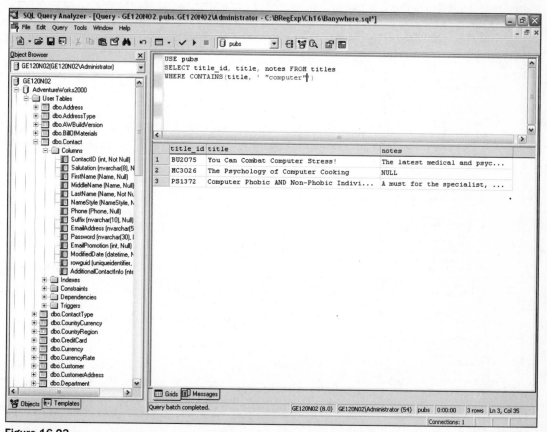

Figure 16-23

3. Type the preceding code into the query pane of the Query Analyzer, and press F5 or click the blue right-pointing arrow to run the code.

Five rows are returned. Three contain the word computer, two contain the plural form computers, and both match the pattern %computer%.

The CONTAINS predicate allows two terms to be searched for using AND logic. For example, suppose you want to find titles that contain both computer and psychology. You can use the following WHERE clause:

```
WHERE CONTAINS(title, ' "computer" AND "psychology" ')
```

4. Type the following code into the query pane:

```
USE pubs
SELECT title_id, title, notes FROM titles
WHERE CONTAINS(title, ' "computer" AND "psychology" ')
```

5. Press F5 or click the blue right-pointing arrow to run the code. Figure 16-24 shows the appearance after this step. Notice that only one row is displayed, whose title contains both the words computer and psychology.

Similarly, OR logic can be used.

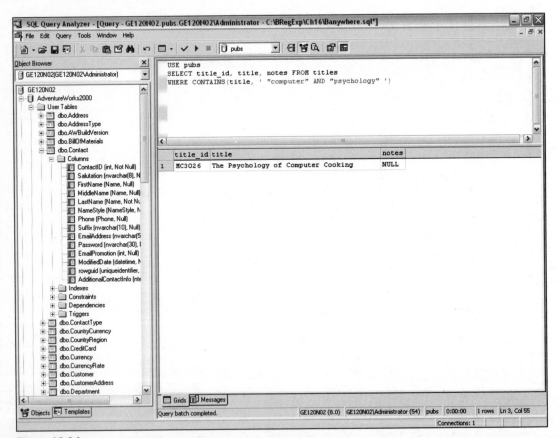

Figure 16-24

6. Type the following code into the query pane:

```
USE pubs
SELECT title_id, title, notes FROM titles
WHERE CONTAINS(title, ' "computer" OR "busy" ')
```

7. Press F5 or click the blue right-pointing arrow to run the code. The three titles that contain the word `computer` are displayed together with the one title that contains the word `busy`.

You can also match words that begin with specified characters. For example, the following `WHERE` clause will cause titles that contain words beginning with `computer` to be displayed:

```
WHERE CONTAINS(title, ' "computer*" ')
```

In the data in the `titles` table, titles containing `computer` or `computers` will be displayed.

Proximity can also be tested using the `NEAR` keyword.

8. Type the following code into the query pane:

```
USE pubs
SELECT title_id, title, notes FROM titles
WHERE CONTAINS(title, ' "computer" NEAR "phobic" ')
```

9. Press F5 or click the blue right-pointing arrow to run the code. The row that contains the title containing both `computer` and `phobic` is displayed.

Inflectional forms can be tested using the `FORMSOF` keyword. Inflectional forms include plurals.

10. Type the following code into the query pane:

```
USE pubs
SELECT title_id, title, notes FROM titles
WHERE CONTAINS(title, ' FORMSOF(INFLECTIONAL,computer)')
```

11. Press F5 or click the blue right-pointing arrow to run the code. Figure 16-25 shows the results. Notice that titles containing `computer` or `computers` are displayed.

Full-text searching has enormous power, particularly when extensive textual data is being manipulated. The `pubs` database allows limited testing only of full-text search.

How It Works

The `CONTAINS` predicate looks for whole words, `computer` in this example:

```
WHERE CONTAINS(title, ' "computer" ')
```

Combinations of words can be searched for using the `AND` keyword inside the `CONTAINS` predicate:

```
WHERE CONTAINS(title, ' "computer" AND "psychology" ')
```

The `OR` keyword provides functionality similar to alternation in standard regular expressions:

```
WHERE CONTAINS(title, ' "computer" OR "busy" ')
```

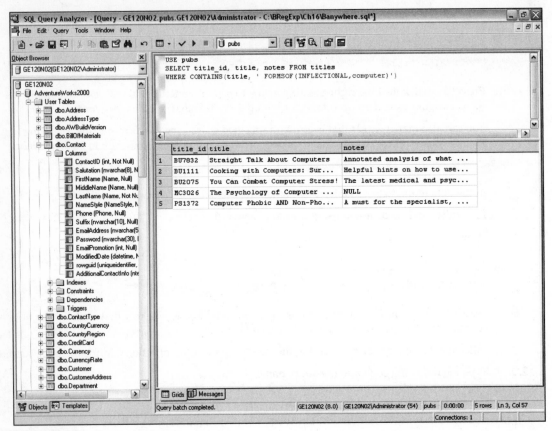

Figure 16-25

The CONTAINS predicate can match words that contain a specified character sequence using the *
metacharacter:

```
WHERE CONTAINS(title, ' "computer*" ')
```

The CONTAINS predicate allows proximity search, which has some resemblance to standard lookaround:

```
WHERE CONTAINS(title, ' "computer" NEAR "phobic" ')
```

The INFLECTIONAL option uses knowledge of word forms to find related words while specifying only
one form of the word:

```
WHERE CONTAINS(title, ' FORMSOF(INFLECTIONAL,computer)')
```

This differs from standard regular expressions where character sequences are matched with no understanding of English word forms being necessary. The INFLECTIONAL keyword operates by using such
knowledge of word forms in English.

Document Filters on Image Columns

In image columns, SQL Server 2000 can store documents of various types. For example, a number of Microsoft Word documents can be stored in such a column. SQL Server has several built-in filters that allow documents contained in image columns to be processed so that their textual content can be indexed and searched.

Storing multiple documents in an image column can be useful to search multiple documents where full-text search functionality is required.

Exercises

The following exercises test your understanding of some of the new material introduced in this chapter:

1. Using the pubs database, create Transact-SQL code that will match only the surnames Green and Greene. Hint: Use the pattern G% to find out which surnames beginning with G are in the pubs database.

2. Using the pubs database, create Transact-SQL code that will match book titles containing the character sequence data. Hint: Book titles are contained in the dbo.titles table in the pubs database.

Using Regular Expressions with MySQL

MySQL is a relational database that aims to compete with longer-established commercial relational database management systems such as IBM's DB2 and Microsoft's SQL Server. While MySQL lacks some features present in the major players in the enterprise relational database management system market, it is a powerful and flexible database management system.

MySQL has extensive regular expression support, which allows powerful and flexible searching of textual data held in a MySQL database.

In this chapter, you will learn the following:

❑ What metacharacters MySQL supports

❑ How to use the SQL metacharacter _ and %

❑ How to use the REGEXP functionality in MySQL

> The functionality described here is present in MySQL version 4.0, the version recommended for production use at the time of this writing. However, a beta of MySQL 4.1 was in development, as well as an alpha of MySQL version 5.0. The regular expression support described in this chapter is anticipated to continue in versions 4.1 and 5.0 but is subject to the usual uncertainties of software in development.

Getting Started with MySQL

The MySQL database product can be downloaded from www.mysql.com. At the time of this writing, the MySQL download page is located at http://dev.mysql.com/downloads.

If you are installing it on Windows, select the desired version (production or an alpha or beta version, according to your interests) suitable for Windows. The examples were run and tested on MySQL 4.0.

Unzip the downloaded file to a temporary directory. From the temporary directory, run the `Setup.exe` file. The examples in this chapter assume that you have installed MySQL to the `c:\mysql` directory. If you install it to some other location, you will need to adjust some of the step-by-step instructions accordingly.

On Windows XP, MySQL runs as a Windows service. Depending on whether you have had earlier versions of MySQL installed, you may find that you need to start the MySQL service manually. From the Start button, select Control Panel. Assuming that you are using the Classic configuration of Control Panel, select Administrative Tools, select Services, and then navigate to the `MySql` service. The status of the service will be displayed. If the status column for the MySql service is blank, with the MySql service highlighted, use the Start link towards the upper-left corner of the Services window to start the MySql service.

Open a command window. Assuming that you installed MySQL to `c:\mysql`, navigate to the `c:\mysql\bin` directory. At the command line, type the following:

```
mysql
```

The `mysql` utility should start. In the examples that follow in this chapter, you will issue SQL commands from the `mysql` utility's command line.

Assuming that MySQL is installed and the MySql service is running, you should see a screen that appears similar to that shown in Figure 17-1 when you type **mysql**.

Figure 17-1

The examples in this chapter will be run against a database called BRegExp. First, you need to create it.

The names of database objects in MySQL on the Windows platform are case sensitive, with the exception of the databases themselves. The reason for this is that MySQL databases are held as operating system files. The Windows operating system does not support case-sensitive filenames; therefore, MySQL, on Windows, behaves as though database names are case insensitive. On Unix and Linux, MySQL database names are case sensitive, so they behave like other MySQL database objects.

To create the BRegExp database, issue the following command at the `mysql` command-line prompt:

```
CREATE DATABASE BRegExp;
```

Be sure to include the semicolon at the end of the command, or the `mysql` utility will wait until you do. For more complex SQL commands, I find it convenient to spread the clauses across several lines, which aids readability.

Incremental versions of MySQL 4.0 have changed the default permissions on database objects from earlier versions. The intent is to improve security, but the concomitant effect is a loss of ease of use. You may find that you need to take time to study the permissions documentation of the version that you download. The instructions in this chapter assume that you have configured MySQL permissions informed by the documentation for the version you are using.

If the BRegExp database has been created successfully, you should see a screen that appears similar to that shown in Figure 17-2.

Figure 17-2

At the mysql command line, issue the following command to switch to using the BRegExp database:

```
USE BRegExp;
```

You should see a message similar to the following:

```
Database Changed
```

You can now create tables in the BRegExp database against which to run SQL queries that contain regular expressions.

Exit the mysql utility by typing **EXIT** at the mysql command line.

The first table you will add to the BRegExp database will allow you to explore some simple SQL regular expression constructs.

The SQL script, People.sql, creates a table People in the BRegExp database and then adds some sample data to the table. Setting the supplied values for the ID column to NULL allows MySQL to provide an autoincremented value for the ID column. It is shown here:

```
USE BRegExp;
CREATE TABLE People
  (ID INT PRIMARY KEY AUTO_INCREMENT,
   LastName VARCHAR(20),
   FirstName VARCHAR(20),
   DateOfBirth DATE);
INSERT INTO People
  (ID, LastName, FirstName, DateOfBirth)
  VALUES
    (NULL, 'Smith', 'George', '1959-11-11'),
    (NULL, 'Armada', 'Francis', '1971-03-08'),
    (NULL, 'Schmidt', 'Georg', '1981-10-09'),
    (NULL, 'Clingon', 'David', '1944-11-01'),
    (NULL, 'Dalek', 'Eve', '1953-04-04'),
    (NULL, 'Bush', 'Harold', '1939-11-08'),
    (NULL, 'Burns', 'Geoffrey', '1960-08-02'),
    (NULL, 'Builth', 'Wellstone', '1947-10-05'),
    (NULL, 'Thomas', 'Dylan', '1984-07-07'),
    (NULL, 'LLareggub', 'Dai', '1950-11-02'),
    (NULL, 'Barns', 'Samuel', '1944-06-01'),
    (NULL, 'Claverhouse', 'Henry', '1931-08-12'),
    (NULL, 'Litmus', 'Susie', '1954-11-03');
```

The following command assumes that you have downloaded the file to a location in the c:\BRegExp\ Ch17 directory and that you have a command window open with the current directory being the bin directory for MySQL. Issue the following command at the operating system command line:

```
mysql <c:\BRegExp\Ch17\People.sql
```

The < character indicates the location of a SQL script that the mysql utility is to execute.

If the script has executed successfully, the command prompt is displayed with no error messages showing.

You can confirm that the table has been successfully created by running the mysql utility. After the mysql utility has started, issue the following commands at the command line:

```
USE BRegExp;
```

Then issue the following:

```
SELECT * FROM People;
```

If the script has run successfully, you should see a screen similar in appearance to that shown in Figure 17-3, with the content of the People table displayed.

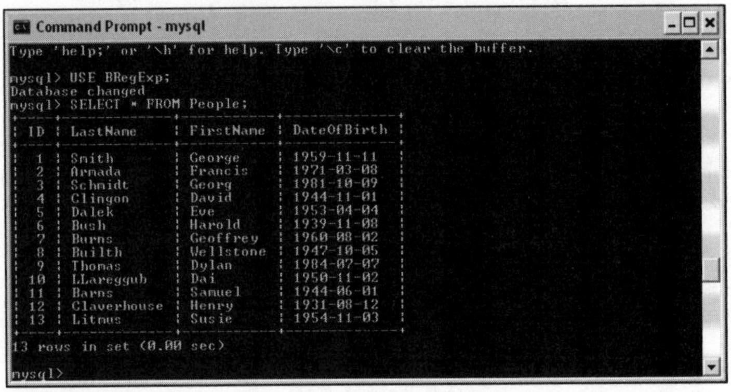

Figure 17-3

The Metacharacters MySQL Supports

MySQL supports a useful range of metacharacters, some derived from SQL syntax and some from regular expressions syntax.

The following tables summarize regular expression support in MySQL 4.0. The first table lists the SQL metacharacters that are used with the LIKE keyword. The second table lists the regular expression metacharacters that are used with the REGEXP keyword.

The following metacharacters are used with the LIKE keyword in an SQL WHERE clause.

Metacharacter	Comment
_	Matches any single character
%	Matches zero or more characters

The following metacharacters are used with the REGEXP keyword in a WHERE clause.

Metacharacter	Comment
^	The beginning-of-field (column) position metacharacter.
$	The end-of-field (column) position metacharacter.
[...]	Character class. Supported, including ranges.
[^ ...]	Negated character class.
?	Quantifier. The preceding character or group is optional.
*	Quantifier. The preceding character or group occurs zero or more times.
+	Quantifier. The preceding character or group occurs one or more times.
{n,m}	Quantifier. The preceding character or group occurs at least n times and no more than m times.
|	Supports alternation. The | metacharacter separates mutually exclusive options.

Lookahead, lookbehind, and back references are not supported in MySQL 4.0.

Using the _ and % Metacharacters

The _ and % metacharacters are SQL metacharacters. They are used in a WHERE clause with the LIKE keyword. The _ metacharacter matches a single character and is similar in meaning to the period metacharacter in standard regular expression syntax. The % metacharacter matches zero or more characters and is equivalent to .* in standard regular expression syntax.

In MySQL, matching using the _ and % metacharacters is case insensitive.

Try It Out   **The _ and % Metacharacters**

The following instructions assume that you have a command window open, with an operating system command prompt, and that the current directory is the MySQL `bin` directory.

1. Start the `mysql` utility, and at the `mysql` command line, issue the following command to switch to the `BRegExp` database:

```
USE BRegExp;
```

First, you will use the _ metacharacter to select rows where the value of the last name begins with B, has any single character, and then has the character sequence rns.

2. Type the following command at the `mysql` command prompt:

```
SELECT LastName, FirstName
FROM People
WHERE LastName LIKE 'B_rns'
;
```

Figure 17-4 shows the results after this step.

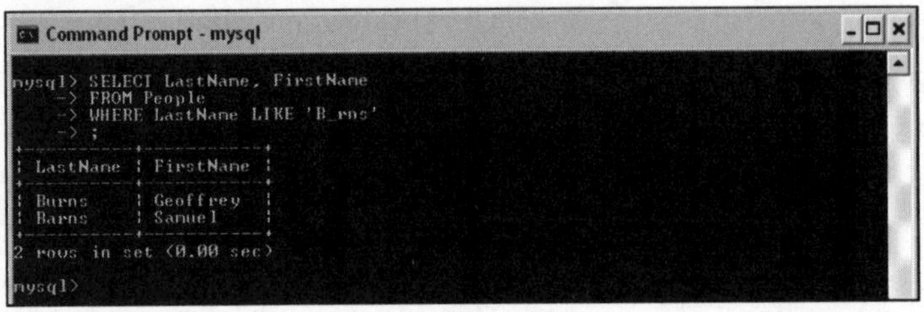

Figure 17-4

3. When the _ metacharacter is used, there are implicitly beginning-of-field and end-of-field metacharacters, too. You can see that if you modify the code to remove the final s in the pattern. At the `mysql` command prompt, type the following:

```
SELECT LastName, FirstName
FROM People
WHERE LastName LIKE 'B_rn'
;
```

As shown in Figure 17-5, the result is now an empty set. In other words, there are no matches. The MySQL regular expression engine treats the pattern B_rn as though it were ^B_rn$.

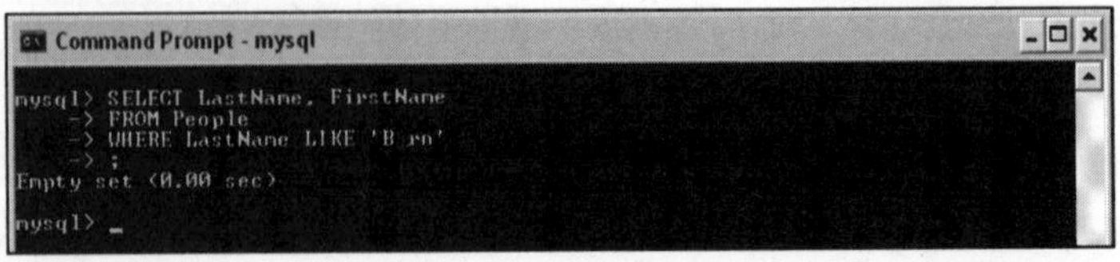

Figure 17-5

4. The % metacharacter can allow you to see only rows where the person's last name begins with the character sequence Cl. At the mysql command prompt, type the following command:

```
SELECT LastName, FirstName
FROM People
WHERE LastName LIKE 'Cl%'
;
```

As you can see in Figure 17-6, only rows where the last name begins with the character sequence Cl are returned.

Figure 17-6

5. You can also use the % metacharacter to match patterns that occur in DATE type columns. You can use this, for example, to match rows where the date of birth is in the 1950s. The pattern 195% allows you to match such dates. On this occasion, use the ORDER BY clause to put the returned rows into date order.

Type the following code at the mysql command prompt:

```
SELECT FirstName, LastName, DateOfBirth
FROM People
WHERE DateOfBirth LIKE '195%'
ORDER BY DateOfBirth
;
```

6. Inspect the results, as shown in Figure 17-7. Only people whose date of birth begins with the character sequence 195 are displayed.

Figure 17-7

Testing Matching of Literals: _ and % Metacharacters

As well as using the LIKE keyword with the _ and % metacharacters to match data already held in a database, you can directly explore whether a character sequence and a pattern matches. This allows you to test whether a desired string is matched by the pattern you are constructing.

The syntax is as follows:

```
SELECT "TheString" LIKE "The Pattern";
```

The delimiters of the string and of the pattern can be paired double quotes, as shown in the preceding code, or can be paired apostrophes, as in the following:

```
SELECT 'TheString' LIKE 'The Pattern';
```

Try It Out   **Selecting Matching of Literals**

Check whether the pattern Fr% matches the character sequence Fred.

1. Type the following at the mysql command line:

```
SELECT "Fred" LIKE "Fr%";
```

2. Type the following at the mysql command line:

```
SELECT "Bid" LIKE "B_d"
```

3. Inspect the results. Figure 17-8 shows the result after Steps 1 and 2. The figure 1 in the result indicates that there is a match, representing a Boolean value of True.

Figure 17-8

When matching is unsuccessful, a value of 0 is displayed in the results.

4. Type the following code at the mysql command line:

```
SELECT "Fred" LIKE "B_d";
```

5. Inspect the results. You can be confident that the character sequence Fred is not matched by the pattern B_d, as when a value of 0 is returned, matching has failed. If you are testing a regular expression that you expect to match, you need to do further work to get it right.

Using the REGEXP Keyword and Metacharacters

MySQL provides an additional keyword that you can use to apply regular expression functionality — the REGEXP keyword. Like the LIKE keyword, the REGEXP keyword is used in a SELECT statement's WHERE clause.

The RLIKE keyword is a synonym for REGEXP.

For the examples in this section, you need to extend the People table created earlier and create an Employees table, which includes SSN, Department, Skills, and Comments columns. The script to create and populate the Employees table is shown here:

```
USE BRegExp;
CREATE TABLE Employees
  (ID INT PRIMARY KEY AUTO_INCREMENT,
  LastName VARCHAR(20),
  FirstName VARCHAR(20),
  DateOfBirth DATE,
  SSN VARCHAR(11),
  Department VARCHAR(18),
  Skills VARCHAR(50),
  Comments VARCHAR(100));
INSERT INTO Employees
  (ID, LastName, FirstName, DateOfBirth, SSN, Department, Skills, Comments)
  VALUES
    (NULL, 'Smith', 'George', '1959-11-11', '123-45-6789', 'Data Management',
'Analysis Services, Business Intelligence, Data Transformation Services', 'Good
skills in SQL Server 2000. Can be grumpy at times.'),
    (NULL, 'Armada', 'Francis', '1971-03-08', '881-32-8913', 'Sales', NULL,
'Effective salesman. Particularly good at relating to the business needs of
clients.'),
    (NULL, 'Schmidt', 'Georg', '1981-10-09', '456-12-1234', 'Admin', NULL,
'Effective head of Admin Department. Good communicator.'),
    (NULL, 'Clingon', 'David', '1944-11-01', '234-59-3489', 'Data Management', 'DBA,
SQL DMO', 'Good database administrator. Lots of experience.'),
    (NULL, 'Dalek', 'Eve', '1953-04-04', '345-19-8822', 'Sales', NULL, 'Good sales
record. Technically informed.'),
    (NULL, 'Bush', 'Harold', '1939-11-08', '378-12-0021', 'Public Relations', NULL,
'An old hand. Handled virus crisis excellently last year.'),
    (NULL, 'Burns', 'Geoffrey', '1960-08-02', '000-12-3872', 'Development', 'C#,
.NET', 'Good .NET programmer. Can lack vision of bigger picture at times.'),
    (NULL, 'Builth', 'Wellstone', '1947-10-05', '009-348-234', 'Development',
'VB.NET, .NET, ADO.NET', 'Sound. Useful member of team.'),
    (NULL, 'Thomas', 'Dylan', '1984-07-07', '310-23-3891', 'Data Management', 'DTS',
'Great guy for those data transformation jobs.'),
    (NULL, 'LLareggub', 'Dai', '1950-11-02', '210-23-4578', 'Data Processing', 'Data
Transformation Services, SQL DMO', 'Good guy. Could be more proactive.'),
    (NULL, 'Barns', 'Samuel', '1944-06-01', '238-12-9999', 'International Sales',
'Good French and German skills.', 'Good salesman.'),
    (NULL, 'Claverhouse', 'Henry', '1931-08-12', '723-123-234', 'International
Sales', NULL, 'Semi-retired now. Still effective though.'),
    (NULL, 'Litmus', 'Susie', '1954-11-03', '123-34-4888', 'Admin', 'Good
organizer.', 'Deputy to Georg Schmidt.');
```

To run the `Employees.sql` script, at an operating system command line, type the following command:

```
mysql <C:\BRegExp\Ch17\Employees.sql
```

If the script has run successfully, the prompt should be displayed with no error messages showing.

For the quantifier examples, use the `Parts` table, which is created by the script `Parts.sql`, shown here:

```
USE BRegExp;
CREATE TABLE Parts
 (ID INT PRIMARY KEY AUTO_INCREMENT,
  PartNum VARCHAR(12),
  Description VARCHAR(50));
INSERT INTO Parts
 (ID, PartNum, Description)
  VALUES
   (NULL, 'ABC123', 'A basic widget.'),
   (NULL, 'AAC123', 'A special widget.'),
   (NULL, 'ABBC1234', 'A green widget.'),
   (NULL, 'AAAAAAC2345', 'A purple thing.'),
   (NULL, 'AAAAADD8899', 'A tartan widget'),
   (NULL, 'BC123', 'A thin widget'),
   (NULL, 'ART987', 'An artistic widget'),
   (NULL, 'XYZ345', 'A recent widget'),
   (NULL, 'AB123', 'A super widget'),
   (NULL, 'AC123', 'An exercise widget'),
   (NULL, 'ABCD234567', 'A long widget'),
   (NULL, 'STUV234', 'A late widget'),
   (NULL, 'VWX7656', 'An automatic widget'),
   (NULL, 'NOP278', 'An opinionated widget'),
   (NULL, 'A2345', 'An numeric widget');
```

At the operating system command line, with the current directory being the MySQL `bin` directory, enter the following command:

```
mysql <C:\BRegExp\Ch17\Parts.sql
```

If the script runs without error messages, it is likely that it has run successfully. However, it makes sense to test that the `Employees` and `Parts` tables have been created and populated successfully.

Run the `mysql` utility. At the `mysql` prompt, type the following command to switch to the `BRegExp` database, which is where the `Employees` and `Parts` tables should have been created:

```
USE BRegExp;
```

Because of the number of columns in the `Employees` table and the length of the Skills and Comments columns, you will display the data in two parts. At the `mysql` command prompt, type the following:

```
SELECT ID, LastName, FirstName, DateOfBirth
FROM Employees
;
```

If the table has been created correctly, 13 rows should be displayed with data in all columns, including the automatically numbered ID column. Figure 17-9 shows the result you should see.

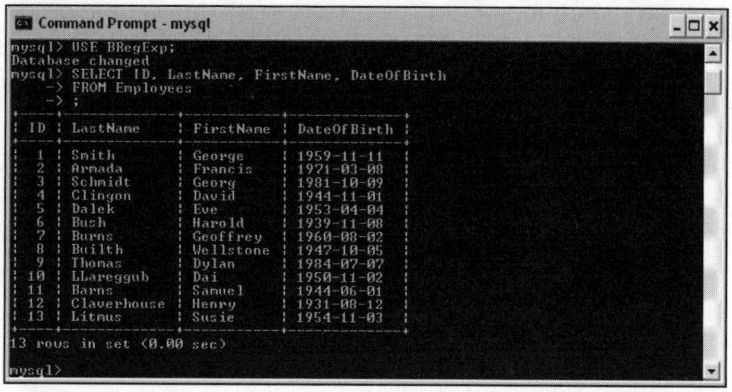

Figure 17-9

Run the following commands to test the other columns. First,

```
SELECT ID, SSN, Department, Skills
FROM Employees
;
```

and then:

```
SELECT ID, Comments
FROM Employees
;
```

Because of the length of the data in the Skills and Employees columns, some of the data will wrap from one line to another, resulting in an untidy appearance. You will have to scroll up a little to confirm that these columns have been correctly populated.

To confirm that the Parts table has been populated correctly, type the following command:

```
SELECT *
FROM Parts
;
```

You don't need to switch databases because, assuming that you have run the code to test the Employees table, you are already using the BRegExp database. Figure 17-10 shows the result if the Parts table has been correctly populated.

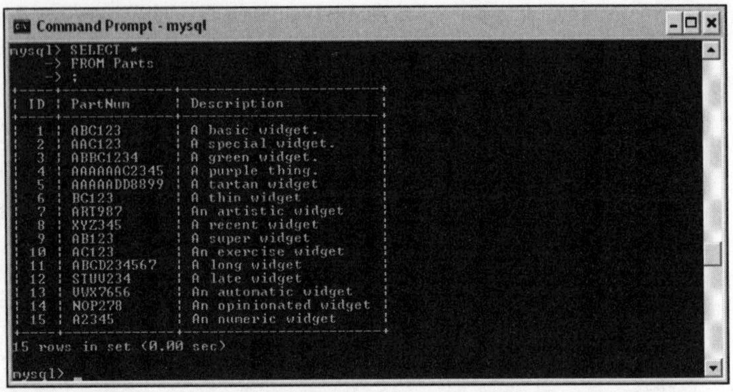

Figure 17-10

Using Positional Metacharacters

MySQL supports both the beginning-of-field (column) metacharacter, ^, and the end-of-field metacharacter, $. If these positional metacharacters are not included in a pattern, the pattern will match if a relevant character sequence occurs anywhere in the field specified in the WHERE clause.

For the following exercise, use the data in the Employees table.

Try It Out   **Positional Metacharacters**

First, you will run code with no positional metacharacters.

1.   At the mysql command prompt, type the following command:

```
USE BRegExp;
```

2.   Then type the following command:

```
SELECT ID, LastName, FirstName, Skills
FROM Employees
WHERE Skills REGEXP 'Data'
;
```

Rows will be displayed where the Skills column includes the character sequence Data. Figure 17-11 shows the result after Step 2. Two rows are displayed: the data for George Smith and Dai LLareggub.

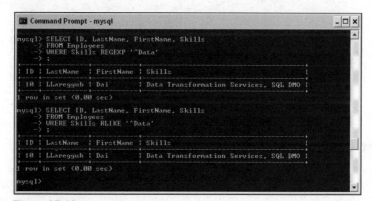

Figure 17-11

Notice that only the data for Dai Llareggub has the character sequence Data at the beginning of the field. So if you add the positional metacharacter ^ to the pattern, only that row should be displayed.

3. Type the following SQL code at the mysql command line:

```
SELECT ID, LastName, FirstName, Skills
FROM Employees
WHERE Skills REGEXP '^Data'
;
```

Notice in Figure 17-12 that only one row of data, the data for Dai Llareggub, is displayed. The data for George Smith is no longer displayed, because the beginning-of-field position specified by the ^ metacharacter is not followed by the character sequence Data.

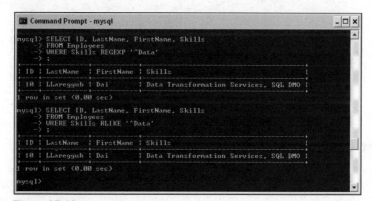

Figure 17-12

4. Next, you will demonstrate that the RLIKE keyword works in the same way as the REGEXP keyword. Type the following command at the mysql command line:

```
SELECT ID, LastName, FirstName, Skills
FROM Employees
WHERE Skills RLIKE '^Data'
;
```

The result from Step 4 is also displayed in Figure 17-12.

5. The $ metacharacter works as the end-of-field (column) metacharacter. You will first attempt to match the character sequence Tra without the $ metacharacter. So you are attempting to match all rows that contain the character sequence Tra anywhere in the Skills column.

Type the following command at the mysql command prompt:

```
SELECT ID, LastName, FirstName, Skills
FROM Employees
WHERE Skills REGEXP 'Tra'
;
```

Two rows are displayed, those for George Smith and Dai LLareggub. When you include the $ metacharacter in the pattern, only one row should be displayed: the row of data for George Smith.

6. Type the following command at the mysql command prompt:

```
SELECT ID, LastName, FirstName, Skills
FROM Employees
WHERE Skills REGEXP 'Tra$'
;
```

Because only the data for George Smith has the character sequence Tra as its final characters, only that row is displayed, as shown in Figure 17-13.

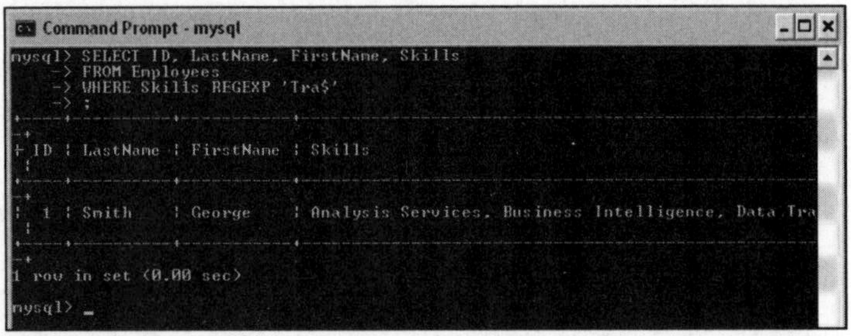

Figure 17-13

Using Character Classes

MySQL supports character classes and negated character classes. The syntax is standard. The pattern [ABCDE] specifies a character class containing the uppercase alphabetic characters A, B, C, D, and E. The character class [A-E] has the same meaning but is expressed using a character class range.

Try It Out   Using Character Classes

This example uses the Parts table.

1. Type the following command at the mysql command prompt:

```
USE BRegExp;
```

2. Type the following command to select parts that begin with A, then B, C, or D:

```
SELECT ID, PartNum, Description
FROM Parts
WHERE PartNum REGEXP 'A[ABCD]'
;
```

Figure 17-14 shows the appearance after Step 2. Eight rows are returned in the results. You will see that each part number begins with the uppercase A and is followed by A, B, C, or D.

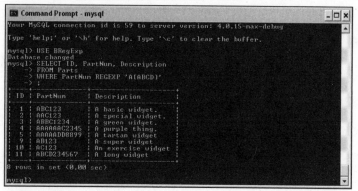

Figure 17-14

3. Character ranges are supported in MySQL. So try using a character class with the range pattern [A-D] to return the same results as in Step 2.

Type the following command at the mysql command prompt:

```
SELECT ID, PartNum, Description
FROM Parts
WHERE PartNum REGEXP 'A[A-D]'
;
```

The results from the preceding code are the same as those shown in Figure 17-14.

4. Negated character classes are also supported. So you can negate the preceding character class to return rows that begin with A and that have a second character that does not match the pattern [A-D].

Type the following SQL code at the mysql command prompt:

```
SELECT ID, PartNum, Description
FROM Parts
WHERE PartNum REGEXP 'A[^A-D]'
;
```

5. Inspect the results, comparing them to the results returned from the preceding character classes. Figure 17-15 shows the appearance after the preceding code has been run. Notice that the rows returned were not returned by code that contained the positive character classes [ABCD] or [A-D].

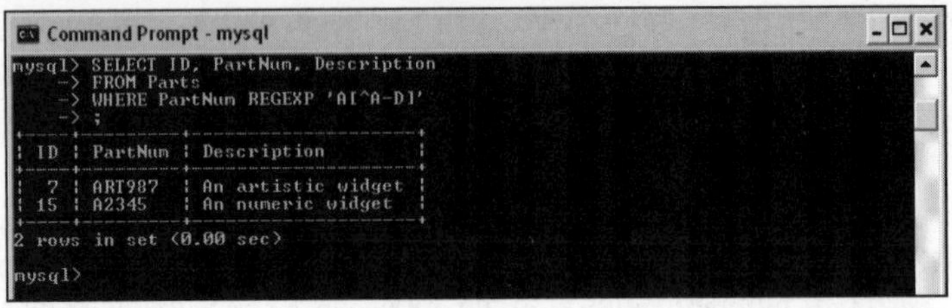

Figure 17-15

Quantifiers

MySQL supports a full range of quantifiers, including the ?, *, and + metacharacters and the {n,m} notation.

Try It Out   Quantifiers in MySQL

For this exercise, use the `Parts` table.

The ? metacharacter matches an optional preceding character or group. The * metacharacter matches zero or more occurrences of the preceding character or group. The + metacharacter matches one or more occurrences of the preceding character or group.

1.   Start the `mysql` utility, and type the following command to switch to the `BRegExp` database:

```
USE BRegExp;
```

2.   Type the following command at the `mysql` command line:

```
SELECT ID, PartNum, Description
FROM Parts
WHERE PartNum REGEXP '^AA?'
;
```

Figure 17-16 shows the result after Step 2. The pattern ^AA? means A as the first character followed by an optional A. In other words, any part number that begins with A will match.

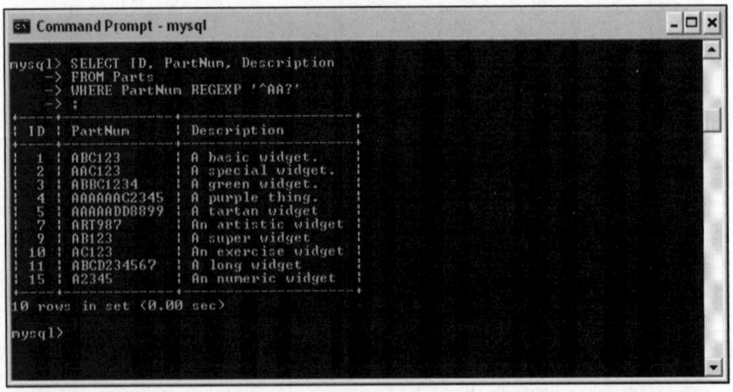

Figure 17-16

408

3. The pattern ^AA* will match zero or more occurrences of the second A. This will return the same rows as the pattern ^AA?, because that latter pattern is the same as the zero or one matches of ^AA*.

Type the following pattern at the mysql command line to confirm the preceding statement:

```
SELECT ID, PartNum, Description
FROM Parts
WHERE PartNum REGEXP '^AA*'
;
```

4. Inspect the results, and compare with those shown in Figure 17-16. The results are the same. However, if you alter the pattern to ^AA+ you now specify one or more occurrences of A after the initial A. Part numbers that do not have A as the second character will no longer match.

5. Type the following pattern at the mysql command line:

```
SELECT ID, PartNum, Description
FROM Parts
WHERE PartNum REGEXP '^AA+'
;
```

6. Inspect the results, and compare them with the results after Step 4. Figure 17-17 shows the result after Step 5. Now only three rows match. Notice that all rows that previously matched but that have a second character that is not A no longer match. The pattern AA+ means that there must be at least one A after the initial A.

Figure 17-17

The full range of quantifier syntax using the {n,m} syntax is supported in MySQL. The {0,} syntax produces the same results as the * quantifier, which is not surprising, because the meanings are identical. Similarly, the pattern ^AA{1,} returns the same results as the pattern ^AA+. Again, this is not surprising, because A{1,} and A+ mean the same.

7. The {n,m} syntax also works when both n and m are specified. To practice, specify between one and three occurrences of A after the initial A. Type the following at the mysql command line:

```
SELECT ID, PartNum, Description
FROM Parts
WHERE PartNum REGEXP '^AA{1,3}'
;
```

8. Inspect the results returned, and compare them to those from earlier examples.

Three rows are returned. They are the same as those shown in Figure 17-17. This is so because you are matching only a character sequence for which you don't specify what comes next. Therefore, if four A characters occur after the initial A, the upper limit of three still matches. The existence of a fourth A doesn't stop three from matching.

409

Social Security Number Example

U.S. Social Security numbers (SSNs) are a classic example of the use of regular expressions for pattern matching. The history of U.S. SSNs is complex. Living people may have had their SSN allocated many years before the current system was implemented.

One relatively simple pattern that you can use to match an SSN is as follows:

```
[0-9]{3}-[0-9]{2}-[0-9]{4}
```

MySQL does not support the \d metacharacter to match numeric digits, so you need to use the character class [0-9] instead.

You can use that pattern to see if all employee records contain a valid Social Security number.

Try It Out   **Matching Social Security Numbers**

These instructions assume that the mysql utility is running and that BRegExp is the current database.

1. At the mysql command prompt, type the following command:

```
SELECT ID, LastName, FirstName, SSN
FROM Employees
WHERE SSN REGEXP '^[0-9]{3}-[0-9]{2}-[0-9]{4}$'
;
```

Because you want to match only if the whole field is a valid SSN, you wrap the pattern shown earlier inside the ^ and $ metacharacters.

2. Inspect the results to identify ID numbers not displayed. Figure 17-18 shows that each row's displayed value in the SSN column conforms to the pattern three digits, a hyphen, two digits, a hyphen, and four digits. So you can confirm that the pattern will match valid SSNs.

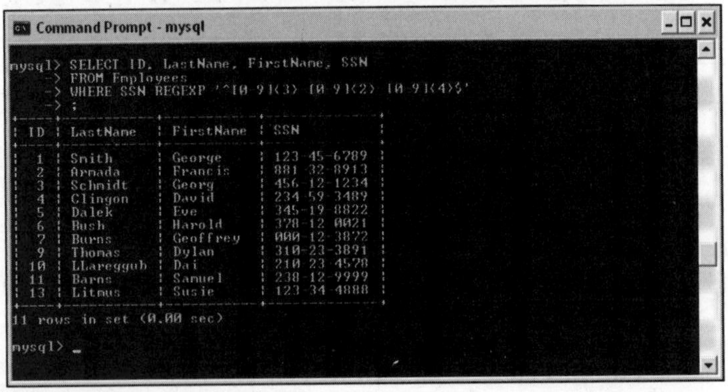

Figure 17-18

The NOT keyword is not supported in association with the REGEXP keyword; therefore, you can't directly identify rows with invalid values in the SSN column.

The lack of support for lookahead and lookbehind limits further refinement of the SSN pattern in MySQL. If lookahead were supported, you could specify, by syntax such as `^(?!000)`, which is not supported in MySQL, that the first three numeric digits of the SSN couldn't be `000`. The official description of the SSN located at `www.ssa.gov/foia/stateweb.html` indicates that the first three digits of a valid SSN will never be `000`. As indicated at the same URL, more area numbers (the first three digits) are likely to be put into use in the near future. If you wish to create a highly specific pattern to match SSNs, you need to monitor that URL to see what the current position is.

Exercises

1. Write a line of SQL code to determine whether the pattern `195%` matches the date `1950-01-01`.

2. Write some SQL code to display employees who have .NET skills. Display the ID, last name, and first name, together with the description of the employee's skills.

Regular Expressions and Microsoft Access

Microsoft Access has provided a popular database management system for small businesses and other users for over a decade.

A fundamental task when using Access is the retrieval of data that is of interest to the user. With small quantities of data, it may be acceptable to return all data and allow the user to scan the data by eye for records that are of interest. However, once the volume of data increases much beyond the trivial, it is more efficient and more reliable to rely on Access's queries, which include several wildcards (regular expression–like metacharacters) to select the desired data for display. Access wildcards can assist in filtering data retrieved by a query and improve the value of Access in many routine data retrieval uses for business.

In this chapter, you will learn the following:

❑ The metacharacters supported in Access

❑ How to use those metacharacters in Access queries

❑ How to create select queries and parameter queries to apply the Access wildcards

To use wildcards in Access, you will need to understand at least a little about each of these aspects. Therefore, the presentation of material in this chapter isn't entirely linear.

The Interface to Metacharacters in Microsoft Access

A principal use of wildcards in Access is in queries to match desired patterns of text. Options for using wildcards include in hard-wired queries where a specific query needs to be run frequently and in parameter queries where the user can enter a parameter that is used in the wildcard search he or she runs.

This chapter explores both approaches and uses them to show examples of the various metacharacters that can be used in Access.

The examples make use of an `AuctionPurchases` sample database where a book collector with very eclectic tastes records his purchases from a fictional online auction house called dBeach. Most of the attention in the worked examples will focus on the ItemTitle and ItemAuthor fields, which, respectively, contain information about the title and author(s) of the purchased books. The book titles and their author(s) are real. All other aspects of the database are fictional, including dates and prices.

> The examples in this chapter have been tested on Microsoft Access 2003. The interface shown in the examples is also the Access 2003 interface. Other versions of Access will appear similar but may not be identical.

Creating a Hard-Wired Query

This example assumes that you want to find item authors whose name includes the character sequence `Hill` or `hill`. Because matching in Access is case insensitive, either pattern will do for attempted literal matching.

The instructions given next are for Access 2003. Earlier versions may vary slightly in the detail of the interface.

Try It Out   Creating a Hard-Wired Query

1. Open Access 2003, and choose the Open option from the File menu.

2. Navigate to `C:\BRegExp\Ch18`, select the `AuctionPurchases.mdb` database, and click the OK button. If you downloaded the sample database to another location, navigate to the relevant directory.

   Figure 18-1 shows the appearance just before the OK button is clicked in Step 2.

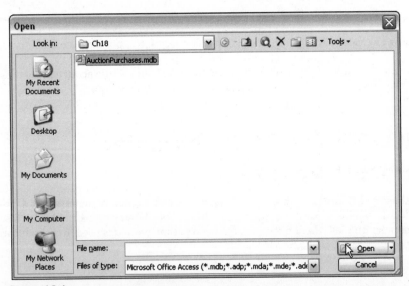

Figure 18-1

3. The `AuctionPurchases` sample database will open. In the Database Object window (see Figure 18-2), click Queries in the left pane, and in the right pane, you will see options to create a query in Design View and to create a query using a wizard. For your purposes here, the Design View option is more useful.

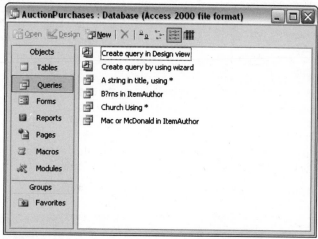

Figure 18-2

4. Double-click the Create Query in Design View option.

5. The Design View, including the Show Table dialog box (shown in Figure 18-3), will open. Highlight the `dBeachPurchases` table, and click the Add button.

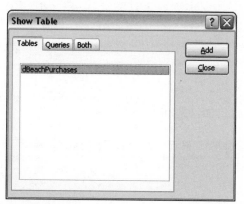

Figure 18-3

6. Click the Close button to hide the Show Table dialog box. The `dBeachPurchases` table should be displayed in the upper part of the design window shown in Figure 18-4. This allows you to add columns from the `dBeachPurchases` table in the lower part of the design window.

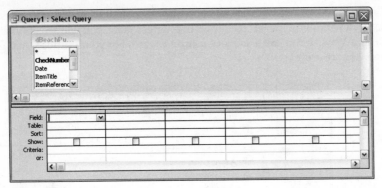

Figure 18-4

7. Click in the leftmost cell in the Field row of the grid in the lower part of the design window. A drop-down list is displayed. Select ItemTitle from the options offered.

    Figure 18-5 shows the appearance while selecting a column in Step 7.

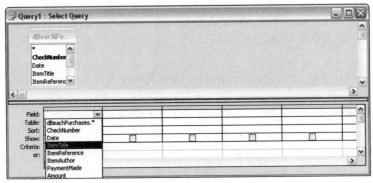

Figure 18-5

8. In the next column, select the ItemAuthor column from the options offered. Figure 18-6 shows the appearance while selecting ItemAuthor.

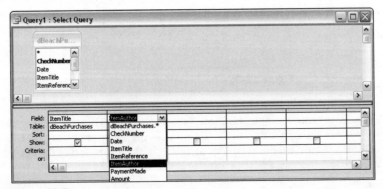

Figure 18-6

9. Switch to SQL View, using the menu shown in Figure 18-7. The menu is above and to the left of the design window. If it's not visible, you may need to display the Query Design toolbar. To do that, go to the View menu, select Toolbars, and ensure that the Query Design Toolbar option is checked.

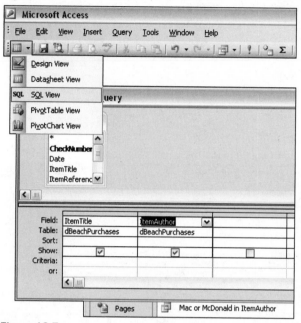

Figure 18-7

As you can see in Figure 18-8, the SQL code for a simple SELECT statement has been created for you.

The two selections that you made in Steps 7 and 8 produced the following SQL code:

```
SELECT dBeachPurchases.ItemTitle, dBeachPurchases.ItemAuthor
FROM dBeachPurchases;
```

If you are proficient in SQL code, you can simply add a WHERE clause to display only the desired rows, as follows:

```
SELECT dBeachPurchases.ItemTitle, dBeachPurchases.ItemAuthor
FROM dBeachPurchases
WHERE dBeachPurchases.ItemTitle LIKE "*Hill*";
```

Sometimes, Access will add extra quotes or parentheses if you write SQL code. Sometimes, they have no effect on what the query does. Occasionally, they appear to significantly change the results that are returned.

However, for the purposes of this example, you will add the regular expression filtering in the design window.

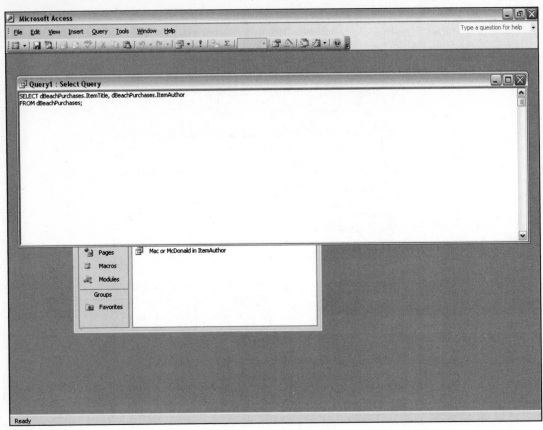

Figure 18-8

10.   Type the following in the Criteria row in the design window:

```
Like "*Hill*"
```

The * metacharacter matches zero or more characters. Therefore, the pattern *Hill* will match zero or more characters occurring before the character sequence Hill (any case combination, because the default matching is case insensitive) and any number of characters occurring after the character sequence Hill. Figure 18-9 shows the result.

11.   Save the query. Name it Hill in ItemTitle.

12.   Open the SQL View, and inspect the code that has been created by the Access designer:

```
SELECT dBeachPurchases.ItemTitle, dBeachPurchases.ItemAuthor
FROM dBeachPurchases
WHERE (((dBeachPurchases.ItemTitle) Like "*Hill*"));
```

Notice how Access adds parentheses, which, to my eye at least, seem unnecessary.

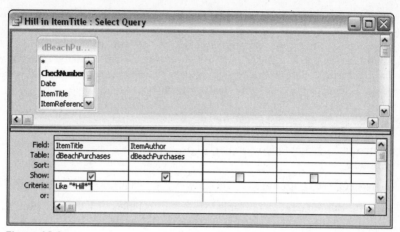

Figure 18-9

13. Close the query.

14. From the database objects window, double-click Hill in ItemTitle. The results shown in Figure 18-10 should be displayed.

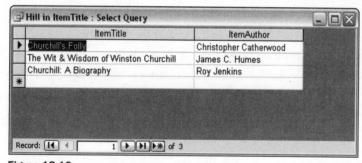

Figure 18-10

Each of the three rows of data displayed contains the character sequence hill. In the sample data, each of the occurrences of hill is part of the character sequences Churchill (twice) or Churchill's. If you create a similar query but specify the LIKE "*Hill*" criterion for the ItemAuthor column, you will see two rows returned with the character sequence Hill as the word Hill and Hills. The query Hill in ItemAuthor is provided in the sample database to allow you to test this.

Creating a Parameter Query

In some settings a hard-wired query as specified in the preceding section can be useful, particularly if it has a little more to it than the simple example just described. For example, a query that retrieves sales data for a particular period is likely to be run many times.

However, rather than hard-wiring the literal part of the regular expression pattern, you can achieve much more flexibility if you allow the user to specify the character sequence that is being searched for. Most of the steps required to create a parameter query are similar to those needed to create a hard-wired query, as described in the preceding section. The similar parts of the following example will, therefore, be described fairly sparsely. Refer to the preceding section, as necessary, for further detail and figures to illustrate what you can expect to see while creating the query.

Try It Out Creating a Parameter Query

1. Open Access, highlight Queries in the left pane of the database objects window, and click the New button.

2. In the New Query window, select Design View, and click OK

3. Click on the dBeachPurchases table to select it, and then click the Add button.

4. Click the Close button.

5. In the leftmost column, select ItemTitle in the Field row, and in the Criteria row, type the following code:

```
LIKE "*" & [Enter a character sequence to search for:] & "*"
```

   Be careful not to enclose the middle part inside paired quotes. In other words, don't put quotation marks outside the square brackets. If you insert quotation marks there, you won't create a parameter query.

6. In the next column, select ItemAuthor in the Field row.

7. Save the query, naming the query Find a sequence in ItemTitle, and close the query.

8. From the database objects window, select Queries in the left pane, and double-click the Find a sequence in ItemTitle query.

   The Enter Parameter Value dialog box should open and should look like the one shown in Figure 18-11.

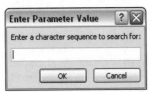

Figure 18-11

9. Type **Love** in the text box in the Enter Parameter Value window. Figure 18-12 shows the appearance after this step. The titles returned include the word Love and Lovers.

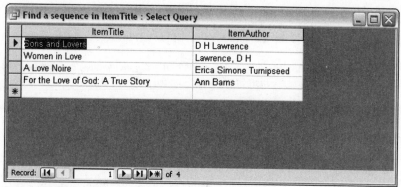

Figure 18-12

10. Double-click the Find a sequence in ItemTitle query, and in the Enter Parameter Value dialog box, enter the character sequence **Men**. Figure 18-13 shows the results.

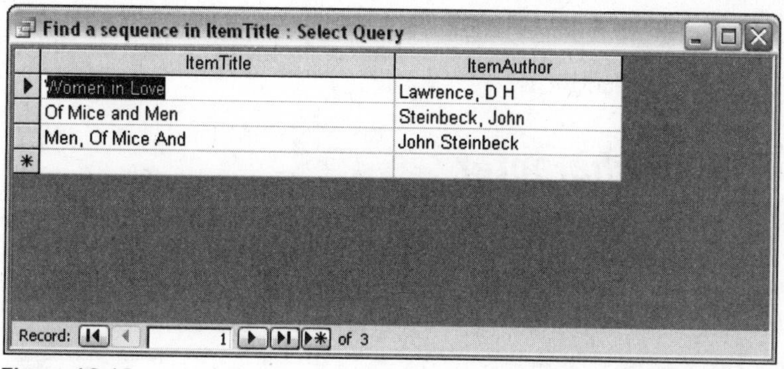

Figure 18-13

Notice in the figure that you match two different rows, each of which refers to the title Of Mice and Men, but which record that title in two different ways. The pattern *Men*, which is the pattern created behind the scenes, will match the character sequence Men wherever it occurs in an ItemTitle field, including as part of the word women in one of the displayed results.

The Metacharacters Supported in Access

Access has a fairly limited range of regular expression support compared to a database management system like MySQL. However, it does provide useful filtering functionality when carrying out queries.

The following table summarizes the metacharacters supported in Access 2003.

If you are accessing data in Access using ADO, a different set of metacharacters, not covered in detail in this chapter, is available. You use % instead of * and _ instead of ?.

Metacharacter	Description
?	Matches a single character
*	Matches zero or more characters
#	Matches any single numeric digit
[...]	Matches any single character among those listed inside the square brackets
[! ...]	Matches any single character *not* among those listed inside the square brackets

The examples that are described and worked through in the following sections all use the `AuctionPurchases.mdb` database.

Using the ? Metacharacter

The ? metacharacter matches a single character.

The following example creates a query that displays rows where the author-name contains H followed by any character followed by the character sequence 11. The pattern to be used in the query is H?11.

Try It Out   **Using the ? Metacharacter**

1. Open Access, highlight Queries in the left pane of the database objects window, and click the New button.

2. In the New Query window, select Design View, and click OK

3. Click the dBeachPurchases table to select it, and then click the Add button.

4. Click the Close button.

5. In the leftmost column, select ItemTitle in the Field row.

6. In the next column, select ItemAuthor in the Field row.

7. In the Criteria row, type the following code:

```
Like "*H?11*"
```

8. Save and close the query you have just created, naming it `Find H?ll in ItemAuthor`.

9. Double-click `Find H?ll in ItemAuthor` to run the query.

Figure 18-14 shows the results. Notice that the names `Heller`, `Hill`, `Hills`, and `Hall` match the pattern `*H?ll*`, because each of those author names contains an `H` character followed by some character (which the `?` metacharacter matches), followed by the character sequence `ll`. The presence of the `*` metacharacter at both the beginning and the end of the pattern specifies that the matching four-character sequences can be preceded or followed by any sequence of characters or none at all.

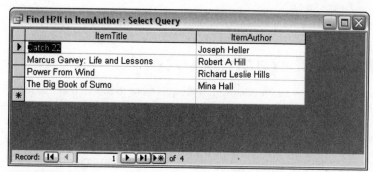

Figure 18-14

Using the * Metacharacter

The `*` metacharacter matches zero or more characters.

The query `Find a sequence in ItemAuthor` is a parameter query that allows the user to enter a string that matches all or part of an author name. The construction of the query is very similar to the parameter query `Find a sequence in ItemTitle` described in detail earlier in this chapter, so the step-by-step creation is not described here for reasons of space.

In the second column from the left in the design window, the ItemAuthor column should be selected, and the following code should be entered in the Criteria row:

```
Like "*" & [Enter a character sequence:] & "*"
```

The regular expression pattern is constructed dynamically after the user enters a character sequence in the text box of the Enter Parameter Value dialog box. So if the user enters the character sequence `Hill`, the pattern becomes `*Hill*`. Or if the user enters the character sequence `Mark`, the pattern becomes `*Mark*`.

Double-click the `Find a sequence in ItemAuthor` query. Enter the character sequence **Mark** in the text box in the Enter Parameter Value dialog box. The results displayed are shown in Figure 18-15.

Each of the returned rows of data contains the character sequence `Mark` in the ItemAuthor column. As it happens, both results consist of the character sequence `Mark Twain`. So the first `*` metacharacter in the pattern `*Mark*` matches exactly zero characters, and the second `*` metacharacter matches the character sequence of space character followed by `Twain`.

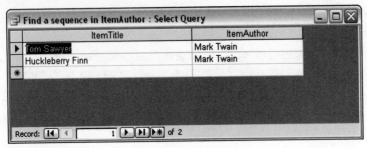

Figure 18-15

Using the # Metacharacter

The # metacharacter matches a numeric digit. It is equivalent to the \d metacharacter in more standard regular expression syntax.

The query Number in ItemTitle demonstrates how the # metacharacter can be used.

Try It Out   Matching a Numeric Digit

1.   Open Access, and open the AuctionPurchases.mdb database.

2.   In the database objects window, select Queries, and click the New button.

3.   Select the dBeachPurchases table, click the Add button, and then click the Close button.

4.   In the leftmost column in the design window, select ItemTitle in the Field row.

5.   In the Criteria row in that column, enter the following code:

```
LIKE "*#*"
```

The # metacharacter will match in any ItemTitle column if a numeric digit is present.

6.   In the next column, select ItemAuthor in the Field row, and save the query as Number in ItemTitle.

7.   Close the query in design view. Double-click the Number in ItemTitle query, and inspect the results, as shown in Figure 18-16.

Notice that the title of each row returned contains one (or more) numeric digits. Because there is only one numeric digit in the pattern *#*, there needs to be only one numeric digit to achieve a successful match and, therefore, for the row to be displayed.

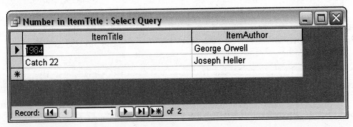

Figure 18-16

Using the # Character with Date/Time Data

The # character has another use in Access queries: to match values of Date/Time. Strictly speaking, this isn't using # as a regular expression character. But you may, nevertheless, find the technique useful when matching dates of interest.

Try It Out   Using the # Character with Date/Time Data

1. Open Access, and open the `AuctionPurchases.mdb` database.

2. In the database objects window, select Queries in the left pane, and click the New button.

3. In the Show Table dialog box, select the `dBeachPurchases` table, and click the Add button.

4. In the left column, select the ItemTitle column in the Field row of the grid.

5. In the next column, select the ItemAuthor column.

6. In the next column, select the Date column.

7. In the Criteria row of that column, enter the following code:

```
Between #4/1/2003# And #4/30/2003#
```

The preceding code assumes U.S.-style dates — that is, month followed by day of the month followed by year. That is simply how Access works; it assumes MM/DD/YYYY format irrespective of locale settings.

8. Save the query as `April 2003 Purchases`, and close the query in design view.

9. Double-click `April 2003 Purchases` in the database objects window, and inspect the results. Figure 18-17 shows the items purchased in April 2003. From the Date column, you can confirm that only purchases made in April 2003 are displayed.

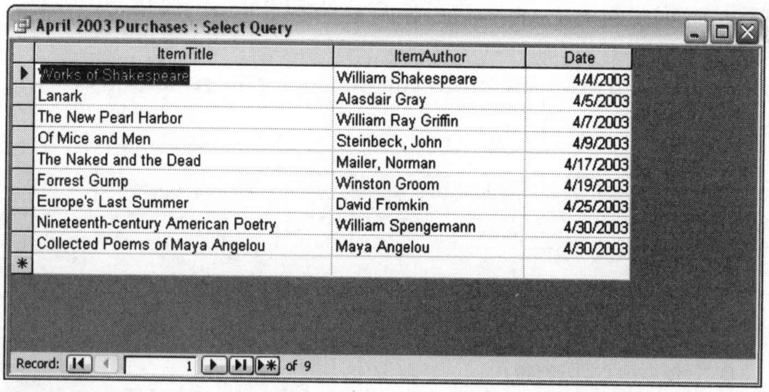

ItemTitle	ItemAuthor	Date
Works of Shakespeare	William Shakespeare	4/4/2003
Lanark	Alasdair Gray	4/5/2003
The New Pearl Harbor	William Ray Griffin	4/7/2003
Of Mice and Men	Steinbeck, John	4/9/2003
The Naked and the Dead	Mailer, Norman	4/17/2003
Forrest Gump	Winston Groom	4/19/2003
Europe's Last Summer	David Fromkin	4/25/2003
Nineteenth-century American Poetry	William Spengemann	4/30/2003
Collected Poems of Maya Angelou	Maya Angelou	4/30/2003

Record: 1 of 9

Figure 18-17

Using Character Classes in Access

Microsoft Access supports character classes, including ranges and negated character classes. The normal syntax of using square brackets to enclose the character class is used in Access. However, negated character classes are indicated by an exclamation mark following the first square bracket. So if you don't want to match the characters N through Z, the negated character class [!N-Z] would be an appropriate pattern. Outside the square brackets that contain a character class, the exclamation mark is simply a literal character.

> **This book uses the term** *character class* **to refer to the collection of characters contained in square brackets. You will also see the term** *character list* **used when referring to character classes in Access.**

Try It Out   Using a Positive Character Class

1. Open the `AuctionPurchases.mdb` database in Access, and select Queries in the left pane of the database objects window.

2. Click the New button, and select Design View from the options offered. Select dBeachPurchases.

3. In the left column, select ItemTitle.

4. In the Criteria row, enter the following code:

```
LIKE "[A-D]*"
```

5. In the next column, select ItemAuthor.

6. Save the query as Titles Beginning A to D, and close the query.

7. Double-click Titles Beginning A to D in the Queries pane to run the query, and inspect the results, as shown in Figure 18-18. Notice that all of the titles displayed have their initial character in the range A through D.

   Adding an ORDER BY clause can aid you in reading the results by ensuring that data is ordered in a specified way.

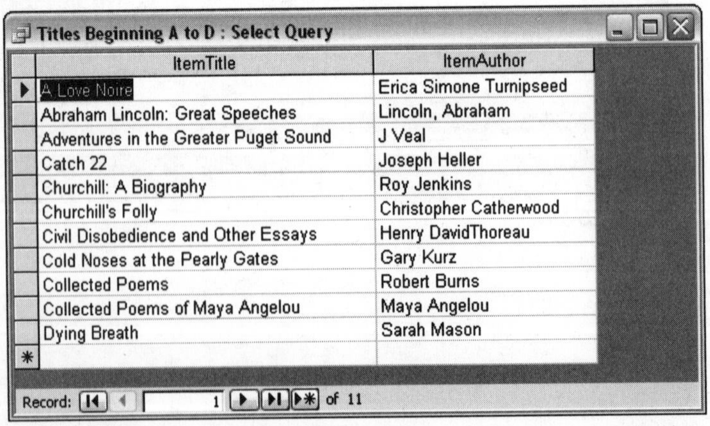

ItemTitle	ItemAuthor
A Love Noire	Erica Simone Turnipseed
Abraham Lincoln: Great Speeches	Lincoln, Abraham
Adventures in the Greater Puget Sound	J Veal
Catch 22	Joseph Heller
Churchill: A Biography	Roy Jenkins
Churchill's Folly	Christopher Catherwood
Civil Disobedience and Other Essays	Henry DavidThoreau
Cold Noses at the Pearly Gates	Gary Kurz
Collected Poems	Robert Burns
Collected Poems of Maya Angelou	Maya Angelou
Dying Breath	Sarah Mason

Record: 1 of 11

Figure 18-18

8. Right-click `Titles Beginning A to D`, and select the Design View option in the context menu.

9. When the design view window opens, use the drop-down list in the toolbar to switch to SQL View. The code will look like this:

```
SELECT dBeachPurchases.ItemTitle, dBeachPurchases.ItemAuthor
FROM dBeachPurchases
WHERE (((dBeachPurchases.ItemTitle) Like "[A-D]*"));
```

10. Immediately before the final semicolon of the SQL code, insert the following code:

```
ORDER BY dBeachPurchases.ItemTitle
```

The completed code should look like this:

```
SELECT dBeachPurchases.ItemTitle, dBeachPurchases.ItemAuthor
FROM dBeachPurchases
WHERE (((dBeachPurchases.ItemTitle) Like "[A-D]*"))
ORDER BY dBeachPurchases.ItemTitle;
```

11. Save (using Ctrl+S) the amended query, and close it.

12. In the database objects window, double-click the `Titles Beginning A to D` query. As you can see in Figure 18-19, the titles are now ordered. It is now apparent that only titles beginning with the characters A through D are displayed.

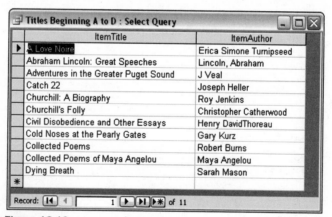

Figure 18-19

Try It Out **Using a Negated Character Class**

Follow the steps for the preceding example with the following amendments.

In Step 4, enter the following code:

```
LIKE "[!A-D]*"
```

This will create the negated character class.

In Step 6, save the query as `Titles NOT beginning A to D`.

In all later steps where a reference is made to `Titles beginning A to D`, substitute the new query.

Figure 18-20 shows the appearance after the new query `Titles NOT beginning A to D` is run.

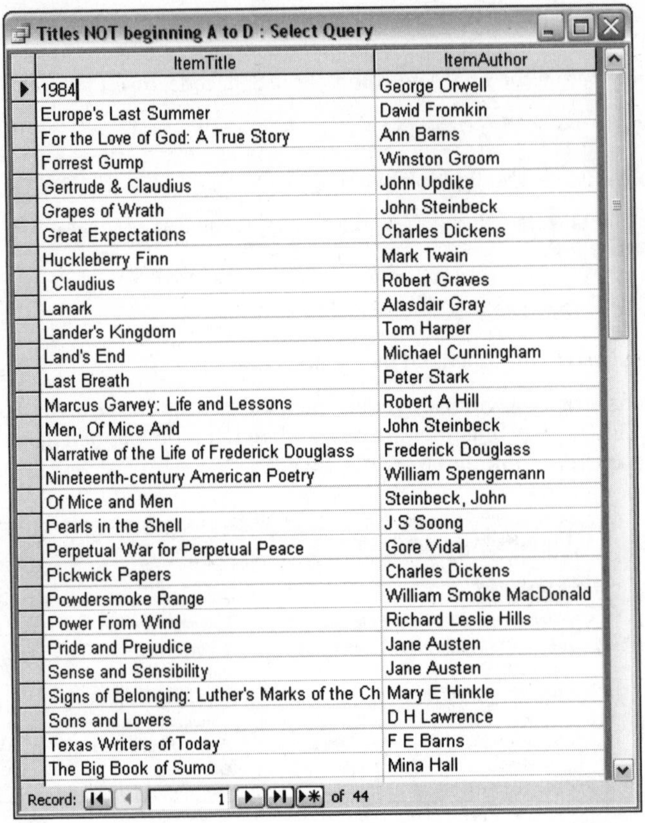

ItemTitle	ItemAuthor
1984	George Orwell
Europe's Last Summer	David Fromkin
For the Love of God: A True Story	Ann Barns
Forrest Gump	Winston Groom
Gertrude & Claudius	John Updike
Grapes of Wrath	John Steinbeck
Great Expectations	Charles Dickens
Huckleberry Finn	Mark Twain
I Claudius	Robert Graves
Lanark	Alasdair Gray
Lander's Kingdom	Tom Harper
Land's End	Michael Cunningham
Last Breath	Peter Stark
Marcus Garvey: Life and Lessons	Robert A Hill
Men, Of Mice And	John Steinbeck
Narrative of the Life of Frederick Douglass	Frederick Douglass
Nineteenth-century American Poetry	William Spengemann
Of Mice and Men	Steinbeck, John
Pearls in the Shell	J S Soong
Perpetual War for Perpetual Peace	Gore Vidal
Pickwick Papers	Charles Dickens
Powdersmoke Range	William Smoke MacDonald
Power From Wind	Richard Leslie Hills
Pride and Prejudice	Jane Austen
Sense and Sensibility	Jane Austen
Signs of Belonging: Luther's Marks of the Ch	Mary E Hinkle
Sons and Lovers	D H Lawrence
Texas Writers of Today	F E Barns
The Big Book of Sumo	Mina Hall

Record: 1 of 44

Figure 18-20

Exercises

1. Specify the SQL for a query that will find names such as `Burns` and `Barns` anywhere in the ItemAuthor field of the `dBeachPurchases` database.

2. Specify a query that will display the ItemTitle and ItemAuthor fields when the ItemTitle field contains the surname `McDonald` or `MacDonald`.

Regular Expressions in JScript and JavaScript

JavaScript and JScript are both dialects of ECMAScript, the official standard (ECMA 262), which is the successor to the original proprietary Netscape JavaScript.

Netscape and Mozilla browsers use JavaScript (currently at version 1.5), and Microsoft Internet Explorer uses JScript (currently at version 5.6). Most of the functionality in each language is also present in the other dialect. Both languages provide significant regular expression functionality, which can be used in a Web browser. There are, however, some differences between the two ECMAScript dialects. This chapter focuses on functionality that is common to both dialects. In addition, there are differences between the object models supported by the Internet Explorer browser and the Mozilla family of browsers, including the Firefox browser.

To run JScript and JavaScript code, you need to have an associated host to interpret the code. When JScript and JavaScript are run in a Web browser, the browser's JScript/JavaScript interpreter runs the scripting code. When run on the server side, JScript code can be run by Active Server Pages (ASP). In addition, JScript code can be run in association with the interpreter in the Windows Script Host (WSH).

JScript and JavaScript are often used to validate data entered into a form on a Web page. Client-side validation of forms data is much faster than server-side validation, and the responsiveness of well-written client-side code gives a significantly better user experience than the older technique of validation, which was carried out only on the server side. Typically, in modern forms scripts, there is server-side validation and processing code to complement the client-side validation scripts. This duplication of validation code has development costs associated with it and also imposes an extra maintenance task to ensure that the client-side code and the server-side code are not in conflict.

> The W3C has created a specification for XForms that uses XML-based validation to provide a newer validation technique for forms data. XForms uses W3C XML Schema for validation. At the time of this writing, XForms is used much less than client-side JavaScript or JScript code.

In this chapter, you will learn the following:

❑   How to use regular expressions in JavaScript and JScript

❑   The metacharacters supported in JavaScript and JScript

❑   How to use the metacharacters in Web-page examples

> **The examples shown in this chapter have been tested in Internet Explorer 6.0 and Mozilla Firefox 0.9.3, as appropriate. Due to the differences in the supported object model, not all code will run in Firefox 0.9.3.**

JScript is not the same language as JScript.NET. The latter language uses the Microsoft .NET Framework, not a JavaScript/JScript interpreter. JScript .NET is not covered in this chapter.

Using Regular Expressions in JavaScript and JScript

One of the principal uses of JScript and JavaScript regular expressions is in processing information entered by end users into Web forms.

JavaScript and JScript code is, for security reasons, typically unable to access files held on the local file system when run in a Web browser. If scripting code were able to access, read, and write to such files when run in a browser, this would pose a significant security threat when the scripting code formed part of a Web page, whose author in many situations would be unknown and might, justifiably, be untrusted. In fact, even with those restrictions on what scripting code can do, many Web browsers offer options to disallow the running of any scripting code to provide an extra layer of reassurance for users who desire it.

If you want to try out the code examples in this chapter, you will need to have JavaScript code enabled for at least some Web pages on your preferred Web browser. Instructions are given here for the configuration of two popular Web browsers, Firefox 0.9.3 and Internet Explorer 6.0.

In Firefox 0.9.3, you can check whether JavaScript is enabled by selecting Tools ➪ Options. In the left pane of the Options window, click Web Features. The screen's appearance will then be similar to that shown in Figure 19-1.

Ensure that the Enable JavaScript check box is checked if you want to run the code for this chapter's examples.

Internet Explorer has more finely grained security settings. The following instructions assume that you will download the example code and run it locally.

Figure 19-1

In Internet Explorer 6, choose Tools ➪ Internet Options. In the Internet Options dialog box, select the Security tab, and click the Local Intranet option in the upper part of the Security tab (see Figure 19-2).

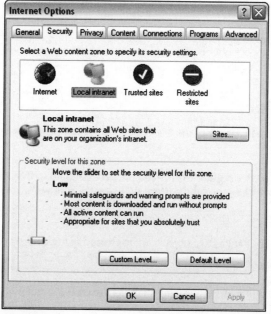

Figure 19-2

Then click the Custom Level button toward the bottom of the Security tab. The Security Settings window opens. Scroll down the options in the Security Settings window until you come to the scripting options shown in Figure 19-3.

Figure 19-3

If you want to run the examples in this chapter, ensure that the scripting options are enabled, as shown in the preceding figure. Enabling scripting of Java applets is not necessary to run this chapter's sample code.

Use of regular expressions in JavaScript and JScript depends on regular expression functionality in the RegExp object and the String object. The RegExp object will be described in full, and aspects of the String object relevant to regular expressions will also be described.

The RegExp Object

Patterns can be used with instances of the RegExp object. Those instances can be created in either of two ways:

❑   A variable can have a regular expression pattern assigned to it. For example, the variable myPattern can be assigned the pattern t$ using the following code:

```
myPattern = /t$/;
```

❑   A new instance of the RegExp object can be created using a RegExp() constructor:

```
myPattern = new RegExp("t$");
```

The pattern t$ will match any string that has the final character t.

JScript statements can be written one statement to a line without using the statement-terminating semicolon. However, the semicolon is required as a statement terminator in JavaScript. Therefore, all code in this chapter, which aims for cross-language compatibility, will use a semicolon routinely as a statement-terminator character.

The following two examples work identically as far as the end user is concerned. However, one uses the forward-slash syntax and the other uses the RegExp() constructor to assign a RegExp object to a variable. The screenshots in one example are from Internet Explorer and in the other from Firefox. The functionality, as far as the end user is concerned, is the same in each browser.

Try It Out   **Creating a RegExp Object Instance Using Forward-Slash Syntax**

1. Either type the following code into your favorite editor or open the sample file FinalT.html:

```
<html>
<head>
<title>Check for Final t in a string</title>
<script language="javascript" type="text/javascript">
var myRegExp = /t$/;

function Validate(entry){
return myRegExp.test(entry);
} // end function Validate()

function ShowPrompt(){
var entry = prompt("This script tests for matches for the regular expression
pattern: " + myRegExp + ".\nType in a string and click on the OK button.", "Type
your text here.");
if (Validate(entry)){
alert("There is a match!\nThe regular expression pattern is: " + myRegExp + ".\n
The string that you entered was: '" + entry + "'.");
} // end if
else{
 alert("There is no match in the string you entered.\n" + "The regular expression
pattern is " + myRegExp + "\n" + "You entered the string: '" + entry + "'." );
} // end else

} // end function ShowPrompt()

</script>
</head>
<body>
<form name="myForm">
<br />
<button type="Button" onclick="ShowPrompt()">Click here to enter text.</button>
</form>
</body>
</html>
```

2. Open FinalT.html in Internet Explorer. Depending on the file associations you have set on your machine, you may be able to do that simply by double-clicking the file. Alternatively, right-click the file in Windows Explorer and use the Open With option, in which Internet Explorer may already be listed in the context menu. If it's not listed, click the Choose Program

option and follow the on-screen instructions to locate Internet Explorer. Another alternative is to open Internet Explorer and use the Open option in the File menu to open FinalT.html. Figure 19-4 shows the screen's appearance when FinalT.html is opened in Internet Explorer.

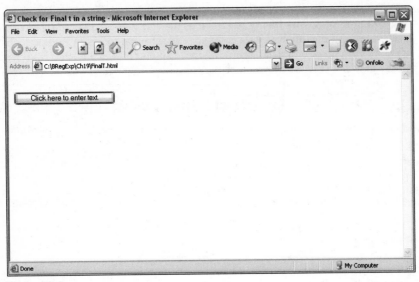

Figure 19-4

3.   Click the Click Here to Enter Text button. Figure 19-5 shows the resulting screen's appearance.

Figure 19-5

4.   Type the character sequence **Test** in the text box, and click the OK button.

Figure 19-6 shows the screen's appearance after you click OK. Because the test character sequence, Test, ends in the character t, there is a match for the pattern t$.

Figure 19-6

If you enter a character sequence that does not match, a message indicating that there is no match will be displayed.

5. Click the OK button again, and the message displayed in Figure 19-6 will no longer be displayed. Then click the Click Here to Enter Text button.

6. Type the nonmatching character sequence **Tess**, and click OK. Figure 19-7 shows the appearance of the resulting message, indicating that there is no match for that test string.

Figure 19-7

How It Works

A global variable, `myRegExp`, is declared. To that variable is assigned a regular expression pattern, `t$`, contained between paired forward slashes:

```
var myRegExp = /t$/;
```

The pattern `t$` matches a single character, `t`, when it is the last character that the user enters. The paired forward slashes are the delimiters for a regular expression pattern, similarly to the way that paired quotation marks are delimiters for a string.

When the Click Here to Enter Text button is clicked, the `ShowPrompt()` function is called:

```
<button type="Button" onclick="ShowPrompt()">Click here to enter text.</button>
```

The `ShowPrompt()` function accepts text from the user:

```
var entry = prompt("This script tests for matches for the regular expression
pattern: " + myRegExp + ".\nType in a string and click on the OK button.", "Type
your text here.");
```

Then an `if` statement uses the `Validate()` function to check whether or not there is a match for the pattern `t$`. If there is a match, an alert box is displayed, as specified in the following code:

```
if (Validate(entry)){
alert("There is a match!\nThe regular expression pattern is: " + myRegExp + ".\n
The string that you entered was: '" + entry + "'.");
} // end if
```

The arguments to the `alert()` function concatenate literal message text with the value for the regular expression pattern, contained in the `myRegExp` variable, and the value entered by the user, contained in the `entry` variable.

If there is no match, the `else` clause causes an alert box with alternative text to appear, indicating that there is no match to be displayed:

```
else{
  alert("There is no match in the string you entered.\n" + "The regular expression
pattern is " + myRegExp + "\n" + "You entered the string: '" + entry + "'." );
} // end else
```

The `Validate()` function uses the following code to test whether the text entered by the user at the prompt matches the regular expression pattern held in the `myRegExp` variable:

```
function Validate(entry){
return myRegExp.test(entry);
} // end function Validate()
```

The `test()` method of the `RegExp` object takes a string as its argument and tests whether there is a match in the string for the regular expression pattern.

As indicated in the preceding paragraphs, if there is a match, an alert box to that effect is displayed. If there is not, match a message indicating as much is displayed instead.

Next, you will use the `RegExp()` constructor in the Firefox browser to achieve the same thing.

Try It Out   Using the RegExp() Constructor

1. Open the Firefox browser, if it is installed on your machine. If Firefox is not available, the code will also run on Internet Explorer.

2. From the File menu, select Open; navigate to the file `FinalTConstructor.html`; and open it. The content is shown here:

```
<html>
<head>
<title>Check for Final t in a string</title>
<script language="javascript" type="text/javascript">
var myRegExp = new RegExp("t$");

function Validate(entry){
return myRegExp.test(entry);
} // end function Validate()

function ShowPrompt(){
var entry = prompt("This script tests for matches for the regular expression
pattern: " + myRegExp + ".\nType in a string and click on the OK button.", "Type
your text here.");
if (Validate(entry)){
alert("There is a match!\nThe regular expression pattern is: " + myRegExp + ".\n
The string that you entered was: '" + entry + "'.");
} // end if
else{
  alert("There is no match in the string you entered.\n" + "The regular expression
pattern is " + myRegExp + "\n" + "You entered the string: '" + entry + "'." );
} // end else
```

```
}  // end function ShowPrompt()

</script>
</head>
<body>
<form name="myForm">
<br />
<button type="Button" onclick="ShowPrompt()">Click here to enter text.</button>
</form>
</body>
</html>
```

3. Click the Click Here to Enter Text button, and enter the character sequence **Test**.

4. Click the OK button, and inspect the alert box that is displayed when there is a match, as shown in Figure 19-8.

Figure 19-8

5. Click the OK button to dismiss the alert box; then click the Click Here to Enter Text button and enter the character sequence **Test.**. Notice that there is a period character as the final character of the test-character sequence.

6. Click the OK button, and inspect the alert box that is displayed.

How It Works

The following code uses the RegExp() constructor to assign a regular expression object containing the pattern t$ to the variable myRegExp:

```
var myRegExp = new RegExp("t$");
```

The rest of the code functions as described in the preceding Try It Out section. When a lowercase t is the last character entered by the user. there is a match; otherwise, there is not.

Personally, I find the following syntax more convenient to use:

```
var myRegExp = /t$/;
```

But the two techniques are functionally equivalent, and if you prefer to use the RegExp() constructor, just substitute that in later examples in this chapter that use the paired-forward-slash syntax.

Attributes of the RegExp Object

The following code (which you have just seen) assigns a pattern t$ to the variable myRegExp using the default settings of the RegExp object:

```
var myRegExp = /t$/;
```

The general form of such an assignment statement allows attributes of the RegExp object to be expressed. The general form is

```
var myVariable = /pattern/attributes
```

where *pattern* is a regular expression pattern and *attributes* is a string that can contain any of the characters m, g, and i. The attribute m indicates multiline matching, the attribute i indicates case-insensitive matching, and the attribute g indicates global matching. In multiline matching, the ^ and $ metacharacters match the positions at the beginning and end of the whole test text, even if it spreads across multiple lines.

If you prefer using the RegExp() constructor, the syntax is as follows:

```
var myVariable = new RegExp(pattern, attributes)
```

The m, g, and i attributes correspond to three of the properties of the RegExp object. The RegExp object's global property indicates whether or not the g attribute has been specified. The RegExp object's ignoreCase property corresponds to the i attribute having been specified. The RegExp object's multiline property indicates whether the m attribute has been sent.

The Other Properties of the RegExp Object

In addition to the global, ignoreCase, and multiline properties, the RegExp object has additional properties.

The lastIndex property indicates the position of the last match. The lastIndex property is used when finding multiple matches in a string. The source property holds the source text for the regular expression — in other words, it holds the regular expression pattern.

The example file NumericDigitsOthersAllowed.html shows how you can access the properties just mentioned. The code for NumericDigitsOthersAllowed.html is shown here:

```
<html>
<head>
<title>RegExp Object Properties</title>
<script language="javascript" type="text/javascript">
var myRegExp = /\d+/;

function Validate(entry){
return myRegExp.test(entry);
} // end function Validate()

function ShowPrompt(){
var entry = prompt("This script tests for matches for the regular expression
pattern: " + myRegExp + ".\nType in a string and click on the OK button.", "Type
your text here.");
if (Validate(entry)){
```

```
displayString = "";
displayString += "There is a match!\nThe regular expression pattern is: " +
myRegExp + ".\nThe string that you entered was: '" + entry +"\n";
displayString += "The global property contained: " + myRegExp.global + "\n";
displayString += "The ignoreCase property contained: " + myRegExp.ignoreCase +
"\n";
displayString += "The multiline property contained: " + myRegExp.multiline + "\n";
displayString += "The source property contained: " + myRegExp.source + "\n";
displayString += "The lastIndex property contained: " + myRegExp.lastIndex;
alert(displayString);
} // end if
else{
 alert("There is no match in the string you entered.\n" + "The regular expression
pattern is " + myRegExp + "\n" + "You entered the string: '" + entry + "'." );
} // end else

} // end function ShowPrompt()

</script>
</head>
<body>
<form name="myForm">
<br />
<button type="Button" onclick="ShowPrompt()">Click here to enter text.</button>
</form>
</body>
</html>
```

Try It Out   Explore RegExp Object Properties

1. Open the file `NumericDigitsOthersAllowed.html` in Internet Explorer.

2. Click the Click Here to Enter Text button, and enter the text **Hello 99** in the text box.

3. Click the OK button, and inspect the information displayed in the alert box, as shown in Figure 19-9.

Figure 19-9

4. Click the OK button to dismiss the alert box, click the Click Here to Enter Text button again, and enter the text **99 Hello** in the text box.

439

5. Click the OK button, and inspect the information displayed in the alert box, as shown in Figure 19-10.

Figure 19-10

6. Compare the appearances of Figure 19-9 (after the sample text `Hello 99` was entered) and Figure 19-10 (after the sample text `99 Hello` was entered). Notice the difference in the values of the `lastIndex` property of the `RegExp` object.

How It Works

The variable `myRegExp` is declared as a global variable:

```
var myRegExp = /\d+/;
```

It is assigned a `RegExp` object containing the pattern `\d+`, which will match one or more numeric digits.

When the Click Here to Enter Text button is clicked, the `ShowPrompt()` function is called.

```
<button type="Button" onclick="ShowPrompt()">Click here to enter text.</button>
```

The Validate() function is called from the `ShowPrompt()` function:

```
function Validate(entry){
return myRegExp.test(entry);
} // end function Validate()
```

If the entry variable is validated, a display string is built up that contains information about the properties of the `RegExp` object assigned to the variable `myRegExp`:

```
if (Validate(entry)){
displayString = "";
displayString += "There is a match!\nThe regular expression pattern is: " +
myRegExp + ".\nThe string that you entered was: '" + entry +"\n";
displayString += "The global property contained: " + myRegExp.global + "\n";
displayString += "The ignoreCase property contained: " + myRegExp.ignoreCase +
"\n";
displayString += "The multiline property contained: " + myRegExp.multiline + "\n";
displayString += "The source property contained: " + myRegExp.source + "\n";
displayString += "The lastIndex property contained: " + myRegExp.lastIndex;
alert(displayString);
} // end if
```

Because the `myRegExp` variable was created with none of the associations specified, each of the `global`, `ignoreCase`, and `multiline` properties contains the Boolean value `false`.

The `source` property contains the value of the pattern, `\d+`, which was contained in the assignment statement for the `myRegExp` variable.

The `lastIndex` property contains the value of the character position following the previous match. When the test text was `Hello 99`, the value of the `lastIndex` property was 8, because the match (the character sequence 99) consisted of character positions 6 and 7. When the test text was `99 Hello`, the value of the `lastIndex` property was 2, because the match, `99`, consisted of character positions 0 and 1, because indexing starts at 0.

The test() Method of the RegExp Object

The `test()` method of the `RegExp` object tests whether or not a string matches a pattern. If there is at least one match, the `test()` method returns the Boolean value `true`. If there is no match, the `test()` method returns the Boolean value `false`.

You saw in the preceding example situations that the value `true` was returned, because both test character sequences, `Hello 99` and `99 Hello`, contained at least one numeric digit and therefore matched the pattern `\d+`, which matches one or more numeric digits.

If you enter a character sequence that contains no numeric digit, the value returned by the `test()` method when matching the pattern `\d+` will be the Boolean value `false`.

The exec() Method of the RegExp Object

The `exec()` method of the `RegExp` object is powerful, flexible, and potentially confusing.

First, let's look at using the `exec()` method when the pattern is used with the `g` attribute. In other words, the value of the global property of the `RegExp` object will contain the Boolean value `true`.

Try It Out   With global Property true

The test file, `RegExpExecExample.html`, contains the following markup and code:

```
<html>
<head>
<title>RegExp exec() Method Example with global attribute set.</title>
<script language="javascript" type="text/javascript">
var myRegExp = /\sthe/ig;
var entry;

function PatternProcess(entry){
var displayString = "";

while ((result = myRegExp.exec(entry)) != null ){
displayString += "Matched '" + result;
displayString += "' at position " + result.index + "\n";
displayString += "The next match attempt begins at position " + myRegExp.lastIndex;
alert(displayString);
displayString = "";
} // end while loop
} // end function Process(entry)
```

```
function ShowPrompt(){
entry = prompt("This script tests for matches for the regular expression pattern: "
+ myRegExp + ".\nType in a string and click on the OK button.", "Type your text
here.");
PatternProcess(entry);
} // end function ShowPrompt()

</script>
</head>
<body>
<form name="myForm">
<br />
<button type="Button" onclick="ShowPrompt()">Click here to enter text.</button>
</form>
</body>
</html>
```

1. Open `RegExpExecExample.html` in Internet Explorer, and click the Click Here to Enter Text button.

2. In the text box, enter the following text: **Hello there, the theatre is nice.**, which contains three matches for the pattern \sthe.

Figure 19-11 shows the sample text entered in the prompt dialog box.

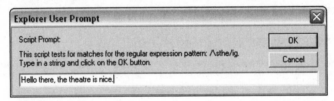

Figure 19-11

3. Click the OK button, and inspect the alert box that is displayed, as shown in Figure 19-12. Notice that the matched text is the, which starts at position 6. Given the test string Hello there, the theatre is nice., I hope you can see that the match the is the first three characters of there.

Figure 19-12

4. Click the OK button, and inspect the next alert box that is displayed, as shown in Figure 19-13. Notice that the position of the matched text now begins at position 12, which indicates that the matching the is the word the in the test string.

Figure 19-13

5. Click the OK button, and inspect the next alert box that is displayed, as shown in Figure 19-14. Notice that the position of the matched text now begins at position 16, which indicates that the matching the is the first three letters of theatre in the test string.

Figure 19-14

How It Works

As written, the code will display all matches in separate alert boxes. If there is no match, no message is displayed.

The pattern to be matched is \sthe, which is a whitespace character followed by the character sequence the.

The test string, Hello there, the theatre is nice., contains three character sequences that match the pattern \sthe.

The first match is the space character after the word Hello followed by the character sequence the in the word there. Numbering of character positions starts at 0. Position 5 is the position before the first matching character, which is a space character. Any further matching would continue after the e of the at position 9.

The second match is the space character after the comma following the word there. The following character sequence the is the word the.

The third match is the space character after the word the, followed by the first three characters of the word theatre.

When the exec() method of the RegExp object is used in a nonglobal matching process, it matches only once. It returns parts of the matching character sequence that correspond to parts of the pattern that are within parentheses in an array. It is, perhaps, easier to demonstrate what is returned, rather than attempt to describe it in isolation.

Try It Out   **The exec() Method in Nonglobal Matching**

The sample file, `RegExpExecNonGlobal.html`, is shown here:

```
<html>
<head>
<title>RegExp exec() Method Example with no global attribute.</title>
<script language="javascript" type="text/javascript">
var myRegExp = /((A|B)(\d{3}))/i;
var entry;

function PatternProcess(entry){
var displayString = "";
result = myRegExp.exec(entry);
for (n=0; n<5; n++){
displayString += "Matched '" + result[n];
displayString += "' in result[" + n + "].\n";
} // end for loop

alert(displayString);displayString = "";
} // end function Process(entry)

function ShowPrompt(){
entry = prompt("This script tests for matches for the regular expression pattern: "
+ myRegExp + ".\nType in a string and click on the OK button.", "Type your text
here.");
PatternProcess(entry);
} // end function ShowPrompt()

</script>
</head>
<body>
<form name="myForm">
<br />
<button type="Button" onclick="ShowPrompt()">Click here to enter text.</button>
</form>
</body>
</html>
```

1. Open `RegExpExecNonGlobal.html` in Internet Explorer, and click the Click Here to Enter Text button.

2. Enter a part number, **A234**, in the text box in the prompt dialog box, and click the OK button.

3. Inspect the alert box that is displayed, as shown in Figure 19-15.

Figure 19-15

How It Works

In `result[0]`, the whole of the matching character sequence is returned — in this case, A234.

In `result[1]`, the matching character sequence contained in the outermost parentheses is returned. In this example, that is also A234.

In `result[2]`, the matching character sequence contained in the next set of nested parentheses is returned. In this case, that is A.

In `result[3]`, the matching character sequence contained in the next set of nested parentheses is returned. In this case, that is 234.

The array element `result[4]` was added to demonstrate that the value `undefined` is returned when there is no further pair of matching parentheses.

The next Try It Out section puts the two situations together to look in more detail at using parentheses and global matching.

Try It Out   Parentheses and Global Matching with exec()

The test file, `RegExpExecExample2.html`, is shown here:

```
<html>
<head>
<title>RegExp exec() Method Example with global attribute set.</title>
<script language="javascript" type="text/javascript">
var myRegExp = /((A|B|C)(\d{3}))/ig;
var entry;

function PatternProcess(entry){
var displayString = "";

while ((result = myRegExp.exec(entry)) != null ){
displayString += "Matched '" + result;
displayString += "' at position " + result.index + "\n";
displayString += "The next match attempt begins at position " + myRegExp.lastIndex
+ "\n";
displayString += "The whole matching string is " + result[0] + "\n";
displayString += "The content of the outer parentheses is " + result[1] + "\n";
displayString += "The content of the first nested parentheses is " + result[2] +
"\n";
displayString += "The content of the second nested parentheses is " + result[3] +
"\n";
alert(displayString);
displayString = "";
} // end while loop
} // end function Process(entry)

function ShowPrompt(){
entry = prompt("This script tests for matches for the regular expression pattern: "
+ myRegExp + ".\nType in a string and click on the OK button.", "Type your text
here.");
PatternProcess(entry);
} // end function ShowPrompt()
```

```
</script>
</head>
<body>
<form name="myForm">
<br />
<button type="Button" onclick="ShowPrompt()">Click here to enter text.</button>
</form>
</body>
</html>
```

The matching is global, as indicated by the g attribute in the declaration of the myRegExp variable. It also includes parentheses.

1. Open RegExpExecExample2.html in Internet Explorer, and click the Click Here to Enter Text button.

2. Enter the test text **A123, B456, C789** in the text box, and click the OK button.

3. Inspect the results displayed in the first alert box, as shown in Figure 19-16. (The results will be discussed in the How It Works section that follows.)

Figure 19-16

4. Click the OK button to dismiss the first alert box, and inspect the results displayed in the second alert box, as shown in Figure 19-17.

Figure 19-17

5. Click the OK button to dismiss the second alert box, and inspect the results displayed in the third alert box, as shown in Figure 19-18.

Figure 19-18

How It Works

The myRegExp variable is declared in the following statement:

```
var myRegExp = /((A|B|C)(\d{3}))/ig;
```

This pattern, ((A|B|C)(\d{3})), will match character sequences that begin with A, B, or C followed by three numeric digits. Not all the parentheses are necessary, but they help illustrate what the exec() method returns in the array of results when parentheses are present.

The following test string contains three matches for the pattern ((A|B|C)(\d{3})): A123, B456, and C789:

```
A123, B456, C789
```

First, look in detail at what is displayed in the first alert box, which you can inspect in Figure 19-16.

The information displayed in that alert box is built up in the following code:

```
displayString += "Matched '" + result;
displayString += "' at position " + result.index + "\n";
displayString += "The next match attempt begins at position " + myRegExp.lastIndex
+ "\n";
displayString += "The whole matching string is " + result[0] + "\n";
displayString += "The content of the outer parentheses is " + result[1] + "\n";
displayString += "The content of the first nested parentheses is " + result[2] +
"\n";
displayString += "The content of the second nested parentheses is " + result[3] +
"\n";
```

It is displayed using the following code:

```
alert(displayString);
```

The first line of the alert box displays each part of the result array separated by commas. As you can see in Figure 19-16, it reads Matched 'A123, A123, A, 123' at position 0. The commas separate the content of result[0], result[1], result[2], and result[3]. Matching begins at position 0.

The next four lines in the alert box in Figure 19-16 spell out how each part of the result array is arrived at.

The next match is B456, and the results for that are displayed in Figure 19-17. Notice that the position is now 6. The elements of the result array are displayed as just described.

The third match is C789. The results are displayed in Figure 19-18. Notice that the position is now 12. The elements of the result array are displayed as described earlier in this How It Works section.

The String Object

In JavaScript/JScript, a string is a sequence of Unicode characters enclosed in paired quotation marks or apostrophes. The JavaScript/JScript String object represents a string. For many purposes, the value of a JavaScript string is the same as a character sequence. A String object represents a programmatic interface to such a sequence of characters.

The following lines of code each contain an example of a JavaScript/JScript string:

```
"Test"
'This is a multicharacter string enclosed in paired apostrophes.'
"99.31"
"This string has two \n lines."
```

A string must be written on a single line. However, a multiline string can be represented using the \n escape sequence notation to represent a newline.

Three methods of the String object are relevant to the use of regular expressions:

- ❑ match()
- ❑ replace()
- ❑ search()

The match() method takes a RegExp object as its argument and tests whether the string is a match for the pattern associated with that object.

Try It Out   The String.match() Method

The test file for the String.match() example is StringObjectMatch.html, whose code is shown here:

```
<html>
<head>
<title>The match() Method of the String Object.</title>
<script language="javascript" type="text/javascript">
var myRegExp = /\d+\.\d+/;
var entryString;
var displayString = "";

function StringProcess(){
```

```
if (entryString.match(myRegExp) != null ){
var result = entryString.match(myRegExp);
displayString += "Matched '" + result + ".\n";
displayString += "result[0] is " + result[0] + ".\n";
displayString += "result[1] is " + result[1] + ".\n";
alert(displayString);
displayString = "";
} // end if statement
else
alert("The string you entered did not match the pattern " + myRegExp);
} // end function StringProcess()

function ShowPrompt(){
entryString = prompt("Type a string which is or contains a decimal number.\nType
and click on the OK button.", "Type a pattern here.");
StringProcess();
}

</script>
</head>
<body>
<form name="myForm">
<br />
<button type="Button" onclick="ShowPrompt()">Click here to enter a decimal
value.</button>
</form>
</body>
</html>
```

The example will accept a string that contains or consists of a decimal number. To match the pattern \d+\.\d+, the decimal number must contain at least one numeric digit before the decimal point and at least one numeric digit after the decimal point.

1. Open StringObjectMatch.html in Internet Explorer, and click the Click Here to Enter a Decimal Value button.

2. In the text box in the prompt dialog box, enter the string **My score is 91.23**, and click the OK button.

3. Inspect the information displayed in the alert box, as shown in Figure 19-19.

Figure 19-19

How It Works

The variable `myRegExp` is assigned the regular expression pattern `\d+\.\d+`:

```
var myRegExp = /\d+\.\d+/;
```

This will match decimal numbers, provided that there is at least one numeric digit both before and after the decimal point.

Clicking the Click Here to Enter a Decimal Value button calls the `ShowPrompt()` function, which requests user input. The user input is assigned to the variable `entryString`:

```
entryString = prompt("Type a string which is or contains a decimal number.\nType
and click on the OK button.", "Type a pattern here.");
```

And then the `ProcessString()` function is called.

First, an `if` statement tests whether there is a match or not:

```
if (entryString.match(myRegExp) != null )
```

If there is no match, `entryString.match(myRegExp)` will return `null`, and the processing of the function will proceed through the `else` clause (shown a little later). If there is a match, `entryString` `.match(myRegExp)` is not `null`, so processing of the `if` statement proceeds.

The result variable is an array (because you know there is a match) where element `result[0]` contains the matching character sequence. The elements `result[1]` and higher contain any components of the match as signified by parentheses in the regular expression pattern. This resembles the behavior of the `exec()` method of the `RegExp` object:

```
if (entryString.match(myRegExp) != null ){
var result = entryString.match(myRegExp);
displayString += "Matched '" + result + ".\n";
displayString += "result[0] is " + result[0] + ".\n";
displayString += "result[1] is " + result[1] + ".\n";
alert(displayString);
displayString = "";
```

The variable `displayString` is declared globally as an empty string:

```
var displayString = "";
```

Then, inside the `if` statement, its content is built up using the value of result, `result[0]`, and `result[1]`. As you can see in Figure 19-19, the value of `result[1]` is undefined, because the pattern `\d+\.\d+` contains no parentheses. Finally, after the alert box is dismissed, the value of `displayString` is again assigned the empty string as its value. This is necessary because you are not submitting the data anywhere.

If `entryString.match(myRegExp)` returns `null`, the `else` clause will be processed, which displays a message stating that there was no match.

Using the g attribute with `String.match()` produces multiple results in the way that you saw earlier with `RegExp.exec()`. If there are parentheses in the pattern, the results have an array of elements for each match, again resembling `RegExp.exec()`.

The `String.search()` method takes a `RegExp` object as its argument. It returns the position of the first match in the string or `-1` if there is no match.

The `String.replace()` method takes two arguments; the first is a `RegExp` object, and the second is the replacement string for matching text in the `String` object. The replacement string can be specified literally or can be a function call.

Metacharacters in JavaScript and JScript

JavaScript and JScript regular expressions are based on Perl regular expressions. Just as Perl regular expression support has evolved over time, so the support for regular expressions has evolved in JScript and JavaScript.

The following table summarizes the metacharacters supported in JavaScript 1.5 and JScript 5.6.

Metacharacter	Description
\d	Matches a single numeric digit.
. (the period metacharacter)	Matches any character except the newline character or another Unicode character for newline.
\w	Matches any ASCII word character — that is [A-Za-z0-9].
\W	Matches any character not matched by \w.
\s	Matches a whitespace character.
\S	Matches any character not matched by \s.
\D	Matches any character not matched by \d — that is, \D is equivalent to [^0-9].
[...]	Character class. Matches any single character inside the square brackets. Ranges are supported.
[^...]	Negated character class.
?	Quantifier. Indicates that zero or one occurrence of the preceding character or group matches.
*	Quantifier. Indicates that zero or more occurrences of the preceding character or group matches.
+	Quantifier. Indicates that one or more occurrences of the preceding character or group match.
{n,m}	Quantifier. Indicates that a minimum of *n* and a maximum of *m* occurrences of the preceding character or group match.

Documenting JavaScript Regular Expressions

A number of languages support the use of extended whitespace for regular expressions. Unfortunately, that feature is not supported in JavaScript or JScript.

I suggest that for anything but fairly trivial regular expression patterns, you document the pattern in comment lines immediately before or after the declaration of the variable to which the RegExp object is assigned.

For example, suppose that you had the following declaration:

```
var myRegExp = /\d{3}-\d{2}-\d{4}/;
```

You might want to document it like this:

```
var myRegExp = /\d{3}-\d{2}-\d{4}/;
// \d{3} matches three numeric digits
// - matches a hyphen
// \d{2} matches two numeric digits
// - matches a hyphen
// \d{4} matches four numeric digits
```

Or, if you prefer, document it like this:

```
var myRegExp = /\d{3}-\d{2}-\d{4}/;
/* \d{3} matches three numeric digits
   - matches a hyphen
   \d{2} matches two numeric digits
   - matches a hyphen
   \d{4} matches four numeric digits
*/
```

Either way, for complex patterns it is useful, particularly when doing code maintenance, to have a step-by-step description of the programmer's intention in the documentation inside the code file. It can also be very useful when creating the code, because having to write documentation like this can sometimes throw up issues that you previously overlooked. Being forced to think formally like this does help you avoid some coding errors.

SSN Validation Example

You can use regular expressions with JavaScript and JScript to validate information entered into a form on a Web page. This example will validate the structure of a U.S. Social Security number (SSN). An SSN has three numeric digits followed by a hyphen, followed by two numeric digits, followed by a hyphen, followed by four numeric digits.

The test file, SSNValidation.html, is intended for use on Internet Explorer:

```html
<html>
<head>
<title>Processing an SSN</title>
<script language="javascript" >
myRegExp = /\d{3}-\d{2}-\d{4}/;
var entry;

function Validate(){
entry = simpleForm.SSNBox.value;
if (myRegExp.test(entry)) {
alert("The value you entered, " + entry + "\n matches the regular expression, " +
myRegExp + ". It is a valid SSN." );
} // end the if statement
else
{
alert("The value you entered," + entry + ",\nis not a valid SSN. Please try
again.");
} // end of else clause
} // end Validate() function

function ClearBox(){
simpleForm.SSNBox.value = "";
// The above line clears the texbox when it receives focus
} // end ClearBox() function
</script>
</head>
<body>
<form name="simpleForm" >
<table>
<tr>
<td width="40%">Enter a valid SSN here:</td>
<td><input name="SSNBox" onfocus="ClearBox()" type="text" value="Enter an SSN
here"></input></td>
</tr>
<tr>
<td><input name="Submit" type="submit" value="Check the SSN" onclick="Validate()"
></input></td>
</tr>
</table>
</form>
</body>
</html>
```

How It Works

A pattern is specified that matches three numeric digits followed by a hyphen, followed by two numeric digits, followed by a hyphen, followed by four numeric digits:

```
myRegExp = /\d{3}-\d{2}-\d{4}/;
```

Whether there is a match or not is determined by using the `RegExp` object's `test()` method:

```
if (myRegExp.test(entry)) {
```

If matching is successful, a message is displayed that shows the user-entered text. If matching fails, the user is informed that the value entered is not an SSN.

Exercises

The following exercises are intended to allow you to test your understanding of some of the material discussed in this chapter:

1. Modify the `FinalT.html` example so that it will match a user entry that contains at least one numeric digit and contains only numeric digits.

2. Modify `SSNValidation.html` so that it will match a 16-digit credit card number that is entered in groups of four numeric digits separated by a whitespace character.

Regular Expressions and VBScript

Regular expressions were introduced to VBScript in version 5.0. They can be used to parse character sequences (strings) and can be used to provide flexible replace functionality.

VBScript can be used on the client side in Web pages when the Internet Explorer browser provides the VBScript interpreter or in the Windows Script Host (WSH).

The VBScript interpreter (vbscript.dll) does not allow file access, but the associated file, scrrun.dll, allows VBScript when used with WSH, for example, to have file access and allows directory manipulation.

In this chapter, you will learn the following:

❑   How to use the properties and methods of the RegExp object

❑   How to use the Match object and the Matches collection

❑   The metacharacters supported in VBScript and how to use them

❑   How to use VBScript regular expressions to solve some text-handling problems

The RegExp Object and How to Use It

The RegExp object, the Match object, and the Matches collection all relate to how regular expressions are used in VBScript. This section focuses on the RegExp object.

The RegExp object has three properties and three methods. The properties are as follows:

❑   Pattern property

❑   Global property

❑   IgnoreCase property

Each of these properties is described in the following sections. The three methods are as follows:

- ❏ Execute method
- ❏ Replace method
- ❏ Test method

Each of these methods is described and demonstrated in the following sections. To carry out simple matching, the Pattern property and the Test() method are often used.

The RegExp Object's Pattern Property

The VBScript RegExp object differs in functionality from the tools and languages discussed earlier in this book. For example, there is no syntax in VBScript like the following JScript declaration and assignment statement:

```
var myRegExp = /\d{3}/;
```

Instead, VBScript uses the value of the RegExp object's Pattern property to hold a string value, which is the regular expression pattern.

So the VBScript equivalent of the preceding JScript code would look like this:

```
Dim myRegExp
Set myRegExp = new RegExp
myRegExp.Pattern = "\d{3}"
```

The following example shows a very simple function that uses the Pattern property as part of a simple replace operation.

Try It Out A Simple Match Operation

The sample file, TestForA.html, shows how the Pattern property is used:

```
<html>
<head>
<title>Test For Upper Case A</title>
<script language="vbscript" type="text/vbscript">
Function MatchTest
Dim myRegExp, TestString
Set myRegExp = new RegExp
myRegExp.Pattern = "A"
TestString = "Andrew"
If myRegExp.Test(TestString) = True Then
  MsgBox "The test string '" & TestString & "' matches the pattern '" &
myRegExp.Pattern & "'."
Else
  MsgBox "There is no match."
End If
End Function
```

```
</script>
</head>
<body onload="MatchTest">

</body>
</html>
```

Open `TestForA.html` in Internet Explorer, and notice the message box that is displayed when the page loads.

Figure 20-1 shows the appearance of the message box that is displayed. It correctly indicates that there is a match for the pattern A in the character sequence `Andrew`.

Figure 20-1

How It Works

When the HTML page loads, the `MatchTest()` function is called:

```
<body onload="MatchTest">
```

The functionality is all contained in the `MatchTest()` function:

```
Function MatchTest
```

First, the variables `myRegExp` (which contains the regular expression pattern in its `Pattern` property) and the `TestString` (which is supplied literally) are dimensioned:

```
Dim myRegExp, TestString
```

Next, in a `Set` statement, a reference to a new `RegExp` object is assigned to the variable `myRegExp`:

```
Set myRegExp = new RegExp
```

Next, a single literal character, A, is assigned to the `myRegExp` object's `Pattern` property:

```
myRegExp.Pattern = "A"
```

Then the character sequence `Andrew` is assigned to the variable `TestString`:

```
TestString = "Andrew"
```

An `If` statement is used to display a message box when matching is successful. Notice that the `Test()` method of the `myRegExp` variable is used in the logical test of the `If` statement. The `Test()` method tests whether or not the string, which is the method's single argument, contains a match for the value of the `Pattern` property of the same `RegExp` object, in this case, the `RegExp` object referenced by the `myRegExp` variable:

```
If myRegExp.Test(TestString) = True Then
```

The message to be displayed is constructed by concatenating literal text with the values of the `TestString` variable and the value of the `myRegExp.Pattern` property:

```
MsgBox "The test string '" & TestString & "' matches the pattern '" &
myRegExp.Pattern & "'."
```

An `Else` clause is also provided with an alternate message indicating that there is no match. However, with the supplied values for `myRegExp.Pattern` and `TestString`, the `Else` clause is never needed in this example. In later examples, where the test string is supplied by the user, you will need an `Else` clause to be in place:

```
Else
   MsgBox "There is no match."
```

Finally, the `End If` and `End Function` statements complete the `MatchTest` function:

```
End If
End Function
```

The RegExp Object's Global Property

The `RegExp` object's `Global` property can have the Boolean values `True` or `False`. The `Global` property's default value is `False`, which means that only a single match for the value of the `Pattern` property is sought. When the value of the `Global` property is `True`, matching continues to be attempted throughout the test string, and multiple matches may be returned.

Try It Out   **The Global Property**

The test file for this example, `MatchGlobal.html`, is shown here:

```
<html>
<head>
<title>Carry out a non-global replace and a global replace.</title>
<script language="vbscript" type="text/vbscript">
Dim myRegExp, InputString, ChangedString

Function MatchGlobal
Set myRegExp = new RegExp
myRegExp.Pattern = "A"
DoReplaceDefault
DoReplaceGlobal
End Function

Function DoReplaceDefault
InputString = InputBox("Enter a string. It will be tested once to see if it
contains" &VBCrLf & "any 'A' characters. Any 'A' will be replaced by 'B'")
myRegExp.Global = False
```

```
ChangedString = myRegExp.Replace(InputString, "B")
If myRegExp.Test(InputString) = True Then
  MsgBox "The test string '" & InputString & "' matches the pattern '" &
myRegExp.Pattern & "'." _& VBCrLf
  & "The changed string is " & ChangedString
Else
  MsgBox "There is no match. '" & InputString & "' does not match " &VBCrLf _
  & "the pattern '" & myRegExp.Pattern & "'."
End If
End Function

Function DoReplaceGlobal
InputString = InputBox("Enter a string. It will be tested to see if it contains"
&VBCrLf & "any 'A' characters. Any 'A' will be replaced by 'B'")
myRegExp.Global = True
ChangedString = myRegExp.Replace(InputString, "B")
If myRegExp.Test(InputString) = True Then
  MsgBox "The test string '" & InputString & "' matches the pattern '" &
myRegExp.Pattern & "'." & VBCrLf _
  & "The changed string is " & ChangedString
Else
  MsgBox "There is no match. '" & InputString & "' does not match " &VBCrLf _
  & "the pattern '" & myRegExp.Pattern & "'."
End If
End Function

</script>
</head>
<body onload="MatchGlobal">

</body>
</html>
```

As well as using the `Global` property, the code makes use of the `RegExp` object's `Replace()` method.

When `MatchGlobal.html` is opened, two message boxes will be displayed. The first attempts only a single match, and the second matches as many times as there are matches in the test string.

1. Open `MatchGlobal.html` in Internet Explorer.

2. In the message box that appears, enter the character sequence **THE APPLE IS A TASTY FRUIT**. Because matching in VBScript is, by default, case sensitive, be sure to use all uppercase characters.

3. Click the OK button, and inspect the message box that is displayed.

Figure 20-2 shows the screen's appearance after Step 3. Notice that only a single occurrence of uppercase A has been replaced.

Figure 20-2

4. Click the OK button in the message box, and reenter the same string, **THE APPLE IS A TASTY FRUIT**, in the input box.

5. Click the OK button, and inspect the result displayed in the message box.

Figure 20-3 shows the screen's appearance after Step 5. Notice that each occurrence of uppercase A has been replaced with uppercase B.

Figure 20-3

How It Works

The code in this example is split into three functions, `MatchGlobal`, `DoReplaceDefault`, and `DoReplaceGlobal`.

Because the `myRegExp` variable is used in multiple functions, it, together with other variables, is declared globally:

```
Dim myRegExp, InputString, ChangedString
```

The `MatchGlobal` function uses the `Set` statement to create a reference, stored in the `myRegExp` variable, to a new `RegExp` object:

```
Function MatchGlobal
Set myRegExp = new RegExp
myRegExp.Pattern = "A"
DoReplaceDefault
DoReplaceGlobal
End Function
```

Assigning the string value A to be the value of the `Pattern` property of `myRegExp` makes it the simple literal pattern that is to be matched.

The following `DoReplaceDefault` function accepts a string typed by the user into an input box:

```
Function DoReplaceDefault
InputString = InputBox("Enter a string. It will be tested once to see if it
contains" &VBCrLf & "any 'A' characters. Any 'A' will be replaced by 'B'")
myRegExp.Global = False
ChangedString = myRegExp.Replace(InputString, "B")
If myRegExp.Test(InputString) = True Then
  MsgBox "The test string '" & InputString & "' matches the pattern '" &
myRegExp.Pattern & "'." _& VBCrLf
  & "The changed string is " & ChangedString
```

```
  Else
    MsgBox "There is no match. '" & InputString & "' does not match " &VBCrLf _
    & "the pattern '" & myRegExp.Pattern & "'."
  End If
End Function
```

The input box is displayed using the VBScript `InputBox()` function. Notice that the information given to the user states that the string will be tested for a match only once.

To carry out the replacement of any (first) occurrence of A in the string that the user enters into the input box, the `RegExp` object's `Replace()` method is used:

```
  ChangedString = myRegExp.Replace(InputString, "B")
```

Notice that it isn't necessary to express the pattern to match as an argument to the `Replace()` method. That pattern was defined earlier when a pattern was assigned to `myRegExp`'s `Pattern` property:

```
  myRegExp.Pattern = "A"
```

The two arguments to the `Replace()` method are, respectively, the string in which the replace operation is to be carried out (in this case, the value of the `InputString` variable) and the character sequence to be used to replace the first occurrence of text that matches the value of the `Pattern` property (in this case, the character A, which is the value of the `Pattern` property, is replaced by the character B, the second argument to the `Replace()` method).

The first occurrence of A in THE APPLE IS A TASTY FRUIT is the initial character of APPLE. That A is replaced by the second argument of the `Replace()` method, B. So the value of the following `ChangedString` variable is THE BPPLE IS A TASTY FRUIT, with the only change being the creation of the character sequence BPPLE in place of the character sequence APPLE:

```
  ChangedString = myRegExp.Replace(InputString, "B")
```

This is the default behavior, to match, and in this case, replace once.

The following `DoReplaceGlobal` function does almost the same thing, except that matching is attempted on the input string an unlimited number of times:

```
Function DoReplaceGlobal
InputString = InputBox("Enter a string. It will be tested to see if it contains"
&VBCrLf & "any 'A' characters. Any 'A' will be replaced by 'B'")
myRegExp.Global = True
ChangedString = myRegExp.Replace(InputString, "B")
If myRegExp.Test(InputString) = True Then
  MsgBox "The test string '" & InputString & "' matches the pattern '" &
myRegExp.Pattern & "'." & VBCrLf _
  & "The changed string is " & ChangedString
Else
  MsgBox "There is no match. '" & InputString & "' does not match " &VBCrLf _
  & "the pattern '" & myRegExp.Pattern & "'."
End If
End Function
```

This change in processing behavior occurs because the value of the `Global` property of the `RegExp` object has been set to `True`:

```
myRegExp.Global = True
```

Each time the value of the `Pattern` property, in this example, the uppercase character A, is matched, it is replaced in the variable `ChangedString` by the uppercase character B:

```
ChangedString = myRegExp.Replace(InputString, "B")
```

Thus, each A in the input string THE APPLE IS A TASTY FRUIT is replaced by B, giving the value of the `ChangedString` variable as THE BPPLE IS B TBSTY FRUIT.

The RegExp Object's IgnoreCase Property

The `RegExp` object's `IgnoreCase` property allows case-insensitive matching to be carried out.

The preceding `MatchGlobal.html` example used an input string that was all uppercase. More naturally, instead of THE APPLE IS A TASTY FRUIT, you might input the string The apple is a tasty fruit..

The following sample file, `CaseReplace.html`, allows you to try out case-sensitive (the default) and case-insensitive replacement:

```
<html>
<head>
<title>Carry out a case-sensitive replace and a case-insensitive replace.</title>
<script language="vbscript" type="text/vbscript">
Dim myRegExp, InputString, ChangedString

Function MatchCaseOptions
Set myRegExp = new RegExp
myRegExp.Pattern = "A"
myRegExp.Global = True
DoReplaceSensitive
DoReplaceInsensitive
End Function


Function DoReplaceSensitive
InputString = InputBox("Enter a string. It will be tested once to see if it
contains" &VBCrLf & "any 'A' characters. Any 'A' will be replaced by 'B'")
ChangedString = myRegExp.Replace(InputString, "B")
If myRegExp.Test(InputString) = True Then
  MsgBox "The test string '" & InputString & "' matches the pattern '" &
myRegExp.Pattern & "'." & VBCrLf _
  & "The changed string is " & ChangedString
Else
  MsgBox "There is no match. '" & InputString & "' does not match " &VBCrLf _
  & "the pattern '" & myRegExp.Pattern & "'."
End If
End Function
```

```
Function DoReplaceInsensitive
myRegExp.IgnoreCase = True
InputString = InputBox("Enter a string. It will be tested to see if it contains"
&VBCrLf & "any 'A' characters. Any 'A' will be replaced by 'B'")
ChangedString = myRegExp.Replace(InputString, "B")
If myRegExp.Test(InputString) = True Then
  MsgBox "The test string '" & InputString & "' matches the pattern '" &
myRegExp.Pattern & "'." & VBCrLf _
  & "The changed string is " & ChangedString
Else
  MsgBox "There is no match. '" & InputString & "' does not match " &VBCrLf _
  & "the pattern '" & myRegExp.Pattern & "'."
End If
End Function

</script>
</head>
<body onload="MatchCaseOptions">

</body>
</html>
```

Try It Out   Using the IgnoreCase Property of the RegExp Object

First, attempt to match an input string using the default value of the IgnoreCase property.

1. Open CaseReplace.html in Internet Explorer, and in the displayed input box, enter the test string **The apple is a tasty fruit.**.

2. Click the OK button, and inspect the information displayed in the message box., as shown in Figure 20-4. Notice that there is no match at this point.

Figure 20-4

Next, attempt to match an input string with the value of the IgnoreCase property set to True. In other words, matching will be case insensitive.

3. Click the OK button to dismiss the message box that was displayed in Figure 20-4.

4. In the displayed input box, enter the test string **The apple is a tasty fruit.**.

5. Click the OK button, and inspect the information displayed in the message box, as shown in Figure 20-5.

Figure 20-5

How It Works

When `CaseReplace.html` is loaded, the function `MatchCaseOptions` is called:

```
<body onload="MatchCaseOptions">
```

Notice that in `MatchCaseOptions`, the value of the `Global` property is set to `True`, so all matches will be replaced:

```
Function MatchCaseOptions
Set myRegExp = new RegExp
myRegExp.Pattern = "A"
myRegExp.Global = True
DoReplaceSensitive
DoReplaceInsensitive
End Function
```

The `DoReplaceSensitive` function does a global attempted match similar to the one you saw in the preceding example.

The `DoReplaceInsensitive` function does a global attempted match but does it case insensitively because the value of the `IgnoreCase` property is set to `True`:

```
Function DoReplaceInsensitive
myRegExp.IgnoreCase = True
```

Every occurrence of the character A (whether lowercase or uppercase) in the input string `The apple is a tasty fruit.` is replaced by uppercase B, as you saw in Figure 20-5.

The RegExp Object's Test() Method

The `Test()` method executes an attempted regular expression match against a specified test string and returns a Boolean value. The Boolean value returned by the `Test()` method can be used in a logical test. For example, you saw in an earlier example the following code, which tested whether the test string held in the `TestString` variable matched the value of the `Pattern` property and, depending on the Boolean value returned, would display a message box indicating a successful match or a failure to match.

```
If myRegExp.Test(TestString) = True Then
  MsgBox "The test string '" & TestString & "' matches the pattern '" &
myRegExp.Pattern & "'."
Else
  MsgBox "There is no match."
End If
```

The RegExp Object's Replace() Method

The Replace() method replaces the part of a string that matches the pattern held in the Pattern property of the RegExp object with another string. The string in which replacement is to take place is the first argument to the Replace() method, and the replacement string is the second argument to the Replace() method.

The Replace() method, when used together with grouping parentheses, can be used to reverse the order of parts of the string in the first argument to the method. The groups captured in the matching string can be used in reverse order in the replacement string.

Try It Out   Using the Replace() Method to Reverse Order

The test file, ReverseName.html, is shown here:

```
<html>
<head>
<title>Reverse Surname and First Name</title>
<script language="vbscript" type="text/vbscript">
Function ReverseName
Dim myRegExp, TestName, Match
Set myRegExp = new RegExp
myRegExp.Pattern = "(\S+)(\s+)(\S+)"
TestString = InputBox("Enter your name below, in the form" & VBCrLf & _
 "first name, then a space then last name." & VBCrLf & "Don't enter an initial or
middle name.")
Match = myRegexp.Replace(TestString, "$3,$2$1")
If Match <> "" Then
  MsgBox "Your name in last name, first name format is:" & VBCrLf & Match
Else
  MsgBox "You didn't enter your name." & VBCrLF & "Press OK then F5 to run the
example again."
End If
End Function

</script>
</head>
<body onload="ReverseName">

</body>
</html>
```

1. Open `ReverseName.html` in Internet Explorer.

2. In the input box that is displayed, enter your name in first name–last name format, with the first and last names separated by at least one space character.

   Figure 20-6 shows the name John Smith input in the desired format.

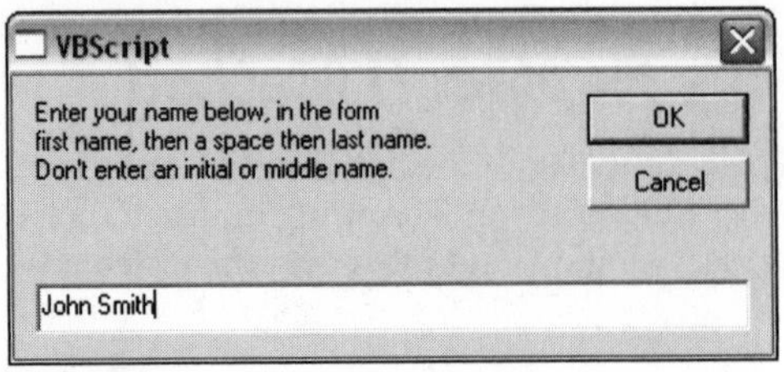

Figure 20-6

3. Click the OK button, and inspect the results, as shown in Figure 20-7.

   If a name has been entered in the requested format, *firstname lastname*, the name is displayed in a message box in the format *lastname, firstname*.

Figure 20-7

How It Works

When the Web page loads, the `ReverseName` function is called:

```
<body onload="ReverseName">
```

The pattern `(\S+)(\s+)(\S+)` is assigned to the `myRegExp` variable's `Pattern` property:

```
myRegExp.Pattern = "(\S+)(\s+)(\S+)"
```

The preceding pattern captures three groups. The first, specified by `(\S+)`, matches and captures one or more nonwhitespace characters. The second, specified by `(\s+)`, matches and captures one or more whitespace characters. The third, specified by `(\S+)`, matches and captures one or more nonwhitespace characters. If the user enters his name in the requested format of *firstname* followed by a space character, followed by *lastname*, there should be a match contained in the `TestString` variable. The groups are held, respectively, in the special variables `$1`, `$2`, and `$3`:

```
TestString = InputBox("Enter your name below, in the form" & VBCrLf & _
  "first name, then a space then last name." & VBCrLf & "Don't enter an initial or
  middle name.")
```

You can use the $3, $2, and $1 variables in the replace operation, as follows:

```
Match = myRegexp.Replace(TestString, "$3,$2$1")
```

Because the last name should be contained in $3 and the first name contained in $1, you can reverse those and add a comma using the pattern $3, $2$1. If you wanted to standardize on a single space character in the output (rather than echoing whatever whitespace the user entered into the input box), you could alter the pattern to $3, $1.

The If statement controls whether a message about a successful match is displayed or a message indicating that the user didn't enter a valid name is displayed:

```
If Match <> "" Then
  MsgBox "Your name in last name, first name format is:" & VBCrLf & Match
Else
  MsgBox "You didn't enter your name." & VBCrLF & "Press OK then F5 to run the
example again."
End If
```

The RegExp Object's Execute() Method

The RegExp object's Execute() method executes regular expression matching against a specified string. The regular expression pattern is held as the value of the RegExp object's Pattern property. The Execute() method returns a Matches collection, which contains a Match object for each match in the string being tested.

Try It Out   The Execute() Method

The test file, ExecuteDemo.html, is shown here:

```
<html>
<head>
<title>Demo of the Execute() Method</title>
<script language="vbscript" type="text/vbscript">
Function ExecuteDemo
Dim myRegExp, TestName, Match, Matches, displayString
displayString = ""
Set myRegExp = new RegExp
myRegExp.Pattern = "[A-Z]\d"
myRegExp.IgnoreCase = True
myRegExp.Global = False
TestString = InputBox("Enter characters and numbers in the text box below.")
Set Matches = myRegexp.Execute(TestString)
  For Each Match in Matches
    displayString = displayString & "Match found at position " & Match.FirstIndex &
VBCrLf
    displayString = displayString & "The match value is '" & Match.Value & "'."
    MsgBox displayString
    displayString = ""
  Next
End Function
```

```
    </script>
    </head>
    <body onload="ExecuteDemo">

    </body>
    </html>
```

1. Open `ExecuteDemo.html` in Internet Explorer, and in the text box within the input box, enter the character sequence **A9**.

2. Click the OK button, and inspect the text displayed in the message box, as shown in Figure 20-8. Notice that the match is said to occur at position 0, indicating that character positions are numbered from zero.

Figure 20-8

3. Click OK, and press F5 to reload the page and run the script again.

4. In the text box within the input box, enter the character sequence **A9 A10 A11 A12 A13**.

5. Click the OK button, and inspect the text displayed in the message box, as shown in Figure 20-9. Notice that the result displayed is the same as before. This is so because the value of the `myRegExp.Global` property is set to `False`. (In a moment, you will repeat this example, but with the `myRegExp.Global` property set to `True`.)

Figure 20-9

How It Works

When the Web page loads, the `ExecuteDemo` function is called:

```
    <body onload="ExecuteDemo">
```

First, the variables used in `ExecuteDemo` are dimensioned:

```
    Function ExecuteDemo
        Dim myRegExp, TestName, Match, Matches, displayString
```

The value of the `displayString` variable is set to the empty string, and a reference to a new `RegExp` object is set:

```
displayString = ""
Set myRegExp = new RegExp
```

The regular expression pattern `[A-Z]\d`, which matches an alphabetic character followed by a numeric digit, is assigned to the `myRegExp` object's `Pattern` property of the `myRegExp` object:

```
myRegExp.Pattern = "[A-Z]\d"
```

The `IgnoreCase` property is set to `True`, which means that the matching process will be case insensitive:

```
myRegExp.IgnoreCase = True
```

The value of the `Global` property is set to `False`. This means that the `Execute()` method will return only one match:

```
myRegExp.Global = False
```

Input from the user is sought using the `InputBox()` function, and the input is assigned to the `TestString` variable:

```
TestString = InputBox("Enter characters and numbers in the text box below.")
```

The `Execute()` method is used to produce a `Matches` collection:

```
Set Matches = myRegexp.Execute(TestString)
```

Each `Match` in the `Matches` collection is then processed in a `For Each` loop. If there is no match, this loop produces no displayed output. The `displayString` variable is used to construct a string for display:

```
For Each Match in Matches
   displayString = displayString & "Match found at position " & Match.FirstIndex & VBCrLf
   displayString = displayString & "The match value is '" & Match.Value & "'."
```

Then the `MsgBox` function is used to display the value of the `displayString` variable:

```
MsgBox displayString
```

Finally, the value of the `displayString` variable is again set to the empty string, ready to be used in the next iteration of the `For Each` loop. If the value of the `displayString` variable was not reset to the empty string, the information from each match would be concatenated into one long display string. You may prefer that approach, which, when the value of the `Global` property is set to `True`, will display the information about all `Match` objects in the `Matches` collection in a single message box:

```
   displayString = ""
Next
End Function
```

The following example modifies the code so that all matches in the test string are returned.

The Execute() Method with Global Equal to True

The test file, `ExecuteDemoGlobal.html`, is shown here:

```
<html>
<head>
<title>Demo of the Execute() Method</title>
<script language="vbscript" type="text/vbscript">
Function ExecuteDemo
Dim myRegExp, TestName, Match, Matches, displayString
displayString = ""
Set myRegExp = new RegExp
myRegExp.Pattern = "[A-Z]\d"
myRegExp.IgnoreCase = True
myRegExp.Global = True
TestString = InputBox("Enter characters and numbers in the text box below.")
Set Matches = myRegexp.Execute(TestString)
  For Each Match in Matches
    displayString = displayString & "Match found at position " & Match.FirstIndex &
"."
    displayString = displayString & "The match value is '" & Match.Value & "'." &
VBCrLf
    'displayString = ""
  Next
  MsgBox displayString
End Function

</script>
</head>
<body onload="ExecuteDemo">

</body>
</html>
```

1. Open the file `ExecuteDemoGlobal.html` in Internet Explorer.

2. Enter the test string **A9 A10 A11 A12 A13** into the input box.

3. Click the OK button, and inspect the results displayed in the message box, as shown in Figure 20-10. Notice that each match in the `Matches` collection is now listed in the message box.

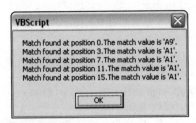

Figure 20-10

How It Works

The code works similarly to the code in `ExecuteDemo.html`. The crucial difference is that the value of the `myRegExp` variable's `Global` property is set to a value of `True`:

```
myRegExp.Global = True
```

This means that the `Execute()` method will return all matches found. For each match, a `Match` object will be returned in the `Matches` collection. As Figure 20-10 shows, there are five matches on this occasion.

Using the Match Object and the Matches Collection

The `Matches` collection and its contained `Match` objects can be created only by using the `Execute()` method, described in the previous section.

Each `Match` object has three read-only properties:

- ❑ **FirstIndex** — The position of the first character in a match
- ❑ **Length** — The length of the match
- ❑ **Value** — The value of the match

These contain information about the value of the match, where its first character is located, and the length of the matching character sequence.

The use of the `FirstIndex` and `Value` properties was demonstrated in the examples using the `Execute()` method in the preceding section.

The test file, `MatchLength.html`, is shown here:

```
<html>
<head>
<title>The Length Property of a Match Object</title>
<script language="vbscript" type="text/vbscript">
Function MatchLength
Dim myRegExp, TestName, Match, Matches, displayString
displayString = ""
Set myRegExp = new RegExp
myRegExp.Pattern = "[A-Z]\d+"
myRegExp.IgnoreCase = True
myRegExp.Global = True
TestString = InputBox("Enter characters and numbers in the text box below.")
Set Matches = myRegexp.Execute(TestString)
  For Each Match in Matches
     displayString = displayString & "Match found at position " & Match.FirstIndex &
"."

     displayString = displayString & "The match value is '" & Match.Value & "'." &
VBCrLf
```

```
        displayString = displayString & "Its length is " & Match.Length & "
characters." &VBCrLf & VBCrLf
        'displayString = ""
  Next
  MsgBox displayString
End Function

</script>
</head>
<body onload="MatchLength">

</body>
</html>
```

The Length Property

1.   Open MatchLength.html in Internet Explorer.

2.   Enter the following character sequence into the text box of the input box: **A9 B10 C110
     D1123456 E1234567890 A3**.

3.   Click the OK button, and inspect the results displayed in the message box, as shown in
     Figure 20-11.

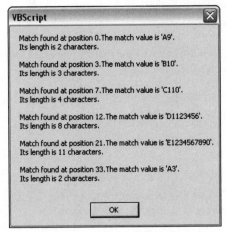

Figure 20-11

How It Works

When the Web page loads, the MatchLength function is called:

```
<body onload="MatchLength">
```

The regular expression pattern assigned to the Pattern property:

```
myRegExp.Pattern = "[A-Z]\d+"
```

matches a single alphabetic character of any case, because the value of the `IgnoreCase` property is set to `True`, followed by one or more numeric digits:

```
myRegExp.IgnoreCase = True
```

The test string, A9 B10 C110 D1123456 E1234567890 A3, contains six matches. Because the value of the `myRegExp` variable's `Global` property is set to `True`, all six matches are represented as `Match` objects in the `Matches` collection:

```
myRegExp.Global = True
```

The `Matches` collection is created when the following line of code is executed:

```
Set Matches = myRegexp.Execute(TestString)
```

The `Execute()` method creates the `Matches` collection, which, in this example, contains six `Match` objects, each of which is processed in the same way as specified in the following `For Each` loop:

```
For Each Match in Matches
    displayString = displayString & "Match found at position " & Match.FirstIndex &
"."
    displayString = displayString & "The match value is '" & Match.Value & "'." &
VBCrLf
    displayString = displayString & "Its length is " & Match.Length & "
characters." &VBCrLf & VBCrLf
    'displayString = ""
  Next
```

The `displayString` variable initially holds the empty string. Each time through the `For Each` loop, information is added to the `displayString` variable about the position of the match (as held in the `FirstIndex` property) and the length of the match (held in the `Length` property).

Finally, the value of the `displayString` variable is displayed in a message box, which displays information about the position and length of each match:

```
MsgBox displayString
```

Supported Metacharacters

The following table summarizes the metacharacters supported in VBScript.

Metacharacter	Description
^	Matches the position at the beginning of an input string.
$	Matches the position at the end of an input string.
?	A quantifier. It matches when there is zero or one occurrence of the preceding character or group.

Table continued on following page

Metacharacter	Description
*	A quantifier. It matches when there are zero or more occurrences of the preceding character or group.
+	A quantifier. It matches when there are one or more occurrences of the preceding character or group.
{n,m}	Quantifier notation. It matches when there is a minimum of *n* and a maximum of *m* occurrences of the preceding character or group.
(...)	Grouping parentheses.
(?: ...)	Nongrouping parentheses.
(?= ...)	Positive lookahead.
(?! ...)	Negative lookahead.
|	Alternation.
[...]	Character class. Character class ranges are supported.
[^ ...]	Negated character class.
\b	Matches the boundary between alphanumeric characters and nonalphanumeric characters. In effect, it can match the boundary at the beginning or end of a "word."
\B	Matches a position that does not match \b.
\d	Matches a numeric digit. It is equivalent to the character class [0-9].
\D	Matches a character that is not a numeric digit. It is equivalent to the negated character class [^0-9].
\s	Matches any whitespace character.
\S	Matches any character that does not match \s.
\t	Matches a tab character.
\w	Matches any alphanumeric "word" character. It is equivalent to the character class [A-Za-z0-9_].
\W	Matches any character that does not match \w. It is equivalent to the negated character class [^A-Za-z0-9_].

Quantifiers

VBScript supports a full range of quantifiers—that is, the ?, *, + metacharacters, together with the {n,m} notation.

The usage of these quantifiers in VBScript is standard.

Positional Metacharacters

The ^ metacharacter is supported and matches the position before the first character of a character sequence. The $ metacharacter is also supported and matches the position after the last character of an input character sequence.

The test file, `Positional.html`, is shown here:

```
<html>
<head>
<title>Positional Metacharacters</title>
<script language="vbscript" type="text/vbscript">
Dim myRegExp, TestString, displayString, MatchOrNot


Function FindMatch
displayString = ""
Set myRegExp = new RegExp
myRegExp.Pattern = "[A-Z]\d{2}"
myRegExp.IgnoreCase = False
myRegExp.Global = False
TestString = InputBox("Enter one alphabetic character and two numbers in the text
box below.")
MatchOrNot = myRegexp.Test(TestString)
If MatchOrNot Then
displayString = "When the pattern is '" & myRegExp.Pattern & "' the input '" _
 & TestString & "' contains a match."
Else
displayString = "When the pattern is '" & myRegExp.Pattern & "' the input '" _
 & TestString & "' does not contain a match."
End If
myRegExp.Pattern = "^[A-Z]\d{2}$"
MatchOrNot = myRegexp.Test(TestString)
If MatchOrNot Then
displayString = displayString & VBCrLf & "When the pattern is '" & myRegExp.Pattern
& "' the input '" _
 & TestString & "' contains a match."
Else
displayString = displayString & VBCrLf & "When the pattern is '" & myRegExp.Pattern
& "' the input '" _
 & TestString & "' does not contain a match."
End If

MsgBox displayString
End Function

</script>
</head>
<body onload="FindMatch">

</body>
</html>
```

The code matches the character sequence entered into the input box against two patterns. The first does not include the positional metacharacters ^ and $. The second pattern includes both metacharacters.

Try It Out   **Positional Metacharacters**

1. Open `Positional.html` in Internet Explorer.

2. In the text box in the input box, enter the character sequence **A99**.

3. Click the OK button, and inspect the information displayed in the message box, as shown in Figure 20-12. The message box shows the results of attempted matching when there are no positional metacharacters present and when both positional metacharacters are present. Notice that there is a match in both situations.

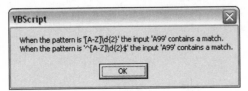

Figure 20-12

4. Click the OK button to dismiss the message box and then press F5 to reload the Web page.

5. In the text box in the input box, enter the character sequence **A999**.

6. Click the OK button, and inspect the information displayed in the message box, as shown in Figure 20-13. Notice that there is a match when no positional metacharacters are present but no match when the positional metacharacters are present in the pattern.

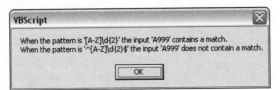

Figure 20-13

7. Click the OK button to dismiss the message box and then press F5 to reload the Web page.

8. In the text box in the input box, enter the character sequence **A2A**.

9. Click the OK button, and inspect the information displayed in the message box, as shown in Figure 20-14. There is no match with either pattern.

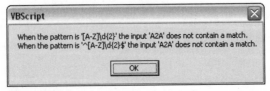

Figure 20-14

How It Works

When the page is loaded, the `FindMatch` function is called:

```
<body onload="FindMatch">
```

The `FindMatch` function twice uses the `RegExp` object's `Test()` method to attempt to match a string input by the user.

Initially, the value assigned to the `Pattern` property is the pattern `[A-Z]\d{2}`, which matches a single alphabetic character followed by two numeric digits:

```
myRegExp.Pattern = "[A-Z]\d{2}"
```

Because the `IgnoreCase` and `Global` properties are each set to `False`, the alphabetic character can be entered in either case, and only one match is attempted:

```
myRegExp.IgnoreCase = False
myRegExp.Global = False
```

The string that is input by the user is assigned to the `TestString` variable:

```
TestString = InputBox("Enter one alphabetic character and two numbers in the text
box below.")
```

And the result of the `Test()` method, with the `TestString` variable as its argument, is assigned to the variable `MatchOrNot`, which contains a Boolean value. The `MatchOrNot` variable either contains a nonzero length string (which is equivalent to Boolean `True`) or the empty string (which is equivalent to the Boolean value `False`):

```
MatchOrNot = myRegexp.Test(TestString)
```

If there is a match, the pattern is output together with the test string it matches:

```
If MatchOrNot Then
displayString = "When the pattern is '" & myRegExp.Pattern & "' the input '" _
 & TestString & "' contains a match."
```

If there is no match, a message that the pattern is not matched by the input string is output:

```
Else
displayString = "When the pattern is '" & myRegExp.Pattern & "' the input '" _
 & TestString & "' does not contain a match."
End If
```

The `displayString` variable now contains the result of the first attempted matching process. Now, however, the value of the `Pattern` property is changed to allow a second attempted match using a pattern that now includes both the `^` and `$` metacharacters:

```
myRegExp.Pattern = "^[A-Z]\d{2}$"
```

Again, the Boolean value returned by the `Test()` method is assigned to the `MatchOrNot` variable:

```
MatchOrNot = myRegexp.Test(TestString)
```

If there is a match, the `MatchOrNot` variable contains a value equivalent to Boolean `True`, so a message specifying the pattern and the match is added to the `displayString` variable:

```
If MatchOrNot Then
displayString = displayString & VBCrLf & "When the pattern is '" & myRegExp.Pattern
& "' the input '" _
 & TestString & "' contains a match."
```

But if there is no match, a message indicating that is added to the `displayString` variable:

```
Else
displayString = displayString & VBCrLf & "When the pattern is '" & myRegExp.Pattern
& "' the input '" _
 & TestString & "' does not contain a match."
End If
```

Finally, the value of the `displayString` variable (which contains information about two attempted matches with two different values of the `Pattern` property) is displayed in a message box:

```
MsgBox displayString
End Function
```

When the test string is A99, it matches the pattern `[A-Z]\d{2}` and also matches the pattern `^[A-Z]\d{2}`.

When the test string is A999, it matches the pattern `[A-Z]\d{2}` because there is an alphabetic character followed by two numeric digits. However, there is no match for the second pattern, `^[A-Z]\d{2}$`, because there are three numeric digits, not two as required by the pattern, before the end-of-line position that matches the $ metacharacter.

The test string A2A fails to match either pattern because there is no alphabetic character followed by two numeric digits, as would be required by both patterns, `[A-Z]\d{2}` and `^[A-Z]\d{2}$`.

Character Classes

VBScript has full support for character classes. The VBScript documentation does, however, refer to character classes as *character sets*.

To match any character from A through L, the character class `[ABCDEFGHIJKL]` can be used. Equally, a range can be used, `[A-L]`.

Negated character classes can be used, too. The character class `[^A-D]` will match any character except A through D.

Word Boundaries

VBScript supports the \b metacharacter to match the position either at the beginning or at the end of a sequence of word characters. Often, the sequence of alphanumeric characters will form what a human reader will view as a word, but regular expression engines do not have knowledge of the concept of a word. The \b metacharacter matches in one of two situations:

❑ A position where the preceding character is contained in [A-Za-z0-9_] and the following character is contained in [^A-Za-z0-9_]. This is equivalent to the end of a word.

❑ A position where the preceding character is contained in [^A-Za-z0-9_] and the following character is contained in [A-Za-z0-9_]. This is equivalent to the beginning of a word.

Lookahead

VBScript supports lookahead. Both positive and negative lookaheads are supported. The syntax for a positive lookahead is (?=theLookahead) and for a negative lookahead is (?!theNegativeLookahead).

The following example demonstrates both positive and negative lookahead. The test file, Lookaheads.html, is shown here:

```
<html>
<head>
<title>Positive and Negative Lookahead</title>
<script language="vbscript" type="text/vbscript">
Function MatchLookaheads
Dim myRegExp, TestName, Match, Matches, displayString
displayString = ""
Set myRegExp = new RegExp
myRegExp.Pattern = "the(?=atre)" 'matches, for example, the in theatre
myRegExp.IgnoreCase = True
myRegExp.Global = True
TestString = InputBox("Enter characters and numbers in the text box below.")
Set Matches = myRegexp.Execute(TestString)
displayString = displayString & "MATCH ATTEMPT 1: 'the' in 'theatre'" & VBCrLf
  For Each Match in Matches
     displayString = displayString & "Match found at position " & Match.FirstIndex &
"."
     displayString = displayString & "The match value is '" & Match.Value & "'." &
VBCrLf
  Next
displayString = displayString & VBCrLf & VBCrLf
'Begin a new match which produces a new Match collection.
myRegExp.Pattern = "the(?!atre)" 'matches the NOT in theatre
Set Matches = myRegexp.Execute(TestString)
displayString = displayString & "MATCH ATTEMPT 2: 'the' not in 'theatre'" & VBCrLf
  For Each Match in Matches
     displayString = displayString & "Match found at position " & Match.FirstIndex &
"."
     displayString = displayString & "The match value is '" & Match.Value & "'." &
VBCrLf
```

```
    Next
    MsgBox displayString
  End Function

</script>
</head>
<body onload="MatchLookaheads">

</body>
</html>
```

Positive and Negative Lookahead

1. Open `Lookaheads.html` in Internet Explorer.

2. In the text box in the input box, enter the character sequence **They love the theatre theatrically.**.

3. Click the OK button, and inspect the result displayed in the message box, as shown in Figure 20-15. The Match 1 section in the message box occurs when the pattern is `the(?=atre)`. The Match 2 section in the message box occurs when the pattern is `the(?!atre)`.

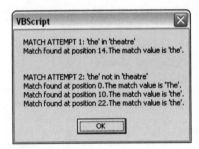

Figure 20-15

How It Works

When the page loads, the `MatchLookaheads` function is called:

```
<body onload="MatchLookaheads">
```

The code uses the `RegExp` object's `Execute()` method twice. First, with the following value in the `Pattern` property:

```
myRegExp.Pattern = "the(?=atre)" 'matches, for example, the in theatre
```

The `Execute()` method is executed:

```
Set Matches = myRegexp.Execute(TestString)
```

The `displayString` variable is assigned a label indicating that this is the first match attempt:

```
displayString = displayString & "MATCH ATTEMPT 1: 'the' in 'theatre'" & VBCrLf
```

For each `Match` object in the `Matches` collection (only one match in this case), information about the match is added to the `displayString` variable:

```
For Each Match in Matches
   displayString = displayString & "Match found at position " & Match.FirstIndex &
"."
   displayString = displayString & "The match value is '" & Match.Value & "'." &
VBCrLf
   'displayString = ""
Next
displayString = displayString & VBCrLf & VBCrLf
```

The pattern being matched is `the(?=atre)`, which matches the character sequence `the` when it is followed by the character sequence `atre`. This is positive lookahead. It matches `the` in, for example, `theatre` or `theatres`.

Then the second attempt at matching is made. The value of the `Pattern` property is assigned a pattern that includes a negative lookahead. This means that matches will occur when the character sequence `the` is not followed by the character sequence `atre`:

```
myRegExp.Pattern = "the(?!atre)" 'matches the NOT in theatre
```

The `Execute()` method means that the former `Matches` collection is replaced with a new one. However, information about the former `Matches` collection has already been captured in the `displayString` variable for later displaying:

```
Set Matches = myRegexp.Execute(TestString)
```

Information about the second `Matches` collection is now added to the `displayString` variable:

```
displayString = displayString & "MATCH ATTEMPT 2: 'the' not in 'theatre'" & VBCrLf
   For Each Match in Matches
      displayString = displayString & "Match found at position " & Match.FirstIndex &
"."
      displayString = displayString & "The match value is '" & Match.Value & "'." &
VBCrLf

   Next
```

The first match attempt matches the pattern `the(?=atre)`, which includes the positive lookahead. In the test character sequence, `They love the theatre theatrically.`, it matches the character sequence `the` in `theatre`. The `Matches` collection contains a single `Match` object.

The second match attempt matches the pattern `the(?!atre)`, which includes the negative lookahead. In the test character sequence, `They love the theatre theatrically.`, there are three matches. The second `Matches` collection, therefore, contains three `Match` objects corresponding to matches in `The` of `They`, the word `the`, and in the word `theatrically`. Notice that while matching is case insensitive, the case of the initial `T` of `They` is preserved.

Grouping and Nongrouping Parentheses

VBScript supports both grouping and nongrouping parentheses. Grouping parentheses are written as (*theGroup*), and nongrouping parentheses as (?:*notGrouped*).

The following example modifies ReverseName.html, so that the whitespace characters are not captured. The test file, NonGrouping.html, is shown here:

```
<html>
<head>
<title>Reverse Surname and First Name, using non-grouping parentheses</title>
<script language="vbscript" type="text/vbscript">
Function ReverseName2
Dim myRegExp, TestName, Match
Set myRegExp = new RegExp
myRegExp.Pattern = "(\S+)(?:\s+)(\S+)"
TestString = InputBox("Enter your name below, in the form" & VBCrLf & _
  "first name, then a space then last name." & VBCrLf & "Don't enter an initial or
middle name.")
Match = myRegexp.Replace(TestString, "$2, $1")
If Match <> "" Then
  MsgBox "Your name in last name, first name format is:" & VBCrLf & Match
Else
  MsgBox "You didn't enter your name." & VBCrLF & "Press OK then F5 to run the
example again."
End If
End Function

</script>
</head>
<body onload="ReverseName2">

</body>
</html>
```

Try It Out   Grouping and Nongrouping Parentheses

1. Open NonGrouping.html in Internet Explorer.

2. In the text box of the input box, enter the string **John Smith**.

3. Click OK, and inspect the information displayed in the message box, as shown in Figure 20-16. The effect is the same as that produced by the ReverseName.html example. The behind-the-scenes grouping differs, as explained in How It Works.

Figure 20-16

How It Works

The ReverseName2 function differs from the ReverseName function that you saw in an earlier example in this chapter in one key respect: It uses nongrouping parentheses to contain the whitespace characters entered between the first name and last name:

```
myRegExp.Pattern = "(\S+)(?:\s+)(\S+)"
```

This means that the first name is in $1 (as before), and the last name is in $2 (it was previously in $3). So when using the Replace() method, you must make appropriate adjustments to ensure that the last name (in $2) is displayed first, then the comma and space character, and then the first name (in $1):

```
Match = myRegexp.Replace(TestString, "$2, $1")
```

Exercises

1. Modify the file TestForA.html so that it tests for a date value entered in the format MM/DD/YYYY.

2. Modify the file ReverseName.html so that it will accept only a sequence of alphabetic characters followed by one or more whitespace characters, followed by a sequence of alphabetic characters in the input box. If there is any additional input in the text box, an error message should be displayed requesting input in the specified format. Hint: As well as needing to modify the value of the Pattern property, you will need to amend the message displayed if there is not a match.

Visual Basic .NET and Regular Expressions

Microsoft Visual Basic .NET provides powerful and flexible regular expression functionality. There are both significant similarities and significant differences between the regular expression support in Visual Basic .NET and that described earlier in VBScript. Visual Basic .NET regular expression support is more powerful and flexible.

The foundation on which Visual Basic .NET regular expression programming rests is the `System.Text.RegularExpressions` namespace, which is part of the .NET Framework Class Library.

In this chapter, you will learn the following:

❑ How to use the classes and objects contained in the `System.Text.RegularExpressions` namespace

❑ The meaning of the metacharacters supported in Visual Basic .NET

> **Examples shown in this chapter have been tested with Visual Studio 2003 and the .NET Framework 1.1. I will assume that you have access to a copy of Visual Studio 2003 and have a working knowledge of at least the basics of Visual Basic .NET. It isn't the intent of this chapter to provide a tutorial on the basics of using Visual Studio .NET 2003. However, if you do not have access to a copy of Visual Studio 2003, there are copies of the .exe files, which you can run, although you won't be able to view and edit the Visual Basic .NET code.**

The System.Text.RegularExpressions namespace

Regular expression functionality in Visual Basic .NET is contained in objects that are part of the System.Text.RegularExpressions namespace. Before looking at those classes, a very simple Visual Basic .NET regular expressions example is laid out.

There are several ways to use regular expressions in Visual Basic .NET. The following example uses one technique to carry out simple matching.

A Simple Visual Basic .NET Example

This example simply tests whether a string entered by the user matches a literal regular expression pattern, Fred.

The sample file, Module1.vb in the FindFred project, contains the following code:

```
Imports System.Text.RegularExpressions
Module Module1

    Sub Main()
        Dim myInput, myRegex
        myRegex = New Regex("Fred")
        Console.WriteLine("Enter a test string")
        Console.WriteLine("Then press the Enter key to continue.")
        myInput = Console.ReadLine()
        Console.WriteLine("The string you entered was: " & myInput)
        Console.WriteLine("The match is: " & myRegex.Match(myInput).Value)
        Console.WriteLine("Press the Return key to continue.")
        Console.ReadLine()
    End Sub
End Module
```

In some examples, the lines of code may break on the printed page when, in the original code, they exist on a single line. This difference is caused by the relatively limited line length on the printed page.

The following instructions assume that you have Visual Studio 2003 installed.

1. Open Visual Studio 2003, and from the File menu, select New; then select Project.

   Figure 21-1 shows the dialog box that opens. The choices specified in Steps 2 through 4 are already made.

2. In the dialog box shown in Figure 21-1, select Visual Basic Projects in the Project Types pane.

3. Select Console Application in the Templates pane, and enter the text **FindFred** in the Name text box.

4. In the Location text box, enter the text **C:\BRegExp\Ch21**. If you wish, you can select another location. Click the OK button.

   Figure 21-2 shows the screen's appearance after clicking OK. The exact appearance may differ from that shown in the figure due to the many customization options available in Visual Studio 2003.

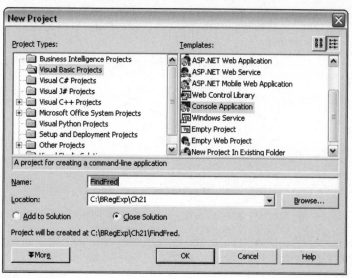

Figure 21-1

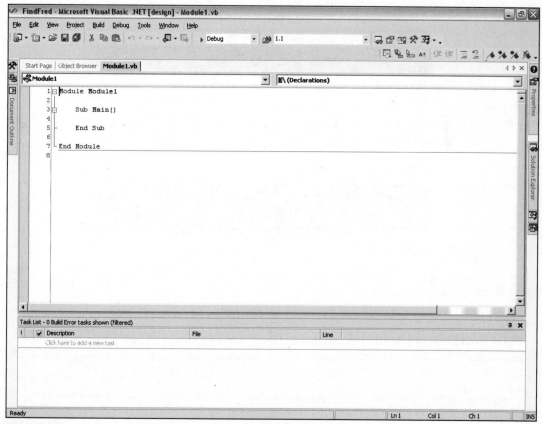

Figure 21-2

The `Regex` object is part of the `System.Text.RegularExpressions` namespace. It is useful for conciseness of the code to import the `System.Text.RegularExpressions` namespace, using the `Imports` statement.

5. Add the following code to the code window, making sure that you add it before the line containing `Module Module1`:

```
Imports System.Text.RegularExpressions
```

6. Add the following code after the line that contains `Sub Main()`:

```
Dim myInput, myRegex
myRegex = New Regex("Fred")
Console.WriteLine("Enter a test string")
Console.WriteLine("Then press the Enter key to continue.")
myInput = Console.ReadLine()
Console.WriteLine("The string you entered was: " & myInput)
Console.WriteLine("The match is: " & myRegex.Match(myInput).Value)
Console.WriteLine("Press the Return key to continue.")
Console.ReadLine()
```

7. From the File menu, select Save All. (You can use the Ctrl+Shift+S keyboard shortcut if you prefer.)

8. Press the F5 key to run the code. If you have entered the code correctly, you should see a console window open with the appearance shown in Figure 21-3.

Figure 21-3

9. At the command line, type **Does anyone here know Fred?**. Then press the Return key, and inspect the information that is displayed, as shown in Figure 21-4.

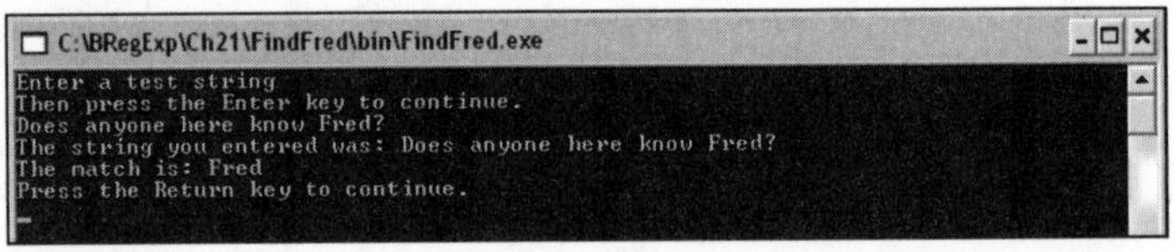

Figure 21-4

How It Works

Steps 1 through 4 create the skeleton for a console (command window) application.

The code added in Step 5 allows the classes contained in the `System.Text.RegularExpressions` namespace to be referred to simply by the name of the class, rather than the fully qualified name, such as `System.Text.RegularExpressions.Regex`:

```
Imports System.Text.RegularExpressions
```

In this example, where the Regex object is used only once, importing the `System.Text` `.RegularExpressions` namespace doesn't save time. In more complex examples, importing the namespace does help to save developer time, because you're writing code such as:

```
myRegex = New Regex("Fred")
```

rather than:

```
myRegex = New System.Text.RegularExpressions.Regex("Fred")
```

Both pieces of code do the same thing, but the first example makes the code easier to write and to read.

The code added inside `Sub Main()` defines what the console application does. First, two variables, `myInput` and `myRegex`, are dimensioned (declared). If `OPTION STRICT` had been set to `ON`, it would have been necessary to specify the type of each variable:

```
Dim myInput, myRegex
```

Next, a `Regex` object is instantiated and is passed the literal pattern `Fred` in the constructor. Instantiating a `Regex` object is one of the ways you can make regular expression functionality available in Visual Basic .NET:

```
myRegex = New Regex("Fred")
```

Then `Console.WriteLine()` is used twice to display simple instructions for the user:

```
Console.WriteLine("Enter a test string")
Console.WriteLine("Then press the Enter key to continue.")
```

Then the user input is read from the command window when the Return key is pressed, using the `Console.ReadLine()` method, and the value is assigned to the variable `myInput`:

```
myInput = Console.ReadLine()
```

Then the string that the user entered, contained in the variable `myInput`, is echoed to the command window using `Console.WriteLine()`:

```
Console.WriteLine("The string you entered was: " & myInput)
```

The `Match()` method of the `Regex` object is used to match against the character sequence held in the `myInput` variable. The `Console.WriteLine()` method is used to display some explanatory text and the result of the matching process, in this case, the character sequence `Fred`:

```
Console.WriteLine("The match is: " & myRegex.Match(myInput).Value)
```

A message is displayed telling the user what to do to move the application on:

```
Console.WriteLine("Press the Return key to continue.")
```

Making the command window wait for user input allows the output of the earlier parts of the application to be displayed until such time as the user is ready to close the application:

```
Console.ReadLine()
```

The Classes of System.Text.RegularExpressions

The following table lists the classes that are contained in the `System.Text.RegularExpressions` namespace. The properties and methods of several of the classes listed are described in detail later in this chapter, together with examples demonstrating how to use some of the properties and methods.

Class	Description
Capture	Represents the text captured by a single set of parentheses surrounding a subexpression
CaptureCollection	Represents a collection of Capture objects
Group	Represents the result of a single capturing group of paired parentheses
GroupCollection	Represents a collection of Group objects
Match	Represents the result of a single regular expression match
MatchCollection	Represents a collection of Match objects
Regex	The class that contains the regular expression pattern
RegexCompilationInfo	Provides information that the compiler uses to compile a regular expression into an assembly

You may find it useful to think of the `Regex` object as containing all the information relating to a regular expression. The `MatchesCollection` object contains all the matches for a matching process, with information about each match being contained in a `Match` object. A `GroupsCollection` object contains information about all the groups in a match, with each group being represented by a `Group` object. The `CapturesCollection` object contains information about all captures for a group, with information about each capture being held in a `Capture` object.

The following sections take a closer look at several of these members of the `System.Text.RegularExpressions` namespace.

In the following sections, classes will be referred to simply by their class name (for example, Regex) rather than using the fully qualified name, such as System.Text.RegularExpressions.Regex.

The Regex Object

The `Regex` object can be instantiated to make its properties and methods accessible to programmatic manipulation. In addition, three of the methods of the `Regex` class are available as shared methods. The use of these shared methods is described and demonstrated later.

The `Regex` object has two public properties, described briefly in the following table.

Property	Description
Options	Contains information about the options passed to the `Regex` object.
RightToLeft	Returns a Boolean value indicating whether or not right-to-left processing of matching is operative. A value of `True` indicates right-to-left matching.

If you are used to creating regular expression objects in JScript or VBScript where the regular expression object is the `RegExp` *object, be careful to spell the .NET* `Regex` *object correctly in your code.*

The following table summarizes the `Regex` object's methods. Some of the concepts and techniques of the `Regex` object are not found in standard regular expressions. Therefore, some of the concepts summarized in the table may usefully be clarified for you when you read following sections that further describe the methods and/or demonstrate how they are used.

Method	Description
CompileToAssembly	Compiles a regular expression to an assembly (the default behavior of a regular expression is not to compile to an assembly)
Equals	Determines whether two objects are equal
Escape	Escapes a set of metacharacters, replacing the metacharacter with the corresponding escaped character
GetGroupNames	Returns an array of capturing group names
GetGroupNumbers	Returns an array of capturing group numbers
GetHashCode	Inherited from the `Object` class
GetType	Gets the type of the current instance
GroupNameFromNumber	Gets a group name that corresponds to the group number supplied as an argument
GroupNumberFromName	Gets a group number that corresponds to the group name supplied as an argument
IsMatch	Returns a Boolean value indicating whether the regular expression pattern is matched in the string that is the argument to the `IsMatch()` method
Match	Returns zero or one `Match` object, depending on whether or not the string supplied to the method as its argument contains a match
Matches	Returns a `MatchCollection` object containing zero or more `Match` objects, which contain all matches (or none) in the string that is the argument to the `Matches()` method

Table continued on following page

Method	Description
Replace	Replaces all occurrences of a regular expression pattern with a specified character sequence
Split	Splits an input string into an array of strings; the split occurs at a position indicated by a regular expression pattern
ToString	Returns a string that contains the regular expression passed into the Regex object in its constructor
Unescape	Unescapes any escaped characters in the input string

Using the Match Object and Matches Collection

The Match() method returns a Match object if there is a successful match. If there are potentially multiple matches, the Match() method only matches once and stops.

Try It Out   **The Match() Method**

The sample code is contained in Module1.vb in the MatchMethodDemo project:

```
Imports System.Text.RegularExpressions
Module Module1
    Dim myRegex = New Regex("[A-Z]\d")
    Sub Main()
        Console.WriteLine("Enter a string on the following line:")
        Dim inputString = Console.ReadLine()
        Dim myMatch = myRegex.Match(InputString)
        Console.WriteLine("The match, '" & myMatch.Value & "' was found.")
        Console.WriteLine("Press Return to close this application.")
        Console.ReadLine()
    End Sub

End Module
```

1. Create a new project in Visual Studio 2003. If you are unused to creating projects, refer to the detailed description in the first example in this chapter.

2. Name the project MatchMethodDemo.

3. Edit Module1.vb so that the content is as shown in the preceding code.

4. Save the project, and press F5 to run it. If you entered the code correctly, you should see a command window displaying the following text:

```
Enter a string on the following line:
```

5. Enter the text **Hello K9 and K10**, and press Return. Inspect the results.

   There are two potential matches for the pattern [A-Z]\d in the string you entered: K9 and K10. Notice in Figure 21-5 that only one match is displayed, K9, which is the first match in the string.

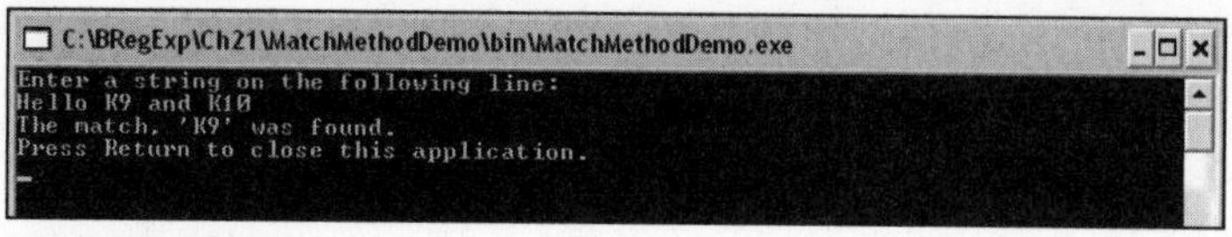

Figure 21-5

How It Works

The variable myRegex is dimensioned and assigned the pattern [A-Z]\d, which matches an uppercase alphabetic character followed by a numeric digit:

```
Dim myRegex = New Regex("[A-Z]\d")
```

After the test string has been read from the command line, the myRegex variable's Match() method is applied to InputString, and the result is assigned to the myMatch variable:

```
Dim myMatch = myRegex.Match(InputString)
```

The value of InputString is the string Hello K9 and K10.. There are two matches for the pattern [A-Z]\d: the character sequences K9 and K1.

The value of the myMatch object's Value property is concatenated to some explanatory text and is written to the display:

```
Console.WriteLine("The match, '" & myMatch.Value & "' was found.")
```

The first match, K9, is displayed. The second potential match K1 is not matched and is not displayed. To match and display all matches in a test string, you need to use the Matches() method of the Regex object.

The Matches() method, however, returns a MatchCollection object, which can contain Match objects for all the matches in the test string. The following example looks at how the Matches() method can be used.

Try It Out   **The Matches() Method**

The sample code is contained in Module1.vb in the MatchesMethodDemo project:

```
Imports System.Text.RegularExpressions
Module Module1

    Sub Main()
        Dim myRegex = New Regex("[A-Z]\d")
        Console.WriteLine("Enter a string on the following line:")
        Dim inputString = Console.ReadLine()
        Dim myMatchCollection = myRegex.Matches(inputString)
        Console.WriteLine()
        Console.WriteLine("There are {0} matches.", myMatchCollection.Count)
        Console.WriteLine()
```

```
            Dim myMatch As Match
            For Each myMatch In myMatchCollection
                Console.WriteLine("At position {0}, the match '{1}' was found",
    myMatch.Index, myMatch.ToString)
            Next
            Console.WriteLine()
            Console.WriteLine("Press Return to close this application.")
            Console.ReadLine()

        End Sub

    End Module
```

1. Create a new Visual Basic .NET console project in Visual Studio 2003. Name the project `MatchesMethodDemo`.

2. Edit the code in `Module1.vb` so that it appears as in the preceding code.

3. Press Ctrl+S to save the code. Press F5 to run it.

4. In the command window, type **Hello K9, K10 and K21.**, and press Return.

5. Inspect the displayed results, as shown in Figure 21-6. Notice that there are now three matches: `K9`, `K1`, and `K2`.

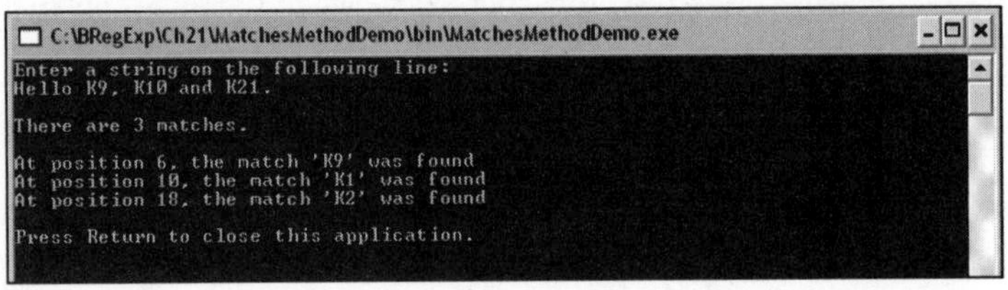

Figure 21-6

How It Works

The `myRegex` variable is dimensioned, and a new `Regex` object is instantiated and is assigned the pattern `[A-Z]\d`:

```
Dim myRegex = New Regex("[A-Z]\d")
```

After the user is invited to enter a string, a `myMatchCollection` variable is dimensioned and assigned the match collection produced by the `Matches()` method with the `inputString` variable as its argument.

```
        Dim myMatchCollection = myRegex.Matches(inputString)
```

A count of the `Match` objects in the match collection represented by the `myMatchCollection` object is displayed, using the `MatchCollection` object's `Count` property:

```
        Console.WriteLine("There are {0} matches.", myMatchCollection.Count)
```

The myMatch variable is dimensioned as a Match object:

```
Dim myMatch As Match
```

Then each Match object in the myMatchCollection variable is processed in the same way using a For Each loop:

```
For Each myMatch In myMatchCollection
```

The Index property of the Match object is used to display the position in the string at which each match occurs. The Match object's ToString() method returns the character sequence contained in a Match object:

```
        Console.WriteLine("At position {0}, the match '{1}' was found",
myMatch.Index, myMatch.ToString)
        Next
```

Using the Match.Success Property and Match.NextMatch Method

The MatchCollection object just described provides one way to iterate through matches in a test string. An alternative approach to looping through the matches in a test string is to use the Match object's Success property together with the Match object's NextMatch method.

Try It Out   The Match.Success Property and Match.NextMatch Method

The content of Module1.vb in the NextMatchDemo project is shown here:

```
Imports System.Text.RegularExpressions
Module Module1

    Sub Main()
        Dim myRegex = New Regex("[A-Z]\d")
        Console.WriteLine("Enter a string on the following line:")
        Dim inputString = Console.ReadLine()
        Dim myMatch = myRegex.Match(inputString)
        Dim myMatchCount As Integer
        Console.WriteLine("The first match is {0}.", myMatch.ToString)
        Do While myMatch.Success
            myMatchCount += 1
            Console.WriteLine("At position {0}, the match '{1}' was found",
myMatch.Index, myMatch.ToString)
            myMatch = myMatch.NextMatch
        Loop
        Console.WriteLine("There were {0} matches.", myMatchCount)
        Console.WriteLine()
        Console.WriteLine("Press Return to close this application.")
        Console.ReadLine()

    End Sub

End Module
```

1. Open Visual Studio, and create a new project. Name the project NextMatchDemo.

2. In the code window for Module1.vb, make edits to produce the content shown in the preceding Module1.vb file.

3. Save the Module1.vb file, and press F5 to run the code.

4. Enter the test text **Hello K9, K10 and K21.** at the command line, and press the Return key. Inspect the results, as shown in Figure 21-7.

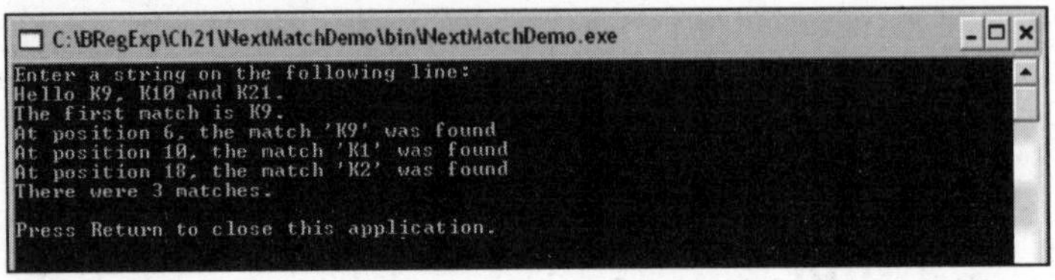

Figure 21-7

How It Works

The same regular expression pattern used in the preceding example is assigned to an instantiated Regex object in the myRegex variable:

```
Dim myRegex = New Regex("[A-Z]\d")
```

The test string is accepted from the user, and that string is assigned to the variable inputString. Then the Match() method of MyRegex is used to match the pattern [A-Z]\d against inputString:

```
Dim myMatch = myRegex.Match(inputString)
```

A variable myMatchCount is dimensioned. It will be used to count how many successful matches there are:

```
Dim myMatchCount As Integer
```

The value of the first match is output:

```
Console.WriteLine("The first match is {0}.", myMatch.ToString)
```

A Do While loop uses the Success property of the myMatch variable to process each successful match:

```
Do While myMatch.Success
```

The loop counter variable, myMatchCount, is incremented by 1:

```
myMatchCount += 1
```

Then the position and value of the match are displayed, using the Index property and ToString() method:

```
Console.WriteLine("At position {0}, the match '{1}' was found",
    myMatch.Index, myMatch.ToString)
```

Then the NextMatch() method is used to test whether or not there is another match. If there is another match, when the myMatch.Success test in the Do While statement is evaluated, the Boolean value

True is returned, and the loop is processed again. If there is no match, `myMatch.Success` returns the Boolean value of `False`, and the loop is exited:

```
        myMatch = myMatch.NextMatch
    Loop
```

After the loop is exited, the value of the `myMatchCount` variable is used to display the number of matches found:

```
    Console.WriteLine("There were {0} matches.", myMatchCount)
```

This technique provides an alternative to using the `MatchCollection` object when iterating through a collection of matches in a test string.

The GroupCollection and Group Classes

The patterns used in the preceding examples in this chapter have been very simple. More typically, parentheses in a pattern create groups. All the groups in a match are contained in a `GroupCollection` object. Each group in the collection is contained in a `Group` object.

Try It Out   The GroupCollection and Group Classes

The content of `Module1.vb` in the `GroupsDemo` project is shown here:

```
Imports System.Text.RegularExpressions
Module Module1

    Sub Main()
        Dim myRegex = New Regex("([A-Z])(\d+)")
        Console.WriteLine("Enter a string on the following line:")
        Dim inputString = Console.ReadLine()
        Dim myMatchCollection = myRegex.Matches(inputString)
        Console.WriteLine()
        Console.WriteLine("There are {0} matches.", myMatchCollection.Count)
        Console.WriteLine()
        Dim myMatch As Match
        Dim myGroupCollection As GroupCollection
        Dim myGroup As Group
        For Each myMatch In myMatchCollection
            Console.WriteLine("At position {0}, the match '{1}' was found",
myMatch.Index, myMatch.ToString)
            myGroupCollection = myMatch.Groups
            For Each myGroup In myGroupCollection
                Console.WriteLine("Group containing '{0}' found at position
'{1}'.", myGroup.Value, myGroup.Index)
            Next
            Console.WriteLine()
        Next
        Console.WriteLine()
        Console.WriteLine("Press Return to close this application.")
        Console.ReadLine()

    End Sub

End Module
```

1. Create a new project in Visual Studio 2003. Name the new project GroupsDemo.

2. In the code window for Module1.vb, make edits to produce the content shown in the preceding Module1.vb file.

3. Save the code, and press F5 to run the code.

4. In the command window, enter the test string **Hello K9, K10, K21 and K999**.

5. Press the Return key, and inspect the displayed results, as shown in Figure 21-8.

```
C:\BRegExp\Ch21\GroupsDemo\bin\GroupsDemo.exe
There are 4 matches.

At position 6, the match 'K9' was found
Group containing 'K9' found at position '6'.
Group containing 'K' found at position '6'.
Group containing '9' found at position '7'.

At position 10, the match 'K10' was found
Group containing 'K10' found at position '10'.
Group containing 'K' found at position '10'.
Group containing '10' found at position '11'.

At position 15, the match 'K21' was found
Group containing 'K21' found at position '15'.
Group containing 'K' found at position '15'.
Group containing '21' found at position '16'.

At position 23, the match 'K999' was found
Group containing 'K999' found at position '23'.
Group containing 'K' found at position '23'.
Group containing '999' found at position '24'.

Press Return to close this application.
```

Figure 21-8

How It Works

The regular expression pattern in this example includes two pairs of parentheses. Notice, too, that the pattern will now match one or more numeric digits, rather than matching exactly one numeric digit:

```
Dim myRegex = New Regex("([A-Z])(\d+)")
```

The user is asked to enter a test string as in the previous examples, and the Regex object's Matches() method is used to match the inputString variable against the pattern contained in the myRegex variable:

```
Dim myMatchCollection = myRegex.Matches(inputString)
```

A variable, myGroupCollection, is dimensioned as a GroupCollection object:

```
Dim myGroupCollection As GroupCollection
```

A variable, myGroup, is dimensioned as a Group object:

```
Dim myGroup As Group
```

Two For Each loops are used. The outer For Each loop is used to iterate through the Match objects in the MatchCollection object:

```
For Each myMatch In myMatchCollection
```

For each `Match` object, the position and value of the match are displayed using the `Index` property and `ToString()` method:

```
        Console.WriteLine("At position {0}, the match '{1}' was found",
    myMatch.Index, myMatch.ToString)
```

The `Match` object's `Groups` property is assigned to the `myGroupCollection` variable:

```
        myGroupCollection = myMatch.Groups
```

The inner `For Each` loop processes each `Group` object contained in the `GroupCollection` object:

```
        For Each myGroup In myGroupCollection
```

The value and position of each group are displayed using the values of the `Group` object's `Value` and `Index` properties:

```
            Console.WriteLine("Group containing '{0}' found at position
   '{1}'.", myGroup.Value, myGroup.Index)
        Next
        Console.WriteLine()
    Next
```

The first group output contains the group corresponding to the entire regular expression pattern. That group is present in all successful matching processes. Additional groups occur in the `GroupCollection` when paired parentheses occur in the regular expression pattern. Because the regular expression pattern `([A-Z])(\d+)` has two pairs of parentheses, each `GroupCollection` contains three groups. You can see in Figure 21-8 that three groups are displayed for each match.

The CaptureCollection and Capture Class

The `CaptureCollection` object contains a collection of one or more `Capture` objects. Each `Capture` object represents the content of one capturing group of paired parentheses.

There is no public constructor for an instance of the `Capture` object. And the `Capture` object is immutable. It can be created only by a matching process, and each `Capture` object is part of the `CaptureCollection` collection.

Try It Out **The CaptureCollection Object and the Capture Class**

The code contained in `Module1.vb` of the `CapturesDemo` project is shown here:

```
Imports System.Text.RegularExpressions
Module Module1

    Sub Main()
        Dim myRegex = New Regex("([A-Z])+(\d)+")
        Console.WriteLine("Enter a string on the following line:")
        Dim inputString = Console.ReadLine()
        Dim myMatchCollection = myRegex.Matches(inputString)
        Console.WriteLine()
```

```
            Console.WriteLine("There are {0} matches.", myMatchCollection.Count)
            Console.WriteLine()
            Dim myMatch As Match
            Dim myGroupCollection As GroupCollection
            Dim myGroup As Group
            For Each myMatch In myMatchCollection
                Console.WriteLine("At position {0}, the match '{1}' was found",
    myMatch.Index, myMatch.ToString)
                Console.WriteLine("This match has {0} groups.", myMatch.Groups.Count)
                myGroupCollection = myMatch.Groups
                For Each myGroup In myGroupCollection
                    Dim myCaptureCollection As CaptureCollection = myGroup.Captures
                    Dim myCapture As Capture
                    Console.WriteLine("Group containing '{0}' found at position
    '{1}'.", myGroup.Value, myGroup.Index)
                    For Each myCapture In myCaptureCollection
                        Console.WriteLine("    Capture: '{0}' at position '{1}'.",
    myCapture.Value, myCapture.Index)
                    Next
                Next
                Console.WriteLine()
            Next
            Console.WriteLine()
            Console.WriteLine("Press Return to close this application.")
            Console.ReadLine()

        End Sub

    End Module
```

1. Create a new project in Visual Studio 2003 based on a console application template. Name the project CapturesDemo.

2. Edit the default module to match the preceding code. Save the code, and press F5 to run it.

3. In the command window, enter the test string **ABC1 A123**.

4. Press Return and inspect the results, as shown in Figure 21-9.

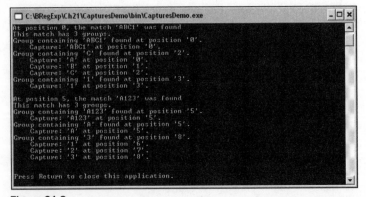

Figure 21-9

How It Works

The regular expression pattern for this example is importantly but subtly changed from the pattern in the preceding example:

```
Dim myRegex = New Regex("([A-Z])+(\d)+")
```

Notice that the character class [A-Z] is enclosed in paired parentheses and that the group is qualified by the + quantifier. That means that there is a group that captures a single character. If there is one upper-case alphabetic character in the test string, one group and one capture are created. If there are multiple alphabetic characters, multiple groups and multiple captures are created.

Similar considerations apply to the numeric part of the pattern, because (\d) creates a group that can occur one or more times, depending on the content of the test string. The pattern (\d)+ creates a group for each numeric digit captured, which is different from the pattern (\d+), which creates one group, whether there is one numeric digit or ten.

After accepting the user's test string, ABC1 A123, the matches, groups, and captures are processed inside three nested For Each loops:

```
For Each myMatch In myMatchCollection
```

First, the value of each match is displayed:

```
        Console.WriteLine("At position {0}, the match '{1}' was found",
    myMatch.Index, myMatch.ToString)
```

Then the number of groups for that match is displayed:

```
        Console.WriteLine("This match has {0} groups.", myMatch.Groups.Count)
```

The myGroupCollection variable is assigned the Groups property of the myMatch variable:

```
        myGroupCollection = myMatch.Groups
```

Each Group object in the GroupCollection object is processed next:

```
        For Each myGroup In myGroupCollection
```

Each capture for the group is assigned to the myCaptureCollection variable:

```
            Dim myCaptureCollection As CaptureCollection = myGroup.Captures
            Dim myCapture As Capture
```

Each group is displayed. You may be surprised to see that only the final occurrence of a group that occurs more than once is displayed:

```
            Console.WriteLine("Group containing '{0}' found at position
    '{1}'.", myGroup.Value, myGroup.Index)
```

Then each capture in the captures collection is displayed. Because each pair of parentheses captures only a single character, a character sequence such as ABC results in three captures being displayed:

```
                For Each myCapture In myCaptureCollection
                    Console.WriteLine("    Capture: '{0}' at position '{1}'.",
    myCapture.Value, myCapture.Index)
```

The For Each loops each conclude with a Next statement:

```
                Next
            Next
            Console.WriteLine()
        Next
```

The RegexOptions Enumeration

The System.Text.RegularExpressions namespace includes a RegexOptions enumeration that controls the modes of operation of regular expression matching.

The following table summarizes the features of the RegexOptions enumeration.

Option	Description
None	Specifies that no options are set.
IgnoreCase	Specifies that matching is case insensitive.
Multiline	Treats each line as a separate string for matching purposes. Therefore, the meaning of the ^ metacharacter is changed (matches the beginning of each line position), as is the $ metacharacter (matches the end of each line position).
ExplicitCapture	Changes the capturing behavior of parentheses.
Compiled	Specifies whether or not the regular expression is compiled to an assembly.
SingleLine	Changes the meaning of the period metacharacter so that it matches every character. Normally, it matches every character except \n.
IgnorePatternWhitespace	Interprets unescaped whitespace as not part of the pattern. Allows comments inline preceded by #.
RightToLeft	Specifies that pattern matching proceeds from right to left.
ECMAScript	Enables (limited) ECMAScript compatibility.
CultureInvariant	Specifies that cultural differences in language are ignored.

Case-Insensitive Matching: The IgnoreCase Option

In Visual Basic .NET regular expressions, the default matching mode is case sensitive. To specify that matching be carried out in a case-insensitive way, the IgnoreCase option is used.

Try It Out   Case-Insensitive Matching

The code in Module1.vb in the IgnoreCaseDemo project is shown here:

```vb
Imports System.Text.RegularExpressions
Module Module1

    Sub Main()
        Dim myPattern As String = "[A-Z]+\d+"
        Console.WriteLine("Enter a string on the following line:")
        Dim inputString = Console.ReadLine()
        Dim myMatchCollection = Regex.Matches(inputString, myPattern)
        Console.WriteLine("This is case sensitive matching.")
        Console.WriteLine("There are {0} matches.", myMatchCollection.Count)
        Console.WriteLine()
        Dim myMatch As Match
        For Each myMatch In myMatchCollection
            Console.WriteLine("At position {0}, the match '{1}' was found",
myMatch.Index, myMatch.ToString)
        Next
        Console.WriteLine()
        myMatchCollection = Regex.Matches(inputString, myPattern,
RegexOptions.IgnoreCase)
        Console.WriteLine("This is case insensitive matching.")
        Console.WriteLine("There are {0} matches.", myMatchCollection.Count)
        Console.WriteLine()
        For Each myMatch In myMatchCollection
            Console.WriteLine("At position {0}, the match '{1}' was found",
myMatch.Index, myMatch.ToString)
        Next
        Console.WriteLine()
        Console.WriteLine("Press Return to close this application.")
        Console.ReadLine()

    End Sub

End Module
```

1. Create a new project in Visual Studio 2003 using the console application template. Name the project CaseInsensitiveDemo.

2. Edit the code so that it reads the same as the preceding Module1.vb.

3. Save the code; then run it using the F5 key.

4. In the command window, enter the test text **ABC123 abc123 DeF234**.

5. Press the Return key, and inspect the results, as shown in Figure 21-10. Notice that when matching is case sensitive, there are two matches, and there are three matches when matching is case insensitive. Notice, too, that the case-sensitive match against DeF234 is F234, while the case-insensitive match is DeF234.

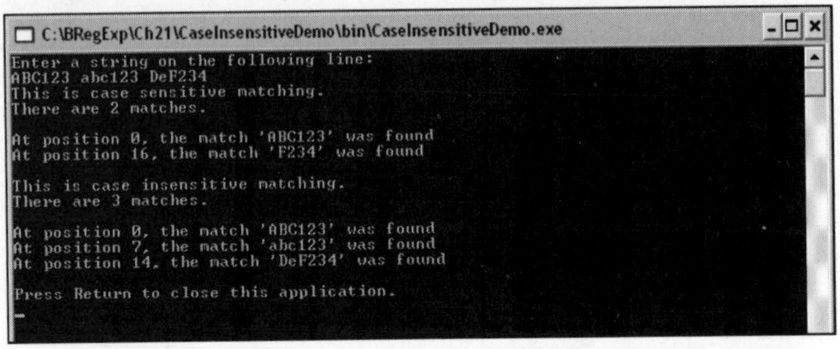

Figure 21-10

How It Works

The pattern assigned to the `myPattern` string (notice that it isn't a `Regex` object) is `[A-Z]+\d+`. This, using the default case-sensitive matching in .NET, would match only when the user entered uppercase alphabetic characters:

```
Dim myPattern As String = "[A-Z]+\d+"
```

The `MatchCollection` object corresponding to the `myMatchCollection` variable is created using the shared `Matches()` method of the `Regex` class. No `Regex` object is instantiated. Notice that the `Matches()` method takes two arguments on this occasion (when case-sensitive matching is applied), the second argument being the string value containing the regular expression pattern:

```
Dim myMatchCollection = Regex.Matches(inputString, myPattern)
```

The character sequence `ABC123` matches because only uppercase alphabetic characters are contained in the character sequence. The character sequence `abc123`, by the same measure, does not match. In the character sequence `DeF234`, the character sequence `F234` matches because it contains one uppercase character followed by three numeric digits.

After the results of case-sensitive matching have been displayed, a new collection of `Match` objects is assigned to the `myMatchCollection` variable. Notice that on this occasion, the `Matches()` method takes three arguments. The third argument specifies one of the properties of the `RegexOptions` object, in this case, the `IgnoreCase` property:

```
myMatchCollection = Regex.Matches(inputString, myPattern,
RegexOptions.IgnoreCase)
```

When matching is case insensitive, the three character sequences, `ABC123`, `abc123`, and `DeF234` all match the pattern `[A-Z]+\d+`.

If you want to specify multiple options, you must separate the options with the word Or. So to specify case-insensitive matching that matches from right to left, you could use code such as the following:

```
        myMatchCollection = Regex.Matches(inputString, myPattern, _
    RegexOptions.IgnoreCase Or RegexOptions.RightToLeft)
```

Multiline Matching: The Effect on the ^ and $ Metacharacters

The ^ metacharacter normally matches the position before the first character at the beginning of a string, and the $ metacharacter normally matches the position after the last character at the end of a string.

When multiline matching is used, the ^ metacharacter matches the position before the first character at the beginning of each line, and the $ metacharacter matches the position after the last character on each line.

Inline Documentation Using the IgnorePatternWhitespace Option

The IgnorePatternWhitespace option allows inline comments to be created that spell out the meaning of each part of the regular expression pattern.

Normally, when a regular expression pattern is matched, any whitespace in the pattern is significant. For example, a space character in the pattern is interpreted as a character to be matched. As a result of setting the IgnorePatternWhitespace option, all whitespace contained in the pattern is ignored, including space characters and newline characters. This allows a single pattern to be laid out to aid readability, to allow comments to be added, and to aid in maintenance of the regular expression pattern. To match a whitespace character, you can use the \s metacharacter.

In Visual Basic .NET, the syntax for adding inline comments is a little cumbersome. If you wanted to use the myRegex variable to match an alphabetic character followed by a numeric digit, you might typically write the following:

```
    Dim myRegex = New Regex("[A-Z]\d")
```

However, to use the IgnorePatternWhitespace option to specify the same regular expression pattern and include comments inline, you must write something like the following:

```
    Dim myRegex = New Regex( _
      "[A-Z] (?# A character class to match an uppercase  alphabetic character)" & _
      "\d    (?# followed by a numeric digit)", & _
      RegexOptions.IgnorePatternWhitespace)
```

The inline comments are preceded by the character sequence (?# and followed by a) character. The Visual Basic .NET concatenation character, &, is used between the components of the pattern, and the line-continuation character (the underscore) is used to indicate that a statement is being continued on the following line.

Try It Out   Using the IgnorePatternWhitespace Option

This example matches a U.S. Social Security number. The code contained in `Module1.vb` in the `IgnorePatternWhitespaceDemo` project is shown here:

```
Imports System.Text.RegularExpressions
Module Module1
    Dim myRegex = _
    New Regex _
        ("^      (?# match the position before the first character)" & _
        "\d{3} (?# Three numeric digits, followed by)" & _
        "-     (?# a literal hyphen)" & _
        "\d{2} (?# then two numeric digits)" & _
        "-     (?# then a literal hyphen)" & _
        "\d{4} (?# then two numeric digits)" & _
        "$     (?# match the position after the last character)", _
        RegexOptions.IgnorePatternWhitespace)
    Sub Main()
        Console.WriteLine("Enter a string on the following line:")
        Dim inputString = Console.ReadLine()
        Dim myMatch = myRegex.Match(inputString)
        If myMatch.ToString.Length Then
            Console.WriteLine("The match, '" & myMatch.Value & "' was found.")
        Else
            Console.WriteLine("There was no match")
        End If
        Console.WriteLine("Press Return to close this application.")
        Console.ReadLine()

    End Sub

End Module
```

1. Create a new console application project in Visual Studio 2003. Name the project `IgnorePatternWhitespaceDemo`.

2. Edit the code in the code window so that it matches the code in the preceding `Module1.vb` file. Save the code, and press F5 to run it.

3. At the command line, enter the test string **123-12-1234**. Press Return, and inspect the results, as shown in Figure 21-11. Notice that there is a successful match.

Figure 21-11

4. In Visual Studio 2005, press F5 to run the code again.

5. At the command line, enter the test string **A123-12-1234**. Press Return, and inspect the results, as shown in Figure 21-12.

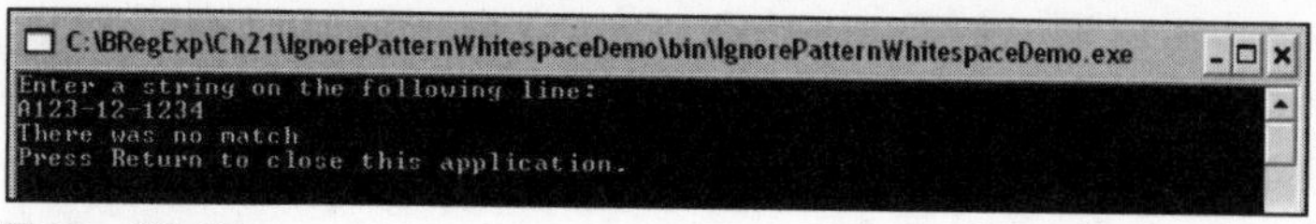

Figure 21-12

How It Works

The pattern to be matched, if written on a single line, is as follows:

```
^\d{3}-\d{2}-\d{4}
```

You may recognize this as a simple pattern that will match a valid U.S. Social Security number (SSN).

In this example, the pattern is written with inline comments when the `myRegex` variable is dimensioned. As you can see, it is much more complex to write the pattern in this way, but the inline comments make it easier for you or another developer to work out precisely what the pattern was intended to do.

The Visual Basic .NET syntax of `(?# ... )` for inline comments is less clean than the simple `#` construct in Visual C# .NET, for example. I find that the Visual Basic .NET syntax tends to get in the way of readability of the comments. Lining up the left parentheses on each line helps maximize readability in Visual Basic .NET:

```
New Regex _
   ("^      (?# match the position before the first character)" & _
   "\d{3} (?# Three numeric digits, followed by)" & _
   "-      (?# a literal hyphen)" & _
   "\d{2} (?# then two numeric digits)" & _
   "-      (?# then a literal hyphen)" & _
   "\d{4} (?# then two numeric digits)" & _
   "$      (?# match the position after the last character)", _
   RegexOptions.IgnorePatternWhitespace)
```

The pattern is equivalent to `^\d{3}-\d{2}-\d{4}$` and so matches an SSN. Therefore, when the test string is 123-12-1234, there is a match, as indicated in Figure 21-11. This is under control of the `If` statement in the following code. When the `Length` property is not 0, a match has been found, so the `myMatch` variable's `Value` property contains the matching sequence of characters:

```
If myMatch.ToString.Length Then
    Console.WriteLine("The match, '" & myMatch.Value & "' was found.")
```

When the `Length` property of `myMatch.ToString` is 0, no match has been found, and a message indicating that is output in the `Else` clause:

```
Else
    Console.WriteLine("There was no match")
End If
```

Right to Left Matching: The RightToLeft Option

When using English, the normal progression of characters along a line is from left to right. In some other languages, the progression of characters is from right to left. To support use of regular expressions in such languages, the .NET Framework provides the functionality to conduct matching from right to left. Unfortunately, my experience and that of others is that when using the `RightToLeft` option, the matching behavior is not fully reliable.

The Metacharacters Supported in Visual Basic .NET

Visual Basic .NET has perhaps a more complete and extensive regular expressions implementation than any of the tools you have seen in earlier chapters of this book.

Much of the regular expression support in Visual Basic .NET can reasonably be termed standard. However, as with many Microsoft technologies, the standard syntax and techniques have been extended or modified in places.

The following table summarizes the metacharacters supported in Visual Basic .NET.

Metacharacter	Description
\d	Matches a numeric digit.
\D	Matches any character except a numeric digit.
\w	Equivalent to the character class [A-Za-z0-9_].
\W	Equivalent to the character class [^A-Za-z0-9_].
\b	Matches the position at the beginning of a sequence of \w characters or at the end of a sequence of \w characters. Colloquially, \b is referred to as a word-boundary metacharacter.
\B	Matches a position that is not a \b position.
\t	Matches a tab character.
\n	Matches a newline character.
\040	Matches an ASCII character, expressed in Octal notation. The metacharacter \040 matches a space character.
\x020	Matches an ASCII character, expressed in hexadecimal notation. The metacharacter \x020 matches a space character.
\u0020	Matches a Unicode character, expressed in hexadecimal notation with exactly four numeric digits. The metacharacter \u0020 matches a space character.
[...]	Matches any character specified in the character class.
[^...]	Matches any character but the characters specified in the character class.
\s	Matches a whitespace character.
\S	Matches any character that is not a whitespace character.
^	Depending on whether the MultiLine option is set, it matches the position before the first character in a line or the position before the first character in a string.

Metacharacter	Description
$	Depending on whether the MultiLine option is set, it matches the position after the last character in a line or the position after the last character in a string.
$number	Substitutes the character sequence matched by the last occurrence of group number *number*.
${name}	Substitutes the character sequence matched by the last occurrence of the group named *name*.
\A	Matches the position before the first character in a string. Its behavior is not affected by the setting of the MultiLine option.
\Z	Matches the position after the last character in a string. Its behavior is not affected by the setting of the MultiLine option.
\G	Specifies that matches must be consecutive, without any intervening nonmatching characters.
?	A quantifier. Matches when there is zero or one occurrence of the preceding character or group.
*	A quantifier. Matches when there are zero or more occurrences of the preceding character or group.
+	A quantifier. Matches when there are one or more occurrences of the preceding character or group.
{n}	A quantifier. Matches when there are exactly *n* occurrences of the preceding character or group.
{n,m}	A quantifier. Matches when there are at least *n* occurrences and a maximum of *m* occurrences of the preceding character or group.
(substring)	Captures the contained substring.
(?<name>substring)	Captures the contained substring and assigns it a name.
(?:substring)	A non-capturing group.
(?=...)	A positive lookahead.
(?!...)	A negative lookahead.
(?<=...)	A positive lookbehind.
(?<!...)	A negative lookbehind.
\N (where N is a number)	A back reference to a numbered group.
\k<name>	A back reference that references a named back reference (same meaning as the following).
\k'name'	A back reference that references a named back reference (same meaning as the preceding).
!	Alternation.
(?imnsx-imnsx)	An alternate technique to specify RegexOptions settings inline.

Lookahead and Lookbehind

Support for positive and negative lookahead and lookbehind in Visual Basic .NET is good. All four options are supported.

Positive lookahead uses the `(?=theLookahead)` syntax. To match the word `Star` when followed by a space character and the character sequence `Training`, you could use the following code:

```
Dim myRegex  = New Regex("Star(?= Training)")
Dim myMatch =  myRegex.Match("The Star Training Company carries out great
training.")
```

Negative lookahead uses the `(?!theLookahead)` syntax. To match the character sequence `Star` when it is not followed by a space character and the character sequence `Training`, you could use the following code:

```
Dim myRegex  = New Regex("Star(?! Training)")
Dim myMatch =  myRegex.Match("The Star Training Company carries out great
training.")
```

Positive lookbehind uses the `(?<=theLookbehind)` syntax. To match the character sequence `Training` when it is preceded by the character sequence `Star` followed by a space character, you could use the following code:

```
Dim myRegex  = New Regex("(?<=Star )Training)")
Dim myMatch =  myRegex.Match("The Star Training Company carries out great
training.")
```

Negative lookbehind uses the `(?<!theLookbehind)` syntax. To match the character sequence `Training` when it is not preceded by the character sequence `Star` followed by a space character, you could use the following code:

```
Dim myRegex  = New Regex("(?<!Star )Training)")
Dim myMatch =  myRegex.Match("The Star Training Company carries out great
training.")
```

Exercises

1. Specify a pattern that will match the character sequence `old` only when it is part of a word such as `cold` or `bold`. Hint: Provide two solutions, one of which uses lookbehind and lookahead.

2. Create a console application that replaces the character sequence `Doctor` or `Doc` with the character sequence `Dr.`.

C# and Regular Expressions

Microsoft Visual C# .NET provides extensive, powerful, and flexible support for regular expression functionality. Visual C# .NET provides support comparable to Perl version 5, plus some extensions that are essentially specific to the .NET Framework (for example, right-to-left matching). The implementations of regular expressions are essentially playing an ongoing game of catch-up, and it is likely that at least some other languages will also implement features such as right-to-left matching in time.

In this chapter, you will learn how to do the following:

❑   Use the objects contained in the `System.Text.RegularExpresssions` namespace

❑   Use the metacharacters supported in C#

> **Examples shown in this chapter have been tested with Visual Studio 2003 and the .NET Framework 1.1. I will assume that you have access to a copy of Visual Studio 2003 and have a working knowledge of at least the basics of Visual C# .NET. It isn't the intent of this chapter to provide a tutorial on the basics of using Visual Studio .NET 2003.**
>
> **However, if you do not have access to a copy of Visual Studio 2003, there are copies of the .exe files you can run, although you won't be able to view and edit the Visual C# .NET code if you use the .exe files.**

The regular expression functionality in C# is based on the classes in the `System.Text .RegularExpressions` namespace. Those classes will be explained in some detail, including several examples of how the classes, their properties, and methods can be used in code.

The Classes of the System.Text .RegularExpressions namespace

The regular expressions support in the .NET Framework class library is contained in the `System.Text.RegularExpressions` namespace.

An Introductory Example

This example demonstrates the basics of one way to use regular expressions when using Visual C#. Other techniques are discussed and demonstrated later in the chapter, when the classes of the `System.Text.RegularExpressions` namespace and their members are discussed in more detail.

Try It Out   **An Introductory C# Console Application Example**

The following code is contained in `Class1.cs` in the `SimpleMatch` project:

```
using System;
using System.Text.RegularExpressions;

namespace SimpleMatch
{
 /// <summary>
 /// This is a simple regular expression example which uses the Regex object.
 /// </summary>
 class Class1
 {
        /// <summary>
        /// The main entry point for the application.
        /// </summary>
        [STAThread]
        static void Main(string[] args)
        {
                Console.WriteLine(@"This will find a match for the regular
expression '[A-Z]\d'.");
                Console.WriteLine("Enter a test string now.");
                Regex myRegex = new Regex(@"[A-Z]\d", RegexOptions.IgnoreCase);
                string inputString;
                inputString = Console.ReadLine();
                Match myMatch = myRegex.Match(inputString);
                Console.WriteLine("You entered the string: '" + inputString +
"'.");
                if (myMatch.Success)
                Console.WriteLine("The match '" + myMatch.ToString() + "' was found
in the string you entered.");
                Console.ReadLine();
        }
 }
}
```

The following instructions walk you through all the steps necessary to create a simple console application in Visual Studio 2003 using Visual C# .NET. If you have done much programming in C#, you will find most of the steps pretty self-evident.

1. Open Visual Studio 2003, and from the File menu, select New; then select Project to create a new solution that contains a single project.

   Figure 22-1 shows the appearance of the Project screen, but with the choices specified in Steps 2 through 5 already made.

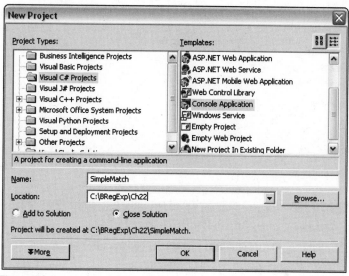

Figure 22-1

2. In the Project Types pane, select Visual C# Projects.

3. In the Templates pane, select Console Application.

4. In the Name text box, type **SimpleMatch** as the name of the project.

5. In the Location text box, type **C:\BRegExp\Ch22** as the location (or select another location, if you prefer).

6. Click the OK button. After a short pause while Visual Studio 2003 is creating the files needed for the project, the code editor will open with the following template code already in place:

```
using System;

namespace SimpleMatch
{
    /// <summary>
    /// Summary description for Class1.
    /// </summary>
    class Class1
    {
            /// <summary>
            /// The main entry point for the application.
            /// </summary>
            [STAThread]
            static void Main(string[] args)
            {
                    //
                    // TODO: Add code to start application here
                    //
            }
    }
}
```

7. Edit the preceding template code so that it contains the code shown earlier in `Class1.cs`.

8. Save the code using Ctrl+Shift+S. Press F5 to run the code.

9. At the command line, enter the test text **K9**. Then press Return. Inspect the results, as shown in Figure 22-2.

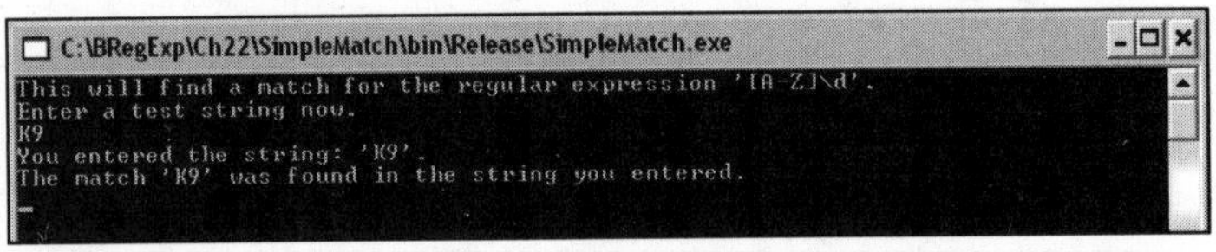

Figure 22-2

How It Works

When using C# you must specify the components of the .NET Framework class library that you are using. Visual Studio 2003 automatically adds the following line when the file `Class1.cs` is created:

```
using System;
```

And because you are using the `Regex` class from the `System.Text.RegularExpresssions` namespace, it is appropriate to add a using statement referencing that namespace, too:

```
using System.Text.RegularExpressions;
```

The alternative approach is to use fully qualified names when referring to an object. For example, with the using System.Text.RegularExpressions; statement in the code, you can simply write the following to declare the myRegex object variable and assign it a value:

```
Regex myRegex = new Regex(@"[A-Z]\d", RegexOptions.IgnoreCase);
```

If the using System.Text.RegularExpressions; statement is missing, and you attempt to run the code, you will receive a bundle of error messages, including the following, because the Regex class is not found in the System namespace, the only namespace that is declared by the default template code created by Visual Studio 2003:

```
The type or namespace name 'Regex' could not be found.
```

So to declare the myRegex variable and assign it a value, you would have to write the following code, using fully qualified names, because the Regex and RegexOptions classes are contained in the System.Text.RegularExpressions namespace:

```
System.Text.RegularExpressions.Regex myRegex = new
System.Text.RegularExpressions.Regex(@"[A-Z]\d",
System.Text.RegularExpressions.RegexOptions.IgnoreCase);
```

Similarly, it would be necessary to write the following to declare the myMatch object variable and assign it a value:

```
System.Text.RegularExpressions.Match myMatch = myRegex.Match(inputString);
```

In all but the most trivial code, it is easier to write and read code when the using System.Text.RegularExpressions; statement is present.

There are automatically generated stubs for documentation comments in Class1.cs and an automatically generated namespace corresponding to the project name and a class name — by default, Class1.

The content of the Main() method is where the work of this simple example is carried out:

```
static void Main(string[] args)
{
```

First, a message is written to the command window using the Console object's WriteLine() method. The Console class is a member of the System namespace, which has already been referenced using the using System; statement, so you can simply write Console.Writeline() with appropriate content between the parentheses:

```
Console.WriteLine(@"This will find a match for the regular expression '[A-Z]\d'.");
```

Notice that the first character inside the parentheses of the WriteLine() method is an @ character. This is used because without it, an error would be reported, because C# is unable to recognize the character sequence \d. In the absence of the @ character, you would have to write the string in the double quotes as "This will find a match for the regular expression '[A-Z]\\d'.". In other words, you must write \\d for C# to recognize this as meaning the regular expression metacharacter \d.

Personally, I prefer adding the @ character, because I can then use the familiar regular expression syntax that I use in other languages. Because I use regular expressions across various languages and tools, I tend to avoid the double-backslash notation.

Next, a straightforward information string is output:

```
Console.WriteLine("Enter a test string now.");
```

Next, an object variable, myRegex, is declared as inheriting from the Regex class. As explained earlier, writing Regex is a convenient abbreviation for the fully qualified name System.Text.RegularExpressions .Regex. The regular expression pattern [A-Z]\d is the first argument for the Regex() constructor and specifies that pattern as the pattern against which matching will take place. The second argument of the Regex() constructor specifies that the option of case-insensitive matching is to be used:

```
Regex myRegex = new Regex(@"[A-Z]\d", RegexOptions.IgnoreCase);
```

Next, a string variable, inputString, is declared:

```
string inputString;
```

The Console class's ReadLine() method is used to read the text entered by the user. The value read is assigned to the inputString variable:

```
inputString = Console.ReadLine();
```

The object variable myMatch is declared as inheriting from the Match class. The value assigned to the myMatch variable is specified using the Regex class's Match() method with the inputString variable as its argument. In other words, the myMatch variable contains the first match found in the inputString variable using the regular expression pattern [A-Z]\d that was assigned earlier to the myRegex variable:

```
Match myMatch = myRegex.Match(inputString);
```

Now that you have a match, you first output the value of the inputString variable to remind or inform the user of the string that was captured using the Console.ReadLine() method:

```
Console.WriteLine("You entered the string: '" + inputString + "'.");
```

An if statement is used that tests the value of the Success property of the myMatch object variable. If a match has been found (as indicated by the value of the Success property), a string is output using Console.WriteLine() to inform the user of the content of the match:

```
if (myMatch.Success)
    Console.WriteLine("The match '" + myMatch.ToString() + "' was found in the string
you entered.");
```

The ReadLine() method is used so that the displayed match remains on-screen until the user presses the Return key:

```
            Console.ReadLine();
    }
```

The Classes of System.Text.RegularExpressions

The following table lists the classes that are contained in the `System.Text.RegularExpressions` namespace. The properties and methods of several of the classes listed are described in detail later in this chapter, together with examples demonstrating how to use them.

Class	Description
Capture	Represents the text captured by a single set of parentheses surrounding a subexpression
CaptureCollection	Represents a collection of `Capture` objects
Group	Represents the result of a single capturing group of paired parentheses
GroupCollection	Represents a collection of `Group` objects
Match	Represents the result of a single regular expression match
MatchCollection	Represents a collection of `Match` objects
Regex	The class that contains the regular expression pattern
RegexCompilationInfo	Provides information that the compiler uses to compile a regular expression into an assembly

The `Regex` class is the most important class in the `System.Text.RegularExpressions` namespace.

The Regex Class

The `Regex` object can be instantiated to make its properties and methods accessible to programmatic manipulation. In addition, three of the methods of the `Regex` class are available as static methods. The use of these shared methods is described and demonstrated later.

The `Regex` object has two public properties, described briefly in the following table.

Property	Description
Options	Contains information about the options passed to the `Regex` object.
RightToLeft	Returns a `Boolean` value indicating whether or not right-to-left processing of matching is operative. A value of `True` indicates right-to-left matching.

If you are used to creating regular expression objects in JScript or VBScript, where the regular expression object is the `RegExp` object, be careful to spell the .NET `Regex` object correctly in your code.

The Options Property of the Regex Class

The Options property contains a value each bit of which corresponds to the options set. The individual bits of the value each contain a 0 or 1, which corresponds to whether a particular option is or is not chosen. When the default value, equivalent to RegexOptions.None, is passed in, for example, a Match() method, the value of the Options property is 0. The available options are described later in the description of the RegexOptions class.

The Regex Class's RightToLeft Property

The .NET Framework allows right-to-left matching to be used. When attempting matching in English and other languages where words and lines are written left to right, regular expression matching also takes place in a left-to-right direction. In languages such as Arabic and Hebrew, writing and reading may take place in a right-to-left direction. The RightToLeft property of the Regex class supports, or is intended to support, matching from right to left.

However, not all of the matching process is reversed. Lookahead still looks at character sequences to the right of the current matching position, and lookbehind still looks at character sequences to the left of the matching position. In practice, matching using the RightToLeft property has proved to be less reliable than I had hoped and, therefore, is not demonstrated here.

Regex Class Methods

The following table summarizes the methods of the Regex object. Some of the concepts and techniques of the Regex object are not found in standard regular expressions. Therefore, some of the concepts summarized in the following table may usefully be clarified for you when you read following sections that further describe the methods and/or demonstrate how they are used.

Method	Description
CompileToAssembly	Compiles a regular expression to an assembly (the default behavior of a regular expression is not to compile to an assembly).
Equals	Determines whether two objects are equal.
Escape	Escapes a set of metacharacters, replacing the metacharacter with the corresponding escaped character.
GetGroupNames	Returns an array of capturing group names.
GetGroupNumbers	Returns an array of capturing group numbers.
GetHashCode	Inherited from the Object class.
GetType	Gets the type of the current instance.
GroupNameFromNumber	Gets a group name that corresponds to the group number supplied as an argument.
GroupNumberFromName	Gets a group number that corresponds to the group name supplied as an argument.

Method	Description
IsMatch	Returns a Boolean value that indicates whether the regular expression pattern is matched in the string, which is the argument to the IsMatch() method.
Match	Returns zero or one Match object, depending on whether the string supplied to the method as its argument contains a match.
Matches	Returns a MatchCollection object containing zero or more Match objects, which contain all matches (or none) in the string that is the argument to the Matches() method.
Replace	Replaces all occurrences of a regular expression pattern with a specified character sequence.
Split	Splits an input string into an array of strings. The split occurs at a position indicated by a regular expression pattern.
ToString	Returns a string containing the regular expression passed into the Regex object in its constructor.
Unescape	Unescapes any escaped characters in the input string.

The CompileToAssembly() Method

The Regex class's CompileToAssembly() method takes two arguments: the RegexCompilationInfo object (which is a member of the System.Text.RegularExpressions namespace and contains the information necessary to specify how compilation is to be carried out) and the name of the assembly to be created.

When the CompileToAssembly() method is used, the startup time can be expected to increase but with the benefit of faster running.

The GetGroupNames() Method

The GetGroupNames() method retrieves the names of any named groups associated with a Match object. The GetGroupNames() method takes no argument.

The GetGroupNumbers() Method

The GetGroupNumbers() method retrieves the numbers of any numbered groups associated with a Match object. There is always at least one group, which matches the entire regular expression pattern. If paired parentheses are included in the regular expression pattern, there may be additional numbered groups. The GetGroupNumbers() method takes no argument.

GroupNumberFromName() and GroupNameFromNumber() Methods

The GroupNumberFromName() method retrieves a group number given a group name as its argument. The group's name is supplied as a string argument. The GroupNameFromNumber() method retrieves a group name, if one exists, for a group number supplied as the method's argument. The group's number is supplied to the method as an int argument.

The IsMatch() Method

The `Regex` object's `IsMatch()` method takes a single `string` argument and tests whether the regular expression pattern is matched in that string argument. It returns a `bool` value. Optionally, the `IsMatch()` method takes a second argument, an `int` value, which specifies the position in the string argument at which the attempt at matching is to begin.

Try It Out — The IsMatch() Method

1. Open Visual Studio 2003, create a new application from a console application template, and name the new project `IsMatchDemo`.

2. Add the following statement after the `using System;` statement:

```
using System.Text.RegularExpressions;
```

3. Edit the content of the `Main()` method as follows:

```
Console.WriteLine(@"This will find a match for the regular expression
'[A-Z]\d'.");
Console.WriteLine("Enter a test string now.");
Regex myRegex = new Regex(@"[A-Z]\d", RegexOptions.IgnoreCase);
string inputString;
inputString = Console.ReadLine();
Match myMatch = myRegex.Match(inputString);
string outputString = "The following option(s) are set: ";
Console.WriteLine(outputString + myRegex.Options.ToString());
Console.WriteLine("You entered the string: '" + inputString + "'.");
if (myRegex.IsMatch(inputString))
        Console.WriteLine("The match '" + myMatch.ToString() + "' was
found in the string you entered.");
    else
        Console.WriteLine("No match was found.");
Console.ReadLine();
```

4. Save the code, and press F5 to run it.

5. Enter the test string **J88** at the command-line prompt; press Return; and inspect the displayed information, as shown in Figure 22-3.

Figure 22-3

The `IsMatch()` method can also be statically overloaded so that you can use it without having to instantiate a `Regex` object.

How It Works

As in the first example in this chapter, a `Regex` object is instantiated and assigned to the object variable `myRegex` with the regular expression pattern `[A-Z]\d`. Because there is a metacharacter that includes a backslash, the `@` character precedes the string argument in the `Regex()` constructor, so you need not double the backslash:

```
Regex myRegex = new Regex(@"[A-Z]\d", RegexOptions.IgnoreCase);
```

After the user has entered a string, the `IsMatch()` method is used to determine whether the entered string does or does not contain a match:

```
if (myRegex.IsMatch(inputString))
```

When the test string contains a match, the `bool` value `True` is returned. In this example, the content of the `if` statement is, therefore, processed. If no match is found, the `bool` value `False` is returned, and the `else` statement is processed:

```
else
        Console.WriteLine("No match was found.");
```

Because the regular expression pattern is `[A-Z]\d`, the match from the test string `J88` is `J8`.

The Match() Method

The `Match()` method has the following overloaded methods:

```
public Match Match(string, inputString);
```

and:

```
public Match Match(string inputString,
            int startAt);
```

and:

```
public Match Match(string inputString,
            int startAt,
            int length);
```

The `inputString` argument is tested to determine whether a match is present for the regular expression pattern contained in the `Regex` object.

As you saw in the first example in this chapter, the `Match()` method returns a `Match` object:

```
Match myMatch = myRegex.Match(inputString);
```

The `Match()` method is used when you want to find out whether or not there is a match in a test string. The `Regex` object's `Match()` method can be used together with the `Match` object's `NextMatch()` method to iterate through all matches in a test string. This usage is further discussed in conjunction with the `Match` object a little later in this chapter.

The `Match()` method can also be used as a static method, as discussed later in this chapter.

The Matches() Method

When you want to find all the matches in a test string, the `Matches()` method is the one to use.

Try It Out   **The Matches() Method**

1. Open Visual Studio 2003, create a new project from the Windows Application template, and name the new project `MatchesDemo`. Figure 22-4 shows the screen's appearance. Depending on how you have set options for Visual Studio 2003, the appearance that you see may differ slightly.

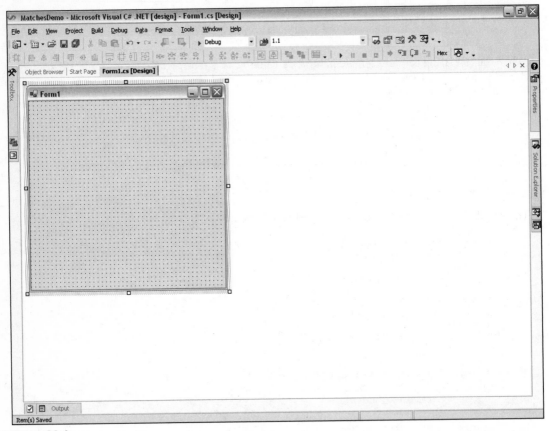

Figure 22-4

2. Drag a Label control from the Toolbox to close to the top of the form, and change its `Text` property to `This form tests against the pattern '[A-Z]\d'`.

3. Drag a Label control from the Toolbox onto the form, and change its `Text` property to `Enter a test string:`

4. Drag a TextBox control from the Toolbox to the form's design surface, and change its `Text` property to be blank.

5.   Drag a Button control to the form, and change its Text property to Click to Find Matches.

6.   Drag a TextBox control to the form, and change its Multline property to True and its Text property to be blank. Figure 22-5 shows the desired appearance after this step. You will likely have to tweak the position and size of the controls to achieve an appearance similar to the one shown.

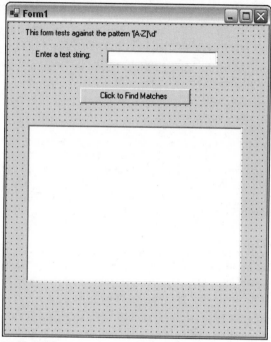

Figure 22-5

At this stage, the form looks reasonably tidy but has no functionality associated with it. Now the code must be created to specify that you are using the System.Text.RegularExpressions namespace.

7.   In the Solution Explorer, right-click Form1.cs and select View Code to open the code editor. Scroll up, if necessary, and you will see several using statements:

```
using System;
using System.Drawing;
using System.Collections;
using System.ComponentModel;
using System.Windows.Forms;
using System.Data;
```

8.   After the final automatically created using statement, add the following new line of code:

```
using System.Text.RegularExpressions;
```

9. Return to the design surface. Double-click the Click to Find Matches button. The code editor will open with the following code automatically created for you:

```
private void button1_Click(object sender, System.EventArgs e)
{

}
```

The `button1_Click` event handler responds to a click on the button. You now need to add code to create some functionality when that button is clicked.

10. In the code editor, add the following code between the opening brace and closing brace of the `button1_Click` event handler:

```
Regex myRegex = new Regex(@"[A-Z]\d");
            string inputString;
            inputString = this.textBox1.ToString();
            MatchCollection myMatchCollection = myRegex.Matches(inputString);
            this.textBox2.Text = "The matches are:" + Environment.NewLine;
            foreach(Match myMatch in myMatchCollection)
            {
                    this.textBox2.Text += myMatch.ToString() +
Environment.NewLine;
            }
```

11. Save the code, and press F5 to run it. If the code does not run, take a look at the error messages that appear in the build errors task list. Note the line number that is mentioned in the first error, and attempt to locate and correct that error. Then press F5 to see whether any subsequent errors have also been remedied by correcting the first error.

    If you entered the code correctly, you should see a screen with an appearance similar to that shown in Figure 22-6. The exact appearance will depend on how you positioned the form controls and sized the form.

12. Enter the test string **K99 L00 M11** in the upper text box.

13. Click the Click to Find Matches button, and inspect the results displayed in the lower text box, as shown in Figure 22-7. Notice that three matches are displayed in the lower text box.

How It Works

To use classes from the `System.Text.RegularExpressions` namespace, you must add an appropriate `using` directive:

```
using System.Text.RegularExpressions;
```

The work of the simple application is carried out by the code inside the `button1_Click` function. First, an object variable, `myRegex`, is declared as inheriting from the `Regex` class and is assigned the regular expression pattern `[A-Z]\d`, using the @ syntax to avoid having to double backslash characters inside the paired double quotes.

```
Regex myRegex = new Regex(@"[A-Z]\d");
```

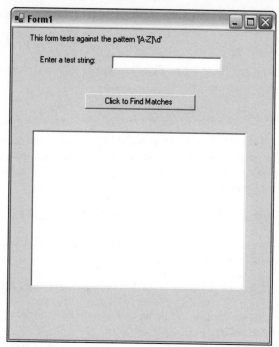

Figure 22-6

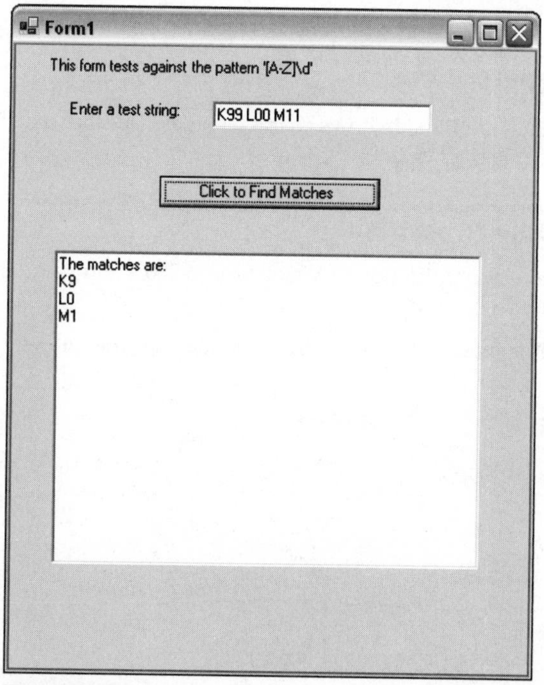

Figure 22-7

Next, a string variable, inputString, is declared:

```
string inputString;
```

Next, the value entered into textBox1 (the single line, upper text box) is assigned to the inputString variable:

```
inputString = this.textBox1.ToString();
```

Next, an object variable, myMatchCollection, is declared to inherit from the MatchCollection class. A MatchCollection object can contain zero or more Match objects. You populate the myMatchCollection variable using the myRegex variable's Matches() method, supplying the inputString variable as the argument to the Matches() method:

```
MatchCollection myMatchCollection = myRegex.Matches(inputString);
```

Next, assign some literal text to the Text property of textBox2. The Environment.Newline is used to cause the display to move to a new line:

```
this.textBox2.Text = "The matches are:" + Environment.NewLine;
```

Then you use a foreach statement to add further text to textBox2 for each Match object contained in the myMatchCollection variable:

```
foreach(Match myMatch in myMatchCollection)
{
    this.textBox2.Text += myMatch.ToString() + Environment.NewLine;
}
```

The Replace() Method

The Regex class's Replace() method allows character sequences that match a pattern to be replaced by a specified pattern or sequence of characters.

Try It Out   the Replace() Method

1. Create a new console application in Visual Studio 2003, and name the new project SimpleReplace.

2. In the code editor, make edits so that the code matches the following, Class1.cs:

```
using System;
using System.Text.RegularExpressions;

namespace SimpleReplace
{

    class Class1
    {

            [STAThread]
            static void Main(string[] args)
            {
```

```
        Console.WriteLine(@"This will find a match for the regular expression 'wrox'");
        Console.WriteLine(@"and replace it with 'Wrox'.");
        Console.WriteLine("Enter a test string now.");
    Regex myRegex = new Regex(@"wrox", RegexOptions.IgnoreCase);
        string inputString;
        inputString = Console.ReadLine();
        string newString = myRegex.Replace(inputString, "Wrox");
        Console.WriteLine("You entered the string '" + inputString + "'.");
        Console.WriteLine("After replacement the new string is '" + newString + "'.");
                    Console.ReadLine();
            }
        }
    }
```

Be sure to include the using System.Text.RegularExpressions; directive. Save the code, and press F5 to run it.

3. In the command window, enter the sample text **This book is published by wrox.**; and then press the Return key and inspect the displayed results, as shown in Figure 22-8. Notice that the character sequence wrox (initial lowercase w) is replaced by Wrox (initial uppercase W).

Figure 22-8

4. Press the Return key to close the command window.

5. In Visual Studio, press F5 to run the code again.

6. In the command window, enter the test string **This book is published by WROX.**; press the Return key; and inspect the results. Because matching is case insensitive, as specified by the IgnoreCase option, the character sequence WROX is matched and is also replaced by the character sequence Wrox.

How It Works

The code, as usual, includes a using System.Text.RegularExpressions; directive.

First, a message is displayed that informs the user of the purpose of the application:

```
        Console.WriteLine(@"This will find a match for the regular expression 'wrox'");
        Console.WriteLine(@"and replace it with 'Wrox'.");
```

The simple literal pattern wrox is assigned to the myRegex object variable. Because the IgnoreCase option is specified, wrox, Wrox, WROX, and so on will be matched:

```
    Regex myRegex = new Regex(@"wrox", RegexOptions.IgnoreCase);
```

Then the user is invited to input a string, which is assigned to the inputString variable.

The myRegex object's Replace() method is used to replace the first occurrence of wrox (matched case insensitively) in the variable inputString with the character sequence Wrox:

```
string newString = myRegex.Replace(inputString, "Wrox");
Console.WriteLine("You entered the string '" + inputString + "'.");
Console.WriteLine("After replacement the new string is '" + newString + "'.");
```

When the input string contains the character sequence wrox, it is replaced with Wrox. When the input string contains WROX, it is also replaced with Wrox.

The Split() Method

The Regex class's Split() method splits a string at a position specified by a regular expression pattern.

The Split() method can be used with an instantiated Regex object or as a static method.

Try It Out   **the Regex.Split() Method**

1. Create a new project in Visual Studio 2003 using the Windows Application template.

2. Drag a label onto the form, and change its Text property to This demonstrates the Regex Split() method..

3. Drag another label onto the form a little lower, and change its Text property to This will split a string when a comma is matched..

4. Drag a third label onto the form a little lower than the second, and change its Text property to Enter a string which includes commas:.

5. Drag a text box onto the form, and make its Text property blank.

6. Drag a button onto the form, and make its Text property Click to split the string..

7. Tidy up the layout of the form so that it resembles that shown in Figure 22-9. Your form may differ a little in appearance without affecting the functionality.

8. Double-click the button, and the code editor should open with the following code displayed:

```
private void button1_Click(object sender, System.EventArgs e)
{

}
```

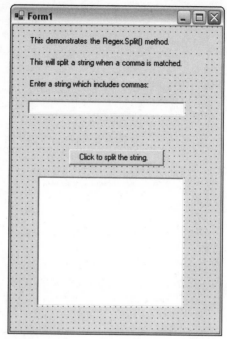

Figure 22-9

9. Scroll up to the top of the code, and below the automatically created `using` directives, insert the following code:

```
using System.Text.RegularExpressions;
```

10. Scroll down to the `button1_Click()` function, and add the following code:

```
Regex myRegex = new Regex(",");
string inputString = this.textBox1.Text;
string[] splitResults;
splitResults = myRegex.Split(inputString);
this.textBox2.Text = "The string contained the following elements:" +
Environment.NewLine + Environment.NewLine;
foreach (string stringElement in splitResults)
this.textBox2.Text += stringElement + Environment.NewLine;
```

11. Save the code, and press F5 to run it.

12. In the upper text box, add the text **A1,B2,C12,D13**; click the button; and inspect the results displayed in the lower (multiline) text box, as shown in Figure 22-10.

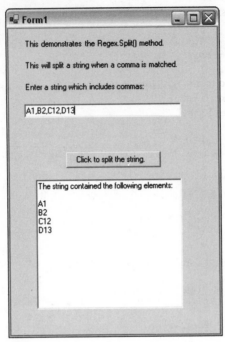

Figure 22-10

How It Works

Looking at the code in the button1_Click() function, first the myRegex variable is declared and is assigned the value of a comma. In other words, myRegex will match on a comma. However, in this example, you will split the test string when you find a match for the regular expression pattern.

```
Regex myRegex = new Regex(",");
```

Next, the variable inputString is declared and is assigned the value of the text entered into the upper of the two text boxes:

```
string inputString = this.textBox1.Text;
```

Next, a string array, splitResults, is declared:

```
string[] splitResults;
```

Then the result of applying the Split() method to the inputString variable is assigned to the splitResults array. Each element in that array contains a character sequence that was originally separated by a comma from its neighboring element:

```
splitResults = myRegex.Split(inputString);
```

Some basic display text is assigned to the `Text` property of `textBox2`:

```
this.textBox2.Text = "The string contained the following elements:" +
Environment.NewLine + Environment.NewLine;
```

Then a `foreach` loop is used to add the value of each string in the `splitResults` array to the value of the `Text` property of `textBox2`. Each element of the array is displayed on a separate line in the text box, due to the `Environment.Newline`:

```
foreach (string stringElement in splitResults)
this.textBox2.Text += stringElement + Environment.NewLine;
```

Using the Static Methods of the Regex Class

Several of the `Regex` class methods can be used as statics without your having to instantiate an instance of the `Regex` class.

Each of the following sections assumes that the following directive is in the code:

```
using System.Text.RegularExpressions;
```

The IsMatch() Method as a Static

Two overloads are available for the `IsMatch()` method:

```
public static bool Regex.IsMatch(string inputString, string pattern);
```

and:

```
public static bool Regex.IsMatch(string inputString, string pattern, RegexOptions
options);
```

The Match() Method as a Static

Two overloads are available for the `Match()` method as a static:

```
public static Match Match(string inputString, string pattern);
```

and:

```
public static Match Match(string inputString, string pattern, RegexOptions
options);
```

The Matches() Method as a Static

Two overloads are available for the `Matches()` method as a static:

```
public static MatchCollection Matches(string inputString, string pattern);
```

and:

```
public static MatchCollection Matches(string inputString, string pattern,
RegexOptions options);
```

The Replace() Method as a Static

Two overloads are available for the Replace() method as a static:

```
public static string Regex.Replace(string inputString, string pattern, string
replacementString);
```

and:

```
public static string Regex.Replace(string inputString, string pattern, string
replacementString, RegexOptions options);
```

The Split() Method as a Static

Two overloads are available for the Split() method as a static:

```
public static string[] Regex.Split(string inputString, string pattern);
```

and:

```
public static string[] Regex.Split(string inputString, string pattern, RegexOptions
options);
```

The Match and Matches Classes

The Match class contains a single match. The MatchCollection class contains a collection of matches.

The Match Class

The Match class has no public constructor. Therefore, it must be accessed from another class. For example, this can be done using the Regex class's Match() method.

A Match object has a Groups property. Every Match object has at least one group. The Match object is equivalent to Match.Groups[0], because the zeroth group contains the entire match.

The Match class has the properties described in the following table.

Property	Description
Captures	Gets a collection of captures captured by a capturing group. There may be zero or more captures in a match.
Empty	Returned if an attempted match fails.
Groups	Gets a collection of groups that make up the match regular expression. Assuming that there is a match, there is at least one group in the collection.
Index	The position in the string at which the first character of a successful match is located.

Property	Description
Length	The length of the matched substring.
Success	A value indicating whether or not the match was successful.
Value	The matched substring.

The `Match` object has the methods described in the following table. Not all are directly relevant to the use of regular expressions.

Method	Description
Equals	Determines whether two objects are equal
GetHashCode	Gets a hash code
GetType	Gets the type of the current object instance
NextMatch	Finds the next match in the test string, if such a match exists
Result	Contains the value after replacement
Synchronized	Returns a `Match` object that can be shared among threads
ToString	Gets the matched substring from the test string

The `NextMatch()` method can be used together with the `Match()` method to iterate through several matches in a test string.

Try It Out   Using the Match() and NextMatch() Methods

1. Open Visual Studio 2003, create a new project using the Windows Application template, and name the new project `MatchNextMatchDemo`.

2. Drag a label onto the form, and change its `Text` property to `Demo of the Match() and NextMatch() methods`..

3. Drag a label onto the form design surface, and change its `Text` property to `This finds matches for the pattern '[A-Z]\d'`..

4. Drag a label onto the form design surface, and change its `Text` property to `Enter a string in the text box below:`.

5. Drag a text box onto the form design surface, and make its `Text` property blank.

6. Drag a button onto the form design surface, and change its `Text` property to `Click to find all matches`..

7. Drag a text box onto the design surface. Change its `Multiline` property to `True`. Change its `Text` property so that it is blank.

8. Size and align the form controls so that they resemble those shown in Figure 22-11.

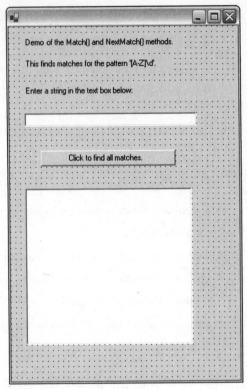

Figure 22-11

9. Add the following code below the other using directives:

```
using System.Text.RegularExpressions;
```

10. Double-click the button to create the `button1_Click()` function, and add the following code:

```
Regex myRegex = new Regex(@"[A-Z]\d");
string inputString = this.textBox1.Text;
Match myMatch = myRegex.Match(inputString);
this.textBox2.Text = "Here are all the matches:" + Environment.NewLine;
while (myMatch.Success)
{
   this.textBox2.Text += myMatch.ToString()+ Environment.NewLine;
   myMatch = myMatch.NextMatch();
```

11. Save the code, and press F5 to run it.

12. In the upper text box, enter the text **A11 B22 C33 D44**; click the button; and inspect the results displayed in the lower text box, as shown in Figure 22-12.

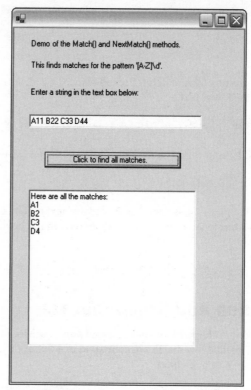

Figure 22-12

How It Works

The following describes how the code inside the button1_Click() function works.

The myRegex variable is declared, and the pattern [A-Z]\d is assigned to it:

```
Regex myRegex = new Regex(@"[A-Z]\d");
```

The variable inputString is declared and is assigned the value entered by the user in the upper text box:

```
string inputString = this.textBox1.Text;
```

The myMatch variable is declared and is assigned the match returned by the Match() method applied to the inputString variable:

```
Match myMatch = myRegex.Match(inputString);
```

Some explanatory text is assigned to the Text property of the lower (multiline) text box:

```
this.textBox2.Text = "Here are all the matches:" + Environment.NewLine;
```

A while loop tests whether there is a successful match, using the Match object's Success property:

```
while (myMatch.Success)
    {
```

Inside the while loop, the value of the match retrieved using the ToString() method is concatenated to the string displayed in the lower text box:

```
this.textBox2.Text += myMatch.ToString()+ Environment.NewLine;
```

The NextMatch() method is used to assign the next match in the test string to the myMatch variable:

```
myMatch = myMatch.NextMatch();
```

The while loop test, Match.Success, is tested again for the next match, and if it is successful, the string value of the next match is concatenated to the string displayed in the lower text box. If the test fails, the while loop exits;

```
    }
```

The GroupCollection and Group Classes

The preceding examples in this chapter have used simple patterns. More typically, parentheses in a pattern create groups. All the groups in a match are contained in a GroupCollection object. Each group in the collection is contained in a Group object.

Try It Out   The GroupCollection and Group Classes

1. Create a new project in Visual Studio 2003 from the console application template, and name the project GroupsDemo.

2. In the code editor, enter the following code in the Main() method. Notice that the regular expression pattern in the first line uses two pairs of parentheses, which will create captured groups.

```
Regex myRegex = new Regex(@"([A-Z])(\d+)");
Console.WriteLine("Enter a string on the following line:");
string inputString = Console.ReadLine();
MatchCollection myMatchCollection = myRegex.Matches(inputString);
Console.WriteLine();
Console.WriteLine("There are {0} matches.", myMatchCollection.Count);
Console.WriteLine();
GroupCollection myGroupCollection;

foreach (Match myMatch in myMatchCollection)
    {
    Console.WriteLine("At position {0}, the match '{1}' was found", myMatch.Index,
myMatch.ToString());
    myGroupCollection = myMatch.Groups;
    foreach (Group myGroup in myGroupCollection)
        {
```

```
        Console.WriteLine("Group containing '{0}' found at position '{1}'.",
    myGroup.Value, myGroup.Index);
        }
    Console.WriteLine();
    }

Console.WriteLine();
Console.WriteLine("Press Return to close this application.");
Console.ReadLine ();
```

3. Save the code; press F5 to run it; and in the command window, enter the test string **A12 B23 C34**.

4. Press the Return key, and inspect the results displayed in the command window, as shown in Figure 22-13.

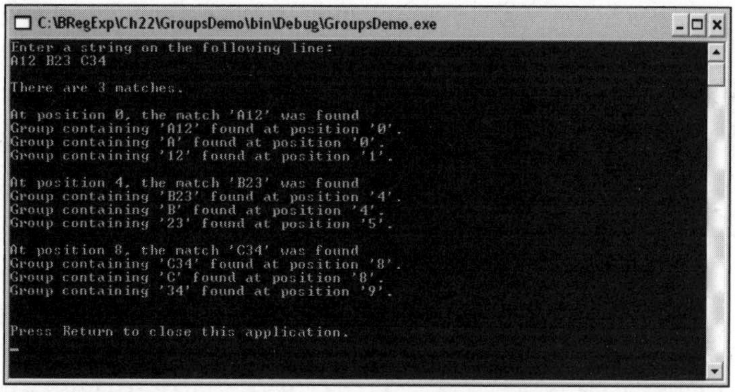

Figure 22-13

How It Works

Let's look in more detail at the code added to the Main() method. The variable myRegex is declared and is assigned the pattern [A-Z]\d+, which matches an uppercase alphabetic character followed by one or more numeric digits:

```
Regex myRegex = new Regex(@"([A-Z])(\d+)");
```

After displaying a prompt for the user to enter a test string, the myMatchCollection variable is declared, and the Matches() method is applied to the inputString. The result is assigned to the myMatchCollection variable:

```
Console.WriteLine("Enter a string on the following line:");
string inputString = Console.ReadLine();
MatchCollection myMatchCollection = myRegex.Matches(inputString);
```

After a spacer blank line is written to the command window, the number of matches in the `Count` property of `myMatchCollection` is displayed:

```
Console.WriteLine();
Console.WriteLine("There are {0} matches.", myMatchCollection.Count);
```

After an additional blank spacer line, the `myGroupCollection` variable is declared as inheriting from the `GroupCollection` class:

```
Console.WriteLine();
GroupCollection myGroupCollection;
```

Then nested `foreach` loops are used to process each match and each group within each match:

```
foreach (Match myMatch in myMatchCollection)
  {
```

The `Match` object's `Index` property is used to display the position of a match in the test string, together with the substring that constitutes the match:

```
Console.WriteLine("At position {0}, the match '{1}' was found", myMatch.Index,
myMatch.ToString());
```

For each match, the `Groups` property, which contains information about all the groups for that match, is assigned to the `myGroupCollection` variable:

```
myGroupCollection = myMatch.Groups;
```

Then each `Group` object in the `myGroupCollection` variable is processed using a nested `foreach` loop:

```
foreach (Group myGroup in myGroupCollection)
  {
```

The content of each group is displayed using the `Group` object's `Value` property together with the position at which the group is found, using the `Index` property of the `Group` object:

```
Console.WriteLine("Group containing '{0}' found at position '{1}'.",
myGroup.Value,
myGroup.Index);
  }
```

Each match has a `zeroth` group containing the value of the whole match. Because the pattern `([A-Z])(\d+)` contained two additional groups, created by the paired parentheses, there are two additional groups displayed each time the inner `foreach` loop is processed. So because the pattern has two visible capturing groups (created by the paired parentheses), there are three groups displayed for each match.

Finally, a further spacing line is output each time round the outer `foreach` loop:

```
Console.WriteLine();
  }
```

The RegexOptions Class

The RegexOptions class, a member of the System.Text.RegularExpressions namespace, specifies which of the available options are or are not set.

The following table summarizes the options available using RegexOptions.

Option	Description
None	Specifies that no options are set.
IgnoreCase	Specifies that matching is case insensitive.
Multiline	Treats each line as a separate string for matching purposes. Therefore, the meaning of the ^ metacharacter is changed (matches the beginning of each line position), as is the $ metacharacter (matches the end of each line position).
ExplicitCapture	Changes the capturing behavior of parentheses.
Compiled	Specifies whether or not the regular expression is compiled to an assembly.
SingleLine	Changes the meaning of the period metacharacter so that it matches every character. Normally, it matches every character except \n.
IgnorePatternWhitespace	Interprets unescaped whitespace as not part of the pattern. Allows comments inline preceded by #.
RightToLeft	Specifies that pattern matching proceeds from the right to the left.
ECMAScript	Enables (limited) ECMAScript compatibility.
CultureInvariant	Specifies that cultural differences in language are ignored.

The IgnorePatternWhitespace Option

The IgnorePatternWhitespace option allows inline comments to be created that spell out the meaning of each part of the regular expression pattern.

Normally, when a regular expression pattern is matched, any whitespace in the pattern is significant. For example, a space character in the pattern is interpreted as a character to be matched. By setting the IgnorePatternWhitespace option, all whitespace contained in the pattern is ignored, including space characters and newline characters. This allows a single pattern to be laid out over several lines to aid readability, to allow comments to be added, and to aid in maintenance of the regular expression pattern.

> The following description assumes that a using System.Text.RegularExpressions; directive is present earlier in the code.

In C#, if you wanted to match a pattern [A-Z] \d using the myRegex variable, you might declare the variable like this:

```
Regex myRegex = new Regex(@"[A-Z]\d");
```

However, if you use the IgnorePatternWhitespace option, you could write it like this:

```
Regex myRegex = new Regex(
  @"[A-Z]   # Matches a single upper case alphabetic character
  \d        # Matches a single numeric digit",
  RegexOptions.IgnorePatternWhitespace);
```

As you can see, you can include a comment, preceded by a # character, on each line and split each logical component of the regular expression onto a separate line so that the way the pattern is made up becomes clearer. This is useful particularly when the regular expression pattern is lengthy or complex.

Try It Out   Using the IgnorePatternWhitespace Option

1. Create a new project in Visual Studio 2003 using the Console Application template, and name the project IgnorePatternWhitespaceDemo.

2. In the code editor, add the following line of code after the default using statement(s):

```
using System.Text.RegularExpressions;
```

3. Enter the following code inside the Main() method:

```
Regex myRegex = new Regex(
@"^ # match the position before the first character
\d{3} # Three numeric digits, followed by
-     # a literal hyphen
\d{2} # then two numeric digits
-     # then a literal hyphen
\d{4} # then two numeric digits
$     # match the position after the last character",
RegexOptions.IgnorePatternWhitespace);
Console.WriteLine("Enter a string on the following line:");
string inputString = Console.ReadLine();
Match myMatch = myRegex.Match(inputString);
if (myMatch.ToString().Length != 0)
  {
  Console.WriteLine("The match, '" + myMatch.Value + "' was found.");
  }
else
{
  Console.WriteLine("There was no match");
}
Console.WriteLine("Press Return to close this application.");
Console.ReadLine();
```

4. Save the code, and press F5 to run it.

5. At the command line, enter the text **123-12-1234** (a U.S. Social Security number [SSN]); press the Return key; and inspect the displayed message, as shown in Figure 22-14.

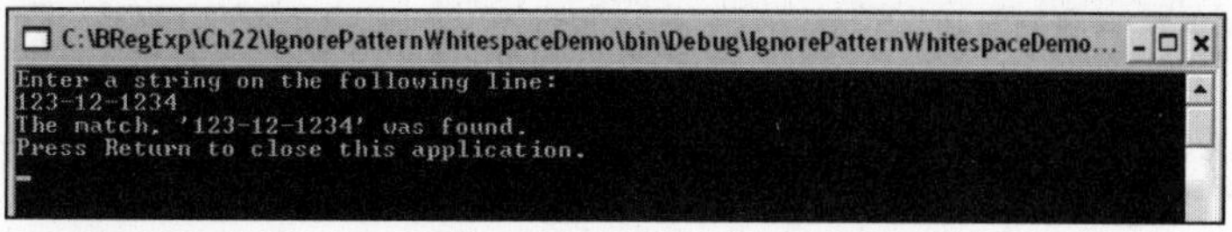

Figure 22-14

6. Press the Return key to close the application, and press F5 in Visual Studio 2003 to run the code again.

7. Enter the text **123-12-1234A** at the command line, press the Return key, and inspect the displayed message. There is no match for the string entered.

How It Works

This code seeks to match lines where a U.S. SSN is matched, and the line contains no other characters.

The interesting part of the code is how the regular expression can be written when the IgnorePatternWhitespace option is selected.

The myRegex variable is declared. Instead of writing:

```
Regex myRegex = new Regex(@"^\d{3}-\d{2}-\d{4}$";
```

when you use the IgnorePatternWhitespace option, the pattern can be written over several lines. The @ character allows you to write the \d component of the pattern without having to double the backslash. Any part of the pattern can be written on its own line, and a comment can be supplied following the # character to document each pattern component:

```
Regex myRegex = new Regex(
@"^    # match the position before the first character
\d{3} # Three numeric digits, followed by
-     # a literal hyphen
\d{2} # then two numeric digits
-     # then a literal hyphen
\d{4} # then two numeric digits
$     # match the position after the last character",
```

Finally, the IgnorePatternWhitespace option is specified:

```
RegexOptions.IgnorePatternWhitespace);
```

The pattern ^\d{3}-\d{2}-\d{4}$ matches the position at the beginning of a line followed by three numeric digits, followed by a hyphen, followed by two numeric digits, followed by a hyphen, followed by four numeric digits, followed by the end-of-line position. Strings matching this pattern contain a character sequence that is likely to be a U.S. SSN. There are more specific patterns that attempt to reject character sequences that are not valid but that do match this pattern. Because the purpose of this example is to show how to use the IgnorePatternWhitespace option, that issue is explored no further here.

Metacharacters Supported in Visual C# .NET

Visual C#.NET has a very complete and extensive regular expressions implementation, which exceeds in functionality many of the tools you saw in earlier chapters of this book.

Much of the regular expression support in Visual C# .NET can reasonably be termed standard. However, as with many Microsoft technologies, the standard syntax and techniques have been extended or modified in places.

The following table summarizes many of the metacharacters supported in Visual C# .NET.

Metacharacter	Description
\d	Matches a numeric digit.
\D	Matches any character except a numeric digit.
\w	Equivalent to the character class [A-Za-z0-9_].
\W	Equivalent to the character class [^A-Za-z0-9_].
\b	Matches the position at the beginning of a sequence of \w characters or at the end of a sequence of \w characters. Colloquially, \b is referred to as a word-boundary metacharacter.
\B	Matches a position that is not a \b position.
\t	Matches a tab character.
\n	Matches a newline character.
\040	Matches an ASCII character expressed in Octal notation. The metacharacter \040 matches a space character.
\x020	Matches an ASCII character expressed in hexadecimal notation. The metacharacter \x020 matches a space character.
\u0020	Matches a Unicode character expressed in hexadecimal notation with exactly four numeric digits. The metacharacter \u0020 matches a space character.
[...]	Matches any character specified in the character class.
[^...]	Matches any character but the characters specified in the character class.
\s	Matches a whitespace character.
\S	Matches any character that is not a whitespace character.
^	Depending on whether the MultiLine option is set, matches the position before the first character in a line or the position before the first character in a string.
$	Depending on whether the MultiLine option is set, matches the position after the last character in a line or the position after the last character in a string.

Metacharacter	Description
`$number`	Substitutes the character sequence matched by the last occurrence of group number *number*.
`${name}`	Substitutes the character sequence matched by the last occurrence of the group named *name*.
`\A`	Matches the position before the first character in a string. Its behavior is not affected by the setting of the `MultiLine` option.
`\Z`	Matches the position after the last character in a string. Its behavior is not affected by the setting of the `MultiLine` option.
`\G`	Specifies that matches must be consecutive, without any intervening nonmatching characters.
`?`	A quantifier. Matches when there is zero or one occurrence of the preceding character or group.
`*`	A quantifier. Matches when there are zero or more occurrences of the preceding character or group.
`+`	A quantifier. Matches when there are one or more occurrences of the preceding character or group.
`{n}`	A quantifier. Matches when there are exactly *n* occurrences of the preceding character or group.
`{n,m}`	A quantifier. Matches when there are at least *n* occurrences and a maximum of *m* occurrences of the preceding character or group.
`(substring)`	Captures the contained substring.
`(?<name>substring)`	Captures the contained substring and assigns it a name.
`(?:substring)`	A non-capturing group.
`(?=...)`	A positive lookahead.
`(?!...)`	A negative lookahead.
`(?<=...)`	A positive lookbehind.
`(?<!...)`	A negative lookbehind.
`\N` where N is a number	A back reference to a numbered group.
`\k<name>`	A back reference that references a named back reference (same meaning as the following).
`\k'name'`	A back reference that references a named back reference (same meaning as the preceding).
`!`	Alternation.
`(?imnsx-imnsx)`	An alternative technique to specify `RegexOptions` settings inline.

Using Named Groups

One of the features supported in the .NET Framework but not supported in many other regular expression implementations is the notion of named groups.

The syntax is `(<nameOfGroup>pattern)`. Naming a group of characters can make understanding and maintenance of code easier than using numbered groups. For example, examine the following pattern:

```
${lastName}, ${firstName}
```

The purpose of this pattern in a replacement string is more easily understood than the purpose of the same replacement operation expressed as numbered, rather than named, groups:

```
${1}, ${2}
```

The following example reverses first name and last name using named groups.

Try It Out   **Using Named Groups**

1. Create a new project in Visual Studio 2003 using the Console Application template, and name the project `NamedGroupsDemo`.

2. In the code editor, add the following line after any default `using` statements:

```
using System.Text.RegularExpressions;
```

3. Enter the following code between the curly braces of the `Main()` method:

```
Console.WriteLine(@"This will find a match for the regular
expression '^(?<firstName>\w+)\s+(?<lastName>\w+)$'.");
Console.WriteLine("Enter a test string consisting of a first name
then a last name.");
string inputString;
inputString = Console.ReadLine();
string outputString = Regex.Replace(inputString,
@"^(?<firstName>\w+)\s+(?<lastName>\w+)$", "${lastName}, ${firstName}");
Console.WriteLine("You entered the string: '" + inputString +
"'.");
Console.WriteLine("The replaced string is '" + outputString +
"'.");
Console.ReadLine();
```

4. Save the code, and press F5 to run it.

5. At the command line, enter the test string **John Smith,** and inspect the displayed result, as shown in Figure 22-15.

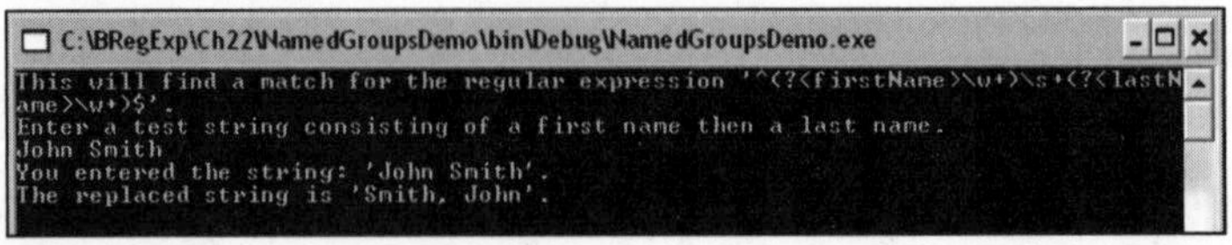

Figure 22-15

How It Works

The content of the `Main()` method is explained here.

First, the pattern to be matched against is displayed, and the user is invited to enter a first name and last name. The pattern to be matched contains two named groups, represented respectively by `(?<firstName>\w+)` and `(?<lastName>\w+)`:

```
Console.WriteLine(@"This will find a match for the regular
expression '^(?<firstName>\w+)\s+(?<lastName>\w+)$'.");
Console.WriteLine("Enter a test string consisting of a first name
then a last name.");
```

The `inputString` variable is declared; then the `Console.ReadLine()` method is used to capture the string entered by the user. That string value is assigned to the `inputString` variable:

```
string inputString;
inputString = Console.ReadLine();
```

The `Regex` class's `Replace()` method is used statically, with three arguments. The first argument specifies the string in which replacement is to take place — in this case, the string specified by the `inputString` variable. The pattern to be used to match is specified by the second argument — in this case, the pattern `^(?<firstName>\w+)\s+(?<lastName>\w+)$`. The third argument, which is formally a `string` value, uses the notation `${namedGroup}` to represent each named group.

The `${firstName}` group, not surprisingly, contains the alphabetic character sequence entered first, and the `${lastName}` group contains the alphabetic character sequence entered second:

```
string outputString = Regex.Replace(inputString,
@"^(?<firstName>\w+)\s+(?<lastName>\w+)$", "${lastName}, ${firstName}");
```

The user is shown the string that was entered and the string produced when the `Replace()` method was applied:

```
Console.WriteLine("You entered the string: '" + inputString +
"'.");
Console.WriteLine("The replaced string is '" + outputString +
"'.");
Console.ReadLine();
```

Using Back References

Back references are supported in C# .NET. A typical use for back references is finding doubled words and removing them. The following example shows this.

Try It Out   **Using Back References**

1.   Create a new project in Visual Studio 2003 using the Console Application template, and name the project `BackReferenceDemo`.

2.   Add a using `System.Text.RegularExpressions;` statement.

3. In the code editor, add the following code between the paired braces of the `Main()` method:

```
Console.WriteLine("This example will find a doubled word.");
Console.WriteLine("Using a backreference and the Replace() method
the doubled word will be removed.");
Console.WriteLine("Enter a test string containing a doubled
word.");
string inputString;
inputString = Console.ReadLine();
string outputString = Regex.Replace(inputString, @"(\w+)\s+(\1)",
"${1}");
Console.WriteLine("You entered the string: '" + inputString +
"'.");
Console.WriteLine("The replaced string is '" + outputString +
"'.");
Console.ReadLine();
```

4. Save the code, and press F5 to run it.

5. Enter the test string **Paris in the the Spring** (note the doubled `the` in the test string); press Return; and inspect the displayed information, as shown in Figure 22-16.

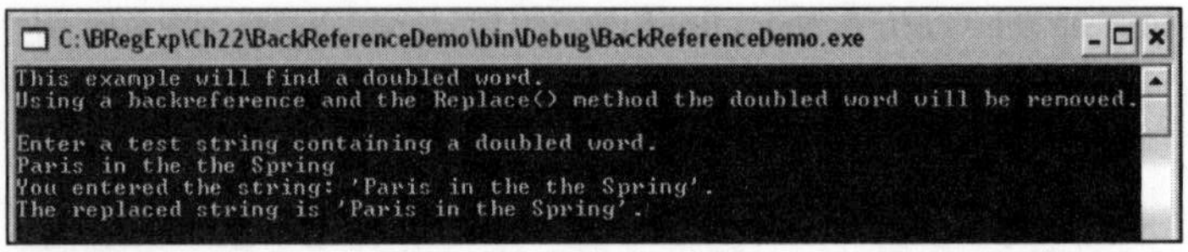

Figure 22-16

6. Press Return to close the application. In Visual Studio, press F5 to run the code again.

7. Enter the test string **Hello Hello**, press Return, and inspect the displayed information. Again, the doubled word is identified and replaced with a single occurrence of the same word.

How It Works

The `Main()` method code begins by displaying information to the user about the use of back references and invites the user to enter a string containing a doubled word:

```
Console.WriteLine("This example will find a doubled word.");
Console.WriteLine("Using a backreference and the Replace() method
the doubled word will be removed.");
Console.WriteLine("Enter a test string containing a doubled
word.");
```

The `inputString` variable is declared. And the string that the user entered is assigned to the `inputString` variable:

```
string inputString;
inputString = Console.ReadLine();
```

The `Regex` class's `Replace()` method is used statically and is applied to the `inputString` variable, and the result is assigned to the `outputString` variable.

The regular expression to be matched is in the second argument of the `Replace()` method, `(\w+)\s+(\1)`. That pattern matches a sequence of word characters equivalent to the character class `[A-Za-z0-9_]` followed by one or more whitespace characters and, as indicated by the `\1` back reference, the same sequence of word characters that has already been matched. In other words, the pattern matches a doubled word separated by whitespace.

The third argument of the `Replace()` method is the pattern to be used to replace any matched text. The matched text contains the doubled word (if one exists). The replacement text uses the numbered group corresponding to the back reference, `${1}`, to replace two occurrences of the word with one:

```
string outputString = Regex.Replace(inputString, @"(\w+)\s+(\1)",
"${1}");
```

Then the original string and the changed string are displayed to the user:

```
Console.WriteLine("You entered the string: '" + inputString +
"'.");
Console.WriteLine("The replaced string is '" + outputString +
"'.");
Console.ReadLine();
```

Exercise

1.   Which of the `RegexOptions` is used to specify case-insensitive matching?

PHP and Regular Expressions

PHP, the PHP Hypertext Processor, is a widely used language for Web-based applications. One common task in Web-based applications, whatever language is used, is the validation of user input either on the client side or on the server side before data is written to a relational database.

PHP is typically used on the server side and has similarities to ASP and ASP.NET. To work through the examples in this chapter, you will need to install PHP on a Web server.

In this chapter, you will learn the following:

❑   How to get started with PHP 5.0

❑   How PHP structures support for regular expressions

❑   How to use the `ereg()` family of functions

❑   What metacharacters are supported in PHP in Perl Compatible Regular Expressions (PCRE)

❑   How to match commonly needed user entries

> This chapter describes the regular expression functionality in PHP version 5.0.

Getting Started with PHP 5.0

To run the examples shown in this chapter, you must install PHP on a Web server. Because this book is focusing on the use of regular expressions on the Windows platforms, the focus will be on installing PHP on a Windows IIS server.

With the advent of PHP 5.0, the recommended methods of installing PHP have changed significantly from those previously recommended on www.php.net.

> The PHP Web site at www.php.net **is the official source of up-to-date information**
> **about PHP. This chapter focuses on PHP 5.0 functionality, but it is possible that rec-**
> **ommendations on installation and/or configuration will change. I suggest that you**
> **check the URL given for the current situation.**
>
> **If you need PHP 4 rather than PHP 5, that can still be downloaded from** www.php.net/
> downloads.php **at the time of this writing. If, for compatibility reasons, you need**
> **PHP 3, it can be downloaded from** http://museum.php.net/.

The following instructions describe how to install PHP 5.0.1 using the Windows installer package. It is assumed that you have already installed IIS. The Windows installer package is the easiest way to install PHP on Windows, but it has limitations. The PHP installation files are also available as a .zip file, which has to be installed manually but does allow full control over how PHP is installed. Because the focus of this chapter is the use of regular expressions with PHP, rather than on a detailed consideration of PHP installation on a Web server, no information on installation and configuration of the .zip file download is provided here.

The following instructions should get you up and running. But be aware that they take no account of how to create a secure PHP installation. If you want to use PHP on a production server, be sure to invest time in fully understanding the security issues relating to the use of PHP on the Internet.

Try It Out   Installing PHP Using the Windows Installer

1. Download the Windows installer from the download page on www.php.net (at the time of this writing, downloads were listed on www.php.net/downloads.php), and double-click the Windows installer package. Figure 23-1 shows the initial screen of the installer package for PHP 5.0.1.

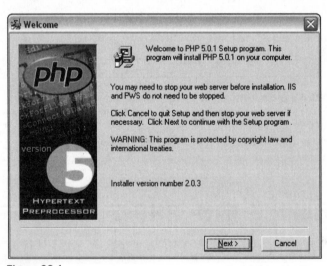

Figure 23-1

2. Click the Next button. Read the License Agreement, and click the I Agree button. If you don't accept the license, you won't be able to use the installer to install PHP 5.0.1.

3. On the next screen, you are offered a choice between Standard and Advanced installation. Select Advanced, and click the Next button.

4. Choose a location for installation. I chose `C:\PHP 5.0.1`. Click the Next button.

5. You are then asked if you want to create backups of any file replaced during installation. Leave the default option, Yes, and click the Next button.

6. Accept the default upload directory, and click the Next button. Accept the default directory for session information, and click the Next button.

7. Accept localhost as your SMTP server location or modify it as appropriate. For the purposes of this test installation, I suggest that you accept localhost; then click the Next button.

8. Accept the default option about warnings and errors, and click the Next button.

9. On the next screen, the installer is likely to recognize the version of IIS or Personal Web Server (PWS) you have installed. Unless you have good reason to do otherwise, accept the default, and click the Next button.

10. Select the file extensions to be associated with PHP. I suggest that you restrict this to .php unless you have a specific need to do otherwise. Click the Next button.

11. On the next screen, you are informed that the installer has the needed information to carry out the installation. Click the Next button. The installer will display messages about progress of the installation. If all has gone well, you should see the message shown in Figure 23-2.

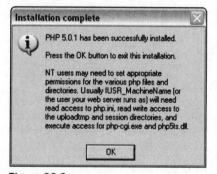

Figure 23-2

Now that PHP appears to have been installed successfully, you need to test whether it works correctly with IIS. The following instructions assume that IIS is installed, that it is running on the local machine, and that the default directory for IIS content is `C:\inetpub\wwwroot\`. If you have a different setup, amend the following instructions accordingly.

12. In Notepad or some other text editor, type the following code:

```
<?php
phpinfo()
?>
```

13. Create a subdirectory PHP in `C:\inetpub\wwwroot\` or an alternative location, if you prefer. That will allow you to access PHP code using the URL `http://localhost/PHP/` plus the relevant PHP filename.

14. Save the file as `phpinfo.php` in the `PHP` directory. If you are saving from Notepad, be sure to enclose the filename in paired double quotes, or Notepad will save the file as `phpinfo.php.txt`, which won't run correctly when accessed from a Web browser.

15. Open Internet Explorer or an alternative browser, and type the URL `http://localhost/` `PHP/phpinfo.php` into the browser.

Figure 23-3 shows the result you should expect to see after this step. Naturally, if you are not using Internet Explorer 6.0 or PHP 5.0.1, the appearance will differ a little from that shown. However, if you see a Web page similar to that in Figure 23-3, you have a successful install of PHP.

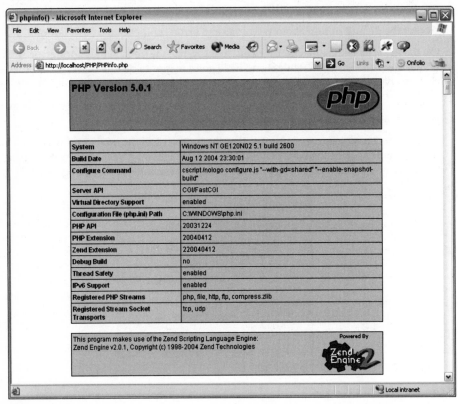

Figure 23-3

16. Use the Ctrl+F keyboard shortcut to search for the text PCRE in the Web page. As shown in Figure 23-4, the PCRE functionality is enabled by default in PHP 5.0.1 installed using the Windows installer option. Because some of the examples in this chapter depend on the presence of PCRE functionality, it is important that you verify that it is enabled.

Now that you know your PHP installation is working, you can move on to take a closer look at the ways in which regular expression functionality is supported in PHP 5.0.

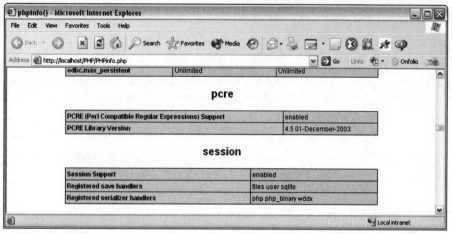

Figure 23-4

How PHP Structures Support for Regular Expressions

Regular expression support in PHP is provided by two different sets of functions. One, `ereg()` and related functions, has been available in PHP for some time (you can use it with PHP3 Web servers if you wish). The other, Perl Compatible Regular Expressions (PCRE), is more recent and has more regular expression functionality. Most of the descriptions and examples in this chapter will focus on the PCRE functionality.

If you need compatibility with older versions of PHP, the `ereg()` set of functions may be your only choice. On the other hand, if you need the functionality that is absent from the `ereg()` family, PCRE may be the most viable option, and if necessary, you may need to upgrade the PHP version on your Web server(s).

The ereg() Set of Functions

The `ereg()` set of functions is based on POSIX regular expressions. The following table summarizes the functions that relate to the `ereg()` function.

Function	Description
`ereg()`	Attempts to match a regular expression pattern against a string case sensitively.
`eregi()`	Attempts to match a regular expression pattern against a string case insensitively.
`ereg_replace()`	Attempts to match a regular expression pattern case sensitively, and if matches are found, they are replaced.

Table continued on following page

Function	Description
eregi_replace()	Attempts to match a regular expression pattern case insensitively, and if matches are found, they are replaced.
split()	Splits a string into an array, based on matching of a regular expression, case-sensitive matching.
spliti()	Splits a string into an array, based on matching of a regular expression, case-insensitive matching.
sql_regcase()	Creates a valid regular expression pattern to attempt case-insensitive matching of a specified string.

The ereg() Function

The `ereg()` function matches case sensitively. The `ereg()` function can be used with two arguments or three. When `ereg()` is used with two arguments, the first argument is a string value, which is a regular expression pattern. The second argument is a test string.

For example, if you wanted to find whether there is a match for the literal pattern `the` in the test string `The theatre is a favorite of thespians.`, you could use the following code:

```
ereg('the', "The theatre is a favorite of thespians");
```

Because `ereg()` matches case sensitively, there are two matches: the first three characters of `theatre` and of `thespians`.

Before looking at how to use `ereg()` with three arguments, work through the following example, which uses the `ereg()` function with two arguments. It shows a very simple use of the `ereg()` function to match a literal regular expression pattern, `Hel`, against a literal string value, `Hello world!`.

Try It Out   A Simple ereg() Example

1. In a text editor, enter the following code. You can use Notepad if you have no other text editor available.

```
<html>
<head>
<title>Simple ereg() Regex Test</title>
</head>
<body>
<?php
if (ereg("Hel", "Hello world!")) echo "<p>A match was found.</p>"
?>
</body>
</html>
```

2. Save the file as `C:\inetpub\PHP\SimpleRegexTest.php`. Modify the location if your Web server is not located on the local machine or you created the PHP directory in a different location.

3.   In your preferred Web browser, enter the URL `http://localhost/PHP/SimpleRegexTest.php;` press the Return key; and inspect the Web page that is displayed, as shown in Figure 23-5. The message `A match was found.` is displayed.

Figure 23-5

How It Works

The file `SimpleRegexTest.php` includes HTML/XHTML markup and PHP code. The PHP code is very simple:

```php
<?php
if (ereg("Hel", "Hello world!")) echo "<p>A match was found.</p>"
?>
```

The `<?php` marks where the PHP code begins, and the `?>` marks where the PHP code ends. The middle line is the PHP code itself.

The `if` statement tests the value returned by the `ereg()` function. The `ereg()` function takes two arguments in this example. The first argument is the string `Hel`, which is interpreted as a literal regular expression pattern. The second argument is the string `Hello world!`, which is the test string. In other words, the PHP processor attempts to find the pattern `Hel` in the string `Hello world!`. Not surprisingly, a match is found, so the `ereg()` function returns the value 1, indicating the presence of a match. The value 1 is interpreted as equivalent to `True`, so the code controlled by the `if` statement is executed:

```php
echo "<p>A match was found.</p>"
```

> **Typically, a PHP statement has to end with a semicolon. Because this very simple example has only one line of PHP code, it isn't necessary to add a semicolon. In other examples in this chapter, your code almost certainly won't run correctly if you omit the semicolon at the end of PHP statements.**

The `echo` statement causes a string to be inserted into the Web page at the position where the PHP code existed in the Web page `SimpleRegexTest.php`. That string, which includes HTML/XHTML markup, is inserted on the server between the start tag, `<body>`, and the end tag, `</body>`. The source code for the Web page, as delivered to the client, is shown in Figure 23-6.

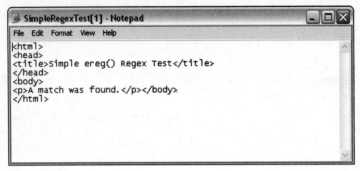

Figure 23-6

This example simply used the `boolean` value returned by the `ereg()` function to control the literal text that was added to the Web page. The next example looks at how the content of individual matches can be manipulated when using the `ereg()` function.

The ereg() Function with Three Arguments

When the `ereg()` function is used with three arguments, the first argument is the regular expression pattern expressed as a string value, the second argument is the test string, and the third argument specifies an array where the matches are to be stored.

Try It Out   The ereg() Function with Three Arguments

1.   In your favorite text editor, enter the following code:

```
<html>
<head>
<title>Splitting a date using ereg()</title>
</head>
<body>
<?php
$myPattern = '([12][0-9]{3}) ([01][0-9]) ([0123][0-9])';
$testString = gmdate("Y m d");
echo "<p>The date is now: $testString</p>";
$myResult = ereg($myPattern, $testString, $matches);
if ($myResult)
{
echo "<p>A match was found when testing case sensitively.</p>";
echo "<p>Expressed in MM/DD/YYYY format the date is now,
$matches[2]/$matches[3]/$matches[1].</p>";
}
else
{
echo "<p>No match was found when testing case sensitively.</p>";
}
?>
</body>
</html>
```

2.   Save the code as `SplitDate.php` in the `PHP` directory in the `wwwroot` directory of your IIS installation. In other words, save the code as `C:\inetpub\wwwroot\PHP\SplitDate.php`.

3.   Enter the URL `http://localhost/PHP/SplitDate.php` in Internet Explorer, and inspect the displayed results, as shown in Figure 23-7. The code was run on September 22, 2004. Notice that on the final line in the Web browser, that date is displayed as `09/22/2004`, having originally been `2004 09 22` when formatted by the `gmdate()` function.

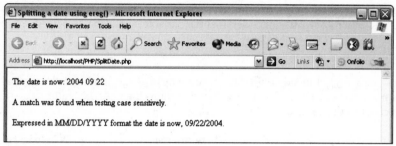

Figure 23-7

How It Works

First, look at the pattern that is used:

```
([12][0-9]{3}) ([01][0-9]) ([0123][0-9])
```

Because the date is created by the PHP `gmdate()` function, you don't, realistically, need to worry much about the function returning invalid dates. So you can use a fairly crude pattern here.

This pattern first matches a single numeric digit: a 1 or 2. This makes sense if the dates you are dealing with are in the twentieth and twenty-first centuries. Then three further numeric digits are matched. This part of the pattern is contained in paired parentheses, so it is captured. You will see a little later how the captured group is handled and retrieved. This pattern component matches a four-digit year from the twentieth or twenty-first century.

A single space character follows. Then comes a further captured group beginning with a 0 or 1, which is followed by a numeric digit. This matches the numeric value of the month. Theoretically, it will match "months" such as the 19th month of a year. However, because the `gmdate()` function is very unlikely ever to return a spurious date like that, it's an issue you don't need to worry about in this example.

Then follows a single space character and a further captured group beginning with a 0, 1, 2, or 3 followed by a numeric digit. This matches the numeric value of the day of the month. Theoretically, it will match "days" such as the 39th of January. Again, because the `gmdate()` function is very unlikely ever to return a spurious date, you don't need to worry about it.

First, you assign the pattern, as a string, to the `$myPattern` variable:

```
$myPattern = '([12][0-9]{3}) ([01][0-9]) ([0123][0-9])';
```

Then you use the `gmdate()` function to assign a string value to the `$testString` variable. The arguments to the `gmdate()` function specify the formatting of the date returned. In this case, `Y` specifies that the year is returned as a four-digit form, `2004`; the `m` specifies that the month is expressed as a number between 1 and 12; and the `d` specifies that the day of the month is expressed as a number from 1 to 31:

```
$testString = gmdate("Y m d");
```

Then you use the echo statement to display the format in which the current date was returned. If you are used to languages such as JavaScript, you may find it surprising that the $testString variable is just written inside the paired double quotes rather than having literal text inside paired double quotes and using the + concatenation operator. In PHP, you simply write a variable inside the paired quotes, and the PHP processor knows it is intended that the variable's value be displayed:

```
echo "<p>The date is now: $testString</p>";
```

Then you use the ereg() function with three arguments to assign a value to the $myResult variable. If one or more matches exist, the $myResult variable contains the boolean value True (1), and if there is no match, it contains the boolean value False (0).

The first argument is a pattern, and the second argument is the test string, as before. The third argument is an array containing the components of the matched text. The elements of that array are determined by the capturing parentheses, which were mentioned when you looked at the components of the regular expression pattern:

```
$myResult = ereg($myPattern, $testString, $matches);
```

You test to see if there was a match:

```
if ($myResult)
```

If there was, you use two echo statements to add content to the Web page:

```
{
```

You simply state that a match was found:

```
echo "<p>A match was found when testing case sensitively.</p>";
```

Then you indicate that the date will be returned in MM/DD/YYYY format, which means that you must reorder the date. This is done using $matches[2]/$matches[3]/$matches[1].

The value of the whole match is in array element 0. The pattern that matched the date contained three pairs of capturing parentheses. The result of the first pair goes in $matches[1], the result of the second pair in $matches[2], and so on. So the year is in $matches[1], the month in $matches[2], and the day in $matches[3].

Because you want to return MM/DD/YYYY, you use the sequence $matches[2]/$matches[3]/$matches[1], which means return the value in $matches[2] (the month) followed by a literal forward-slash character, followed by the value in $matches[3] (the day), followed by a literal forward-slash character, followed by the value in $matches [1] (the year).

So the value that was originally displayed as 2004 09 20 is transformed into 09/20/2004:

```
echo "<p>Expressed in MM/DD/YYYY format the date is now,
$matches[2]/$matches[3]/$matches[1].</p>";
```

If no match were present, you would simply display a message indicating that

```
}
else
{
echo "<p>No match was found when testing case sensitively.</p>";
}
```

So groups that are captured using paired parentheses are, if you specify a variable as the third argument to the ereg() function, each stored in the elements of the array specified by the third argument.

The eregi() Function

The eregi() function does almost the same as the ereg() function, except that it matches case insensitively.

The following example shows the results when using ereg() and eregi() on the same test text.

Try It Out   The eregi() Function

1.   In a text editor, enter the following code:

```
<html>
<head>
<title>ereg() and eregi() Test to match [A-Z][0-9]</title>
</head>
<body>
<?php
$myPattern = '[A-Z][0-9]';
$testString = "a9";
$myResult = ereg($myPattern, $testString);
if ($myResult)
{
echo "<p>A match was found when testing case sensitively.</p>";
}
else
{
echo "<p>No match was found when testing case sensitively.</p>";
}
$myResult2 = eregi($myPattern, $testString);
if ($myResult2)
{
echo "<p>A match was found when testing case insensitively.</p>";
}
else
{
echo "<p>No match was found when testing case insensitively.</p>";
}
?>
</body>
</html>
```

2.   Save the code to C:\inetpub\wwwroot\PHP\EregEregiTest.php.

3. Enter the URL `http://localhost/PHP/EregEregiTest.php` in Internet Explorer, and inspect the displayed results, as shown in Figure 23-8. When using `ereg()`, there is no match, as indicated by the first displayed message, and when using `eregi()`, there is a match, as indicated by the second displayed message.

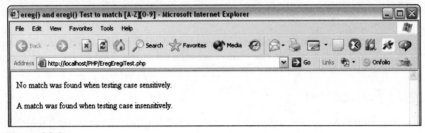

Figure 23-8

How It Works

The pattern `[A-Z][0-9]` is assigned to the variable `$myPattern`. You can't use the `\d` metacharacter to match a numeric digit because it is not recognized inside `ereg()`:

```
$myPattern = '[A-Z][0-9]';
```

The test string is a9, and it is assigned to the `$testString` variable:

```
$testString = "a9";
```

The result of `ereg()` is assigned to the `$myResult` variable, with `$myPattern` as the first argument of `ereg()` and `$testString` the second. Thus, you are testing whether the pattern `[A-Z][0-9]` has a match in the test string a9:

```
$myResult = ereg($myPattern, $testString);
```

If there is a match, `$myResult` contains the `boolean` value `True` (1). If there is no match, it contains the `boolean` value `False` (0). You use that `boolean` value to control what is displayed to the user:

```
if ($myResult)
```

The first character of the test string, a9, is not contained in the character class `[A-Z]`, because matching is case sensitive.

When using `ereg()`, the `$myResult` variable returns `False`. Therefore, the message `No match was found when testing case sensitively.` is displayed:

```
else
{
echo "<p>No match was found when testing case sensitively.</p>";
}
```

However, when the `eregi()` function is used matching is case insensitive; so the first character of the test string, a9, is matches the character class `[A-Z]`. And the second character of the test string is matches the character class `[0-9]` because there is a match for each component of the pattern. The value contained in the variable `$myResult2` is, therefore, the `boolean` value `True`.

Because the value contained in `$myResult2` is `True`, the message `A match was found when testing case insensitively.` is displayed:

```
if ($myResult2)
{
echo "<p>A match was found when testing case insensitively.</p>";
}
```

The ereg_replace() Function

The `ereg_replace()` function attempts to match a pattern case insensitively. If a match is found, the match is replaced by the specified replacement text. If multiple matches exist, each is replaced.

The `ereg_replace()` function takes three arguments. The first argument is the pattern to be used in attempted matching. The second argument is the text used to replace any match. The third argument is the test string.

Try It Out   Using the ereg_replace() Function

1.   In a text editor, enter the following code:

```
<html>
<head>
<title>ereg_replace() Demo</title>
</head>
<body>
<?php
$myPattern = "Hello";
$myReplacement = "Hi";
$myString = "Hello world!";
echo "<p>The original string was '$myString'.</p>";
echo "<p>The pattern is '$myPattern'.</p>";
echo "<p>The replacement text is '$myReplacement'.</p>";
$replacedString = ereg_replace($myPattern, $myReplacement, $myString);
$displayString = "<p>After replacement the string becomes: ' ";
$displayString = $displayString . $replacedString . "'.</p>";
echo $displayString;
?>
</body>
</html>
```

2.   Save the code as `C:\inetpub\wwwroot\ereg_replaceDemo.php`.

3.   Enter the URL `http://localhost/PHP/ereg_replaceDemo.php` in Internet Explorer, and inspect the displayed results, as shown in Figure 23-9. The character sequence `Hello` in the original sequence has been replaced by the character sequence `Hi`.

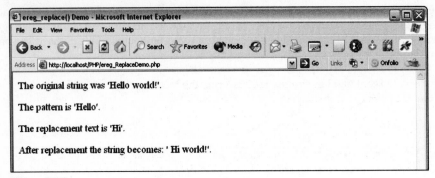

Figure 23-9

How It Works

Three variables, $myPattern, $myReplacement, and $myString, are declared and assigned string values:

```
$myPattern = "Hello";
$myReplacement = "Hi";
$myString = "Hello world!";
```

Then the original values of those variables are echoed to the user:

```
echo "<p>The original string was '$myString'.</p>";
echo "<p>The pattern is '$myPattern'.</p>";
echo "<p>The replacement text is '$myReplacement'.</p>";
```

The variable $replacedString is declared and assigned a value returned by the ereg_replace() function. Notice the order of the arguments of the ereg_replace() function; the test string is the third argument, not the second, as you might have expected from familiarity with the ereg() function:

```
$replacedString = ereg_replace($myPattern, $myReplacement, $myString);
```

Finally, the $displayString variable is declared. The value of $displayString is created by concatenating literal text and the value of $replacedString. Notice that the period character is used to concatenate strings in PHP:

```
$displayString = "<p>After replacement the string becomes: ' ";
$displayString = $displayString . $replacedString . "'.</p>";
echo $displayString;
```

If no match existed for the pattern, the original string would have been returned.

The eregi_replace() Function

The `eregi_replace()` function matches in a case-insensitive way and replaces any match found in the test string using the replacement string.

The `eregi_replace()` function takes three arguments. The first is a string value that represents the regular expression pattern. The second is the replacement string that replaces each match found in the test string. The third argument is the test string.

Try It Out   **Using the eregi_replace() Function**

1.   Enter the following code in a text editor:

```
<html>
<head>
<title>eregi_replace() Demo</title>
</head>
<body>
<?php
$myPattern = "Doctor";
$myReplacement = "Dr.";
$myString = "Doctor Smith spoke with another doctor.";
echo "<p>The original string was '$myString'.</p>";
echo "<p>The pattern is '$myPattern'.</p>";
echo "<p>The replacement text is '$myReplacement'.</p>";
$replacedString = eregi_replace($myPattern, $myReplacement, $myString);
$displayString = "<p>After replacment the string becomes: ' ";
$displayString = $displayString . $replacedString . "'.</p>";
echo $displayString;
?>
</body>
</html>
```

2.   Save the code as `C:\inetpub\wwwroot\PHP\eregi_replaceDemo.php`.

3.   In Internet Explorer, enter the URL `http://localhost/PHP/eregi_replaceDemo.php`, and inspect the displayed results, as shown in Figure 23-10. Notice that two occurrences of the word `Doctor` (one `Doctor` and the other `doctor`) have been replaced. In all likelihood, it would be undesirable to replace the second occurrence.

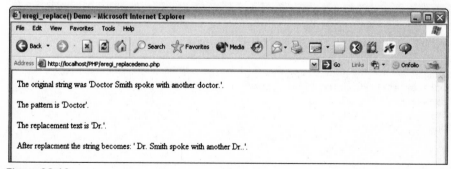

Figure 23-10

How It Works

The example aims to replace all occurrences of the string `Doctor`, matched case insensitively, with the abbreviated form `Dr.`.

You first assign values to the variables `$myPattern`, `$myReplacement`, and `$myString`:

```
$myPattern = "Doctor";
$myReplacement = "Dr.";
$myString = "Doctor Smith spoke with another doctor.";
```

After displaying the values of the preceding variables to the user, the `eregi_replace()` function is used to replace all occurrences of `Doctor`, matched case insensitively, with the form `Dr.`:

```
$replacedString = eregi_replace($myPattern, $myReplacement, $myString);
```

This causes the occurrences of `Doctor` and `doctor` (in the test string) to be replaced, because matching against the pattern `Doctor` is case insensitive. This reduces the specificity of matching because character sequences such as `DocTOr`, `dOCtor`, and so on would also be matched. In all likelihood, the replacing of `doctor` by `Dr.` is inappropriate. For this particular task, the case-sensitive matching of the `ereg_replace()` function would have been more appropriate. However, the example does demonstrate how case-insensitive matching works.

The split() Function

The `split()` function can split a string into component substrings, with the point where the string is split determined by a regular expression pattern. This can be useful when handling comma-separated values in files or handling dates that have different separators. The following example illustrates how the `split()` function can be used to split dates that use the hyphen, forward slash, and period character as separators.

The `split()` function can take two or three arguments. The first argument is the regular expression pattern at which a split is to take place. If a match is found, the character sequence that matches the pattern is discarded. This makes sense as default behavior when, for example, you have comma-separated data and want only the data and not the commas. The second argument is the test string. The third (optional) argument is an `int` value, which specifies the maximum number of times matching and splitting is to take place.

Try It Out   Using the split() Function

1.   Type the following code into a code editor:

```
<html>
<head>
<title>split() Function Demo</title>
</head>
<body>
<?php
```

```
$myString1 = "2004/09/23";
$myString2 = "2004.09.23";
$myString3 = "2004-09-23";
$myPattern = "[-/.]";
list($year, $month, $day) = split($myPattern, $myString1);
echo "<p>String was: $myString1. <br />Year: $year <br />Month: $month <br />Day:
$day</p>";
list($year, $month, $day) = split($myPattern, $myString2);
echo "<br /><br /><p>String was: $myString2. <br />Year: $year <br />Month: $month
<br />Day: $day</p>";
list($year, $month, $day) = split($myPattern, $myString3);
echo "<br /><br /><p>String was: $myString3. <br />Year: $year <br />Month: $month
<br />Day: $day</p>";
?>
</body>
</html>
```

2. Save the code as C:\inetpub\wwwroot\PHP\splitdemo.php.

3. In Internet Explorer, type the URL http://localhost/PHP/splitdemo.php, and inspect the displayed results, as shown in Figure 23-11.

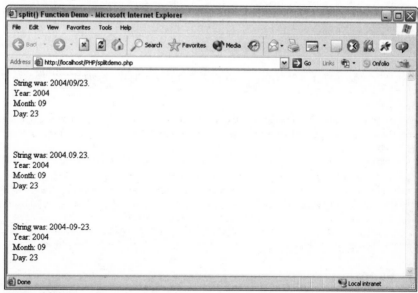

Figure 23-11

How It Works

This example demonstrates how three strings, which represent dates, can be split using three possible separators: the forward slash, the period character, and the hyphen.

First, three variables are declared, each of which holds the date September 23, 2004. Each of the variables — $myString1, $myString2, and $myString3 — uses a different separator character.

```
$myString1 = "2004/09/23";
$myString2 = "2004.09.23";
$myString3 = "2004-09-23";
```

Then the variable $myPattern is declared and is assigned a string that represents a character class containing the hyphen, the forward slash, and the period character. The hyphen character is the first character in the character class, so this is not specifying a character class range:

```
$myPattern = "[-/.]";
```

A list is created, containing the component parts of the date represented in myString1. The forward slash in the character class [-/.] matches twice, so the string myString1 is split into three parts, which are represented in the list by $year, $month, and $day:

```
list($year, $month, $day) = split($myPattern, $myString1);
```

The variables $year, $month, and $day are output:

```
echo "<p>String was: $myString1. <br />Year: $year <br />Month: $month <br />Day:
$day</p>";
```

The process of creating a list that contains the component parts of a string is repeated with the variables $myString2 (which uses a period character as separator) and $myString3 (which uses a hyphen as separator):

```
list($year, $month, $day) = split($myPattern, $myString2);
echo "<br /><br /><p>String was: $myString2. <br />Year: $year <br />Month: $month
<br />Day: $day</p>";
list($year, $month, $day) = split($myPattern, $myString3);
echo "<br /><br /><p>String was: $myString3. <br />Year: $year <br />Month: $month
<br />Day: $day</p>";
```

The spliti() Function

The spliti() function does the same thing as the split() function, except that it matches case insensitively. If an alphabetic character is used as a separator, spliti() will match case insensitively, while split() matches case sensitively. However, because the most likely separators used are the comma, the hyphen, the forward slash, the semicolon, and the period character, the two functions will often behave identically in practical use.

The spliti() function, like the split() function, takes two or three arguments. The first argument is the regular expression pattern at which splitting is to take place. The second argument is the test string. The third (optional) argument is an int value, which specifies the maximum number of times matching and splitting are to take place. In the absence of a third argument, matching and splitting proceed through the whole string.

The sql_regcase() Function

The `sql_regcase()` function is different from all the other functions in the `ereg()` family because it is used to create a regular expression pattern, rather than use one, as all the other functions do.

Using the sql_regcase() Function

1. Type the following code in a text editor:

```html
<html>
<head>
<title>sql_regcase() Demo</title>
</head>
<body>
<?php
$sequenceToMatch = "Doctor";
$myPattern = sql_regcase($sequenceToMatch);
echo "<p>To match '$sequenceToMatch' the sql_regcase() function produces:
'$myPattern'.</p>";
?>
</body>
</html>
```

2. Save the code as `C:\inetpub\wwwroot\PHP\sql_regcaseDemo.php`.

3. In Internet Explorer, enter the URL `http://localhost/PHP/sql_regcaseDemo.php`, and inspect the displayed results, as shown in Figure 23-12. The result produced is a sequence of character classes that allow case-insensitive matching.

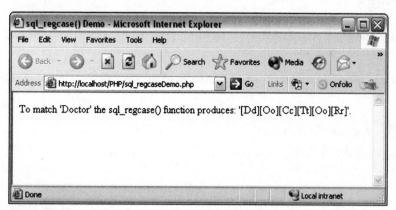

Figure 23-12

How It Works

For each character in `$sequenceToMatch` a character class containing both an uppercase and lowercase character is created. So, for example, for the D of doctor, a character class `[Dd]` is created.

Perl Compatible Regular Expressions

Perl Compatible Regular Expressions (PCRE) provides more modern and more powerful regular expression support in PHP than do ereg() and associated functions.

The following table summarizes the family of functions supported in PCRE in PHP. Each of these functions is covered in more detail a little later in the chapter.

Function	Description
preg_match()	Attempts to match a specified pattern in a specified test string
preg_match_all()	Attempts to match a specified pattern as many times as possible in a specified test string
preg_grep()	This function finds matches for a regular expression pattern in an array
preg_quote()	This function takes a regular expression pattern and escapes each character in it using a backslash
preg_replace()	Attempts to match a regular expression pattern in a string and replaces any matches using a specified replacement string
preg_replace_callback()	Similar to preg_replace(), except that a callback is used to define the replacement string
preg_split()	Splits a test string into an array of substrings, using a specified pattern to define where splitting should take place

Pattern Delimiters in PCRE

PCRE includes support for developer-specified delimiters of regular expression patterns. The default delimiters are paired forward-slash characters. To supply a regular expression, you enclose it in paired delimiters inside the paired double quotes.

You can use any paired nonalphanumeric character as a delimiter, or you can use matched characters such as {}, <>, or ().

Try It Out   Various Delimiters

1.   Type the following code into a text editor:

```
<html>
<head>
<title>Simple preg_match() Regex Test</title>
</head>
<body>
<?php
if (preg_match("/Hel/", "Hello world!")) echo "<p>A match was found using paired
'/' as delimiter.</p>";
if (preg_match(".Hel.", "Hello world!")) echo "<p>A match was found using paired
'.' as delimiter.</p>";
```

```
if (preg_match("{Hel}", "Hello world!")) echo "<p>A match was found using matched
'{' and '}' as delimiters.</p>";
if (preg_match("(Hel)", "Hello world!")) echo "<p>A match was found using matched
'(' and ')' as delimiters.</p>";
if (preg_match("<Hel>", "Hello world!")) echo "<p>A match was found using matched
'<' and '>' as delimiters.</p>";
?>
</body>
</html>
```

2. Save the code as `C:\inetpub\wwwroot\PHP\DelimiterTest.php`.

3. Type the URL `http://localhost/PHP/DelimiterTest.php` into Internet Explorer, and inspect the displayed results, as shown in Figure 23-13.

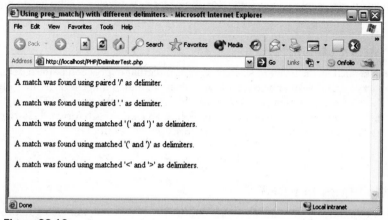

Figure 23-13

How It Works

There are five examples of using the `preg_match()` function in this example. Each does basically the same thing, testing whether there is a match for the literal pattern `Hel` in the test string `Hello world!`, and if there is (there is in each of the examples), a message stating that there is a match and what delimiter was used is displayed.

The first example uses paired forward slashes as delimiters. I prefer using these because they are the default delimiters in Perl too:

```
if (preg_match("/Hel/", "Hello world!")) echo "<p>A match was found using paired
'/' as delimiter.</p>";
```

However, you can also use other paired nonalphanumeric delimiters. The second example uses paired period characters as the pattern delimiters:

```
if (preg_match(".Hel.", "Hello world!")) echo "<p>A match was found using paired
'.' as delimiter.</p>";
```

The other three examples use matched pairs of characters. They are matched in the sense that a left curly brace, {, is matched with a right curly brace, }. The other matched pairs are ordinary parentheses, (and), and left and right angled brackets, < and >.

```
if (preg_match("{Hel}", "Hello world!")) echo "<p>A match was found using matched
'{' and '}' as delimiters.</p>";
if (preg_match("(Hel)", "Hello world!")) echo "<p>A match was found using matched
'(' and ')' as delimiters.</p>";
if (preg_match("<Hel>", "Hello world!")) echo "<p>A match was found using matched
'<' and '>' as delimiters.</p>";
```

I suggest that unless there is good reason to vary from using the forward slash, you use that. Most developers will be familiar with the use of paired forward slashes as regular expression delimiters, so using them is least likely to cause confusion for others reading your code. If you use another delimiter, I suggest that you add a comment to document your choice for any developer who has to maintain your code.

Escaping Pattern Delimiters

When a character such as the forward slash is used as a regular expression pattern delimiter in PHP, it is necessary to escape that delimiter character if you desire to match that character literally. For example, if the forward slash is used as a pattern delimiter, and you want to match an HTTP URL that references the com, net, org, info, and biz top-level domains, you must escape each forward slash in the pattern, which is the first argument of the preg_match() function. For example:

```
preg_match('/http:\/\/.*\.(com|net|org|info|biz)\/.*/', $testString)
```

Matching Modifiers in PCRE

It will come as little surprise that the matching modifiers in Perl Compatible Regular Expressions are based on those in Perl. The following table summarizes the matching modifiers available in the PCRE functionality in PHP.

Matching Modifier	Description
i	Causes matching to be case insensitive.
m	Multiline. Alters the effect of the ^ and $ metacharacters. With multiline chosen, ^ matches the position at the beginning of a line, and $ matches the position at the end of a line.
s	Modifies what the period metacharacter matches. With the s modifier selected, the period metacharacter matches all characters. Without s being selected, the period metacharacter matches all characters except newline.
x	Modifies how whitespace inside a pattern is processed. With x selected unescaped, whitespace characters are ignored.
A	Constrains matching to the beginning of the test string.
D	If the D modifier is set, the $ metacharacter matches only at the end of the test string. If the m matching modifier is set, the D modifier is ignored.

Matching Modifier	Description
S	Affects how a pattern is processed. If the S modifier is set, further analysis of how best to process the regular expression takes place.
U	The U modifier alters the "greediness" behavior of patterns. With U set, the default behavior becomes nongreedy ("lazy"). Matching becomes greedy with (? ...).
X	Turns on Perl-incompatible behavior.
e	Applies to preg_replace() function only.

Matching modifiers are written after the second of the paired or matched delimiters and immediately before the second of the paired double quote characters. So to match the pattern Hel case insensitively against the test string Hello world! using the preg_match() function, you would write the following:

```
preg_match("/Hel/i", "Hello world!")
```

Several of these matching modifiers are used in examples later in the chapter.

Using the preg_match() Function

The preg_match() function attempts to match a pattern against a test string and is very similar to the ereg() function you used earlier. However, it is often faster than ereg() and so is to be preferred to ereg() when using versions of PHP that support PCRE functionality.

The preg_match() function can take two or three arguments. The first argument is a regular expression pattern. However, unlike ereg(), where you would write:

```
ereg("Hel", "Hello world!");
```

to match the character sequence Hel in the string Hello world!, when you use the preg_match() function you must enclose the pattern in paired delimiters, such as paired forward slashes, inside the paired double quote characters. So when using preg_match(), you would write the following to match the character sequence Hel in Hello world!:

```
preg_match("/Hel/", Hello world!");
```

The second argument is the test string. The optional third argument is a variable into which an array of groups will be returned, assuming that a match is found.

Try It Out   A preg_match() Example

1. Type the following code in a text editor:

```
<html>
<head>
<title>Simple preg_match() Regex Test</title>
</head>
<body>
<?php
```

```
if (preg_match("/Hel/", "Hello world!")) echo "<p>A match was found.</p>"
?>
</body>
</html>
```

2. Save the code as `C:\inetpub\wwwroot\PHP\SimplePregTest.php`.

3. In Internet Explorer, enter the URL `http://localhost/PHP/SimplePregTest.php`, and inspect the displayed result, as shown in Figure 23-14. Because the pattern `Hel` is matched, the message `A match was found.` is displayed.

Figure 23-14

How It Works

The `preg_match()` function is used to produce a `boolean` value that can be tested in an `if` statement:

```
if (preg_match("/Hel/", "Hello world!")) echo "<p>A match was found.</p>"
```

Notice that paired forward slashes are used as the delimiters for the regular expression pattern in the first argument of the `preg_match()` function:

The next example uses the `preg_match()` function with three arguments and manipulates the array elements specified in the third argument to the function. Array elements are numbered beginning at zero. Element `[0]` contains the whole match.

Try It Out   **Using the preg_match() Function with Groups**

1. Type the following code in a text editor:

```
<html>
<head>
<title>Using preg_match() with 3 arguments</title>
</head>
<body>
<?php
$dateToday = gmdate("Y m d");
$myDate = preg_match("/(\d{4})\s(\d{2}) (\d{2})/", $dateToday, $dateComponents);
if ($myDate)
{
```

```
echo "<p>The original date was: $dateToday</p>";
echo "<p>In MM/DD/YYYY format today is:
$dateComponents[2]/$dateComponents[3]/$dateComponents[1]</p>";
}
?>
</body>
</html>
```

2. Save the code as `C:\inetpub\wwwroot\PHP\preg_match_3args.php`.

3. Type the URL `http://localhost/PHP/preg_match_3args.php` in Internet Explorer, and inspect the displayed results, as shown in Figure 23-15. The upper line of the Web page shows the original format of the date. The lower line shows the date expressed in MM/DD/YYYY format, with the new format being created using the `$dateComponents` array, which was created because `$dateComponents` was the third argument of the `preg_match()` function.

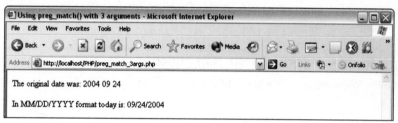

Figure 23-15

How It Works

The variable `$dateToday` is assigned a value returned from the `gmdate()` function. The arguments to the `gmdate()` function specify that the date is returned in YYYY MM DD format, with all values being expressed as numeric digits:

```
$dateToday = gmdate("Y m d");
```

The `$myDate` variable is assigned the value returned by the `preg_match()` function. Because there is a match for the pattern `(\d{4})\s(\d{2}) (\d{2})` in the value of `$dateToday`, the `$myDate` variable holds the equivalent of the boolean value True. Notice that there is a space character between the second and third sets of paired parentheses.

The `preg_match()` function has three arguments, and the pattern in the first argument has groups created using parentheses. The `$dateComponents` variable is assigned array elements corresponding to each group created by the matched parentheses:

```
$myDate = preg_match("/(\d{4})\s(\d{2}) (\d{2})/", $dateToday, $dateComponents);
```

Because there is a match, the `$myDate` variable holds the value of True, so the statements contained in the `if` statement are executed:

```
if ($myDate)
```

The original format of the date is displayed using the value of the $dateToday variable. The elements of the $dateComponents array are reordered to display the date in MM/DD/YYYY format:

```
{
echo "<p>The original date was: $dateToday</p>";
echo "<p>In MM/DD/YYYY format today is:
$dateComponents[2]/$dateComponents[3]/$dateComponents[1]</p>";

}
```

The preg_match() function answers the question of whether or not a match is present. If you want to find and manipulate multiple matches (if they are present in the test string), you need to use the preg_match_all() function.

Using the preg_match_all() Function

The preg_match_all() function matches all character sequences in the test string that are matches for the specified regular expression.

Try It Out   **Using the preg_match_all() Function**

1. Type the following code in a text editor:

```
<html>
<head>
<title>Using preg_match_all()</title>
</head>
<body>
<?php
$testString = "A99 B888 C234 D123 E45678 f2345";
$myMatches = preg_match_all("/[A-Z]\d{1,5}/", $testString, $partNumbers);
if ($myMatches)
{
  for($counter=0; $counter < $myMatches; $counter++)
  {
   echo "<p>" . $partNumbers[0][$counter]. "</p>";
  }
}
?>
</body>
</html>
```

2. Save the code as C:\inetpub\wwwroot\PHP\preg_match_all.php.

3. In Internet Explorer, type the URL http://localhost/PHP/preg_match_all.php, and inspect the displayed results, as shown in Figure 23-16.

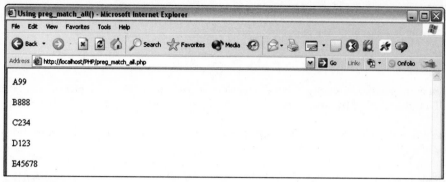

Figure 23-16

4. Edit the following line

```
$myMatches = preg_match_all("/[A-Z]\d{1,5}/", $testString, $partNumbers);
```

so that it matches case insensitively:

```
$myMatches = preg_match_all("/[A-Z]\d{1,5}/i", $testString, $partNumbers);
```

5. Save the amended code as C:\inetpub\wwwroot\PHP\preg_match_all_Insensitive.php.

6. Type the URL http://localhost/PHP/preg_match_all_Insensitive.php in Internet Explorer, and inspect the displayed results, as shown in Figure 23-17. Notice that there is an additional match displayed, f2345.

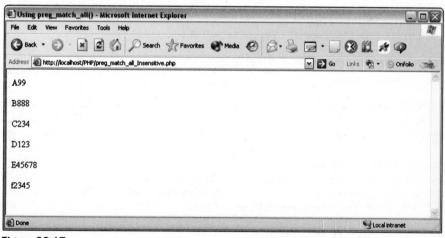

Figure 23-17

How It Works

The test string is assigned to the variable $testString:

```
$testString = "A99 B888 C234 D123 E45678 f2345";
```

The $myMatches variable is assigned the int value returned from the preg_match_all() function. You will use the value of the $myMatches variable when looping through array values a little later.

The $partNumbers variable is the third argument of the preg_match_all() function and is assigned an array of matches:

```
$myMatches = preg_match_all("/[A-Z]\d{1,5}/", $testString, $partNumbers);
```

To display all the results, use an if statement with a for loop nested inside it. The test of the if statement is whether $myMatches is unequal to 0; in other words, if there is at least one match, the test for the if statement returns True:

```
if ($myMatches)
{
```

The for loop starts at 0 and counts up to the value of the $myMatches variable:

```
for($counter=0; $counter < $myMatches; $counter++)
{
```

The echo statement is used to concatenate literal text with the value of an array element, determined by $counter and a further piece of literal text.

You want to return the whole match, so use element 0 for each match The other dimension of the array is determined by the current value of the $counter variable:

```
    echo "<p>" . $partNumbers[0][$counter]. "</p>";
}
```

At Step 4, the pattern [A-Z]\d{1,5} is matched. This matches any character sequence where an upper-case alphabetic character is followed by between one and five numeric digits. The default matching is case sensitive. Therefore, the matches are A99, B888, C234, D123, and E45678 (as displayed in Figure 23-16).

After you edit the first argument of the preg_match_all() function to "/[A-Z]\d{1,5}/i", matching is case insensitive. Now the pattern [A-Z]\d{1,5} matches an alphabetic character of either case followed by between one and five numeric digits. All the previous matches still match. In addition, there is a match f2345, which has a lowercase alphabetic character.

Using the preg_grep() Function

The preg_grep() function matches a regular expression pattern against the elements in an array. The preg_grep() function takes two arguments. The first argument is a regular expression pattern. The second argument is an array.

So to assign the matches in an array $myArray for a pattern $myPattern to a variable $myMatches, you would write the following:

```php
$myMatches = preg_grep($myPattern, $myArray);
```

Try It Out   **Using the preg_grep() Function**

1.   Type the following code in a text editor:

```php
<html>
<head>
<title>A preg_grep() Test</title>
</head>
<body>
<?php
$myArray = array("Hello", "Help", "helper", "shell", "satchel", "Camera");
$myMatchesSensitive = preg_grep("/Hel/", $myArray);
echo "<p>Matching case sensitively:</p>";
if ($myMatchesSensitive)
{
  print_r (array_values($myMatchesSensitive));
}
$myMatchesInsensitive = preg_grep("/Hel/i", $myArray);
echo "<br /><p>Matching case insensitively:</p>";
if ($myMatchesInsensitive)
{
  print_r (array_values($myMatchesInsensitive));
}
?>
</body>
</html>
```

2.   Save the code as `C:\inetpub\wwwroot\PHP\preg_grep.php`.

3.   In Internet Explorer, enter the URL `http://localhost/PHP/preg_grep.php`, and inspect the displayed results, as shown in Figure 23-18. Compare the matches with case-sensitive and case-insensitive matching.

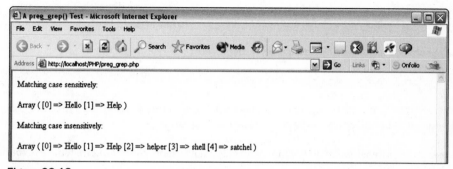

Figure 23-18

How It Works

The example uses the `preg_grep()` method twice: — first to match case sensitively (the default), and second to match case insensitively.

The array that is matched is $myArray, which is assigned an array of values shown here:

```
$myArray = array("Hello", "Help", "helper", "shell", "satchel", "Camera");
```

First, the case-sensitive matching is carried out. The $myMatchesSensitive variable is assigned the array returned from the `preg_grep()` function, using the literal pattern `"/Hel/"` as its first argument and $myArray as its second argument:

```
$myMatchesSensitive = preg_grep("/Hel/", $myArray);
```

A message about case-sensitive matching is displayed:

```
echo "<p>Matching case sensitively:</p>";
```

Then the value of the $myMatchesSensitive variable is used as a test for an `if` statement. If the $myMatchesSensitive variable contains a nonempty array, the statement in the `if` statement is executed:

```
if ($myMatchesSensitive)
```

The `print_r()` function is used to display the key and values of the array elements in $myArray. The `print_r()` function prints human-readable information about a function.

Only two elements containing matches, `Hello` and `Help`, are found when matching is case sensitive:

```
{
    print_r (array_values($myMatchesSensitive));
}
```

The process is repeated for case-insensitive matching. The $myMatchesInsensitive variable is assigned the array returned from the `preg_grep()` function. Notice in the first argument that the i matching modifier is used to specify case-insensitive matching:

```
$myMatchesInsensitive = preg_grep("/Hel/i", $myArray);
```

A message about case-insensitive matching is displayed:

```
echo "<br /><p>Matching case insensitively:</p>";
```

Then the `if` statement tests if $myMatchesInsensitive is empty. If not, the `print_r()` function is used to output information about the case-insensitive matches.

When using case-insensitive matching, three additional elements containing matches are found: `helper`, `shell`, and `satchel`.

```
if ($myMatchesInsensitive)
{
    print_r (array_values($myMatchesInsensitive));
}
```

Using the preg_quote() Function

The `preg_quote()` function is used to escape strings produced at runtime that may contain values that would be misinterpreted without escaping. You could use `preg_quote()` to match a period character, for example. In the output string, the period character would be escaped, being written as \..

Using the preg_replace() Function

The `preg_replace()` function attempts to match a regular expression as many times as possible in a test string. Each substring that is a match is replaced by specified replacement text.

The `preg_replace()` function takes three or more arguments. The first argument is a regular expression pattern. The second is the replacement text. The third is the test string. The optional fourth argument is an `int` value that indicates a maximum number of times that replacement should take place.

The e matching modifier causes back references in the replacement text to be interpreted as PHP code and uses the result to replace the test string.

Try It Out   Using the preg_replace() Function

The following illustrates how you can use the `preg_replace()` function to replace the literal text Star with the literal text Moon.

1. Type the following code in a text editor:

```
<html>
<head>
<title>A preg_replace() Demo</title>
</head>
<body>
<?php
$myString = "Star Training Company.";
$newString = preg_replace("/Star/", "Moon", $myString);
echo "<p>The original string was: '$myString'.</p>";
echo "<p>After replacement the string is: '$newString'.</p.>";
?>
</body>
</html>
```

2. Save the code as `C:\inetpub\wwwroot\PHP\replaceDemo.php`.

3. In Internet Explorer, enter the URL `http://localhost/PHP/replaceDemo.php`, and inspect the displayed results, as shown in Figure 23-19.

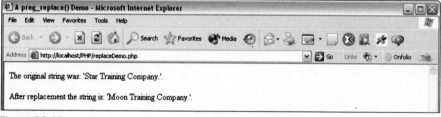

Figure 23-19

How It Works

The original string `Star Training Company` is assigned to the `$myString` variable:

```
$myString = "Star Training Company.";
```

The string value returned by the `preg_replace()` function is assigned to the `$newString` variable. The pattern used in the `preg_replace()` function is a literal pattern `Star`. The replacement text is `Moon`. Replacement is to take place in the string specified by the `$myString` variable. Essentially, any occurrence of `Star` is replaced by `Moon`:

```
$newString = preg_replace("/Star/", "Moon", $myString);
```

The original and replaced strings are displayed to the user:

```
echo "<p>The original string was: '$myString'.</p>";
echo "<p>After replacement the string is: '$newString'.</p.>";
```

Using the preg_replace_callback() Function

The `preg_replace_callback()` function behaves essentially identically to the `preg_replace()` function, except that the second argument to the `preg_replace_callback()` function is a callback to another function. The callback can be to any user-specified function.

Using the preg_split() Function

The `preg_split()` function splits a test string according to a regular expression pattern. It returns an array. It takes two mandatory arguments and two optional arguments. The two mandatory arguments are a regular expression pattern and a test string. The third (optional) argument is an `int` value that specifies the maximum number of splits. The fourth (optional) argument is an `int` value that indicates the flags that are set.

Try It Out   The preg_split() Function

1. Type the following code in a text editor:

```
<html>
<head>
<title>A preg_split() Example</title>
</head>
<body>
<?php
$myCSV = "Oranges, Apples, Bananas, Kiwi Fruit, Mangos";
$myArray = preg_split("/,/", $myCSV);
echo "<p>The original string was: '$myCSV'.</p>";
echo "<p>After splitting the array contains the following values:</p.><br />";
print_r(array_values($myArray));
?>
</body>
</html>
```

2. Save the code as C:\inetpub\wwwroot\PHP\preg_split.php.

3. Type the following URL in Internet Explorer: http://localhost/PHP/preg_split.php. Inspect the displayed results, as shown in Figure 23-20.

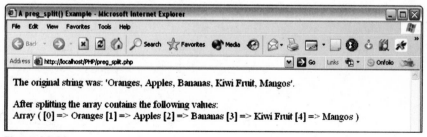

Figure 23-20

How It Works

The example splits a comma-separated list of values that are contained in a single string into an array. First, the test string is assigned to the $myCSV variable:

```
$myCSV = "Oranges, Apples, Bananas, Kiwi Fruit, Mangos";
```

Then the array returned by the preg_split() function is assigned to the $myArray variable. The first argument to preg_split() is a regular expression pattern containing a comma, so the test string $myCSV is split at each comma. Splitting takes place at each occurrence of the comma because no third argument to the preg_split() function is specified:

```
$myArray = preg_split("/,/", $myCSV);
```

Two echo statements are used to display the original string and information to the user. The print_r() function is used with the array_values() function to display the values in the $myArray variable:

```
echo "<p>The original string was: '$myCSV'.</p>";
echo "<p>After splitting the array contains the following values:</p.><br />";
print_r(array_values($myArray));
```

The Metacharacters Supported in PHP

This description of the supported metacharacters will treat the ereg() and preg() sets of functions separately. So if you wish to use one of these sets of functions only, you can easily see which functionality is supported in your chosen set of functions.

Supported Metacharacters with ereg()

The following table summarizes the metacharacters supported in PHP when you are using the ereg() family of functions.

Metacharacter	Description
\d	Not supported. Use the character class [0-9] instead.
\D	Not supported. Use the negated character class [^0-9] instead.
\w	Not supported. Use the character class [A-Za-z0-9_] or the POSIX character class [:alnum:] instead with ereg().
\W	Not supported. Use the negated character class [^A-Za-z0-9_] instead with ereg().
?	Quantifier. Matches zero or one occurrence of the preceding character or group.
*	Quantifier. Matches zero or more occurrences of the preceding character or group.
+	Quantifier. Matches one or more occurrences of the preceding character or group.
{n,m}	Quantifier. Matches at least n occurrences and no more than m occurrences of the preceding character or group.
. (period character)	Matches any character except newline.
^	Matches the position at the beginning of a string.
$	Matches the position at the end of a string.
[...]	Character class. Matches a single occurrence of any character contained between the square brackets.
[^...]	Negated character class. Matches a single occurrence of any character not contained between the square brackets.

Using POSIX Character Classes with PHP

The ereg() functionality is based on POSIX. Therefore, you can use POSIX character classes such as [:alnum:] with ereg() and associated functions.

The following table lists the most commonly used POSIX character classes.

Character Class	Description
[:alnum:]	Matches alphabetic or numeric characters
[:alpha:]	Matches alphabetic characters
[:space:]	Matches whitespace characters
[:blank:]	Matches a space character or a tab character
[:digit:]	Matches a numeric digit
[:lower:]	Matches a lowercase alphabetic character
[:upper:]	Matches an uppercase alphabetic character

Try It Out   Using [:alnum:] with ereg()

1.   Enter the following code in your favorite text editor:

```
<html>
<head>
<title>ereg() [:alnum:] Test</title>
</head>
<body>
<?php
$match = ereg('[[:alnum:]]+', "Hello world!", $matches);
if ($match)
{
 echo "<p>A match was found.</p>";
 echo "<p>$matches[0]</p>";
}
?>
</body>
</html>
```

2.   Save the file as EregAlnumTest.php.

3.   In Internet Explorer, enter the URL http://localhost/PHP/EregAlnumTest.php, and
      inspect the displayed result, as shown in Figure 23-21.

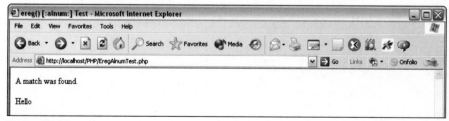

Figure 23-21

How It Works

The POSIX character class [:alnum:] matches alphabetic characters and numeric digits. Unlike the \w metacharacter, it does not match the underscore character.

The first argument to the ereg() function matches one or more alphanumeric characters. Notice that in PHP, the [:alnum:] character class is contained inside another pair of square brackets.

Matching is attempted against the test string, Hello world!. The ereg() function has three arguments, so the value of groups in the first match, if there is one, is returned in the $matches array:

```
$match = ereg('[[:alnum:]]+', "Hello world!", $matches);
```

The if statement tests if there is a match, using the value of the $match variable:

```
if ($match)
```

In this case, the user is informed that there is a match:

```
{
  echo "<p>A match was found.</p>";
```

The matched text is contained in the zeroth group in the $matches array. That matched character sequence is displayed to the user:

```
  echo "<p>$matches[0]</p>";
}
```

The next example uses the POSIX [:space:] character class, which matches whitespace characters.

Try It Out   Using the [:space:] Character Class

1.   Enter the following code in a text editor:

```
<html>
<head>
<title>ereg() [:space:] Test</title>
</head>
<body>
<?php
$match = ereg('o[[:space:]]+w', "Hello world!", $matches);
if ($match)
{
  echo "<p>A match was found.</p>";
  echo "<p>$matches[0]</p>";
}
?>
</body>
</html>
```

2. Save the code as `C:\inetpub\wwwroot\PHP\EregSpaceTest.php`.

3. Enter the URL `http://localhost/PHP/EregSpaceTest.php` in Internet Explorer, and inspect the results, as shown in Figure 23-22.

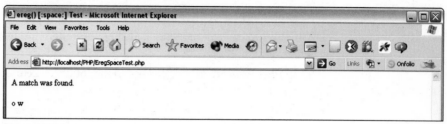

Figure 23-22

How It Works

The `ereg()` function's first argument matches a literal o followed by a space character, followed by a literal w. In the test string `Hello world!`, the matched text is the final o of `Hello` followed by a space character, followed by the initial w of `world`:

```
$match = ereg('o[[:space:]]+w', "Hello world!", $matches);
```

The user is informed that a match exists, and the `zeroth` element of the `$matches` array is used to display the matched value to the user:

```
echo "<p>A match was found.</p>";
echo "<p>$matches[0]</p>";
```

Supported Metacharacters with PCRE

The following table summarizes the metacharacters that are supported with PCRE. If you compare this with the table showing the metacharacters supported in the `ereg()` family of functions, you will see that there is much more functionality in PCRE.

Metacharacter	Description
^	Matches the position at the beginning of a string (or line in multiline mode).
$	Matches the position at the end of a string (or line in multiline mode).
. (period character)	Matches any character except newline (by default).
[...]	Character class. Matches any character contained inside the square brackets once.

Table continued on following page

Metacharacter	Description
`[^...]`	Negated character class. Matches any character once except those contained inside the square brackets.
`|`	Alternation.
`()`	Groups the character sequence matching the pattern inside the paired parentheses.
`?`	Quantifier. Matches zero or one occurrence of the preceding character or group.
`*`	Quantifier. Matches zero or more occurrences of the preceding character or group.
`+`	Quantifier. Matches one or more occurrences of the preceding character or group.
`{n,m}`	Quantifier. Matches at least n occurrences and at most m occurrences of the preceding character or group.
`\d`	Matches a numeric digit.
`\D`	Matches any character except a numeric digit.
`\s`	Matches a whitespace character.
`\S`	Matches any character except a whitespace character.
`\w`	Matches any Perl "word" character. Equivalent to the character class `[A-Za-z0-9_]`.
`\W`	Matches any character except a Perl "word" character. Equivalent to the negated character class `[^A-Za-z0-9_]`.
`\b`	Matches a position between a `\w` character and a `\W` character.
`\B`	Matches a position that is not between a `\w` character and a `\W` character.
`\A`	Matches the position at the beginning of a string. Its operation is not affected by multiline mode.
`\z`	Matches the position at the end of a string. Its operation is not affected by multiline mode.

Positional Metacharacters

The ^ and $ metacharacters allow matching of the position at the beginning of a test string and the end of a test string, respectively. If the m matching modifier is used, the ^ metacharacter matches the position at the beginning of a line, and the $ metacharacter matches the position at the end of a line.

Character Classes In PHP

The PCRE functionality in PHP supports a full range of character class functionality, including ranges and negated character classes.

The following example illustrates how a negated character class can be used to test that only a desired type of character is present in a string.

Using a Negated Character Class

1. Enter the following code in a text editor:

```
<html>
<head>
<title>Negated Character Class Example</title>
</head>
<body>
<?php
$sequenceToMatch1 = "12345";
$sequenceToMatch2 = "123 45";
$negCharClass = "/[^0-9]/";
$nonNumMatch = preg_match($negCharClass, $sequenceToMatch1);
if ($nonNumMatch)
{
echo "<p>There was a non-numeric character in $sequenceToMatch1.</p>";
}
else
{
echo "<p>All characters were numeric in $sequenceToMatch1.</p>";
}
$nonNumMatch = preg_match($negCharClass, $sequenceToMatch2);
if ($nonNumMatch)
{
echo "<p>A non-numeric character was found in $sequenceToMatch2.</p>";
}
else
{
echo "<p>All characters were numeric in $sequenceToMatch2.</p>";
}
?>
</body>
</html>
```

2. Save the code as `C:\inetpub\wwwroot\PHP\NegatedCharacterClass.php`.

3. In Internet Explorer, enter the URL `http://localhost/PHP/NegatedCharacterClass.php`, and inspect the results displayed, as shown in Figure 23-23.

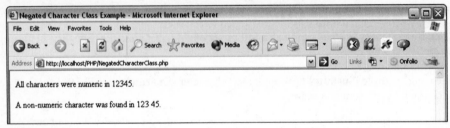

Figure 23-23

How It Works

This example tests two strings to see if any undesired character is present in the string—in this case, a character that is not a numeric digit.

First, the two test strings are assigned to the variables $sequenceToMatch1 and $sequenceToMatch2. As you can see, $sequenceToMatch2 contains a space character, which is not a numeric digit. The $sequenceToMatch1 variable contains only numeric digits:

```
$sequenceToMatch1 = "12345";
$sequenceToMatch2 = "123 45";
```

The regular expression pattern is assigned to the $negCharClass variable and consists of the negated character class [^0-9], which will match any character that is not a numeric digit:

```
$negCharClass = "/[^0-9]/";
```

The preg_match() function is used to test whether there is a character that is not a numeric digit in the $sequenceToMatch1 variable. Because the non-numeric character is not matched, the else clause is executed:

```
$nonNumMatch = preg_match($negCharClass, $sequenceToMatch1);
if ($nonNumMatch)
{
echo "<p>There was a non-numeric character in $sequenceToMatch1.</p>";
}
else
{
echo "<p>All characters were numeric in $sequenceToMatch1.</p>";
}
```

Next, the preg_match() function is used to test $sequenceToMatch2. In this case, there is a non-numeric character, so $nonNumMatch contains a match:

```
$nonNumMatch = preg_match($negCharClass, $sequenceToMatch2);
```

So the test for the `if` statement returns `True`. The user is informed that there is a non-numeric character in `$sequenceToMatch2`, whose value is displayed to the user:

```
if ($nonNumMatch)
{
echo "<p>A non-numeric character was found in $sequenceToMatch2.</p>";
}
else
{
echo "<p>All characters were numeric in $sequenceToMatch2.</p>";
}
```

Documenting PHP Regular Expressions

The x matching modifier can be used to cause the matching engine to ignore whitespace in the regular expression that is the first argument to a function — for example, the `preg_match()` function.

Try It Out — Using the x Matching Modifier in Documentation

1. Type the following code in a text editor:

```
<html>
<head>
<title>The x matching modifier in use.</title>
</head>
<body>
<?php
$US_SSN = "123-12-1234";
$myMatch = preg_match("/
 \d{3} # Matches three numeric digits
 -      # Matches a literal hyphen
 \d{2} # Matches two numeric digits
 -      # Matches a literal hyphen
 \d{4} # Matches four numeric digits
/x", "123-12-1234", $theMatch);
echo "<p>The test string was: '$US_SSN'.</p>";
echo "<p>This matches the pattern /\d{3}-\d{2}-\d{4}/</p>";
?>
</body>
</html>
```

2. Save the code as `C:\inetpub\wwwroot\PHP\XModifier.php`.

3. In Internet Explorer, enter the URL `http://localhost/PHP/XModifier.php`, and inspect the results displayed, as shown in Figure 23-24.

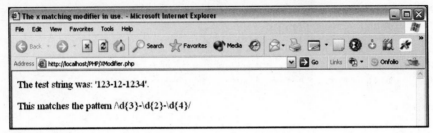

Figure 23-24

How It Works

First, a value that could be a U.S. Social Security number (SSN) is assigned to the variable $US_SSN:

```
$US_SSN = "123-12-1234";
```

The preg_match() function is used to establish if there is a match against the pattern \d{3}-\d{2}-\d{4}. However, because the x matching modifier is used, you can spread the pattern over several lines, using the # character to enter comments about the meaning of the pattern's individual components:

```
$myMatch = preg_match("/
 \d{3} # Matches three numeric digits
 -      # Matches a literal hyphen
 \d{2} # Matches two numeric digits
 -      # Matches a literal hyphen
 \d{4} # Matches four numeric digits
```

The x modifier is written after the second forward slash, which delimits the regular expression pattern. The value of the match is returned in the $theMatch array:

```
/x", "123-12-1234", $theMatch);
```

Then the user is informed of the result of the attempted matching:

```
echo "<p>The test string was: '$US_SSN'.</p>";
echo "<p>This matches the pattern /\d{3}-\d{2}-\d{4}/</p>";
```

Exercises

1. Are Perl Compatible Regular Expressions usable with all versions of PHP?

2. Which matching modifier is used to allow multiline comments inside a pattern?

Regular Expressions in W3C XML Schema

Increasing volumes of data are being stored or transmitted as Extreme Markup Language (XML). Establishing whether that data is valid or not can be very useful. In addition, when an XML data structure holds data such as a credit card number, a Social Security number, or a postal code, it can be useful to apply regular expressions to establish whether the content of the XML data structure corresponds to the desired structure of the data. W3C XML Schema supports several constructs that provide support for controlling the content of parts of an XML document.

In this chapter, you will learn the following:

❑ Basics of how W3C XML Schema works and how a W3C XML Schema document is associated with an XML instance document

❑ How regular expressions and other constraints on content of an XML instance document are expressed

❑ How Unicode affects how W3C XML Schema is used

❑ What metacharacters are supported in W3C XML Schema

> In this chapter, the term *W3C XML Schema* is used to refer to the XML schema definition language specified by the World Wide Web Consortium (W3C).

Details of the W3C XML Schema specifications and an introductory primer are located at www.w3.org/TR/xmlschema-0, www.w3.org/TR/xmlschema-1, and www.w3.org/TR/xmlschema-2. Apart from the primer, you will likely find it useful to refer to books on W3C XML Schema such as *XML Schema Essentials,* by R. Allen Wyke and Andrew Watt (Wiley 2002).

W3C XML Schema Basics

When XML version 1.0 was released early in 1998, it already had a schema language associated with it. The schema for an XML 1.0 document was a document type definition (DTD). The DTD had several limitations, not least of which was that it had very limited facilities to specify the type of XML data and that it lacked functionality to further constrain XML content.

A schema, in the context of XML documents, is a document that specifies the permitted structure and content of a class of XML documents.

There are two fundamental ways in which W3C XML Schema can work to constrain values. It can constrain the *value space* or constrain the *lexical space*. To help distinguish between these two concepts, consider the idea of a value of 100. The value is the same whether you write it as 100.0, 100.00, 100.000, and so on. There is one *value* in the *value space* and three (shown here but there are many more) representations of that value in the *lexical space*. Regular expressions in W3C XML Schema operate on the lexical space, not on the value space.

Tools for Using W3C XML Schema

This chapter illustrates the use of XML editors to create XML instance documents and their corresponding W3C XML Schema documents. Validating the XML instance documents against the schema will allow you to look at the regular expression support in W3C XML Schema.

You can create XML documents and the associated W3C XML Schema documents using a simple text editor. However, using specialized XML editors provides support for some or all of the following functionality: syntax color coding, checking of well-formedness, validation of XML instance documents, association of XML instance documents with a schema, and creation of a W3C XML Schema document from an XML instance document.

> The examples of XML documents and associated W3C XML Schema documents shown in this chapter have been created using XMLSpy, XMLWriter, and StylusStudio. Other XML editors have similar facilities that support W3C XML Schema creation from an instance document (or allow you to author a schema from scratch) and test whether or not an instance XML document does or does not validate against a schema, whether that is a DTD or a W3C XML Schema document.

When using XMLSpy or StylusStudio, you can create an XML instance document and then create a W3C XML Schema document from the XML instance document. Of course, depending on how typical the XML instance document is of the class of XML instance documents, you may have to do some editing of the W3C XML Schema document that is created for you.

Trial downloads of XMLSpy, XMLWriter, and StylusStudio are available from
www.xmlspy.com/download.html, www.xmlwriter.com/download/download.
shtml, and www.stylusstudio.com/xml_download.html, respectively.

Comparing XML Schema and DTDs

If you had a simple XML document, PersonDataForDTD.xml, like the following, the line with the DOCTYPE declaration would indicate the location of a DTD for the XML instance document:

```
<!DOCTYPE PersonData SYSTEM "C:\BRegExp\Ch24\PersonData.dtd">
<PersonData>
  <Person>
    <LastName>Smith</LastName>
    <FirstName>John</FirstName>
  </Person>
</PersonData>
```

If you are unfamiliar with the syntax for the DOCTYPE declaration and have a tool like XMLSpy or Stylus Studio, you can use the software to create the DTD and associate the XML instance document with the DTD.

The first line of PersonDataForDTD.xml references a DTD located at C:\BRegExp\Ch24\
PersonData.dtd. *If you have downloaded the code files to a different location, you will need to edit the code to be able to validate the XML in XMLSpy or a similar XML editor.*

The DTD, PersonData.dtd, for that instance document is shown here:

```
<?xml version="1.0" encoding="UTF-8"?>
<!ELEMENT FirstName (#PCDATA)>
<!ELEMENT LastName (#PCDATA)>
<!ELEMENT Person (LastName, FirstName)>
<!ELEMENT PersonData (Person)>
```

The PersonData element is shown, in the final line, to contain Person elements. In turn, on the second-to-last line, the Person element is shown to contain LastName and FirstName elements. In the second and third lines, the FirstName and LastName are shown to contain PCDATA (parsed character data). Essentially, all that says is that the content of the FirstName and LastName elements is a sequence of Unicode characters that will be parsed by the XML parser.

DTDs can't, for example, specify that an element is to contain a character sequence that is a valid credit card number, phone number, e-mail address, and so on. That limitation of DTDs was one of the reasons why W3C XML Schema was developed.

XMLSpy and StylusStudio can create, on request, a W3C XML Schema document to reflect the structure in a sample XML instance document. In XMLSpy, you can create a W3C XML Schema document automatically.

Figure 24-1 shows how to create a schema in XMLSpy for a sample XML instance document, `PersonDataForSchema.xml`:

```
<?xml version="1.0" encoding="UTF-8"?>
<PersonData >
  <Person>
    <LastName>Smith</LastName>
    <FirstName>John</FirstName>
  </Person>
</PersonData>
```

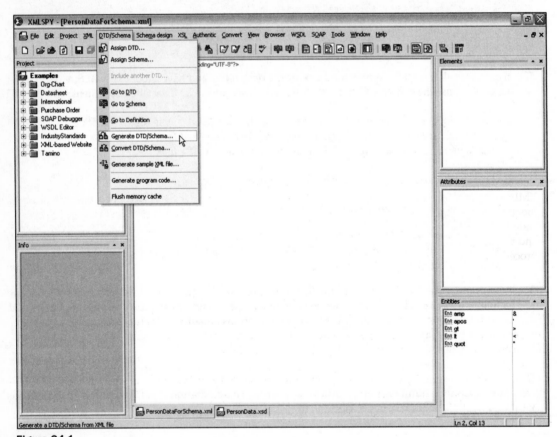

Figure 24-1

A dialog box is then displayed, as shown in Figure 24-2. To create a W3C XML Schema document, select the radio button for W3C Schema, as shown in the figure.

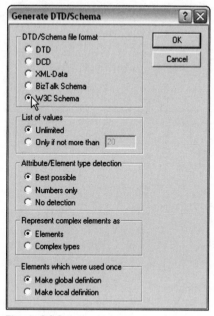

Figure 24-2

XMLSpy asks if you want to associate the XML instance document with the W3C XML Schema document it has created. Figure 24-3 shows the dialog box. If you want that, XMLSpy adds the necessary code to the PersonData element to allow a validating parser, which tools such as XMLSpy, XMLWriter, and StylusStudio have built in, to locate the W3C XML Schema document and carry out the validation process.

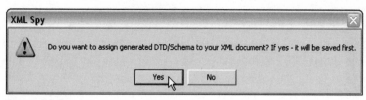

Figure 24-3

The created W3C XML Schema document, `PersonData.xsd`, is shown here:

```
<?xml version="1.0" encoding="UTF-8"?>
<xs:schema xmlns:xs="http://www.w3.org/2001/XMLSchema"
elementFormDefault="qualified">
  <xs:element name="FirstName" type="xs:string"/>
  <xs:element name="LastName" type="xs:string"/>
  <xs:element name="Person">
    <xs:complexType>
      <xs:sequence>
        <xs:element ref="LastName"/>
        <xs:element ref="FirstName"/>
      </xs:sequence>
    </xs:complexType>
  </xs:element>
  <xs:element name="PersonData">
    <xs:complexType>
      <xs:sequence>
        <xs:element ref="Person"/>
      </xs:sequence>
    </xs:complexType>
  </xs:element>
</xs:schema>
```

If you compare this W3C XML Schema document to the DTD `PersonData.dtd` shown earlier, you will see that the corresponding W3C XML Schema document is much longer. The verbosity of W3C XML Schema attracted criticism but must simply be accepted now that the specification has been finalized.

The reason for the W3C XML Schema document being saved first, as shown in Figure 24-3, is that information about the location of the saved W3C XML Schema file is added to the XML instance file.

The modified file, `PersonDataAssocSchema.xml`, is shown here:

```
<?xml version="1.0" encoding="UTF-8"?>
<PersonData xmlns:xsi="http://www.w3.org/2001/XMLSchema-instance"
xsi:noNamespaceSchemaLocation="C:\BRegExp\Ch24\PersonData.xsd">
  <Person>
    <LastName>Smith</LastName>
    <FirstName>John</FirstName>
  </Person>
</PersonData>
```

XMLSpy adds a namespace declaration for the XML Schema instance namespace:

```
xmlns:xsi="http://www.w3.org/2001/XMLSchema-instance"
```

The `xsi:noNamespaceSchemaLocation` attribute, which is in the XML Schema instance namespace, is also added to the document element, with its value, a URI, indicating the location of the W3C XML Schema document. In this case, the W3C XML Schema document is located at `C:\BRegExp\Ch24\`

`PersonData.xsd`. If you want to validate the XML document and the schema is in some other location, you will need to change the value of the `xsi:noNamespaceSchemaLocation` attribute appropriately:

```
xsi:noNamespaceSchemaLocation="C:\BRegExp\Ch24\PersonData.xsd"
```

After XMLSpy has associated a W3C XML Schema document with an XML instance document, you can use XMLSpy to validate the XML instance document. The cursor in Figure 24-3 is hovering over the relevant toolbar button. Toward the bottom of Figure 24-3, you can see the message indicating that the document is valid according to the schema.

You can similarly validate an XML instance document, `PersonDataAssocSchema.xml`, in Stylus Studio (shown in Figure 24-4) or XMLWriter (shown in Figure 24-5). The arrow cursor in each figure shows you the relevant toolbar button to validate an XML instance document.

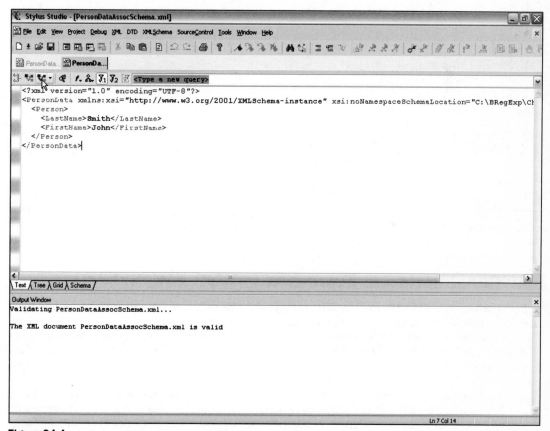

Figure 24-4

Whether you already have an XML editor or choose to use the trial downloads for XMLSpy, StylusStudio, or XMLWriter, you should now be in a position to validate an XML instance document against its schema. So you can now try out the examples in this chapter.

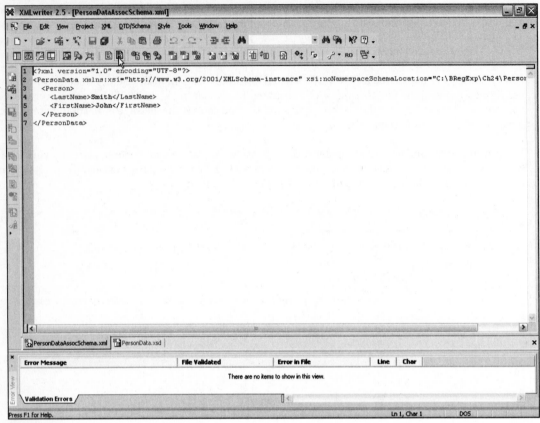

Figure 24-5

How Constraints Are Expressed in W3C XML Schema

In one sense, W3C XML Schema is all about applying constraints. One type of constraint is limiting how elements and attributes can be structured inside an XML instance document belonging to the class of XML documents to which the schema applies. Another aspect of W3C XML Schema constraining the content of a class of XML documents is in constraining the content allowed as the value contained in an element or attribute.

Two kinds of types can exist as the content of an element: a complex type (indicated by an xs:complexType element in the schema) and a simple type (which may be indicated by an xs:simpleType element in the schema). This chapter focuses on constraining the values allowed in simple types in an XML instance document.

W3C XML Schema Datatypes

In the other uses of regular expressions you have seen in this book, the regular expression has been applied to a string value. In W3C XML Schema, it is possible to use regular expressions together with other datatypes.

The following table summarizes the datatypes built into W3C XML Schema. Datatypes are shown as having the xs namespace prefix as an indication that they belong to the XML namespace http://www.w3.org/ 2001/XMLSchema. Datatypes can be viewed as primitive or derived built-in datatypes.

Datatype	Description
xs:anyType	Functions as the root of the type hierarchy. Types derived from xs:anyType can be a complex type or a simple type.
xs:anySimpleType	The base type for all simple types.
xs:string	A sequence of XML characters of finite length.
xs:boolean	Expresses the binary notion of true and false.
xs:base64Binary	Represents base-64 encoded binary data.
xs:hexBinary	Represents hexadecimal encoded binary data.
xs:float	Represents an IEEE single-precision 32-bit floating-point number.
xs:decimal	Represents arbitrary precision decimal numbers.
xs:double	Represents an IEEE double-precision 64-bit floating-point number.
xs:anyURI	Represents a Uniform Resource Identifier, whether absolute or relative, and may include a fragment identifier.
xs:QName	An XML namespace-qualified name.
xs:NOTATION	Represents an XML 1.0 NOTATION.
xs:duration	Represents a duration with Gregorian year, month, day, hour, minute, and seconds components.
xs:dateTime	Represents a specific instant of time.
xs:time	Represents a specific instant of time that recurs every day.
xs:date	Represents a specified calendar day.
xs:gYearMonth	Represents the year and month parts of an xs:dateTime.
xs:gMonthDay	Represents a specified day of the year, such as September 25.
xs:gDay	Represents a specified day of the month, such as the 25th.
xs:gMonth	Represents a specified Gregorian calendar month.

In addition to the datatypes already listed, there are datatypes derived, directly or indirectly, from the xs:string and xs:decimal datatypes.

The following table summarizes the datatypes that are derived from `xs:string`.

Derived Datatype	Description
`xs:normalizedString`	The base type is `xs:string`. The `xs:normalizedString` type is the set of strings that does not contain the characters carriage return (#xD), linefeed (#xA), and tab (#x9).
`xs:token`	The base type is `xs:string`. This datatype is the set of strings that does not contain the linefeed (#xA) or tab (#x9) characters, nor any leading or trailing space characters (#x20) or any doubled internal space characters.
`xs:language`	The base type is `xs:token`. This datatype is the set of `xs:token` values that are language identifiers in the XML 1.0 (second edition) specification.
`xs:Name`	The base type is `xs:token`. This datatype is the set of strings that are legal XML names, as defined in the XML 1.0 (second edition) specification.
`xs:NCName`	The base type is `xs:Name`. This datatype is the set of strings that are XML names but do not contain a colon character.
`xs:ID`	The base type is `xs:NCName`. This datatype represents values of ID type that are also NCNames.
`xs:IDREF`	The base type is `xs:NCName`. This datatype is the set of strings that represent values of type IDREF, which are NCNames.
`xs:IDREFS`	The item type is `xs:IDREF`. This datatype is a list of whitespace-separated values, each of which is of type `xs:IDREF`.
`xs:NMTOKEN`	The base type is `xs:token`. This datatype is the set of `xs:token` values that match the NMTOKEN definition in XML 1.0 (second edition).
`xs:NMTOKENS`	The item type is `xs:NMTOKEN`. This datatype is a list of whitespace-separated values, each of which is of type `xs:NMTOKEN`.
`xs:ENTITY`	The base type is `xs:NCName`. This datatype represents values that are of ENTITY type, as defined in the XML 1.0 (second edition) specification.
`xs:ENTITIES`	The item type is `xs:ENTITY`. This datatype is a list of whitespace-separated values, each of which is of type `xs:ENTITY`.

The following table summarizes the built-in datatypes that are derived, directly or indirectly, from the `xs:decimal` datatype.

Derived Datatype	Description
xs:integer	The base type is xs:decimal. This datatype represents positive and negative integer values.
xs:nonPositiveInteger	The base type is xs:integer. This datatype represents negative integers and zero.
xs:negativeInteger	The base type is xs:nonPositiveInteger. This datatype represents negative integers.
xs:long	The base type is xs:integer. This datatype represents integer values from −9223372036854775808 to 9223372036854775807.
xs:int	The base type is xs:long. This datatype represents integer values from −2147483648 to 2147483647 inclusive.
xs:short	The base type is xs:int. This datatype represents integer values from −32768 to 32767 inclusive.
xs:byte	The base type is xs:short. This datatype represents integer values from −128 to 127 inclusive.
xs:nonNegativeInteger	The base type is xs:integer. This datatype represents integer values that are positive integers and zero.
xs:unsignedLong	The base type is xs:nonNegativeInteger. This datatype represents integer values from 0 to 18446744073709551615.
xs:unsignedInt	The base type is xs:unsignedLong. This datatype represents integer values from 0 to 4294967295 inclusive.
xs:unsignedShort	The base type is xs:unsignedInt. This datatype represents integer values from 0 to 65535 inclusive.
xs:unsignedByte	The base type is xs:unsignedShort. This datatype represents integer values from 0 to 255 inclusive.
xs:positiveInteger	The base type is xs:nonNegativeInteger. This datatype represents integer values of 1 and greater.

Fuller details on how the built-in datatypes are specified can be found in XML Schema Part 2 at www.w3.org/TR/2001/REC-xmlschema-2-20010502, **XML 1.0 (second edition) at** www.w3.org/TR/2000/WD-xml-2e-20000814, **and Namespaces in XML at** www.w3.org/TR/REC-xml-names.

The programmer can develop custom types from these built-in types by any of the three mechanisms in the following list:

❑ **Derivation by restriction**—Values of an existing datatype are constrained by restricting the allowed values.

❑ **Derivation by list**—A list of values of a built-in or user-defined datatype.

❑ **Derivation by union**—The user-defined datatype is the union of two other datatypes (which can be built-in datatypes or user-defined datatypes).

Derivation by Restriction

When using W3C XML Schema, there are often several ways to specify a specific desired structure. Of the methods of derivation in the preceding list, derivation by restriction is the most commonly used.

One method of restriction is to specify an enumeration. The following XML instance document, `BookEnum.xml`, is associated with a W3C XML Schema document that contains an enumeration:

```
<?xml version="1.0" encoding="UTF-8"?>
<Book xmlns:xsi="http://www.w3.org/2001/XMLSchema-instance"
xsi:noNamespaceSchemaLocation="C:\BRegExp\Ch24\BookEnum.xsd">
  <Chapter number="1">Some content</Chapter>
  <Chapter number="2">Some content</Chapter>
  <Chapter number="3">Some content</Chapter>
  <Chapter number="4">Some content</Chapter>
  <Chapter number="5">Some content</Chapter>
</Book>
```

The associated W3C XML Schema document, `BookEnum.xsd`, created by XMLSpy, constrains the values of the `number` attribute of the `Chapter` element to be an enumeration of values from 1 through 5:

```
<?xml version="1.0" encoding="UTF-8"?>
<xs:schema xmlns:xs="http://www.w3.org/2001/XMLSchema"
elementFormDefault="qualified">
  <xs:element name="Book">
    <xs:complexType>
      <xs:sequence>
        <xs:element ref="Chapter" maxOccurs="unbounded"/>
      </xs:sequence>
    </xs:complexType>
  </xs:element>
  <xs:element name="Chapter">
    <xs:complexType>
      <xs:simpleContent>
        <xs:extension base="xs:string">
          <xs:attribute name="number" use="required">
            <xs:simpleType>
              <xs:restriction base="xs:NMTOKEN">
                <xs:enumeration value="1"/>
                <xs:enumeration value="2"/>
                <xs:enumeration value="3"/>
                <xs:enumeration value="4"/>
                <xs:enumeration value="5"/>
              </xs:restriction>
            </xs:simpleType>
          </xs:attribute>
        </xs:extension>
      </xs:simpleContent>
    </xs:complexType>
  </xs:element>
</xs:schema>
```

The value of the `number` attribute is a simple type value. The schema document that XMLSpy creates uses the `xs:NMTOKEN` datatype, because the sample values of 1, 2, 3, 4, and 5 in the XML instance document allow for that datatype. However, the same constraint on values could be applied using the `xs:pattern` element as in `BookPattern.xsd`, shown here:

```
<?xml version="1.0" encoding="UTF-8"?>
<xs:schema xmlns:xs="http://www.w3.org/2001/XMLSchema"
elementFormDefault="qualified">
  <xs:element name="Book">
    <xs:complexType>
      <xs:sequence>
        <xs:element ref="Chapter" maxOccurs="unbounded"/>
      </xs:sequence>
    </xs:complexType>
  </xs:element>
  <xs:element name="Chapter">
    <xs:complexType>
      <xs:simpleContent>
        <xs:extension base="xs:string">
          <xs:attribute name="number" use="required">
            <xs:simpleType>
              <xs:restriction base="xs:NMTOKEN">
               <xs:pattern value="(1|2|3|4|5)" />
              </xs:restriction>
            </xs:simpleType>
          </xs:attribute>
        </xs:extension>
      </xs:simpleContent>
    </xs:complexType>
  </xs:element>
</xs:schema>
```

An XML instance document associated with `BookPattern.xsd` is provided as `BookPattern.xml` in the code download. The only change from `BookEnum.xml` is that the `xsi:noNamespaceSchemaLocation` attribute points to the `BookPattern.xsd` file:

```
<Book xmlns:xsi="http://www.w3.org/2001/XMLSchema-instance"
xsi:noNamespaceSchemaLocation="C:\BRegExp\Ch24\BookPattern.xsd">
```

The `xs:pattern` element is featured prominently in the remainder of this chapter, because it is the W3C XML Schema element that uses regular expressions. The value of the `xs:pattern` element's `value` attribute is a regular expression pattern—hence, the name of the element.

In the pattern shown in the preceding code listing, notice that the value of the `value` attribute is a fairly simple example of alternation, `(1|2|3|4|5)`, which allows the value to be any one value of 1, 2, 3, 4, or 5.

Before looking at the range of metacharacters supported in W3C XML Schema and how those metacharacters can be used, read about how Unicode is relevant to regular expressions in W3C XML Schema documents.

Unicode and W3C XML Schema

XML documents consist of sequences of Unicode characters. Unicode contains many thousands of characters. In reality, few, if any, applications can display all Unicode characters, and very few human beings could easily understand all Unicode characters. To make Unicode more manageable, the characters are divided into *Unicode character classes* and *Unicode blocks*. Each of these is discussed later in this section.

> **Full information about Unicode is located at** www.unicode.org. **At the time of this writing, the current version of the Unicode Standard is version 4.0.1. Further information about the Unicode Standard is located at** www.unicode.org/ standard/standard.html.

Unicode Overview

The Unicode Standard defines the universal character set. The aim of Unicode is to allow the interchange of text content across all the languages of planet Earth. Unicode specifies a text encoding for most characters of most languages, as well as characters to assist in interoperability with older character encodings.

The Windows Character Map utility provides a convenient way to examine the Unicode codes for many individual characters. Figure 24-6 shows the uppercase A selected. Notice in the lower part of the figure that uppercase A is U+0041. The number following the U and the + sign must consist of at least four numeric digits. The number is a sequence of hexadecimal digits. In this example, uppercase A is hexadecimal 0041, which is 65 in decimal notation.

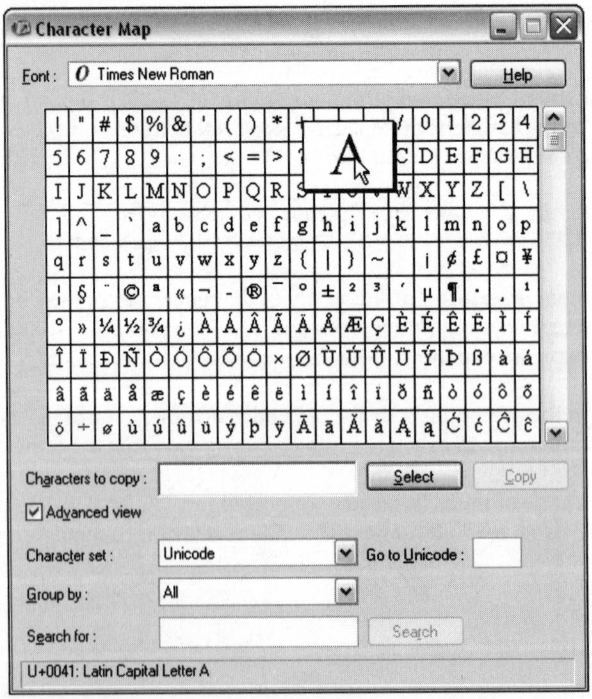

Figure 24-6

In XML, uppercase A can also be written as A. In most situations, it is simpler to express characters commonly used in English literally.

A Unicode character class indicates the type of usage for a set of characters—for example, lowercase letters. A Unicode character block indicates a language or other means of expression associated with that block of characters.

Using Unicode Character Classes

When using a Unicode character class in W3C XML Schema documents, the character class is specified as follows:

```
\p{characterClass}
```

The following table summarizes the Unicode character classes supported in W3C XML Schema.

Unicode Character Class	Description
C	Other characters
Cc	Control characters
Cf	Format characters
Cn	Unassigned code points
L	Letters
Ll	Lowercase letters
Lm	Modifier letters
Ln	Other letters
Lt	Title-case letters
Lu	Uppercase letters
M	All marks
Mc	Space-combining marks
Me	Enclosing marks
Mn	Nonspacing marks
N	Numbers
Nd	Decimal digits
Nl	Number letters
No	Other numbers
P	Punctuation
Pc	Connector punctuation

Table continued on following page

Unicode Character Class	Description
Pd	Dashes
Pe	Closing punctuation
Pf	Final quotes
Pi	Initial quotes
Po	Other forms of punctuation
Ps	Opening punctuation
S	Symbols
Sc	Currency symbols
Sk	Modifier symbols
Sm	Mathematical symbols
So	Other symbols
Z	Separators
Zl	Line breaks
Zp	Paragraph breaks
Zs	Spaces

The following sections briefly illustrate the use of several Unicode character classes.

Matching Decimal Numbers

The Nd character class matches decimal numbers. So if you have a simple document such as the following DocumentUnicode.xml, you can use that Unicode character class to specify allowed values of the Section element's number attribute:

```
<?xml version="1.0" encoding="UTF-8"?>
<Document xmlns:xsi="http://www.w3.org/2001/XMLSchema-instance"
xsi:noNamespaceSchemaLocation="C:\BRegExp\Ch24\DocumentUnicode.xsd">
  <Section number="1">Content</Section>
  <Section number="2">Content</Section>
  <Section number="3">Content</Section>
</Document>
```

The corresponding schema document, DocumentUnicode.xsd, uses the Nd Unicode character class :

```
<?xml version="1.0" encoding="UTF-8"?>
<xs:schema xmlns:xs="http://www.w3.org/2001/XMLSchema"
elementFormDefault="qualified">
  <xs:element name="Document">
    <xs:complexType>
      <xs:sequence>
        <xs:element ref="Section" maxOccurs="unbounded"/>
      </xs:sequence>
```

```
          </xs:complexType>
        </xs:element>
        <xs:element name="Section">
          <xs:complexType>
            <xs:simpleContent>
              <xs:extension base="xs:string">
                <xs:attribute name="number" use="required">
                  <xs:simpleType>
                    <xs:restriction base="xs:NMTOKEN">
                      <xs:pattern value="\p{Nd}" />
                    </xs:restriction>
                  </xs:simpleType>
                </xs:attribute>
              </xs:extension>
            </xs:simpleContent>
          </xs:complexType>
        </xs:element>
      </xs:schema>
```

Notice that the value of the xs:pattern element's value attribute is \p{Nd}, which specifies that the value of the Section element's number attribute is a single decimal number.

Mixing Unicode Character Classes with Other Metacharacters

It is possible to mix Unicode character classes with other metacharacters in the same regular expression. The following example illustrates how this can be done (in a rather contrived way) to match a U.S. Social Security number. The XML instance file, PersonsSSNUnicode.xml, is shown here:

```
<?xml version="1.0" encoding="UTF-8"?>
<PersonsSSN xmlns:xsi="http://www.w3.org/2001/XMLSchema-instance"
xsi:noNamespaceSchemaLocation="C:\BRegExp\Ch24\PersonsSSNUnicode.xsd">
  <Person>
    <Name>Peter Schmidt</Name>
    <SSN>123-45-6789</SSN>
  </Person>
  <Person>
    <Name>Yasmin Brown</Name>
    <SSN>987-65-4321</SSN>
  </Person>
</PersonsSSN>
```

The corresponding W3C XML Schema document, PersonsSSNUnicode.xsd, is shown here:

```
<?xml version="1.0" encoding="UTF-8"?>
<xs:schema xmlns:xs="http://www.w3.org/2001/XMLSchema"
elementFormDefault="qualified">
  <xs:element name="Name" type="xs:string"/>
  <xs:element name="Person">
    <xs:complexType>
      <xs:sequence>
        <xs:element ref="Name"/>
        <xs:element ref="SSN"/>
      </xs:sequence>
    </xs:complexType>
  </xs:element>
```

```
<xs:element name="PersonsSSN">
  <xs:complexType>
    <xs:sequence>
      <xs:element ref="Person" maxOccurs="unbounded"/>
    </xs:sequence>
  </xs:complexType>
</xs:element>
<xs:element name="SSN">
  <xs:simpleType>
    <xs:restriction base="xs:string">
      <xs:pattern value="\p{Nd}{3}-[0-9]{2}-\d{4}" />
    </xs:restriction>
  </xs:simpleType>
</xs:element>
</xs:schema>
```

Notice the pattern specified as the value of the xs:pattern element's value attribute. It uses three different ways of expressing numeric digits: a Unicode character class, a regular expression character class, and the metacharacter \d. The \p{Nd}{3} matches three numeric digits, using a Unicode character class. It is followed by a literal hyphen. Then [0-9]{2} uses a range in a conventional character class to match two numeric digits. Again, it is followed by a literal hyphen. Finally, the \d{4} matches four numeric digits.

Unicode Character Blocks

Unicode character blocks refer to blocks of Unicode characters that are relevant to a particular use. A Unicode character block may refer to a language or group of languages, or may refer to a specialized use, such as box drawing or geometric elements.

The following table illustrates some of the many Unicode character blocks available for use.

Block Name	Start Code	End Code
BasicLatin	#x0000	#x007F
Latin-1 Supplement	#x0080	#x00FF
LatinExtended-A	#x0100	#x017F
Cyrillic	#x0400	#x04FF
Hebrew	#x0590	#x05FF
Arabic	#x0600	#x06FF
Greek	#x0370	#x03FF
Cherokee	#x13A0	#x13FF
SuperscriptsAndSubscripts	#x2070	#x209F
Mathematical Operators	#x2200	#x22FF

Using Unicode Character Blocks

This example illustrates the effect of combining a Unicode character block with a Unicode character class.

Using a Unicode Character Block

1. Type the following XML markup or open the file `WordUnicode.xml` in the code download:

```xml
<?xml version="1.0" encoding="UTF-8"?>
<Word xmlns:xsi="http://www.w3.org/2001/XMLSchema-instance"
xsi:noNamespaceSchemaLocation="C:\BRegExp\Ch24\WordUnicode.xsd">Führer</Word>
```

2. Type the following W3C XML Schema document or open the file `WordUnicode.xsd` in the code download:

```xml
<?xml version="1.0" encoding="UTF-8"?>
<xs:schema xmlns:xs="http://www.w3.org/2001/XMLSchema"
elementFormDefault="qualified">
  <xs:element name="Word" type="UnicodeType"/>
  <xs:simpleType name="UnicodeType">
    <xs:restriction base="xs:string">
      <xs:pattern value="\w+"/>
    </xs:restriction>
  </xs:simpleType>
</xs:schema>
```

3. Attempt to validate `WordUnicode.xml` against `WordUnicode.xsd`. Figure 24-7 shows the appearance when validating in XMLSpy. As you can see in the lower part of the figure, the XML instance document is valid according to its associated schema document.

4. Type the following XML markup or open the file `WordUnicode2.xml` in the code download:

```xml
<?xml version="1.0" encoding="UTF-8"?>
<Word xmlns:xsi="http://www.w3.org/2001/XMLSchema-instance"
xsi:noNamespaceSchemaLocation="C:\BRegExp\Ch24\WordUnicode2.xsd">Führer</Word>
```

5. Type the following W3C XML Schema document or open the file `WordUnicode2.xsd` in the code download:

```xml
<?xml version="1.0" encoding="UTF-8"?>
<xs:schema xmlns:xs="http://www.w3.org/2001/XMLSchema"
elementFormDefault="qualified">
  <xs:element name="Word" type="UnicodeLetterType"/>
  <xs:simpleType name="UnicodeLetterType">
    <xs:restriction base="xs:string">
      <xs:pattern value="\p{L}+"/>
    </xs:restriction>
  </xs:simpleType>
</xs:schema>
```

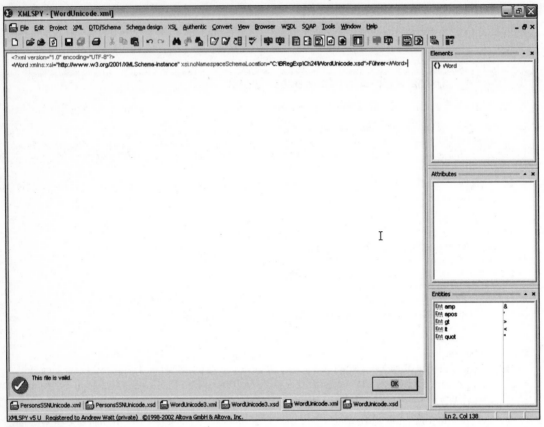

Figure 24-7

6. Attempt to validate `WordUnicode2.xml` against `WordUnicode2.xsd`. Figure 24-8 shows the screen's appearance. This attempts to match Führer against the pattern `\p{L}`, which is all Unicode letters. There is a match.

   Next, attempt to match the word Führer against Basic Latin letters. It won't match, because the character ü is Unicode U+00FC, which is outside the range U+0000 to U+007F for the `BasicLatin` code group.

7. Type the following XML markup or open the file `WordUnicode3.xml` in the code download:

```
<?xml version="1.0" encoding="UTF-8"?>
<Word xmlns:xsi="http://www.w3.org/2001/XMLSchema-instance"
xsi:noNamespaceSchemaLocation="C:\BRegExp\Ch24\WordUnicode3.xsd">Führer</Word>
```

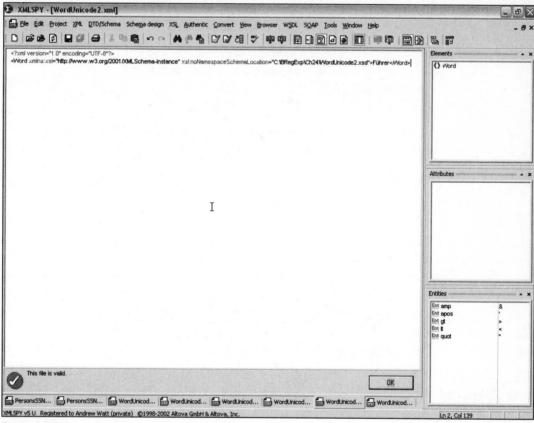

Figure 24-8

8. Type the following W3C XML Schema document or open the file WordUnicode3.xsd in the code download:

```xml
<?xml version="1.0" encoding="UTF-8"?>
<xs:schema xmlns:xs="http://www.w3.org/2001/XMLSchema"
elementFormDefault="qualified">
  <xs:element name="Word" type="UnicodeBasicLatinType" />
  <xs:simpleType name="UnicodeBasicLatinType" >
    <xs:restriction base="xs:string">
    <xs:simpleType>
      <xs:restriction base="xs:string">
       <xs:pattern value="\p{IsBasicLatin}" />
      </xs:restriction>
    </xs:simpleType>
     <xs:pattern value="\p{L}"/>
    </xs:restriction>
  </xs:simpleType>
</xs:schema>
```

Notice how you specify the intersection of the Unicode character class specified by the pattern \p{L} and the Unicode character block specified by \p{IsBasicLatin}.

611

9. Attempt to validate `WordUnicode3.xml` against `WordUnicode3.xsd` (see Figure 24-9). On this occasion, there is no match.

Figure 24-9

How It Works

The files `WordUnicode.xml` and `WordUnicode.xsd` attempt to validate the German word Führer (leader) against the pattern `\w+`. This shows that in W3C XML Schema, the metacharacter matches some letters that aren't used in English.

The files `WordUnicode2.xml` and `WordUnicode2.xsd` attempt to validate the German word Führer (leader) against the pattern `\p{L}`. Because the word Führer contains only Unicode letters, there is a match.

The files `WordUnicode3.xml` and `WordUnicode3.xsd` attempt to validate the German word Führer against the pattern `\p{L}` while also specifying the use of the Unicode character block `BasicLatin`, indicated by the pattern `\p{IsBasicLatin}`. Because the word Führer contains the letter ü, which is not in the range U+0000 through U+007F (it is U+00FC), there is no match, and validation fails.

Metacharacters Supported in W3C XML Schema

The metacharacters supported in W3C XML Schema include a few that relate directly to XML and are not implemented in most other regular expression implementations.

The following table summarizes the metacharacters supported in W3C XML Schema version 1.0. See also information in the preceding section about Unicode support in W3C XML Schema.

Metacharacter	Description
^	Not supported outside negated character classes (see discussion on positional metacharacters).
$	Not supported (see discussion on positional metacharacters).
\d	Matches a numeric digit.
\D	Matches a character that is not a numeric digit.
\s	Matches a whitespace character.
\S	Matches a character that is not a whitespace character.
\w	Matches a "word" character.
\W	Matches a character that is not a "word" character.
| (Pipe character)	Alternation. Allows a choice among two or more options of the preceding and following groups or characters.
?	Quantifier. Specifies that there is zero or one occurrence of the preceding character or group.
*	Quantifier. Specifies that there are zero or more occurrences of the preceding character or group.
+	Quantifier. Specifies that there are one or more occurrences of the preceding character or group.
{n,m}	Quantifier. Specifies that there is a minimum of n occurrences and a maximum of m occurrences of the preceding character or group.
. (period character)	Matches any character or any character except the newline character.
[...]	Positive character class. One character contained between the square brackets is matched once.
[^...]	Negated character class. One character not contained between the square brackets is matched once.
\i	Matches a character allowed as a first character in an XML name. Equivalent to the character class [A-Za-z_].
\I	Matches a character not allowed as a first character in an XML name. Equivalent to the character class [^A-Za-z_].
\c	Matches an XML 1.0 name character. Includes the character class [A-Za-z0-9.:_].
\C	Matches a character that is not an XML 1.0 name character.

Positional Metacharacters

In W3C XML Schema, the positional metacharacters, ^ and $, are not supported as beginning-of-line (or beginning-of-string) or end-of-line (or end-of-string) positional metacharacters due to a difference in how matching takes place in W3C XML Schema compared to many other regular expression implementations.

613

In many regular expression implementations, the pattern [A-Z][0-9] will match any string containing an uppercase alphabetic character followed by a numeric digit. However, in W3C XML Schema, there is a match only if the whole string is matched by the pattern. In other words, when matching in W3C XML Schema, the pattern [A-Z][0-9] is interpreted as though it were ^[A-Z][0-9]$.

Because all W3C XML Schema regular expression patterns are interpreted as though both the ^ and $ metacharacters were already present, they are not supported separately from that implicit mechanism.

The ^ metacharacter can, however, be used in a negated character class.

Matching Numeric Digits

The \d metacharacter can be used to match a numeric digit. For example, the sample document Document.xml contains a number attribute that must be a single numeric digit:

```
<?xml version="1.0" encoding="UTF-8"?>
<Document xmlns:xsi="http://www.w3.org/2001/XMLSchema-instance"
xsi:noNamespaceSchemaLocation="C:\BRegExp\Ch24\Document.xsd">
  <Section number="1">Content</Section>
  <Section number="2">Content</Section>
  <Section number="3">Content</Section>
</Document>
```

The corresponding W3C XML Schema document, Document.xsd, uses the \d metacharacter in an xs:pattern element to specify that the value of the Section element's number attribute is a single numeric digit:

```
<?xml version="1.0" encoding="UTF-8"?>
<xs:schema xmlns:xs="http://www.w3.org/2001/XMLSchema"
elementFormDefault="qualified">
  <xs:element name="Document">
    <xs:complexType>
      <xs:sequence>
        <xs:element ref="Section" maxOccurs="unbounded"/>
      </xs:sequence>
    </xs:complexType>
  </xs:element>
  <xs:element name="Section">
    <xs:complexType>
      <xs:simpleContent>
        <xs:extension base="xs:string">
          <xs:attribute name="number" use="required">
            <xs:simpleType>
              <xs:restriction base="xs:NMTOKEN">
                <xs:pattern value="\d" />
              </xs:restriction>
            </xs:simpleType>
          </xs:attribute>
        </xs:extension>
      </xs:simpleContent>
    </xs:complexType>
  </xs:element>
</xs:schema>
```

The value of the xs:restriction element's base attribute is shown as the type xs:NMTOKEN, but other types could be used in this situation, such as xs:byte.

Alternation

Alternation is supported in W3C XML Schema. The example using BookPattern.xml and BookPattern. xsd earlier in this chapter shows how alternation can be used with the xs:pattern element.

Using the \w and \s Metacharacters

The \w metacharacter represents word characters, including uppercase and lowercase A through Z. The \s metacharacter represents a whitespace character.

The pattern \w+\s+\w+ can be used to represent a name displayed as the first name followed by a space character(s), followed by last name. A sample document, Name.xml, is shown here:

```
<?xml version="1.0" encoding="UTF-8"?>
<Names xmlns:xsi="http://www.w3.org/2001/XMLSchema-instance"
xsi:noNamespaceSchemaLocation="C:\BRegExp\Ch24\Name.xsd">
  <Name>John Smith</Name>
  <Name>Alicia Manton</Name>
  <Name>Pierre Laval</Name>
</Names>
```

A corresponding schema, Name.xsd, uses the pattern \w+\s+\w+ to specify how the value of the Name element is to be constructed:

```
<?xml version="1.0" encoding="UTF-8"?>
<xs:schema xmlns:xs="http://www.w3.org/2001/XMLSchema"
elementFormDefault="qualified">
  <xs:element name="Names">
    <xs:complexType>
      <xs:sequence>
        <xs:element ref="Name" maxOccurs="unbounded">
         <xs:simpleType>
          <xs:restriction base="xs:string">
           <xs:pattern value="\w+\s+\w+" />
          </xs:restriction>
         </xs:simpleType>
        </xs:element>
      </xs:sequence>
    </xs:complexType>
  </xs:element>
</xs:schema>
```

The pattern matches a sequence of word characters followed by one or more whitespace characters, followed by a sequence of word characters.

The pattern specified wouldn't match names such as Maria Von Trapp because \w+\s+\w+ means, in effect, ^\w+\s+\w+$.

Escaping Metacharacters

When you want to match characters that are used as metacharacters in regular expression patterns, it is necessary to escape the metacharacter using a preceding backslash character.

The following table summarizes the escaped character combinations in W3C XML Schema and the character that is matched when the escaped character combination is used.

Escaped Character Combination	Character Matched
\n	Newline
\r	Carriage return
\\	\ (backslash)
|	| (pipe)
\.	. (period)
\-	- (hyphen)
\^	^ (caret)
\?	?
*	*
\+	+
\(	(
\)	)
\[	[
\]	]
\{	{
\}	}

Exercises

1. Modify Name.xsd so that the file Name2.xml, shown here, can be validated against it. Notice that the last two Name elements have content that does not match the existing pattern, \w+\s+\w+. A solution is provided in the file Name2.xsd as indicated by the value of the Names element's xsi:noNamespaceSchemaLocation attribute:

```
<?xml version="1.0" encoding="UTF-8"?>
<Names xmlns:xsi="http://www.w3.org/2001/XMLSchema-instance"
xsi:noNamespaceSchemaLocation="C:\BRegExp\Ch24\Name2.xsd">
  <Name>John Smith</Name>
  <Name>Alicia Manton</Name>
  <Name>Pierre Laval</Name>
```

```
<Name>Maria Von Trapp</Name>
  <Name>John James Manton</Name>
</Names>
```

2. Specify a pattern using Unicode character classes that will match the following part numbers:

- ❏ A99

- ❏ BC9933

- ❏ DEF88125

- ❏ Z1

A sample document, `PartNumbers.xml`, is shown here for convenience:

```
<?xml version="1.0" encoding="UTF-8"?>
<PartNumbers xmlns:xsi="http://www.w3.org/2001/XMLSchema-instance"
xsi:noNamespaceSchemaLocation="C:\BRegExp\Ch24\PartNumbers.xsd">
  <PartNumber>A99</PartNumber>
  <PartNumber>BC9933</PartNumber>
  <PartNumber>DEF88125</PartNumber>
  <PartNumber>Z1</PartNumber>
</PartNumbers>
```

Regular Expressions in Java

Java is a widely used programming language that can be used on a variety of platforms in addition to Windows. Several packages written in or for Java support regular expression functionality. However, because the `java.util.regex` package is now part of Java 2 and has an excellent spectrum of functionality, this chapter focuses only on the `java.util.regex` package, which is part of the official Sun Java downloads.

The regular expression support in Java allows validation of text, as well as searching and replacement of text. Java supports a particularly rich range of character classes, including standard regular expression character classes, POSIX character classes, and Unicode character classes. Other aspects of the `java.util.regex` package also provide rich functionality.

> **This chapter assumes that you have at least a basic understanding of Java coding. The examples are intended to demonstrate the use of the regular expression functionality in Java. The examples have deliberately been kept short and simple. If you have programmed in any modern programming language, the Java aspects of the examples in this chapter should be easy to follow. If you have no experience at all in Java, I suggest that you use a book such as Ivor Horton's *Beginning Java 2* (Wrox Press 2002) to provide the necessary foundational information.**

In this chapter, you will learn the following:

- ❑ About the `java.util.regex` package in Java 2 Standard Edition
- ❑ The metacharacters supported in the `java.util.regex` package
- ❑ How to use many of the metacharacters to match and replace text
- ❑ How to use methods of the `String` class to apply regular expression functionality

> **The examples in this chapter have been tested against Java 5.0. The regular expression functionality in Java 5.0 is essentially unchanged from that previously supported.**

Introduction to the java.util.regex Package

The `java.util.regex` package was introduced in Java 2 Standard Edition version 1.4. So the examples described in this chapter will not work in versions prior to Java 1.4.

The `java.util.regex` package has three classes: `Pattern`, `Matcher`, and `PatternSyntaxException`. Each of those classes is described later in this section. First, look at how to obtain and set up a version of Java that supports the `java.util.regex` package.

Obtaining and Installing Java

If you don't have Java but want to work with the examples in this chapter, you will need to download and install a recent version of Java 2 Standard Edition, which supports `java.util.regex`. At the time of this writing, you have two choices: Java 1.4.2 and Java 5.0. Each of those versions belongs to the broad category of Java 2.

Java 2 Standard Edition can be downloaded from the Sun Java site at `http://java.sun.com`. At the time of this writing, information about the currently available versions of Java 2 Standard Edition can be found at `http://java.sun.com/j2se/`.

Installation instructions are provided online on Sun's Java site for 32-bit and 64-bit platforms. At the time of this writing, installation information can be accessed from `http://java.sun.com/j2se/1.5.0/install.html`.

> *The naming of Java 5.0 or 1.5 is inconsistent in Sun's documentation. For example, the preceding URL uses the term 1.5.0 to refer to what the Web page calls Java 5.0. The two terms Java 1.5 and Java 5.0 refer to the same version of Java.*

Installing Java on the Windows platform is straightforward. An executable installer requires only a few simple choices to be made. At the time of this writing, the installer can be downloaded from `http://java.sun.com/j2se/1.5.0/download.jsp`. There is also an extensive bundle of Java 5.0 documentation available for download from the same URL.

The Pattern Class

The `java.util.regex.Pattern` class is a compiled representation of a regular expression. The `Pattern` class has no public constructor. To create a pattern object, you must use the class's static `compile()` method.

A regular expression pattern is expressed as a string. The regular expression is compiled into an instance of the `Pattern` class using the `compile()` method. The `Pattern` object can then be used to create a `Matcher` object, which can match any arbitrary character sequence against the regular expression pattern associated with the `Pattern` object.

Use of the `Pattern` and `Matcher` objects typically follows this sort of pattern:

```
Pattern myPattern = Pattern.compile("someRegularExpression");
Matcher myMatcher = myPattern.matcher("someString");
boolean myBoolean = myMatcher.matches();
```

The preceding code assumes the existence in the code of the following `import` statement:

```
import java.util.regex;
```

Instances of the `Pattern` class are immutable and are, therefore, safe for use by multiple threads.

Using the matches() Method Statically

If you want to use a regular expression pattern only once, the option exists to use the `matches()` method statically. Using the `matches()` method statically is a convenience when matching is to be carried out once only.

The `matches()` method takes two arguments. The first argument is a regular expression pattern, expressed as a `String`. The second argument is a character sequence, a `CharSequence`, which is the string against which matching is to be attempted.

To use the `matches()` method statically, you would write code such as the following:

```
Pattern.matches(somePattern, someCharacterSequence);
```

So if you wanted to match the pattern `[A-Z]` against the string `George W. Bush and John Kerry were the US Presidential candidates in 2004 for the two main political parties`, you could do so as follows:

```
boolean myBoolean = Pattern.matches("[A-Z]", "George W. Bush and John Kerry were
   the US Presidential candidates in 2004 for the two main political parties");
```

Because the character sequence, the second argument to the `matches()` method, contains at least one uppercase alphabetic character, the `myBoolean` variable would contain the value `true`.

Two Simple Java Examples

The aim of the first example is to find any occurrence of the character sequence `the` and the following characters of the word containing it. The test string is as follows:

```
The theatre is the greatest form of live entertainment according to thespians.
```

The problem statement can be written as follows:

Match words that contain the character sequence t followed by h, followed by e, and the rest of the word, until a word boundary is found.

A pattern to allow you to solve the problem statement is:

```
the[a-z]*\b
```

First, you simply match the literal character sequence `the`. Then you match zero or more lowercase alphabetic characters, indicated by the pattern `[a-z]`. Finally, a word boundary, indicated by `\b`, is matched.

When you write the pattern the[a-z]*\b in an assignment statement, it is necessary to escape the \b metacharacter. So you write the pattern as the[a-z]*\\b. If you retrieve the value for a pattern from a text file, it isn't necessary to escape metacharacters in this way.

The following instructions assume that you have installed Java so that it can be accessed from any directory on your computer.

Try It Out   Using the Pattern and Matcher Classes

1. In a text editor, type the following Java code:

```
import java.util.regex.*;

public class Find_the{
  public static void main(String args[])
  throws Exception{

  String myTestString = "The theatre is the greatest form of live entertainment
according to thespians.";

  String myRegex = "the[a-z]*\\b";

  Pattern myPattern = Pattern.compile(myRegex);

  Matcher myMatcher = myPattern.matcher(myTestString);
  String myGroup = "";

  System.out.println("The test string was: '" + myTestString + "'.");
  System.out.println("The regular expression was '" + myRegex  + "'.");
  while (myMatcher.find())
        {
         myGroup = myMatcher.group();
         System.out.println("A match '" + myGroup + "' was found.");
        } // end while

        if (myGroup == ""){
          System.out.println("There were no matches.");
        } // end if


  } // end main()
  }
```

2. Save the code as Find_the.java.

3. At the command line, type the command **javac Find_the.java** to compile the source code into a class file.

4. At the command line, type the command **java Find_the** to run the code, and inspect the results, as shown in Figure 25-1.

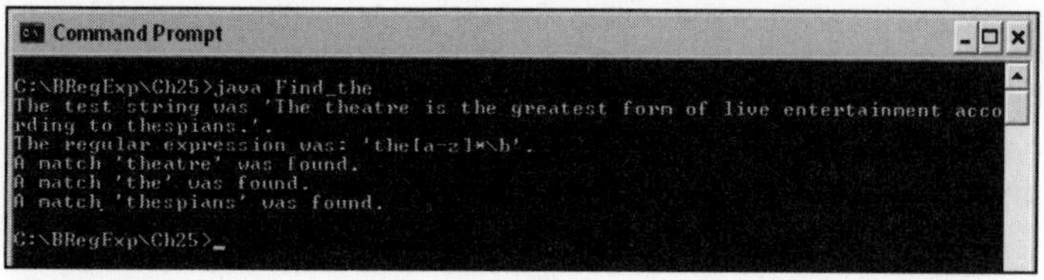

Figure 25-1

How It Works

The Java compiler, javac, is used to compile the code. Be sure to type the filename correctly, including the .java file suffix, or the code most likely won't compile.

The Java interpreter, java, is used to run the code.

To be able to conveniently use the classes of the java.util.regex package, it is customary to import the package into your code:

```
import java.util.regex.*;
```

This enables the developer to write code such as the following:

```
Pattern myPattern = Pattern.compile(myRegex);
```

If there were no import statement, it would be necessary to write the fully qualified name of the Pattern class in each line of code, as follows:

```
java.util.regex.Pattern myPattern = java.util.regex.Pattern.compile(myRegex);
```

Even in simple code like this, the readability benefit of the shorter lines should be clear to you.

The test string is specified and assigned to the myTestString variable:

```
String myTestString = "The theatre is the greatest form of live entertainment
according to thespians.";
```

A string value is assigned to the regex variable:

```
String myRegex = "the[a-z]*\\b";
```

The way in which you write the regular expression pattern is different from the syntax needed in the programs and languages you have seen so far in this book. The \b metacharacter matches the position between a word character and a nonword character. However, to convey to the Java compiler that you intend \b, you need to escape the initial backslash character and write \\b.

If you attempt to declare the myRegex variable and assign it a value as follows:

```
String myRegex = "the[a-z]*\b";
```

the result will not be what you expect. The \b will be interpreted as a backspace character. Figure 25-2 shows the result if you compile and run the Java code in the file UnescapedFind_the.java.

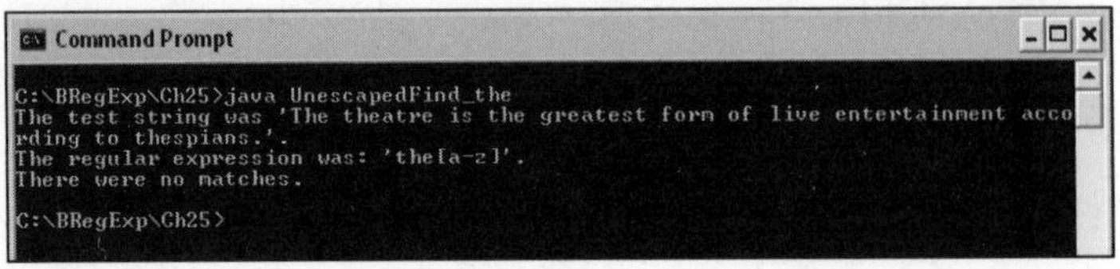

Figure 25-2

The myPattern variable is declared as a Pattern object that is created by using the compile() method with the myRegex variable as its argument:

```
Pattern myPattern = Pattern.compile(myRegex);
```

A myMatcher variable, which is a Matcher object, is declared and assigned the object created by using the myPattern object's matcher() method with the myTestString variable as its argument. There is no public constructor for a Matcher object, so if you want to create a Matcher object, you must use the technique shown:

```
Matcher myMatcher = myPattern.matcher(myTestString);
```

The value of the test string contained in the myTestString variable and the regular expression contained in the myRegex variable are displayed using the println() method of System.out:

```
System.out.println("The test string was '" + myTestString + "'.");
System.out.println("The regular expression was: '" + myRegex + "'.");
```

Then a while loop is used to test whether or not there are any matches. If there is a match, the value returned by myMatcher.find() is true. Therefore, the code contained in the while loop is executed for each match found:

```
while (myMatcher.find())
    {
```

The value returned by the group() method is assigned to the myGroup variable:

```
myGroup = myMatcher.group();
```

And the println() method is used to display the value of the match that is found during the present iteration of the while loop:

```
System.out.println("A match '" + myGroup + "' was found.");
} // end while
```

If no match is found, the value of the myGroup variable is the empty string, and then a message is displayed using the println() method to indicate that no matches have been found:

```
if (myGroup == ""){
  System.out.println("There were no matches.");
} // end if
```

The effect of the code just described is to display each occurrence in the test string of a character sequence beginning with the.

If you review the value of the myTestString variable, you will see that there are four possible occurrences of the character sequence the in the test string: The, theatre, the, and thespians.

```
String myTestString = "The theatre is the greatest form of live entertainment
according to thespians.";
```

Matching in Java is, by default, case sensitive, so the character sequence The is not a match, because the first character is an uppercase alphabetic character.

However, the word theatre matches. The pattern component [a-z]* matches the character sequence atre. The word the matches. The pattern component [a-z]* matches zero characters. And the word thespians matches. The pattern component [a-z]* matches the character sequence spians.

The second example uses a text file to hold the regular expression pattern and another text file to hold the test text.

Try It Out   Retrieving Data from a File

1. Type the following code in a text editor:

```java
import java.io.*;
import java.util.regex.*;

public final class RegexTester {
 private static String myRegex;
 private static String testString;
 private static BufferedReader myPatternBufferedReader;
 private static BufferedReader myTestStringBufferedReader;
 private static Pattern myPattern;
 private static Matcher myMatcher;
 private static boolean foundOrNot;

 public static void main(String[] argv) {
  findFiles();
  doMatching();
  tidyUp(); }

  private static void findFiles() {
   try {
    myPatternBufferedReader = new BufferedReader(new FileReader("Pattern.txt"));
     }
   catch (FileNotFoundException fnfe) {
    System.out.println("Cannot find the Pattern input file! "+fnfe.getMessage());
```

```
     System.exit(0); }
     try { myRegex = myPatternBufferedReader.readLine();
      }
     catch (IOException ioe) {}

// Find and open the file containing the test text
     try {
    myTestTextBufferedReader = new BufferedReader(new FileReader("TestText.txt"));
       }
    catch (FileNotFoundException fnfe) {
    System.out.println("Cannot locate Test Text input file! "+fnfe.getMessage());
    System.exit(0); }
     try {
     testString = myTestTextBufferedReader.readLine();
      }
     catch (IOException ioe) {}

     myPattern = Pattern.compile(myRegex);
     myMatcher = myPattern.matcher(testString);
     System.out.println("The regular expression is: " + myRegex);
     System.out.println("The test text is: " + testString);
     } // end of findFiles()

     private static void doMatching()
     {
      while(myMatcher.find())
       {
       System.out.println("The text \""
        + myMatcher.group() + "\" was found, starting at index "
        + myMatcher.start() + " and ending at index "
        + myMatcher.end() + ".");
       foundOrNot = true; }
       if(!foundOrNot){ System.out.println("No match was found.");
       }
     } // end of doMatching()

     private static void tidyUp()
      {
       try{
          myPatternBufferedReader.close();
          myTestTextBufferedReader.close();
      }catch(IOException ioe){}
     } // end of tidyUp()
   }
```

2. Save the code as `RegexTester.java`; to compile the code, type **javac RegexTester.java** at the command line.

3. Type the following code in a text editor, and save it as `Pattern.txt`:

```
\d\w
```

Then type the following code in a text editor, and save it as `TestText.txt`.

```
3D 2A 5R
```

4. Run the code by typing **java RegexTester** at the command line. Notice in Figure 25-3 that each of the three character sequences in `TestText.txt` is matched.

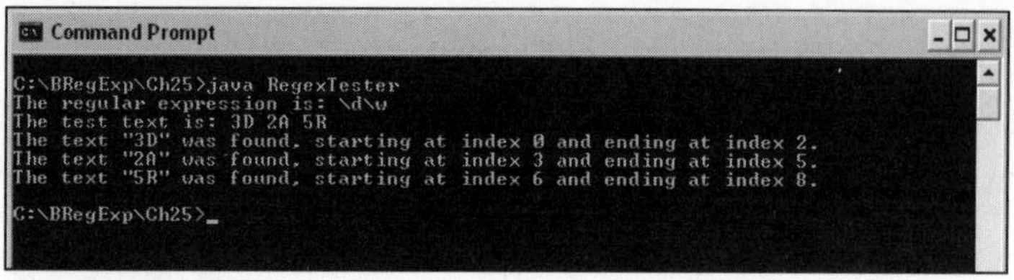

Figure 25-3

How It Works

This example performs file access, so you need to import the `java.io` package as well as the `java.util.regex` package:

```
import java.io.*;
import java.util.regex.*;
```

As assortment of variables is declared, each of which is used later in the code:

```
private static String myRegex;
private static String testString;
private static BufferedReader myPatternBufferedReader;
private static BufferedReader myTestTextBufferedReader;
private static Pattern myPattern;
private static Matcher myMatcher;
private static boolean foundOrNot;
```

The `main()` method consists of three methods: `findFiles()`, `doMatching()`, and `tidyUp()`.

```
public static void main(String[] argv) {
  findFiles();
  doMatching();
  tidyUp(); }
```

The `findFiles()` method uses a `try . . . catch` block to test whether the file `Pattern.txt` exists:

```
private static void findFiles() {
  try {
   myPatternBufferedReader = new BufferedReader(new FileReader("Pattern.txt"));
     }
```

If it doesn't exist, an error message is displayed, and the program terminates:

```
catch (FileNotFoundException fnfe) {
   System.out.println("Cannot find the Pattern input file! "+fnfe.getMessage());
   System.exit(0); }
```

If the file `Pattern.txt` is found (meaning that no error interrupts program flow), the `myPattern` `BufferedReader` object's `readLine()` method (which instantiates the `BufferedReader` class) is used to read in one line of `Pattern.txt` and assign the text in that first line to the `myRegex` variable:

```
try { myRegex = myPatternBufferedReader.readLine();
```

The `myTestTextBufferedReader` object is used to process the test text file, `TestText.txt`, in a similar way. The content of its first line is assigned to the `testString` variable.

Having read in values for the `myRegex` and `testString` variables, a `Pattern` object, `myPattern`, is created using the `Pattern` class's `compile()` method:

```
myPattern = Pattern.compile(myRegex);
```

Then the `myPattern` object's `matcher()` method is used to create a `Matcher` object, `myMatcher`:

```
myMatcher = myPattern.matcher(testString);
```

The `findFiles()` method is completed by displaying the values of the `myRegex` and `testString` variables, which confirms successful loading of both files:

```
System.out.println("The regular expression is: " + myRegex);
System.out.println("The test text is: " + testString);
}
```

Then the `doMatching()` method is executed:

```
private static void doMatching()
{
```

It uses a `while` loop to process each match found:

```
while(myMatcher.find())
{
```

For each match, the `group()`, `start()`, and `end()` methods of the `myMatcher` object are used to display the match, where it starts, and where it ends, respectively:

```
System.out.println("The text \""
 + myMatcher.group() + "\" was found, starting at index "
 + myMatcher.start() + " and ending at index "
 + myMatcher.end() + ".");
```

If any match is found, the value of the `foundOrNot` variable is set to `true` in the final line of the `while` loop:

```
foundOrNot = true; }
```

Then the value of the `foundOrNot` variable is tested as the condition controlling an `if` statement. If it is not `true`, the message `No match found.` is displayed:

```
if(!foundOrNot){ System.out.println("No match found.");
}
}
```

Finally, the `tidyUp()` method tidies up.

The pattern used is defined in the file `Pattern.txt`:

```
\d\w
```

The pattern matches a numeric digit followed by a word character (meaning an alphabetic character of either case, an underline character, or a numeric digit).

The test string is located in the file `TestText.txt`:

```
3D 2A 5R
```

There are three matches for the pattern \d\w: 3D, 2A, and 5R.

The Properties (Fields) of the Pattern Class

The following table summarizes information about the properties (fields) of the `Pattern` class.

Property (Field)	Description
`CANON_EQ`	Enables canonical equivalence when matching.
`CASE_INSENSITIVE`	Enables case-insensitive matching.
`COMMENTS`	Enables whitespace and comments to be included in the pattern.
`DOTALL`	With this flag set, the . (period) metacharacter matches all characters.
`MULTILINE`	Alters the behavior of the ^ (caret) and $ (dollar) positional metacharacters.
`UNICODE_CASE`	In this mode, case-insensitive matching is applied to all Unicode alphabetic characters (as appropriate).
`UNIX_LINES`	In this mode, only the \n line terminator affects the behavior of the . (period), ^ (caret), and $ (dollar) metacharacters.

The CASE_INSENSITIVE Flag

The `CASE_INSENSITIVE` flag applies only to U.S. ASCII characters. If you need case-insensitive matching to apply to other characters, you will likely need the `UNICODE_CASE` flag.

The `CASE_INSENSITIVE` flag can also be specified using the embedded flag expression `(?i)`.

Using the COMMENTS Flag

When the COMMENTS flag is set, it is possible to include whitespace in a regular expression pattern that is not matched against the test character sequence. In other words, whitespace included in a pattern is ignored, enabling the pattern (and the comments describing the meaning of the pattern's components) to be displayed in a way that assists a human reader in reading and understanding it.

The # character is used at the beginning of a comment. All characters following the # character are ignored (as far as matching is concerned) by the regular expression engine.

Comments mode can also be enabled using the embedded flag expression (?x).

The following example shows how comments can be used when attempting to match a U.S. Zip code when the Pattern.COMMENTS flag is set.

Try It Out   Using the COMMENTS Flag

1.   Type the following code into a text editor:

```java
import java.util.regex.*;

public class MatchZipComments{
    public static void main(String args[])
    throws Exception{

    String myTestString = "12345-1234 23456 45678 01234-1234";

    // Attempt to match US Zip codes.
    // The pattern matches five numeric digits followed by a hyphen followed by four
    numeric digits.
    String myRegex =
    "\\d{5} " +
    "# Matches five numeric digits" +
    "\n(-\\d{4})* " +
    "# Matches four numeric digits and a hyphen, all of which are optional";

    Pattern myPattern = Pattern.compile(myRegex, Pattern.COMMENTS);

    Matcher myMatcher = myPattern.matcher(myTestString);
    String myMatch = "";

    System.out.println("The test string was '" + myTestString + "'.");
    System.out.println("The pattern was '\\d{5}-\\d{4}'.");
    while (myMatcher.find())
            {
            myMatch = myMatcher.group();
            System.out.println("A match '" + myMatch + "'was found.");
            } // end while

            if (myMatch == ""){
             System.out.println("There were no matches.");
            } // end if

    } // end main()
    }
```

2. Save the code as `MatchZipComments.java`. To compile it at the command line, type **javac MatchZipComments.java**.

3. Run the code. At the command line, type **java MatchZipComments**, and inspect the results, as shown in Figure 25-4.

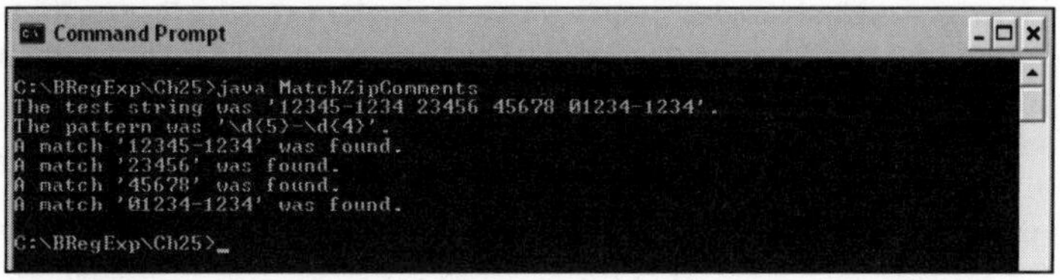

Figure 25-4

How It Works

The variable `myTestString` is assigned a string that contains four character sequences that could be U.S. Zip codes:

```
String myTestString = "12345-1234 23456 45678 01234-1234";
```

Conventional Java comments can be used to indicate the purpose of the regular expression:

```
// Attempt to match US Zip codes.
```

Similarly, conventional Java comments can be used to specify how the pattern is constructed:

```
// The pattern matches five numeric digits followed by a hyphen followed by four
numeric digits.
```

The `Pattern.COMMENTS` flag is set in the following statement; therefore, the value of the `myRegex` variable can be written across several lines, with comments interwoven between the components of the regular expression pattern. Notice that the comments follow the # character:

```
String myRegex =
 "\\d{5} " +
 "# Matches five numeric digits" +
 "\n(-\\d{4})* " +
 "# Matches four numeric digits and a hyphen, all of which are optional";
```

When the value of the variable `myPattern` is assigned the result of the `Pattern` class's `compile()` method, the second argument of the `compile()` method, `Pattern.COMMENTS`, sets the `COMMENTS` flag. When the `COMMENTS` flag is set, whitespace inside the pattern is ignored, and characters from the # character to the next-line terminator character are treated as comments:

```
Pattern myPattern = Pattern.compile(myRegex, Pattern.COMMENTS);
```

Matching takes place against the `myTestString` variable using the `myPattern` object's `matcher()` method:

```
Matcher myMatcher = myPattern.matcher(myTestString);
```

There are four matches in the `myTestString` variable. Character sequences `12345-1234` and `01234-1234` match when the optional part of the pattern, `(-\d{4})*`, matches once; and `23456` and `45678` match when `(-\d{4})*` matches zero occurrences of the pattern.

The DOTALL Flag

By default, the `.` (period) metacharacter matches any character except a line terminator. In Java regular expressions, the term *line terminator* refers to those characters (or combinations of characters) specified in the following list. When the `DOTALL` flag is set, the `.` (period) metacharacter matches all characters, including line terminators:

- ❏ **\n** — A newline (linefeed) character
- ❏ **\r\n** — A carriage-return character followed immediately by a newline character
- ❏ **\r** — A carriage return not followed by a newline character
- ❏ **\u0085** — A next-line character
- ❏ **\u2028** — A line-separator character
- ❏ **\u2029** — A paragraph-separator character

The `DOTALL` mode can also be specified using the embedded flag expression `(?s)`.

The MULTILINE Flag

By default, the positional metacharacters `^` and `$`, respectively, match the position just before the first character in the test character sequence and the position just after the last character in the character sequence. When `MULTILINE` mode is specified, the `^` metacharacter matches the position just before the first character on each line, and the `$` metacharacter matches the position just after the final character (ignoring line terminators) on each line.

The `MULTILINE` flag can also be specified using the embedded flag expression `(?m)`.

The UNICODE_CASE Flag

The `CASE_INSENSITIVE` flag causes matching of U.S. ASCII characters to be carried out in a case-insensitive way. To use case-insensitive matching with other characters, the `UNICODE_CASE` flag is set. It is likely that using the `UNICODE_CASE` flag will impose a performance penalty, so you should use it only when it is essential to the purpose of the regular expression.

The `UNICODE_CASE` flag can also be specified using the embedded flag expression `(?u)`.

The UNIX_LINES Flag

The `UNIX_LINES` flag is set when you are dealing with multiline text originating from a Unix or related operating system where only the \n line terminator is used. Only \n is recognized as affecting the behavior of the `.` (period), `^` (caret), and `$` (dollar) metacharacters.

The `UNIX_LINES` flag can also be specified using the embedded flag expression `(?d)`.

The Methods of the Pattern Class

The following table summarizes the methods that are specific to the `Pattern` class. Methods inherited from the `Object` class are not described here.

Method	Description
compile()	This static method compiles a regular expression pattern into a `Pattern` object.
flags()	Returns the flags set on a `Pattern` object.
matcher()	Creates a `Matcher` object that will match a regular expression against the test string.
matches()	This static method attempts to match a regular expression against a test string.
pattern()	Returns the regular expression pattern from which the `Pattern` object was compiled.
split()	Splits the test string at each occurrence of a match for a regular expression.

The compile() Method

There are two forms of the `compile()` method, each of which is static. One form takes a single argument, a `String` value containing a regular expression pattern. Any metacharacters, such as \d, must be written as \\d. The method throws a `PatternSyntaxException`.

The second form takes two arguments. The first argument is a `String` value containing a regular expression pattern. Any metacharacters, such as \d, must be written as \\d. The second argument is an `int` value indicating which flags are set. The method throws a `PatternSyntaxException`. if the regular expression is invalid and an `IllegalArgumentException` if the `int` value does not correspond to a permitted combination of flags.

The flags() Method

The `flags()` method takes no argument. It returns an `int` value corresponding to the flags (if any) that were set when the `Pattern` object was compiled.

The matcher() Method

The `matcher()` method takes one argument, a `CharSequence` value, which is the test string. A new `Matcher` object is returned that will match the `CharSequence` argument against the regular expression pattern specified for the `Pattern` object.

The matches() Method

This static method takes two arguments. The first argument is a `String` value containing the regular expression pattern. The second argument is a `CharSequence` value containing the test string. The `matches()` method returns a `boolean` value indicating whether or not matching was successful. The `matches()` method throws a `PatternSyntaxException`.

The pattern() Method

The pattern() method takes no argument and returns a String value containing the regular expression pattern that was used to compile the Pattern object.

The split() Method

The split() method can take two forms. The first form has a single CharSequence value as its argument, which contains the test string. A String[] is returned. The CharSequence is split at each occurrence of the regular expression pattern. If the regular expression pattern matches the final character(s) in the CharSequence, the empty string following the match is not returned as part of the string array.

The second form behaves like the first except that it has an int value as its second argument. The int value specifies the maximum number of times that the CharSequence value may be split.

The Matcher Class

The Matcher class is where most of the work is done. The Matcher object interprets the regular expression and performs the matching operations.

The Matcher class provides no public constructor. To create a Matcher object, you must call the public matcher() method on a Pattern object (as shown earlier):

```
Matcher myMatcher = myPattern.matcher("someString");
```

The matcher() method takes a single argument, a string.

The methods of the Matcher class are summarized in the following table.

Method	Description
appendReplacement()	Appends a replacement string to a string buffer when a match is found.
appendTail()	Appends the remaining character sequence to a string buffer after the final match is found (or the whole character sequence, if no match is found).
end()	Returns the index (plus one) of the last character matched.
find()	Attempts to find a substring of the test string that matches the regular expression pattern.
group()	Used with no argument, it returns the matching substring. Used with one argument, it returns the matching substring for a specified capturing group.
groupCount()	Returns the number of capturing groups in a regular expression pattern.
lookingAt()	Attempts to find a match for the regular expression pattern in the test string.

Method	Description
matches()	Attempts to match the whole test string against the regular expression pattern.
pattern()	Returns the Pattern object used in matching.
replaceAll()	Returns a string in which all occurrences of a regular expression pattern have been replaced by a replacement string.
replaceFirst()	Returns a string in which the first occurrence of a regular expression pattern has been replaced by a replacement string.
reset()	Resets a Matcher object.
start()	Returns the index of the first character in a match.

The appendReplacement() Method

The appendReplacement() method is intended for use with the find() and appendTail() methods. The following example uses the appendReplacement(), find(), and appendTail() methods together with a StringBuffer object to replace occurrences of the character sequence Star with the character sequence Moon.

Try It Out   The appendReplacement() Method

1.   Type the following code in a text editor:

```java
import java.io.*;
import java.util.regex.*;

public final class MatcherMethods {
 private static String myRegex;
 private static String testString;
 private static BufferedReader myBufferedReader;
 private static Pattern myPattern;
 private static Matcher myMatcher;

 public static void main(String[] argv) {
  initResources();
  processTest();
  closeResources(); }

  private static void initResources() {
   try {
   myBufferedReader = new BufferedReader(new FileReader("MatcherMethods.txt"));
     }
   catch (FileNotFoundException fnfe) {
    System.out.println("Cannot locate input file! "+fnfe.getMessage());
    System.exit(0); }
    try { myRegex = myBufferedReader.readLine();
     testString = myBufferedReader.readLine();
     }
    catch (IOException ioe) {}
```

```
myPattern = Pattern.compile(myRegex);
myMatcher = myPattern.matcher(testString);
System.out.println("Current myRegex is: "+myRegex);
System.out.println("Current testString is: "+testString);
}

private static void processTest()
{
  StringBuffer myStringBuffer = new StringBuffer();
  while (myMatcher.find())
  {
    myMatcher.appendReplacement(myStringBuffer, "Moon");
  } // end while loop
  myMatcher.appendTail(myStringBuffer);
  System.out.println();
  System.out.println(myStringBuffer.toString());
}

  private static void closeResources()
  {
    try{ myBufferedReader.close();
  }catch(IOException ioe){}
  }
}
```

2. Save the code as `MatcherMethods.java`; compile it; and at the command line, type **javac MatcherMethods.java**.

3. Type the following text in a text editor:

```
Star
Star Training Company is well known for high quality training. Star Training is
currently offering special value training packages.
```

The preceding information other than the first word is all on one line in the file `MatcherMethods.txt`. It is shown wrapped on two lines for the convenience of printing.

4. Save the text as `MatcherMethods.txt`.

5. Run the Java code. At the command line, type **java MatcherMethods**, and inspect the results, as shown in Figure 25-5. Notice that each occurrence of the character sequence `Star` in the test string has been replaced by the character sequence `Moon`.

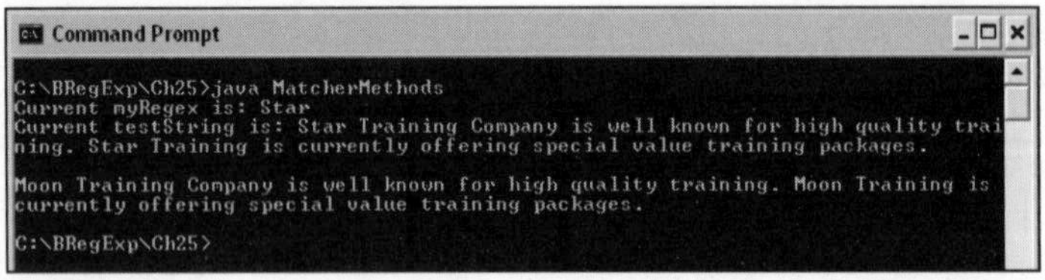

Figure 25-5

How It Works

The key part of this example, as far as the `Matcher` object's methods are concerned, is the use of the `appendReplacement()`, `find()`, and `appendTail()` methods.

A `BufferedReader` is used to accept the contents of `MatcherMethods.txt`:

```
myBufferedReader = new BufferedReader(new FileReader("MatcherMethods.txt"));
```

The code in the `processTest()` method uses the `appendReplacment()`, `find()`, and `appendTail()` methods.

A `myStringBuffer` object is declared and instantiated as a new `StringBuffer` object:

```
StringBuffer myStringBuffer = new StringBuffer();
```

A `while` loop is used to progress through the test string. If a match is found, the `myMatcher.find()` method returns the `boolean` value of `true`, so the code in the `while` loop is executed:

```
while (myMatcher.find())
{
```

The `appendReplacement()` method progresses through the test character sequence, adding characters to the `StringBuffer`. If a match is found, the characters constituting the match are not added to the `StringBuffer`. Instead, the replacement text is appended to the string buffer. Matching continues in the test character sequence from a position immediately after the character sequence that was a match:

```
myMatcher.appendReplacement(myStringBuffer, "Moon");
```

When no further matches are found, the `while` loop is exited:

```
} // end while loop
```

At this point, the string buffer contains the characters from the test character sequence up to the last match. The `appendTail()` method is used to append the remaining, nonmatching characters from the test character sequence to the `StringBuffer`:

```
myMatcher.appendTail(myStringBuffer);
```

A blank line is displayed to separate the test character sequence from the character sequence containing the replaced character sequence (assuming that a match was found). If there was no match, the original test character sequence and the "replaced" character sequence contain the same sequences of characters:

```
System.out.println();
```

The `myStringBuffer` object's `toString()` method is used to allow the replaced string to be displayed using the `println()` method:

```
System.out.println(myStringBuffer.toString());
```

The appendTail() Method

The appendTail() method is intended for use in conjunction with the appendReplacement() and find() methods. An example of using the appendTail() method was given in the preceding section on the appendReplacement() method.

The end() Method

The end() method can be used with no arguments or with one argument. When used with no arguments, the end() method returns the index (or position), plus one, of the last character matched. When used with one argument, the end() method takes an int argument that represents a group captured in the regular expression. The index, plus one, of the last character in the matched group is returned.

When used with zero or one arguments, the end() method can throw an IllegalStateException if no match has been attempted or if the most recent attempt at matching failed. When used with one argument, the end() method can throw an IndexOutOfBoundsException if the int argument does not correspond to a captured group.

The find() Method

The find() method attempts to match the next substring of the test string. If a match is found, the boolean value true is returned. If no (further) match is found, the boolean value false is returned. If the match succeeds, additional information about the match is available via the start(), end(), and group() methods.

The find() method can be used with zero or one arguments. When used with no argument, matching starts at the beginning of the test string, or if a previous match has been found, it starts at the character immediately following the final character of the preceding match.

When used with one argument, which is an int value representing an index at which matching should start, the Matcher object is reset, and the index is calculated from the beginning of the test string. The find() method can throw an IndexOutOfBoundsException if the int value is greater than the length of the test string.

The group() Method

The group() method can be used with no argument or one argument. When used with no argument, the group() method returns the match found by the preceding matching operation. The value returned is a String. In principle, the group() method can return the empty string if the pattern specifies characters or metacharacters that are all optional. The group() method can throw an IllegalStateException if matching has not yet been attempted or the preceding attempt at matching failed.

When used with one argument, the group() method takes an int argument, indicating a group captured in the preceding attempt at matching. It returns the matching substring captured by the correspondingly numbered group. It can throw an IllegalStateException if matching has not yet been attempted or if the preceding attempt at matching failed. It can throw an IndexOutOfBoundsException if the int value supplied as the method's argument does not correspond with a capturing group.

The groupCount() Method

The groupCount() method takes no argument and returns an int value. The value returned represents the number of capturing groups in the regular expression, excluding group zero, which represents the whole match.

The lookingAt() Method

The lookingAt() method attempts to find a match in the test string for a regular expression pattern. Matching begins at the beginning of the test string. The lookingAt() method takes no argument. If a match is found, further information about the match can be accessed by using the Matcher object's start(), end(), and group() methods. The lookingAt() method returns a boolean value of true if any character sequence in the test string matches the regular expression pattern.

The following example attempts to match a name entered at the command line against a pattern that looks for a word followed by a comma, followed by one or more space characters, followed by another word. That pattern is used to match a name entered in the format LastName, FirstName.

Try It Out   **The lookingAt() Method**

1.   Type the following code in a text editor:

```
import java.util.regex.*;
```

```java
public class lookingAt{
 public static void main(String args[]){
  isMatchPresent(args[0]);
 } // end main()

 public static boolean isMatchPresent(String testString){
  boolean testResult = false;
  String LastNameFirstName = "\\w+,\\s+\\w+";

  Pattern myPattern = Pattern.compile(LastNameFirstName);
  Matcher myMatcher = myPattern.matcher(testString);
  testResult = myMatcher.lookingAt();
  String matchIs = myMatcher.group();

  System.out.println("The test string is: " + testString);
  System.out.println("It is " + testString.length() + " characters long.");

  if (testResult){
   System.out.println("There was a match: " + myMatcher.group() );
   System.out.println("It started at: " + myMatcher.start() );
   System.out.println("It ended at: " + myMatcher.end() );
  }
  else
  {
   System.out.println("No match was found.");
  }
 return testResult;
 } // end isMatchPresent()

}
```

2. Save the code as `lookingAt.java`; compile it; and at the command line, type **javac lookingAt.java**.

3. Run the code. At the command line, type **java lookingAt "Smith, John"**. Be sure to insert a space character after the comma, or you will receive an error message.

4. Inspect the displayed results; then run the code again.

5. At the command line, type **java lookingAt "Smith, John James"**, and inspect the results, as shown in Figure 25-6. Notice that the results after Step 4 are also displayed in the upper part of the figure.

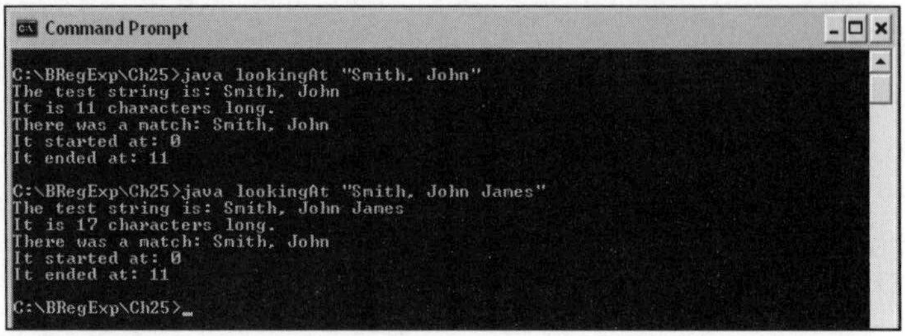

Figure 25-6

How It Works

This example captures and processes a string argument input from the command line. The `main()` method, as always, accepts an array of `String` objects. However, the code inside the `main()` method takes the first of those string arguments, `args[0]`, as the argument to the `isMatchPresent()` method:

```
public static void main(String args[]){
 isMatchPresent(args[0]);
} // end main()
```

The `isMatchPresent()` method makes use of several of the methods of the `Matcher` class.

The `args[0]` argument passed to the `isMatchPresent()` method is referred to as `testString` inside the `isMatchPresent()` method, as indicated by the method's signature:

```
public static boolean isMatchPresent(String testString){
```

First, a `boolean` variable `testResult` is assigned a default value of `false`:

```
boolean testResult = false;
```

Then the pattern you want to match is assigned to the `LastNameFirstName` string variable. Notice that the metacharacters `\w` and `\s` are written as `\\w` and `\\s`:

```
String LastNameFirstName = "\\w+,\\s+\\w+";
```

The myPattern variable is assigned the pattern created using the Pattern class's compile() method. Then a Matcher object, myMatcher, is created using the matcher() method of myPattern:

```
Pattern myPattern = Pattern.compile(LastNameFirstName);
Matcher myMatcher = myPattern.matcher(testString);
```

The boolean value returned by the lookingAt() method is assigned to the testResult variable (which had previously been assigned the value false. If there is a match, the testResult variable now holds the boolean value of true:

```
testResult = myMatcher.lookingAt();
```

The matchIs variable is assigned the value of myMatcher.group(). If there is a match, its value is now assigned to matchIs:

```
String matchIs = myMatcher.group();
```

The original string and its length, retrieved using the String class's length() method, are now displayed. When the argument at the command line is Smith, John, the length is 11 characters. When the argument is Smith, John James, the length is 17 characters:

```
System.out.println("The test string is: " + testString);
System.out.println("It is " + testString.length() + " characters long.");
```

An if statement uses the value of the testResult variable to display information about the match. If information about a match is displayed, you know that the lookingAt() method returned the boolean value of true:

```
if (testResult){
```

The Matcher class's group() method causes the match to be displayed. Notice that the match is the same for both command-line arguments — Smith, John and Smith, John James — because the pattern \w+, \s+\w+ will match as far as the final n or John.

```
System.out.println("There was a match: " + myMatcher.group() );
```

The Matcher class's start() method returns the position of the first character in the match:

```
System.out.println("It started at: " + myMatcher.start() );
```

The Matcher class's end() method returns the position, plus one, of the last characters in the match:

```
System.out.println("It ended at: " + myMatcher.end() );
}
```

If the value of testResult were false, the following message would be displayed:

```
else
{
System.out.println("No match was found.");
}
return testResult;
```

The matches() Method

The matches() method attempts to match a regular expression pattern against the whole of the test string. It returns a boolean value of true if the whole test string matches the regular expression pattern.

The pattern() Method

The pattern() method takes no argument. It returns a Pattern object. The Pattern object contains the regular expression pattern that the Matcher object uses in matching.

The replaceAll() Method

The replaceAll() method replaces every occurrence of a character sequence in the test string that matches the regular expression pattern with a specified replacement string. The replacement string is the replaceAll() method's sole argument. The return value is a String.

Try It Out   **Using the replaceAll() Method**

1.   Type the following code in a text editor:

```
import java.util.regex.*;

public class replaceAll{
 public static void main(String args[]){
  myReplace(args[0]);
 } // end main()

 public static boolean myReplace(String testString){
  String myMatch = "Star";

  Pattern myPattern = Pattern.compile(myMatch);
  Matcher myMatcher = myPattern.matcher(testString);
  String testResult = myMatcher.replaceAll("Moon");

  System.out.println("The test string is: \n'" + testString + "'.");
  System.out.println();

 if (testResult.length() > 0)
   {
    System.out.println("After replacement the string is: \n'" + testResult + "'." );
   }
   else
   {
    System.out.println("No match was found.");
   }
  return true;
 } // end myReplace()

}
```

2.   Save the code as replaceAll.java; compile the code; and at the command line, type **javac replaceAll.java**.

3. Run the code. At the command line, type **java replaceAll "Star training is great. Star Training Company is well known."** Inspect the results, as shown in Figure 25-7. Notice that each occurrence of the character sequence `Star` has been replaced by the character sequence `Moon`.

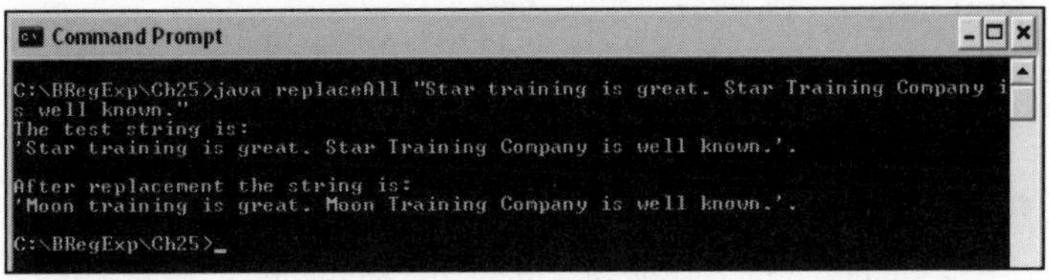

Figure 25-7

How It Works

The code in the `main()` method calls the `myReplace()` method, passing a string entered on the command line:

```
myReplace(args[0]);
```

In the `myReplace()` method, a literal pattern, `Star`, is assigned to the `myMatch` variable:

```
String myMatch = "Star";
```

Then a `Pattern` object and a `Matcher` object are created:

```
Pattern myPattern = Pattern.compile(myMatch);
Matcher myMatcher = myPattern.matcher(testString);
```

The `replaceAll()` method of the `Matcher` object is called with the replacement string `Moon`. The result is assigned to the `testResult` variable:

```
String testResult = myMatcher.replaceAll("Moon");
```

The original test string and a blank line as a separator are displayed:

```
System.out.println("The test string is: \n'" + testString + "'.");
System.out.println();
```

The `String` class's `length()` method is used to determine the length of `testResult`. If there is a match, the length of `testResult` will be greater than zero characters; therefore, the test for the `if` statement returns `true`, and the information about the replacement string is displayed:

```
if (testResult.length() > 0)
  {
  System.out.println("After replacement the string is: \n'" + testResult + "'." );
  }
```

If the length of `testResult` is zero characters, a message is displayed indicating that no match was found:

```
    else
    {
      System.out.println("No match was found.");
    }
  return true;
  } // end myReplace()
```

The replaceFirst() Method

The `replaceFirst()` method replaces the first matching character sequence in the test string with a specified replacement string. The replacement string is the sole argument of the `replaceFirst()` method. The value returned is a `String`.

The reset() Method

The `reset()` method resets state information on a `Matcher` object. It can be used with no argument or with one argument. When the `reset()` method is used with no argument, the state information is reset. Any matching takes place from the beginning of the test string. The test string remains the same as previously. The value returned is a `Matcher` object.

When the `reset()` method is used with a single argument, the state information is reset. The `reset()` method's argument is a `String`, which then becomes the test string for any future matching. The value returned is a `Matcher` object.

The start() Method

The `start()` method takes no argument. It returns an `int` value, which is the index of the first character in the most recent match.

The `start()` method can throw an `IllegalStateException` if matching has not started or if the most recent attempt at matching failed.

The PatternSyntaxException Class

A `PatternSyntaxException` object is an unchecked exception that indicates that there is an error in the syntax of a regular expression pattern.

The `PatternSyntaxException` class has methods that allow information about the exception to be accessed. The following table summarizes information about the methods of the `PatternSyntax Exception` class.

Method	Description
getDescription()	Retrieves the description of the error
getIndex()	Retrieves the error index in the pattern
getMessage()	Returns a multiline string that contains the description, pattern, and index
getPattern()	Retrieves the regular expression pattern that caused the error

Metacharacters Supported in the java.util.regex Package

The `java.util.regex` package supports an extensive range of metacharacters, which are briefly described in several tables in this section. Some of the metacharacters and character classes are described in more detail later in the section, with examples of how they can be used.

The following table summarizes many of the metacharacters supported in the Java `java.util.regex` package. The POSIX metacharacters supported in `java.util.regex` are listed in a later section in this chapter.

Metacharacter	Description
. (period character)	Matches any character. May or may not match line-terminator characters.
\d	Matches a numeric digit. Equivalent to the character class [0-9].
\D	Matches a character that is not a numeric digit. Equivalent to the character class [^0-9].
\s	Matches a whitespace character.
\S	Matches any character that is not a whitespace character.
\w	Matches a word character. Equivalent to the character class [A-Za-z0-9_].
\W	Matches a character that is not a word character. Equivalent to the negated character class [^A-Za-z0-9_].
[...]	Character class. Matches any single character contained between the square brackets.
[a-d[w-z]]	The union of two character classes. Equivalent to [a-dw-z].
[a-m[h-z]]	The intersection of two character classes. Equivalent to [h-m].
[a-z[^h-m]]	The intersection of a character class and a negated character class. The overall effect is subtraction of one character class from another. Equivalent to [a-gn-z].
[^...]	Negated character class. Matches any single character, except those characters contained between the square brackets.

Using the \d Metacharacter

The \d metacharacter matches a single numeric digit. The following example attempts to match U.S. Zip codes. A simple pattern `\d{5}-\d{4}*` can match abbreviated and extended U.S. Zip codes.

sing the \d Metacharacter

1. Type the following code into a text editor:

```
import java.util.regex.*;

public class MatchZip{
  public static void main(String args[])
  throws Exception{

  String myTestString = "12345-1234 23456 45678 01234-1234";

  // Attempt to match US Zip codes.
  // The pattern matches five numeric digits followed by a hyphen followed by four
numeric digits.
  String myRegex = "\\d{5}(-\\d{4})*";

  Pattern myPattern = Pattern.compile(myRegex);

  Matcher myMatcher = myPattern.matcher(myTestString);
  String myMatch = "";

  System.out.println("The test string was '" + myTestString + "'.");
  System.out.println("The pattern was '" + myRegex + "'.");
  while (myMatcher.find())
      {
        myMatch = myMatcher.group();
        System.out.println("The match '" + myMatch + "' was found.");
      } // end while

        if (myMatch == ""){
          System.out.println("There were no matches.");
        } // end if


  } // end main()
}
```

2. Save the code as MatchZip.java.

3. Compile the code by typing **javac MatchZip.java** at the command line.

4. Run the code by typing java **MatchZip** at the command line, and inspect the results, as shown in Figure 25-8.

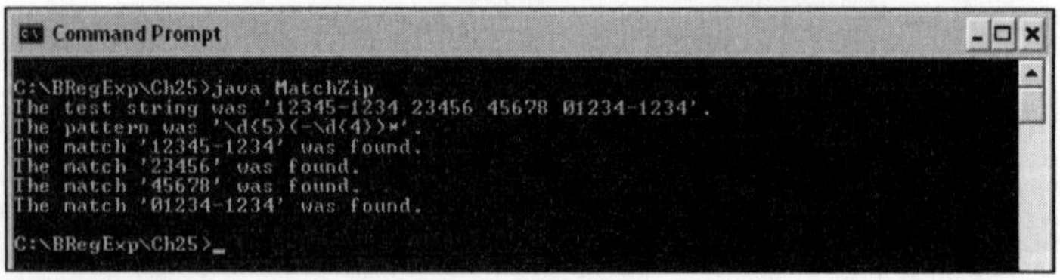

Figure 25-8

How It Works

The test string is assigned to the `myTestString` variable:

```
String myTestString = "12345-1234 23456 45678 01234-1234";
```

A pattern that can match U.S. Zip codes is assigned to the `myRegex` variable:

```
String myRegex = "\\d{5}(-\\d{4})*";
```

The `myRegex` and `myTestString` variables are used in the creation of a `Pattern` object, `myPattern`, and a `Matcher` object, `myMatcher`:

```
Pattern myPattern = Pattern.compile(myRegex);
Matcher myMatcher = myPattern.matcher(myTestString);
```

The empty string is assigned to the variable `myMatch`. This will allow you to test later whether there has been a match or not. If the value of `myMatch` is still the empty string, there has been no match:

```
String myMatch = "";
```

The original values of the test string, `myTestString`, and the regular expression pattern, `myRegex`, are displayed:

```
System.out.println("The test string was '" + myTestString + "'.");
System.out.println("The pattern was '" + myRegex + "'.");
```

A `while` loop uses the `find()` method as a test to determine whether or not a match has been found. If there is no match at all, the code in the `while` loop is never executed. For each match, the value of the match is displayed. After the final match, the test `myMatcher.find()` returns `false`, so the `while` loop exits:

```
while (myMatcher.find())
    {
     myMatch = myMatcher.group();
     System.out.println("The match '" + myMatch + "' was found.");
    } // end while
```

If the value of `myMatch` is still the empty string, there has been no match, so you can safely output a message indicating that there was no match. If there has been a match, the value of the `myMatch` variable will be something other than the empty string, and the following message will not be displayed:

```
if (myMatch == ""){
 System.out.println("There were no matches.");
} // end if
```

Character Classes

Support for character classes in `java.util.regex` includes the character classes, negated character classes, and character class ranges (discussed in the introductory chapters of this book). However, there is some useful additional functionality in `java.util.regex` that is unsupported in many regular expression implementations.

The following example demonstrates basic character class functionality.

Try It Out   Character Class

1.   Type the following code in a text editor:

```
import java.util.regex.*;

public class CharClass{
 public static void main(String args[]){
  findMatches(args[0]);
 } // end main()

 public static boolean findMatches(String testString){
  String myRegex = "[A-D]\\d";

  Pattern myPattern = Pattern.compile(myRegex);
  Matcher myMatcher = myPattern.matcher(testString);
  String myMatch = null;

  System.out.println("The test string was: " + testString);
  System.out.println("The regular expression pattern was:" + myRegex);
  while (myMatcher.find())
        {
         myMatch = myMatcher.group();
         System.out.println("Match found: " + myMatch);
        } // end while

        if (myMatch == null){
           System.out.println("There were no matches.");
        } // end if

  return true;
 } // findMatches()

}
```

2.   Save the code as CharClass.java.

3.   Compile the code. At the command line, type **javac CharClass.java**.

4.   Run the code. At the command line, type **java CharClass "A1 B2 C3 D9 E8 F3 G5"**, and inspect the results, as shown in Figure 25-9. Notice that the character sequences E8, F3, and G5 do not match.

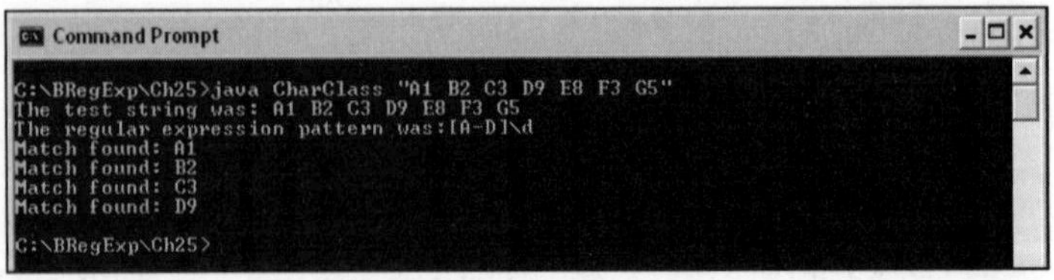

Figure 25-9

How It Works

The `myRegex` variable is assigned the pattern `[A-D]\d`:

```
String myRegex = "[A-D]\\d";
```

The test string `A1 B2 C3 D9 E8 F3 G5` is input at the command line and is assigned to the `args[0]` array element, which is used as the `findMatches()` method's argument:

```
findMatches(args[0]);
```

A `while` loop is used to display each match that is found. While the test for the `while` statement returns `true`, the code in the `while` loop is executed. When there are no more matches, the `find()` method returns the `boolean` value `false`, and the `while` loop exits:

```
while (myMatcher.find())
        {
         myMatch = myMatcher.group();
         System.out.println("Match found: " + myMatch);
        } // end while
```

Java supports the use of unions of character classes, as demonstrated in the following example.

Try It Out   Union of Character Classes

1. Type the following code in a text editor:

```
import java.util.regex.*;

public class CharClassUnion{
 public static void main(String args[]){
  findMatches(args[0]);
 } // end main()

 public static boolean findMatches(String testString){
  String myRegex = "[A-D[H-M]]\\d";

  Pattern myPattern = Pattern.compile(myRegex);
  Matcher myMatcher = myPattern.matcher(testString);
  String myMatch = null;

  System.out.println("The test string was: " + testString);
  System.out.println("The regular expression pattern was:" + myRegex);
  while (myMatcher.find())
          {
           myMatch = myMatcher.group();
           System.out.println("Match found: " + myMatch);
          } // end while

          if (myMatch == null){
           System.out.println("There were no matches.");
          } // end if
```

```
    return true;
  } // findMatches()

}
```

2. Save the code as `CharClassUnion.java`.

3. Compile the code. At the command line, type **javac CharClassUnion.java**.

4. Run the code. At the command line, type **java CharClassUnion "A1 B2 C3 D4 E5 H9 I2 J3 N4"**, and inspect the results, as displayed in Figure 25-10. Notice that the character sequences E5 and N4 are not matched.

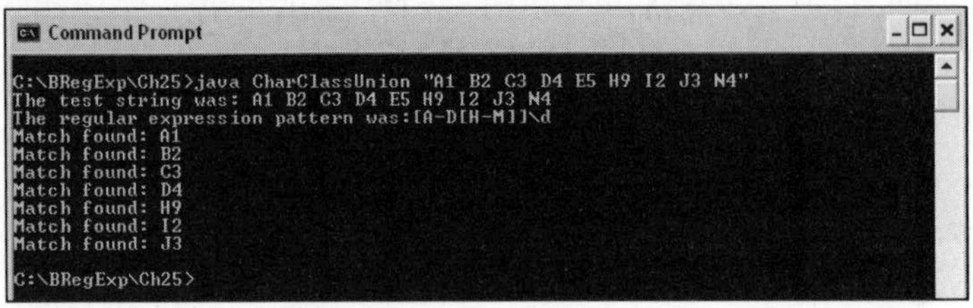

```
Command Prompt                                          _ □ ×

C:\BRegExp\Ch25>java CharClassUnion "A1 B2 C3 D4 E5 H9 I2 J3 N4"
The test string was: A1 B2 C3 D4 E5 H9 I2 J3 N4
The regular expression pattern was:[A-D[H-M]]\d
Match found: A1
Match found: B2
Match found: C3
Match found: D4
Match found: H9
Match found: I2
Match found: J3

C:\BRegExp\Ch25>
```

Figure 25-10

How It Works

The string assigned to the `myRegex` variable specifies the union of two character classes, `[A-D]` and `[H-M]`. The union operator is implicit. The character class is equivalent to `[A-DH-M]`:

```
String myRegex = "[A-D[H-M]]\\d";
```

Each match is displayed using the `while` loop as previously described.

If the alphabetic character is in the character class `[A-DH-M]`, together with the following numeric digit, there is a match.

<hr>

Try It Out   **Subtraction of Character Classes**

1. Type the following code in a text editor:

```
import java.util.regex.*;
```

```
public class CharClassSubtraction{
  public static void main(String args[]){
  String testString = args[0];
   findMatches(testString);
  } // end main()

  public static boolean findMatches(String testString){
    String myRegex = "[A-Z&&[^H-M]]\\d";

    Pattern myPattern = Pattern.compile(myRegex);
    Matcher myMatcher = myPattern.matcher(testString);
    String myMatch = null;
```

```
        System.out.println("The test string was: " + testString);
        System.out.println("The regular expression pattern was: " + myRegex);
        while (myMatcher.find())
            {
             myMatch = myMatcher.group();
             System.out.println("Match found: " + myMatch);
            } // end while

            if (myMatch == null){
             System.out.println("There were no matches.");
            } // end if

    return true;
    } // findMatches()

}
```

2. Save the code as `CharClassSubtraction.java`.

3. Compile the code. At the command line, type **javac CharClassSubtraction.java**.

4. Run the code. At the command line, type **java CharClassSubtraction "A1 B2 H3 I2 J4 M5 N6"**, and inspect the results, as shown in Figure 25-11. Notice that H3, I2, and J4 are not matched.

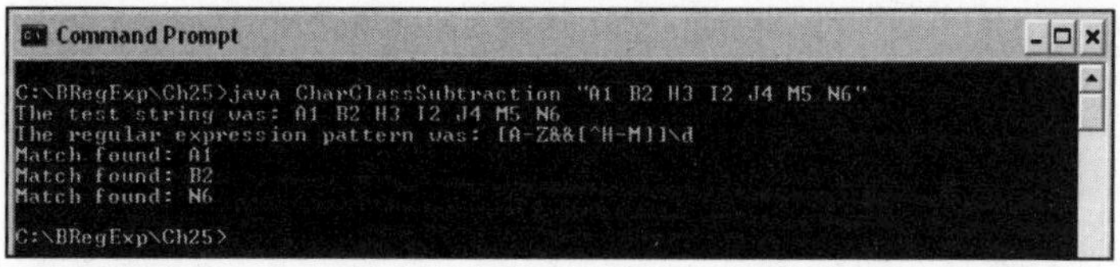

```
Command Prompt                                                    _ □ ×

C:\BRegExp\Ch25>java CharClassSubtraction "A1 B2 H3 I2 J4 M5 N6"
The test string was: A1 B2 H3 I2 J4 M5 N6
The regular expression pattern was: [A-Z&&[^H-M]]\d
Match found: A1
Match found: B2
Match found: N6

C:\BRegExp\Ch25>
```

Figure 25-11

How It Works

On this occasion, the regular expression pattern is `[A-Z&&[^H-M]]\d`. The `&&` operator inside the character class finds the intersection of two character classes — in this case, `[A-Z]` and `[^H-M]`. The intersection is uppercase alphabetic characters not between H and M. So `[A-Z&&[^H-M]]` is equivalent to `[A-GN-Z]`:

```
        String myRegex = "[A-Z&&[^H-M]]\\d";
```

The character sequences H3, I2, and J4 fail to match because alphabetic characters from H to M do not match the combined character class.

The POSIX Character Classes in the java.util.regex Package

The Java `java.util.regex` package supports several POSIX character classes but uses a syntax different from the one you have seen in OpenOffice.org, for example. The `java.util.regex` syntax for POSIX character classes resembles in some respects the syntax used in W3C XML Schema for Unicode character classes and character blocks. The following table lists the POSIX character classes supported in the `java.util.regex` package.

Metacharacter	Description
\p{Lower}	Equivalent to the character class [a-z].
\p{Upper}	Equivalent to the character class [A-Z].
\p{ASCII]	Matches all ASCII characters. Equivalent to U+0000 through U+007F.
\p{Alpha}	Matches any alphabetic character. Equivalent to either the [\p{Upper}\p{Lower}] or [A-Za-z] character classes.
\p{Digit}	Equivalent to the character class [0-9].
\p{Punct}	Equivalent to the character class [!"#$%&'()*+,-./:;<=>?@[\]^_`{|}~].
\p{Graph}	Visible characters. Equivalent to the character class [\p{Alpha}\p{Punct}].
\p{Print}	Printable characters. Equivalent to the character class [\p{Graph}].
\p{Blank}	A space character or tab character.
\p{Cntrl}	A control character. Equivalent to the character class [\x00-\x1F\x7F].
\p{XDigit}	A hexadecimal digit. Equivalent to the character class [0-9a-fA-F].
\p{Space}	A whitespace character. Equivalent to the character class [\t\n\x0B\f\r].

Unicode Character Classes and Character Blocks

Strings in Java are sequences of Unicode characters. Each character is represented by a 2-byte number. If you are unfamiliar with how English-language characters and other characters map to Unicode code points, the Windows Character Map utility can be useful. Figure 25-12 shows e with a circumflex selected in Character Map. Notice in the lower left of the figure that the character can be expressed as U+00EA. In Java, you would write that as \u00EA.

To match characters in the Basic Latin character block, for example, use a lowercase p as in the pattern \p{InBasicLatin}.

To match characters not in the Basic Latin character block, use an uppercase P as in the pattern \P{InBasicLatin}.

> Full information about Unicode is located at www.unicode.org. At the time of this writing, the current version of the Unicode Standard is version 4.0.1. Further information about the Unicode Standard is located at www.unicode.org/standard/standard.html.

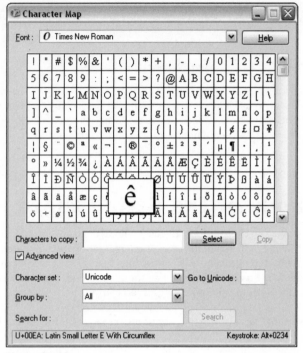

Figure 25-12

Using Escaped Characters

To match characters that are used for special purposes as regular expression metacharacters, it is necessary to escape such characters. The following table lists some of the more commonly used escaped characters in Java.

Escaped Character Sequence	Matches
\\	\ (the backslash)
\(	((opening parenthesis)
\)	) (closing parenthesis)
\[	[(opening square bracket)
\]	] (closing square bracket)
\^	^ (caret); used only outside a character class
\$	$ (dollar)
\?	? (question mark)
*	* (asterisk)

Table continued on following page

Escaped Character Sequence	Matches
\+	+ (plus sign)
\.	. (period character)

There is an alternative way to use a metacharacter without having to escape it in the way shown in the preceding table. A metacharacter or sequence of metacharacters can be enclosed between two other metacharacters: \Q (which starts a sequence of quoted characters) and \E (which ends a sequence of quoted characters).

Using Methods of the String Class

Several methods of the String class support the use of regular expression functionality. The matches() method tests whether there is a match in the string for a regular expression pattern. The replaceFirst() and replaceAll() methods replace one or all substrings that match a regular expression with a specified replacement string. The String class also has a replace() method, but it makes no use of regular expression functionality, simply matching and replacing a literal string.

The following table summarizes information about the methods of the String class that support regular expression functionality. There are, of course, many other methods of the String class that do not use regular expressions; they are not discussed here.

Method	Description
matches()	Tests whether or not a string contains a match for a given regular expression
replaceFirst()	Replaces the first substring in the string that matches a regular expression pattern with the specified replacement string
replaceAll()	Replaces all substrings in the string that match a regular expression pattern with the specified replacement string
split()	Splits a string into substrings at each match for a specified regular expression

Using the matches() Method

The String class's matches() method tests whether the whole string matches a regular expression. The matches() method takes a single argument, which is a String representing the regular expression pattern.

Try It Out   The matches() Method of the String Class

1.   Type the following code in a text editor:

```
import java.util.regex.*;
```

```
public class stringMatches{
 public static void main(String args[]){
  findMatch(args[0]);
 } // end main()
```

```
 public static boolean findMatch(String testString){
  String myRegex = "\\b[a-z]*hip[a-z]*\\b";
  boolean testResult = testString.matches(myRegex);
```

```
  System.out.println("The string was: " + testString);
  System.out.println("The regular expression pattern was:" + myRegex);
  if (testResult)
       {
       System.out.println("There was a match.");
       } // end if
       else
       {
       System.out.println("There was no match.");
       }
       return true;
 } // findMatch()
```

```
}
```

2.   Save the code as `stringMatches.java`.

3.   Compile the code. At the command line, type **javac stringMatches.java**.

4.   Run the code. At the command line, type **java stringMatches "ship"**, and inspect the displayed results.

5.   Run the code again. At the command line, type **java stringMatches "The ship was large."** Inspect the results, as shown in Figure 25-13. Notice that the character sequence `ship` matches, but the character sequence `The ship was large.` does not match.

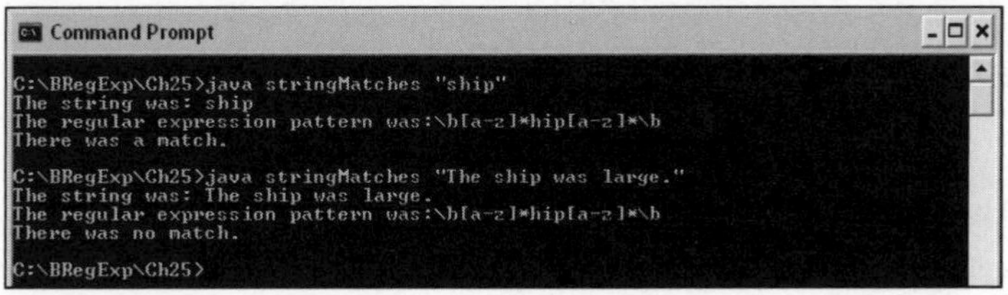

Figure 25-13

How It Works

The regular expression pattern assigned to the `myRegex` variable matches any word containing the character sequence `hip`:

```
String myRegex = "\\b[a-z]*hip[a-z]*\\b";
```

The `String` class's `matches()` method is used to assign a value to the `boolean` variable `testResult`. Notice that the `matches()` method's argument is the regular expression assigned to the `myRegex` variable:

```
boolean testResult = testString.matches(myRegex);
```

Because the `matches()` method simply returns a `boolean` value, you are confined to testing the value of the `testResult` variable to see if it is `true` or `false`. In this example, the value of the `testResult` variable is used to control the display of a message indicating whether or not there is a match:

```
if (testResult)
    {
    System.out.println("There was a match.");
    } // end if
    else
    {
    System.out.println("There was no match.");
    }
```

Because the pattern `\b[a-z]*hip[a-z]*\b` matches case sensitively, it will match the character sequence `ship` but not `Ship`, for example. Because the `String` class's `matches()` method must match the whole string, the pattern will not match strings such as `The ship was large.`, which contain other characters in addition to the character sequence that would match the pattern in other circumstances.

Using the replaceFirst() Method

The `String` class's `replaceFirst()` method takes two arguments. The first argument is a `String` containing the regular expression pattern. The second argument is a `String` containing the replacement string.

The `replaceFirst()` method can throw a `PatternSyntaxException` if there is an error in the regular expression pattern.

The following example uses the `replaceFirst()` method to replace the first occurrence of the character sequence `twinkle` with the character sequence `TWINKLE`.

Try It Out   Using the String Class's replaceFirst() Method

1.   Type the following code in a text editor:

```
import java.util.regex.*;

public class stringReplaceFirst{
  public static void main(String args[]){
    myReplaceFirst(args[0]);
```

```
    } // end main()

public static boolean myReplaceFirst(String testString){
  String myRegex = "twinkle";
  String testResult = testString.replaceFirst(myRegex, "TWINKLE");

  System.out.println("The string was: '" + testString + "'.");
  System.out.println("The regular expression pattern was: '" + myRegex +"'.");
  System.out.println("After replacement the string was: '" + testResult +"'.");
      return true;
  } // myReplaceFirst()

}
```

2. Save the code as `stringReplaceFirst.java`.

3. Compile the code. At the command line, type **javac stringReplaceFirst.java**.

4. Run the code. At the command line, type **java stringReplaceFirst "twinkle, twinkle little star"**, and inspect the displayed results, as shown in Figure 25-14.

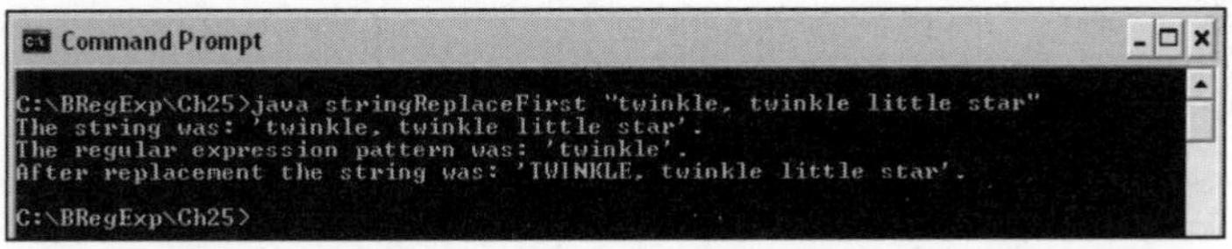

Figure 25-14

How It Works

A simple literal pattern, `twinkle`, is assigned to the `myRegex` variable:

```
String myRegex = "twinkle";
```

The `replaceFirst()` method is used to assign a value to the `testResult` variable, which is a `String`. The second argument of the `replaceFirst()` method specifies that the character sequence `TWINKLE` is the replacement string:

```
String testResult = testString.replaceFirst(myRegex, "TWINKLE");
```

The value of the string, the regular expression, and the replaced string are displayed:

```
System.out.println("The string was: '" + testString + "'.");
System.out.println("The regular expression pattern was: '" + myRegex +"'.");
System.out.println("After replacement the string was: '" + testResult +"'.");
```

The value of `testString` was `twinkle, twinkle little star`. The first occurrence of `twinkle` is replaced. So after replacement, the string is `TWINKLE, twinkle little star`..

Using the replaceAll() Method

The String class's replaceAll() method replaces all matches for a regular expression with a specified replacement string. The first argument of replaceAll() is a String containing the regular expression pattern. The second argument is a String containing the replacement string.

Using the split() Method

The String class's split() method may be used with one argument or two. It is used to split a string into substrings. The place of the split is defined by the regular expression. It returns a String array.

When used with one argument, the argument is a String containing a regular expression pattern. At each occurrence of the pattern, the test string is split into substrings. When used with two arguments, the first argument is a String containing a regular expression. The second argument is an int value that specifies a maximum number of splits to take place. Subject to the limit imposed by the second argument, the test string is split into substrings at each occurrence of the pattern. If the regular expression pattern contains an error, a PatternSyntaxException is raised.

Exercises

The following exercises allow you to test your understanding of some aspects of the material covered in this chapter:

1. Modify the replaceAll.java code so that only the first occurrence of a match for the regular expression pattern is replaced.

2. Modify the stringReplaceFirst.java code so that all occurrences of the character sequence twinkle are replaced.

Regular Expressions in Perl

Perl is a powerful and sometimes cryptic scripting language with particular strengths in the realm of text manipulation, system administration, and dynamic Web-content generation. Regular expression support in Perl is a key strength of the language, contributing significant power to Perl's text manipulation functionality.

Because of its compact syntax, Perl can be a cryptic, sometimes impenetrable programming language for programmers with little or no Perl experience. Combining Perl with regular expressions, with their own potential for compact, cryptic syntax, can be an intimidating experience for the unprepared. However, if the components of the Perl and regular expression syntax are considered in their component parts, the worst of the potential for intimidating compactness can be avoided. By the time you have finished working through the content and examples in this chapter, you should have taken significant steps toward making Perl do useful text manipulation using regular expressions.

In this chapter, you will learn the following:

❑ To obtain a Perl download and install it on Windows

❑ To use Perl for basic regular expression tasks

❑ To use the Perl regular expression operators

❑ What metacharacters are supported in Perl

❑ To use many of the Perl metacharacters

❑ To specify and use regular expression modes in Perl

Obtaining and Installing Perl

This book is focused primarily on the Windows platform. However, Perl is available for use on a wide range of platforms.

To obtain a copy of a current version of Perl for a range of operating system platforms, visit www.perl.com/download.csp or http://www.perl.org/get.html, where currently available

Perl downloads are listed. If you are using a platform other than Windows, choose the appropriate download from those offered and follow any installation information provided.

The Perl 5.8 download for Windows is available from www.activestate.com/ActivePerl/. ActivePerl is produced by a commercial company, ActiveState.com, but is recommended by Perl.com and is, at the time of this writing, available for free. To download the ActivePerl installer, you will first need to provide a name and e-mail address.

After downloading the ActivePerl MSI installer, simply double-click it and follow the on-screen instructions. If you are using Windows XP or Windows Server 2003 and have administrator rights, installation should be straightforward. If you are using another version of Windows, check the ActivePerl installation information at http://aspn.activestate.com/ASPN/docs/ActivePerl/install.html. On the installation screen, shown in Figure 26-1, leave all options checked unless you have specific reasons to do otherwise.

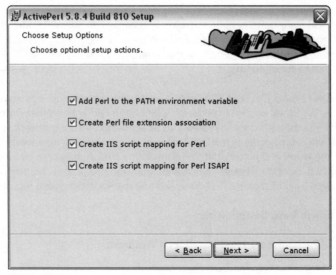

Figure 26-1

> **The installation instructions assume that you are installing Perl on a development machine used for testing purposes only. If you intend to install Perl on a production server, you should take the time to fully understand the relevant security issues.**

ActivePerl will be installed to C:\Perl (no other option for installation location is given). If you have a previous version of ActivePerl installed it will be overwritten without your being informed. Unless you want to compare individual versions of ActivePerl, this default behavior doesn't cause any problems, in my experience.

The ActivePerl installation includes a wealth of Perl documentation. The ActivePerl User Guide can be opened in a browser at `C:\Perl\html\index.html` and is shown in the Firefox browser in Figure 26-2. The left frame of the User Guide has several screens of information vertically and is well worth scrolling down. In particular, the left frame contains links to the Perl core documentation. An alternative way to access the ActivePerl User Guide is, on Windows XP, to select Start ➪ All Programs ➪ ActiveState ActivePerl 5.8 ➪ Documentation. The ActivePerl User Guide will open in a browser window.

If you prefer using the `perldoc` utility rather than the ActivePerl User Guide to explore the documentation, you can simply type the relevant `perldoc` command at the Windows command line, because the installer adds the needed information to the `PATH` environment variable. Figure 26-3 shows some of the information from `perldoc` about the Perl `strict` pragma accessed using the command `perldoc strict` at the Windows command line. To navigate forward by a screen, use the spacebar. To navigate forward one line, press the Return key.

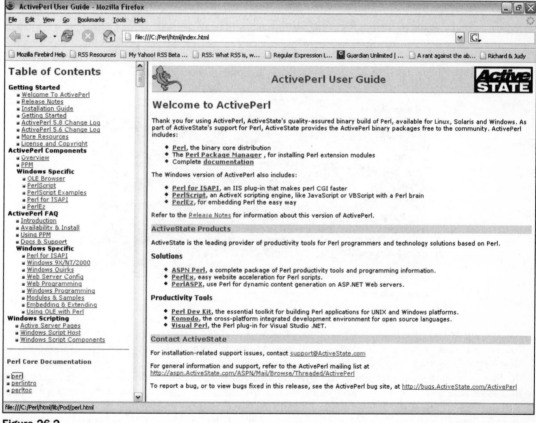

Figure 26-2

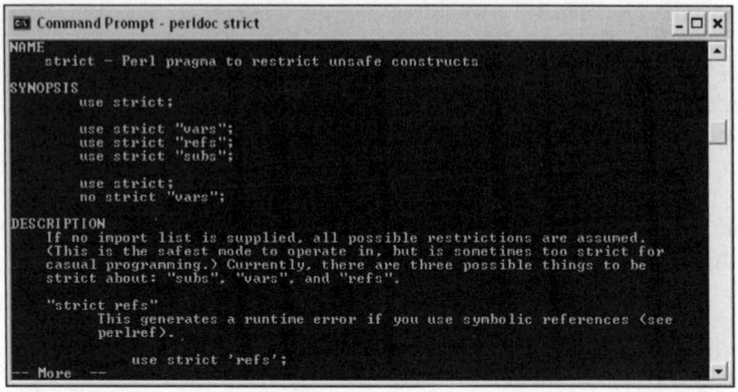

Figure 26-3

Now that you know where to find the Perl documentation in an ActivePerl installation, you will also want to be sure that Perl has installed correctly. You can check that the `perl` command is working by entering the command `perl -v` at the command line, which will display information about the version of Perl that you have installed. Figure 26-4 shows the appearance with ActivePerl 5.8.4.

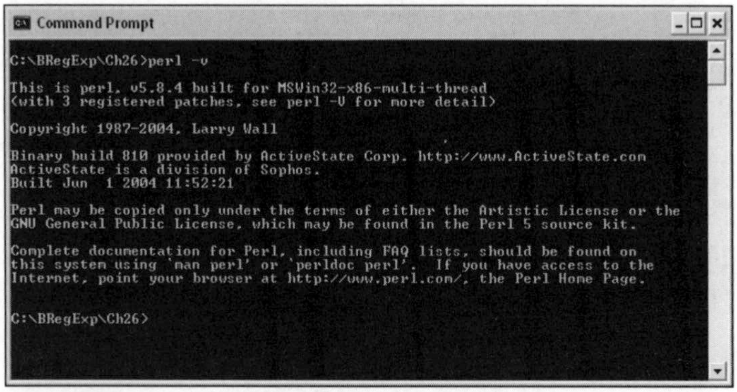

Figure 26-4

You can create Perl code using any text editor or integrated development environment that you prefer. Examples in this chapter are developed using the ActiveState Komodo 3.0 development environment. A time-limited, free trial download of Komodo is available from `www.activestate.com/Products/Komodo`. To download the evaluation edition, you must provide a name and e-mail address. Be careful that the e-mail address is entered correctly, because a small executable is needed to create a functioning version of Komodo, and the URL to download the executable is sent to the e-mail address you provide. Komodo 3.0 is available as an MSI installer. In my experience, installation of Komodo has been straightforward and simply a matter of following the on-screen instructions.

Creating a Simple Perl Program

You are now ready to create and run a first, simple Perl program using Komodo 3.0 and ActivePerl. If you prefer to use a different text editor, I assume that you are familiar with the necessary commands to enter and edit Perl code in that editor.

Try It Out   Creating a Simple Perl Program

1. In Komodo 3.0, select New from the File menu; then select New File.

2. In the New File dialog box(shown in Figure 26-5), select the Perl option, then click the Open button.

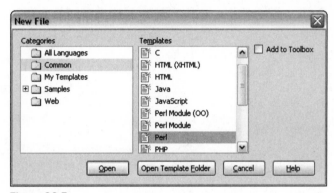

Figure 26-5

The file `Perl-1.pl` will open in Komodo 3.0 with brief template code, as shown in Figure 26-6. The significance of those lines is explained in the How It Works section that follows.

3. Edit the Perl code so that it reads as follows:

```
#!/usr/bin/perl -w
use strict;
my $myString = "Hello world!";
print "$myString\n";
print "The preceding line printed the variable \$myString.\n";
print "This program has run without errors.";
```

4. Save the code as `C:\BRegExpr\Ch26\Simple.pl`.

5. In Komodo 3.0, press F5; then press the Return key (accepts the default of no script arguments) to run the code in debug mode.

> If this is the first code file you have created in Komodo, following the preceding instruction should be all you need to do. If you have been running other code inside Komodo, you will need to take the extra step of selecting which file to run between pressing the F5 and Return keys. Click the Browse button to select the file you want to run.

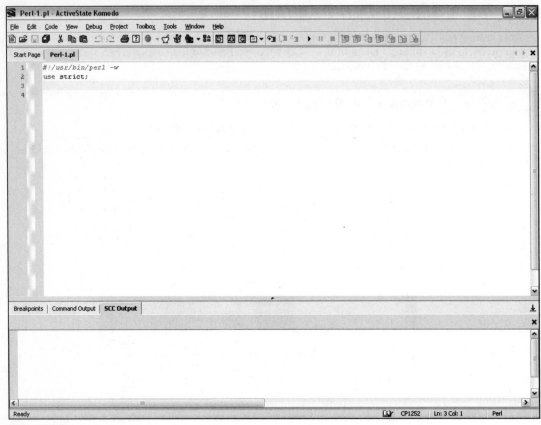

Figure 26-6

6. Inspect the results displayed in the Output pane in the lower-right corner of the Komodo screen, as shown in Figure 26-7. Notice that three lines of text are displayed in the Output pane.

> The Perl examples in this chapter were tested using ActivePerl 5.8.4. It is likely that the examples will run unchanged on all versions of Perl 5.8, but this has not been tested.

If you have chosen not to use the Komodo 3.0 development environment, you can run the file Simple.pl from the command line. Simply type the following command, and the file will be run, assuming that you installed ActivePerl (which sets up the PATH environment variable) or added the perl engine to your machine's path:

```
perl Simple.pl
```

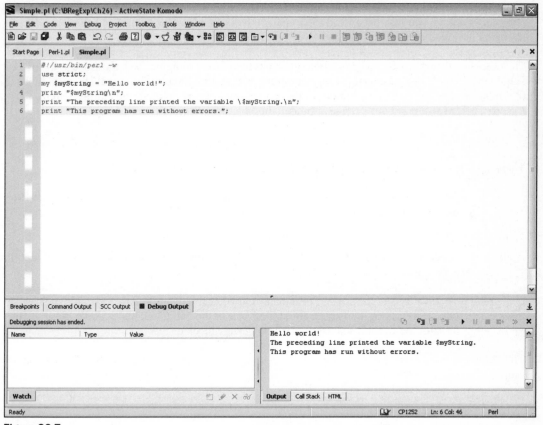

Figure 26-7

Figure 26-8 shows the screen's appearance after running Simple.pl in a Windows XP command window.

Figure 26-8

How It Works

The first line added to Perl files by Komodo 3.0 is as follows:

```
#!/usr/bin/perl -w
```

The # character indicates a Perl comment. All characters from the # character to the end of the line are normally treated as a Perl comment. However, when the #! character sequence constitutes the first two characters of the first line of a program on Unix platforms, it indicates the location of the program that will run that code. If, like me, you are running Perl on Windows, you can ignore this line. On Unix-like operating systems, you may need to edit that line if the perl program is located in a directory different from that indicated by the first line.

The other line that Komodo 3.0 adds automatically is the strict pragma. This indicates to the perl engine that potentially questionable programming practices should not be allowed. The form in the line that follows indicates that all the options of the strict pragma are applied. Put simply, that means that the perl engine will point out a range of potential problems with your code:

```
use strict;
```

There are three more narrowly scoped versions of the strict pragma:

❑ **use strict "vars";** —Generates an error if you access a variable that wasn't declared via our or use vars, was localized via my, or wasn't fully qualified

❑ **use strict "refs";** —Generates an error if you use symbolic references

❑ **use strict "subs";** —Generates a compile-time error if you try to use a bareword identifier that is not a subroutine

One of the practical effects of the strict pragma is that you cannot simply use a variable such as $myString without indicating something about the scope of the variable. This example uses my. The my keyword declares the variable to be local to the enclosing block or file.

The following line assigns the string value Hello world! to the $myString variable that has local scope:

```
my $myString = "Hello world!";
```

The print operator is used to print the value held in the $myString variable to the command window and then prints a newline character, as indicated by \n. You may find the inclusion of $myString inside paired double quotes surprising. In Perl, you simply include a variable inside paired quotes when you want to display its value using print:

```
print "$myString\n";
```

That raises the question of how you print the $ sign. You simply precede it with a backslash character so that you can display which variable's value was printed:

```
print "The preceding line printed the variable \$myString.\n";
```

You can also use the print operator to display literal text:

```
print "This program has run without errors.";
```

Of course, there is much more to Perl than this simple example, but it gives you some notion of how output can be displayed.

Basics of Perl Regular Expression Usage

This section illustrates straightforward uses of regular expressions in Perl, for those readers who are not fluent in Perl. This chapter does not provide a full tutorial on how to use Perl. If you have little or no knowledge of Perl, I suggest that if you want to use regular expressions in real Perl applications, you take time to study a book such as *Perl For Dummies*, by Paul Hoffman (Wiley 2003).

To use regular expressions in Perl, you must use one or more of the regular expression operators.

Using the Perl Regular Expression Operators

The Perl regular expression operators interact intimately with regular expression patterns. The following table lists and briefly describes the regular expression operators.

Operator	Description
m//	Used when matching a string against a regular expression
s///	Used when matching and then substituting a pattern
q// etc	Generalized quotes
split//	Splits a string into a list of strings

The simplest operator is the m// operator, which is used to test if there is a match between a string and a regular expression. As you will see later, the m of the m// operator isn't essential in Perl code. However, I suggest that you use it routinely, because it makes clearer what is happening in the matching process.

Using the m// Operator

The m// operator is used together with the =~ operator to test whether a string contains a match for a specified regular expression.

Try It Out   Using the m// Operator

1. Create a new Perl file in Komodo 3.0 or in your chosen text editor, and edit the code to read as follows:

```
#!/usr/bin/perl -w
use strict;
my $myString = "Hello world!";
if ($myString =~ m/world/)
{
 print "There was a match.";
}
```

```
else
{
 print "There was no match.";
}
```

2. Save the code as SimpleMatch.pl.

3. Press F5, use the Browse button to select SimpleMatch.pl, and press Return to run the code in debug mode.

4. Inspect the results displayed in the Output pane (in the lower-right corner of the Komodo window), as shown in Figure 26-9. The displayed message simply states that a match was found.

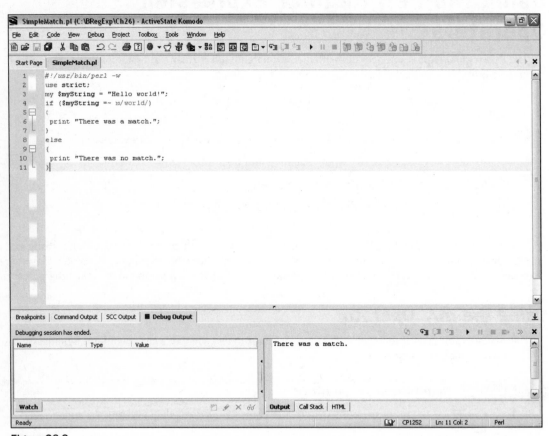

Figure 26-9

How It Works

First, the string value Hello world! was assigned to the $myString variable, as before. Because the strict pragma is in force, you add a my before the variable name:

```
my $myString = "Hello world!";
```

Then an `if` statement is used to determine whether a message indicating successful matching or failed matching is to be displayed. The test of the `if` statement is whether or not the `$myString` variable contains a match for the literal regular expression pattern `world`. The combination of the `=~` operator and the `m//` operator can be read as matches.

Perl doesn't have a Boolean datatype, but it behaves as though it does:

```
if ($myString =~ m/world/)
```

By default, matching in Perl is case sensitive.

If a match is found (there is a match, given the code in this example file), a message is displayed indicating that matching was successful. In Perl, the paired curly braces are required to enclose the statement block that is executed when the test returns the equivalent of `true`, even if only a single statement is to be executed:

```
{
  print "There was a match.";
}
```

If no match is found, a message to that effect is displayed. Again, the paired curly braces of the `else` clause are required, even though there is only a single statement in the `else` statement block:

```
else
{
  print "There was no match.";
}
```

The `m//` operator can be used with any of the regular expression matching modes that Perl supports. The following example shows how matching can be carried out case insensitively. The case-insensitive matching mode is indicated by a lowercase `i` following the second forward slash of the paired forward slashes that delimit the regular expression pattern:

```
$myTestString =~ m/world/i;
```

The example also introduces a very useful function, `chomp`, which you will use often in code that accepts input from the user.

Try It Out   Matching Case Insensitively

1. Type the following code in Komodo or your chosen text editor, and save the code as `MatchInsensitive.pl`:

```
#!/usr/bin/perl -w
use strict;
print "Enter a string. It will be matched against the pattern '/Star/i'.\n\n";
my $myTestString = <STDIN>;
chomp($myTestString);
if ($myTestString =~ m/Star/i)
{
```

```
      print "There is a match for '$myTestString'.";
}
else
{
   print "No match was found in '$myTestString'.";
}
```

2.   Either run the code inside Komodo 3.0 (by pressing F5, selecting `MatchInsensitive.pl` using the Browse button, and then pressing the Return key) or type **perl MatchInsensitive.pl** at the command line.

3.   The first time that the code is run, enter the test string **Startle**, and press the Return key. Inspect the displayed message, as shown in Figure 26-10.

> When entering text in the Komodo 3.0 Output pane, be sure that the focus has gone to the desired line. It is easy to type characters unintentionally into the Code pane, rather than the Output pane, with a resulting avalanche of syntax errors the next time you attempt to run the code.

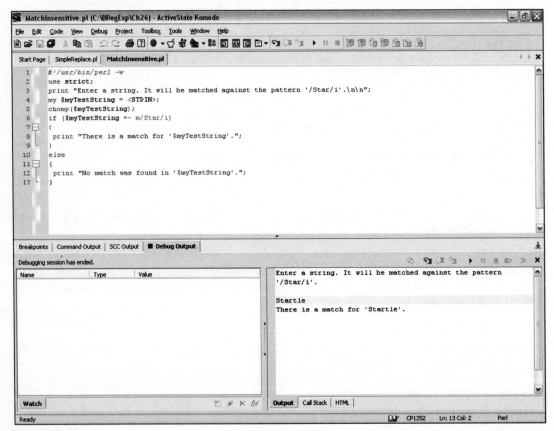

Figure 26-10

4. Run the code again, enter the test string **startle**, and press the Return key. Inspect the displayed message. Again, a match is found, because the pattern `Star`, when matched case insensitively, matches the initial `star` of `startle`.

5. Run the code again, enter the test string **Hello**, and press the Return key. Inspect the displayed message, as shown in Figure 26-11.

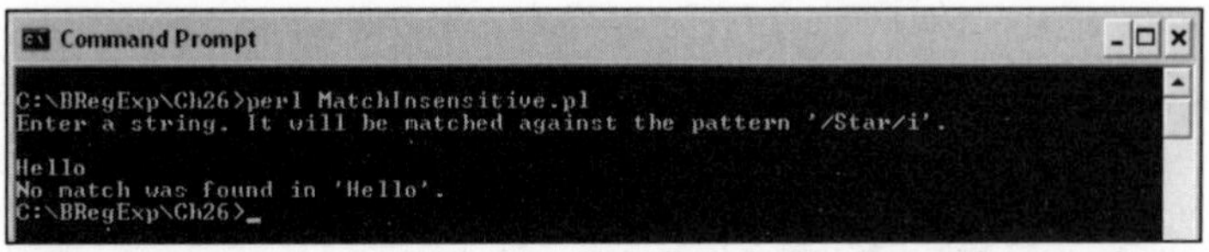

Figure 26-11

How It Works

First, the `print` operator is used to display a message inviting the user to enter a test string:

```
print "Enter a string. It will be matched against the pattern '/Star/i'.\n\n";
```

The variable `$myTestString` is assigned the sequence of characters that the user enters at the command line. The `<STDIN>` operator reads in a line of characters from the standard input. Typically, the standard input device is the keyboard. So `<STDIN>` reads a line of characters from the keyboard, ending when you press the Return key. One of the minor inconveniences about the line of characters provided by the standard input is that it includes the newline character. Perl treats a newline character as part of the character sequence to be matched. So the newline needs to be removed to achieve the matching behavior that you would likely expect:

```
my $myTestString = <STDIN>;
```

Perl provides the `chomp` operator to remove the newline character from the end of the sequence of characters that have been read in from the standard input:

```
chomp($myTestString);
```

The code file `MatchInsensitiveLengths.pl`, shown here and also included in the code download, displays the length of `$myTestString` before and after the `chomp()` function is used. Notice that when the test string is `Startle`, the length of the string is 8, one more than the number of visible characters. The newline character is the eighth character:

```
#!/usr/bin/perl -w
use strict;
print "Enter a string. It will be matched against the pattern '/Star/i'.\n\n";
my $myTestString = <STDIN>;
my $myLength = length($myTestString);
print "The length before chomp() is $myLength.\n\n";
chomp($myTestString);
$myLength = length($myTestString);
print "The length after chomp() is $myLength.\n\n";
```

```
if ($myTestString =~ m/Star/i)
{
 print "There is a match for '$myTestString'.\n\n";
}
else
{
 print "No match was found in '$myTestString'.";
}
```

Figure 26-12 shows the screen's appearance when you run `MatchInsensitiveLengths.pl` from the command line. Notice the length of the `$myTestString` before and after `chomp()` is used.

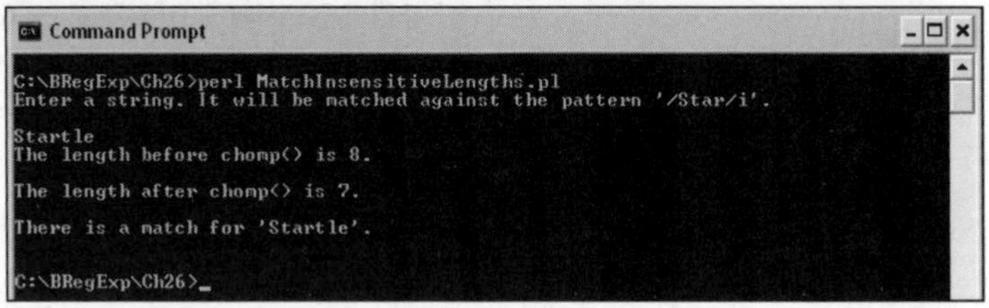

Figure 26-12

One of the difficulties for beginners when using Perl is that many constructs can be written in more than one way. The next couple of examples illustrate some of these variations, which you may meet when you have to handle code created by other developers.

The character m in the m// operator is, in fact, optional. I suggest, for the sake of clarity (the m hints at the idea of matching), that you use m// rather than just //, as in the following example.

Try It Out   **Optional "m"**

1.   Type the following code in Komodo 3.0 or an alternative text editor, and save the code as `SimpleMatchNoM.pl`:

```
#!/usr/bin/perl -w
use strict;
my $myString = "Hello world!";
if ($myString =~ /world/)
{
 print "There was a match.";
}
else
{
 print "There was no match.";
}
```

2.   Press F5 and then press the Return key to run the code.

3.   Inspect the result. Because the behavior of matching with // instead of m// is no different, the screen's appearance is the same as was shown in Figure 26-9.

The `chomp()` function is something you are likely to use frequently, because it is useful to remove the newline character that ends a line of user input. The following example shows an alternative syntax for `chomp()` which, while less obvious to occasional Perl programmers, is more succinct.

An Alternative chomp() Syntax

1. Type the following code in Komodo 3.0 or an alternative text editor, and save the code as `MatchAlternativeChomp.pl`:

```perl
#!/usr/bin/perl -w
use strict;
print "Enter a string. It will be matched against the pattern '/Star/i'.\n\n";
chomp (my $myTestString = <STDIN>);
if ($myTestString =~ m/Star/i)
{
 print "There is a match for '$myTestString'.";
}
else
{
 print "No match was found in '$myTestString'.";
}
```

2. Run the code inside Komodo or, at the command line, type **perl MatchAlternativeChomp.pl**.

3. Enter the test string **Star Training**, and press the Return key. Inspect the displayed results, as shown in Figure 26-13.

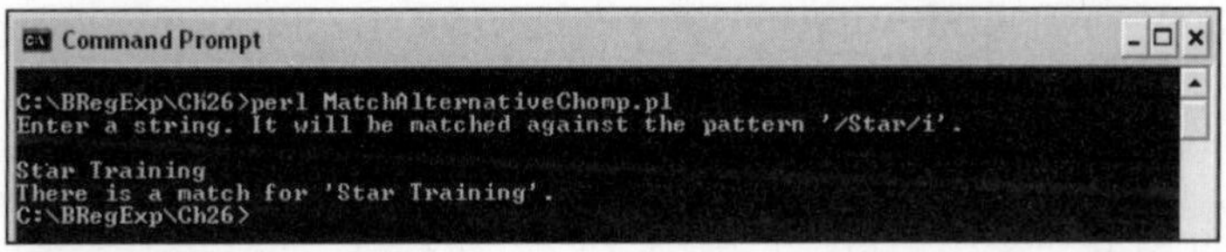

Figure 26-13

How It Works

The line of code:

```perl
chomp (my $myTestString = <STDIN>);
```

is functionally equivalent to:

```perl
my $myTestString = <STDIN>;
chomp ($myTestString);
```

The precedence of the assignment operator, =, means that the assignment happens first; then, when that assignment has taken place, the `chomp()` function is applied.

There are also variants in how the `print` function can be used. It is possible to use the `print` operator conditionally in the following way. The following code is included in the file `MatchAlternativeChomp2.pl` in the code download:

```
print "Enter a string. It will be matched against the pattern '/Star/i'.\n\n";
chomp (my $myTestString = <STDIN>);
```

The `if` statement is included in the same line as the `print` operator after the string to be printed:

```
print "There is a match for '$myTestString'." if ($myTestString =~ m/Star/i);
```

The `!~` operator in the test for the if statement means "There is not a match":

```
print "There is no match for '$myTestString'." if ($myTestString !~ m/Star/i);
```

It isn't necessary to express the pattern to match against as a string. You have the option to match against a variable. Matching against a variable is useful when you want to match against the same pattern more than once in your code.

Try It Out   Matching Against a Variable

1. Type the following code in your chosen editor, and save the code as `MatchUsingVariable.pl`:

```
#!/usr/bin/perl -w
use strict;
my $myPattern = "^\\d{5}(-\\d{4})?\$";
print "Enter a US Zip Code: ";
my $myTestString = <STDIN>;
chomp ($myTestString);
print "You entered a Zip code.\n\n" if ($myTestString =~ m/$myPattern/);
print "The value you entered wasn't recognized as a US Zip code." if ($myTestString
!~ m/$myPattern/);
```

2. Run the code in Komodo or at the command line. When prompted, enter the test string **12345**, and inspect the displayed result.

3. Run the code again (F3 if you are using the Windows command line). When prompted, enter the test string **12345-6789**, and inspect the displayed result.

4. Run the code again. When prompted, enter the test string **Hello world!** and inspect the result, as shown in Figure 26-14.

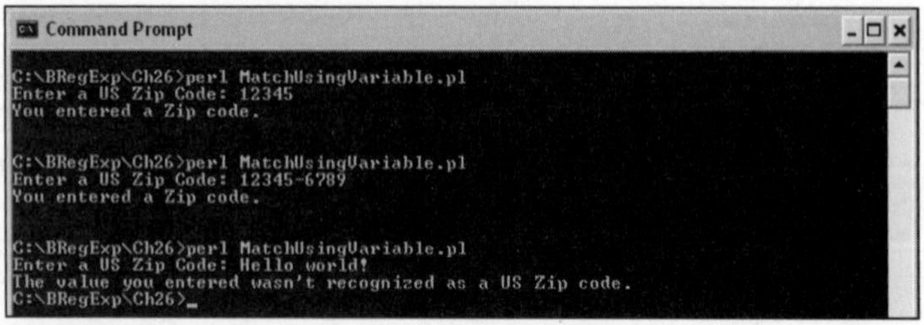

Figure 26-14

How It Works

First, the variable $myPattern is declared and assigned the pattern ^\d{5}(-\d{4})?$. Notice that when you use the \d metacharacter and the $ metacharacter, you must precede them with an extra backslash character.

The pattern uses the positional metacharacters ^ and $ to indicate that the pattern must match all of the test string. The pattern matches either a test string of five numeric digits, as indicated by \d{5}, which is the abbreviated form of a U.S. Zip code, or a sequence of five numeric digits, optionally followed by a hyphen and four numeric digits, as indicated by (-\d{4})?, which matches the extended version of a U.S. Zip code. The -\d{4} is grouped inside paired parentheses, so the ? quantifier indicates that all of -\d{4} is optional:

```
my $myPattern = "^\\d{5}(-\\d{4})?\$";
```

Next, the user is invited to enter a Zip code. The input is captured from the standard input using <STDIN>. And chomp() is used to remove the newline character at the end of $myTestString:

```
print "Enter a US Zip Code: ";
my $myTestString = <STDIN>;
chomp ($myTestString);
```

Then two print statements are used, each with an if statement and corresponding test that determines whether or not anything is displayed. The if statement on the first of the following lines means that the message is output if there is a match. The if statement on the last line causes the text to be displayed if there is no match:

```
print "You entered a Zip code.\n\n" if ($myTestString =~ m/$myPattern/);
print "The value you entered wasn't recognized as a US Zip code." if ($myTestString
!~ m/$myPattern/);
```

Using Other Regular Expression Delimiters

The flexibility of Perl also includes a syntax to specify alternative characters to delimit a regular expression pattern.

The default regular expression delimiters in Perl are paired forward slashes, as in the following:

```
my $myTestString = "Hello world!";
$myTestString =~ /world/;
```

However, Perl allows developers to use other characters as regular expression delimiters, if the m is specified. Personally, I find it easiest to stick with the paired forward slashes almost all the time, but because Perl provides the flexibility to use other characters, it can be confusing interpreting matches or substitutions that use delimiters other than paired forward slashes, if you aren't aware that Perl allows this flexibility.

The following example shows how matched curly braces, paired exclamation marks, and paired period (dot) characters can be used as regular expression delimiters.

Try It Out   Using Nondefault Delimiters

1.   Type the following code into your chosen text editor, and save the code as NonDefaultDelimiters.pl:

```
#!/usr/bin/perl -w
use strict;
print "This example uses delimiters other than the default /somePattern/.\n\n";
my $myTestString = "Hello world!";
print "It worked using paired { and }\n\n" if $myTestString =~ m{world};
print "It worked using paired ! and !\n\n" if $myTestString =~ m!world!;
print "It worked using paired . and .\n\n" if $myTestString =~ m.world.;
```

2.   Run the code inside or Komodo or at the command line by typing **perl NonDefaultDelimiters.pl**.

3.   Inspect the displayed results, as shown in Figure 26-15. Notice that matched { and }, or paired ! and ! or paired period characters, have all worked, in the sense that they have been used to achieve a successful match.

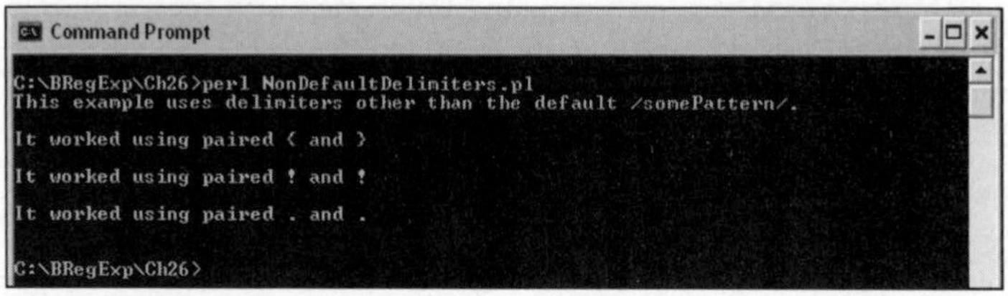

Figure 26-15

How It Works

After a brief informational message, the string Hello world! is assigned to the variable $myTestString:

```
my $myTestString = "Hello world!";
```

Then the print operator is used three times to print out a message indicating matching using specified delimiters, if the test of an if statement has been satisfied, which it has been in this case.

Matching Using Variable Substitution

If you are new to Perl programming, it may have been surprising that you can include variables inside paired double quotes. You may be even more surprised to learn that you can also include variables inside regular expression patterns.

There are two ways variables can be included in patterns, depending on whether or not the variable comes at the end of the pattern.

If the variable comes at the end of the pattern, you can write the following:

```
/some characters$myPattern/
```

However, if you want to use the variable at any other position in the pattern, you need to write something like this:

```
/${myPattern}some other characters/
```

Try It Out   Matching Using Variable Substitution

1. Type the following code in a text editor:

```
#!/usr/bin/perl -w
use strict;
my $myTestString = "shells";
my $myPattern = "she";
print "$myPattern is found in $myTestString.\n\n" if ($myTestString =~
m/${myPattern}ll/);
$myTestString = "scar";
$myPattern = "car";
print "$myPattern is found in $myTestString.\n\n" if ($myTestString =~
m/s$myPattern/);
```

2. Save the code as MatchingVariableSubstitution.pl.

3. Run the code and inspect the results, as shown in Figure 26-16.

Figure 26-16

How It Works

First, look at the variable substitution syntax that can be placed anywhere inside a pattern. You assign values to the $myTestString and $myPattern variables:

```
my $myTestString = "shells";
my $myPattern = "she";
```

The following line is split only for reasons of presentation on page. Notice the syntax used in the pattern in the test for the if statement. The $myPattern variable is used inside the pattern and is written as ${myPattern}. The paired curly braces allow the name of the pattern to be unambiguously delineated:

```
print "$myPattern is found in $myTestString.\n\n" if ($myTestString =~
m/${myPattern}ll/);
```

The second part of this example uses the syntax that can be used only at the end of the pattern. The $myPattern variable is written exactly like that: $myPattern. Because the only use of the second of the paired forward slashes is to delimit the end of the pattern, the meaning is clear:

```
$myTestString = "scar";
$myPattern = "car";
print "$myPattern is found in $myTestString.\n\n" if ($myTestString =~
m/s$myPattern/);
```

As you have seen in this section on matching, there is enormous flexibility in the syntax you can use to achieve matching in Perl.

Using the s/// Operator

The s/// operator is used when a match in the test string is to be replaced by (or substituted with) a replacement string. Search-and-replace syntax takes the following general form:

```
s/pattern/replacmentText/modifiers
```

If there is a match, s/// returns the numeric value corresponding to the number of successful matches. The number of matches attempted depends on whether or not the s/// operator is modified by the g (global) modifier. If the g modifier is present, the regular expression engine attempts to find all matches in the test string.

In the following example, the literal pattern Star is replaced by the replacement (substitution) string Moon.

Try It Out   **Using the s/// Operator**

1. Type the following code in Komodo or another text editor:

```
#!/usr/bin/perl -w
use strict;
my $myString = "I attended a Star Training Company training course.";
my $oldString = $myString;
$myString =~ s/Star/Moon/;
print "The original string was: \n'$oldString'\n\n";
print "After replacement the string is: \n'$myString'\n\n";
if ($oldString =~ m/Star/)
{
print "The string 'Star' was matched and replaced in the old string";
}
```

2. Save the code as SimpleReplace.pl.

3. Either run the code inside Komodo 3.0 or type **perl SimpleReplace.pl** at the command line, assuming that the file is saved in the current directory or a directory on your machine's PATH. Inspect the displayed results, as shown in Figure 26-17.

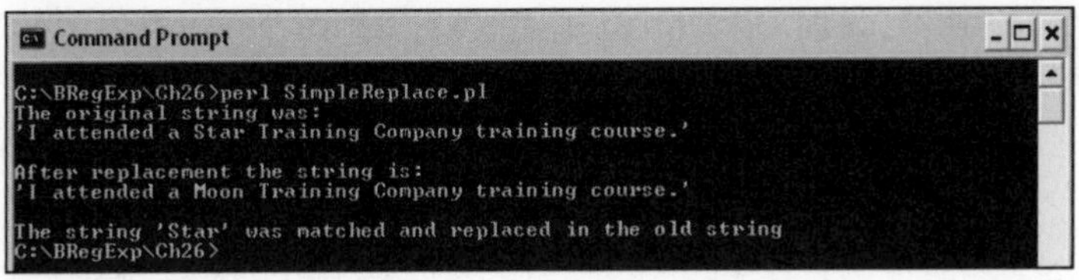

Figure 26-17

How It Works

The test string is assigned to the variable $myString:

```
my $myString = "I attended a Star Training Company training course.";
```

The variable $oldString is used to hold the original value for later display:

```
my $oldString = $myString;
```

The first occurrence of the character sequence Star in the test string is replaced by the character sequence Moon:

```
$myString =~ s/Star/Moon/;
```

The user is informed of the original and replaced strings:

```
print "The original string was: \n'$oldString'\n\n";
print "After replacement the string is: \n'$myString'\n\n";
if ($oldString =~ m/Star/)
{
print "The string 'Star' was matched and replaced in the old string";
}
```

Using s/// with the Global Modifier

Often, you will want to replace all occurrences of a character sequence in the test string. The example of the Star Training Company earlier in this book is a case in point. To specify that all occurrences of a pattern are replaced, the global modifier, g, is used.

To achieve global replacement, you write the following:

```
$myTestString =~ s/pattern/replacementString/g
```

The g modifier after the third forward slash indicates that global replacement is to take place.

Try It Out   **Using s/// with the Global Modifier**

   1.   Type the following code in a text editor:

```
#!/usr/bin/perl -w
use strict;
```

```
print "This example uses the global modifier, 'g'\n\n";
my $myTestString = "Star Training Company courses are great. Choose Star for your
training needs.";
my $myOnceString = $myTestString;
my $myGlobalString = $myTestString;
my $myPattern = "Star";
my $myReplacementString = "Moon";
$myOnceString =~ s/$myPattern/$myReplacementString/;
$myGlobalString =~ s/$myPattern/$myReplacementString/g;
print "The original string was '$myTestString'.\n\n";
print "After a single replacement it became '$myOnceString'.\n\n";
print "After global replacement it became '$myGlobalString'.\n\n";
```

2. Save the code as `GlobalReplace.pl`.

3. Run the code and inspect the results, as shown in Figure 26-18. Notice that without the g modifier, only one occurrence of the character sequence `Star` has been replaced. With the g modifier present, all occurrences (in this case, there are two) are replaced.

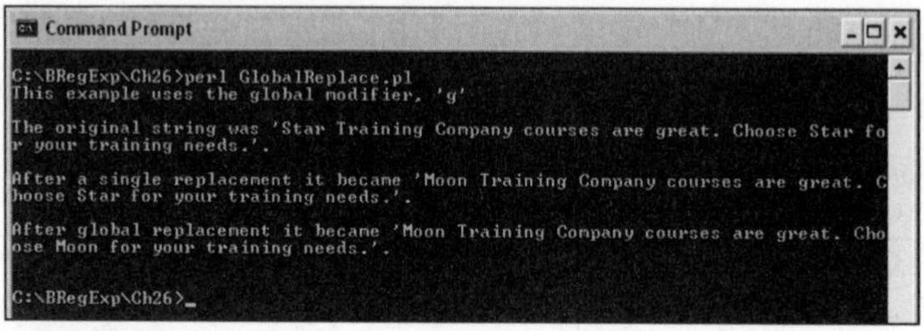

Figure 26-18

How It Works

The test string is assigned to the variable $myTestString:

```
my $myTestString = "Star Training Company courses are great. Choose Star for your
training needs.";
```

The value of the original test string is copied to the variables $myOnceString and $myGlobalString:

```
my $myOnceString = $myTestString;
my $myGlobalString = $myTestString;
```

The pattern `Star` is assigned to the variable $myPattern:

```
my $myPattern = "Star";
```

The replacement string, Moon, is assigned to the variable $myReplacementString:

```
my $myReplacementString = "Moon";
```

One match is replaced in $myOnceString:

```
$myOnceString =~ s/$myPattern/$myReplacementString/;
```

All matches (two, in this example) are replaced in $myGlobalString, because the g modifier is specified:

```
$myGlobalString =~ s/$myPattern/$myReplacementString/g;
```

Then the original string, the string after a single replacement, and the string after global replacement are displayed:

```
print "The original string was '$myTestString'.\n\n";
print "After a single replacement it became '$myOnceString'.\n\n";
print "After global replacement it became '$myGlobalString'.\n\n";
```

Using s/// with the Default Variable

The default variable, $_, can be used with s/// to search and replace the value held in the default variable.

Two forms of syntax can be used. You can use the normal s/// syntax, with the variable name, the =~ operator and the pattern and replacement text:

```
$_ =~ s/pattern/replacementText/modifiers;
```

The alternative, more succinct, syntax allows the name of the default variable and =~ operator to be omitted. So you can simply write the following:

```
s/pattern/replacementText/modifiers
```

Try It Out   Using s/// with the Default Variable

1.   Type the following code in a text editor:

```
#!/usr/bin/perl -w
use strict;
$_ = "I went to a training course from Star Training Company.";
print "The default string, \$_, contains '$_'.\n\n";
if (s/Star/Moon/)
{
  print "A replacement has taken place using the default variable.\n";
  print "The replaced string in \$_ is now '$_'.";
}
```

2.   Save the code as ReplaceDefaultVariable.pl.

3.   Run the code, and inspect the displayed result, as shown in Figure 26-19.

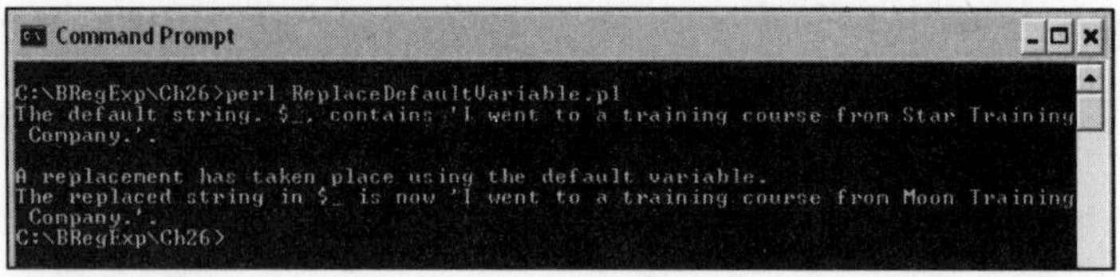

Figure 26-19

How It Works

The test string is assigned to the default variable, $_:

```
$_ = "I went to a training course from Star Training Company.";
```

The value contained in the default variable is displayed:

```
print "The default string, \$_, contains '$_'.\n\n";
```

The test of the `if` statement uses the abbreviated syntax for carrying out a replacement on the default variable:

```
if (s/Star/Moon/)
```

You might prefer to use the full syntax:

```
if ($_ =~ s/Star/Moon/)
```

Whichever syntax you use, the user is then informed that a replacement operation has taken place and is informed of the value of the string after the replacement operation:

```
print "A replacement has taken place using the default variable.\n";
 print "The replaced string in \$_ is now '$_'.";
```

Using the split Operator

The `split` operator is used to split a test string according to the match for a regular expression.

The following example shows how you can separate a comma-separated sequence of values into its component parts.

Try It Out   Using the split Operator

1. Type the following code into a text editor:

```
#!/usr/bin/perl -w
use strict;
my $myTestString = "A, B, C, D";
print "The original string was '$myTestString'.\n";
my @myArray = split/,\s?/, $myTestString;
```

```
print "The string has been split into four array elements:\n";
print "$myArray[0]\n";
print "$myArray[1]\n";
print "$myArray[2]\n";
print "$myArray[3]\n";
print "Displaying array elements using the 'foreach' statement:\n";
foreach my $mySplit (split/,\s?/, $myTestString)
{
 print "$mySplit\n";
}
```

2. Save the code as SplitDemo.pl.

3. Run the code, and inspect the displayed results, as shown in Figure 26-20.

Figure 26-20

How It Works

A sequence of values separated by commas and a space character is assigned to the variable $myTestString:

```
my $myTestString = "A, B, C, D";
```

The value of the original string is displayed:

```
print "The original string was '$myTestString'.\n";
```

The @myArray array is assigned the result of using the split operator. The pattern that is matched against is a comma optionally followed by a whitespace character. The target of the split operator is the variable $myTestString:

```
my @myArray = split/,\s?/, $myTestString;
```

Then you can use array indices to display the components into which the string has been split:

```
print "The string has been split into four array elements:\n";
print "$myArray[0]\n";
print "$myArray[1]\n";
print "$myArray[2]\n";
print "$myArray[3]\n";
```

Or, more elegantly, you can use a `foreach` statement to display each result of splitting the `$myTestString` variable:

```
print "Displaying array elements using the 'foreach' statement:\n";
foreach my $mySplit (split/,\s?/, $myTestString)
{
  print "$mySplit\n";
}
```

The Metacharacters Supported in Perl

Perl supports a useful range of metacharacters, as summarized in the following table.

Metacharacter	Description
. (period character)	Matches any character (with the exception, according to mode, of the new-line character).
\w	Matches a character that is alphabetic, numeric, or an underscore character. Sometimes called a "word character." Equivalent to the character class [A-Za-z0-9_].
\W	Matches a character that is not alphabetic, numeric, or an underscore character. Equivalent to the character class [^A-Za-z0-9_] or [^\w].
\s	Matches a whitespace character.
\S	Matches a character that is not a whitespace character.
\d	Matches a character that is a numeric digit. Equivalent to the character class [0-9].
\D	Matches a character that is not a numeric digit. Equivalent to the character class [^0-9].
?	Quantifier. Matches if the preceding character or group occurs zero or one time.
*	Quantifier. Matches if the preceding character or group occurs zero or more times.
+	Quantifier. Matches if the preceding character or group occurs one or more times.
{n,m}	Quantifier. Matches if the preceding character or group occurs a minimum of n times and a maximum of m times.
(...)	Capturing parentheses.
$1 etc	Variables that allow access to captured groups
|	Alternation character.

Metacharacter	Description
\b	Matches a word boundary—in other words, the position between a word character ([A-Za-z0-9_]) and a nonword character.
[...]	Character class. It matches one character of the set of characters inside the square brackets.
[^...]	Negated character class. It matches one character that is not in the set of characters inside the square brackets.
\A	A positional metacharacter that always matches the position before the first character in the test string.
\Z	A positional metacharacter that matches after the final non-newline character on a line or in a string.
\z	A positional metacharacter that always matches the position after the last character in a string, irrespective of mode.
(?= ...)	Positive lookahead.
(?! ...)	Negative lookahead.
(?<= ...)	Positive lookbehind.
(?<! ...)	Negative lookbehind.
\p{charClass}	Matches a character that is in a specified Unicode character class or block.
\P{charClass}	Matches a character that is not in a specified Unicode character class or block.

Using Quantifiers in Perl

Perl supports a fairly typical range of quantifiers.

The ? metacharacter matches the preceding character or group zero or one times. In other words, the preceding character or group is optional. To match bat and bats, you can use the pattern bats?. The ? metacharacter indicates that the s is optional.

The * metacharacter matches the preceding character or group zero or more times. In other words, the character or group can occur zero times or any number of times greater than zero. The pattern AB* will match the following character sequences, A, AB, ABB, ABBB, and so on.

The + metacharacter matches the preceding character or group one or more times. In other words, the character or group must occur at least one time but can occur any number of times greater than one. The pattern AB+ will match the character sequences AB, ABB, ABBB, and so on. But it will not match A, because there must be at least one B character for matching to succeed.

To match any of the ?, *, or + metacharacters, simply add a backslash character before the quantifier. So you would write \?, *, and \+, respectively.

The quantifier syntax, which uses curly braces, is also available. The pattern [A-Z]\d{3} will match if there are exactly three numeric digits following an uppercase alphabetic character. The pattern [A-Z]\d{1,3} will match between one and three digits following an uppercase alphabetic character. So it will match A1, A12, and A123.

The pattern [A-Z]\d{2,} will match an uppercase alphabetic character followed by two or more numeric digits. So it will match A12, A123, A1234, A12345, and so on. But it will not match A1, because there must be at least two numeric digits for a successful match.

Using Positional Metacharacters

Perl supports both the ^ and $ positional metacharacters. The ^ metacharacter matches the position immediately before the first character of a line or string. The $ metacharacter matches the position immediately after the last non-newline character of a line or string.

The \A positional metacharacter matches the position immediately before the start of a string.

The \z positional metacharacter matches the position immediately after the last character of a string.

Try It Out   **Using Positional Metacharacters**

1. Type the following code into your chosen text editor:

```
#!/usr/bin/perl -w
use strict;
print "\nThis example demonstrates the use of the ^ and \$ positional
metacharacters.\n\n";
my $myPattern = "cape";
my $myTestString = "escape";
print "In '$myTestString' there is a match for the pattern '$myPattern'.\n\n" if
($myTestString =~ m/$myPattern/);

$myPattern = "^cape";
print "When the pattern is '$myPattern' there is no match for '$myTestString'.\n\n"
if ($myTestString !~ m/$myPattern/);
$myPattern = "cape\$";
print "But there is a match for '$myTestString' when the pattern is
'$myPattern'.\n\n" if ($myTestString =~ m/$myPattern/);
```

2. Save the code as PositionalMetacharacters.pl.

3. Run the code, and inspect the displayed results, as shown in Figure 26-21.

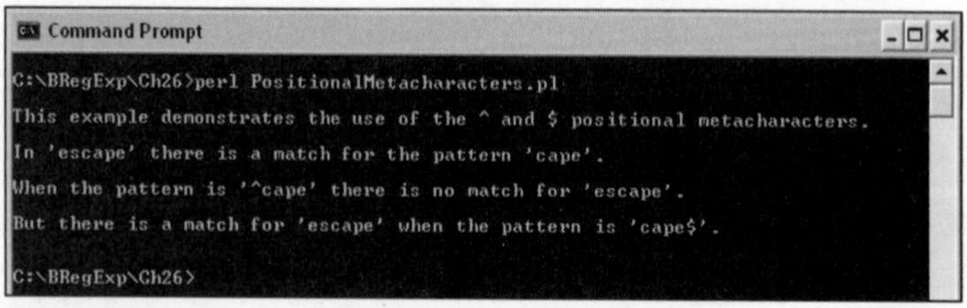

Figure 26-21

How It Works

First, a simple informational message is displayed to the user:

```
print "\nThis example demonstrates the use of the ^ and \$ positional
metacharacters.\n\n";
```

Then the first pattern to be used is defined. It is a simple character sequence without any positional metacharacters:

```
my $myPattern = "cape";
```

The test string is defined:

```
my $myTestString = "escape";
```

Then matching takes place. The `if` statement ensures that a message is displayed only when there is a successful match:

```
print "In '$myTestString' there is a match for the pattern '$myPattern'.\n\n" if
($myTestString =~ m/$myPattern/);
```

The pattern is modified so that it includes a ^ positional metacharacter. It will now match only when the character sequence has cape as its first four characters:

```
$myPattern = "^cape";
```

So a message is displayed indicating that matching failed:

```
print "When the pattern is '$myPattern' there is no match for '$myTestString'.\n\n"
if ($myTestString !~ m/$myPattern/);
```

The pattern is changed again. Now it will match only if cape appears as the last four characters of the test string:

```
$myPattern = "cape\$";
```

There is a match when matching against escape, so a message indicating a successful match is displayed:

```
print "But there is a match for '$myTestString' when the pattern is
'$myPattern'.\n\n" if ($myTestString =~ m/$myPattern/);
```

Captured Groups in Perl

In Perl, captured groups are specified using paired parentheses. The first captured group is produced by the paired parentheses with the leftmost opening parenthesis. Additional captured groups are added for each pair of parentheses, with the numbering corresponding to the order of the opening parenthesis of a pair.

Captured groups can be accessed from outside the regular expression using the numbered variables $1, $2, and so on.

In Perl, the whole match is available in the $& variable.

1. Type the following code in your chosen text editor:

```perl
#!/usr/bin/perl -w
use strict;
my $myPattern = "([A-Z])(\\d)";
my $myTestString = "B99";
$myTestString =~ m/$myPattern/;
print "The pattern is '$myPattern'.\n";
print "The test string is '$myTestString'.\n";
print "The whole match is '$&', contained in the \$& variable.\n";
print "The first captured group is '$1', contained in '\$1'.\n";
print "The second captured group is '$2', contained in '\$2'\n";
```

2. Save the code as CapturedGroupsDemo.pl.

3. Run the code, and inspect the displayed results, as shown in Figure 26-22. Notice that the whole match for the pattern (([A-Z])(\d)) is retrieved using the $1 variable.

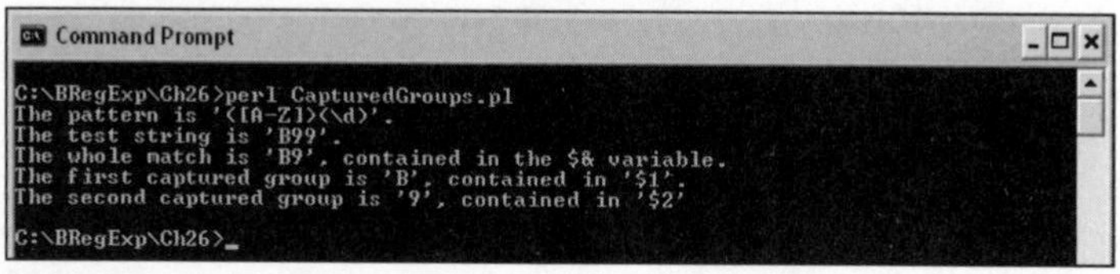

```
Command Prompt                                              _ □ x

C:\BRegExp\Ch26>perl CapturedGroups.pl
The pattern is '([A-Z])(\d)'.
The test string is 'B99'.
The whole match is 'B9', contained in the $& variable.
The first captured group is 'B', contained in '$1'.
The second captured group is '9', contained in '$2'

C:\BRegExp\Ch26>_
```

Figure 26-22

How It Works

The pattern to be matched against is assigned to the $myPattern variable:

```perl
my $myPattern = "([A-Z])(\\d)";
```

The test string is assigned to the $myTestString variable:

```perl
my $myTestString = "B99";
```

The $myTestString variable is matched against the $myPattern variable:

```perl
$myTestString =~ m/$myPattern/;
```

The values of the test string and pattern are displayed to the user:

```perl
print "The pattern is '$myPattern'.\n";
print "The test string is '$myTestString'.\n";
```

The $& variable is used to display the whole match, in this case, the character sequence B9:

```
print "The whole match is '$&', contained in the \$& variable.\n";
```

The group captured by the first pair of parentheses matches the character class [A-Z]. In this case, the variable $1 holds the single character B:

```
print "The first captured group is '$1', contained in '\$1'.\n";
```

The group captured by the second pair of parentheses matches against the metacharacter \d. In this case the variable $2 holds the value 9:

```
print "The second captured group is '$2', contained in '\$2'\n";
```

Using Back References in Perl

Perl supports the use of back references, which are references to captured groups that can be used from inside the regular expression pattern.

A classic example of the use of back references is in the identification and correction of doubled words in text. The following example illustrates the use of back references for that purpose.

Try It Out   Using Back References to Detect Doubled Words

1. Type the following code into a text editor:

```
#!/usr/bin/perl -w
use strict;
my $myPattern = "(\\w+)(\\s+\\1\\b)";
my $myTestString = "Paris in the the Spring Spring.";
print "The original string was '$myTestString'.\n";
$myTestString =~ s/$myPattern/$1/g;
print "The captured group was: '$1'.\n";
print "Any doubled word has now been removed.\n";
print "The string is now '$myTestString'.\n";
```

2. Save the code as DoubledWord.pl.

3. Run the code, and inspect the displayed result, as shown in Figure 26-23. Notice in the original test string that two words were doubled: the and Spring. In the replacement string, both doubled words have been removed.

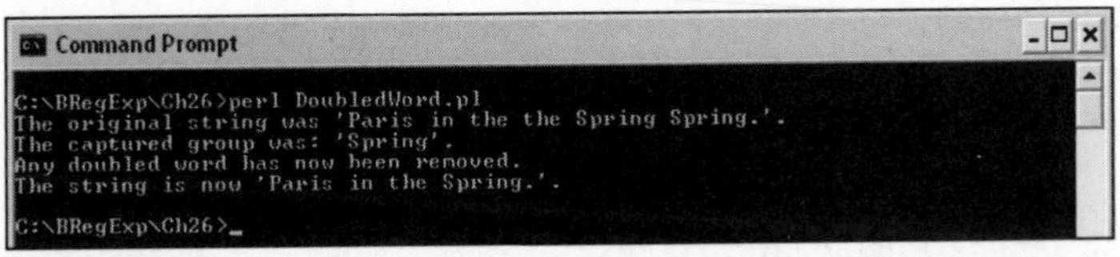

Figure 26-23

How It Works

The pattern is assigned to the variable $myPattern. The metacharacters \w, \s, and \b have to be written with an extra backslash.

Note that the back reference \1 must also be written with an extra backslash:

```
my $myPattern = "(\\w+)(\\s+\\1\\b)";
```

The test string Paris in the the Spring Spring. has two pairs of doubled words:

```
my $myTestString = "Paris in the the Spring Spring.";
```

The original string containing the doubled words is displayed to the user:

```
print "The original string was '$myTestString'.\n";
```

The back reference $1 is used with the s/// operator.

In the pattern, the component (\w+) captures the first word in $1. The remainder of the match is in $2, which is discarded.

The g modifier means that all occurrences of doubled words will be replaced:

```
$myTestString =~ s/$myPattern/$1/g;
```

Information about the first captured group, the effect of the replacement, and the result of the replacement is displayed to the user:

```
print "The captured group was: '$1'.\n";
print "Any doubled word has now been removed.\n";
print "The string is now '$myTestString'.\n";
```

Using Alternation

Alternation allows specific options to be matched. The pipe character, |, is used to express alternation.

Try It Out   Using Alternation

1.   Type the following code into a text editor, and save it as Alternation.pl:

```
#!/usr/bin/perl -w
use strict;
my $myPattern = "(Jim|Fred|Alice)";
print "Enter your first name here: \n";
my $myTestString = <STDIN>;
chomp($myTestString);
if ($myTestString =~ m/$myPattern/)
{
  print "Hello $&. How are you?";
}
else
```

```
    {
        print "I am sorry, $myTestString. I don't know you.";
    }
```

2. Run the code, enter the name **Alice**, and inspect the displayed results.

3. Run the code again; enter the name **Andrew**; and inspect the displayed results, as shown in Figure 26-24.

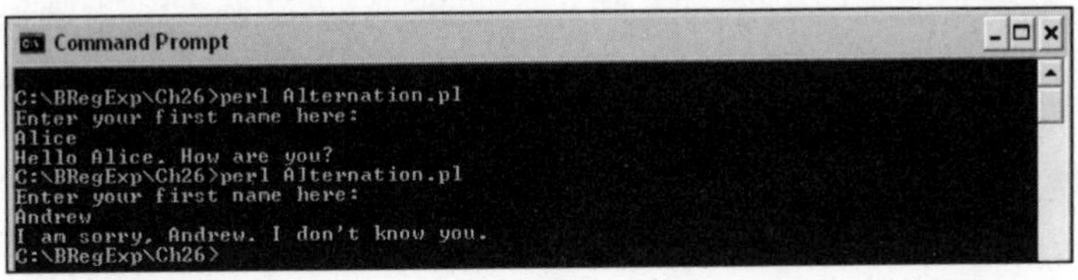

Figure 26-24

How It Works

The $myPattern variable is assigned a pattern that uses the pipe character to specify three literal patterns as options:

```
    my $myPattern = "(Jim|Fred|Alice)";
```

The user is asked to enter his or her first name:

```
    print "Enter your first name here: \n";
```

A line of characters from the standard input is assigned to the $myTestString variable:

```
    my $myTestString = <STDIN>;
```

The chomp() operator is used to remove the newline character at the end of $myTestString:

```
    chomp($myTestString);
```

If the name entered by the user is one of the three specified options, a message greeting the user is displayed:

```
    if ($myTestString =~ m/$myPattern/)
    {
      print "Hello $&. How are you?";
    }
```

However, if the name entered is not one of the three permitted options, the user is told that he or she is not known:

```
    else
    {
      print "I am sorry, $myTestString. I don't know you.";
    }
```

Using Character Classes in Perl

Perl supports an extensive range of character class functionality. If you want to specify individual characters to be matched, you simply list those inside a character class.

Metacharacters inside character classes are different from metacharacters outside them. Outside a character class, the ^ metacharacter matches a position before the first character of a string or line (depending on settings). Inside a character class, the ^ metacharacter, when it is the first character after the left square bracket, indicates a negated character class. All the characters after the ^ are characters that do not match.

Try It Out   Using a Character Class

1. Type the following code in a text editor, and save it as `CharacterClass.pl`:

```
#!/usr/bin/perl -w
use strict;
print "Enter a character class to be used as a pattern: ";
my $myPattern = <STDIN>;
print "\n\nEnter a string to test against the character class: ";
my $myTestString = <STDIN>;
chomp ($myPattern);
chomp ($myTestString);
print "\n\nThe string you entered was: '$myTestString'.\n";
print "The pattern you entered was: '$myPattern'.\n";
if ($myTestString =~ m/$myPattern/)
{
 print "There was a match: '$&'.\n";
}
else
{
 print "There was no match.";
}
```

2. Run the code.

3. Enter the pattern **[A-Z][a-z]***.

4. Enter the test string **Hello world!**, and inspect the displayed results.

5. Run the code again.

6. Enter the pattern **[A-E][a-z]***.

7. Enter the test string **Hello Ethel. How are you?**, and inspect the displayed results, as shown in Figure 26-25.

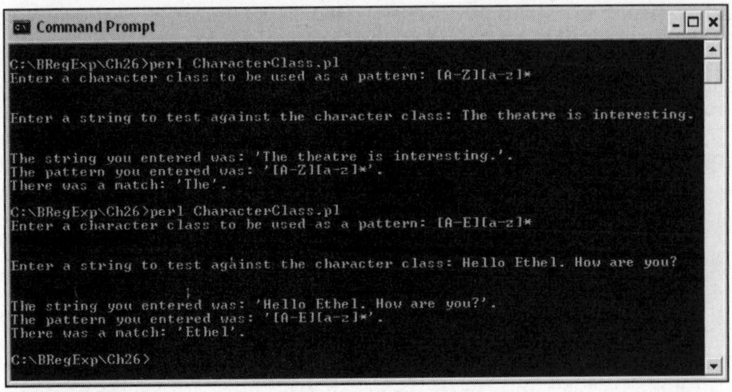

Figure 26-25

How It Works

The user is invited to enter a pattern to be matched against:

```
print "Enter a character class to be used as a pattern: ";
```

A line of characters from the standard input is assigned to the $myPattern variable:

```
my $myPattern = <STDIN>;
```

The user is then invited to enter a test string. The test string is captured from the standard input and is assigned to the $myTestString variable:

```
print "\n\nEnter a string to test against the character class: ";
my $myTestString = <STDIN>;
```

Then the chomp() operator is used to remove the terminal newline character from $myPattern and from $myTestString:

```
chomp ($myPattern);
chomp ($myTestString);
```

The pattern and test string are displayed to ensure that the user is aware of both. The user should identify any typos from that information:

```
print "\n\nThe string you entered was: '$myTestString'.\n";
print "The pattern you entered was: '$myPattern'.\n";
```

An if statement uses a matching process to determine whether a message about success or failure of matching has occurred:

```
if ($myTestString =~ m/$myPattern/)
{
```

If the match is successful, the content of the match, which is contained in the `$&` variable, is displayed:

```
    print "There was a match: '$&'.\n";
    }
```

If matching is unsuccessful, the statement specified by the `else` clause is executed:

```
    else
    {
    print "There was no match.";
    }
```

When the pattern is `[A-Z][a-z]*`, it matches an uppercase alphabetic character followed by zero or more lowercase alphabetic characters. In the test string `Hello world!`, the first matching character sequence is `Hello`. Matching is greedy, in that it matches as many characters as possible.

When the pattern is `[A-E][a-z]*`, the initial uppercase alphabetic character must be in the range `A` through `E`. Therefore, the `H` of `Hello` does not match. However, the `E` of `Ethel` does match against `[A-E]`. The `E` is followed by lowercase alphabetic characters, so the entire match is `Ethel`, as shown in Figure 26-25.

Negated character classes specify that a character class matches a character that is not one of those contained between the square brackets. The `^` metacharacter specifies that it is a negated character class if it is the first character after the opening square bracket.

Try It Out   Using a Negated Character Class

1. Type the following code in a text editor:

```perl
#!/usr/bin/perl -w
use strict;
my $myPattern = "[^A-D]\\d{2}";
my $myTestString = "A99 B23 C34 D45 E55";
print "The test string is: '$myTestString'.\n";
print "The pattern is: '$myPattern'.\n";
if ($myTestString =~ m/$myPattern/)
{
 print "There was a match: '$&'.\n";
}
else
{
 print "There was no match.";
}
```

2. Save the code as `NegatedCharacterClass.pl`.

3. Run the code, and inspect the displayed results, as shown in Figure 26-26.

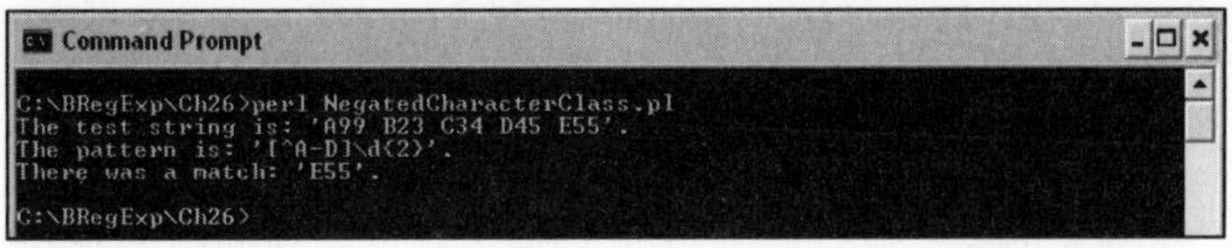

Figure 26-26

How It Works

The pattern assigned to the $myPattern variable is [^A-D]\d{2}. Remember, it is necessary to double the backslash to ensure that the \d metacharacter is correctly recognized. The pattern [^A-D]\d{2} matches a character that is not A through D, followed by two numeric digits:

```
my $myPattern = "[^A-D]\\d{2}";
```

The test string is assigned to the $myTestString variable. Notice that the first four character sequences include an uppercase alphabetic character in the range A through D, which the negated character class will not match:

```
my $myTestString = "A99 B23 C34 D45 E55";
```

The test string and pattern are displayed:

```
print "The test string is: '$myTestString'.\n";
print "The pattern is: '$myPattern'.\n";
```

The if statement uses a test that determines whether or not there is a match:

```
if ($myTestString =~ m/$myPattern/)
```

Because the negated character class [^A-D] won't match an uppercase character A through D, the first match is E55. That value is, therefore, displayed using the $& variable:

```
print "There was a match: '$&'.\n";
```

You saw earlier in this chapter how variable substitution can be used in other settings. Variable substitution can also be used in character classes.

Try It Out   **Using Variable Substitution in a Character Class**

1.   Type the following code in a text editor:

```
#!/usr/bin/perl -w
use strict;
my $toBeSubstituted = "A-D";
my $myPattern = "[$toBeSubstituted]\\d{2}";
my $myTestString = "A99 B23 C34 D45 E55";
print "The test string is: '$myTestString'.\n";
print "The pattern is: '$myPattern'.\n";
if ($myTestString =~ m/$myPattern/)
```

```
{
 print "There was a match: '$&'.\n";
}
else
{
 print "There was no match.";
}
```

2. Save the code as `VariableSubstitutionCharClass.pl`.

3. Run the code, and inspect the displayed result, as shown in Figure 26-27. Notice that the match is `A99`.

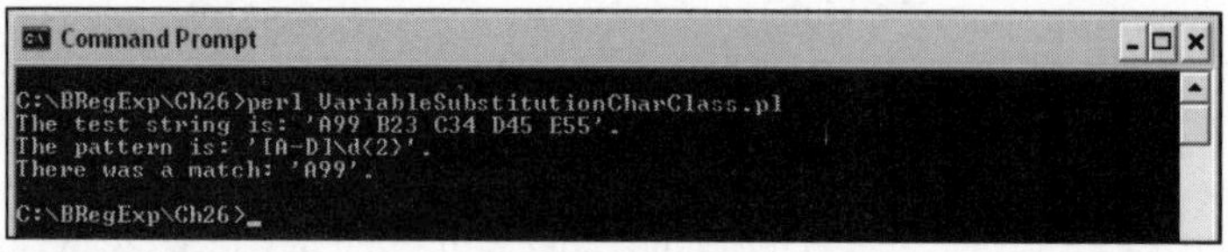

```
C:\BRegExp\Ch26>perl VariableSubstitutionCharClass.pl
The test string is: 'A99 B23 C34 D45 E55'.
The pattern is: '[A-D]\d{2}'.
There was a match: 'A99'.

C:\BRegExp\Ch26>_
```

Figure 26-27

How It Works

This example is similar to `NegatedCharacterClass.pl`. However, the value for the character class is supplied by variable substitution using the `$toBeSubstituted` variable. First, a value that would be interpretable between square brackets is assigned to the `$toBeSubstituted` variable:

```
my $toBeSubstituted = "A-D";
```

Then the value assigned to the `$myPattern` variable uses the `$toBeSubstituted` variable to specify the character class at the beginning of the pattern:

```
my $myPattern = "[$toBeSubstituted]\\d{2}";
```

The remainder of the example follows the code used in `NegatedCharacterClass.pl`. Because the operative character class is `[A-D]`, the value `A99` matches the pattern `[A-D]\d{2}`.

Using Lookahead

Lookahead tests the character sequence that follows some other part of a pattern. Both positive lookahead and negative lookahead are supported in Perl.

The positive lookahead syntax, `(?= ... )`, is used to specify what is being looked for after the other component of the regular expression pattern matches. The character(s) inside the lookahead are not captured.

The negative lookahead syntax, `(?! ...)`, is used to specify what must not come after another component if the regular expression pattern is matched.

Try It Out **Using Positive Lookahead**

1. Type the following code in a text editor, and save it as `Lookahead.pl`:

```perl
#!/usr/bin/perl -w
use strict;
print "Enter a test string here: ";
my $myTestString = <STDIN>;
chomp($myTestString);
if ($myTestString =~ m/Star(?= Training)/)
{
 print "There was a match which was '$&'.";
}
else
{
 print "There was no match.";
}
```

2. Run the code. Enter **I work for Star.** as the test text, and press Return. Inspect the result.

3. Run the code again. Enter **I work for Star Training.** as the test text, and press Return. Inspect the result, as shown in Figure 26-28. Notice that with test text of I work for Star. there is no match, but when the test text is I work for Star Training. there is a match, which is the character sequence Star.

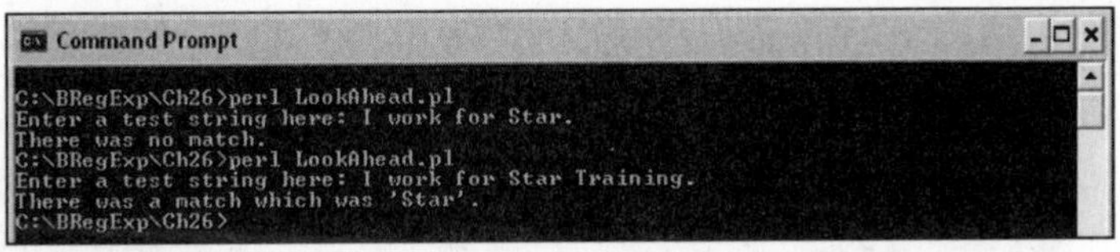

Figure 26-28

How It Works

The user enters a test string that is assigned to the variable $myTestString:

```perl
print "Enter a test string here: ";
my $myTestString = <STDIN>;
```

The chomp() operator removes the terminal newline character:

```perl
chomp($myTestString);
```

The if statement tests whether the value of $myTestString matches the pattern Star(?= Training):

```perl
if ($myTestString =~ m/Star(?= Training)/)
```

If the character sequence Star is matched (which it is in this example), the lookahead, (?= Training), tests whether Star is followed by a space character followed by the character sequence Training. Because it is, there is a match.

The following example shows how negative lookahead can be used.

Try It Out   **Using Negative Lookahead**

1. Type the following code in a text editor, and save it as `NegativeLookahead.pl`:

```perl
#!/usr/bin/perl -w
use strict;
print "Enter a test string here: ";
my $myTestString = <STDIN>;
chomp($myTestString);
if ($myTestString =~ m/Star(?! Training)/)
{
 print "There was a match which was '$&'.";
}
else
{
 print "There was no match.";
}
```

2. Run the code. Enter **I work for Star.** as the test text, and press Return. Inspect the result.

3. Run the code again. Enter **I work for Star Training.** as the test text, and press Return. Inspect the result, as shown in Figure 26-29. Notice that now the first test string matches and the second test string doesn't. This is so because, not surprisingly, negative lookahead produces the opposite result to positive lookahead.

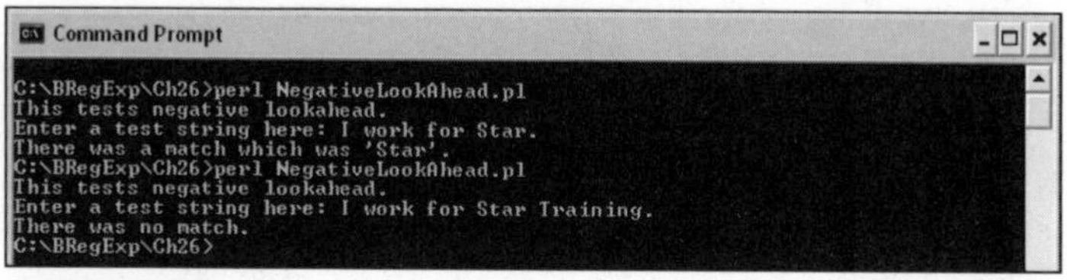

Figure 26-29

How It Works

The key change in the code is you now use a negative lookahead:

```perl
if ($myTestString =~ m/Star(?! Training)/)
```

When the test string is `I work for Star.` there is a match, because the character sequence `Star` is not followed by a space character and the character sequence `Training`. However, when the test string is `I work for Star Training.` there is no match, because the forbidden lookahead occurs.

Using Lookbehind

Lookbehind works similarly to lookahead, except that a character sequence that precedes another component of the regular expression pattern is the focus of interest.

Positive lookbehind is signified by the syntax `(?<= ...)`. Negative lookbehind is signified by `(?<!...)`.

Try It Out   **Using Lookbehind**

1. Type the following code in a text editor, and save it as `LookBehind.pl`:

```perl
#!/usr/bin/perl -w
use strict;
print "This tests positive lookbehind.\n";
print "Enter a test string here: ";
my $myTestString = <STDIN>;
chomp($myTestString);
if ($myTestString =~ m/(?<=Star )Training/)
{
 print "There was a match which was '$&'.";
}
else
{
 print "There was no match.";
}
```

2. Run the code. Enter the test string **Training is great!**, and press the Return key. Inspect the displayed result.

3. Run the code again. Enter the test string **Star Training is great!**, and press the Return key. Inspect the displayed result, as shown in Figure 26-30. Notice that the character sequence `Training` is matched only when the character sequence `Star` followed by a space character comes before `Training`, as specified by the positive lookbehind.

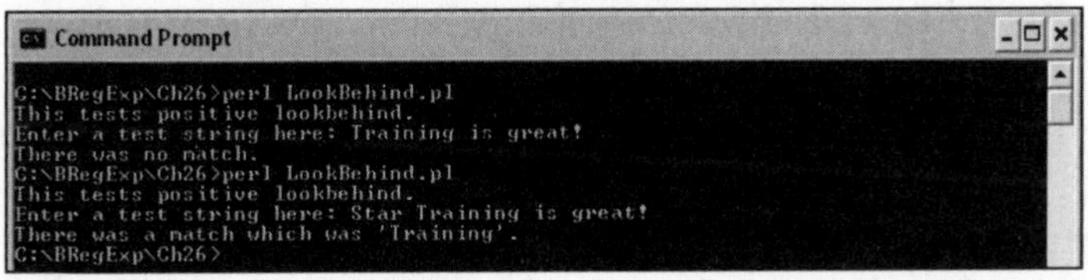

Figure 26-30

How It Works

The key change is in the pattern to be matched. Notice that the pattern's lookbehind component, `(?<=Star )`, comes before the character sequence `Training`:

```perl
if ($myTestString =~ m/(?<=Star )Training/)
```

When the test string is `Star Training is great!` there is a match, because the necessary character sequence (`Star` followed by a space character) precedes the character sequence `Training`.

Using the Regular Expression Matching Modes in Perl

The regular expression matching modes allow developers to control useful aspects of how regular expression patterns are applied.

The following table summarizes the regular expression matching modes in Perl.

Mode	Description
i	Matching is case insensitive.
x	Allows whitespace to be ignored.
g	Matching is global.
m	Matching treats the test text as multiple lines.
s	Matching treats the test text as a single line.

You have seen earlier in this chapter examples of using the i (case-insensitive matching) and g (global matching) modifiers. The following example illustrates the use of the x modifier to assist in documentation of complex regular expression patterns.

Try It Out   **Using the x Modifier**

1.   Type the following code in a text editor, and save it as xModifier.pl:

```perl
#!/usr/bin/perl -w
use strict;
print "This matches a US Zip code.\n";
print "Enter a test string here: ";
my $myTestString = <STDIN>;
chomp($myTestString);
if ($myTestString =~
    m/\d{5} # Match five numeric digits
    (-\d{4})? # Optionally match a hyphen followed by four numeric digits
    /x)
{
 print "There was a match which was '$&'.";
}
else
{
 print "There was no match.";
}
```

2.   Run the code. Enter **12345** as a test string, and press the Return key. Inspect the displayed result.

3.   Run the code again. Enter **12345-6789** as a test string, and press the Return key. Inspect the displayed result, as shown in Figure 26-31.

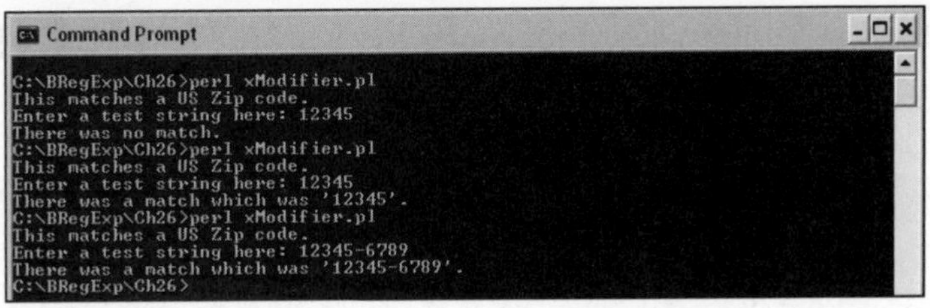

Figure 26-31

How It Works

The key part of xModifier.pl is how the content of the m// operator is laid out in the code. Notice in the last of the following lines that the x modifier is specified. That means unescaped whitespace inside the paired forward slashes of m// is ignored. Also, any characters from # to the end of a line are treated as comments.

This allows the pattern to be spread over several lines, and on each line, a comment can be added that explains the purpose of the component of the regular expression pattern on that line:

```
if ($myTestString =~
    m/\d{5} # Match five numeric digits
    (-\d{4})? # Optionally match a hyphen followed by four numeric digits
    /x)
```

Escaping Metacharacters

When you want to literally match characters that are used as metacharacters, you must escape the metacharacter using a preceding backslash character.

The following table summarizes the escaping needed for commonly used metacharacters, assuming that paired forward slashes are used to delimit a regular expression pattern.

Escaped Metacharacter	Unescaped Metacharacter
\/ (backslash followed by a forward slash)	/ (forward slash)
\?	?
*	*
\+	+

In Perl, because you can specify the delimiters for a regular expression pattern, the use of escaping can vary depending on what delimiter you have specified, as you will see in the next example.

Try It Out	Using Escaped Metacharacters

1. Type the following code in your chosen text editor:

```perl
#!/usr/bin/perl -w
use strict;
my $myTestString = "http://www.w3.org/";
print "The test string is '$myTestString'.\n";
print "There is a match.\n\n" if ($myTestString =~ m/http:\/\/.*/);
print "The test string hasn't changed but the pattern has.\n";
print "Also the delimiter character is now paired '!' characters.\n";
print "There is a match.\n\n" if ($myTestString =~ m!http://!);
print "The test string hasn't changed and the pattern is the original one.\n";
print "Also the delimiter character is still paired '!' characters.\n";
print "There is a match.\n\n" if ($myTestString =~ m!http:\/\/!);
```

2. Save the code as EscapedMetacharacters.pl.

3. Run the code, and inspect the results, as shown in Figure 26-32.

Figure 26-32

How It Works

The first line assigns a URL (for the World Wide Web Consortium) to the $myTestString variable. Notice that the URL contains forward slash characters, as many URLs do:

```perl
my $myTestString = "http://www.w3.org/";
```

The test string is output for the user's information:

```perl
print "The test string is '$myTestString'.\n";
```

If there is a match in the test string for the specified pattern, a message is displayed. Notice how the pattern is constructed. Each forward-slash character is escaped by a preceding backslash character. If you try to run the code with the pattern http://.* but fail to escape the forward slashes, an error message will be displayed:

```perl
print "There is a match.\n\n" if ($myTestString =~ m/http:\/\/.*/);
print "The test string hasn't changed but the pattern has.\n";
print "Also the delimiter character is now paired '!' characters.\n";
print "There is a match.\n\n" if ($myTestString =~ m!http://!);
print "The test string hasn't changed and the pattern is the original one.\n";
print "Also the delimiter character is still paired '!' characters.\n";
print "There is a match.\n\n" if ($myTestString =~ m!http:\/\/!);
```

A Simple Perl Regex Tester

You have seen a range of techniques used to explore some of the ways Perl regular expressions can be used. You may find it useful to have a simple Perl tool to test regular expressions against test strings. `RegexTester.pl` is intended to provide you with straightforward functionality to do that.

The code for `RegexTester.pl` is shown here (the file is available in the code download):

```perl
#!/usr/bin/perl -w
use strict;
print "This is a simple Regular Expression Tester.\n";
print "First, enter the pattern you want to test.\n";
print "Remember NOT to escape metacharacters like \\d with an extra \\ when you
supply a pattern on the command line.\n";
print "Enter your pattern here: ";
my $myPattern = <STDIN>;
chomp($myPattern);
print "The pattern being tested is '$myPattern'.";
print "Enter a test string:\n";
while (<>)
{
 chomp();
 if (/$myPattern/)
 {
  print "Matched '$&' in '$_'\n";
  print "\nEnter another test string (or Ctrl+C to terminate):";
 }
 else
 {
  print "No match was found for '$myPattern' in '$_'.\n";
  print "\nEnter another test string (or Ctrl+C to terminate):";
 }
}
```

Try It Out   **Using the Simple Perl Regex Tester**

1. Run `RegexTester.pl` from the command line, using the command `perl RegexTester.pl`.

2. Enter the pattern **\d{5}-\d{4}**, which matches an extended U.S. Zip code but does not match the abbreviated Zip code form.

3. Enter the test string **12345-6789**, and inspect the displayed result.

4. Enter the test string **12345**, and inspect the result, as shown in Figure 26-33.

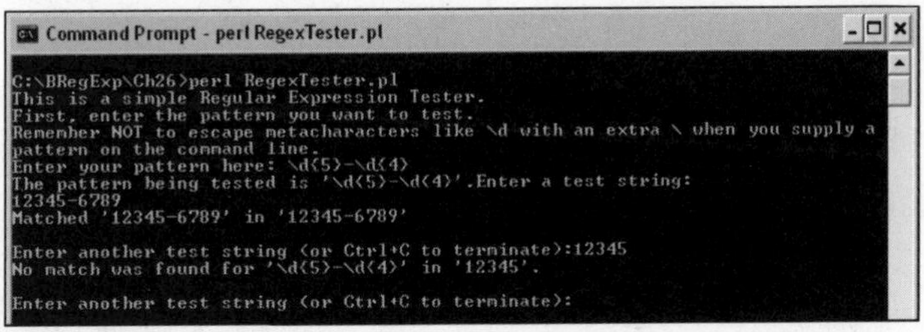

Figure 26-33

How It Works

First, some straightforward information is displayed to remind the user what the program does:

```
print "This is a simple Regular Expression Tester.\n";
print "First, enter the pattern you want to test.\n";
```

Paradoxically, in the message that tells the user not to escape metacharacters, such as \d, you have to escape the \d to get it to display correctly. The same applies to displaying the backslash character:

```
print "Remember NOT to escape metacharacters like \\d with an extra \\ when you
supply a pattern on the command line.\n";
```

Then instruct the user to enter a pattern:

```
print "Enter your pattern here: ";
```

Use the <STDIN> to capture the line of input from the user. It contains the pattern that the user specified plus a newline character:

```
my $myPattern = <STDIN>;
```

Use chomp() to remove the undesired newline character:

```
chomp($myPattern);
```

Tell the user the pattern that was entered, so the user can check for any typos before wasting time matching against a pattern that is different from the pattern he or she thinks is being matched against:

```
print "The pattern being tested is '$myPattern'.";
```

Ask the user to enter a test string:

```
print "Enter a test string:\n";
```

Then use <> to indicate to keep looping while there is another line of input from the user:

```
while (<>)
{
```

The test string that the user has input has an undesired newline character at the end of it, so you use chomp() to get rid of the newline:

```
chomp();
```

Then the test for the if statement tests whether there is a match in the input line (after chomp() has been used) against the pattern $myPattern:

```
if (/$myPattern/)
{
```

If there is a match, the special variable $& contains it. So you tell the user what character sequence matched the pattern:

```
print "Matched '$&' in '$_'\n";
```

Then you invite the user to either input another test string or terminate the program:

```
print "\nEnter another test string (or Ctrl+C to terminate):";
}
```

If no match is found, the statement block for the `else` clause is executed. The user is informed that there is no match and that he or she has a choice to enter another test string or terminate the program:

```
else
{
print "No match was found for '$myPattern' in '$_'.\n";
print "\nEnter another test string (or Ctrl+C to terminate):";
}
}
```

Exercises

1. Create a pattern for a 16-digit credit card number, allowing the user the option to split the numeric digits into groups of four. Assume for the purposes of this exercise that all numeric digits are acceptable in all positions where a numeric digit is expected. Use the `RegexTester.pl` to test the test strings 1234 5678 9012 3456 and 1234567890123456.

2. Modify the example `LookBehind.pl` so that it matches `Training` when it is *not* preceded by the character sequence `Star` followed by a space character. Make sure that the code you create is working by testing it with the test strings `Training is great!` and `Star Training is great!`.

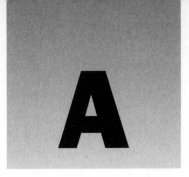

Exercise Answers

Chapter 3

1. You can match a doubled s using the pattern ss or s{2}. To match doubled m, use the pattern mm or m{2}.

2. The pattern AB\d\d or AB\d{2} would match the specified text.

3. You need to change only one line in UpperL.html to achieve the desired result. For tidiness you should also change the content of the title element to reflect the changed functionality.

The modified file UpperLmodified.html is shown here. The edited lines are highlighted. The second highlighted line causes the variable myRegExp to attempt to match the pattern the:

```
<html>
<head>
<title>Check for character sequence 'the'.</title>
<script language="javascript" type="text/javascript">
var myRegExp = /the/;

function Validate(entry){
return myRegExp.test(entry);
} // end function Validate()

function ShowPrompt(){
var entry = prompt("This script tests for matches for the regular expression
pattern: " + myRegExp + ".\nType in a string and click on the OK button.",
"Type your text here.");
if (Validate(entry)){
alert("There is a match!\nThe regular expression pattern is: " + myRegExp +
".\n The string that you entered was: '" + entry + "'.");
} // end if
else{
 alert("There is no match in the string you entered.\n" + "The regular
expression pattern is " + myRegExp + "\n" + "You entered the string: '" +
entry + "'." );
```

```
} // end else

} // end function ShowPrompt()

</script>
</head>
<body>
<form name="myForm">
<br />
<button type="Button" onclick="ShowPrompt()">Click here to enter text.</button>
</form>
</body>
</html>
```

Chapter 4

1. The . metacharacter matches all characters except a newline character. The \w metacharacter matches only ASCII alphabetic character (both uppercase and lowercase A through Z).

2. The line with the revised pattern is as follows:

```
var myRegExp = /<Person DateOfBirth\s*=\s*".*"\s*>/;
```

The revised pattern adds the pattern \s* on both sides of the = character.

Chapter 5

1. The problem definition to match license and licence should be something like this:

> Match a lowercase **l** followed by a lowercase **i**, followed by a lowercase **c**, followed by a lowercase **e**, followed by a lowercase **n**, followed by a choice of either lowercase **s** or lowercase **c**, followed by a lowercase **e**.

Two regular expression patterns are correct. The regular expression pattern needed is either:

```
licen[cs]e
```

or:

```
licen[sc]e
```

These are identical in meaning.

2. Let's break the solution for this question into two parts.

For the month, there are two situations: when the first digit is 0 and when the first digit is 1.

When the first digit is 0, you want the second digit to be 1 through 9. You can write a pattern to reflect that as follows:

```
0[1-9]
```

When the first digit of the month is 1, the second digit must be 0, 1, or 2. You can use the following patterns to reflect that:

```
1[012]
```

or:

```
1[0-2]
```

Because you want either of those choices, you can use parentheses with a bar character, |, between them to specify months 01 through 12:

```
(0[1-9]|1[012])
```

For the day part of the problem, you first have the situation where the first digit is 0. In that situation, the second digit must be in the range 1 through 9. A suitable pattern is:

```
0[1-9]
```

When the first digit of the day is 1, the second digit must be 0 through 9. A suitable pattern is:

```
1[0-9]
```

Similarly, when the first digit of the day is 2, the second digit must be 0 through 9. A suitable pattern is:

```
2[0-9]
```

You can combine those two patterns as follows:

```
[12][0-9]
```

Finally, when the first digit of the day is 3, the second digit must be 0 or 1. A suitable pattern is:

```
3[01]
```

The patterns for the day are mutually exclusive choices, so you can combine them using the bar, |, character as follows:

```
(0[1-9]|[12][0-9]|3[01])
```

The whole pattern then becomes the following:

```
(20|19)[0-9]{2}[-./](0[1-9]|1[012])[-./](0[1-9]|[12][0-9]|3[01])
```

This pattern is an improvement on the previous one, but not perfect. It does not, for example, recognize that there is something wrong with a date 2004/02/30. Because there is no such day as February 30, you might not want to allow that to match. Whether you want to develop the pattern further would depend on how important it is to you to ensure that all spurious dates be identified.

Chapter 6

1. The pattern `the\>` matches occurrences of the sequence of characters `the` when they occur at the end of a word. The corresponding pattern using the `\b` metacharacter is `the\b`.

2. The pattern asked for won't match a word boundary before the sequence of characters `the` (because it won't match `the` in `then`); neither will it match a word boundary after the sequence of characters `the` (because it won't match `the` in `lathe`). Therefore, you need a pattern that matches something that isn't a word boundary followed by the sequence of characters `the`, followed by something that isn't a word boundary.

The problem definition could be expressed as follows:

> **Match a position that isn't a word boundary followed by the sequence of characters t, h, and e, followed by a position that isn't a word boundary.**

A suitable pattern is:

```
\Bthe\B
```

Figure A-1 shows the solution in the Komodo Regular Expressions Toolkit.

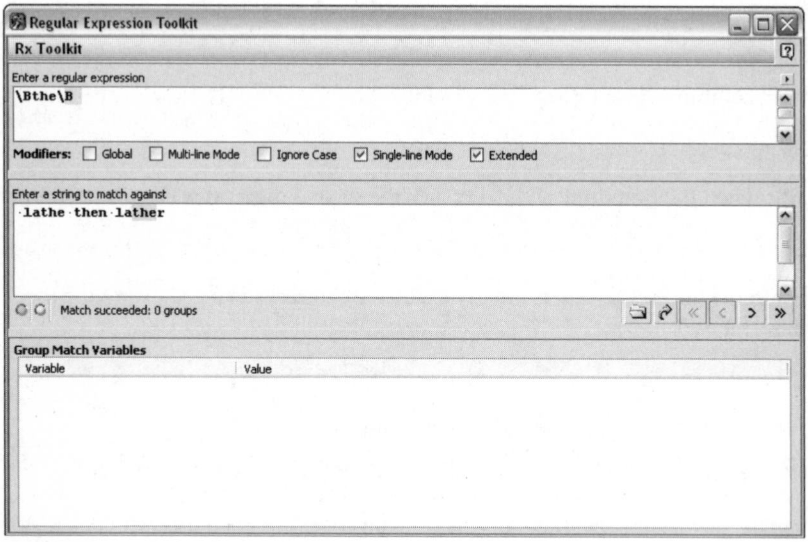

Figure A-1

Chapter 7

1. Three patterns that will match each of the two desired sequences of characters follow:

```
(licence|license)
```

or:

```
licen(c|s)e
```

or:

```
licen[cs]e
```

In each of the three options shown, reversal of the order of options inside the parentheses also gives correct answers.

2. The following pattern is the only solution:

```
(Fear|fear) \1
```

The following pattern captures only the initial f or F, so it doesn't detect whether the second word is fear or, for example, Fred:

```
(F|f)ear \1
```

The following pattern won't work, because there are no parentheses; nothing is captured. Therefore, the \1 back reference won't work:

```
[Ff]ear \1
```

Chapter 8

1. The alphabetic characters can match the pattern [A-Za-z]+, assuming that both uppercase and lowercase characters are to be matched. To specify that the alphabetic characters must be followed by a comma, simply add a literal comma inside the appropriate lookahead parentheses, (?=,). The whole pattern is [A-Za-z]+(?=,).

2. The pattern (?<=\W)sheep(?=\W) will match the word sheep. The lookbehind (?<=\W) specifies that the character preceding the s of sheep must not be a word character. The lookahead (?=\W) specifies that the character following the p of sheep must not be a word character. The overall effect is that the word sheep is matched.

The pattern (?<=[^A-Za-z])sheep(?=[^A-Za-z]) would also match the word sheep.

Chapter 9

1. The original pattern was ^\w*(?<=\w)\.?\w+@(?=[\w\.]+\W)\w+\.\w{3,4}$. The necessary modification is straightforward. Instead of using \w{3,4} to match three-character or four-character sequences after the final period character of the e-mail address, you can use alternation to offer the desired choice of specific domains.

That is matched by the pattern (com|net|org). Remember not to include any space characters inside the parentheses, or you will lose matches, because there is no space character in the e-mails in the test data.

The full pattern is:

```
^\w*(?<=\w)\.?\w+@(?=[\w\.]+\W)\w+\.(com|net|org)$
```

2. One approach would be to add further alternative specific lookaheads. The following pattern will match the additional characters that occur in the test text:

```
Star((?= Training)|(?=\.)|(?=\?)|(?=!))
```

Chapter 11

1. The pattern pe[ae]k will do what is required. Character classes are supported in Word.

2. Assuming that you use the pattern ([0-9]{2})[./-]([0-9]{2})[./-]([0-9]{4}) to match dates, only a small change is needed to replace U.K. dates.

   U.K. dates are in DD/MM/YY format. So to output international date format, you can use the pattern:

   ```
   \3-\2-\1
   ```

   to order the components of the original date in the desired order.

Chapter 12

1. The pattern [A-V] is the most convenient solution.

2. The pattern [a-ht-z] is a convenient solution.

   Figure A-2 shows the solution applied to the test file ClassTest.txt.

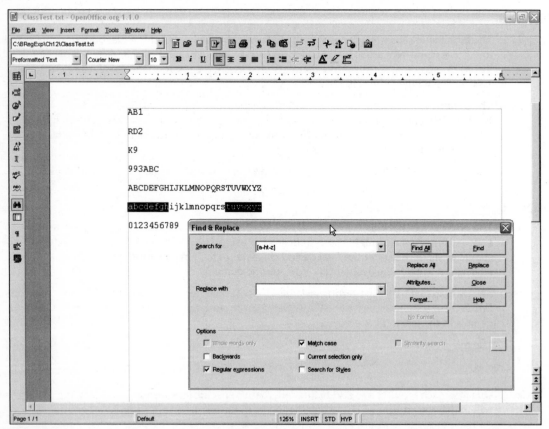

Figure A-2

Chapter 13

1. The following command would find lines that contain the desired matches:

```
findstr "[A-Z][A-KO-Z][A-Z][0-9][0-9][0-9]" filename*.extension
```

2. Either of the following will find the desired matches:

```
findstr /i "^the" filename*.extension
```

or:

```
findstr /i /b "the" filename*.extension
```

Chapter 14

1. The reason that regexp is never matched is that the option regexp occurs earlier among the options in the following and in the other alternate regular expressions:

```
(regular expression|regex|regexp)
```

If the character sequence regexp occurs, the option regex always matches; therefore, the pattern regexp is never matched.

The problem is solved very simply, by moving the pattern regexp before the pattern regexp in the options, as follows:

```
(regular expression|regexp|regex)
```

Similar simple reordering solves the problem in the second alternate pattern, giving you the following:

```
reg(ular expression|exp|ex)
```

However, the following third option cannot be similarly changed:

```
reg(ular expression|(ex)p?)
```

It could be changed to the option shown earlier:

```
reg(ular expression|exp|ex)
```

If you provide options that are very similar, ensure that the more difficult-to-match options precede similar but simpler options if you want to avoid this class of problem.

2. The following pattern would match:

```
\$\d{2}\.\d{2}
```

Remember that the $ metacharacter, if not escaped, matches the end-of-line position. So to match the dollar sign, the escaped \$ is used. Remember, too, that to match the decimal point the \. metacharacter matches only the period character.

If you used a pattern such as the following, using the period metacharacter (unescaped) would match, for example, $12345, which is not the desired result:

```
\$\d{2}.\d{2}
```

Chapter 15

1. Assuming that the filter has already been created, select the Custom menu option from the first-name drop-down list (cell C3). Select the Begins With option from the top-left drop-down list in the Custom AutoFilter dialog box. Enter the pattern **Kar*** in the top-right text box, and click the OK button. Only the rows for Karen Peters and Kara Stelman should be displayed.

2. Use Ctrl+F to open the Find and Replace dialog box. Enter the pattern **Ju?** in the Find What text box. Check the Match Entire Cell Contents check box. Click the Find All button.

Chapter 16

1. There is only one surname, `Gringlesby`, in the `authors` table that is not desired as a match. There are several options for a solution, given the existing data. One option is:

```
USE pubs
SELECT au_lname, au_fname FROM dbo.authors
WHERE au_lname LIKE 'Gre%'
ORDER BY au_lname
```

The pattern `Gre%` will match `Green` and `Greene` and not match `Gringlesby`.

Other options include the following:

```
WHERE au_lname LIKE 'Gree%'
```

and:

```
WHERE au_lname LIKE 'Green%'
```

2. The following Transact-SQL code will achieve the specified results:

```
USE pubs
SELECT title_id, title, pubdate FROM dbo.titles
WHERE title LIKE '%data%'
ORDER BY title
```

The pattern `%data%` will match a value for the `title` column that has zero or more characters preceding the character sequence `data` and has zero or more characters following the character sequence. In other words, any title containing the character sequence `data` is matched.

Chapter 17

1. The following lines of code are functionally equivalent, and each is a suitable answer to the question:

```
SELECT "1950-01-01" LIKE "195%";
```

or:

```
SELECT '1950-01-01' LIKE '195%';
```

2. The following code would do what is required:

```
USE BRegExp;
SELECT ID, LastName, FirstName, Skills
FROM Employees
WHERE Skills REGEXP '\.NET'
;
```

Be careful to escape the period character as \ .; otherwise, (depending on the data), you might get undesired matches on words such as Ethernet, because the period metacharacter (if it wasn't escaped) would match the r or Ethernet.

Chapter 18

1. The following code will meet the requirements of the question:

```
SELECT dBeachPurchases.ItemTitle, dBeachPurchases.ItemAuthor
FROM dBeachPurchases
WHERE dBeachPurchases.ItemAuthor LIKE '*B?rns*';
```

The query has been created for you in the B?rns in ItemAuthor query in the AuctionPurchases.mdb database.

Alternatively, the ? metacharacter could be replaced by the _ metacharacter, and/or the * metacharacter could be replaced by the % metacharacter, giving the following code if both replacements are made:

```
SELECT dBeachPurchases.ItemTitle, dBeachPurchases.ItemAuthor
FROM dBeachPurchases
WHERE dBeachPurchases.ItemAuthor LIKE '%B_rns%';
```

2. When attempting to answer this question, you will probably notice that Access lacks a quantifier, which signifies that the preceding character is optional. In many regular expression implementations, the pattern Ma?cDonald would be what you need to match McDonald or MacDonald. Because Access doesn't have such a metacharacter, which is an optional quantifier, you need to take a different approach.

You need code that will match McDonald anywhere in the ItemAuthor field and code that will match MacDonald anywhere in the ItemAuthor field. The following code in a WHERE clause does the first:

```
WHERE dBeachPurchases.ItemAuthor LIKE "*McDonald*"
```

The next piece of code in a WHERE clause does the second:

```
WHERE dBeachPurchases.ItemAuthor LIKE "*McDonald*"
```

Because you want to match both possibilities, you can use the OR keyword to produce a compound WHERE clause like this:

```
WHERE dBeachPurchases.ItemAuthor LIKE "*McDonald*" OR  dBeachPurchases.ItemAuthor
LIKE "*MacDonald*"
```

If the WHERE clause is the final line of the SQL code, you will need to add a terminating semicolon to the line:

   a.   From the Database Objects window, select Queries, and click the New button.

   b.   Select Design View from the New Query dialog window. Figure A-3 shows the screen's appearance at that point.

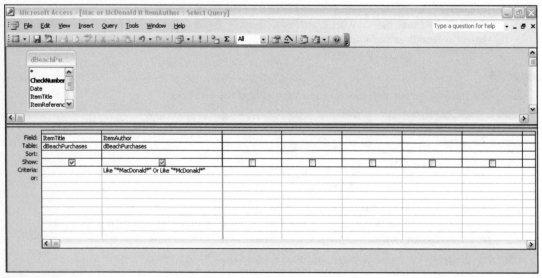

Figure A-3

   c.   Click the Add button to make the dBeachPurchases table available to query. In the left column of the grid, select ItemTitle in the leftmost Field drop-down list.

   d.   In the next column, select ItemAuthor in the Field drop-down list. In the same column, add the following to the Criteria cell:

```
LIKE "*McDonald*" OR LIKE  "*MacDonald"
```

   e.   Use Ctrl+S to save the new query; name it Mac or McDonald in ItemAuthor. Close the window in which you created the query.

If you open the window later in Design view, it will look like Figure 18-21. Notice that LIKE has been replaced, by Access, with Like. Because SQL is case insensitive, this change made by Access is purely cosmetic but can be a little confusing if you consistently use uppercase for SQL keywords.

Similarly, depending on what you hand-code or produce in Design view, you may find that Access adds paired parentheses, which are not strictly necessary, as in the following code, which is what I saw in the SQL view:

```
SELECT dBeachPurchases.ItemTitle, dBeachPurchases.ItemAuthor
FROM dBeachPurchases
WHERE (((dBeachPurchases.ItemAuthor) Like "*MacDonald*")) OR
(((dBeachPurchases.ItemAuthor) Like "*McDonald*"));
```

Chapter 19

1. The only part of `FinalT.html` that you need to change is the line where the `myRegExp` variable is declared:

```
var myRegExp = /^\d+$/;
```

The pattern `^\d+$` matches the beginning-of-string position (using the `^` metacharacter) and then matches one or more (using the `+` metacharacter) numeric digits (signified by the `\d` metacharacter), followed by the end-of-string position (signified by the `$` metacharacter).

The complete file, `NumericDigitsOnly.html`, is included in the code download.

2. Apart from modifying minor cosmetic details, for example, in the `title` element of the Web page, you will need to alter only the assignment statement for the `myRegExp` global variable.

The problem definition can be stated as follows:

> **Match a sequence of four numeric digits followed by a whitespace character, followed by a sequence of four numeric digits, followed by a whitespace character, followed by a sequence of four numeric digits, followed by a whitespace character, followed by a sequence of four numeric digits.**

So the pattern is as follows:

```
\d{4}\s\d{4}\s\d{4}\s\d{4}
```

And the declaration of the `myRegExp` variable together with its documentation would look like this:

```
var myRegExp = /\d{4}\s\d{4}\s\d{4}\s\d{4}/;
// \d{4} match four numeric digits
// \s match a whitespace character
// \d{4} match four numeric digits
// \s match a whitespace character
// \d{4} match four numeric digits
// \s match a whitespace character
// \d{4} match four numeric digits
```

The modified file, `CreditCard.html`, is in the code download. Its content is shown here for convenience:

```
<html>
<head>
<title>Processing a 16 digit credit card number.</title>
<script language="ecmascript" >
var myRegExp = /\d{4}\s\d{4}\s\d{4}\s\d{4}/;
// \d{4} match four numeric digits
// \s match a whitespace character
// \d{4} match four numeric digits
// \s match a whitespace character
// \d{4} match four numeric digits
// \s match a whitespace character
// \d{4} match four numeric digits

var entry;
```

```
function Validate(){
entry = document.simpleForm.CCNBox.value;
if (myRegExp.test(entry)) {
alert("The value you entered, " + entry + "\nmatches the regular expression, " +
myRegExp + ". \nIt is a valid 16 digit credit card number." );
} // end of the if statement
else
{
alert("The value you entered," + entry + ",\nis not a valid 16 digit credit card
number. Please try again.");
} // end of else clause
} // end Validate() function

function ClearBox(){
document.simpleForm.CCNBox.value = "";
// The above line clears the textbox when it receives focus
} // end ClearBox() function
</script>
</head>
<body>
<form name="simpleForm" >
<table>
<tr>
<td width="50%">Enter a valid 16 digit credit card number here, separating the
groups of four numbers by spaces:</td>
<td width="40%"><input name="CCNBox" width="50" onfocus="ClearBox()" type="text"
value="Enter a credit card number here"></input></td>
</tr>
<tr>
<td><input name="Submit" type="submit" value="Check the Credit Card Number"
onclick="Validate()" ></input></td>
</tr>
</table>
</form>
</body>
</html>
```

Chapter 20

1. The modified file, `TestForDate.html` is shown here:

```
<html>
<head>
<title>Test For A Date</title>
<script language="vbscript" type="text/vbscript">
Function MatchDate
Dim myRegExp, TestString, InputString
Set myRegExp = new RegExp
InputString = InputBox("Enter a Date in the format MM/DD/YYYY")
myRegExp.Pattern = "(0[1-9]|1[012])[-/.](0[1-9]|[12][0-9]|3[01])[-/.]\d{4}"
TestString = InputString
If myRegExp.Test(TestString) = True Then
  MsgBox "The test string '" & TestString & "' matches the pattern '" &
myRegExp.Pattern & "'."
```

```
Else
  MsgBox "There is no match. '" & InputString & "' does not match " &VBCrLf _
  & "the pattern '" & myRegExp.Pattern & "'."
End If
End Function

</script>
</head>
<body onload="MatchDate">

</body>
</html>
```

This is one way to achieve a solution as desired by the exercise. There are many other possible approaches.

The name of the function is changed to MatchDate. An additional variable, InputString, is declared that will accept the input text from a VBScript InputBox() function:

```
InputString = InputBox("Enter a Date in the format MM/DD/YYYY")
```

The InputBox() function simply accepts a string from the user. The instructions to the user specify a MM/DD/YYYY format.

The Pattern property of the myRegExp object is assigned a pattern that will match a date in the desired format:

```
myRegExp.Pattern = "(0[1-9]|1[012])[-/.](0[1-9]|[12][0-9]|3[01])[-/.]\d{4}"
```

The month part of the date has to match the following pattern:

```
(0[1-9]|1[012])
```

This allows dates of 1 through 9 inclusive in the first option and 10 through 12 in the second.

The separator can be a hyphen, a forward slash, or a period character, as specified in the following character class:

```
[-/.]
```

Be careful not to use the following character class, because that is a range that will not specify the correct values:

```
[/-.]
```

The day part of the date has to match the following pattern:

```
(0[1-9]|[12][0-9]|3[01])
```

The first option matches days 1 through 9. The second option matches days 10 through 29. The third option matches days 30 through 31.

In the regular expression assigned to the Pattern property, the year part of the date is expressed simply as \d{4}, which would allow years from 0000 through 9999. Likely, you might wish to restrict allowed dates to a more contemporary range and provide a more specific pattern to match the year component of the date.

719

2. The file `NameReverseStricter.html`, which is one possible answer to the exercise, is shown here. Some of the changes in the code are essentially cosmetic and won't be discussed further. The focus is on the processing of the regular expression and how that interacts with the properties of the `RegExp` object:

```
<html>
<head>
<title>Reverse Surname and First Name</title>
<script language="vbscript" type="text/vbscript">
Function ReverseName
Dim myRegExp, TestName, Match
Set myRegExp = new RegExp
myRegExp.Pattern = "^([A-Za-z]+)(\s+)([A-Za-z]+)$"
TestString = InputBox("Enter your name below, in the form" & VBCrLf & _
 "first name, then a space then last name." & VBCrLf & "Don't enter an initial or
middle name."_
 & "Any extra information will result in an error.")
Match = myRegexp.Replace(TestString, "$3,$2$1")
If Match <> TestString Then
   MsgBox "Your name in last name, first name format is:" & VBCrLf & Match
Else
   MsgBox "You didn't enter your name in the format requested." & VBCrLF _
   & "You may have entered no data, omitted part of your name," & VBCrLf _
   & "or entered extra data." & VBCrLf & VBCrLf _
   & "Press OK then F5 to run the example again."
End If
End Function

</script>
</head>
<body onload="ReverseName">

</body>
</html>
```

The main change that you need to make is the character sequence that is assigned to the `myRegExp` variable:

```
myRegExp.Pattern = "^([A-Za-z]+)(\s+)([A-Za-z]+)$"
```

The exercise specified that only a sequence of alphabetic characters is to be allowed. Therefore, the `\w` metacharacter is unsuitable, because it would allow numeric digits, and the underscore character as part of what was assumed to be a name. To allow only alphabetic characters, you could use the preceding pattern shown.

An alternative approach would be to set the value of the `IgnoreCase` property to `True` and use a character class with only one case of alphabetic characters (or either case), such as in the following code, which uses the character class `[A-Z]` twice:

```
myRegExp.IgnoreCase = True
myRegExp.Pattern = "^([A-Z]+)(\s+)([A-Z]+)$"
```

You will also need to amend the following line:

```
If Match <> TestString Then
```

which previously was

```
If Match <> "" Then
```

By changing the condition that governs the If statement to make a comparison between the value of the Match variable and the TestString variable, you can determine whether a successful match was found and then, as appropriate, either display the reordered name (when there is a successful match) or display a message indicating that the input was not in the desired format (when there is no match).

Chapter 21

1. The more complex solution uses both lookahead and lookbehind for practice.

The pattern (?<=\b[A-Za-z])old\b will match the character sequence old only when it is preceded by a single alphabetic character (of either case) and is not followed by any alphabetic characters — that is, it is immediately followed by a word-boundary metacharacter \b. This will match only words such as bold, cold, fold, gold, hold, and so on.

To also match words such as scold or scolds, the pattern (?<=\b[A-Za-z]+)old(?=[A-Za-z]*\b) could be used.

To additionally match old in words such as golden, the pattern could be modified to (?<=\b[A-Za-z]*)old(?=[A-Za-z]*\b).

The simpler solution uses the \B metacharacter, which matches a position that is not between word characters and a nonword character. So the pattern \Bold matches a position that is not a word boundary followed by the character sequence old. Because \B matches a position that is not a word boundary, the character before the o of old must be a word character; so old in words such as cold and bold will match.

2. There are many ways to solve this problem using back references. The following instructions provide one way to solve the exercise:

    a.   Create a new console application project in Visual Studio 2003. Name the project ReplaceDemo.

    b.   Edit the code so that it reads:

```
Imports System.Text.RegularExpressions
Module Module1
    Dim myPattern As String = "(Doctor|Doc)"
    Dim myRegex = New Regex(myPattern)
    Sub Main()
        Console.WriteLine("This example replaces 'Doctor' or 'Doc' with 'Dr.'.")
        Console.WriteLine("Enter a string on the following line:")
        Dim inputString = Console.ReadLine()
        Dim myMatch = myRegex.Match(inputString)
        Dim myReplacedString = myRegex.Replace(inputString, "Dr.")
        Console.WriteLine("The match '" & myMatch.Value & "' was found.")
        Console.WriteLine("The amended string is: " & myReplacedString)
        Console.WriteLine("Press Return to close this application.")
        Console.ReadLine()
    End Sub

End Module
```

c. Save the code, and press F5 to run it.

d. Test the code with the strings `I know Doc Smith.` and `I know Doctor Smith.`

In the pattern, which includes alternation, be sure to put the longer pattern first; otherwise, only `Doc` will be matched, and `Doctor` never will be:

```
Dim myPattern As String = "(Doctor|Doc)"
```

The replacement is carried out using the `Replace()` method of the `Regex` object:

```
Dim myReplacedString = myRegex.Replace(inputString, "Dr.")
```

The matching pattern is specified when the `myRegex` variable is dimensioned:

```
Dim myPattern As String = "(Doctor|Doc)"
```

In the use of the `Replace()` method itself, the two arguments, when used in this way, are the input string and the replacement text:

Chapter 22

1. The `IgnoreCase` option is used to specify case-insensitive matching.

Chapter 23

1. No. Perl Compatible Regular Expressions were introduced in PHP version 3.0.9. They are enabled by default in versions since PHP 4.2.

2. The `x` modifier causes unescaped whitespace inside a pattern to be ignored. This enables a pattern to be written across several lines, with a comment on each line explaining the intended effect of the pattern component on that line.

Chapter 24

1. The file `Name2.xsd`, shown here, is one possible solution to allow names such as `Maria Von Trapp` and `John James Manton` to be the content of a `Name` element:

```
<?xml version="1.0" encoding="UTF-8"?>
<xs:schema xmlns:xs="http://www.w3.org/2001/XMLSchema"
elementFormDefault="qualified">
  <xs:element name="Names">
    <xs:complexType>
      <xs:sequence>
        <xs:element ref="Name" maxOccurs="unbounded">
         <xs:simpleType>
           <xs:restriction base="xs:string">
            <xs:pattern value="\w+\s+\w+(\s+\w+)?" />
           </xs:restriction>
         </xs:simpleType>
        </xs:element>
      </xs:sequence>
    </xs:complexType>
  </xs:element>
</xs:schema>
```

The pattern has been modified to \w+\s+\w+(\s+\w+)?. The (\s+\w+)? matches an optional character sequence containing one or more whitespace characters followed by one or more word characters. When the content of the Name element is a name such as John Smith, the (\s+\w+)? pattern matches the zero-length string. When the content of the Name element is a name such as John James Manton, the (\s+\w+)? pattern matches the whitespace after James and the character sequence Manton.

2. The example part numbers indicate between one and three alphabetic characters followed by between one and five numeric digits.

A possible W3C XML Schema document, PartNumbers.xsd, is shown here:

```
<?xml version="1.0" encoding="UTF-8"?>
<xs:schema xmlns:xs="http://www.w3.org/2001/XMLSchema"
elementFormDefault="qualified">
  <xs:element name="PartNumber">
    <xs:simpleType>
      <xs:restriction base="xs:string">
  <xs:pattern value="\p{L}{1,3}\p{Nd}{1,5}" />
      </xs:restriction>
    </xs:simpleType>
  </xs:element>
  <xs:element name="PartNumbers">
    <xs:complexType>
      <xs:sequence>
        <xs:element ref="PartNumber" maxOccurs="unbounded"/>
      </xs:sequence>
    </xs:complexType>
  </xs:element>
</xs:schema>
```

The pattern \p{L}{1,3}\p{Nd}{1,5} assumes that both uppercase and lowercase letters are acceptable. The \p{L} will match any Unicode letter, uppercase or lowercase. The \p{Nd} will match a numeric digit. With the quantifiers shown in the preceding code, each of the sample part numbers will match.

If you assumed that only uppercase alphabetic characters were acceptable, a pattern, \p{Lu}{1,3}\p{Nd}{1,5}, would also be an acceptable answer.

If you assumed that only BasicLatin characters were acceptable, you could find the intersection of \p{IsBasicLatin} and either \p{L}{1,3}\p{Nd}{1,5} or \p{Lu}{1,3}\p{Nd}{1,5}, as demonstrated earlier in the chapter.

Chapter 25

1. The replaceAll.java code uses the Matcher class's replaceAll() method to replace all matches. To replace only the first occurrence of a match, you simply use the replaceFirst() method instead of the replaceAll() method.

So you need to edit only one line of the code:

```
String testResult = myMatcher.replaceAll("Moon");
```

so that it uses the replaceFirst() method:

```
String testResult = myMatcher.replaceFirst("Moon");
```

I saved the amended code as `replaceFirst.java`, so I also had to modify the name of the class:

```
public class replaceFirst{
```

Running the code produced the result shown in Figure A-4. Notice that only the first occurrence of the character sequence `Star` has been replaced.

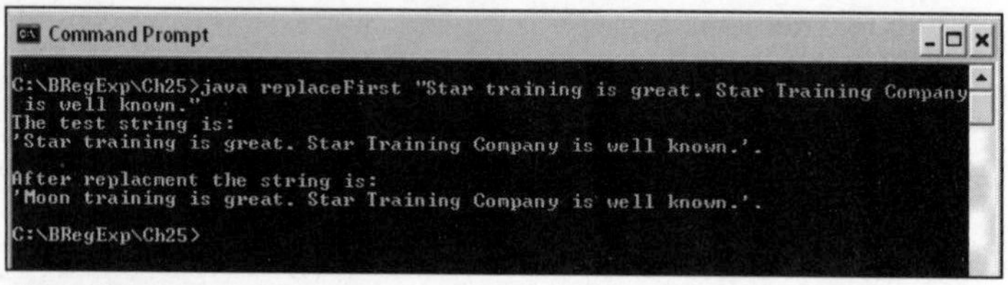

Figure A-4

2. Again, the modification is simply a replacement of a single line of code (apart from minor tidying) — in this case, replacement of the `String` class's `replaceFirst()` method with the `replaceAll()` method.

The key line needs to be changed to the following:

```
String testResult = testString.replaceAll(myRegex, "TWINKLE");
```

The code would run as desired, but I have changed method names and so on to reflect the changed functionality.

The modified code is shown here. I saved the modified code as `stringReplaceAll.java`:

```
import java.util.regex.*;

public class stringReplaceAll{
 public static void main(String args[]){
  myReplaceAll(args[0]);
 } // end main()

 public static boolean myReplaceAll(String testString){
  String myRegex = "twinkle";
  String testResult = testString.replaceAll(myRegex, "TWINKLE");

 System.out.println("The string was: '" + testString + "'.");
 System.out.println("The regular expression pattern was: '" + myRegex +"'.");
 System.out.println("After replacement the string was: '" + testResult + "'.");
        return true;
 } // myReplaceAll()

}
```

If the following command is entered at the command line, after `stringReplaceAll.java` is compiled, the appearance will reflect that shown in Figure A-5:

```
java stringReplaceAll "twinkle, twinkle little star."
```

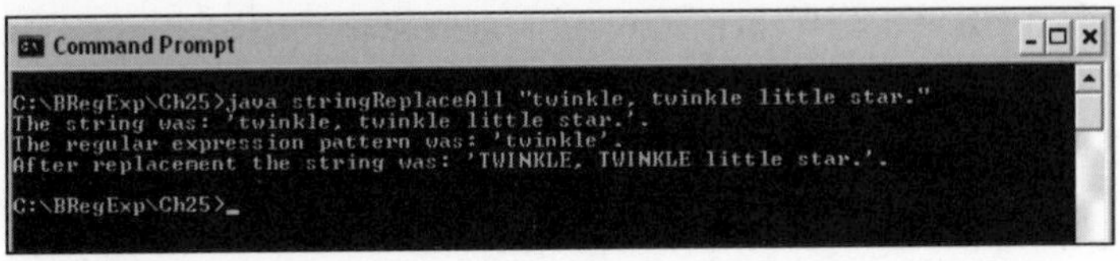

Figure A-5

Chapter 26

1. The first thing that is helpful to do is try to break the requirements for the example down into a problem definition. A credible problem definition follows:

Match a sequence of four numeric digits followed by an optional space character, followed by four numeric digits, followed by an optional space character, followed by four numeric digits, followed by an optional space character, followed by four numeric digits.

There is an obvious repeating pattern in the problem definition, "a sequence of four numeric digits followed by an optional space character," which occurs three times. A credible pattern for the repeating part of the pattern is as follows:

```
(\d{4}\s*){3}
```

The final part of the pattern is simply four numeric digits:

```
\d{4}
```

You don't want anything other than the credit card number to be entered, so you can use the ^ and $ metacharacters to ensure that only the desired characters are accepted.

Putting the parts together gives you the following pattern:

```
^(\d{4}\s*){3}\d{4}$
```

Figure A-6 shows the screen's appearance after both the required test strings have been entered, as well as a further test string that includes two successive space characters between one quartet of numeric digits.

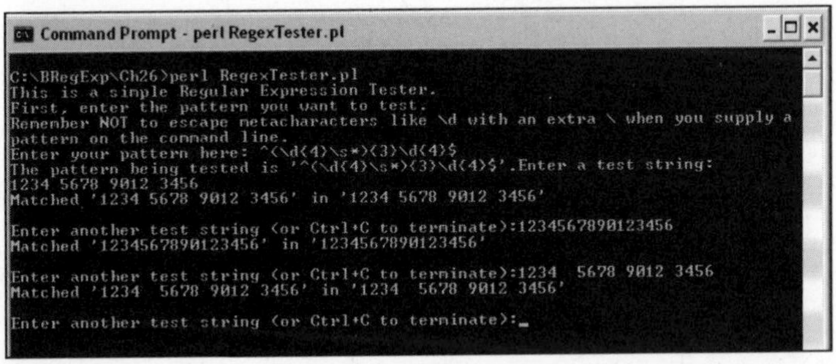

Figure A-6

2. To produce code that does what is required, you need to change only one character in the LookBehind.pl code.

The line that is:

```
if ($myTestString =~ m/(?<=Star )Training/)
```

in LookBehind.pl needs to read:

```
if ($myTestString =~ m/(?<!Star )Training/)
```

to produce negative lookbehind.

The amended code is in the code download as NegativeLookBehind.pl. Figure A-7 shows the appearance after the two test strings have been tested when running the code from the command line.

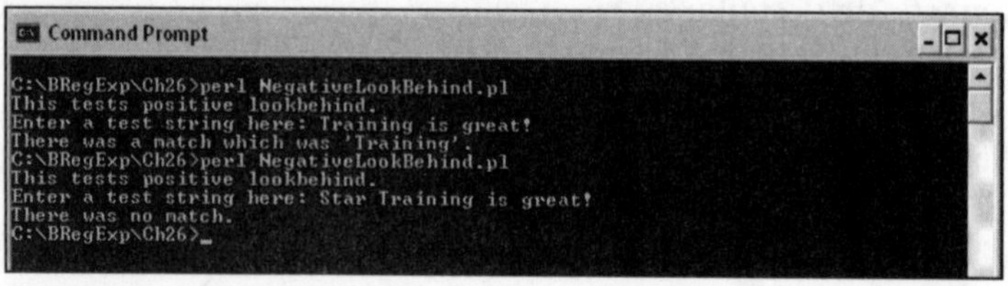

Figure A-7

Index

X

Z